1995-1996 CHURCH ALMANAC

GENERAL AUTHORITIES

OFFICERS

WORLDWIDE CHURCH

MISSIONS

TEMPLES

CHRONOLOGY

NEWS IN REVIEW

FACTS, STATISTICS

Pictured on the cover are, top left, the First Presidency, July 1994: President Howard W. Hunter, center; President Gordon B. Hinckley, left, and President Thomas S. Monson. Top right, Cambodian members attend San Diego Temple dedication in April 1993. Below left, LDS volunteers prepare for massive clean-up in Georgia floods of July 1994. Below right is Orlando Florida Temple at dedication, October 1994.

Photos are by Tom Smart, Dell Van Orden, Todd Stone and Gerry Avant.

GENERAL AUTHORITIES, OFFICERS

WORLDWIDE CHURCH

MISSIONS, TEMPLES

CHRONOLOGY, NEWS IN REVIEW

FACTS, STATISTICS

FOREWORD

Keeping informed is vital in today's fast-moving world. To provide the facts, data and knowledge required, there are numerous information systems and networks that are being developed almost daily.

Staying up to date in the Church is equally important, and for more than 20 years the *Deseret News Church Almanac* has been a key source of information about the growth and progress of the Church.

First published in 1973, this biannual almanac has become the authoritative printed source of Church data. An electronic on-line version will follow soon.

This new volume for 1995-1996 contains vital information, details and statistics, including a chronological account of important events in the Church since 1830. More complete information is given on the period from October 1992 to October 1994. New in this year's publication are historical accounts of the Church auxiliary organizations, plus details of extensive Church growth in Africa and the Eastern European nations.

This almanac is a cooperative effort of the staffs of the *Church News* supplement to the *Deseret News* and the Historical Department of the Church. Sincere appreciation is expressed to all who have worked so well together to prepare the material in this volume and to ensure its accuracy.

We at the *Deseret News* hope that this volume will be instructive, enlightening and educational for you, the reader and user.

**Wm. James Mortimer,
Publisher, Deseret News**

**Copyright © Deseret News 1994
Post Box 1257
Salt Lake City, Utah 84110
Second printing, 1996**

The *Deseret News Church Almanac* is prepared and edited by the staff of the *Church News*, a section of the *Deseret News*, in cooperation with the staff of the Historical Department of The Church of Jesus Christ of Latter-day Saints.

Deseret News

Deseret News President and Publisher	Wm. James Mortimer
Deseret News Managing Editor	Don C. Woodward
Church News Editor	Dell Van Orden
Church News Assistant Editor	Gerry Avant
Almanac Coordinating Editor	John L. Hart
Church News Staff	R. Scott Lloyd
	Mike Cannon
	Julie Dockstader
	Greg Hill
	Linda Hamilton
Deseret News	Robert Noyce
Art Department	Craig Holyoak
	LouAnn England
	Cory Maylett
	Reed McGregor
	Christie Jackson Meyer
	Heather Tuttle
Deseret News photo staff	
	Tom Smart
	Ravell Call
	Jeffrey D. Allred
	Paul Barker
	Garry Bryant
	Don Grayston
	Kristan Jacobsen
	Gary M. McKellar
	Gerald W. Silver
Deseret News Pagination	Jean M. Cassidy
	B. Douglas Osborn
Typesetting Manager	Shirl R. Lake

Historical Department

Executive Director	Elder Stephen D. Nadauld
Assistant Executive Director	Elder Alexander B. Morrison
Managing Director	Richard E. Turley Jr.
Almanac Chairman	Grant A. Anderson
Staff contributions	Melvin L. Bashore
	Karen S. Bolzendahl
	Kim B. Farr
	Mary S. Gifford
	James L. Kimball
	Pauline K. Musig
	Veneese C. Nelson
	William W. Slaughter
	Larry R. Skidmore
	Brian Sokolowsky
	Vivian D. Wellman

CONTENTS

Statistical profile 6

Major events

Administrative and policy changes 7
Changes in leadership 8
Appointments 9
Awards and honors 10
Deaths 10
News events 11

General Authorities (current)

First Presidency 14
Council of the Twelve photo 16
Council of the Twelve 17
Presidency of the Quorums of the Seventy 21
First Quorum of the Seventy 23
Second Quorum of the Seventy 33
Presiding Bishopric 41

General Authorities (past and present)

Presidents of the Church 42
Assistant Presidents of the Church 44
First Counselors in the First Presidency 44
Second Counselors in the First Presidency 47
Other Counselors in the First Presidency 48
Assistant Counselors in the First Presidency 50
Council of the Twelve 50
Other Apostles 57
Patriarchs to the Church 57
First Council of the Seventy 58
Assistants to the Twelve 63
Presidency of the Seventy 65
First Quorum of the Seventy 66
Second Quorum of the Seventy 73
Presiding Bishops 75
First Counselors to Presiding Bishops 76
Second Counselors to Presiding Bishops 77
Length of Service in First Presidency and the Twelve 79

General Officers of the Church

Sunday School 81
Sunday School general superintendencies, presidencies ... 82
Young Men 84
Young Men and Young Men's Mutual Improvement Association
    general superintendencies, presidencies 85
Primary 87
General presidencies of the Primary Association 88
Young Women 90
Young Women and Young Women's Mutual Improvement
    Association general presidencies 92
Relief Society 93
Relief Society general presidencies 95

Worldwide Church

Maps of areas of the world 98
United States (includes stakes) 108
Countries of the world (includes stakes) 192

Missions, temples of the Church

Missions in chronological order..306
First stake organized in each state of the United States..........................326
First stake organized in each country...327
Temples of the world, map...328
Temples listed by order of completion..329
Temples, pictures and information, listed alphabetically............................330
Microfilm rolls in Granite Mountain Records Vault......................................359
Temples in use, chart...359
Church growth, chart..360
Nations, territories, chart...360
Stakes, chart...360

Historical Chronology of the Church..362

News in Review...396
Progress during administrations of the presidents....................................410

Statistics, Facts

Membership and units by Church area..412
Membership and units by lands...413
Membership and units in the United States, Canada..................................416
Church statistics...418

Index 421

A statistical profile of

THE CHURCH OF JESUS CHRIST OF LATTER-DAY SAINTS
Dec. 31, 1993

CHURCH MEMBERSHIP

Total membership 8,688,000

CHURCH UNITS

Stakes 1,968
Districts 647
Missions 295
Wards, branches 21,002
Nations and territories with wards, branches 149

CHURCH GROWTH

Children of record baptized in 1993 76,312
Converts baptized in 1993 304,808

TEMPLES

Temples in use 45
Temples approved or under construction 12

LANGUAGES

Established languages spoken by members 28
Languages in developing nations spoken by members 144
Complete translations of Book of Mormon in print 38
Translated selections of Book of Mormon in print 48
Total number of language translations 86

MISSIONARIES

Total missionaries serving 48,708

EDUCATION
(1992-93 school year)

Cumulative total of continuing education enrollment 440,193
Students in seminary 325,304
(1993-94 total) 342,088
Students in institute 158,433
(1993-94 total) 177,377
Students in primary and secondary Church schools 9,303
(1993-94 total) 8,956
Students in Church colleges and universities (Fall, 1992) 37,468

Oct. 1, 1994

Total membership 8,960,000
Stakes 1,992
Missions 303
Temples in use 45
Temples planned, or under construction 12
Missionaries 48,567

President Howard W. Hunter and counselors, President Gordon B. Hinckley and President Thomas S. Monson, sustain themselves in solemn assembly Oct. 1, 1994.

MAJOR EVENTS
OCTOBER 1992 — OCTOBER 1994

For a more detailed listing, see News in Review section

Administrative and policy changes

● The First Presidency announced Aug. 27, 1993, that Sunday School opening exercises and the hymn practice would no longer be held, effective Jan. 1, 1994.

● *A Member's Guide to Temple and Family History Work* was introduced to general and local Church officers with an accompanying announcement letter from the First Presidency Nov. 8, 1993. The new book replaces *Come Unto Christ through Temple Ordinances and Covenants.*

● The First Presidency and Council of the Twelve reaffirmed the Church's policy on discipline Nov. 2, 1993, saying, "We have the responsibility to preserve the doctrinal purity of the Church. . . ." The letter explained that apostasy refers to Church members who "repeatedly act in clear, open and deliberate public opposition to the Church or its leaders; or persist in teaching as Church doctrine information that is not Church doctrine after being corrected by their bishops or higher authority; or continue to follow the teachings of apostate cults (such as those that advocate plural marriage) af-

ter being corrected by their bishops or higher authority."

● The First Presidency issued a statement Nov. 23, 1993, calling for the continued emphasis on keeping the Sabbath Day holy. "Throughout generations of time, the sacred law of the Sabbath has been upheld by the prophets of God as a holy observance to help sanctify and bring joy to those who would keep the commandments of the Lord."

● The First Presidency issued a statement Feb. 1, 1994, opposing efforts to give legal authorization to marriages between persons of the same gender.

● The First Presidency on Feb. 1, 1994, said that unwed parents, who are "unable or unwilling to marry, should be encouraged to place the child for adoption, preferably through LDS Social Services. . . . The best interests of the child should be the paramount consideration."

● In a letter to general and local Church officers on Feb. 1, 1994, President Howard W. Hunter of the Council of the Twelve announced the consolidation of the Stake Record Extraction and Family Record Extraction programs to create a single, simplified organization called Family Record Extraction.

• A man who has been previously sealed and later divorced, who desires to be married and sealed in the temple, must first obtain a clearance from the First Presidency, the First Presidency stated Feb. 3, 1994.

• Priesthood leaders in the United States and Canada were notified of the uniform curriculum April 21, 1994, which will be implemented worldwide Jan. 1, 1995. Implemented over a two-year-period from 1993-95, the new curriculum focuses on the scriptures and combines various age groups in the auxiliaries. A modified curriculum to provide a uniform approach for teaching the gospel Churchwide was announced to international priesthood leaders April 6, 1992, to begin the transition.

Changes in leadership

GENERAL AUTHORITIES
First Presidency

• President Howard W. Hunter was ordained and set apart as the 14th president of the Church on June 5, 1994, following the death of President Ezra Taft Benson on May 30, 1994.

• President Gordon B. Hinckley, first counselor to President Ezra Taft Benson, was called June 5, 1994, as first counselor to President Howard W. Hunter.

• President Thomas S. Monson, second counselor to President Ezra Taft Benson, was called June 5, 1994, as second counselor to President Howard W. Hunter.

Council of the Twelve

• President Hinckley was also called and set apart as president of the Council of the Twelve June 5, 1994. Elder Boyd K. Packer was called to serve as acting president of the Twelve.

• Elder Robert D. Hales, Presiding Bishop from 1985 to 1994 and a General Authority since 1975, was ordained an apostle April 7, 1994, succeeding Elder Marvin J. Ashton, who died Feb. 25, 1994.

• Elder Jeffrey R. Holland, called to the First Quorum of the Seventy on April 1, 1989, was ordained an apostle June 23, 1994. He filled a vacancy in left in the Council of the Twelve after President Howard W. Hunter became president of the Church.

Presidency of the Seventy

• Elders Joe J. Christensen, Monte J. Brough and W. Eugene Hansen were called to the Presidency of the Seventy, effective Aug. 15, 1993. They succeeded Elders Dean L. Larsen, James M. Paramore and J. Richard Clarke, who were called as area presidents.

First Quorum of the Seventy

• Members of the Second Quorum of the Seventy sustained to the First Quorum of the Seventy were Elders F. Melvin Hammond, Kenneth Johnson and Lynn A. Mickelsen on April 3, 1993, Elder Cree-L Kofford on April 2, 1994, and Elder Dennis B. Neuenschwander on Oct. 1, 1994.

• Sustained to the First Quorum of the Seventy on April 3, 1993, were Elders Neil L. Andersen and D. Todd Christofferson. Sustained on Oct. 1, 1994, were Elders Andrew W. Peterson and Cecil O. Samuelson Jr.

Emeritus General Authorities

• Elders Jacob de Jager, Adney Y. Komatsu and H. Burke Peterson of the First Quorum of the Seventy were given emeritus status Oct. 2, 1993. Elder Hartman Rector Jr. of the First Quorum of the Seventy received emeritus status Oct. 1, 1994.

Second Quorum of the Seventy

Five new members of the Second Quorum of the Seventy were sustained on April 2, 1994: Elders Claudio R. M. Costa, W. Don Ladd, James O. Mason, Dieter F. Uchtdorf, and Lance B. Wickman.

• Released from the Second Quorum of the Seventy Oct. 1, 1994, were Elders Albert Choules Jr., Lloyd P. George, Malcolm S. Jeppsen, Richard P. Lindsay, Merlin R. Lybbert, Gerald E. Melchin and Horacio A. Tenorio.

Presiding Bishopric

● Sustained April 2, 1994, as Presiding Bishop was Elder Merrill J. Bateman of the Second Quorum of the Seventy. He succeeded Presiding Bishop Robert D. Hales, who was called to the the Council of the Twelve.

● Sustained as counselors to Bishop Bateman on April 2, 1994, were Bishops H. David Burton and Richard C. Edgley, who had previously served as first and second counselors, respectively, to Presiding Bishop Hales.

General Authority Deaths

● President Ezra Taft Benson, ordained an apostle Oct. 7, 1943, and ordained and set apart as president of the Church Nov. 10, 1985, died May 30, 1994, in Salt Lake City, Utah, at age 94.

● Elder Marvin J. Ashton, ordained an apostle Dec. 2, 1971, died Feb. 25, 1994, in Salt Lake City, Utah, at age 78.

● Elder Robert E. Sackley, 70, of the Second Quorum of the Seventy, died Feb. 22, 1993, in Australia, while serving as first counselor in the Pacific Area presidency. He had been a General Authority since April 2, 1988.

● Elder Clinton L. Cutler, 64, a member of the Second Quorum of the Seventy since March 31, 1990, and a counselor in the Sunday School general presidency, died April 9, 1994, in South Jordan, Utah.

● Elder Sterling W. Sill, 91, called as a General Authority on April 6, 1954, and an emeritus member of the Seventy since Dec. 31, 1978, died in Salt Lake City, Utah, on May 25, 1994.

AUXILIARIES

● Elder Vaughn J Featherstone of the Seventy was called as second counselor in the Young Men general presidency, effective Aug. 15, 1993, succeeding Elder L. Lionel Kendrick.

● Elder Charles Didier was called as Sunday School general president, with Elder F. Burton Howard as first counselor and Elder J Ballard Washburn as second counselor, effective Aug. 15, 1994. They succeeded Elder Merlin R. Lybbert and his second counselor Elder Ronald E. Poelman. His first counselor, Elder Clinton L. Cutler, died April 9, 1994.

● Patricia P. Pinegar was sustained as Primary general president Oct. 1, 1994, along with her counselors, Anne G. Wirthlin and Susan L. Warner. They succeeded Michaelene P. Grassli and her counselors, Sisters Betty Jo N. Jepsen and Ruth B. Wright. Sister Pinegar had been second counselor in the Young Women general presidency.

● Bonnie D. Parkin was sustained Oct. 1, 1994, as second counselor in the Young Women general presidency, succeeding Sister Pinegar.

Appointments

● Professional Scouter Hart Bullock of Centerville, Utah, was appointed director of LDS relationships for the Boy Scouts of America, as of December 1992. Brother Bullock also serves as director of BSA's Area 2, which includes Utah, Idaho and Wyoming.

● Betty Jo N. Jepsen, first counselor in the Primary general presidency, was appointed to serve on the National Boy Scout Committee of the Boy Scouts of America, effective May 20, 1993.

● BYU professor of ancient scripture S. Kent Brown was named director of BYU's Jerusalem Center for Near Eastern Studies, effective mid-June 1993.

● Richard K. Circuit of San Diego, California, was named president of the 1994 Thrifty Car Rental Holiday Bowl, the Western Athletic Conference football bowl played annually Dec. 30.

● Eric B. Shumway, vice president for academics, was named president of BYU-Hawaii, it was announced April 14, 1994. Brad W. Farnsworth, BYU-Hawaii vice president for administrative services, succeeds Dee F. Andersen, who retired August, 1994, as administrative vice president at BYU. BYU-Hawaii appointed the first female university vice president in the history of the Church Educational System when V. Napua Baker was named vice president of University Advancement in November 1992.

● Carolyn B. Przekurat of Albuquerque, N.M., was appointed in August

1994 to a four-year term as chief dietitian officer in the United States Department of Health and Human Services by U.S. Surgeon General Jocelyn Elders.

Awards and honors

• San Francisco 49ers football team quarterback Steve Young was named to the Associated Press 1992 All-Pro first team, it was announced Dec. 29, 1992. The former BYU all-American also became the first National Football League quarterback to win three consecutive passing titles.

• Olympic distance runner/road racer Ed Eyestone of Layton, Utah, was named U.S. Road Athlete of the Year for 1992 by Track & Field News. This was his fourth consecutive year to receive the honor.

• In 1993, for the fifth consecutive year, Brigham Young University was named to the Honor Roll sponsored by the John Templeton Foundation, honoring colleges and universities that promote high integrity as well as education.

• Michelle Kay Waite of Peru, Ind., was named the 1993 National Mother of Young Children at the 58th annual American Mothers National Convention April 22-25, 1993, in Raleigh, N.C.

• Two returned missionaries were selected in the 1993 National Basketball Association draft June 30, 1993. Shawn Bradley of BYU was drafted No. 2 overall by Philadelphia in the first round, the highest any LDS basketball player has ever been drafted. Josh Grant of the University of Utah was drafted in the second round (43rd overall) by Denver.

• University of Wisconsin quarterback Darrell Bevell led the Badgers to a 26-16 win against UCLA in the Jan. 1, 1994, Rose Bowl.

• David W. Checketts, president of the New York Knicks basketball team, was honored as one of the 1994 National Fathers of the Year at the Sheraton Manhattan Hotel in New York City in May 1994.

• The Polish Genealogical Society of America presented the Wiglia Award to the Church on May 14, 1994, for its efforts to microfilm eastern European records in areas that once belonged to the Polish Commonwealth.

• Coach Tom Peterson led the Penn State Nittany Lions to the 1994 NCAA Men's Volleyball Championship for the first time in 25 years of NCAA men's volleyball that a team outside California has claimed the title. Coach Peterson, 40, was named American Volleyball Coaches Association Coach of the Year.

• President Ezra Taft Benson was inducted into the University of Idaho Alumni Association's Alumni Hall of Fame. He was among five alumni inducted into the Hall of Fame at commencement exercises May 13, 1994.

• Archibald F. Bennett, who pioneered acquisition of genealogical materials for the Church, was posthumously elected to the National Genealogy Hall of Fame on June 3, 1994. He is the first Church member and ninth person to receive the honor given annually for significant contributions to the field of genealogy in the United States.

Deaths

• Dr. James LeRoy Kimball, 90, president of Nauvoo Restoration Inc., from 1963-87, and instrumental in the restoration of Nauvoo, Ill., as a Church historic site, died Oct. 18, 1992, in Salt Lake City.

• Lowell Marsden Durham, 75, a well-known composer for the Mormon Tabernacle Choir, the Utah Symphony, the Philadelphia Orchestra and the New York Philharmonic Orchestra, and a former Sunday School general board member, died Nov. 10, 1992, in Salt Lake City.

• Burton Stafford (Buzz) Tingey, 67, manager of risk retention and insurance for the Church, died Nov. 25, 1992, in Salt Lake City. He had served as regional representative and president of the Australia Sydney Mission from 1985-88.

• Joseph T. Bentley, 87, general superintendent of the Young Men's Mutual Improvement Association from 1958-62, and former president of the Northern

Mexican Mission, from 1956-58, and the Argentina Rosario Mission, from 1972-75, died June 15, 1993, in Provo, Utah.

● Ada Strong Van Dam, 85, the first matron of the Jordan River Temple and a former member of the Primary general board, died Sept. 11, 1993, in Salt Lake City.

● David Lawrence McKay, the eldest son of the late President David O. McKay and Emma Ray Riggs McKay, former president of the Eastern States Mission from 1971-1974 and general Sunday School superintendent from 1966-1971, died Oct. 27, 1993, at age 92 in Salt Lake City.

● William Edwin Berrett, 91, author of *The Restored Church*, and former administrator of Church seminaries and institutes and a vice president at BYU, died Nov. 30, 1993, in Provo, Utah.

● Wallace F. Bennett, 95, who served in U.S. Senate from Utah for 24 years, and member of the Sunday School general board from 1936-1966, died in Salt Lake City Dec. 19, 1993. He married Frances Grant, youngest daughter of President Heber J. Grant.

● William Roberts, 86, the first New Zealander to serve as a stake president in his homeland, died Jan. 12, 1994, in Hamilton, New Zealand.

● Keith Maurice Engar, 70, former member of the YMMIA general board and the first chairman of the Church's general activities committee, died Feb. 9, 1994, in Salt Lake City.

● D. Arthur Haycock, 77, personal secretary to five Church presidents and missionary, mission president and temple president in Hawaii, died Feb. 25, 1994. He was secretary to Presidents George Albert Smith, Joseph Fielding Smith, Harold B. Lee, Spencer W. Kimball and Ezra Taft Benson.

● Evert Wilford Perciwall, 71, the first stake president in Sweden, died April 24, 1994, at his home in Stockholm.

● Armis Joseph Ashby, 72, pioneer in the development of audiovisual programming of temple services, died Aug. 10, 1994, in Salt Lake City.

News events

● Italy granted legal status to the Church May 12, 1993, following formal registration with the courts. The decree was signed on Feb. 22, 1993, by Italy's president, Oscar Luigi Scalfaro.

● On Oct. 18-20, 1992, the London Temple was rededicated and on Oct. 23-25, 1992, the Swiss Temple was rededicated. Both temples were extensively remodeled and refurbished.

● On Nov. 8, 1992, Elaine L. Jack, Relief Society general president, made the first visit to India by a Church auxiliary president.

● The Church reached a milestone of 20,000 wards and branches with the creation of the Harvest Park Ward in the Salt Lake Granger South Stake on Dec. 6, 1992.

● The nation of Belize, on the Yucatan Peninsula in Central America, was dedicated Dec. 7, 1992, completing the dedication of all seven nations in Central America.

● A worldwide gospel literacy effort by the Relief Society was announced by Elaine L. Jack, Relief Society general president. A letter to leaders from the First Presidency was sent Dec. 15, 1992.

● A historic tour of the Holy Land was concluded Jan. 6, 1993, by the Tabernacle Choir.

● Four Church-service missionaries entered Vietnam Jan. 6, 1993, the first Church presence there in two decades.

● A man threatening to detonate a bomb interrupted a BYU 19-stake fireside address by President Howard W. Hunter Feb. 7, 1993. President Hunter refused to sign the man's statement, and the man was subdued by security officers and members of the congregation, and taken into custody.

● Seventeen new missions were announced March 6 and 13, 1993, in the U.S., South America, and eastern Europe.

● Elder James E. Faust of the Council of the Twelve dedicated Latvia March 17, 1993.

● The centennial of the Salt Lake Temple was observed April 6, 1993, with a video, museum exhibit, and addresses in general conference.

• Elder Neal A. Maxwell of the Council of the Twelve dedicated Mongolia on April 15, 1993.

• Elder Dallin H. Oaks dedicated Albania April 23, 1993.

• President Gordon B. Hinckley, first counselor in the First Presidency, dedicated the San Diego California Temple April 25, 1993.

• Elder Russell M. Nelson dedicated Belarus May 11, 1993.

• Elder M. Russell Ballard dedicated Lithuania May 20, 1993.

• The former Hotel Utah in Salt Lake City was dedicated June 27, 1993, and renamed the Joseph Smith Memorial Building.

• The Church was formally registered by the government of Mexico June 29, 1993, receiving all the rights of a religious organization, including the right to own property.

• Flooding of rivers in the Midwest in July 1993 caused severe damage, and Church members volunteered for service during the last two weeks of the month.

• More than 16 tons of clothing and shoes arrived in St. Petersburg, Russia, in August as part of the Church's humanitarian aid efforts.

• Elder Russell M. Nelson of the Council of the Twelve represented the Church at the 1993 Parliament of the World's Religions in Chicago, Ill., on Aug. 28-Sept. 5, 1993.

• Elder Joseph B. Wirthlin of the Council of the Twelve dedicated the Mediterranean island of Cyprus on Sept. 14, 1993.

• The long-awaited software, TempleReady, which makes it possible to rapidly clear names for temple work, was announced in a letter to priesthood leaders from the First Presidency on Nov. 8, 1993.

• On Nov. 16, 1993, President Bill Clinton signed into law the the Religious Freedom Restoration Act passed Oct. 27 by the U.S. Senate, May 11 by the House of Representatives. Church leaders hailed the legislation as "the most historic piece of legislation dealing with religious freedom in our lifetime."

• The first temple in the Caribbean was announced Dec. 4, 1993, by the First Presidency to be built in Santo Domingo, Dominican Republic.

• On Jan. 17, 1994, an earthquake in Southern California measuring 6.6 on the Richter Scale destroyed 15 homes of Church members and displaced an estimated 500-600 members.

• The First Presidency announced Feb. 13, 1994, that the 87-year-old Uintah Stake Tabernacle in Vernal, Utah, will be renovated and dedicated as Utah's 10th temple. It is the first existing building to be renovated into a temple.

• The government of Cambodia officially recognized the Church, announced President Gordon B. Hinckley, first counselor in the First Presidency, on March 6, 1994.

• Elder Russell M. Nelson of the Council of the Twelve dedicated the islands of French Polynesia in Papeete, Tahiti, May 8 during the 150th anniversary of the arrival of LDS missionaries in Tahiti.

• President Howard W. Hunter, President Gordon B. Hinckley and Elder M. Russell Ballard spoke at programs held in Nauvoo and Carthage, Ill., on June 26, 1994, commemorating the 150th anniversary of the martyrdom of the Prophet Joseph Smith.

• Massive relief efforts by the Church and LDS volunteers July 2-12, 1994, helped in the aftermath of the worst flooding in history in 43 counties in Georgia. The homes of 35 LDS families were damaged.

• The First Presidency announced July 28, 1994, that a relief package for the amount of $760,000 was sent to Rwanda, including emergency supplies and funds to deliver the supplies. It was also announced that Church assistance has been distributed in more than 50 countries during recent years.

• The Utah Central Area was consolidated with the Utah North Area, effective Aug. 15, 1994, reducing the number of areas from 23 to 22.

• President Howard W. Hunter addressed full-time missionaries Sept. 13, 1994, over the satellite system.

• Elder Dallin H.Oaks of the Council of the Twelve dedicated the Republic of Cape Verde, islands 400 miles west of Senegal on the Africa Coast, Sept. 14, 1994.

GENERAL
AUTHORITIES,
OFFICERS

GENERAL AUTHORITIES
(Current as of Oct. 1, 1994)

THE FIRST PRESIDENCY

President Howard W. Hunter

President Howard W. Hunter was ordained and set apart as the 14th president of the Church on June 5, 1994, at age 86, after serving nearly 35 years in the Council of the Twelve. He is the first Church president born in the 20th century.

President Hunter immediately began a busy schedule of speaking and traveling. He emphasized the importance of more fully following the example of the Savior. Every adult member of the Church was urged to be temple worthy, hold a current recommend and use it as often as possible.

A lifetime of discipleship to the Savior prepared President Hunter for his calling as prophet and president of the Church. He was born Nov. 14, 1907, in Boise, Idaho, to John William and Nellie Rasmussen Hunter, the eldest of two children. During his childhood he developed a reputation for helping others. He had a strong work ethic. At 15 he earned the Eagle Scout award, the second Scout in Boise to receive the award.

In 1928 he moved to Southern California where he worked for a bank and attended evening classes. He met Clara Jeffs at a Church social and they were married June 10, 1931. They became the parents of three children. One died in early childhood. Sister Hunter died Oct. 9, 1983. On April 12, 1990, he married Inis Bernice Egan.

In 1934, he began schooling for a law degree, which he received in 1939, graduating cum laude from Southwestern University. He passed the bar examination in October 1939 and became a leading corporate attorney.

On Aug. 27, 1940, at age 32, he was called as the first bishop of the newly created El Sereno Ward. A decade later, on Feb. 25, 1950, he was called as the president of the Pasadena Stake. While stake president, he took part in many fund raising and building projects, including a stake center, a welfare farm and the Los Angeles Temple. He served as chairman of the Los Angeles Welfare Region and the Southern California Welfare Region.

A little less than a decade later, on Oct. 9, 1959, he was called by President David O. McKay to be a member of the Council of the Twelve and ordained an apostle Oct. 15, 1959. Among his other assignments, he was involved with the New World Archaeological Foundation, a BYU-based research organization working in Mesoamerica; in the Holy Land with the Orson Hyde Memorial Gardens, which was dedicated in 1979; and at the BYU Jerusalem Center, which he dedicated May 16, 1989.

In more recent years, his perseverance and courage in the face of health difficulties became legendary. In mid-1987 he lost the use of his legs through a combination of health problems. He later regained his ability to walk with the help of a walker.

President Hunter was set apart as acting president of the Twelve on Nov. 10, 1985, at the death of President Spencer W. Kimball. He was set apart as president of the Council of the Twelve June 2, 1988, following the death of President Marion G. Romney. President Hunter died March 3, 1995, at age 87.

Gordon B. Hinckley

President Gordon B. Hinckley was set apart as first counselor to President Howard W. Hunter on June 5, 1994. He served previously in the First Presidency as a counselor to President Spencer W. Kimball from 1981 until President Kimball's death, and as first counselor to President Ezra Taft Benson from 1985 until President Benson's death.

President Hinckley is a vice chairman of the Church Board of Education, a vice chairman of the boards of trustees of BYU and Ricks College, and has served as chairman of the executive committees of these boards. He is chairman of the budget, human resource and audio-visual committees.

He is also chairman of the board of Deseret Management Corporation, Bonneville International Corporation, and other entities.

Born June 23, 1910, in Salt Lake City, to Bryant S. and Ada Bitner Hinckley, President Hinckley was sustained an Assistant to the Twelve April 6, 1958, and ordained an apostle Oct. 5, 1961, at age 51.

He served for 20 years as executive secretary of the Radio, Publicity and Literature Committee of the Church, pioneering the public relations work of the Church, and was one of the pioneers in adapting modern electronic media to Church uses. He was president of the East Millcreek Stake, and is a graduate of the University of Utah.

President Hinckley and his wife, the former Marjorie Pay, have five children.

Thomas S. Monson

President Thomas S. Monson was set apart as second counselor to President Howard W. Hunter on June 5, 1994. He also served as second counselor to President Ezra Taft Benson from Nov. 10, 1985, until President Benson's death. President Monson previously served 22 years in the Council of the Twelve, being called as an apostle on Oct. 4, 1963, at age 36.

He is vice chairman of the General Welfare Services Committee and is chairman of the Welfare Services Executive Committee. He is chairman of the Information and Communications Committee, a vice chairman of the Church Board of Education and a vice chairman of the BYU and Ricks College boards of trustees. He is also on the National Executive Board of Boy Scouts of America.

He is chairman of the board of *Deseret News* Publishing Co., and a director of Newspaper Agency Corp. Before being called as a General Authority, he was general manager of Deseret Press.

Born Aug. 21, 1927, in Salt Lake City, to G. Spencer and Gladys Condie Monson, he graduated cum laude from the University of Utah in business management, and received an MBA degree from BYU. He served in the Navy during World War II.

He was ordained a bishop of a Salt Lake City ward at age 22. President Monson served in the presidency of the Temple View Stake in Salt Lake City and he was called as president of the Canadian Mission in 1959 at age 31. He and his wife, the former Frances Beverly Johnson, are parents of three children.

The Council of the Twelve
(As of October, 1994)

Front row, from left, President Boyd K. Packer, and Elders L. Tom Perry, David B. Haight and James E. Faust. Back row, from left, Elders Neal A. Maxwell, Russell M. Nelson, Dallin H. Oaks, M. Russell Ballard, Joseph B. Wirthlin, Richard G. Scott, Robert D. Hales and Jeffrey R. Holland.

THE COUNCIL OF THE TWELVE

Boyd K. Packer

Set apart as acting President of the Council of the Twelve on June 5, 1994. Sustained an Assistant to the Twelve Sept. 30, 1961; sustained to the Council of the Twelve April 5, 1970, and ordained an apostle April 9, 1970, at age 45. Former supervisor of Seminaries and Institutes of Religion. Former president of the New England Mission. Received his bachelor's and master's degrees from Utah State University, and Ph.D. in educational administration from BYU. Pilot in the Pacific Theater during World War II. Born Sept. 10, 1924, in Brigham City, Utah, a son of Ira Wright and Emma Jensen Packer. Wife, Donna Smith Packer, parents of 10 children.

Serves on the Church Board of Education. Sustained as Assistant to the Twelve Oct. 6, 1972; sustained to the Council of the Twelve on April 6, 1974, and ordained an apostle April 11, 1974, at age 51. Served in the Marines in the Pacific during World War II. Graduated from Utah State University with a B.S. degree in finance; was vice president and treasurer of department store chain in Boston, Mass. Born Aug. 5, 1922, in Logan, Utah, to L. Tom and Nora Sonne Perry. Married Virginia Lee, parents of three children. She died in 1974. Married Barbara Dayton in 1976.

L. Tom Perry

David B. Haight

Serves on the board of directors and executive committee of Bonneville International Corp. and Deseret Management Corp. Sustained an Assistant to the Twelve April 6, 1970; ordained an apostle Jan. 8, 1976, at age 69, and sustained to the Council of the Twelve April 3, 1976. Former regional representative, president of Scottish Mission and stake president. Attended Utah State University. Former mayor of Palo Alto, Calif., district and regional manager of large retail store chain, assistant to president of BYU; a commander in the Navy during World War II. Born Sept. 2, 1906, at Oakley, Idaho, to Hector C. and Clara Tuttle Haight. Wife, Ruby Olson Haight, parents of three children.

James E. Faust

Serves as vice chairman of board and chairman of executive committee of the *Deseret News*. Sustained Assistant to the Twelve Oct. 6, 1972, and to the Presidency of the First Quorum of the Seventy Oct. 1, 1976; sustained to the Council of the Twelve Sept. 30, 1978, and ordained an apostle Oct. 1, 1978, at age 58. Attorney and former state legislator. Served as regional representative and stake president; served in Air Force during World War II. Graduated from University of Utah with B.A. and juris doctorate; was president of Utah Bar Association. Born July 31, 1920, in Delta, Utah, a son of George A. and Amy Finlinson Faust. Wife, Ruth Wright Faust, parents of five children.

Serves on Church Board of Education and BYU Board of Trustees executive committees. Called as Assistant to the Twelve April 6, 1974, and to the Presidency of the First Quorum of the Seventy Oct. 1, 1976; ordained an apostle July 23, 1981, at age 55, and sustained to Council of the Twelve Oct. 3, 1981. Received bachelor's degree in political science and master's degree from the University of Utah; has received four honorary doctorates. Former Church commissioner of education, former YMMIA general board member and regional representative. Former executive vice president of the University of Utah. Born in Salt Lake City, Utah, on July 6, 1926, to Clarence H. and Emma Ash Maxwell. Wife, Colleen Hinckley Maxwell, parents of four children.

Neal A. Maxwell

Russell M. Nelson

Sustained to the Council of the Twelve April 7, 1984, and ordained an apostle April 12, 1984, at age 59. Former Sunday School general president, regional representative and stake president. Renowned surgeon and medical researcher. Received B.A. and M.D. degrees from University of Utah, and Ph.D. from University of Minnesota. Former president of the Society for Vascular Surgery and former chairman of the Council on Cardiovascular Surgery for the American Heart Association. Born in Salt Lake City, Utah, on Sept. 9, 1924, a son of Marion C. and Edna Anderson Nelson. Wife, Dantzel White Nelson, parents of 10 children.

Chairman of the board of the Polynesian Cultural Center in Laie, Hawaii. Sustained to Council of the Twelve April 7, 1984, and ordained apostle on May 3, 1984, at age 51. Graduate of BYU in accounting; received juris doctorate cum laude from University of Chicago; was law clerk to U.S. Supreme Court Chief Justice Earl Warren, practiced law in Chicago, and was professor of law at University of Chicago for 10 years, and was executive director of the American Bar Foundation for a year. Served nine years as president of BYU, and three years as Utah Supreme Court justice. Born Aug. 12, 1932, in Provo, Utah, a son of Dr. Lloyd E. and Stella Harris Oaks. Wife, June Dixon Oaks, parents of six children.

Dallin H. Oaks

M. Russell Ballard

Serves on the Church Board of Education and its board of trustees, and is chairman of the board of Deseret Book. Sustained to the First Quorum of the Seventy April 3, 1976, and to the presidency of the quorum Feb. 21, 1980. Sustained to the Council of the Twelve Oct. 6, 1985, and ordained an apostle Oct. 10, 1985, at age 57. Attended the University of Utah; previously engaged in various business enterprises, including automotive, real estate and investments. Was president of the Canada Toronto Mission; also served as counselor in a mission presidency. The grandson of Apostles Melvin J. Ballard and Hyrum Mack Smith, he was born in Salt Lake City, Utah, on Oct. 8, 1928, to Melvin Russell Sr. and Geraldine Smith Ballard. Wife, Barbara Bowen Ballard, parents of seven children.

Sustained as an Assistant to the Twelve April 4, 1975, to the First Quorum of the Seventy on Oct. 1, 1976, and to the presidency of the quorum on Aug. 28, 1986; sustained to the Council of the Twelve Oct. 4, 1986, and ordained an apostle Oct. 9, 1986, at age 69. Served in the Sunday School general presidency, former stake president's counselor. Graduate of University of Utah in business management; former president of trade association in Utah. Born June 11, 1917, in Salt Lake City, Utah, to Joseph L. and Madeline Bitner Wirthlin. Wife, Elisa Young Rogers Wirthlin, parents of eight children.

Joseph B. Wirthlin

Richard G. Scott

Sustained to the First Quorum of the Seventy April 2, 1977, and to the presidency of the quorum on Oct. 1, 1983; sustained to the Council of the Twelve on Oct. 1, 1988, and ordained an apostle Oct. 6, 1988, at age 59. Received B.S. degree in mechanical engineering from George Washington University, and completed post-graduate work in nuclear engineering at Oakridge, Tenn. Worked 12 years on the staff of Adm. Hyman Rickover, developing military and private nuclear power reactors; subsequently consultant to nuclear power industry. Born Nov. 7, 1928, in Pocatello, Idaho, to Kenneth Leroy and Mary Eliza Whittle Scott. Wife, Jeanene Watkins Scott, parents of seven children, five of whom are living.

Sustained an Assistant to the Twelve April 4, 1975, and to the First Quorum of the Seventy Oct. 1, 1976; sustained as Presiding Bishop April 6, 1985; sustained to the Council of the Twelve April 2, 1994, and ordained an apostle April 7, 1994, at age 61. Former first counselor in the Sunday School general presidency, president of the England London Mission, regional representative, and served in various leadership positions, including stake president's counselor in the United States, England, Germany and Spain. Earned bachelor's degree from the University of Utah, and master of business administration degree from Harvard; served in the U.S. Air Force as a jet fighter pilot; was an executive with four major national companies. Born Aug. 24, 1932, in New York City, N.Y., to John Rulon and Vera Marie Holbrook Hales. Wife, Mary Elene Crandall Hales, parents of two sons.

Robert D. Hales

Jeffrey R. Holland

Sustained to the First Quorum of the Seventy on April 1, 1989, while serving as president of Brigham Young University in Provo, Utah; ordained an apostle June 23, 1994, at age 53; sustained to the Council of the Twelve Oct. 1, 1994. Former Church commissioner of education and director or instructor at many institutes of religion. Received bachelor's degree in English and master's degree in religious education from Brigham Young University, and received master's degree and doctorate in American studies from Yale University. Born Dec. 3, 1940, in St. George, Utah, a son of Frank D. and Alice Bentley Holland. Wife, Patricia Terry Holland, parents of three children.

PRESIDENCY OF THE QUORUMS OF THE SEVENTY

Rex D. Pinegar

Sustained to First Council of the Seventy Oct. 6, 1972, at age 41; sustained to First Quorum of the Seventy Oct. 1, 1976, and to the quorum presidency on Sept. 30, 1989. Served as counselor in the Young Men general presidency from 1979-85. Received bachelor's degree from BYU, a master's degree from San Francisco State College, and a doctorate in education from the University of Southern California. Former chairman of the Educational Psychology Department at BYU. Born Sept. 18, 1931, in Orem, Utah, to John F. and Grace Murl Ellis Pinegar. Wife, Bonnie Lee Crabb Pinegar, parents of six children.

Sustained to the First Quorum of the Seventy April 3, 1976, at age 49; served in the Presidency of the First Quorum of the Seventy, 1980-1986, and sustained to the presidency for the second time Oct. 1, 1989. Former president of the Texas North Mission, and served on the Sunday School general board. Received bachelor's degree and doctorate in educational administration from University of Utah. Was professor of education at BYU and assistant dean at BYU-Hawaii. Born June 12, 1926, in Sutherland, (Millard Co.), Utah, to A.E. Lyle and Elsie Egan Asay. Wife, Colleen Webb Asay, parents of eight children, seven of whom are living.

Carlos E. Asay

Charles Didier

Sunday School general president. Sustained to the First Quorum of the Seventy Oct. 3, 1975, at age 39; called to the Presidency of the Seventy Aug. 15, 1992, and sustained Oct. 3, 1992. Was president of France Switzerland Mission and regional representative; converted to Church in 1957; fluent in five languages, Flemish, French, German, Spanish and English. Received bachelor's degree in economics from University of Liege in Belgium; served as officer in the Belgian Air Force Reserve. Born Oct. 5, 1935, at Ixelles, Belgium, to Andre and Gabrielle Colpaert Didier. Wife, Lucie Lodomez Didier, parents of two sons.

L. Aldin Porter

Sustained to the First Quorum of the Seventy April 4, 1987, at age 55, and sustained to the Second Quorum of the Seventy on April 1, 1989; sustained to the First Quorum of the Seventy April 6, 1992; called to the Presidency of the Seventy Aug. 15, 1992, and sustained Oct. 3, 1992. Former counselor in the Boise Idaho Temple presidency, president of the Louisiana Baton Rouge Mission, regional representative, stake president, and bishop. A graduate of BYU, he was an executive of a financial planning company. Born June 30, 1931, in Salt Lake City, Utah, to J. Lloyd and Revon Hayward Porter; wife, Shirley Palmer Porter, parents of six children.

Sustained to the First Quorum of the Seventy April 1, 1989, at age 59, while serving as president of Ricks College in Rexburg, Idaho; called to the Presidency of the Seventy Aug. 15, 1993, and sustained Oct. 2, 1993. Former mission president in Mexico, president of the Missionary Training Center in Provo, Utah, counselor in the Young Men and Melchizedek Priesthood MIA; active in Scouting, serving as council commissioner and a member of the National Exploring Standing Committee. Received bachelor's degree from BYU, doctorate in education from Washington State University. Served as associate commissioner of education for the Church Educational System and has been director of several institutes of religion. Born July 21, 1929, in Banida, Idaho, to Joseph A. and Goldie Miles Christensen. Wife, Barbara Kohler Christensen, parents of six children.

Joe J. Christensen

Monte J. Brough

Sustained to the First Quorum of the Seventy Oct. 1, 1988, at age 49; sustained to the Second Quorum of the Seventy April 1, 1989; sustained to the First Quorum of the Seventy April 6, 1991; called to the Presidency of the Seventy Aug. 15, 1993, and sustained Oct. 2, 1993. Former regional representative, president of the Minnesota Minneapolis Mission, member of the Young Men General Board, and bishop. Received bachelor's degree and doctorate in business administration from University of Utah; former president and founder of financial management company. Born June 11, 1939, in Randolph, Utah, to Richard Muir and Gwendolyn Kearl Brough. Wife, Lanette Barker Brough, parents of seven children.

Sustained to the First Quorum of the Seventy April 1, 1989, at age 60; called to the Presidency of the Seventy Aug. 15, 1993, and sustained Oct. 2, 1993. Former stake president, stake Young Men president, and bishop. Graduate of Utah State University, where he received bachelor's degree in agricultural economics; received juris doctorate from the University of Utah; former trial lawyer, president of the Utah State Bar Association; served on active duty in the Army during the Korean War, and in the U.S. Army Reserve from 1950-1980. Born Aug. 23, 1928, in Tremonton, Utah, to Warren E. and Ruth Steed Hansen. Wife, Jeanine Showell Hansen, parents of six children.

W. Eugene Hansen

FIRST QUORUM OF THE SEVENTY

President of the Mexico North Area. Sustained to the First Quorum of the Seventy April 4, 1981, at age 47; first Argentine General Authority. Former president of Argentina Rosario Mission and the Buenos Aires Argentina Temple, stake president and regional representative. Graduate of University of Buenos Aires; certified public accountant; served as secretary of the treasury in San Miguel, Argentina. Born Sept. 13, 1933, in Buenos Aires, Argentina, to Edealo and Zulema Estrada Abrea. Wife, Maria Victoria Chiapparino de Abrea, parents of three daughters.

Angel Abrea

President of the Central America Area. Sustained to the Second Quorum of the Seventy April 1, 1989, at age 44; called to the First Quorum of the Seventy June 6, 1992, and sustained Oct. 3, 1992. Former president of the Guatemala Guatemala City Mission, where he was assigned to reopen the El Salvador San Salvador Mission, chairman of the Guatemala City Temple Committee, former regional representative, stake president and counselor, bishop, and branch president. Received degree from the Technical Vocational Institute of Guatemala City; former technical draftsman, and later became an area director for the Church Educational System. Born Sept. 25, 1944, in Guatemala City, Guatemala, to Carlos and Rosario Funes de Amado. Wife, Mayavel Pineda Amado, parents of five children.

Carlos H. Amado

Second counselor in the Europe Mediterranean Area presidency. Sustained to the First Quorum of the Seventy April 3, 1993, at age 41. President of the France Bordeaux Mission from 1989-1992, former stake president and stake president's counselor. Graduated cum laude with a bachelor's degree from BYU, master of business from Harvard Graduate School of Business. Vice president of Morton Plant Health System; former partner in and later owner of advertising agencies. Born Aug. 9, 1951, in Logan, Utah, to Lyle P. and Kathryn Andersen. Wife, Kathy Sue Williams Andersen, parents of four children.

Neil L. Andersen

President of the Philippines/Micronesia Area. Sustained to the Second Quorum of the Seventy on April 1, 1989, at age 56; called to the First Quorum of the Seventy June 6, 1992, and sustained Oct. 3, 1992. Former president of the Scotland Edinburgh Mission, was stake president, and bishop of three different wards. Attended the University of Utah and was owner and president of lumber company; formerly employed by two road machinery equipment companies. Born April 4, 1932, in Murray, Utah, to Ben F. and Samantha Berry Banks. Wife, Susan Kearnes Banks, parents of seven children and one foster child.

Ben B. Banks

William R. Bradford

First counselor in the North America Central Area presidency. Sustained to the First Quorum of the Seventy Oct. 3, 1975, at age 41, while president of Chile Mission; lived in Latin America and Asia for several years while in Church leadership positions. Was in fruit growing and shipping business in Texas, and owner of a company that grew citrus and tropical fruits in Texas, Mexico and Central America for distribution in the United States and other countries; attended BYU. Born Oct. 25, 1933, in Springville, Utah, to Rawsel W. and Mary Waddoups Bradford. Wife, Mary Ann Bird Bradford, parents of six children.

President of the North America Northwest Area. Sustained to the First Quorum of the Seventy Sept. 30, 1978, at age 53. Former president of Central American Mission, and has lived for several years in Latin America on Church assignments. Former regional representative, stake president and stake president's counselor. Graduate of University of Alberta in pharmacology; former pharmacist in Calgary, Alberta, area; veteran of the Royal Canadian Air Force during World War II. Born March 30, 1925, at Raymond, Alberta, to Lee and Jane Fisher Brewerton. Wife, Dorothy Hall Brewerton, parents of six children.

Ted E. Brewerton

F. Enzio Busche

Second counselor in the North America Southwest Area presidency. Sustained to the First Quorum of the Seventy Oct. 1, 1977, at age 47. Former president of Frankfurt Germany Temple, Germany Munich Mission, regional representative and district president; converted to the Church in 1958. Graduate in economics and management from Bonn and Freiburg universities, and did graduate studies in technical printing; former chief executive officer of large printing and publishing company in Germany. Born April 5, 1930, at Dortmund, Germany, to Friedrich and Anna Weber Busche. Wife, Jutta Baum Busche, parents of four children.

President of the Asia Area. Sustained to the First Quorum of the Seventy April 7, 1984, at age 52, while president of Idaho Boise Mission. Former regional representative, stake president. Received B.A. degree from BYU, law degree from University of California at Los Angeles; an attorney, he was legislative assistant in California Legislature; was president of a law firm in Los Angeles and past president of Westwood Bar Association. Born May 10, 1931, in Winslow, Ariz., to Cecil E. and Gladys Bushman Carmack. Wife, Shirley Fay Allen Carmack, parents of five children.

John K. Carmack

Second counselor in the Mexico South Area presidency. Sustained to the First Quorum of the Seventy April 3, 1993, at age 48. Former regional representative, stake president, stake president's counselor, bishop. Received bachelor's degree from BYU, juris doctorate from Duke University. Associate general counsel of NationsBank Corp. in Charlotte, N.C.; practiced law in Washington D.C. and was volunteer chairman of Middle Tennessee Literacy Coalition, and Affordable Housing of Nashville, Tenn. Born Jan. 24, 1945, in American Fork, Utah, to Paul V. and Jeanne Swenson Christofferson. Wife, Katherine Thelma Jacob Christofferson, parents of five children.

D. Todd Christofferson

President of the Africa Area. Sustained as second counselor in Presiding Bishopric Oct. 1, 1976, at age 49, to the First Quorum of the Seventy April 6, 1985, and to the Presidency of the First Quorum of the Seventy Oct. 1, 1988, serving until Aug. 15, 1993. Former president of the South Africa Cape Town Mission, regional representative, stake president, counselor in a stake presidency. Graduate of BYU with B.S. in marketing, did graduate work at Stanford University; former agency manager for life insurance company in Boise, Idaho. Born April 4, 1927, at Rexburg, Idaho, to John Roland and Nora L. Redford Clark. Wife, Barbara Jean Reed Clarke, parents of eight children.

J. Richard Clarke

First counselor in the the North America Northwest Area presidency. Sustained to the Second Quorum of the Seventy April 1, 1989, at age 48; called to the First Quorum of the Seventy June 6, 1992, and sustained Oct. 3, 1992. Former president of the Austria Vienna Mission, regional representative, stake president and bishop of two wards. Former professor of sociology and ancient scripture at Brigham Young University; has received the Karl G. Maeser Distinguished Teaching Award and Honors Program professor-of-the-year honors. Born Aug. 27, 1940, in Preston, Idaho, to Spencer C. and Josie Peterson Condie. Wife, Dorthea Speth Condie, parents of five children.

Spencer J. Condie

First counselor in the North America Southwest Area presidency. Sustained to First Council of the Seventy Oct. 3, 1975, at age 34, and to the First Quorum of the Seventy Oct. 1, 1976. Former executive secretary to the First Council of the Seventy, president of Uruguay-Paraguay Mission, and lived in Latin American countries for many years while on Church assignments. Previously was consultant, agency manager and trainer for life insurance firm, was management trainer for Church employment. Received bachelor's and master's degrees in business administration from Arizona State University. Born Sept. 1, 1941, at Lehi, Utah, to Clarence H. and Myrl Johnson Cook. Wife, Janelle Schlink Cook, parents of eight children.

Gene R. Cook

Robert K. Dellenbach

First counselor in the Europe Area presidency. Sustained to the Second Quorum of the Seventy March 31, 1990, at age 52; called to the First Quorum of the Seventy June 6, 1992, and sustained Oct. 3, 1992. Former president of the Germany Duesseldorf and Germany Munich missions, regional representative, stake president and bishop. Former president, vice president, and business manager of various universities; has worked for the Salk Institute and was involved with a company that assisted agencies and scientific institutes in the Soviet Union. Born May 10, 1937, in Salt Lake City, Utah, to Frank and Leona Conshafter Dellenbach. Wife, Mary-Jayne Broadbent Dellenbach, parents of three sons.

President of the North America West Area. Sustained to the First Council of the Seventy April 6, 1968, at age 37, and to the First Quorum of the Seventy Oct. 1, 1976; has lived in Brazil, Australia, Philippines and New Zealand while in Church leadership positions. Former counselor in mission presidency. Received degree in journalism and economics from BYU and M.S. in public relations from Boston University; former executive with economic development board in Boston, where he was noted for his work in regional economic planning. Born June 12, 1930, in Tooele, Utah, to Alex F. and Carol Horsfall Dunn. Wife, Sharon Longden Dunn, parents of five children.

Loren C. Dunn

Henry B. Eyring

Second counselor in the North America West Area presidency and serves as Commissioner of Education for the Church Educational System. Sustained first counselor in the Presiding Bishopric April 6, 1985, at age 51; sustained to the First Quorum of the Seventy Oct. 3, 1992. Former regional representative, member of the Sunday School General Board and bishop. Received bachelor's degree from University of Utah, and master's and doctorate from Harvard University. Former commissioner and deputy commissioner of education for Church Educational System, and former president of Ricks College. Born May 31, 1933, in Princeton, N.J., to Henry and Mildred Bennion Eyring. Wife, Kathleen Johnson Eyring, parents of six children.

Second counselor in the North America Northeast Area presidency, second counselor in the Young Men general presidency. Sustained as second counselor in Presiding Bishopric April 6, 1972, at age 41; sustained to the First Quorum of the Seventy Oct. 1, 1976. Former Young Men general president, president of Texas San Antonio Mission, member of the YMMIA General Board and stake president; member, Boy Scouts of America National Executive Board, recipient of Silver Antelope and Silver Buffalo awards; former corporate training manager of supermarket chain based in Boise, Idaho. Born March 26, 1931, at Stockton, Utah, to Stephen E. and Emma M. Johnson Featherstone. Wife, Merlene Miner Featherstone, parents of seven children.

Vaughn J Featherstone

Young Men general president and first counselor in the Utah South Area presidency. Sustained to the First Quorum of the Seventy Sept. 30, 1978, at age 50, and served in the Presidency of the Seventy, 1985-87. Former counselor in Aaronic Priesthood MIA general presidency, former president of the Arizona Tempe Mission, regional representative, stake president and bishop. Graduate of University of Utah; was vice president of a metals corporation, also served as officer in U.S. Air Force. Born April 18, 1928, in Salt Lake City, Utah, to Jack H. and Anita Jack Goaslind. Wife, Gwen Caroline Bradford Goaslind, parents of six children.

Jack H Goaslind

Second counselor in the Asia Area presidency. Sustained to the First Quorum of the Seventy April 3, 1976, at age 41. Former president of the Tonga Mission, regional representative and bishop. Has lived in South America and Hawaii while in Church leadership positions. Received bachelor's degree from BYU, master of business administration degree from Indiana University, where he also taught; formerly in real estate, development, and construction; was vice president of Idaho State Real Estate Association. Born June 17, 1934, in Idaho Falls, Idaho, to Delbert V. and Jennie Holbrook Groberg. Wife, Jean Sabin Groberg, parents of 11 children.

John H. Groberg

Second counselor in the North America Central Area presidency. Sustained to the Second Quorum of the Seventy April 1, 1989, at age 55; sustained to the First Quorum of the Seventy April 3, 1993. Former president of the Bolivia Cochabamba Mission, stake president, bishop and temple worker in the Idaho Falls Temple. Was professor of religion at Ricks College; served eight terms in the Idaho State Legislature and was minority leader for three terms. Born Dec. 19, 1933, in Blackfoot, Idaho, to Floyd Milton and Ruby Hoge Hammond. Wife, Bonnie Sellers Hammond, parents of six children.

F. Melvin Hammond

President of the Brazil Area. Sustained to the Second Quorum of the Seventy March 31, 1990, at age 54; sustained to the First Quorum of the Seventy April 6, 1991. Former regional representative, and was president of the Portugal Lisbon Mission, stake president and counselor. An orthodontist, he has been president of the Idaho Falls (Idaho) Dental Society, Idaho State Orthodontic Society, president of the Rocky Mountain Society of Orthodontists, and president of the Teton Peaks Council, Boy Scouts of America. Born Sept. 1, 1935, at Sugar City, Idaho, to Gordon R. and Florence Evelyn Skidmore Hillam. Wife, Carol Lois Rasmussen Hillam, parents of seven children.

Harold G. Hillam

First counselor in the North America Southeast Area presidency and second counselor in the Sunday School general presidency. Sustained to the First Quorum of the Seventy Sept. 30, 1978, at age 45. Former president of Uruguay Montevideo Mission and stake president; was special representative for First Presidency in Latin American affairs. Graduate of Utah State University, received law degree from the University of Utah; former assistant attorney general for Utah, chief counsel for Utah Tax Commission, legal counsel for Mexico in Intermountain Area and managing partner of Salt Lake City law firm. Born March 24, 1933, at Logan, Utah, to Fred P. and Beatrice Ward Howard. Wife, Caroline Heise Howard, parents of five children.

F. Burton Howard

President of the New York Rochester Mission. Sustained to the First Quorum of the Seventy April 1, 1989, at age 46. Former regional representative, stake president and bishop. Received bachelor's degree in German from Brigham Young University and juris doctorate from the University of Utah; was attorney specializing in business and estate planning. Born May 18, 1942, in Ogden, Utah, to Keith G. and Lula Hill Jensen. Wife, Kathleen Bushnell Jensen, parents of eight children.

Marlin K. Jensen

President of the Europe North Area. Sustained to the Second Quorum of the Seventy March 31, 1990, at age 49; sustained to First Quorum of the Seventy April 3, 1993. Former regional representative and stake president; converted to the Church in 1959. Graduated from Norwich City College in England and did graduate work at the City and Guilds of London Institute of Printing; former college instructor and partner in a British insurance brokerage firm. Born July 5, 1940, at Norwich, England, to Bertie A.M. and Ada Hutson Johnson. Wife, Pamela Wilson Johnson, parents of a son.

Kenneth Johnson

Sustained to the First Quorum of the Seventy April 2, 1988, at age 56; sustained to the Second Quorum of the Seventy April 1, 1989; sustained to the First Quorum of the Seventy April 6, 1991. Former president of Florida Tampa Mission, regional representative, and stake president; converted to the Church while in the U.S. Air Force in 1954. Received bachelor's, master's and doctoral degrees of education from Louisiana State University; was professor of health education and director of the Regional Training Center at East Carolina University. Born Sept. 19, 1931, in Baton Rouge, La., to Bonnie Delen and Edna Campbell Forbes Kendrick. Wife, Myrtis Lee Noble Kendrick, parents of four children.

L. Lionel Kendrick

President of Tokyo Temple. Sustained to the First Quorum of the Seventy Oct. 1, 1977, at age 36; first native-born Japanese called as General Authority. Former president of Hawaii Honolulu Mission, was stake president and counselor to mission president; converted to the Church in 1955. Graduated from Asia University of Tokyo in business psychology and management; former sales manager over Japan for a cookware company, president of a Japanese food storage company. Born July 25, 1941, to Hatsuo and Koyo Ideda Kikuchi at Hokkaido, Japan. Wife, Toshiko Koshiya Kikuchi, parents of four children.

Yoshihiko Kikuchi

President of the North America Northeast Area. Sustained to the Second Quorum of the Seventy April 6, 1991, at age 57, and to the First Quorum April 2, 1994. Former regional representative, president of the New York New York Mission, stake president twice and bishop. Was managing partner in a law firm. Received bachelor's degree from University of Utah, juris doctorate from the University of Southern California. Born July 11, 1933, in Santaquin, Utah, to Cree Clarence and Melba Nelson Kofford. Wife, Ila Macdonald, parents of five children.

Cree-L Kofford

President of the Europe/Mediterranean Area. Sustained to the First Quorum of the Seventy Oct. 1, 1976, at age 49, and to the quorum presidency Feb. 22, 1980, serving until Aug. 15, 1993. Served as president of the Texas South Mission, regional representative, member of the Sunday School general board, secretary of Adult Correlation Committee, member of Priesthood Missionary Committee. Graduated from Utah State University in English, was basketball coach and seminary teacher. Born May 24, 1927, at Hyrum, Utah, to Edgar Niels and Gertrude Prouse Larsen. Wife, Geneal Johnson Larsen, parents of five children.

Dean L. Larsen

President of the South America South Area. Sustained to the Second Quorum of the Seventy March 31, 1990, at age 54, and to the First Quorum April 3, 1993. Former president of the Colombia Cali Mission, regional representative, stake president and bishop. Attended Ricks College and graduated from BYU. Served on a hospital board and in farm associations; formerly self-employed as a farmer and potato shipper. Born July 21, 1935, at Idaho Falls, Idaho, to Lloyd P. and Reva Faye Willmore Mickelsen. Wife, Jeanine Andersen Mickelsen, parents of nine children.

Lynn A. Mickelsen

Alexander B. Morrison

Second counselor in the Utah North Area presidency. Sustained to the First Quorum of the Seventy April 4, 1987, at age 56; sustained to the Second Quorum of the Seventy April 1, 1989; sustained to the First Quorum of the Seventy April 6, 1991. Former regional representative, bishop, and branch president. Received master's degrees from University of Alberta and University of Michigan, and doctorate at Cornell University, formerly professor and chairman of Food Sciences Department at University of Guelph in Canada, and was assistant deputy minister of National Health and Welfare for Canada, honored for humanitarian work. Born Dec. 22, 1930, in Edmonton, Alberta, to Alexander S. and Christina Wilson Morrison. Wife, Shirley Brooks Morrison, parents of eight children.

President of the Europe Area. Sustained to the Second Quorum of the Seventy April 6, 1991, at age 51; sustained to First Quorum of the Seventy Oct. 1, 1994. Former president of the Austria Vienna East Mission and counselor in mission presidency. Was manager of International Area of Acquisitions Division of the Church Genealogical Department. Received bachelor's degree from BYU, master's degree and doctorate in Russian literature from Syracuse University in New York. Born Oct. 6, 1939, at Salt Lake City, Utah, to George Henry and Genevieve Bramwell Neuenschwander. Wife, LeAnn Clement Neuenschwander, parents of four sons.

Dennis B. Neuenschwander

Glenn L. Pace

President of the Australia Sydney North Mission. Sustained as second counselor in the Presiding Bishopric April 6, 1985, at age 45; sustained to the First Quorum of the Seventy Oct. 3, 1992. Former bishop's counselor, stake clerk, and elders quorum president. Received bachelor's and master's degrees in accounting from BYU; was a certified public accountant, employed by a national accounting firm and was chief financial officer for a land development company; managing director of Church Welfare Services for nearly four years. Born March 21, 1940, in Provo, Utah, to Kenneth LeRoy and Elizabeth A. Wilde Pace. Wife, Jolene Clayson Pace, parents of six children.

President of the North America Central Area. Sustained to the First Quorum of the Seventy April 2, 1977, at age 48, and to the quorum presidency Aug. 15, 1987, serving until Aug. 15, 1993. Former executive secretary to the Council of the Twelve, president of the Franco-Belgian (now Belgium Brussels) Mission. Graduate of BYU, former executive director of Utah Committee on Children and Youth, and was on board of directors of National Committee on Children and Youth. Born May 6, 1928, in Salt Lake City, Utah, to James F. and Ruth C. Martin Paramore. Wife, Helen Heslington Paramore, parents of six children.

James M. Paramore

Sustained to the First Quorum of the Seventy Oct. 1, 1994, at age 47. Fotmer regional representative, president of the Mexico Merida Mission from 1981-84, and stake president. Received bachelor's degree from the University of Utah, and graduated from the University of Pacific Dental School; practiced dentistry in Salt Lake City for 20 years. Did volunteer work with the Lowell Bennion Community Service Center and Utah Bolivia Partners. Born June 8, 1947, in San Francisco, Calif., to Wayne Leo and Virginia Parker Peterson. Wife, Christine Ann Swensen Peterson, parents of eight children.

Andrew W. Peterson

First counselor in the Europe North Area presidency. Sustained to the First Quorum of the Seventy Oct. 1, 1977, at age 43, and served in the quorum presidency from Oct. 4, 1986-Oct. 1, 1989; served twice as general president of the Sunday School, 1979-86 and 1989-92. Former regional representative and president of Pennsylvania Harrisburg Mission. Graduate of University of Utah, former area general agent for insurance company, president of Deseret Foundation of LDS Hospital, was appointed to serve on several governmental boards. Born Jan. 15, 1934, in Salt Lake City, Utah, to Lawrence Sylvester and Florence Boden Pinnock. Wife, Anne Hawkins Pinnock, parents of six children.

Hugh W. Pinnock

Second counselor in the Utah South Area presidency. Sustained to the First Quorum of the Seventy April 1, 1978, at age 49; served in Sunday School general presidency, 1979-81, and from Oct. 3, 1992 to Aug. 15, 1994. Graduate of the University of Utah with juris doctorate; also graduated from Harvard University's Graduate School of Business Administration, Advanced Management Program; was vice president, secretary and director of trucking company. Born May 10, 1928, in Salt Lake City, Utah, to Hendrick and Ella May Perkins Poelman. Married Claire Howell Stoddard, parents of four children; she died May 5, 1979. Married Anne G. Osborn June 29, 1982.

Ronald E. Poelman

First counselor in the Europe/Mediterranean Area presidency. Sustained to the First Quorum of the Seventy April 6, 1985, at age 59. First native of Switzerland to become a General Authority; was regional representative and stake president in Zurich, Switzerland, and bishop. Retired colonel in the Swiss army; was electrical engineer, architect, industrial designer and planner for laboratories and factories. Born Nov. 2, 1925, in Zurich, Switzerland, to Carl and Maria Reif Ringger. Wife, Helen Suzy Zimmer Ringger, parents of four children.

Hans B. Ringger

Cecil O. Samuelson Jr.

Sustained to the First Quorum of the Seventy on Oct. 1, 1994, at age 53. Former regional representative and stake president. He received bachelor's and master's degrees and medical degree from the University of Utah; was a physician and senior vice president of Intermountain Health Care and former vice president for health sciences and dean of the School of Medicine at the University of Utah; served as director of the Utah Chapter of the American Red Cross and Catholic Heathcare West in San Francisco. Born Aug. 1, 1941, to Cecil Osborn Samuelson Sr. and Janet Brazier Mitchell Samuelson. Wife, Sharon Giauque Samuelson; parents of five children.

President of the Utah South Area. Called to the First Quorum of the Seventy Jan. 1, 1991, and sustained April 6, 1991, at age 56. Former regional representative, president of the Australia Sydney Mission, counselor in the presidencies of the Eastern States, Utah North and Utah Ogden missions, and bishop. Formerly corporate attorney for Kennecott Copper Corp.; graduated from the University of Utah Law School and earned a master's degree from New York University. Born June 11, 1934, in Bountiful, Utah, to William W. and Sylvia Carr Tingey. Wife, Joanne Wells Tingey, parents of four children.

Earl C. Tingey

Robert E. Wells

First counselor in the Central America Area presidency. Sustained to the First Quorum of the Seventy Oct. 1, 1976, at age 48. Former mission president in Mexico and served as branch president, district president, regional representative in Latin America. Graduate of BYU; was former head of Central Purchasing for the Church, and former banking executive in South America for 18 years for a New York City-based bank. Born Dec. 28, 1927, in Las Vegas, Nev., to Robert Stephen and Zella Verona Earl Wells. Married Meryl Leavitt, who died in 1960. Wife, Helen Walser, parents of seven children, including Sharlene Wells Hawkes, Miss America of 1985.

THE SECOND QUORUM OF THE SEVENTY

President of the Mexico South Area. Called to the Second Quorum of the Seventy June 6, 1992, at age 47, and sustained Oct. 3, 1992. Former regional representative, president of the Mexico Mexico City South Mission, patriarch, stake president's counselor twice and bishop. Church Educational System coordinator for Mexico. Received bachelor's degree in education from Superior School of Mexico. Born July 18, 1944, in Arteaga, Couhiula, Mexico, to Lino and Margarita Vasquez Alvarez. Wife, Argelia de Villanueva de Alvarez, parents of three children.

Lino Alvarez

Dallas N. Archibald

Second counselor in the Brazil Area presidency. Called to the Second Quorum of the Seventy June 6, 1992, at age 53, and sustained Oct. 3, 1992. Former regional representative, president of the Spain Seville Mission and bishop. Was vice president of an international industrial chemical company and lived in seven other countries. Received bachelor's degree in Spanish from Weber State College, master's degree from Thunderbird Graduate School of International Management. Born July 24, 1938, in Logan, Utah, to Ezra Wilson and Marguerite Nielsen Archibald. Wife, Linda Ritchie Archibald, parents of one daughter.

Second counselor in the South America North Area presidency. Sustained to the Second Quorum of the Seventy March 31, 1990, at age 52. Former president of the Uruguay Montevideo Mission, regional representative, sealer in the Santiago Chile Temple, president of two stakes, and district president; converted to the Church in 1969. Former administrator of an electrical company in Santiago, Chile, and director of seminaries and institutes for the Church Educational System. Born May 3, 1937, in Coronel, Chile, to Magdonio and Maria Aburto Ayala. Wife, Blanca Espinoza de Ayala, parents of three children.

Eduardo Ayala

C. Max Caldwell

Second counselor in the Philippines/Micronesia Area presidency. Called to the Second Quorum of the Seventy June 6, 1992, at age 58, and sustained Oct. 3, 1992. Former regional representative, president of the Louisiana Baton Rouge Mission, stake president's counselor and bishop. Former associate professor of Church history at BYU. Received bachelor's degree from the University of Utah in business management and master's degree from BYU in Church history and doctrine. Born Dec. 4, 1933, in Salt Lake City, Utah, to Chellus M. and Electa J. Caldwell. Wife, Bonnie Adamson Caldwell, parents of five children.

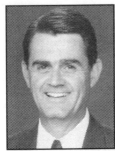

Gary J. Coleman

First counselor in the Mexico South Area presidency. Called to the Second Quorum of the Seventy June 6, 1992, at age 50, and sustained Oct. 3, 1992. Former president of the California Arcadia Mission, counselor in the Utah Ogden Mission, stake president's counselor and bishop. Was associate director and instructor at Weber State University Institute of Religion. Received bachelor's degree in physical education from Washington State University, master's degree and doctorate from BYU in counseling and guidance. Born Sept. 18, 1941, Wenatchee, Wash., to Benton Joseph and Evalin Barrett Coleman. Wife, Judith Renee England Coleman, parents of six children.

Second counselor in the South America South Area presidency. Sustained to the Second Quorum of the Seventy April 2, 1994, at age 45. Served as president of the Brazil Manaus Mission 1990-93, regional representative, stake president's counselor and bishop. Graduated from Colegio Pio XII, attended Paulista School of Marketing, Paulista Institute of Gems and Precious Metals. Former Church Educational System associate area director, diamond cutter, manager of jewelry store chain and finance director of diversified Almeida Prado Co. Born March 25, 1949, in Santos, Brazil, to Nelson Mendes Costa and Luzia Tassar Simoes Costa. Wife, Margareth Fernandes Morgado Mendes Costa; parents of four children.

Claudio R. M. Costa

Rulon G. Craven

Second counselor in the North America Southeast Area presidency. Called to the Second Quorum of the Seventy Dec. 5, 1990, at age 66, and sustained April 6, 1991. Former president of the New Zealand North Mission, regional representative, member of the Sunday School general board, stake president's counselor and bishop. Secretary to the Council of the Twelve from 1974-1990. Received bachelor's degree from BYU. Born Nov. 11, 1924, in Murray, Utah, to Gerald and Susie Craven. Wife, Donna Lunt Craven, parents of six children.

Second counselor in North America Northwest Area presidency. Sustained to the Second Quorum of the Seventy March 31, 1990, at age 66. Former counselor in the general presidency of the Aaronic Priesthood MIA and Young Men general presidency, president of the Florida Tallahassee Mission, regional representative, stake president and bishop. Was dentist; attended University of Utah, received master's degree and doctorate in dentistry and orthodontics from the University of Missouri at Kansas City. Served in the Army from 1943-44. Born May 22, 1924, in Salt Lake City, Utah, to Alexander R. and Genevieve Raine Curtis. Wife, Patricia Glade Curtis, parents of eight children.

LeGrand R. Curtis

First counselor in the South America North Area presidency. Sustained to the Second Quorum of the Seventy April 6, 1991, at age 58. Former regional representative twice, president of the Colombia Cali Mission, stake president and branch president. Printing business owner and Church employee. Converted to the Church in 1968. Educated in Bogota, Colombia, trade schools. Born May 23, 1932, in Bucaramunga, Colombia, to Julio E. Davila Villamicar and Rita Penalosa de Davila. Wife, Mary Zapata Davila, parents of two daughters.

Julio E. Davila

First counselor in the South America South area presidency. Called to the Second Quorum of the Seventy June 6, 1992, at age 48, and sustained Oct. 3, 1992. Former president of the Mexico City Mexico North Mission, stake president and stake president's counselor. Was vice president of sawmill and timber company. Received bachelor's degree from Brigham Young University in business administration. Born July 12, 1943, in Tacoma, Wash., to John H. and Helen Baird Dickson. Wife, Deloris Jones Dickson, parents of eight children.

John B. Dickson

Second counselor in the Europe North Area presidency. Sustained to the Second Quorum of the Seventy April 6, 1991, at age 64. Former counselor in the Young Men general presidency, 1977-79, president of the Missouri Independence Mission, stake president and bishop. Formerly president of a real estate management firm. Received bachelor's degree in business administration from University of Utah, did post-graduate work. Born March 30, 1927, in Salt Lake City, Utah, to Graham H. and Leone Watson Doxey. Wife, Mary Lou Young Doxey, parents of 12 children.

Graham W. Doxey

President of the Utah North Area. Called to the Second Quorum of the Seventy June 6, 1992, at age 47, and sustained Oct. 3, 1992. Former regional representative, president of the Georgia Atlanta Mission, stake president and stake president's counselor. Was consultant and financial adviser to international oil and gas company. Received bachelor's and master's degrees in accounting from BYU. Born Nov. 10, 1944, in Redding, Calif., to R. Walter and Lois Manita Clayton Fowler. Wife, Marie S. Spilsbury Fowler, parents of six children.

John E. Fowler

First counselor in the Asia North Area presidency. Called to the Second Quorum of the Seventy June 1, 1991, at age 52, and sustained Oct. 5, 1991. He is the first Korean General Authority. Former president of the Korea Pusan Mission, regional representative, district president and branch president; converted in 1957. Was regional manager for Church Temporal Affairs in Seoul and former dairy products company employee. Graduated from Hongik University in Seoul, Korea. Born Dec. 10, 1938, in Seoul, Korea, to Han Chang Soo and Lee Do Ho. Wife, Kyu In Lee, parents of five children.

In Sang Han

President of the South America North Area. Called to the Second Quorum of the Seventy June 6, 1992, at age 50, and sustained Oct. 3, 1992. Former president of the Colombia Cali Mission, counselor in the Missionary Training Center presidency, stake president's counselor and bishop. Formerly director of scriptures coordination for the Church Curriculum Department. Received bachelor's, and master's degrees and doctorate in Spanish and history, Church history and doctrine, and education, respectively, from BYU. Born Feb. 5, 1942, in Payson, Utah, to Ruel W. and Ethel Otte Jensen. Wife, Lona Lee Child Jensen, parents of six children.

Jay E. Jensen

Second counselor in the North America Northeast Area presidency. Sustained to the Second Quorum of the Seventy April 2, 1994, at age 60. Former regional representative, stake president and counselor, bishop and branch president. Was vice president for government affairs for Marriott International, Inc., in Washington, D.C.; also served as adviser to the Church on international and governmental affairs. Born July 14, 1933, in San Mateo, Fla., to Joseph Donald and Phyllis Rose Anderson Ladd. Wife, Ruth Lynne Pearson Ladd, parents of four children.

W. Don Ladd

President of the North America Southwest Area. Called to the Second Quorum of the Seventy Jan. 1, 1991, at age 64, and sustained April 6, 1991. Former regional representative, stake president's counselor and bishop. Formerly vice president and chief executive officer in Utah for US West telephone company. Received bachelor's degree in business from the University of Utah. Born Oct. 28, 1926, in Salt Lake City, Utah, to Richard Sterling and Thelma McKenzie Lawrence. Wife, Jacqueline Young Lawrence, parents of three children.

W. Mack Lawrence

First counselor in the Philippines/Micronesia Area presidency. Called to the Second Quorum of the Seventy June 6, 1992, at age 58 and sustained Oct. 3, 1992. First Filipino General Authority. Former president of the Philippines Naga Mission, regional representative, stake president, temple sealer and mission president's counselor; converted in 1964. An attorney and law professor, he received bachelor of law degree from Silliman University at Dumaguete City, Philippines. Born May 4, 1934, in Santa Cruz, Philippines, to Leon B. and Beatriz R. Alandy Lim. Wife, Myrna Garcia Morillo Lim, parents of eight children.

Augusto A. Lim

Second counselor in the Mexico North Area presidency. Called to the Second Quorum of the Seventy June 6, 1992, at age 53, and sustained Oct. 3, 1992. Former president of the England Southwest Mission, member of the Melchizedek Priesthood MIA general board and Young Men general board and regional representative. Was BYU religion professor. Received bachelor's in zoology from Washington State University, master's degree and doctorate in education from BYU. Born April 24, 1939, in Washington D.C. to Louis L. and Edith Louise Gundersen Madsen. Wife, Diane Dursteler Madsen, parents of six children.

John M. Madsen

First counselor in the Brazil Area presidency. Sustained to the Second Quorum of the Seventy March 31, 1990, at age 59, while serving as president of the Brazil Fortaleza Mission. Former counselor to two stake presidents and bishop. Converted in 1972. Former assistant professor at Rio de Janeiro State University, financial management controller for Petrobras, S.A., and financial director of Liderbras, S.A. Born July 27, 1930, in Rio de Janeiro, Brazil, to Honorio and Benedicta Francisca Martins. Wife, Ruda Tourinho de Assis Martins, parents of four children.

Helvecio Martins

Second counselor in the Africa Area presidency. Sustained to the Second Quorum of the Seventy April 2, 1994, at age 63. Served as regional representative, member of the Young Men general board, stake president, and bishop. Received bachelor's and medical degrees from the University of Utah, master's degree and doctorate of public health from Harvard University. Was assistant secretary for health and head of U.S. Public Health Service in the U.S. Department of Health and Human Services, director of Centers for Disease Control, executive director of Utah Department of Health and Church commissioner of Health Services. Born June 19, 1930, in Salt Lake City, Utah, to A. Stanton and Neoma Thorup Mason. Wife, Marie Smith Mason, parents of seven children.

James O. Mason

First counselor in the Pacific Area presidency. Called to the Second Quorum of the Seventy June 6, 1992, at age 56, and sustained Oct. 3, 1992. Former president of the Utah South Mission, regional representative, stake president's counselor and bishop. Was president and founder of leadership and consulting companies, and family and taxpayer political action organizations; candidate for U.S. Senate in Maryland. Received bachelor's and master's degrees from BYU, doctorate from University of Southern California in management and public affairs. Born Jan. 25, 1936, in Basalt, Idaho, to Victor Lybbert and Beatrice Jensen Merrell. Wife, Karen Dixon Merrell, parents of nine children.

V. Dallas Merrell

Second counselor in the Central America Area presidency. Sustained to the Second Quorum of the Seventy April 6, 1991, at age 55. Former president of the San Jose Costa Rica Mission, temple sealer, stake president's counselor and served on various general Church writing committees. Converted in 1957. Was director of Temporal Affairs for the United Kingdom for the Church. Received bachelor's and master's degrees from San Jose State University, doctorate from University of Southern California in business administration. Born Feb. 5, 1936, in Richmond, Calif., to Joseph S. and Alba Maria Cairo Muren. Wife, Gladys Smith Muren, parents of six children.

Joseph C. Muren

President of the North America Southeast Area and first counselor in the Young Men general presidency. Called to the Second Quorum of the Seventy June 1, 1991, at age 49, and sustained Oct. 5, 1991. Former regional representative, stake president's counselor and bishop. Former president of Weber State University. Received bachelor's degree from BYU, master's degree from Harvard University and doctorate from University of California at Berkeley in finance and economics. Born May 31, 1942, in Idaho Falls, Idaho, to Sterling Dwaine and Lois Madsen Nadauld Corey. Wife, Margaret Dyreng Nadauld, parents of seven sons.

Stephen D. Nadauld

First counselor in the Mexico North Area presidency. Sustained to the Second Quorum of the Seventy April 6, 1991, at age 50. Former president of the Mexico Guadalajara Mission, regional representative, stake president and stake president's counselor. Was language translation business owner, former Presiding Bishopric Area Office manager. Received dual bachelor's degrees in education and physical education from University of Chihuahua and Chihuahua Normal College, and did graduate studies at the University of New Mexico. Born Sept. 27, 1940, in Delicias, Chihuahua, Mexico, to Rodolfo and Hilaria Ornelas Rojas. Wife, Marcela Burgos Perez de Rojas, parents of five children.

Jorge A. Rojas

Second counselor in the Asia North Area presidency. Called to the Second Quorum of the Seventy July 13, 1991, at age 66, and sustained Oct. 5, 1991. Former president of the Japan Sendai Mission, president of the Tokyo Temple, stake president and bishop. Former government employee, government contractor. Received bachelor's degree from the University of Hawaii in public administration. Born June 7, 1925, in Waipahu, Hawaii, to Kame and Ushi Nakasone Shimabukuro. Wife, Amy Michiko Hirose Shimabukuro, parents of one child.

Sam K. Shimabukuro

David E. Sorensen

President of the Asia North Area presidency. Called to the Second Quorum of the Seventy June 6, 1992, at age 58, and sustained Oct. 3, 1992. Former president of the Canada Halifax Mission, stake president and counselor and bishop. Was chairman and chief executive officer of North American Health Care, a hospital chain and board vice chairman of Nevada Community Bank in Las Vegas, Nev. Attended BYU, Utah State University and University of Utah. Born June 29, 1933, in Aurora, Utah, to Alma and Metta Amelia Helquist Sorensen. Wife, Verla Anderson Sorensen, parents of seven children.

First counselor in the Africa Area presidency. Called to the Second Quorum of the Seventy June 6, 1992, at age 56, and sustained Oct. 3, 1992. Former president of the Boise Idaho Mission, regional representative, temple sealer, Young Men general board member, stake president, stake president's counselor and bishop. Was vice president and general manager of contracting company. Attended University of Utah. Born Sept. 11, 1935, in Salt Lake City, Utah, to O. Frank and Winifred Parker Stanley. Wife, Annette Shewell Stanley, parents of eight children.

F. David Stanley

Kwok Yuen Tai

First counselor in the Asia Area presidency. Called to the Second Quorum of the Seventy June 6, 1992, at age 50, and sustained Oct. 3, 1992. Former president of the Hong Kong Mission, regional representative, stake president's counselor and branch president. Was self-employed in the import/export business, and in real estate development. Graduated from the University of Sydney in Australia in chemical engineering, graduate study in management at the University of Hong Kong. Born June 30, 1941, in Hong Kong to Lung Hing and Yau Yin Chu Tai. Wife, Hui Hua Tai, parents of three children.

Dieter F. Uchtdorf

Second counselor in the Europe Area presidency. Sustained to the Second Quorum of the Seventy April 2, 1994, at age 53. Former stake president and stake mission president. Senior vice president for flight operations and chief pilot for Lufthansa German Airlines, and check and training captain for Boeing 747s; received wings as a jet fighter pilot in the German Air Force in 1962. Born Nov. 6, 1940, in Ostrava, Czechoslovakia, to Karl Albert and Hilde Else Opelt Uchtdorf. Wife, Harriett Reich Uchtdorf, parents of two children.

First counselor in the Utah North Area presidency. Sustained to the Second Quorum of the Seventy March 31, 1990, at age 61. Former president of the Arizona Phoenix Mission, regional representative and stake president. Graduated from Brigham Young University and the University of Utah Medical School, practiced medicine for 28 years in Page, Ariz., doing much work among the Indian population. Born Jan. 18, 1929, at Blanding, Utah, to Alvin Lavell and Wasel Black Washburn. Wife, Barbara Harries Washburn, parents of 10 children.

J Ballard Washburn

Lance B. Wickman

First counselor in the North America West Area presidency. Sustained to the Second Quorum of the Seventy April 2, 1994, at age 53. Served as regional representative, stake president and bishop. Received bachelor's degree from University of California at Berkeley and juris doctorate from Stanford University. Partner in the international law firm of Latham and Watkins in San Diego, Calif. Born Nov. 11, 1940, in Seattle, Wash., to Alton C. and Irene Marilyn Carlson Wickman. Wife, Patricia Farr Wickman, parents of five children.

President of the Pacific Area. Called to the Second Quorum of the Seventy June 6, 1992, at age 59; sustained Oct. 3, 1992. Former president of the South Africa Johannesburg Mission, stake president's counselor, bishop and branch president. Formerly director of temporal affairs for Asia and Philippines, helped found Ezra Taft Benson Food and Agricultural Institute. Received bachelor's degree from BYU, master's degree from Montana State University and doctorate from University of California at Berkeley in agricultural economics. Born Jan. 23, 1933, in Cardston, Alberta, to Wm. Dale and Donna Wolf Wood. Wife, Lorna Cox Wood, parents of five children.

Lowell D. Wood

Second counselor in the Pacific Area presidency. Sustained to the Second Quorum of the Seventy March 31, 1990, at age 63. Former president of the Arizona Tempe Mission, stake president and counselor. Former businessman and founder of Woolsey Oil Inc. of Stockton, Calif.; served as president of the Taft Chamber of Commerce and Rotary Club in Taft, Calif. Born June 12, 1926, at Escalante, Utah, to Willis A. and Ruby Riddle Woolsey. Wife, LaRae Wood Woolsey, parents of three children.

Durrel A. Woolsey

THE PRESIDING BISHOPRIC

Called to the Second Quorum of the Seventy June 6, 1992, at age 55, and sustained Oct. 3, 1992; sustained as Presiding Bishop April 2, 1994. Former regional representative and stake president twice. Owner of two management companies; former dean of BYU College of Business, and served as business consultant to nations in West Africa. Received bachelor's degree from University of Utah and doctorate in economics from Massachusetts Institute of Technology. Born June 19, 1936, in Lehi, Utah, to Joseph Frederic and Belva Smith Bateman. Wife, Marilyn Scholes Bateman, parents of seven children.

Merrill J. Bateman

Sustained as first counselor to Presiding Bishop Robert D. Hales on Oct. 3, 1992, at age 54, and first counselor to Presiding Bishop Merrill J. Bateman on April 2, 1994. Former stake president and temple sealer. Former secretary to the Presiding Bishopric for 14 years. Received bachelor's degree in economics from the University of Utah, master's degree from University of Michigan in business administration. Born April 26, 1938, in Salt Lake City, Utah, to Harold Nelson and Blanche Mabel Swanson Burton. Wife, Barbara Matheson Burton, parents of five children.

H. David Burton

Sustained as second counselor to Presiding Bishop Robert D. Hales on Oct. 3, 1992, at age 56, and as second counselor to Presiding Bishop Merrill J. Bateman on April 2, 1994. Former stake president and bishop. Was managing director of the Church's Finance and Records Department, board member on various Church-related corporations. Received bachelor's degree in political science from BYU, master's degree in business administration from Indiana University. Born Feb. 6, 1936, in Preston, Idaho, to Phenoi Harrison and Ona Crockett Edgley. Wife, Pauline Nielson Edgley, parents of six children.

Richard C. Edgley

HISTORICAL LISTING OF GENERAL AUTHORITIES
PRESIDENTS OF THE CHURCH

1. Joseph Smith Jr. — Born Dec. 23, 1805, in Sharon, Windsor Co., Vermont, to Joseph Smith Sr. and Lucy Mack. Married Emma Hale Jan. 18, 1827, seven children.  Received the Melchizedek Priesthood (ordained apostle) in May 1829 by Peter, James and John (D&C 20:2, 27:12); sustained as First Elder of the Church April 6, 1830, at age 24; ordained high priest June 3, 1831, by Lyman Wight, sustained as president of the High Priesthood Jan. 25, 1832, at age 26 at a conference at Amherst, Loraine Co., Ohio; martyred June 27, 1844, at Carthage Jail, Carthage, Hancock Co., Illinois, at age 38.

2. Brigham Young — Born June 1, 1801, at Whitingham, Windham Co., Vermont, to John Young and Abigail Howe. Ordained apostle Feb. 14, 1835, at age 33 by the Three Witnesses to the Book of Mormon: Oliver Cowdery, David Whitmer and Martin Harris;  sustained as president of the Quorum of the Twelve Apostles April 14, 1840; sustained as president of the Church Dec. 27, 1847, at age 46; died Aug. 29, 1877, in Salt Lake City, Salt Lake Co., Utah, at age 76.

3. John Taylor — Born Nov. 1, 1808, at Milnthrop, Westmoreland Co., England, to James Taylor and Agnes Taylor. Ordained apostle Dec. 19, 1838, under the hands of Brigham Young and Heber C. Kimball at age 30; sustained as president of the Quorum of  the Twelve Apostles Oct. 6, 1877; sustained as president of the Church Oct. 10, 1880, at age 71; died July 25, 1887, in Kaysville, Davis Co., Utah, at age 78.

4. Wilford Woodruff — Born March 1, 1807, at Avon (Farmington), Hartford Co., Connecticut, to Aphek Woodruff and Beulah Thompson. Ordained apostle April 26, 1839, at age 32 by Brigham Young; sustained as president of the Quorum of the Twelve  Apostles Oct. 10, 1880; sustained as president of the Church April 7, 1889, at age 82; died Sept. 2, 1898, in San Francisco, San Francisco Co., California, at age 91.

5. Lorenzo Snow — Born April 3, 1814, at Mantua, Portage Co., Ohio, to Oliver Snow and Rosetta Leonora Pettibone. Ordained apostle Feb. 12, 1849, at age 34 by Heber C. Kimball; sustained as counselor to President Brigham Young April 8, 1873;  sustained as assistant counselor to President Brigham Young May 9, 1874; sustained as president of the Quorum of the Twelve Apostles April 7, 1889; ordained and set apart as president of the Church Sept. 13, 1898, at age 84; died Oct. 10, 1901, in Salt Lake City, Salt Lake Co., Utah, at age 87.

6. Joseph Fielding Smith — Born Nov. 13, 1838, at Far West, Caldwell Co., Missouri, to Hyrum Smith and Mary Fielding. Ordained apostle and named counselor to the First Presidency July 1, 1866, at age 27 by Brigham Young; set apart as a member of  the Quorum of the Twelve Apostles Oct. 8, 1867; released as counselor to the First Presidency at the death of President Young Aug. 29, 1877; sustained as second counselor to President John Taylor Oct. 10, 1880; released at the death of President Taylor July 25, 1887; sustained as second counselor to President Wilford Woodruff April 7, 1889; sustained as second counselor to President Lorenzo Snow Sept. 13, 1898; sustained as first counselor to Lorenzo Snow Oct. 6, 1901, not set apart to this position; released at the death of President Snow Oct. 10, 1901; ordained and set apart as president of the Church Oct. 17, 1901, at age 62; died Nov. 19, 1918, in Salt Lake City; Salt Lake Co., Utah, at age 80.

7. Heber Jeddy Grant — Born Nov. 22, 1856, in Salt Lake City, Salt Lake Co., Utah, to Jedediah Morgan Grant and Rachel Ridgeway Ivins. Ordained apostle Oct. 16, 1882, at age 25 by George Q. Cannon; became president of the Quorum of the Twelve  Apostles Nov. 23, 1916; ordained and set apart as president of the Church Nov. 23, 1918, at age 62; died May 14, 1945, in Salt Lake City, Salt Lake Co., Utah, at age 88.

8. George Albert Smith — Born April 4, 1870, in Salt Lake City, Salt Lake Co., Utah, to John Henry Smith and Sarah Farr. Married Lucy Emily Woodruff May 25, 1892 (she died Nov. 5, 1937); they had three children. Ordained apostle Oct. 8, 1903, at age 33 by  Joseph F. Smith; sustained as president of the Quorum of the Twelve Apostles July 1, 1943; ordained and set apart as president of the Church May 21, 1945, at age 75; died April 4, 1951, in Salt Lake City, Salt Lake Co., Utah, at age 81.

9. David Oman McKay — Born Sept. 8, 1873, at Huntsville, Weber Co., Utah, to David McKay and Jennette Eveline Evans. Married to Emma Ray Riggs Jan. 2, 1901 (she died Nov. 14, 1970); they had seven children. Ordained apostle April 9, 1906, at age 32  by Joseph F. Smith; sustained as sec-

ond counselor to President Heber J. Grant Oct. 6, 1934; sustained as second counselor to President George Albert Smith May 21, 1945; sustained as president of the Quorum of the Twelve Apostles Sept. 30, 1950; sustained as president of the Church April 9, 1951, at age 77; died Jan. 18, 1970, in Salt Lake City, Salt Lake Co., Utah, at age 96.

10. Joseph Fielding Smith — Born July 19, 1876, in Salt Lake City, Salt Lake Co., Utah, to Joseph Fielding Smith and Julina Lambson. Married Louie E. Shurtliff April 26, 1898 (she died March 30, 1908); they had two children. Married Ethel G. Reynolds  Nov. 2, 1908 (she died Aug. 26, 1937); they had nine children. Married Jessie Ella Evans April 12, 1938 (she died Aug. 3, 1971). Ordained apostle April 7, 1910, at age 33 by Joseph F. Smith; sustained as acting president of the Quorum of the Twelve Apostles Sept. 30, 1950; sustained as president of the Quorum of the Twelve Apostles April 9, 1951; sustained as counselor in the First Presidency Oct. 29, 1965; ordained and set apart as president of the Church Jan. 23, 1970, at age 93; died July 2, 1972, in Salt Lake City, Salt Lake Co., Utah, at age 95.

11. Harold Bingham Lee — Born March 28, 1899, at Clifton, Oneida Co., Idaho, to Samuel M. Lee and Louisa Bingham. Married Fern Lucinda Tanner Nov. 14, 1923 (she died Sept. 24, 1962); they had two children. Married Freda Joan Jensen June 17, 1963.  Ordained apostle April 10, 1941, at age 42 by Heber J. Grant; sustained as president of the Quorum of the Twelve Apostles Jan. 23, 1970; sustained as first counselor to President Joseph Fielding Smith Jan. 23, 1970; ordained and set apart as president of the Church July 7, 1972, at age 73; died Dec. 26, 1973, in Salt Lake City, Salt Lake Co., Utah, at age 74.

12. Spencer Woolley Kimball — Born March 28, 1895, in Salt Lake City, Salt Lake Co., Utah, to Andrew and Olive Woolley Kimball. Married Camilla Eyring on Nov. 16, 1917 (she died Sept. 20, 1987); they had four children. Ordained apostle Oct. 7, 1943, at

age 48 by President Heber J. Grant; became acting president of the Quorum of the Twelve Apostles after the death of President David O. McKay in 1970; became president of the Quorum of the Twelve Apostles July 7, 1972; ordained and set apart as president of the Church Dec. 30, 1973, at age 78; died Nov. 5, 1985, in Salt Lake City, Salt Lake Co., Utah, at age 90.

13. Ezra Taft Benson — Born Aug. 4, 1899, at Whitney, Franklin County, Idaho, to George T. and Sarah Dunkley Benson. Married Flora Smith Amussen Sept. 10, 1926 (she died Aug. 14, 1992); they had six children. Ordained an apostle Oct. 7, 1943, at age 44

by President Heber J. Grant; served as U.S. Secretary of Agriculture, 1953-61. Became president of the Quorum of the Twelve Apostles Dec. 30, 1973; ordained and set apart as president of the Church on Nov. 10, 1985, at age 86; died May 30, 1994, in Salt Lake City, Salt Lake Co., Utah, at age 94.

14. Howard William Hunter — See current FIRST PRESIDENCY.

ASSISTANT PRESIDENTS OF THE CHURCH

1. Oliver Cowdery — Born Oct. 3, 1806, at Wells, Rutland Co., Vermont, to William Cowdery and Rebecca Fuller. Received Melchizedek Priesthood (ordained apostle) in May 1829, by Peter, James and John (D&C 20:2, 27:12); sustained as Second Elder

of the Church April 6, 1830, at age 23; ordained high priest Aug. 28, 1831, by Sidney Rigdon; ordained assistant president of the High Priesthood Dec. 5, 1834, at age 28; sustained as assistant counselor in the First Presidency Sept. 3, 1837; excommunicated April 11, 1838; rebaptized Nov. 12, 1848; died March 3, 1850, at Richmond, Ray Co., Missouri, at age 43.

2. Hyrum Smith — Born Feb. 9, 1800, at Tunbridge, Orange Co., Vermont, to Joseph Smith Sr. and Lucy Mack. Ordained high priest in June 1831 by Joseph Smith; sustained as assistant counselor to the First Presidency Sept. 3, 1837, at age 37; sus-

tained as second counselor to President Joseph Smith Nov. 7, 1837; given all the priesthood formerly held by Oliver Cowdery (including apostle); ordained Patriarch to the Church and assistant president Jan. 24, 1841, by Joseph Smith, at age 40; martyred June 27, 1844, at Carthage Jail, Carthage, Hancock Co., Illinois, at age 44.

FIRST COUNSELORS IN THE FIRST PRESIDENCY

1. Sidney Rigdon — Born Feb. 19, 1793, at Saint Clair Township, Allegheny Co., Pennsylvania, to William Rigdon and Nancy Bryant. Ordained high priest in June 1831 by Lyman Wight; set apart as first counselor to President Joseph

Smith March 18, 1833, at age 40; excommunicated Sept. 8, 1844; died July 14, 1876, at Friendship, Allegany Co., New York, at age 83.

2. Heber Chase Kimball — Born June 14, 1801, at Sheldon, Franklin Co., Vermont, to Solomon Farnham Kimball and Anna Spaulding. Ordained apostle Feb. 14, 1835, under the hands of Oliver Cowdery, David Whitmer and Martin Harris at age 33; sustained as first counselor to President Brigham Young Dec. 27, 1847, at age 46; died June 22, 1868, at Salt Lake City, Salt Lake Co., Utah, at age 67.

3. George Albert Smith — Born June 26, 1817, at Potsdam, Saint Lawrence Co., New York, to John Smith and Clarissa Lyman. Ordained apostle April 26, 1839, by Heber C. Kimball at age 21; sustained as first counselor to President Brigham Young Oct. 7, 1868, at age 51; died Sept. 1, 1875, at Salt Lake City, Salt Lake Co., Utah, at age 58.

4. John Willard Young — Born Oct. 1, 1844, at Nauvoo, Hancock Co., Illinois, to Brigham Young and Mary Ann Angell. Sustained as counselor to President Brigham Young April 8, 1873, at age 28; sustained as assistant counselor to President Young May 9, 1874; sustained as first counselor to President Young Oct. 7, 1876, at age 32; released at death of President Young Aug. 29, 1877; sustained as a counselor to the Twelve Apostles Oct. 6, 1877; released Oct. 6, 1891; died Feb. 11, 1924, at New York City, New York, at age 79.

5. George Quayle Cannon — Born Jan. 11, 1827, at Liverpool, Lancashire Co., England, to George Cannon and Ann Quayle. Ordained an apostle Aug. 26, 1860, by Brigham Young at age 33; sustained as counselor to President Young April 8, 1873, at age 46; sustained as assistant counselor to President Young May 9, 1874; released at death of President Young Aug. 29, 1877; sustained as first counselor to President John Taylor Oct. 10, 1880; released at death of President Taylor July 25, 1887; sustained as first counselor to President Wilford Woodruff April 7, 1889; sustained as first counselor to President Lorenzo Snow Sept. 13, 1898; died April 12, 1901, at Monterey, Monterey Co., California, at age 74.

6. Joseph Fielding Smith — See PRESIDENTS OF THE CHURCH, No. 6.

7. John Rex Winder — Born Dec. 11, 1821, at Biddenham, Kent Co., England, to Richard Winder and Sophia Collins. Ordained high priest March 4, 1872, by Edward Hunter; sustained as second counselor to Presiding Bishop William B. Preston April 8, 1887, at age 65; sustained as first counselor to President Joseph F. Smith Oct. 17, 1901, at age 79; died March 27, 1910, at Salt Lake City, Salt Lake Co., Utah, at age 88.

8. Anthon Henrik Lund — Born May 15, 1844, at Aalborg, Jutland, Denmark, to Henrik Lund and Anne C. Andersen. Ordained apostle Oct. 7, 1889, by George Q. Cannon at age 45; sustained as second counselor to President Joseph F. Smith Oct. 17, 1901, at age 57; sustained as first counselor to President Smith April 7, 1910; sustained as first counselor to President Heber J. Grant Nov. 23, 1918; died March 2, 1921, at Salt Lake City, Salt Lake Co., Utah, at age 76.

9. Charles William Penrose — Born Feb. 4, 1832, at London, Surrey Co., England, to Richard Penrose and Matilda Sims.  Ordained apostle July 7, 1904, by Joseph F. Smith at age 72; sustained as second counselor to President Smith Dec. 7, 1911, at age 79; sustained as second counselor to President Heber J. Grant Nov. 23, 1918; sustained as first counselor to President Grant March 10, 1921; died May 15, 1925, at Salt Lake City, Salt Lake Co., Utah, at age 93.

10. Anthony Woodward Ivins — Born Sept. 16, 1852, at Toms River, Ocean Co., New Jersey, to Israel Ivins and Anna Lowrie. Ordained apostle Oct. 6, 1907, by Joseph F. Smith at age 55; sustained as second counselor to President Heber J. Grant  March 10, 1921, at age 68; sustained as first counselor to President Grant May 28, 1925; died Sept. 23, 1934, at Salt Lake City, Salt Lake Co., Utah, at age 82.

11. Joshua Reuben Clark Jr. — Born Sept. 1, 1871, at Grantsville, Tooele Co., Utah, to Joshua Reuben Clark and Mary Louise Woolley. Sustained as second counselor to President Heber J. Grant, April 6, 1933, at age 61; sustained as first counselor  to President Grant, Oct. 6, 1934; ordained apostle Oct. 11, 1934, at age 63, by President Grant; sustained as first counselor to President George Albert Smith May 21, 1945; sustained as second counselor to President David O. McKay April 9, 1951; sustained as first counselor to President McKay June 12, 1959; died Oct. 6, 1961, at Salt Lake City, Salt Lake Co., Utah, at age 90.

12. Stephen L Richards — Born June 18, 1879, at Mendon, Cache Co., Utah, to Stephen Longstroth Richards and Emma Louise Stayner. Ordained apostle Jan. 18, 1917, by Joseph F. Smith at age 37; sustained as first counselor to President David O.  McKay April 9, 1951, at age 71; died May 19, 1959, at Salt Lake City, Salt Lake Co., Utah, at age 79.

13. Joshua Reuben Clark Jr. — See No. 11 above.

14. Henry Dinwoodey Moyle — Born April 22, 1889, at Salt Lake City, Salt Lake Co., Utah, to James H. Moyle and Alice E. Dinwoodey. Ordained apostle April 10, 1947, by George Albert Smith at age 57; sustained as second counselor to President David  O. McKay June 12, 1959 at age 70; sustained as first counselor to President McKay Oct. 12, 1961; died Sept. 18, 1963, at Deer Park, Osceola Co., Florida, at age 74.

15. Hugh Brown Brown — Born Oct. 24, 1883, at Granger, Salt Lake Co., Utah, to Homer Manly Brown and Lydia Jane Brown. Sustained as Assistant to the Twelve Oct. 4, 1953, at age 69; ordained an apostle April 10, 1958, at age 74 by David O. McKay; sustained  as counselor in the First Presidency June 22, 1961; sustained as second counselor to President McKay Oct. 12, 1961; sustained as first counselor to President McKay Oct. 4, 1963; released at death of President McKay Jan. 18, 1970, and resumed position in the Quorum of the Twelve Apostles; died Dec. 2, 1975, at Salt Lake City, Salt Lake Co., Utah, at age 92.

16. Harold Bingham Lee — See PRESIDENTS OF THE CHURCH, No. 11.

17. Nathan Eldon Tanner — Born May 9, 1898, at Salt Lake City, Salt Lake Co., Utah, to Nathan William Tanner and Sarah Edna Brown. Sustained as Assistant to the Twelve Oct. 8, 1960, at age 62; ordained apostle Oct. 11, 1962, at age 64; sus-

tained as second counselor to President David O. McKay Oct. 4, 1963; sustained as second counselor to President Joseph Fielding Smith Jan. 23, 1970; sustained as first counselor to President Harold B. Lee July 7, 1972; sustained as first counselor to President Spencer W. Kimball Dec. 30, 1973; died Nov. 27, 1982, at Salt Lake City, Salt Lake Co., Utah, at age 84.

18. Marion George Romney — Born Sept. 19, 1897, in Colonia Juarez, Mexi-

co, to George Samuel Romney and Teressa Artemesia Redd. Sustained as Church's first Assistant to the Twelve April 6, 1941, at age 43; ordained apostle Oct. 11, 1951, at age 54; sustained as second counselor to President

Harold B. Lee July 7, 1972; sustained as second counselor to President Spencer W. Kimball on Dec. 30, 1973; sustained as first counselor to President Kimball Dec. 2, 1982; released at the death of President Kimball Nov. 5, 1985; became president of the Quorum of the Twelve Apostles Nov. 10, 1985; died May 20, 1988, at Salt Lake City, Salt Lake Co., Utah, at age 90.

19. Gordon Bitner Hinckley — See current FIRST PRESIDENCY.

SECOND COUNSELORS IN THE FIRST PRESIDENCY

1. Frederick Granger Williams — Born Oct. 28, 1787, at Suffield, Hartford, Co., Connecticut, to William Wheeler Williams and Ruth Granger. Called by revelation March 1832 to be a high priest and counselor to President Joseph Smith (D&C 81:1); ordained

high priest by Miles H. Jones; set apart as second counselor to President Smith March 18, 1833, at age 45; rejected Nov. 7, 1837; excommunicated March 17, 1839; restored to fellowship April 8, 1840; died Oct. 10, 1842, at Quincy, Adams Co., Illinois, at age 54.

2. Hyrum Smith — See ASSISTANT PRESIDENTS OF THE CHURCH, No. 2.

3. William Law — Born Sept. 8, 1809. Set apart as second counselor to President Joseph Smith Jan. 24, 1841, at age 31; excommunicated April 18, 1844; died Jan. 19, 1892, at Shullsburg, Lafayette Co., Wisconsin, at age 82.

4. Willard Richards — Born June 24, 1804, at Hopkinton, Middlesex Co., Massachusetts, to Joseph Richards and Rhoda Howe. Ordained apostle April 14,

1840, by Brigham Young at age 35; sustained as second counselor to President Young Dec. 27, 1847, at age 43; died March 11, 1854, at Salt Lake City, Salt Lake Co., Utah, at age 49.

5. Jedediah Morgan Grant — Born Feb. 21, 1816, at Windsor, Broome Co., New York, to Joshua Grant and Athalia Howard. Set apart as one of the First Seven Presidents of the Seventy Dec. 2, 1845, at age 29; ordained apostle April 7, 1854, at age 38 by

Brigham Young; sustained as second counselor to President Young April 7, 1854; died Dec. 1, 1856, at Salt Lake City, Salt Lake Co., Utah, at age 40.

6. Daniel Hanmer Wells — Born Oct. 27, 1814, at Trenton, Oneida Co., New York, to Daniel Wells and Catherine Chapin. Set apart as second counselor to President Young Jan. 4, 1857, at age

42; released at death of President Young Aug. 29, 1877; sustained as a counselor to the Twelve Apostles Oct. 6, 1877; died March 24, 1891, at Salt Lake City, Salt Lake Co., Utah, at age 76.

7. Joseph Fielding Smith — See PRESIDENTS OF THE CHURCH, No. 6.

8. Rudger Clawson — Born March 12, 1857, at Salt Lake City, Salt Lake Co., Utah, to Hiram Bradley Clawson and Margaret Gay Judd. Ordained apostle Oct. 10, 1898, by Lorenzo Snow, at age 41; sustained as second counselor to President Snow Oct. 6, 1901, at age 44, not set apart to this position; released at death of President Snow Oct. 10, 1901, and resumed position in the Quorum of the Twelve Apostles; sustained as president of the Quorum of the Twelve Apostles March 17, 1921; died June 21, 1943, in Salt Lake City, Salt Lake Co., Utah at age 86.

9. Anthon Henrik Lund — See FIRST COUNSELORS IN THE FIRST PRESIDENCY, No. 8.

10. John Henry Smith — Born Sept. 18, 1848, at Carbunca (now part of Council Bluffs), Pottawattamie Co., Iowa, to George Albert Smith and Sarah Ann Libby. Ordained apostle Oct. 27, 1880, by Wilford Woodruff at age 32; sustained as second counselor to President Joseph F. Smith April 7, 1910, at age 61; died Oct. 13, 1911, at Salt Lake City, Salt Lake Co., Utah, at 63.

11. Charles William Penrose — See FIRST COUNSELORS IN THE FIRST PRESIDENCY, No. 9.

12. Anthony Woodward Ivins — See FIRST COUNSELORS IN THE FIRST PRESIDENCY, No. 10

13. Charles Wilson Nibley — Born Feb. 15, 1849, at Hunterfield, Midlothian Region, Scotland, to James Nibley and Jane Wilson. Ordained high priest June 9, 1901, by Joseph F. Smith; sustained as Presiding Bishop of the Church Dec. 4, 1907, at age 58; sustained as second counselor to President Heber J. Grant, May 28, 1925, at age 76; died Dec. 11, 1931, at Salt Lake City, Salt Lake Co., Utah, at age 82.

14. Joshua Reuben Clark Jr. — See FIRST COUNSELORS IN THE FIRST PRESIDENCY, No. 11.

15. David Oman McKay — See PRESIDENTS OF THE CHURCH, No. 9.

16. Joshua Reuben Clark Jr. — See FIRST COUNSELORS IN THE FIRST PRESIDENCY, No. 11.

17. Henry Dinwoodey Moyle — See FIRST COUNSELORS IN THE FIRST PRESIDENCY, No. 14.

18. Hugh Brown Brown — See FIRST COUNSELORS IN THE FIRST PRESIDENCY, No. 15.

19. Nathan Eldon Tanner — See FIRST COUNSELORS IN THE FIRST PRESIDENCY, No. 17.

20. Marion George Romney — See FIRST COUNSELORS IN THE FIRST PRESIDENCY, No. 18.

21. Gordon Bitner Hinckley — See current FIRST PRESIDENCY.

22. Thomas Spencer Monson — See current FIRST PRESIDENCY.

OTHER COUNSELORS IN THE FIRST PRESIDENCY

1. Jesse Gause — Born about 1784 at East Marlborough, Chester Co., Virginia, to William and Mary Beverly Gause. Converted from the Shaker sect, he was baptized about the end of 1831. Set apart as counselor to Joseph Smith March 8, 1832; sent on a mission Aug. 1, 1832. Excommunicated Dec. 3, 1832. Died about 1836.

2. John Cook Bennett — Born Aug.

3, 1804, at Fair Haven, Bristol Co., Massachusetts, to J. and N. Bennett.  Presented as assistant president with the First Presidency April 8, 1841, at age 36 (See *Documentary History of the Church* 4:341); disfellowshipped May 25, 1842; excommunicated latter part of 1842; died in Polk City, Polk Co., Iowa.

3. Amasa Mason Lyman — Born March 30, 1813, at Lyman, Crafton Co., New Hampshire, to Roswell Lyman and Martha Mason. Ordained apostle Aug. 20, 1842, by Brigham Young at age 29; replaced in the Quorum of the Twelve Apostles Jan. 20, 1843,  due to reinstatement of Orson Pratt; appointed counselor to the First Presidency about Feb. 4, 1843; retired from the First Presidency with death of Joseph Smith June 27, 1844; returned to the Quorum of the Twelve Apostles Aug. 12, 1844; deprived of apostleship Oct. 6, 1867; excommunicated May 12, 1870; died Feb. 4, 1877, at Fillmore, Millard Co., Utah, at age 63. Blessings restored after death.

4. Joseph Fielding Smith — See PRESIDENTS OF THE CHURCH, No. 6.

5. Lorenzo Snow — See PRESIDENTS OF THE CHURCH, No. 5.

6. Brigham Young Jr. — Born Dec. 18, 1836, at Kirtland, Geauga Co., Ohio, to Brigham Young and Mary Ann Angell. Ordained apostle Feb. 4, 1864, at age 27, by President Brigham Young; sustained to the Quorum of the Twelve Apostles Oct. 9, 1868;  sustained as counselor to President Young April 8, 1873, at age 36; sustained as assistant counselor to President Young May 9, 1874; released at President Young's death Aug. 29, 1877, and resumed position in the Quorum of the Twelve Apostles; sustained as president of the Quorum of the Twelve Apostles Oct. 17, 1901; died April 11, 1903, in

Salt Lake City, Salt Lake Co., Utah, at age 66.

7. Albert Carrington — Born Jan. 8, 1813, at Royalton, Windsor Co., Vermont, to Daniel Van Carrington and Isabella Bowman. Ordained apostle July 3, 1870, by Brigham Young at age 57; sustained as counselor to President Young April 8, 1873, at  age 60; sustained as assistant counselor to President Young May 9, 1874; released at death of President Young Aug. 29, 1877; excommunicated Nov. 7, 1885; rebaptized Nov. 1, 1887; died Sept. 19, 1889, at Salt Lake City, Salt Lake Co., Utah, at age 76.

8. John Willard Young — See FIRST COUNSELORS IN THE FIRST PRESIDENCY, No. 4.

9. George Quayle Cannon — See FIRST COUNSELORS IN THE FIRST PRESIDENCY, No. 5.

10. Hugh Brown Brown — See FIRST COUNSELORS IN THE FIRST PRESIDENCY, No. 15.

11. Joseph Fielding Smith — See PRESIDENTS OF THE CHURCH, No. 10.

12. Henry Thorpe Beal Isaacson — Born Sept. 6, 1898, at Ephraim, Sanpete Co., Utah, to Martin Isaacson and Mary Jemima Beal. Ordained high priest Oct. 1, 1941, by Charles A. Callis; sustained as second counselor to Presiding Bishop LeGrand Richards  Dec. 12, 1946, at age 48; sustained as first counselor to Presiding Bishop Joseph L. Wirthlin April 6, 1952; sustained as Assistant to the Twelve Sept. 30, 1961; sustained as counselor in the First Presidency Oct. 28, 1965, at age 67; released at death of President David O. McKay Jan. 18, 1970; resumed position as Assistant to the Twelve Jan. 23, 1970; died Nov. 9, 1970, at Salt Lake City, Salt Lake Co., Utah, at age 72.

13. Alvin Rulon Dyer — Born Jan. 1, 1903, at Salt Lake City, Salt Lake Co., Utah, to Alfred R. Dyer and Harriet Walsh. Ordained high priest Oct. 2,

1927, by Joseph Fielding Smith; sustained an Assistant to the Twelve Oct. 11, 1958, at age 55; ordained apostle Oct. 5, 1967, by David O. McKay at age 64; sustained as counselor in the First Presidency April 6, 1968; released at death of President McKay Jan. 18, 1970; resumed position as Assistant to the Twelve Apostles Jan. 23, 1970; sustained a member of First Quorum of the Seventy Oct. 1, 1976; died March 6, 1977, at Salt Lake City, Salt Lake Co., Utah, at age 74.

14. Gordon Bitner Hinckley — See current FIRST PRESIDENCY.

ASSISTANT COUNSELORS IN THE FIRST PRESIDENCY

1. Oliver Cowdery — See ASSISTANT PRESIDENTS OF THE CHURCH, No. 1.

2. Joseph Smith Sr. — Born July 12, 1771, at Topsfield, Essex Co., Massachusetts, to Asael Smith and Mary Duty. Ordained high priest June 3, 1831, by Lyman Wight; ordained Patriarch to the Church Dec. 18, 1833, at age 62; sustained as assistant counselor to the First Presidency Sept. 3, 1837, at age 66; died Sept. 14, 1840, at Nauvoo, Hancock Co., Illinois, at age 69.

3. Hyrum Smith — See ASSISTANT PRESIDENTS OF THE CHURCH, No. 2.

4. John Smith — Born July 16, 1781, at Derryfield, Hillsboro Co., New Hampshire, to Asael Smith and Mary Duty. Ordained high priest June 3, 1833, by Lyman Wight; sustained as assistant counselor to the First Presidency Sept. 3, 1837, at age 56; re-

leased at the death of Joseph Smith June 27, 1844; set apart as Patriarch to the Church Jan. 1, 1849, at age 67; died May 23, 1854, at Salt Lake City, Salt Lake Co., Utah, at age 72.

5. Lorenzo Snow — See PRESIDENTS OF THE CHURCH, No. 5.

6. Brigham Young Jr. — See OTHER COUNSELORS IN THE FIRST PRESIDENCY, No. 6.

7. Albert Carrington — See OTHER COUNSELORS IN THE FIRST PRESIDENCY, No. 7.

8. John Willard Young — See FIRST COUNSELORS IN THE FIRST PRESIDENCY, No. 4.

9. George Quayle Cannon — See FIRST COUNSELORS IN THE FIRST PRESIDENCY, No. 5.

THE COUNCIL OF THE TWELVE

1. Thomas Baldwin Marsh — Born Nov. 1, 1799, at Acton, Middlesex Co., Massachusetts, to James Marsh and Molly Law. Ordained apostle April 25, 1835, under the hands of Oliver Cowdery, David Whitmer and Martin Harris, at Kirtland, Ohio, at age 35; sustained as president of the Quorum of the Twelve Apostles May 2, 1835; excommunicated March 17, 1839; rebaptized in July 1857; died January 1866, at Ogden, Weber Co., Utah, at age 66.

2. David Wyman Patten — Born Nov. 14, 1799, at Theresa, Jefferson Co., New York, to Benenio Patten and Abigail Cole. Ordained apostle Feb. 15, 1835, under the hands of Oliver Cowdery, David Whitmer and Martin Harris, at Kirtland, Ohio, at age 35; killed Oct. 25, 1838, at the Battle of Crooked River, Missouri, at age 38.

3. Brigham Young — See PRESIDENTS OF THE CHURCH, No. 2.

4. Heber Chase Kimball — See FIRST COUNSELORS IN THE FIRST PRESIDENCY, No. 2.

5. Orson Hyde — Born Jan. 8, 1805, at Oxford, New Haven Co., Connecticut, to Nathan Hyde and Sally Thorp. Ordained apostle Feb. 15, 1835, under the hands of Oliver Cowdery, David Whitmer and Martin Harris, at Kirtland, Ohio, at age 30;  dropped from Quorum May 4, 1839; restored to Quorum June 27, 1839; sustained as president of the Quorum of the Twelve Apostles Dec. 27, 1847; Brigham Young, on April 10, 1875, took Hyde from his original position in the Quorum and placed him in the order he would have been in when he was restored to fellowship had he come into the Quorum at that time (See *"Succession in the Priesthood"* by John Taylor, p. 16.); died Nov. 28, 1878, at Spring City, Sanpete Co., Utah, at age 73.

6. William E. M'Lellin — Born 1806 in Tennessee. Ordained apostle Feb. 15, 1835, under the hands of Oliver Cowdery, David Whitmer and Martin Harris, at Kirtland, Ohio, at age 29; excommunicated May 11, 1838; died April 24, 1883, at Independence, Jackson Co., Missouri, at age 77.

7. Parley Parker Pratt — Born April 12, 1807, at Burlington, Otsego Co., New York, to Jared Pratt and Charity Dickinson. Ordained apostle Feb. 21, 1835, under the hands of Joseph Smith, Oliver Cowdery and David Whitmer, at Kirtland, Ohio, at age 27; assassinated May 13, 1857, at Van Buren, Crawford Co., Arkansas, at age 50.

8. Luke Johnson — Born Nov. 3, 1807, at Pomfret, Windsor Co., Vermont, to John Johnson and Elsa Jacobs. Ordained apostle Feb. 15, 1835, under the hands of Oliver Cowdery, David Whitmer and Martin Harris, at Kirtland, Ohio, at age 27; excommuni-  cated April 13, 1838; rebaptized in 1846 at Nauvoo, Illinois; died Dec. 9, 1861, at Salt Lake City, Salt Lake Co., Utah, at age 54.

9. William Smith — Born March 13, 1811, at Royalton, Windsor Co., Vermont, to Joseph Smith Sr. and Lucy Mack. Ordained apostle Feb. 15, 1835, under the hands of Oliver Cowdery, David Whitmer and Martin Harris, at Kirtland, Ohio, at age 23; dropped  from the Quorum May 4, 1839; restored to Quorum May 25, 1839; dropped from the Quorum Oct. 6, 1845; excommunicated Oct. 19, 1845; died Nov. 13, 1893, at Osterdock, Clayton Co., Iowa, at age 82.

10. Orson Pratt — Born Sept. 19, 1811, at Hartford, Washington, Co., New York, to Jared Pratt and Charity Dickinson. Ordained apostle April 26, 1835, under the hands of Oliver Cowdery, David Whitmer and Martin Harris, at Kirtland, Ohio, at age 23; excommuni-  cated Aug. 20, 1842; rebaptized Jan. 20, 1843, and ordained to former office in the Quorum of the Twelve Apostles. Brigham Young took him from his original position in the Quorum in 1875 and placed him in the order he would have been in when he was restored to fellowship had he come into the Quorum at that time; died Oct. 3, 1881, at Salt Lake City, Salt Lake Co., Utah, at age 70.

11. John Farnham Boynton — Born Sept. 20, 1811, at Bradford, Essex Co., Massachusetts, to Eliphalet Boynton and Susannah Nichols. Ordained apostle Feb. 15, 1835, under the hands of Oliver Cowdery, David Whitmer and Martin Harris, at Kirtland, Ohio,  at age 23; disfellowshipped Sept. 3, 1837; excommunicated 1837; died Oct. 20, 1890, at Syracuse, Onondaga Co., New York, at age 79.

12. Lyman Eugene Johnson — Born Oct. 24, 1811, at Pomfret, Windsor Co., Vermont, to John Johnson and Elsa Jacobs. Ordained apostle Feb. 14, 1835, under the hands of Oliver Cowdery, David Whitmer and Martin Harris, at Kirtland, Ohio, at age 23; excommunicated April 13, 1838; died December 1856, at Prairie du Chien, Crawford Co., Wisconsin, at age 45.

13. John Edward Page — Born Feb. 25, 1799, at Trenton  Township, Oneida Co., New York, to Ebenezer and Rachel Page. Ordained apostle Dec. 19, 1838, under the hands of Brigham Young and Heber C. Kimball at Far West, Missouri, at age 39; disfellowshipped Feb. 9, 1846; excommunicated June 27, 1846; died in the autumn of 1867, at De Kalb Co., Illinois, at age 68.

14. John Taylor — See PRESIDENTS OF THE CHURCH, No. 3.

15. Wilford Woodruff — See PRESIDENTS OF THE CHURCH, No. 4.

16. George Albert Smith — See FIRST COUNSELORS IN THE FIRST PRESIDENCY, No. 3.

17. Willard Richards — See SECOND COUNSELORS IN THE FIRST PRESIDENCY, No. 4.

18. Lyman Wight — Born May 9, 1796, at Fairfield, Herkimer Co., New York, to Levi Wight and Sarah Corbin. Ordained apostle April 8, 1841, by Joseph Smith, at Nauvoo, Illinois, at age 44. Excommunicated Dec. 3, 1848; died March 31, 1858, in Mountain Valley, Texas, at age 63.

19. Amasa Mason Lyman — See OTHER COUNSELORS IN THE FIRST PRESIDENCY, No. 3.

20. Ezra Taft Benson — Born Feb. 22, 1811, at Mendon, Worcester Co., Massachusetts, to John Benson and Chloe Taft. Ordained apostle July 16, 1846, by Brigham Young at Council Bluffs, Iowa, at age 35;

died Sept. 3, 1869, at Ogden, Weber Co., Utah, at age 58.

21. Charles Coulsen Rich — Born Aug. 21, 1809, at Campbell Co., Kentucky, to Joseph Rich and Nancy O. Neal. Ordained apostle Feb. 12, 1849, by Brigham Young, at Salt Lake City, Utah, at age 39; died Nov. 17, 1883, at Paris, Bear Lake Co., Idaho, at age 74.

22. Lorenzo Snow — See PRESIDENTS OF THE CHURCH, No. 5.

23. Erastus Snow — Born Nov. 9, 1818, at Saint Johnsbury, Caledonia Co., Vermont, to Levi Snow and Lucina Streeter. Ordained apostle Feb. 12, 1849, by Brigham Young, at age 30; died May 27, 1888, at Salt Lake City, Salt Lake Co., Utah, at age 69.

24. Franklin Dewey Richards — Born April 2, 1821, at Richmond, Berkshire Co., Massachusetts, to Phinehas Richards and Wealthy Dewey. Ordained apostle Feb. 12, 1849, by Heber C. Kimball, at age 27; sustained as president of the Quorum of the Twelve Apostles Sept. 13, 1898; died Dec. 9, 1899, at Ogden, Weber Co., Utah, at age 78.

25. George Quayle Cannon — See FIRST COUNSELORS IN THE FIRST PRESIDENCY, No. 5.

26. Joseph Fielding Smith — See PRESIDENTS OF THE CHURCH, No. 6.

27. Brigham Young Jr. — See OTHER COUNSELORS IN THE FIRST PRESIDENCY, No. 6.

28. Albert Carrington — See OTHER COUNSELORS IN THE FIRST PRESIDENCY, No. 7.

29. Moses Thatcher — Born February 1842, Sangamon Co., Illinois, to Hezekiah Thatcher and Alley Kitchen. Ordained apostle April 9, 1879, by John Taylor, at age 37; dropped from the Quorum of the Twelve Apostles April 6, 1896; died Aug. 21, 1909, at Logan, Cache Co., Utah, at age 67.

30. Francis Marion Lyman — Born Jan. 12, 1840, at Good Hope, McDonough Co., Illinois, to Amasa Mason Lyman and Maria Louisa Tanner. Ordained apostle Oct. 27, 1880, by John Taylor, at age 40; sustained as president of the Quorum of the Twelve Apostles Oct. 6, 1903; died Nov. 18, 1916, at Salt Lake City, Salt Lake Co., Utah, at age 76.

31. John Henry Smith — See SECOND COUNSELORS IN THE FIRST PRESIDENCY, No. 10.

32. George Teasdale — Born Dec. 8, 1831, at London Middlesex Co., England, to William Russell Teasdale and Harriett H. Tidey. Ordained apostle Oct. 16, 1882, by John Taylor, at age 50; died June 9, 1907, at Salt Lake City, Salt Lake Co., Utah, at age 75.

33. Heber Jeddy Grant — See PRESIDENTS OF THE CHURCH, No. 7.

34. John Whittaker Taylor — Born May 15, 1858, at Provo, Utah Co., Utah, to John Taylor and Sophia Whittaker. Ordained apostle April 9, 1884, by John Taylor, at age 25; resigned Oct. 28, 1905; excommunicated March 28, 1911; died Oct. 10, 1916, at Salt Lake City, Salt Lake Co., Utah, at age 58. Blessings restored after death.

35. Marriner Wood Merrill — Born Sept. 25, 1832, at Sackville, Westmoreland Co., New Brunswick, Canada, to Nathan Alexander Merrill and Sarah Ann Reynolds. Ordained apostle Oct. 7, 1889, by Wilford Woodruff, at age 57; died Feb. 6, 1906, at Richmond, Cache Co., Utah, at age 73.

36. Anthon Henrik Lund — See FIRST COUNSELORS IN THE FIRST PRESIDENCY, No. 8.

37. Abraham Hoagland Cannon — Born March 12, 1859, at Salt Lake City, Salt Lake Co., Utah, to George Quayle Cannon and Elizabeth Hoagland. Sustained as one of the First Seven Presidents of the Seventy Oct. 8, 1882, at age 23; ordained apostle Oct. 7, 1889, by Joseph F. Smith, at age 30; died July 19, 1896, at Salt Lake City, Salt Lake Co., Utah, at age 37.

38. Matthias Foss Cowley — Born Aug. 25, 1858, at Salt Lake City, Salt Lake Co., Utah, to Matthias Cowley and Sarah Elizabeth Foss. Ordained apostle Oct. 7, 1897, by George Q. Cannon, at age 39; resigned Oct. 28, 1905; priesthood suspended May 11, 1911; restored to full membership April 3, 1936; died June 16, 1940, at Salt Lake City, Salt Lake Co., Utah, at age 81.

39. Abraham Owen Woodruff — Born Nov. 23, 1872, at Salt Lake City, Salt Lake Co., Utah, to Wilford Woodruff and Emma Smith. Ordained apostle Oct. 7, 1897, by Wilford Woodruff, at age 24; died June 20, 1904, at El Paso, El Paso Co., Texas, at age 31.

40. Rudger Clawson — See SECOND COUNSELORS IN THE FIRST PRESIDENCY, No. 8.

41. Reed Smoot — Born Jan. 10, 1862, at Salt Lake City, Salt Lake Co., Utah, to Abraham Owen Smoot and Anne Kestine Morrison. Ordained apostle April 8, 1900, by Lorenzo Snow, at age 38; served in the U.S. Senate, 1903-1933; died Feb. 9, 1941, at St. Petersburg, Pinellas Co., Florida, at age 79.

42. Hyrum Mack Smith — Born March 21, 1872, at Salt Lake City, Salt Lake Co., Utah, to Joseph Fielding Smith and Edna Lambson. Ordained apostle Oct. 24, 1901, by Joseph F. Smith, at age 29; died Jan. 23, 1918, at Salt Lake City, Salt Lake Co., Utah, at age 45.

43. George Albert Smith — See PRESIDENTS OF THE CHURCH, No. 8.

44. Charles William Penrose — See FIRST COUNSELORS IN THE FIRST PRESIDENCY, No. 9.

45. George Franklin Richards — Born Feb. 23, 1861, at Farmington, Davis Co., Utah, to Franklin Dewey Richards and Nanny Longstroth. Ordained apostle April 9, 1906, by Joseph F. Smith, at age 45; sustained as acting Patriarch to the Church Oct. 8, 1937; released from this position Oct. 3, 1942; sustained as president of the Quorum of the Twelve Apostles May 21, 1945; died Aug. 8, 1950, at Salt Lake City, Salt Lake Co., Utah, at age 89.

46. Orson Ferguson Whitney — Born July 1, 1855, at Salt Lake City, Salt Lake Co., Utah, to Horace Kimball Whitney and Helen Mar Kimball. Ordained apostle April 9, 1906, by Joseph F. Smith, at age 50; died May 16, 1931, at Salt Lake City, Salt Lake Co., Utah, at age 75.

47. David Oman McKay — See

PRESIDENTS OF THE CHURCH, No. 9.

48. Anthony Woodward Ivins — See FIRST COUNSELORS IN THE FIRST PRESIDENCY, No. 10.

49. Joseph Fielding Smith — See PRESIDENTS OF THE CHURCH, No. 10.

50. James Edward Talmage — Born Sept. 21, 1862, at Hungerford, Berkshire Co., England, to James J. Talmage and Susannah Preater. Ordained apostle Dec. 8, 1911, by Joseph F. Smith, at age 49; died July 27, 1933, at Salt Lake City, Salt Lake Co., Utah, at age 70.

51. Stephen L Richards — See FIRST COUNSELORS IN THE FIRST PRESIDENCY, No. 12.

52. Richard Roswell Lyman — Born Nov. 23, 1870, at Fillmore, Millard Co., Utah, to Francis Marion Lyman and Clara Caroline Callister. Ordained apostle April 7, 1918, by Joseph F. Smith, at age 47; excommunicated Nov. 12, 1943; rebaptized Oct. 27, 1954; died Dec. 31, 1963, at Salt Lake City, Salt Lake Co., Utah, at age 93.

53. Melvin Joseph Ballard — Born Feb. 9, 1873, at Logan, Cache Co., Utah, to Henry Ballard and Margaret Reid McNeil. Ordained apostle Jan. 7, 1919, by Heber J. Grant, at age 45; died July 30, 1939, at Salt Lake City, Salt Lake Co., Utah, at age 66.

54. John Andreas Widtsoe — Born Jan. 31, 1872, at Daloe, Island of Froyen, Trondhjem, Norway, to John A. Widtsoe and Anna Karine Gaarden. Ordained apostle March 17, 1921, by Heber J. Grant, at age 49; died Nov. 29, 1952, at Salt Lake City, Salt Lake Co., Utah, at age 80.

55. Joseph Francis Merrill — Born Aug. 24, 1868, at Richmond, Cache Co., Utah, to Marriner Wood Merrill and Mariah Loenza Kingsbury. Ordained apostle Oct. 8, 1931, by Heber J. Grant, at age 63; died Feb. 3, 1952, at Salt Lake City, Salt Lake Co., Utah, at age 83.

56. Charles Albert Callis — Born May 4, 1865, at Dublin, Dublin Co., Ireland, to John Callis and Susanna Charlotte Quillam. Ordained apostle Oct. 12, 1933, by Heber J. Grant, at age 68. Died Jan. 21, 1947, in Jacksonville, Duval Co., Florida, at age 81.

57. Joshua Reuben Clark Jr. — See FIRST COUNSELORS IN THE FIRST PRESIDENCY, No. 11.

58. Alonzo Arza Hinckley — Born April 23, 1870, at Cove Fort, Millard Co., Utah, to Ira Nathaniel Hinckley and Angeline Wilcox Noble. Ordained apostle Oct. 11, 1934, by Heber J. Grant, at age 64; died Dec. 22, 1936, at Salt Lake City, Salt Lake Co., Utah, at age 66.

59. Albert Ernest Bowen — Born Oct. 31, 1875, at Henderson Creek, Oneida Co., Idaho, to David Bowen and Annie Schackelton. Ordained apostle April 8, 1937, by Heber J. Grant, at age 61; died July 15, 1953, at Salt Lake City, Salt Lake Co., Utah, at age 77.

60. Sylvester Quayle Cannon — Born June 10, 1877, at Salt Lake City, Salt Lake Co., Utah, to George Quayle Cannon and Elizabeth Hoagland. Sustained as Presiding Bishop of the Church June 4,

1925, at age 47; sustained as Associate to the Quorum of the Twelve Apostles April 6, 1938; ordained apostle April 14, 1938, by Heber J. Grant; sustained as a member of the Quorum of the Twelve Apostles Oct. 6, 1939, at age 62; died May 29, 1943, at Salt Lake City, Salt Lake Co., Utah, at age 65.

61. Harold Bingham Lee — See PRESIDENTS OF THE CHURCH, No. 11.

62. Spencer Woolley Kimball — See PRESIDENTS OF THE CHURCH, No. 12.

63. Ezra Taft Benson — See PRESIDENTS OF THE CHURCH, No. 13.

64. Mark Edward Petersen — Born Nov. 7, 1900, at Salt Lake City, Salt Lake Co., Utah, to Christian Petersen and Christine M. Andersen. Ordained apostle April 20, 1944, by Heber J. Grant, at age 43; died Jan. 11, 1984, at Salt Lake City, Salt Lake Co., Utah, at age 83.

65. Matthew Cowley — Born Aug. 2, 1897, at Preston, Franklin Co., Idaho, to Matthias Foss Cowley and Abbie Hyde. Ordained apostle Oct. 11, 1945, by George Albert Smith, at age 48; died Dec. 13, 1953, at Los Angeles, Los Angeles Co., California, at age 56.

66. Henry Dinwoodey Moyle — See FIRST COUNSELORS IN THE FIRST PRESIDENCY, No. 14.

67. Delbert Leon Stapley — Born Dec. 11, 1896, at Mesa, Maricopa Co., Arizona, to Orley S. Stapley and Polly M. Hunsaker. Ordained apostle Oct. 5, 1950, by George Albert Smith, at age 53; died Aug. 19, 1978, at Salt Lake City, Salt Lake Co., Utah, at age 81.

68. Marion George Romney — See FIRST COUNSELORS IN THE FIRST PRESIDENCY, No. 18.

69. LeGrand Richards — Born Feb. 6, 1886, at Farmington, Davis Co., Utah, to George Franklin Richards and Alice Almira Robinson. Sustained Presiding Bishop of the Church April 6, 1938, at age 52; ordained apostle April 10, 1952, by David O. McKay, at age 66; died Jan. 11, 1983, at Salt Lake City, Salt Lake Co., Utah, at age 96.

70. Adam Samuel Bennion — Born Dec. 2, 1886, at Taylorsville, Salt Lake Co., Utah, to Joseph Bennion and Mary A. Sharp. Ordained apostle April 9, 1953, by David O. McKay, at age 66; died Feb. 11, 1958, at Salt Lake City, Salt Lake Co., Utah, at age 71.

71. Richard Louis Evans — Born March 23, 1906, at Salt Lake City, Salt Lake Co., Utah, to John A. Evans and Florence Neslen. Sustained as member of the First Council of the Seventy Oct. 7, 1938, at age 32; ordained apostle Oct. 8, 1953, by David O. McKay, at age 47; died Nov. 1, 1971, at Salt Lake City, Salt Lake Co., Utah, at age 65.

72. George Quayle Morris — Born Feb. 20, 1874, at Salt Lake City, Salt Lake Co., Utah, to Elias Morris and Mary L. Walker. Sustained as Assistant to the Quorum of the Twelve Apostles Oct. 6, 1951, at age 77; ordained apostle April 8, 1954, by David O. McKay, at age 80; died April 23, 1962, at Salt Lake City, Salt Lake Co., Utah, at age 88.

73. Hugh Brown Brown — See FIRST COUNSELORS IN THE FIRST PRESIDENCY, No. 15.

74. Howard William Hunter — See current FIRST PRESIDENCY.

75. Gordon Bitner Hinckley — See current FIRST PRESIDENCY.

76. Nathan Eldon Tanner — See FIRST COUNSELORS IN THE FIRST PRESIDENCY, No. 17.

77. Thomas Spencer Monson — See current FIRST PRESIDENCY.

78. Boyd Kenneth Packer — See current COUNCIL OF THE TWELVE.

79. Marvin Jeremy Ashton — Born May 6, 1915, in Salt Lake City, Salt Lake Co., Utah, to Marvin O. Ashton and Rachel Jeremy. Sustained Assistant to the Twelve Oct. 3, 1969, at age 54; ordained apostle on Dec. 2, 1971, by Harold B. Lee at age 56. Died Feb. 25, 1994, at Salt Lake City, Salt Lake Co., Utah, at age 78.

80. Bruce Redd McConkie — Born July 29, 1915, at Ann Arbor, Washtenaw Co., Michigan, to Oscar Walter McConkie and Vivian Redd. Sustained to First Council of the Seventy Oct. 6, 1946, at age 31; ordained apostle Oct. 12, 1972, by Harold B. Lee, at age 57; died April 19, 1985, at Salt Lake City, Salt Lake Co., Utah, at age 69.

81. Lowell Tom Perry — See current COUNCIL OF THE TWELVE.

82. David Bruce Haight — See current COUNCIL OF THE TWELVE.

83. James Esdras Faust — See current COUNCIL OF THE TWELVE.

84. Neal Ash Maxwell — See current COUNCIL OF THE TWELVE.

85. Russell Marion Nelson — See current COUNCIL OF THE TWELVE.

86. Dallin Harris Oaks — See current COUNCIL OF THE TWELVE.

87. Melvin Russell Ballard Jr. — See current COUNCIL OF THE TWELVE.

88. Joseph Bitner Wirthlin — See current COUNCIL OF THE TWELVE.

89. Richard Gordon Scott — See current COUNCIL OF THE TWELVE.

90. Robert Dean Hales — See current COUNCIL OF THE TWELVE.

91. Jeffrey Roy Holland — See current COUNCIL OF THE TWELVE.

OTHER APOSTLES

1. Joseph Smith Jr. — See PRESIDENTS OF THE CHURCH, No. 1.

2. Oliver Cowdery — See ASSISTANT PRESIDENTS OF THE CHURCH, No. 1.

3. Hyrum Smith — See ASSISTANT PRESIDENTS OF THE CHURCH, No. 2.

4. Amasa Mason Lyman — See OTHER COUNSELORS IN THE FIRST PRESIDENCY, No. 3.

5. Jedediah Morgan Grant — See SECOND COUNSELORS IN THE FIRST PRESIDENCY, No. 5.

6. John Willard Young — See FIRST COUNSELORS IN THE FIRST PRESIDENCY, No. 4.

7. Daniel Hanmer Wells — See SECOND COUNSELORS IN THE FIRST PRESIDENCY, No. 6.

8. Joseph Angell Young — Born Oct. 14, 1834, in Kirtland, Geauga Co., Ohio, to Brigham Young and Mary Ann Angell. Ordained apostle Feb. 4, 1864, by Brigham Young, at age 29; died Aug. 5, 1875, at Manti, Sanpete Co., Utah, at age 40.

9. Brigham Young Jr. — See OTHER COUNSELORS IN THE FIRST PRESIDENCY, No. 6.

10. Joseph Fielding Smith — See PRESIDENTS OF THE CHURCH, No. 6.

11. Sylvester Quayle Cannon — See COUNCIL OF THE TWELVE, No. 60.

12. Alvin Rulon Dyer — See OTHER COUNSELORS IN THE FIRST PRESIDENCY, No. 13.

PATRIARCHS TO THE CHURCH

1. Joseph Smith Sr. — See ASSISTANT COUNSELORS IN THE FIRST PRESIDENCY, No. 2.

2. Hyrum Smith — See ASSISTANT PRESIDENTS OF THE CHURCH, No. 2.

William Smith — See COUNCIL OF THE TWELVE, No. 9. Ordained Patriarch to the Church May 24, 1845, by the Quorum of the Twelve and then gave patriarchal blessings, but was rejected by the Church membership at the General Conference held Oct. 6, 1845.

3. John Smith — See ASSISTANT COUNSELORS IN THE FIRST PRESIDENCY, No. 4.

4. John Smith — Born Sept. 22, 1832, at Kirtland, Geauga Co., Ohio, the eldest son of Hyrum Smith and Jerusha Barden. Ordained Patriarch to the Church Feb. 18, 1855, by Brigham Young, at age 22; died Nov. 5, 1911, at Salt Lake City, Salt Lake Co., Utah, at age 79.

5. Hyrum Gibbs Smith — Born July 8, 1879, at South Jordan, Salt Lake Co., Utah, the eldest son of Hyrum Fisher Smith and Annie Maria Gibbs. Ordained high priest and Patriarch to the Church May 9, 1912, by Joseph F. Smith, at age 32; died Feb. 4, 1932, at Salt Lake City, Salt Lake Co., Utah, at age 52.

(From 1932 to 1937, no Patriarch to the Church was sustained.)

George Franklin Richards — (Served as acting Patriarch) See COUNCIL OF THE TWELVE, No. 45.

6. Joseph Fielding Smith — Born Jan. 30, 1899, at Salt Lake City, Salt Lake Co., Utah, the eldest son of Hyrum Mack Smith and Ida E. Bowman. Ordained high priest and Patriarch to the Church Oct. 8, 1942, by Heber J. Grant, at age 43; re-

leased Oct. 6, 1946, due to ill health; died Aug. 29, 1964, in Salt Lake City, Salt Lake Co., Utah, at age 65.

7. Eldred Gee Smith — Born Jan. 9, 1907, at Lehi, Utah Co., Utah, the eldest son of Hyrum Gibbs Smith and Martha Electa Gee. Ordained high priest May 23, 1938, by J. Reuben Clark Jr.; ordained Patriarch to the Church April 10,

1947, by George Albert Smith, at age 40; named emeritus General Authority Oct. 6, 1979.

(No Patriarch to the Church has been sustained since Oct. 6, 1979.)

FIRST COUNCIL OF THE SEVENTY
(Functioned from February 1835 to October 1976)

1. Hazen Aldrich — Chosen and ordained one of the First Seven Presidents Feb. 28, 1835; released April 6, 1837, having previously been ordained high priest.

2. Joseph Young — Born April 7, 1797, at Hopkinton, Middlesex Co., Massachusetts, to John Young and Abigail Howe. Ordained seventy Feb. 28, 1835, under the hands of Joseph Smith, Sidney Rigdon and Frederick G. Williams; chosen and ordained one of the First Seven Presidents Feb. 28, 1835, at age 37; died July 16, 1881, at Salt Lake City, Salt Lake Co., Utah, at age 84.

3. Levi Ward Hancock — Born April 7, 1803, at Springfield, Hampden, Co., Massachusetts, to Thomas Hancock and Amy Ward. Ordained seventy Feb. 28, 1835, under the hands of Joseph Smith, Sidney Rigdon and Frederick G. Williams; chosen and ordained one of the First Seven Presidents Feb. 28, 1835, at age 31; released April 6, 1837, having supposedly previously been ordained high priest; restored to former place in the First Council Sept. 3, 1837, as he had not been ordained high priest; died June 10, 1882, at Washington, Washington Co., Utah, at age 79.

4. Leonard Rich — Chosen and ordained one of the First Seven Presidents Feb. 28, 1835; released April 6, 1837, having previously been ordained high priest.

5. Zebedee Coltrin — Born Sept. 7, 1804, at Ovid, Seneca Co., New York, to John Coltrin Jr. and Sarah Graham. Chosen and ordained one of the First Seven Presidents Feb. 28, 1835, at age 30; released April 6, 1837, having previously been ordained high priest; died July 20, 1887, at Spanish Fork, Utah Co., Utah, at age 82.

6. Lyman Royal Sherman — Born May 22, 1804, at Salem, Essex Co., Massachusetts, to Elkanah Sherman and Asenath Hulbert. Chosen and ordained one of the First Seven Presidents Feb. 28, 1835, at age 30; released April 6, 1837, having previously been ordained high priest; died Jan. 27, 1839, at age 34.

7. Sylvester Smith — Chosen and ordained one of the First Seven Presidents Feb. 28, 1835; released April 6, 1837, having previously been ordained high priest.

8. John Gould — Born May 11, 1808. Ordained seventy and set apart as one of the First Seven Presidents April 6, 1837, by Sidney Rigdon and Hyrum Smith, at age 28; released Sept. 3, 1837, to be ordained high priest. Died May 9, 1851, at age 42.

9. James Foster — Born April 1, 1775, at Morgan Co., New Hampshire. Ordained seventy April 6, 1837, under the hands of Sidney Rigdon and Hyrum Smith; set apart as one of the First Seven Presidents April 6, 1837, at age 62; died Dec. 21, 1841, at Morgan Co., Illinois, at age 66.

10. Daniel Sanborn Miles — Born July 23, 1772, at Sanbornton, Belknap Co., New Hampshire, to Josiah Miles and Marah Sanborn. Ordained seventy April 6, 1837, by Hazen Aldrich; set apart as one of the First Seven Presidents April 6, 1837, by Sidney Rigdon and Hyrum Smith, at age 64; died in autumn of 1845, at Hancock Co., Illinois, at age 73.

11. Josiah Butterfield — Born March 13 or 18, 1795, at Saco, York Co., Maine, to Abel Butterfield and Mary or Mercy -----. Ordained seventy April 6, 1837, under the hands of Sidney Rigdon and Hyrum Smith; set apart as one of the First Seven Presidents April 6, 1837, at age 42; excommunicated Oct. 7, 1844; died in April 1871 at Monterey Co., California, at age 76.

12. Salmon Gee — Born Oct. 16, 1792, at Lyme, New London Co., Connecticut, to Zopher Gee and Esther Beckwith. Ordained seventy April 6, 1837, under the hands of Sidney Rigdon and Hyrum Smith; set apart as one of the First Seven Presidents April 6, 1837, at age 44; fellowship withdrawn March 6, 1838; died Sept. 13, 1845, at Ambrosia, Lee Co., Iowa, at age 52; posthumously reinstated Sept. 14, 1967.

13. John Gaylord — Born July 12, 1797, in Pennsylvania, to Chauncey Gaylord. Ordained seventy Dec. 20, 1836, by Hazen Aldrich; set apart as one of the First Seven Presidents April 6, 1837, at age 39, by Sidney Rigdon and others; excommunicated Jan. 13, 1838; rejoined the Church at Nauvoo, Illinois, Oct. 5, 1839; died July 17, 1878, at age 81.

14. Henry Harriman — Born June 9, 1804, at Rowley, Essex Co., Massachusetts, to Enoch Harriman and Sarah Brocklebank. Ordained seventy March 1835, under the hands of Joseph Smith and Sidney Rigdon; set apart as one of the First Seven Presidents Feb.  6, 1838, by Joseph Young and others, at age 33; died May 17, 1891, at Huntington, Emery Co., Utah, at age 86.

15. Zera Pulsipher — Born June 24, 1789, at Rockingham, Windham Co., Vermont, to John Pulsipher and Elizabeth Dutton. Ordained seventy March 6, 1838, under the hands of Joseph Young and James Foster; set apart as one of the First Seven Presidents March 6, 1838, at age 48; re-  leased April 12, 1862; died Jan. 1, 1872, at Hebron, Washington Co., Utah, at age 82.

Roger Orton was excommunicated Nov. 30, 1837; returned to the Church; sustained as one of the First Seven Presidents April 7, 1845, but was never set apart and did not function; dropped from this position Oct. 6, 1845.

16. Albert Perry Rockwood — Born June 5, 1805, at Holliston, Middlesex Co., Massachusetts, to Luther Rockwood and Ruth Perry. Ordained seventy Jan. 5, 1839, under the hands of Joseph Young, Henry Harriman and Zera Pulsipher; set apart as one  of the First Seven Presidents Dec. 2, 1845, by Brigham Young and others, at age 40; died Nov. 26, 1879, at Sugar House, Salt Lake Co., Utah, at age 74.

17. Benjamin Lynn Clapp — Born Aug. 19, 1814, at West Huntsville, Madison Co., Alabama, to Ludwig Lewis Clapp and Margaret Ann Loy. Ordained seventy Oct. 20, 1844, under the hands of Joseph Young and Levi W. Hancock; set apart as one of the First  Seven Presidents Dec. 2, 1845, by Brigham Young and others, at age 31; excommunicated April 7, 1859; died in 1860 in California, at age 46.

18. Jedediah Morgan Grant — See SECOND COUNSELORS IN THE FIRST PRESIDENCY, No. 5.

19. Horace Sunderlin Eldredge —
Born Feb. 6, 1816, at Brutus, Cayuga Co., New York, to Alanson Eldredge and Esther Sunderlin. Ordained seventy Oct. 13, 1844, by Joseph Young; sustained as one of the First Seven Presidents Oct. 7, 1854, at age 38;  died Sept. 6, 1888, at Salt Lake City, Salt Lake Co., Utah, at age 72.

20. Jacob Gates — Born March 9, 1811, at Saint Johnsbury, Caledonia Co., Vermont, to Thomas Gates and Patty Plumley. Ordained seventy Dec. 19, 1838, under the hands of Joseph Smith and Sidney Rigdon; sustained as one  of the First Seven Presidents April 6, 1860, at age 49; set apart Oct. 8, 1862, by Orson Hyde; died April 14, 1892, at Provo, Utah Co., Utah, at age 81.

21. John Van Cott — Born Sept. 7, 1814, at Canaan, Columbia Co., New York, to Losee Van Cott and Lovinia Pratt. Ordained seventy Feb. 25, 1847, by Joseph Young; sustained as one of the First Seven Presidents Oct. 8, 1862, at age 48;  set apart by John Taylor; died Feb. 18, 1883, at Salt Lake City, Salt Lake Co., Utah, at age 68.

22. William Whittaker Taylor —
Born Sept. 11, 1853, at Salt Lake City, Salt Lake Co., Utah, to John Taylor and Harriet Whittaker. Ordained seventy Oct. 11, 1875, by Orson Pratt; sustained as one of the First Seven Presidents April 7, 1880, at age 26; set  apart by John Taylor; died Aug. 1, 1884, at Salt Lake City, Salt Lake Co., Utah, at age 30.

23. Abraham Hoagland Cannon —
See COUNCIL OF THE TWELVE, No. 37.

Theodore Belden Lewis — Born Nov. 18, 1843, at St. Louis, St. Louis Co., Missouri, to Thomas Anderson Lewis and Martha J. O. Belden. Ordained high priest at Nephi, Utah (date not known); sustained as one of the First Seven Presidents Oct. 8,  1882, at age 38; on Oct. 9, when he was to be set apart, he reported that he was already a high priest, so he was not set apart and did not function in this position.

24. Seymour Bicknell Young —
Born Oct. 3, 1837, at Kirtland, Geauga Co., Ohio, to Joseph Young and Jane Adeline Bicknell. Ordained seventy Feb. 18, 1857, by Edmund Ellsworth; set apart by Franklin D. Richards as one of the First Seven Presidents  Oct. 14, 1882, at age 45; sustained April 8, 1883; died Dec. 15, 1924, at Salt Lake City, Salt Lake Co., Utah, at age 87.

25. Christian Daniel Fjelsted —
Born Feb. 20, 1829, at Amagar, Sundbyvester Co., Denmark, to Hendrick Ludvig Fjelsted and Ann Catrine Hendriksen. Ordained seventy Feb. 5, 1859, by William H. Walker; sustained as one of the First Seven Presidents  April 6, 1884, at age 55; set apart by Wilford Woodruff; died Dec. 23, 1905, at Salt Lake City, Salt Lake Co., Utah, at age 76.

26. John Morgan — Born Aug. 8, 1842, at Greensburg, Decatur Co., Indiana, to Gerrard Morgan and Ann Eliza Hamilton. Ordained seventy Oct. 8, 1875, by Joseph Young; sustained as one of the First Seven Presidents Oct. 5,  1884, at age 42; set apart by Wilford Woodruff; died Aug. 14, 1894, at Preston, Franklin Co., Idaho, at age 52.

27. Brigham Henry Roberts — Born March 13, 1857, at Warrington, Lancashire Co., England, to Benjamin Roberts and Ann Everington. Ordained seventy March 8, 1877, by Nathan T. Porter. Sustained as one of the First Seven Presidents Oct. 7,  1888, at age 31; set apart by Lorenzo Snow; died Sept. 27, 1933, at Salt Lake City, Salt Lake Co., Utah, at age 76.

28. George Reynolds — Born Jan. 1, 1842, at Marylebone, London Co., London, England, to George Reynolds and Julia Ann Tautz. Ordained seventy March 18, 1866, by Israel Barlow; sustained as one of the First Seven Presidents April 5, 1890, at  age 48; set apart by Lorenzo Snow; died Aug. 9, 1909, at Salt Lake City, Salt Lake Co., Utah, at age 67.

29. Jonathan Golden Kimball — Born June 9, 1853, at Salt Lake City, Salt Lake Co., Utah, to Heber Chase Kimball and Christeen Golden. Ordained seventy July 21, 1886, by William M. Allred; sustained as one of the First Seven Presidents April 5,  1892, at age 38; set apart by Francis M. Lyman; killed in an automobile accident Sept. 2, 1938, near Reno, Nevada, at age 85.

30. Rulon Seymour Wells — Born July 7, 1854, at Salt Lake City, Salt Lake Co., Utah, to Daniel Hanmer Wells and Louisa Free. Ordained seventy Oct. 22, 1875, by Brigham Young; sustained as one of the First Seven Presidents April 5, 1893, at age 38;  set apart by George Q. Cannon; died May 7, 1941, at Salt Lake City, Salt Lake Co., Utah, at age 86.

31. Edward Stevenson — Born May 1, 1820, at Gibraltar, Spain, to Joseph Stevenson and Elizabeth Stevens. Ordained seventy May 1, 1844, by Joseph Young; sustained as one of the First Seven Presidents Oct. 7, 1894, at age 74; set apart by Brigham  Young; died Jan. 27, 1897, at Salt Lake City, Salt Lake Co., Utah, at age 76.

32. Joseph William McMurrin — Born Sept. 5. 1858, at Tooele, Tooele Co., Utah, to Joseph McMurrin and Margaret Leaning. Ordained seventy April 21, 1884, by Royal Barney; sustained as one of the First Seven Presidents Oct. 5, 1897, at age 39;  set apart Jan. 21, 1898, by Anthon H. Lund; died Oct. 24, 1932, at Los Angeles, Los Angeles Co., California, at age 74.

33. Charles Henry Hart — Born July 5, 1866, at Bloomington, Bear Lake Co., Idaho, to James Henry Hart and Sabina Scheib. Ordained seventy Aug. 10, 1890, by John Henry Smith; sustained as one of the First Seven Presidents April 9, 1906, at age 39;  set apart by Joseph F. Smith; died Sept. 29, 1934, at Salt Lake City, Salt Lake Co., Utah, at age 68.

34. Levi Edgar Young — Born Feb. 2, 1874, at Salt Lake City, Salt Lake Co., Utah, to Seymour Bicknell Young and Ann Elizabeth Riter. Ordained seventy June 18, 1897, by Seymour B. Young; sustained as one of the First Seven Presidents Oct. 6,  1909, at age 35; set apart Jan. 23, 1910, by John Henry Smith; died Dec. 13, 1963, at Salt Lake City, Salt Lake Co., Utah, at age 89.

35. Rey Lucero Pratt — Born Oct. 11, 1878, at Salt Lake City, Salt Lake Co., Utah, to Helaman Pratt and Emeline Victoria Billingsley. Ordained seventy Sept. 23, 1911, by Rulon S. Wells; sustained as one of the First Seven Presidents Jan. 29,  1925, at age 46; set apart April 7, 1925, by Anthony W. Ivins; died April 14, 1931, at Salt Lake City, Salt Lake Co., Utah at age 52.

36. Antoine Ridgeway Ivins — Born May 11, 1881, at St. George, Washington Co., Utah, to Anthony Woodward Ivins and Elizabeth A. Snow. Ordained seventy Dec. 28, 1913, by Fred E. Barker; sustained as one of the First Seven Presidents Oct. 4,  1931, at age 50; ordained high priest June 11, 1961, by David O. McKay; died Oct. 18, 1967, at Salt Lake City, Salt Lake Co., Utah, at age 86.

37. Samuel Otis Bennion — Born June 9, 1874, at Taylorsville, Salt Lake Co., Utah, to John Rowland Bennion and Emma Jane Terry. Ordained seventy March 14, 1904, by Samuel Gerrard; sustained as one of the First Seven Presidents April 6, 1933, at  age 58; set apart by Heber J. Grant; died March 8, 1945, at Salt Lake City, Salt Lake Co., Utah, at age 70.

38. John Harris Taylor — Born June 28, 1875, at Salt Lake City, Salt Lake Co., Utah, to Thomas E. Taylor and Emma L. Harris. Ordained seventy Jan. 24, 1896, by Heber J. Grant; sustained as one of the First Seven Presidents Oct. 6, 1933, at age 58;  set apart by Heber J. Grant; died May 28, 1946, at Salt Lake City, Salt Lake Co., Utah, at age 70.

39. Rufus Kay Hardy — Born May 28, 1878, at Salt Lake City, Salt Lake Co., Utah, to Rufus H. Hardy and Annie Kay. Ordained seventy July 2, 1897, by John Henry Smith; sustained to the First Council of the Seventy Oct. 6, 1934, at age 56; set apart  Feb. 7, 1935, by Heber J. Grant; died March 7, 1945, at Salt Lake City, Salt Lake Co., Utah, at age 66.

40. Richard Louis Evans — See COUNCIL OF THE TWELVE, No. 71.

41. Oscar Ammon Kirkham — Born Jan. 22, 1880, at Lehi, Utah Co., Utah, to James Kirkham and Martha Mercer. Ordained seventy Feb. 26, 1905, by Joseph W. McMurrin; sustained to the First Council of the Seventy Oct. 5, 1941, at age 61; set apart by  Heber J. Grant; died March 10, 1958, at Salt Lake City, Salt Lake Co., Utah, at age 78.

42. Seymour Dilworth Young — See FIRST QUORUM OF THE SEVENTY, No. 24.

43. Milton Reed Hunter — Born Oct. 25, 1902, at Holden, Millard Co., Utah, to John E. Hunter and Margaret Teeples. Ordained seventy Aug. 31, 1928, by Rulon S. Wells; sustained to the First Council of the Seventy April 6, 1945, at age 42; ordained  high priest June 11, 1961, by David O. McKay; died June 27, 1975, at Salt Lake City, Salt Lake Co., Utah, at age 72.

44. Bruce Redd McConkie — See COUNCIL OF THE TWELVE, No. 80.

45. Marion Duff Hanks — See PRESIDENCY OF THE SEVENTY, No. 6.

46. Albert Theodore Tuttle — See PRESIDENCY OF THE SEVENTY, No. 4.

47. Paul Harold Dunn — See PRESIDENCY OF THE SEVENTY, No. 7.

48. Hartman Rector Jr. — See FIRST QUORUM OF THE SEVENTY, No. 25.

49. Loren Charles Dunn — See current FIRST QUORUM OF THE SEVENTY.

50. Rex Dee Pinegar — See current PRESIDENCY OF THE SEVENTY.

51. Gene Raymond Cook — See current FIRST QUORUM OF THE SEVENTY.

On Oct. 3, 1975, the First Quorum of the Seventy was reconstituted with the sustaining of three members, Elders Charles Didier, William R. Bradford and George P. Lee. Four additional members, Elders Carlos E. Asay, M. Russell Ballard, John H. Groberg and Jacob de Jager, were sustained April 3, 1976.

On Oct. 1, 1976, the members of the First Council of the Seventy and the Assistants to the Quorum of the Twelve Apostles were released, and sustained to the First Quorum of the Seventy. A Presidency of the First Quorum of the Seventy was sustained, and the position of the members of the quorum revised.

ASSISTANTS TO THE TWELVE
(Functioned from April 1941 to October 1976)

1. Marion George Romney — See FIRST COUNSELORS IN THE FIRST PRESIDENCY, No. 18.

2. Thomas Evans McKay — Born Oct. 29, 1875, at Huntsville, Weber Co., Utah, to David McKay and Jennette Eveline Evans. Ordained high priest July 26, 1908, by George F. Richards; sustained as Assistant to the Quorum of the Twelve Apostles April  6, 1941, and set apart May 23, 1941, by Heber J. Grant, at age 65; died Jan. 15, 1958, at Salt Lake City, Salt Lake Co., Utah, at age 82.

3. Clifford Earl Young — Born Dec. 7, 1883, at Salt Lake City, Salt Lake Co., Utah, to Seymour Bicknell Young and Ann Elizabeth Riter. Ordained high priest July 1, 1928, by Heber J. Grant; sustained as Assistant to the Quorum of the Twelve Apostles  April 6, 1941, and set apart May 23, 1941, by President Grant, at age 57; died Aug. 21, 1958, at Salt Lake City, Salt Lake Co., Utah, at age 74.

4. Alma Sonne — See FIRST QUORUM OF THE SEVENTY, No. 8.

5. Nicholas Groesbeck Smith — Born June 20, 1881, at Salt Lake City, Salt Lake Co., Utah, to John Henry Smith and Josephine Groesbeck. Ordained high priest Aug. 1, 1921, by Rudger Clawson; sustained an Assistant to the Quorum of the Twelve  Apostles April 6, 1941; set apart Oct. 1, 1941, by Heber J. Grant, at age 60; died Oct. 27, 1945, at Salt Lake City, Salt Lake Co., Utah, at age 64.

6. George Quayle Morris — See COUNCIL OF THE TWELVE, No. 72.

7. Stayner Richards — Born Dec. 20, 1885, at Salt Lake City, Salt Lake Co., Utah, to Stephen Longstroth Richards and Emma Louise Stayner. Ordained high priest Feb. 24, 1914, by George F.  Richards; sustained as Assistant to the Quorum of the Twelve Apostles Oct. 6, 1951, and set apart Oct. 11, 1951, by David O. McKay, at age 65; died May 28, 1953, at Salt Lake City, Salt Lake Co., Utah, at age 67.

8. ElRay LaVar Christiansen — Born July 13, 1897, at Mayfield, Sanpete Co., Utah, to Parley Christiansen and Dorthea C. Jensen. Ordained high priest Oct. 22, 1933, by George F. Richards; sustained as Assistant to the Quorum of the Twelve Apostles Oct. 6,  1951, and set apart Oct. 11, 1951, by Stephen L Richards, at age 54; died Dec. 1, 1975, at Salt Lake City, Salt Lake Co., Utah, at age 78.

9. John Longden — Born Nov. 4, 1898, at Oldham, Lancashire Co., England, to Thomas Johnson Longden and Lizetta Taylor. Ordained high priest Sept. 27, 1925, by Rudger Clawson; sustained as Assistant to the Quorum of the Twelve Apostles Oct. 6,  1951, and set apart Oct. 11, 1951, by J. Reuben Clark Jr., at age 52; died Aug. 30, 1969, at Salt Lake City, Salt Lake Co., Utah, at age 70.

10. Hugh Brown Brown — See FIRST COUNSELORS IN THE FIRST PRESIDENCY, No. 15.

11. Sterling Welling Sill — See FIRST QUORUM OF THE SEVENTY, No. 9.

12. Gordon Bitner Hinckley — See current FIRST PRESIDENCY.

13. Henry Dixon Taylor — See FIRST QUORUM OF THE SEVENTY, No. 10.

14. William James Critchlow Jr. — Born Aug. 21, 1892, at Brigham City, Box Elder Co., Utah, to William James Critchlow and Anna C. Gregerson. Ordained high priest Dec. 16, 1934, by George F. Richards; sustained as Assistant to the Quorum of the Twelve  Apostles Oct. 11, 1958, and set apart Oct. 16, 1958, by David O. McKay, at age 66; died Aug. 29, 1968, at Ogden, Weber Co., Utah, at age 76.

15. Alvin Rulon Dyer — See OTHER COUNSELORS IN THE FIRST PRESIDENCY, No. 13.

16. Nathan Eldon Tanner — See FIRST COUNSELORS IN THE FIRST PRESIDENCY, No. 17.

17. Franklin Dewey Richards — See PRESIDENCY OF THE SEVENTY, No. 1.

18. Theodore Moyle Burton — See FIRST QUORUM OF THE SEVENTY, No. 12.

19. Henry Thorpe Beal Isaacson — See OTHER COUNSELORS IN THE FIRST PRESIDENCY, No. 12.

20. Boyd Kenneth Packer — See current COUNCIL OF THE TWELVE.

21. Bernard Park Brockbank — See FIRST QUORUM OF THE SEVENTY, No. 13.

22. James Alfred Cullimore — See FIRST QUORUM OF THE SEVENTY, No. 14.

23. Marion Duff Hanks — See PRESIDENCY OF THE SEVENTY, No. 6.

24. Marvin Jeremy Ashton — See COUNCIL OF THE TWELVE, No. 79.

25. Joseph Anderson — See FIRST QUORUM OF THE SEVENTY, No. 15.

26. David Bruce Haight — See current COUNCIL OF THE TWELVE.

27. William Hunter Bennett — See FIRST QUORUM OF THE SEVENTY, No. 16.

28. John Henry Vandenberg — See PRESIDING BISHOPS, No. 9.

29. Robert Leatham Simpson — See FIRST QUORUM OF THE SEVENTY, No. 18.

30. Oscar Leslie Stone — See FIRST QUORUM OF THE SEVENTY, No. 19.

31. James Esdras Faust — See current COUNCIL OF THE TWELVE.

32. Lowell Tom Perry — See current COUNCIL OF THE TWELVE.

33. John Thomas Fyans — See PRESIDENCY OF THE SEVENTY, No. 3.

34. Neal Ash Maxwell — See current COUNCIL OF THE TWELVE.

35. William Grant Bangerter — See PRESIDENCY OF THE SEVENTY, No. 8.

36. Robert Dean Hales — See current COUNCIL OF THE TWELVE.

37. Adney Yoshio Komatsu — See FIRST QUORUM OF THE SEVENTY, No. 22.

38. Joseph Bitner Wirthlin — See current COUNCIL OF THE TWELVE.

PRESIDENCY OF THE SEVENTY

(Since April 1, 1989, serves as the Presidency of both the First Quorum of the Seventy and the Second Quorum of the Seventy)

1. Franklin Dewey Richards — Born Nov. 17, 1900, in Og-den, Weber Co., Utah, to Charles C. Richards and Louisa L. Peery. Sustained as Assistant to the Quorum of the Twelve Apostles Oct. 8, 1960, at age 59; sustained to First Quorum of the Seventy Oct. 1,  1976; served in Presidency of the First Quorum of the Seventy, Oct. 1, 1976, to Oct. 1, 1983; died Nov. 13, 1987, at Salt Lake City, Salt Lake Co., Utah, at age 86.

2. James Esdras Faust — See current COUNCIL OF THE TWELVE.

3. John Thomas Fyans — Born May 17, 1918, at Moreland, Bingham Co., Idaho, to Joseph Fyans and Mae Farnsworth. Sustained as Assistant to the Quorum of the Twelve Apostles April 6, 1974, at age 55; sustained to First Quorum of the Seventy Oct. 1, 1976;  served in Presidency of the First Quorum of the Seventy, Oct. 1, 1976, to Oct. 6, 1985; named emeritus General Authority Oct. 1, 1989.

4. Albert Theodore Tuttle — Born March 2, 1919, in Manti, Sanpete Co., Utah, to Albert M. Tuttle and Clarice Beal. Sustained to First Council of the Seventy April 6, 1958, at age 39; sustained to First Quorum of the Seventy Oct. 1, 1976;  served in Presidency of the First Quorum of the Seventy, Oct. 1, 1976, to Feb. 22, 1980; died Nov. 28, 1986, at Salt Lake City, Salt Lake Co., Utah, at age 67.

5. Neal Ash Maxwell — See current COUNCIL OF THE TWELVE.

6. Marion Duff Hanks — Born Oct. 13, 1921, in Salt Lake City, Salt Lake Co., Utah, to Stanley Alonzo Hanks and Maude Frame. Sustained to First Council of the Seventy Oct. 4, 1953, at age 31, and as Assistant to the Quorum of the Twelve Apostles  April 6, 1968; sustained to the First Quorum of the Seventy Oct. 1, 1976; served in the Presidency of the First Quorum of the Seventy from Oct. 1, 1976-April 5, 1980, and from Oct. 6, 1984-Aug. 15, 1992; named emeritus General Authority Oct. 3, 1992.

7. Paul Harold Dunn — Born April 24, 1924, at Provo, Utah Co., Utah, to Joshua Harold Dunn and Geneve Roberts. Sustained to First Council of the Seventy April 6, 1964, at age 39; sustained to First Quorum of the Seventy Oct. 1, 1976; served in Presi-  dency of the First Quorum of the Seventy, Oct. 1, 1976, to Feb. 22, 1980; named emeritus General Authority Oct. 1, 1989.

8. William Grant Bangerter — Born June 8, 1918, at Granger, Salt Lake Co., Utah, to William Henry Bangerter and Isabelle Bawden. Sustained as Assistant to the Quorum of the Twelve Apostles April 4, 1975, at age 56; sustained to First Quorum of the Seventy Oct.  1, 1976; served in Presidency of the First Quorum of the Seventy from Sept. 30,

1978, to April 5, 1980, and from Feb. 17, 1985, to Oct. 1, 1989; named emeritus General Authority Oct. 1, 1989.

9. Carlos Egan Asay — See current PRESIDENCY OF THE SEVENTY.

10. Melvin Russell Ballard Jr. — See current COUNCIL OF THE TWELVE.

11. Dean LeRoy Larsen — See current FIRST QUORUM OF THE SEVENTY.

12. Royden Glade Derrick — Born Sept. 7, 1915 at Salt Lake City, Salt Lake Co., Utah, to Hyrum H. Derrick and Margaret Glade. Sustained to First Quorum of the Seventy Oct. 1, 1976, at age 61; served in Presidency of the First Quorum of the Seventy,  April 5, 1980, to Oct. 6, 1984; named emeritus General Authority Oct. 1, 1989.

13. George Homer Durham — Born Feb. 4, 1911, at Parowan, Iron Co., Utah, to George H. Durham and Mary Ellen Marsden. Sustained to First Quorum of the Seventy April 2, 1977, at age 66; served in Presidency of the First Quorum of the Seventy,  Oct. 1, 1981, until his death on Jan. 10, 1985, at Salt Lake City, Salt Lake Co., Utah, at age 73.

14. Richard Gordon Scott — See current COUNCIL OF THE TWELVE.

15. Marion Duff Hanks — See PRESIDENCY OF THE SEVENTY, No. 6.

16. William Grant Bangerter — See PRESIDENCY OF THE SEVENTY, No. 8.

17. Jack H Goaslind Jr. — See current FIRST QUORUM OF THE SEVENTY.

18. Robert LeGrand Backman — Born March 22, 1922, in Salt Lake City, Salt Lake Co., Utah, to LeGrand P. and Edith Price Backman. Sustained to the First Quorum of the Seventy April 1, 1978, at age 56; served in the Presidency of the Seventy, Oct.  6, 1985, to Aug. 15, 1992; named emeritus General Authority Oct. 3, 1992.

19. Joseph Bitner Wirthlin — See current COUNCIL OF THE TWELVE.

20. Hugh Wallace Pinnock — See current FIRST QUORUM OF THE SEVENTY.

21. James Martin Paramore — See current FIRST QUORUM OF THE SEVENTY.

22. John Richard Clarke — See current FIRST QUORUM OF THE SEVENTY.

23. Rex Dee Pinegar — See current PRESIDENCY OF THE SEVENTY.

24. Carlos Egan Asay — See current PRESIDENCY OF THE SEVENTY.

25. Charles Amand Andre Didier — See current PRESIDENCY OF THE SEVENTY.

26. Lloyd Aldin Porter — See current PRESIDENCY OF THE SEVENTY.

27. Joe Junior Christensen — See current PRESIDENCY OF THE SEVENTY.

28. Monte James Brough — See current PRESIDENCY OF THE SEVENTY.

29. Warren Eugene Hansen — See current PRESIDENCY OF THE SEVENTY.

FIRST QUORUM OF THE SEVENTY

1. Franklin Dewey Richards — See PRESIDENCY OF THE SEVENTY, No. 1.

2. James Esdras Faust — See current COUNCIL OF THE TWELVE.

3. John Thomas Fyans — See PRESIDENCY OF THE SEVENTY, No. 3.

4. Albert Theodore Tuttle — See PRESIDENCY OF THE SEVENTY, No. 4.

5. Neal Ash Maxwell — See current COUNCIL OF THE TWELVE.

6. Marion Duff Hanks — See PRESIDENCY OF THE SEVENTY, No. 6.

7. Paul Harold Dunn — See PRESIDENCY OF THE SEVENTY, No. 7.

8. Alma Sonne — Born March 5, 1884, at Logan, Cache Co., Utah, to Niels C. Sonne and Elisa Peterson. Sustained as Assistant to the Quorum of the Twelve Apostles April 6, 1941, at age 57; sustained to First Quorum of the Seventy Oct. 1, 1976; died Nov. 27,  1977, at Logan, Cache Co., Utah, at age 93.

9. Sterling Welling Sill — Born March 31, 1903, at Layton, Davis Co., Utah, to Joseph Albert Sill and Marcetta Welling. Sustained as Assistant to the Quorum of the Twelve Apostles April 6, 1954, at age 51; sustained to First Quorum of the Seventy Oct. 1, 1976;  named emeritus General Authority Dec. 31, 1978. Died in Salt Lake City, Salt Lake Co., Utah, on May 25, 1994, at age 91.

10. Henry Dixon Taylor — Born Nov. 22, 1903, in Provo, Utah Co., Utah, to Arthur N. Taylor and Maria Dixon. Sustained as Assistant to the Quorum of the Twelve Apostles April 6, 1958, at age 54; sustained to First Quorum of the Seventy Oct. 1, 1976;  named emeritus General Authority Sept. 30, 1978; died Feb. 24, 1987, at Salt Lake City, Salt Lake Co., Utah, at age 83.

11. Alvin Rulon Dyer — See OTHER COUNSELORS IN THE FIRST PRESIDENCY, No. 13.

12. Theodore Moyle Burton — Born March 27, 1907, at Salt Lake City, Salt Lake Co., Utah, to Theodore T. Burton and Florence Moyle. Sustained as Assistant to the Quorum of the Twelve Apostles Oct. 8, 1960, at age 53; sustained to First Quorum of the  Seventy Oct. 1, 1976; named emeritus General Authority Oct. 1, 1989; died

Dec. 22, 1989, at Salt Lake City, Salt Lake Co., Utah, at age 82.

13. Bernard Park Brockbank — Born May 24, 1909, at Salt Lake City, Salt Lake Co., Utah, to Taylor P. Brockbank and Sarah LeCheminant. Sustained as Assistant to the Quorum of the Twelve Apostles Oct. 6, 1962, at age 53; sustained to First Quorum  of the Seventy Oct. 1, 1976; named emeritus General Authority Oct. 4, 1980.

14. James Alfred Cullimore — Born Jan. 17, 1906, at Lindon, Utah Co., Utah, to Albert Lorenzo Cullimore and Luella Keetch. Sustained an Assistant to the Quorum of the Twelve Apostles April 6, 1966, at age 60; sustained to First Quorum of the  Seventy Oct. 1, 1976; named emeritus General Authority Sept. 30, 1978; died June 14, 1986, at Salt Lake City, Salt Lake Co., Utah, at age 80.

15. Joseph Anderson — Born Nov. 20, 1889, at Salt Lake City, Salt Lake Co., Utah, to George Anderson and Isabella Watson. Sustained as Assistant to the Quorum of the Twelve Apostles April 6, 1970, at age 80; sustained to First Quorum of the Seventy  Oct. 1, 1976; named emeritus General Authority Dec. 31, 1978; died March 13, 1992, at Salt Lake City, Salt Lake Co., Utah, at age 102.

16. William Hunter Bennett — Born Nov. 5, 1910, at Taber, Alberta, Canada, to William Alvin Bennett and Mary Walker. Sustained as Assistant to the Quorum of the Twelve Apostles April 6, 1970, at age 59; sustained to First Quorum of the Seventy Oct. 1,  1976; named emeritus General Authority Dec. 31, 1978; died July 23, 1980, at Bountiful, Davis Co., Utah, at age 69.

17. John Henry Vandenberg — See PRESIDING BISHOPS, No. 9.

18. Robert Leatham Simpson — Born Aug. 8, 1915, at Salt Lake City, Salt Lake Co., Utah, to Heber C Simpson and Lillian Leatham. Sustained as first counselor to Presiding Bishop John H. Vandenberg Sept. 30, 1961, at age 46; sustained as Assistant to the Quorum of the Twelve Apostles April 6, 1972; sustained to First Quorum of the Seventy Oct. 1, 1976; named emeritus General Authority Oct. 1, 1989.

19. Oscar Leslie Stone — Born May 28, 1903, at Chapin, Idaho, to Frank J. Stone and Mable Crandall. Sustained as Assistant to the Quorum of the Twelve Apostles, Oct. 6, 1972, at age 69; sustained to First Quorum of the Seventy, Oct. 1, 1976; named emeritus General Authority Oct. 4, 1980; died April 26, 1986, at Salt Lake City, Salt Lake Co., Utah, at age 82.

20. William Grant Bangerter — See PRESIDENCY OF THE SEVENTY, No. 8.

21. Robert Dean Hales — See current COUNCIL OF THE TWELVE.

22. Adney Yoshio Komatsu — Born Aug. 2, 1923, at Honolulu, Honolulu Co., Hawaii, to Jizaemon Komatsu and Misao Tabata. Sustained as Assistant to the Quorum of the Twelve Apostles, April 4, 1975, at age 51; sustained to the First Quorum of the Seventy Oct. 1, 1976; named emeritus General Authority Oct. 2, 1993.

23. Joseph Bitner Wirthlin — See current COUNCIL OF THE TWELVE.

24. Seymour Dilworth Young — Born Sept. 7, 1897, at Salt Lake City, Salt Lake Co., Utah, to Seymour Bicknell Young Jr. and Carlie Louine Clawson. Sustained to the First Council of the Seventy April 6, 1945, at age 47; sustained to the First Quorum of the Seventy Oct. 1, 1976; named emeritus General Authority Sept. 30, 1978; died July 9, 1981, at Salt Lake City, Salt Lake Co., Utah, at age 83.

25. Hartman Rector Jr. — Born Aug. 20, 1924, at Moberly, Randolph Co., Mo., to Hartman Rector and Vivian Fay Garvin. Sustained to the First Council of the Seventy April 6, 1968, at age 43; sustained to the First Quorum of the Seventy Oct. 1, 1976; named emeritus General Authority Oct. 1, 1994.

26. Loren Charles Dunn — See current FIRST QUORUM OF THE SEVENTY.

27. Rex Dee Pinegar — See current PRESIDENCY OF THE SEVENTY.

28. Gene Raymond Cook — See current FIRST QUORUM OF THE SEVENTY.

29. Charles Amand Andre Didier — See current PRESIDENCY OF THE SEVENTY.

30. William Rawsel Bradford — See current FIRST QUORUM OF THE SEVENTY.

31. George Patrick Lee — Born March 23, 1943, at Towaoc, Ute Mountain Indian Reservation, Colorado, to Pete Lee and Mae K. Asdzaatchii. Sustained to First Quorum of the Seventy Oct. 3, 1975, at age 32; excommunicated Sept. 1, 1989.

32. Carlos Egan Asay — See current PRESIDENCY OF THE SEVENTY.

33. Melvin Russell Ballard Jr. — See current COUNCIL OF THE TWELVE.

34. John Holbrook Groberg — See current FIRST QUORUM OF THE SEVENTY.

35. Jacob de Jager — Born Jan. 16, 1923, at The Hague, South Holland, Netherlands, to Alexander Philippis de Jager and Maria Jacoba Cornelia Scheele. Sustained to the First Quorum of the Seventy April 3, 1976, at age 53; named emeritus General Authority Oct. 2, 1993.

36. Vaughn J Featherstone — See current FIRST QUORUM OF THE SEVENTY.

37. Dean LeRoy Larsen — See current FIRST QUORUM OF THE SEVENTY.

38. Royden Glade Derrick — See PRESIDENCY OF THE SEVENTY, No. 12.

39. Robert Earl Wells — See current FIRST QUORUM OF THE SEVENTY.

40. George Homer Durham — See PRESIDENCY OF THE SEVENTY, No. 13.

41. James Martin Paramore — See current FIRST QUORUM OF THE SEVENTY.

42. Richard Gordon Scott — See current COUNCIL OF THE TWELVE.

43. Hugh Wallace Pinnock — See current FIRST QUORUM OF THE SEVENTY.

44. Friedrich Enzio Busche — See current FIRST QUORUM OF THE SEVENTY.

45. Yoshihiko Kikuchi — See current FIRST QUORUM OF THE SEVENTY.

46. Ronald Eugene Poelman — See current FIRST QUORUM OF THE SEVENTY.

47. Derek Alfred Cuthbert — Born Oct. 5, 1926, at Nottingham, Derbyshire Co., England, to Harry Cuthbert and Hilda May Freck. Sustained to the First Quorum of the Seventy April 1, 1978, at age 51; died April 7, 1991, at Salt Lake City, Salt Lake Co., Utah, at age 64.

48. Robert LeGrand Backman — See PRESIDENCY OF THE SEVENTY, No. 18.

49. Rex Cropper Reeve Sr. — Born Nov. 23, 1914, at Hinckley, Millard Co., Utah, to Arthur H. Reeve and Mary A. Cropper. Sustained to First Quorum of the Seventy April 1, 1978, at age 63; named emeritus General Authority Oct. 1, 1989.

50. Fred Burton Howard — See current FIRST QUORUM OF THE SEVENTY.

51. Teddy Eugene Brewerton — See current FIRST QUORUM OF THE SEVENTY.

52. Jack H Goaslind Jr. — See current FIRST QUORUM OF THE SEVENTY.

53. Angel Abrea — See current FIRST QUORUM OF THE SEVENTY.

54. John Kay Carmack — See current FIRST QUORUM OF THE SEVENTY.

55. Russell Carl Taylor — Born Nov. 25, 1925, at Red Mesa, Conejos Co., Colorado, to Leo Sanford Taylor and Florence Stella Dean. Sustained to First Quorum of the Seventy April 7, 1984, at age 58; sustained to Second Quorum of the Seventy April 1, 1989; released Oct. 1, 1989.

56. Robert B Harbertson — Born April 19, 1932, at Ogden, Weber Co. Utah, to Brigham Y. Harbertson and Gladys Venice Lewis; sustained to First Quorum of the Seventy April 7, 1984, at age 51; sustained to Second Quorum of the Seventy April 1, 1989; released Oct. 1, 1989.

57. Devere Harris — Born May 30, 1916, at Portage, Box Elder Co. Utah, to Robert Crumbell Harris and Sylvia Green. Sustained to First Quorum of the Seventy April 7, 1984, at age 67; sustained to Second Quorum of the Seventy April 1, 1989; released Oct. 1, 1989.

58. Spencer Hamlin Osborn — Born July 8, 1921, at Salt Lake City, Salt Lake Co., Utah, to William W. Osborn and Alice M. Hamlin. Sustained to First Quorum of the Seventy April 7, 1984, at age 62; sustained to Second Quorum of the Seventy April 1, 1989; released Oct. 1, 1989.

59. Phillip Tadje Sonntag — Born July 13, 1921, at Salt Lake City, Salt Lake Co., Utah, to Richard Peter Sonntag and Lena Emma Tadje. Sustained to First Quorum of the Seventy April 7, 1984, at age 62; sustained to Second Quorum of the Seventy April 1, 1989; released Oct. 1, 1989.

60. John Sonnenberg — Born April 11, 1922, at Schneidemuhle, Germany, to Otto Paul Sonnenberg and Lucille Mielke. Sustained to First Quorum of the Seventy Oct. 6, 1984, at age 62; sustained to Second Quorum of the Seventy April 1, 1989; released Oct. 1, 1989.

61. Ferril Arthur Kay — Born July 15, 1916, at Annabella, Sevier Co., Utah, to Samuel Arthur Kay and Medora Hooper. Sustained to First Quorum of the Seventy Oct. 6, 1984, at age 68; sustained to Second Quorum of the Seventy April 1, 1989; released Oct. 1, 1989.

62. Keith Wilson Wilcox — Born May 15, 1921, at Hyrum, Cache Co., Utah, to Irving C. Wilcox and Nancy Mary Wilson. Sustained to First Quorum of the Seventy Oct. 6, 1984, at age 63; sustained to Second Quorum of the Seventy April 1, 1989; released Oct. 1, 1989.

63. Victor Lee Brown — See PRESIDING BISHOPS, No. 10.

64. Harold Burke Peterson — Born Sept. 19, 1923, in Salt Lake City, Salt Lake Co., Utah, to Harold A. Peterson and Juna Tye. Sustained as first counselor in Presiding Bishopric April 6, 1972, at age 48; sustained to the First Quorum of the Seventy April 6, 1985: named emeritus General Authority Oct. 2, 1993.

65. John Richard Clarke — See current FIRST QUORUM OF THE SEVENTY.

66. Hans Benjamin Ringger — See current FIRST QUORUM OF THE SEVENTY.

67. Waldo Pratt Call — Born Feb. 5, 1928, at Colonia Juarez, Chihuahua, Mexico, to Charles Helaman Call and Hannah Skousen. Sustained to First Quorum of the Seventy April 6, 1985, at age 57; sustained to Second Quorum of the Seventy April 1, 1989; released Oct. 6, 1990.

68. Helio Da Rocha Camargo — Born Feb. 1, 1926, at Resende, Rio de Janeiro, Brazil, to Jose Medeiros de Camargo and Else Ferreira da Rocha. Sustained to First Quorum of the Seventy April 6, 1985, at age 59; sustained to Second Quorum of the Seventy on April 1, 1989; released on Oct. 6, 1990.

69. Hans Verlan Andersen — Born Nov. 6, 1914, in Logan, Cache Co., Utah, to Hans Andersen and Mynoa Richardson. Sustained to the First Quorum of the Seventy April 6, 1986, at age 71; sustained to the Second Quorum of the Seventy April 1, 1989; released Oct. 5, 1991; died July 16, 1992, at Orem, Utah Co., Utah, at age 76.

70. George Ivins Cannon — Born March 9, 1920, in Salt Lake City, Salt Lake Co., Utah, to George J. Cannon and Lucy Grant. Sustained to the First Quorum of the Seventy April 6, 1986, at age 66; sustained to the Second Quorum of the Seventy April 1, 1989; released Oct. 5, 1991.

71. Francis Marion Gibbons — Born April 10, 1921, in St. Johns, Apache Co., Ariz., to Andrew S. Gibbons and Adeline Christensen. Sustained to the First Quorum of the Seventy April 6, 1986, at age 64; sustained to the Second Quorum of the Seventy April 1, 1989; released Oct. 5, 1991.

72. Gardner Hale Russell — Born Aug. 12, 1920, in Salt Lake City, Salt Lake Co., Utah, to Harry J. Russell and Agnes Gardner. Sustained to the First Quorum of the Seventy April 6, 1986, at age 65; sustained to the Second Quorum of the Seventy April 1, 1989; released Oct. 5, 1991.

73. George Richard Hill III — Born Nov. 24, 1921, in Ogden, Weber Co., Utah, to George Richard Hill Jr. and Elizabeth O. McKay. Sustained to the First Quorum of the Seventy April 4, 1987, at age 65; sustained to the Second Quorum of the Seventy April 1, 1989; released Oct. 3, 1992.

74. John Roger Lasater — Born Dec. 8, 1931, in Farmington, Davis Co., Utah, to Robert B. Lasater and Rowena Saunders. Sustained to the First Quorum of the Seventy April 4, 1987, at age 55; sustained to the Second Quorum of the Seventy April 1, 1989; released Oct. 3, 1992.

75. Douglas James Martin — Born April 20, 1927, in Hastings, New Zealand, to George Martin and Jesse Jamieson. Sustained to the First Quorum of the Seventy April 4, 1987, at age 59; sustained to the Second Quorum of the Seventy April 1, 1989; released Oct. 3, 1992.

76. Alexander Baillie Morrison — See current FIRST QUORUM OF THE SEVENTY.

77. Lloyd Aldin Porter — See current PRESIDENCY OF THE SEVENTY.

78. Glen Larkin Rudd — Born May 18, 1918, in Salt Lake City, Salt Lake Co., Utah, to Charles P. Rudd and Gladys Thomas. Sustained to First Quorum of the Seventy April 4, 1987, at age 68; sustained to the Second Quorum of the Seventy April 1, 1989; released Oct. 3, 1992.

79. Douglas Hill Smith — Born May 11, 1921, in Salt Lake City, Salt Lake

Co., Utah, to Virgil H. Smith and Winifred Pearl Hill. Sustained to the First Quorum of the Seventy April 4, 1987, at age 65; sustained to the Second Quorum of the Seventy April 1, 1989; released Oct. 3, 1992.

80. Lynn Andrew Sorensen — Born Sept. 25, 1919, in Salt Lake City, Salt Lake Co., Utah, to Ulric Andrew Sorensen and Ferny Boam. Sustained to the First Quorum of the Seventy April 4, 1987, at age 67; sustained to the Second Quorum of the Seventy April 1, 1989; released Oct. 3, 1992.

81. Robert Edward Sackley — Born Dec. 17, 1922, in Lismore, New South Wales, Australia, to Cecil James Sackley and Mary Duncan. Sustained to the First Quorum of the Seventy April 2, 1988, at age 65; sustained to the Second Quorum of the Seventy April 1, 1989; died Feb. 22, 1993, near Brisbane, Austrailia, at age 70.

82. Larry Lionel Kendrick — See current FIRST QUORUM OF THE SEVENTY.

83. Monte James Brough — See current PRESIDENCY OF THE SEVENTY.

84. Albert Choules Jr. — Born Feb. 15, 1926, in Driggs, Teton Co., Idaho, to Albert Choules and Rula Wilson. Sustained to the First Quorum of the Seventy Oct. 1, 1988, at age 62; sustained to the Second Quorum of the Seventy April 1, 1989; released Oct. 1, 1994.

85. Lloyd Preal George Jr. — Born Sept. 17, 1920, in Kanosh, Millard Co., Utah, to Preal George and Artemesia Palmer. Sustained to the First Quorum of the Seventy Oct. 1, 1988, at age 68; sustained to the Second Quorum of the Seventy April 1, 1989; released Oct. 1, 1994.

86. Gerald Eldon Melchin — Born May 24, 1921, in Kitchener, Ontario, to Arthur and Rosetta Willis Melchin. Sustained to the First Quorum of the Seventy on Oct. 1, 1988, at age 67; sustained to the Second Quorum of the Seventy on April 1, 1989; released Oct. 1, 1994.

87. Joe Junior Christensen — See current PRESIDENCY OF THE SEVENTY.

88. Warren Eugene Hansen Jr. — See current PRESIDENCY OF THE SEVENTY.

89. Jeffrey Roy Holland — See current COUNCIL OF THE TWELVE.

90. Marlin Keith Jensen — See current FIRST QUORUM OF THE SEVENTY.

91. Earl Carr Tingey — See current FIRST QUORUM OF THE SEVENTY.

92. Harold Gordon Hillam — See current FIRST QUORUM OF THE SEVENTY.

93. Carlos Humberto Amado — See current FIRST QUORUM OF THE SEVENTY.

94. Benjamin Berry Banks — See current FIRST QUORUM OF THE SEVENTY.

95. Spencer Joel Condie — See current FIRST QUORUM OF THE SEVENTY.

96. Robert Kent Dellenbach — See current FIRST QUORUM OF THE SEVENTY.

97. Henry Bennion Eyring — See current FIRST QUORUM OF THE SEVENTY.

98. Glenn Leroy Pace - See current FIRST QUORUM OF THE SEVENTY.

99. Floyd Melvin Hammond — See current FIRST QUORUM OF THE SEVENTY.

100. Kenneth Johnson — See current FIRST QUORUM OF THE SEVENTY.

101. Lynn Alvin Mickelsen — See current FIRST QUORUM OF THE SEVENTY.

102. Neil Linden Andersen — See current FIRST QUORUM OF THE SEVENTY.

103. David Todd Christofferson — See current FIRST QUORUM OF THE SEVENTY.

104. Cree-L Kofford — See current FIRST QUORUM OF THE SEVENTY.

105. Dennis Bramwell Neuenschwander — See current FIRST QUORUM OF THE SEVENTY.

106. Andrew Wayne Peterson — See current FIRST QUORUM OF THE SEVENTY.

107. Cecil Osborn Samuelson Jr. — See current FIRST QUORUM OF THE SEVENTY.

SECOND QUORUM OF THE SEVENTY

The Second Quorum of the Seventy was created April 1, 1989, in response to the "continued rapid growth of the Church." (*Church News,* April 8, 1989.)

The initial members of the Second Quorum were those General Authorities serving under a five-year call (called from April 1984 to October 1988) in the First Quorum of the Seventy. General Authorities in the Second Quorum are called for five years.

1. Russell Carl Taylor — See FIRST QUORUM OF THE SEVENTY No. 55.

2. Robert B Harbertson — See FIRST QUORUM OF THE SEVENTY No. 56.

3. Devere Harris — See FIRST QUORUM OF THE SEVENTY No. 57.

4. Spencer Hamlin Osborn — See FIRST QUORUM OF THE SEVENTY No. 58.

5. Philip Tadje Sonntag — See FIRST QUORUM OF THE SEVENTY No. 59.

6. John Sonnenberg — See FIRST QUORUM OF THE SEVENTY No. 60.

7. Ferril Arthur Kay — See FIRST QUORUM OF THE SEVENTY No. 61.

8. Keith Wilson Wilcox — See FIRST QUORUM OF THE SEVENTY No. 62.

9. Waldo Pratt Call — See FIRST QUORUM OF THE SEVENTY, No. 67.

10. Helio Da Rocha Camargo — See FIRST QUORUM OF THE SEVENTY, No. 68.

11. Hans Verlan Andersen — See FIRST QUORUM OF THE SEVENTY, No. 69.

12. George Ivins Cannon — See FIRST QUORUM OF THE SEVENTY, No. 70.

13. Francis Marion Gibbons — See FIRST QUORUM OF THE SEVENTY, No. 71.

14. Gardner Hale Russell — See FIRST QUORUM OF THE SEVENTY, No. 72.

15. George Richard Hill III — See FIRST QUORUM OF THE SEVENTY, No. 73.

16. John Roger Lasater — See FIRST QUORUM OF THE SEVENTY, No. 74.

17. Douglas James Martin — See FIRST QUORUM OF THE SEVENTY, No. 75.

18. Alexander Baillie Morrison — See current FIRST QUORUM OF THE SEVENTY.

19. Lloyd Aldin Porter — See current PRESIDENCY OF THE SEVENTY.

20. Glen Larkin Rudd — See FIRST QUORUM OF THE SEVENTY, No. 78.

21. Douglas Hill Smith — See FIRST QUORUM OF THE SEVENTY, No. 79.

22. Lynn Andrew Sorensen — See FIRST QUORUM OF THE SEVENTY, No. 80.

23. Robert Edward Sackley — See FIRST QUORUM OF THE SEVENTY, No. 81.

24. Larry Lionel Kendrick — See current FIRST QUORUM OF THE SEVENTY.

25. Monte James Brough — See

current PRESIDENCY OF THE SEVENTY.

26. Albert Choules Jr. — See FIRST QUORUM OF THE SEVENTY, No. 84.

27. Lloyd Preal George — See FIRST QUORUM OF THE SEVENTY, No. 85.

28. Gerald Eldon Melchin — See FIRST QUORUM OF THE SEVENTY, No. 86.

29. Carlos Humberto Amado — See current FIRST QUORUM OF THE SEVENTY.

30. Benjamin Berry Banks — See current FIRST QUORUM OF THE SEVENTY.

31. Spencer Joel Condie — See current FIRST QUORUM OF THE SEVENTY.

32. Floyd Melvin Hammond — See current FIRST QUORUM OF THE SEVENTY.

33. Malcolm Seth Jeppsen — Born Nov. 1, 1924, in Mantua, Box Elder Co., Utah, to Conrad Jeppsen and Laurine Nielsen. Sustained to the Second Quorum of the Seventy April 1, 1989, at age 64. Released Oct. 1, 1994.

34. Richard Powell Lindsay — Born March 18, 1926, in Salt Lake City, Salt Lake Co., Utah, to Samuel Bennion Lindsay and Mary Alice Powell. Sustained to the Second Quorum of the Seventy April 1, 1989, at age 63. Released Oct. 1, 1994.

35. Merlin Rex Lybbert — Born Jan. 31, 1926, in Cardston, Alberta, to Charles Lester Lybbert and Delvia Reed. Sustained to the Second Quorum of the Seventy April 1, 1989, at age 63. Released Oct. 1, 1994.

36. Horacio Antonio Tenorio — Born March 6, 1935, in Mexico City, Distrito Federal, Mexico, to Leopoldo Horacio Tenorio and Blanca Otilia Oriza Arenas. Sustained to the Second Quorum of the Seventy April 1, 1989, at age 54. Released Oct. 1, 1994.

37. Eduardo Ayala — See current SECOND QUORUM OF THE SEVENTY.

38. LeGrand Raine Curtis — See current SECOND QUORUM OF THE SEVENTY.

39. Clinton Louis Cutler — Born Dec. 27, 1929, in Salt Lake City, Salt Lake Co., Utah, to Benjamin Lewis Cutler and Hellie Helena Sharp. Sustained to the Second Quorum of the Seventy March 31, 1990, at age 60. Died April 9, 1994, at South Jordan, Salt Lake Co., Utah, at age 64.

40. Robert Kent Dellenbach — See current FIRST QUORUM OF THE SEVENTY.

41. Harold Gordon Hillam — See current FIRST QUORUM OF THE SEVENTY.

42. Kenneth Johnson — See current FIRST QUORUM OF THE SEVENTY.

43. Helvecio Martins — See current SECOND QUORUM OF THE SEVENTY.

44. Lynn Alvin Mickelsen — See current FIRST QUORUM OF THE SEVENTY.

45. J Ballard Washburn — See current SECOND QUORUM OF THE SEVENTY.

46. Durrel Arden Woolsey — See current SECOND QUORUM OF THE SEVENTY.

47. Rulon Gerald Craven — See current SECOND QUORUM OF THE SEVENTY.

48. William McKenzie Lawrence — See current SECOND QUORUM OF THE SEVENTY.

49. Julio Enrique Davila — See current SECOND QUORUM OF THE SEVENTY.

50. Graham Watson Doxey — See current SECOND QUORUM OF THE SEVENTY.

51. Cree-L Kofford — See current FIRST QUORUM OF THE SEVENTY.

52. Joseph Carl Muren — See current SECOND QUORUM OF THE SEVENTY.

53. Dennis Bramwell Neuenschwander — See current FIRST QUORUM OF THE SEVENTY.

54. Jorge Alfonso Rojas — See current SECOND QUORUM OF THE SEVENTY.

55. In Sang Han — See current SECOND QUORUM OF THE SEVENTY.

56. Stephen Douglas Nadauld — See current SECOND QUORUM OF THE SEVENTY.

57. Sam Koyei Shimabukuro — See current SECOND QUORUM OF THE SEVENTY.

58. Lino Alvarez — See current SECOND QUORUM OF THE SEVENTY.

59. Dallas Nielsen Archibald — See current SECOND QUORUM OF THE SEVENTY.

60. Merrill Joseph Bateman — See current PRESIDING BISHOPRIC.

61. Chellus Max Caldwell — See current SECOND QUORUM OF THE SEVENTY.

62. Gary Jerome Coleman — See current SECOND QUORUM OF THE SEVENTY.

63. John Baird Dickson — See current SECOND QUORUM OF THE SEVENTY.

64. John Emerson Fowler — See current SECOND QUORUM OF THE SEVENTY.

65. Jay Edwin Jensen — See current SECOND QUORUM OF THE SEVENTY.

66. Augusto Alandy Lim — See current SECOND QUORUM OF THE SEVENTY.

67. John Max Madsen — See current SECOND QUORUM OF THE SEVENTY.

68. Victor Dallas Merrell — See current SECOND QUORUM OF THE SEVENTY.

69. David Eugene Sorensen — See current SECOND QUORUM OF THE SEVENTY.

70. Frank David Stanley — See current SECOND QUORUM OF THE SEVENTY.

71. Kwok Yuen Tai — See current SECOND QUORUM OF THE SEVENTY.

72. Lowell Dale Wood — See current SECOND QUORUM OF THE SEVENTY.

PRESIDING BISHOPS

1. Edward Partridge — Born Aug. 27, 1793, at Pittsfield, Berkshire Co., Massachusetts, to William Partridge and Jemima Bidwell. Ordained high priest June 6, 1831, by Lyman Wight; called by revelation to be the First Bishop of the Church Feb. 4, 1831, at age 37 (D&C 41:9); died May 27, 1840, at Nauvoo, Hancock Co., Illinois, at age 46.

2. Newel Kimball Whitney — Born Feb. 5, 1795, at Marlborough, Windham Co., Vermont, to Samuel Whitney and Susanna Kimball. Called by revelation to be the First Bishop of Kirtland (D&C 72:8); sustained as First Bishop of the Church Oct. 7, 1844, at age 49; sustained as Presiding Bishop of the Church April 6, 1847; died Sept. 23, 1850, at Salt Lake City, Salt Lake Co., Utah, at age 55.

George Miller — Born Nov. 25, 1794, at Orange Co., Virginia, to John Miller and Margaret Pfeiffer. Sustained as Second Bishop of the Church Oct. 7, 1844, at age 49; dropped prior to 1847; disfellowshipped Oct. 20, 1848.

3. Edward Hunter — Born June 22, 1793, at Newton, Delaware Co., Pennsylvania, to Edward Hunter and Hannah Maris. Ordained high priest Nov. 23, 1844, by Brigham Young; sustained as Presiding Bishop of the Church April 7, 1851, at age 57; died Oct. 16, 1883, at Salt Lake City, Salt Lake Co., Utah, at age 90.

4. William Bowker Preston — Born Nov. 24, 1830, at Halifax, Franklin Co., Virginia, to Christopher Preston and Martha Mitchell Clayton. Ordained high priest Nov. 14, 1859, by Orson Hyde; sustained as Presiding Bishop of the Church April 6, 1884, at age 53; released due to ill health Dec. 4, 1907; died Aug. 2, 1908, at Salt Lake City, Salt Lake Co., Utah, at age 77.

5. Charles Wilson Nibley — See SECOND COUNSELORS IN THE FIRST PRESIDENCY, No. 13.

6. Sylvester Quayle Cannon — See COUNCIL OF THE TWELVE, No. 60.

7. LeGrand Richards — See COUNCIL OF THE TWELVE, No. 69.

8. Joseph Leopold Wirthlin — Born Aug. 14, 1893, at Salt Lake City, Salt Lake Co., Utah, to Joseph Wirthlin and Emma Hillstead. Ordained high priest Feb. 24, 1926, by Charles W. Nibley; sustained as second coun-

selor to Presiding Bishop LeGrand Richards April 6, 1938, at age 44; sustained as first counselor to Bishop Richards Dec. 12, 1946; sustained as Presiding Bishop of the Church April 6, 1952, at age 58; released Sept. 30, 1961; died Jan. 25, 1963, at Salt Lake City, Salt Lake Co., Utah, at age 69.

9. John Henry Vandenberg — Born Dec. 18, 1904, at Ogden, Weber Co., Utah, to Dirk Vandenberg and Maria Alkema. Sustained as Presiding Bishop of the Church Sept. 30, 1961, at age 56; sustained as Assistant to the Quorum of the Twelve Apostles April 6, 1972; sustained to First Quorum of the Seventy Oct. 1, 1976; named emeritus General Authority Dec. 31, 1978; died June 3, 1992, at Sandy, Salt Lake Co., Utah, at age 87.

10. Victor Lee Brown — Born July 31, 1914, at Cardston, Alberta, Canada, to Gerald Stephen Brown and Maggie Calder Lee. Sustained as second counselor to Presiding Bishop John H. Vandenberg Sept. 30, 1961, at age 47; sustained as Presiding Bishop of the Church April 6, 1972; sustained to First Quorum of the Seventy April 6, 1985; named emeritus General Authority Oct. 1, 1989.

11. Robert Dean Hales — See current COUNCIL OF THE TWELVE.

12. Merrill Joseph Bateman See current PRESIDING BISHOPRIC.

FIRST COUNSELORS TO PRESIDING BISHOPS

1. Isaac Morley — Born March 11, 1786, at Montague, Hampshire Co., Massachusetts, to Thomas Morley and Editha Marsh. Ordained high priest June 3, 1831, by Lyman Wight; set apart as first counselor to Presiding Bishop Edward Partridge June 6, 1831,

at age 45; released at the death of Bishop Partridge May 27, 1840; died June 24, 1865, at Fairview, Sanpete Co., Utah, at age 79.

2. Leonard Wilford Hardy — Born Dec. 31, 1805, at Bradford, Essex Co., Massachusetts, to Simon Hardy and

Rhoda Hardy. Ordained high priest April 6, 1856, by John Taylor; sustained as first counselor to Presiding Bishop Edward Hunter Oct. 6, 1856, at age 50; died July 31, 1884, at Salt Lake City, Salt Lake Co., Utah, at age 78.

3. Robert Taylor Burton — Born Oct. 25, 1821, at Amhertsburg, Ontario, Canada, to Samuel Burton and Hannah Shipley. Ordained high priest Sept. 2, 1875, by Edward Hunter; sustained as second counselor to Presiding Bishop Edward Hunter Oct. 9, 1874, at age 52; sustained as first counselor to Presiding Bishop William B. Preston Oct. 5, 1884; died Nov. 11, 1907, at Salt Lake City, Salt Lake Co., Utah, at age 86.

4. Orrin Porter Miller — Born Sept. 11, 1858, at Mill Creek, Salt Lake Co., Utah, to Reuben G. Miller and Ann Craynor. Ordained high priest Aug. 8, 1886, by Angus M. Cannon; sustained as second counselor to Presiding Bishop William B. Preston Oct. 24, 1901, at age 43; sustained as first counselor to Presiding Bishop Charles W. Nibley Dec. 4, 1907, at age 49; died July 7, 1918, at Salt Lake City, Salt Lake Co., Utah at age 59.

5. David Asael Smith — Born May 24, 1879, at Salt Lake City, Salt Lake Co., Utah, to Joseph Fielding Smith and Julina Lambson. Ordained high priest Dec. 11, 1907, by Anthon H. Lund; sustained as second counselor to Presiding Bishop Charles W. Nibley Dec. 4, 1907, at age 28; sustained as first counselor to Bishop Nibley July 18, 1918, at age 39; sustained as first counselor to Presiding Bishop Sylvester Q.

Cannon June 4, 1925; released April 6, 1938; died April 6, 1952, at Salt Lake City, Salt Lake Co., Utah, at age 72.

6. Marvin Owen Ashton — Born April 8, 1883, at Salt Lake City, Salt Lake Co., Utah, to Edward T. Ashton and Effie W. Morris. Ordained high priest June 22, 1917, by Heber J. Grant; sustained as first counselor to Presiding Bishop LeGrand Richards April 6, 1938, at age 54; died Oct. 7, 1946, at Salt Lake City, Salt Lake Co., Utah, at age 63.

7. Joseph Leopold Wirthlin — See PRESIDING BISHOPS, No., 8.

8. Henry Thorpe Beal Isaacson — See OTHER COUNSELORS IN THE FIRST PRESIDENCY, No. 12.

9. Robert Leatham Simpson — See FIRST QUORUM OF THE SEVENTY, No. 18.

10. Harold Burke Peterson — See FIRST QUORUM OF THE SEVENTY, No. 64.

11. Henry Bennion Eyring — See current FIRST QUORUM OF THE SEVENTY.

12. Harold David Burton — See current PRESIDING BISHOPRIC.

SECOND COUNSELORS TO PRESIDING BISHOPS

1. John Corrill — Born Sept. 17, 1794, at Worcester Co., Massachusetts. Ordained high priest June 6, 1831, by Edward Partridge; set apart as second counselor to Presiding Bishop Edward Partridge June 6, 1831, at age 36; released Aug. 1, 1837; excommunicated March 17, 1839.

2. Titus Billings — Born March 25, 1793, at Greenfield, Franklin Co., Massachusetts, to Ebenezer Billings and Esther Joyce. Ordained high priest Aug. 1, 1837, by Edward Partridge; set apart as second counselor to Presiding Bishop Edward Partridge

Aug. 1, 1837, at age 44; released at the death of Bishop Partridge May 27, 1840; died Feb. 6, 1866, at Provo, Utah Co., Utah, at age 72.

3. Jesse Carter Little — Born Sept. 26, 1815, at Belmont, Waldo Co., Maine, to Thomas Little and Relief White. Ordained high priest April 17, 1845, by Parley P. Pratt; sustained as second counselor to Presiding Bishop Edward Hunter Oct. 6, 1856, at age 41; resigned summer of 1874; died Dec. 26, 1893, at Salt Lake City, Salt Lake Co., Utah, at age 78.

4. Robert Taylor Burton — See FIRST COUNSELORS IN THE PRESIDING BISHOPRIC, No. 3.

5. John Quayle Cannon — Born April 19, 1857, at San Francisco, San Francisco Co., California, to George Quayle Cannon and Elizabeth Hoagland. Ordained high priest October 1884 by John Taylor; sustained as second counselor to Presiding Bishop William B. Preston Oct. 5, 1884, at age 27; excommunicated Sept. 5, 1886; rebaptized May 6, 1888; died Jan. 14, 1931, at Salt Lake City, Salt Lake Co., Utah, at age 73.

6. John Rex Winder — See FIRST COUNSELORS IN THE FIRST PRESIDENCY, No. 7.

7. Orrin Porter Miller — See FIRST COUNSELORS IN THE PRESIDING BISHOPRIC, No. 4.

8. David Asael Smith — See FIRST COUNSELORS IN THE PRESIDING BISHOPRIC, No. 5.

9. John Wells — Born Sept. 16, 1864, at Carlton, Nottinghamshire, England, to Thomas Potter Wells and Sarah Cook. Ordained high priest Feb. 12, 1911, by Richard W. Young; sustained as second counselor to Presiding Bishop Charles W. Nibley July 18, 1918, at age 53; sustained as second counselor to Presiding Bishop Sylvester Q. Cannon June 4, 1925; released April 6, 1938; died April 18, 1941, at Salt Lake City, Salt Lake Co., Utah, at age 76.

10. Joseph Leopold Wirthlin — See PRESIDING BISHOPS, No. 8.

11. Henry Thorpe Beal Isaacson — See OTHER COUNSELORS IN THE FIRST PRESIDENCY, No. 12.

12. Carl William Buehner — Born Dec. 27, 1898, at Stuttgart, Wuerttemberg, Germany, to Carl F. Buehner and Anna B. Geigle. Ordained high priest Dec. 9, 1935, by Richard R. Lyman; sustained as second counselor to Presiding Bishop Joseph L. Wirthlin April 6, 1952, at age 53; released Sept. 30, 1961; died Nov. 18, 1974, at Salt Lake City, Salt Lake Co., Utah, at age 75.

13. Victor Lee Brown — See PRESIDING BISHOPS, No. 10.

14. Vaughn J Featherstone — See current FIRST QUORUM OF THE SEVENTY.

15. John Richard Clarke — See current FIRST QUORUM OF THE SEVENTY.

16. Glenn Leroy Pace — See current FIRST QUORUM OF THE SEVENTY.

17. Richard Crockett Edgley — See current PRESIDING BISHOPRIC.

LENGTH OF SERVICE IN THE
FIRST PRESIDENCY AND COUNCIL OF THE TWELVE
(As of October 1994)

Name	Date of service, Age at time	Length of service	Total Years as General Authority†
David O. McKay	Apr 1906 (32) - Jan 1970 (96)	63 yrs 9 mos	
Heber J. Grant	Oct 1882 (25) - May 1945 (88)	62 yrs 7 mos	
Joseph Fielding Smith	Apr 1910 (33) - Jul 1972 (95)	62 yrs 3 mos	
Wilford Woodruff	Apr 1839 (32) - Sep 1898 (91)	59 yrs 5 mos	
***Lorenzo Snow**	Feb 1849 (34) - Oct 1901 (87)	52 yrs 8 mos	
Joseph Fielding Smith	Jul 1866 (27) - Nov 1918 (80)	52 yrs 4 mos	
Franklin D. Richards	Feb 1849 (27) - Dec 1899 (78)	50 yrs 10 mos	
Ezra Taft Benson	Oct 1943 (44) - May 1994 (94)	50 yrs 7 mos	
John Taylor	Dec 1838 (30) - Jul 1887 (78)	48 yrs 7 mos	
George Albert Smith	Oct 1903 (33) - Apr 1951 (81)	47 yrs 6 mos	
Orson Pratt	Apr 1835 (23) - Aug 1842 Jan 1843 -Oct 1881 (70)	46 yrs 1 mo	
Rudger Clawson	Oct 1898 (41) - Jun 1943 (86)	44 yrs 8 mos	
George F. Richards	Apr 1906 (45) - Aug 1950 (89)	44 yrs 4 mos	
Orson Hyde	Feb 1835 (30) - May 1837 June 1837 - Nov 1878 (73)	43 yrs 9 mos	
Brigham Young	Feb 1835 (33) - Aug 1877 (76)	42 yrs 6 mos	
Stephen L Richards	Jan 1917 (37) - May 1959 (79)	42 yrs 4 mos	
Spencer W. Kimball	Oct 1943 (48) - Nov 1985 (90)	42 yrs 1 mo	
Reed Smoot	Apr 1900 (38) - Feb 1941 (79)	40 yrs 10 mos	
*George Q. Cannon	Aug 1860 (33) - Apr 1901 (74)	40 yrs 8 mos	
Mark E. Petersen	Apr 1944 (43) - Jan 1984 (83)	39 yrs 9 mos	
Erastus Snow	Feb 1849 (30) - May 1888 (69)	39 yrs 3 mos	
Marion G. Romney	Oct 1951 (54) - May 1988 (90)	36 yrs 7 mos	47 yrs 1 mo
George A. Smith	Apr 1839 (21) - Sep 1875 (58)	36 yrs 5 mos	
Francis M. Lyman	Oct 1880 (40) - Nov 1916 (76)	36 yrs 1 mo	
● **Howard W. Hunter**	Oct 1959 (51) - present	35 yrs	
Charles C. Rich	Feb 1849 (39) - Nov 1883 (74)	34 yrs 9 mos	
*Brigham Young Jr.	Oct 1868 (31) - April 1903 (66)	34 yrs 6 mos	
# Daniel H. Wells	Jan 1857 (42) - Mar 1891 (76)	34 yrs 2 mos	
Heber C. Kimball	Feb 1835 (33) - Jun 1868 (67)	33 yrs 4 mos	
● Gordon B. Hinckley	Oct 1961 (51) - present	33 yrs	36 yrs 6 mos
Harold B. Lee	Apr 1941 (42) - Dec 1973 (74)	32 yrs 8 mos	
John A. Widtsoe	Mar 1921 (49) - Nov 1952 (80)	31 yrs 8 mos	
Anthon H. Lund	Oct 1889 (45) - Mar 1921 (76)	31 yrs 5 mos	
● Thomas S. Monson	Oct 1963 (36) - present	31 yrs	
John Henry Smith	Oct 1880 (32) - Oct 1911 (63)	31 yrs	
LeGrand Richards	Apr 1952 (66) - Jan 1983 (96)	30 yrs 9 mos	44 yrs 9 mos
J. Reuben Clark Jr.	Apr 1933 (61) - Oct 1961 (90)	28 yrs 6 mos	
Delbert L. Stapley	Oct 1950 (53) - Aug 1978 (81)	27 yrs 10 mos	
Anthony W. Ivins	Oct 1907 (55) - Sep 1934 (82)	26 yrs 11 mos	
Richard R. Lyman	Apr 1918 (47) - Nov 1943 (72)	25 yrs 7 mos	
Amasa M. Lyman	Aug 1842 (29) - Oct 1867 (54)	25 yrs 2 mos	
Orson F. Whitney	Apr 1906 (50) - May 1931 (75)	25 yrs 1 mo	
George Teasdale	Oct 1882 (50) - Jun 1907 (75)	24 yrs 8 mos	
● Boyd K. Packer	Apr 1970 (45) - present	24 yrs 6 mos	33 yrs
Ezra T. Benson	Jul 1846 (35) - Sep 1869 (58)	23 yrs 2 mos	
Parley P. Pratt	Feb 1835 (27) - May 1857 (50)	22 yrs 3 mos	
Marvin J. Ashton	Dec 1971 (56) - Feb 1994 (78)	22 yrs 2 mos	24 yrs 4 mos
James E. Talmage	Dec 1911 (49) - Jul 1933 (70)	21 yrs 7 mos	
John W. Taylor	Apr 1884 (25) - Oct 1905 (47)	21 yrs 6 mos	
Charles W. Penrose	Jul 1904 (72) - May 1925 (93)	20 yrs 10 mos	
● L. Tom Perry	Apr 1974 (51) - present	20 yrs 6 mos	22 yrs
Melvin J. Ballard	Jan 1919 (45) - Jul 1939 (66)	20 yrs 6 mos	
Joseph F. Merrill	Oct 1931 (63) - Feb 1952 (83)	20 yrs 4 mos	
N. Eldon Tanner	Oct 1962 (64) - Nov 1982 (84)	20 yrs 1 mo	22 yrs 1 mo

Name	Date of service, Age at time	Length of service	Total Years as General Authority†
● David B. Haight	Jan 1976 (69) - present	18 yrs 9 mos	24 yrs 6 mos
* # John Willard Young	Apr 1873 (28) - Oct 1891 (47)	18 yrs 6 mos	
Richard L. Evans	Oct 1953 (47) - Nov 1971 (65)	18 yrs 1 mo	33 yrs 1 mo
Hugh B. Brown	Apr 1958 (74) - Dec 1975 (92)	17 yrs 8 mos	22 yrs 2 mos
Moses Thatcher	Apr 1879 (37) - Apr 1896 (54)	17 yrs	
Henry D. Moyle	Apr 1947 (57) - Sep 1963 (74)	16 yrs 5 mos	
Marriner W. Merrill	Oct 1889 (57) - Feb 1906 (73)	16 yrs 4 mos	
Hyrum Mack Smith	Oct 1901 (29) - Jan 1918 (45)	16 yrs 3 mos	
Albert E. Bowen	Apr 1937 (61) - Jul 1953 (77)	16 yrs 3 mos	
● James E. Faust	Oct 1978 (58) - present	16 yrs	22 yrs
Joseph Smith	Apr 1830 (24) - Jun 1844 (38)	14 yrs 2 mos	
Willard Richards	Apr 1840 (35) - Mar 1854 (49)	13 yrs 11 mos	
● Neal A. Maxwell	Jul 1981 (55) - present	13 yrs 3 mos	20 yrs 6 mos
Charles A. Callis	Oct 1933 (68) - Jan 1947 (81)	13 yrs 3 mos	
Bruce R. McConkie	Oct 1972 (57) - Apr 1985 (69)	12 yrs 6 mos	38 yrs 6 mos
Sidney Rigdon	Mar 1833 (40) - Jun 1844 (51)	11 yrs 3 mos	
William Smith	Feb 1835 (23) - Oct 1845 (34)	10 yrs 8 mos	
● Russell M. Nelson	Apr 1984 (59) - present	10 yrs 6 mos	
● Dallin H. Oaks	Apr 1984 (51) - present	10 yrs 6 mos	
● M. Russell Ballard	Oct 1985 (57) - present	9 yrs	18 yrs 6 mos
John R. Winder	Oct 1901 (79) - Mar 1910 (88)	8 yrs 5 mos	22 yrs 11 mos
Matthew Cowley	Oct 1945 (48) - Dec 1953 (56)	8 yrs 2 mos	
● Joseph B. Wirthlin	Oct 1986 (69) - present	8 yrs	19 yrs 6 mos
Matthias F. Cowley	Oct 1897 (39) - Oct 1905 (47)	8 yrs	
George Q. Morris	Apr 1954 (80) - Apr 1962 (88)	8 yrs	10 yrs 6 mos
*Oliver Cowdery	Apr 1830 (23) - Apr 1838 (31)	8 yrs	
Lyman Wight	Apr 1841 (44) - Dec 1848 (52)	7 yrs 8 mos	
John E. Page	Dec 1838 (39) - Feb 1846 (47)	7 yrs 2 mos	
Abraham H. Cannon	Oct 1889 (30) - Jul 1896 (37)	6 yrs 9 mos	13 yrs 9 mos
*Hyrum Smith	Sep 1837 (37) - Jun 1844 (44)	6 yrs 9 mos	
* John Smith	Sep 1837 (56) - Jun 1844 (62)	6 yrs 9 mos	
Abraham O. Woodruff	Oct 1897 (24) - Jun 1904 (31)	6 yrs 8 mos	
Charles W. Nibley	May 1925 (76) - Dec 1931 (82)	6 yrs 7 mos	24 yrs
● Richard G. Scott	Oct 1988 (59) - present	6 years	17 yrs 6 mos
Sylvester Q. Cannon	Apr 1938 (60) - May 1943 (65)	5 yrs 1 mo	18 yrs
Adam S. Bennion	Apr 1953 (66) - Feb 1958 (71)	4 yrs 10 mos	
Frederick G. Williams	Mar 1833 (45) - Nov 1837 (50)	4 yrs 8 mos	
*Albert Carrington	Apr 1873 (60) - Aug 1877 (64)	4 yrs 4 mos	
Thorpe B. Isaacson	Oct 1965 (67) - Jan 1970 (71)	4 yrs 3 mos	23 yrs 1 mo
Thomas B. Marsh	Apr 1835 (35) - Mar 1839 (39)	3 yrs 11 mos	
David W. Patten	Feb 1835 (35) - Oct 1838 (38)	3 yrs 8 mos	
William E. M'Lellin	Feb 1835 (29) - May 1838 (32)	3 yrs 3 mos	
William Law	Jan 1841 (31) - Apr 1844 (34)	3 yrs 3 mos	
Luke Johnson	Feb 1835 (27) - Apr 1838 (30)	3 yrs 2 mos	
Lyman E. Johnson	Feb 1835 (23) - Apr 1838 (26)	3 yrs 2 mos	
* Joseph Smith Sr.	Sep 1837 (66) - Sep 1840 (69)	3 yrs	6 yrs 9 mos
Jedediah M. Grant	Apr 1854 (38) - Dec 1856 (40)	2 yrs 8 mos	11 yrs
John F. Boynton	Feb 1835 (23) - Sep 1837 (25)	2 yrs 7 mos	
Alonzo A. Hinckley	Oct 1934 (64) - Dec 1936 (66)	2 yrs 2 mos	
Alvin R. Dyer	Apr 1968 (65) - Jan 1970 (67)	1 yr 9 mos	18 yrs 5 mos
● Robert D. Hales	April 1994 (61) - present	6 mos	19 yrs 6 mos
● Jeffrey R. Holland	Jun 1994 (53) - present	4 mos	5 yrs 6 mos

Bold Face denotes Church president
● Currently serving
† Includes service in the First Council of the Seventy, Assistants to the Twelve, First Quorum of the Seventy, Presiding Bishopric or as Church Patriarch
* Served as assistant counselor in the First Presidency
# Served in the First Presidency under Brigham Young; after his death sustained as counselor to Twelve Apostles

GENERAL OFFICERS OF THE CHURCH

SUNDAY SCHOOL

Though a few small Sunday School groups met regularly in Latter-day Saint communities before the Saints' westward exodus, Sunday School did not begin as a Church institution until after their arrival in the Salt Lake Valley in 1847.

Richard Ballantyne was a convert to the Church who, as a Presbyterian in his native Scotland, had organized a Sunday School. In Salt Lake City, disturbed by observing the children at play on the Sabbath day, he saw the need for a Sunday School.

In May 1849, he began plans to start a Sunday School. He built a structure on the northeast corner of 100 West and 300 South streets in Salt Lake City to serve both as his home and a place to hold the Sunday School. A monument on that corner today (now 200 West) commemorates the location of the first Sunday School.

On Sunday, Dec. 9, 1849, the first Sunday School was held, involving 50 children. The following year, a meetinghouse was built for the Salt Lake 14th Ward, in which Richard Ballantyne was second counselor in the bishopric. The expanded Sunday School was moved into the new building and divided into a number of smaller classes, with additional teachers and two assistant superintendents.

Other wards in the valley and elsewhere followed the example of Richard Ballantyne and started Sunday Schools. They were somewhat autonomous, devising their own curricula and administration, but functioned under the direction of the ward bishop.

With the coming of Johnston's Army to Utah, the Sunday School movement was suspended as many of the Saints moved south, but with the lessening of tensions in 1860, the Sunday School was resumed. By 1870, more than 200 Sunday Schools had been formed.

On Nov. 11, 1867, the Deseret Sunday School Union was organized by interested Church leaders, including President Brigham Young. Elder George Q. Cannon of the Quorum of the Twelve became the first general superintendent of the Sunday School. Its functions were to determine lesson topics and source materials and to address topics of punctuality, grading, prizes and rewards, recording and increasing attendance, music, elementary catechism, and libraries. The general Sunday School fostered uniformity in the theretofore disparate and independent Sunday Schools in the Church.

In 1866, prior to formation of the general Sunday School, a publication called the *Juvenile Instructor* was founded privately by Elder George Q. Cannon of the Twelve, who served as editor. It featured material on the scriptures, musical compositions and aids to gospel instruction. It became the official voice of the Deseret Sunday School Union, which purchased it from the Cannon family in January 1901. In 1929 the name was changed to *Instructor*. It was discontinued in 1970 when the Church magazine structure was changed.

In early 1877, the sacrament was instituted as part of Sunday School. The practice continued until 1980, when Sunday meetings were consolidated in a three-hour block, with sacrament administered only during sacrament meeting.

The Deseret Sunday School Union continued to grow through the 1900s. Stake Sunday School superintendencies were designated to supervise ward Sunday Schools. General meetings of the Sunday School were held twice a year in connection with general conference. Five new classes for older children and youth were added in the early 1900s, followed shortly by the introduction of adult classes.

A Sunday School general board was introduced in the 1870s. In the 1900s, it was expanded and members traveled extensively to provide advice and support for local Sunday School programs.

An effort in 1971 to correlate all Church functions under priesthood leadership affected the Sunday School. Dynamic changes followed, including centralized curriculum planning and writing, and an eight-year cycle of scripture instruction, later shortened to four years, for adult classes, focusing in turn on the Old Testament and Pearl of Great Price, the New Testament, the Book of Mormon, and the Doctrine and Covenants and Church History. The size of the general board was reduced, and stake boards were discontinued.

With the introduction of the consolidated meeting schedule in 1980, children's Sunday School classes were discontinued, that function being filled by the Primary. In recent years, Sunday School curriculum for adults has included a gospel essentials class and elective courses on family history, teacher development and family relations.

A modified Church curriculum announced for implementation Jan. 1, 1995, provides that classes for youth ages 14-18 study the scriptures using the *Gospel Principles* or *Gospel Doctrine* courses of study. Under the modified plan, youth ages 12-13 on alternate years study presidents of the Church and preparing for exaltation.

Sources: *Encyclopedia of Mormonism; Jubilee History of Latter-day Saints Sunday Schools* published by the Deseret Sunday School Union; First Presidency letter to General Authorities and priesthood leaders, April 21, 1994.

SUNDAY SCHOOL OFFICERS

President

Charles Didier, 15 Aug 1994 — present. See current PRESIDENCY OF THE SEVENTY.

First Counselor

J Ballard Washburn, 15 Aug 1994 — present. See current SECOND QUORUM OF THE SEVENTY.

Second Counselor

F. Burton Howard, 15 Aug 1994 — present. See current FIRST QUORUM OF THE SEVENTY.

HISTORICAL LISTING OF GENERAL SUPERINTENDENCIES AND PRESIDENCIES OF THE SUNDAY SCHOOL
(Presidents, superintendents pictured)

Superintendent, George Q. Cannon — Nov 1867 - Apr 1901 (See FIRST COUNSELORS IN THE FIRST PRESIDENCY, No. 5).

First Assistants, George Goddard — Jun 1872 - Jan 1899, Karl G. Maeser — Jan 1899 - Feb 1901.

Second Assistants, John Morgan — Jun 1883 - Jul 1894, Karl G. Maeser — Jul 1894 - Jan 1899, George Reynolds — Jan 1899 - May 1901.

Superintendent, Lorenzo Snow (As president of the Church) — May 1901 - Oct 1901 (See PRESIDENTS OF THE CHURCH, No. 5).

First Assistant, George Reynolds — May 1901 - Oct 1901.

Second Assistant, Jay M. Tanner — May 1901 - Oct 1901.

Superintendent, Joseph F. Smith (As president of the Church) — Nov 1901 - Nov 1918 (See PRESIDENTS OF THE CHURCH, No. 6).

First Assistants, George Reynolds — Nov 1901 - May 1909, David O. McKay — May 1909 - Nov 1918.

Second Assistants, Jay M. Tanner — Nov 1901 - April 1906, David O. McKay — Jan 1907 - May 1909, Stephen L Richards — May 1909 - Nov 1918.

Superintendent, David O. McKay — Dec 1918 - Oct 1934 (See PRESIDENTS OF THE CHURCH, No. 9).

First Assistant, Stephen L Richards — Dec 1918 - Oct 1934.

Second Assistant, George D. Pyper — Dec 1918 - Oct 1934.

Superintendent, George D. Pyper — Oct 1934 - Jan 1943.

First Assistant, Milton Bennion — Oct 1934 - May 1943.

Second Assistant, George R. Hill — Oct 1934 - May 1943.

Superintendent, Milton Bennion — May 1943 - Sep 1949.

First Assistant, George R. Hill — May 1943 - Sep 1949.

Second Assistant, Albert Hamer Reiser — May 1943 - Sep 1949.

Superintendent, George R. Hill — Sep 1949 - Nov 1966.

First Assistants, Albert Hamer Reiser — Sep 1949 - Oct 1952, David Lawrence McKay — Oct 1952 - Nov 1966.

Second Assistants, David Lawrence McKay — Sep 1949 - Oct 1952, Lynn S. Richards — Oct 1952 - Nov 1966.

Superintendent, David Lawrence McKay — Nov 1966 - Jun 1971.

First Assistant, Lynn S. Richards — Nov 1966 - Jun 1971.

Second Assistant, Royden G. Derrick — Nov. 1966 - Jun 1971.

President, Russell M. Nelson — Jun 1971 - Oct 1979 (See current COUNCIL OF THE TWELVE).

First Counselors, Joseph B. Wirthlin — Jun 1971 - Apr 1975, B. Lloyd Poelman — Apr 1975 - Mar 1978, Joe J. Christensen — Mar 1978 - Aug 1979, William D. Oswald — Aug 1979 - Oct 1979.

Second Counselors, Richard L. Warner — Jun 1971 - Apr 1975, Joe J. Christensen — Apr 1975 - Mar 1978, William D. Oswald — May 1978 - Aug 1979, J. Hugh Baird — Aug 1979 - Oct 1979.

President, Hugh W. Pinnock — Oct 1979 - Aug 1986 (See current FIRST QUORUM OF THE SEVENTY).

First Counselors, Ronald E. Poelman — Oct 1979 - Jul 1981, Robert D. Hales — Jul 1981 - Jul 1985, Adney Y. Komatsu — Jul 1985 - Aug 1986.

Second Counselors, Jack H Goaslind Jr. — Oct 1979 - Jul 1981, James M. Paramore — Jul 1981 - Jan 1983, Loren C. Dunn — Jan 1983 - Jul 1985, Ronald E. Poelman — Jul 1985 - Aug 1986.

President, Robert L. Simpson — Aug 1986 - 30 Sep 1989 (See FIRST QUORUM OF THE SEVENTY, No. 18).

First Counselors, Adney Y. Komatsu — Aug 1986 - Aug. 1987, Devere Harris — Aug 1987 - 30 Sep 1989.

Second Counselors, A. Theodore Tuttle — Aug 1986 - Nov 1986, Devere Harris — Jan 1987 - Aug 1987, Phillip T. Sonntag — Aug 1987 - Aug 1988, Derek A. Cuthbert — Aug 1988 - 30 Sep 1989.

President, Hugh W. Pinnock — 30 Sep 1989 - 15 Aug 1992 (See current FIRST QUORUM OF THE SEVENTY).

First Counselors, Derek A. Cuthbert — 15 Aug 1988 - 1 Jan 1991, H. Verlan Andersen — 1 Jan 1991 - 5 Oct 1991, Hartman Rector Jr. — 5 Oct 1991- 15 Aug 1992.

Second Counselors, Ted E. Brewerton — 30 Sep 1989 - 1 Oct 1990, H. Verlan Andersen — 6 Oct 1990 - 1 Jan 1991, Rulon G. Craven — 1 Jan 1991 - 5 Oct 1991, Clinton L. Cutler — 5 Oct 1991 - 15 Aug 1992.

President, Merlin R. Lybbert — 15 Aug 1992 - 15 Aug 1994 (See SECOND QUORUM OF THE SEVENTY, No. 35).

First Counselor, Clinton L. Cutler — 15 Aug 1992 - April 9, 1994.

Second Counselor, Ronald E. Poelman — 15 Aug 1992- 15 Aug 1994.

YOUNG MEN

Today's Young Men organization has been significantly streamlined and simplified since its inception in 1875 as the Young Men's Mutual Improvement Association and has as its primary purpose furthering the work of the Aaronic Priesthood.

The YMMIA was established by President Brigham Young, who called Junius F. Wells to organize Mutual Improvement Associations in wards throughout the Church, under the direction of ward superintendencies. It was intended that the YMMIA help young men develop spiritually and intellectually and provide supervised recreational opportunities.

On June 10, 1875, Brother Wells called a meeting in the 13th Ward chapel in Salt Lake City and the first ward YMMIA was organized.

In fall 1875, John Henry Smith, Milton H. Hardy and B. Morris Young were called by the First Presidency to assist Brother Wells in visiting the settlements of Saints and promoting the YMMIA. By April 1876, there were 57 ward YMMIAs in existence with a membership of about 1,200 youth. That same year, a YMMIA central committee was formed with Brother Wells as president. The committee later became the General Board of the YMMIA, which has continued through the years and is now known as the Young Men General Board.

From 1876 to 1905, young men were called to serve YMMIA missions to increase membership and assist local superintendencies. Initially, all of the young men met together regardless of age. Later, the YMMIA adopted four grades or classes: Scouts (ages 12-14), Vanguards (15-16), M Men (17-23) and Adults. As the programs developed and as needs of the youth changed, further refinements were made to the class structure. Today, Young Men classes correspond with the deacons, teachers and priests quorums in the Aaronic Priesthood.

In October 1879, the monthly *Contributor* was launched with Brother Wells as editor. It served as the publication of the YMMIA until October 1899, at which time the publication of the *Improvement Era* began by the General Board.

The YMMIA met separately from the Young Women's Mutual Improvement Association (YWMIA) until around 1900 when the two joined to form the Mutual Improvement Association.

In 1913, the Church formed a formal partnership with Boy Scouts of America and was granted a national charter on May 21 of that year. Scouting exists today as a major component of the Young Men organization to help accomplish the purposes of the Aaronic Priesthood and to compliment Sunday quorum instruction. Besides its partnership with BSA, the Church has established affiliations with other national Scouting organizations throughout the world whose programs, values, goals and ideals are compatible with those of the Church.

In addition to Scouting, YMMIA activities in the early and mid-1900s included sports, dance, drama and music. Athletics became a major part of the program, and stake tournament winners progressed to the All-Church tournaments in Salt Lake City, which were discontinued in the early 1970s.

In the mid-1900s, the general level organization consisted of a superintendency of five men and a general board of 60 to 70 men. The general level was supported by a general fund, paid into by stakes based on YMMIA membership, sale of YMMIA materials and investments. Besides planning and organizing major sports and cultural events, general board members would regularly travel with General Authorities and provide training for local YMMIA leaders.

In the 1960s under priesthood correlation, responsibility for training shifted to local priesthood leaders, the general fund was discontinued, production and sale of materials were centralized and the size and scope of the general superintendency and board were greatly reduced.

The Aaronic Priesthood-MIA was organized in 1972, with efforts centering more fully around the Aaronic Priesthood quorums. In June 1974 the name Aaronic Priesthood-MIA was shortened to Aaronic Priesthood and conducted under the direction of the Presiding Bishopric. In May 1977 the name was changed to Young Men and a general presidency was reinstated. In October 1979 it was announced that the Young Men General Presidency would be comprised of three members of the Seventy. Since 1989, the General Board has been comprised of less than a dozen men who continue to assist the presidency with curriculum development and Aaronic Priesthood and Scouting training.

Sources: *Encyclopedia of Mormonism; Encyclopedic History of the Church* by Andrew Jenson, p. 969.

YOUNG MEN OFFICERS

President
Jack H Goaslind Jr., 6 Oct 1990 - present. See current FIRST QUORUM OF THE SEVENTY

First Counselors
Stephen D. Nadauld, 15 Aug 1992 - present. See current SECOND QUORUM OF THE SEVENTY

Robert K. Dellenbach, 5 Oct 1991 - 15 Aug 1992

LeGrand R. Curtis, 6 Oct 1990 - 5 Oct 1991

Second Counselors
Vaughn J Featherstone, 15 Aug 1993 - present. See current FIRST QUORUM OF THE SEVENTY

L. Lionel Kendrick, 15 Aug 1992 - 15 Aug 1993

Stephen D. Nadauld, 5 Oct 1991 - 15 Aug 1992

Robert K. Dellenbach, 6 Oct 1990 - 5 Oct 1991

HISTORICAL LISTING OF GENERAL SUPERINTENDENCIES AND PRESIDENCIES OF THE YOUNG MEN'S MUTUAL IMPROVEMENT ASSOCIATION AND YOUNG MEN
(Presidents, superintendents pictured)

Superintendent, Junius F. Wells — 1876-1880.

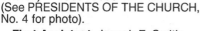

First Counselor, M. H. Hardy.

Second Counselor, Rodney C. Badger.

Superintendent, Wilford Woodruff (As president of the Church) — 1880 - 1898 (See PRESIDENTS OF THE CHURCH, No. 4 for photo).

First Assistant, Joseph F. Smith.

Second Assistant, Moses Thatcher.

Superintendent, Lorenzo Snow (As president of the Church) — 1898 - 1901 (See PRESIDENTS OF THE CHURCH, No. 5).

First Assistant, Joseph F. Smith.

Second Assistant, Heber J. Grant.

Assistant, B. H. Roberts.

Superintendent, Joseph F. Smith (As president of the Church) — 1901 - 1918 (See PRESIDENTS OF THE CHURCH, No. 6).

First Assistant, Heber J. Grant, **Sec-**ond Assistant, B. H. Roberts.

Superintendent, Anthony W. Ivins, (As counselor in First Presidency) — 1918 - 1921 (See FIRST COUNSELORS IN THE FIRST PRESIDENCY, No. 10).

First Assistant, B. H. Roberts.

Second Assistant, Richard R. Lyman.

Superintendent, George Albert Smith (As apostle — 1921 - 1935 (See PRESIDENTS OF THE CHURCH, No. 8).

First Assistant, B. H. Roberts.

Second Assistants, Richard R. Lyman, Melvin J. Ballard.

Superintendent, Albert E. Bowen (as apostle) — 1935 - 1937 (See COUNCIL OF THE TWELVE, No. 59).

First Assistant, George Q. Morris.

Second Assistant, Franklin West.

Superintendent, George Q. Morris (as apostle)— 1937 - 1948 (See COUNCIL OF THE TWELVE, No. 72.).

First Assistants, Joseph J. Cannon, John D. Giles.

Second Assistants, Burton K. Farnsworth, Lorenzo H. Hatch.

Superintendent, Elbert R. Curtis — 1948-1958.

First Assistant, A. Walter Stevenson.

Second Assistants, Ralph W. Hardy, David S. King.

Superintendent, Joseph T. Bentley — 2 Jul 1958 - 6 Oct 1962.

First Assistants, Alvin R. Dyer — 2 Jul 1958 - 6 Dec 1958, G. Carlos Smith — 6 Dec 1958 - 9 Jun 1961, Marvin J. Ashton, 9 Jun 1961 - 6 Oct 1962.

Second Assistants, Marvin J. Ashton, 6 Dec 1958 - 9 Jun 1961, Verl F. Scott, 9 Jun 1961 - 4 Oct 1961, Carl W. Buehner, 25 Oct 1961 - Oct 1962.

Superintendent, G. Carlos Smith —

6 Oct 1962 - 17 Sep 1969.

First Assistant, Marvin J. Ashton — 6 Oct 1962 - 17 Sep 1969.

Second Assistants, Carl W. Beuhner — 6 Oct 1962 - Oct 1967, George Richard Hill — 6 Oct 1967 - 17 Sep 1969.

Superintendent, W. Jay Eldredge — 17 Sep 1969 - 25 Jun 1972.

First Assistants, George Richard Hill — 17 Sep 1969 - 24 Jun 1972.

Second Assistant, George I. Cannon — 17 Sep 1969 - 25 Jun 1972.

President, W. Jay Eldredge — 25 Jun 1972 - 9 Nov 1972 (see photo above).

First Counselor, George I. Cannon — 25 Jun 1972 - 9 Nov 1972.

Second Counselor, Robert L. Backman, 25 Jun 1972 - 9 Nov 1972.

AARONIC PRIESTHOOD MIA

President, Robert L. Backman — 9 Nov 1972 - 23 Jun 1974 (See PRESIDENCY OF THE SEVENTY, No. 18).

First Counselor, LeGrand R. Curtis — Nov 1972 - 23 Jun 1974.

Second Counselor, Jack H Goaslind Jr. — 9 Nov 1972 - 23 Jun 1974.

Note: On June 23, 1974, the Aaronic

Priesthood MIA was dissolved and was replaced by the Aaronic Priesthood and the Young Women coming directly under the stewardship of the Presiding Bishop.

In April 1977, it was renamed the Young Men, and both it and the Young Women came under the direction of the Priesthood Department.

YOUNG MEN

President, Neil D. Schaerrer — 7 Apr 1977 - Oct 1979.

First Counselor, Graham W. Doxey — 7 Apr 1977 - Oct 1979.

Second Counselor, Quinn G. McKay — 7 Apr 1977 - Oct 1979.

President, Robert L. Backman — Oct 1979 - Nov 1985 (See

PRESIDENCY OF THE SEVENTY, No. 18).

First Counselor, Vaughn J Featherstone — Oct 1979 - Nov 1985.

Second Counselor, Rex D. Pinegar — Oct 1979 - Nov 1985.

President, Vaughn J Featherstone — Nov 1985 - 6 Oct 1990 (See current FIRST QUORUM OF THE SEVENTY).

First Counselors, Rex D. Pinegar — Nov 1985 - 30 Sep 1989, Jeffrey R. Holland — 30 Sep 1989 - 6 Oct 1990.

Second Counselors, Robert L. Simpson — Nov 1985 - 15 Aug 1986, Hartman Rector Jr. — 15 Aug 1986 - Oct 1988, Robert B Harbertson, Oct 1988 - 30 Sep 1989, Monte J. Brough, 30 Sep 1989 - 6 Oct 1990.

PRIMARY

Noting the rough and careless behavior of the boys in her Farmington, Utah, neighborhood, Aurelia Spencer Rogers asked, "What will our girls do for good husbands, if this state of things continues?" Then she continued, "Could there not be an organization for little boys, and have them trained to make better men?"

The answer was, "Yes." With the approval of President John Taylor, the encouragement of Relief Society general president Eliza R. Snow, and after receiving a calling from her bishop, Sister Rogers began planning for the first meeting of the Primary Association, and it was an overwhelming success. On Sunday, August 25, 1878, she stood at the entrance to the meetinghouse and greeted 224 boys and girls to Primary. Girls were invited because Sister Rogers thought they could help with the singing that she thought was necessary. During the first meeting, Sister Rogers instructed the children to be obedient and to be kind to one another.

Sister Rogers was not only the first Farmington Ward Primary president, but also the first Davis Stake Primary president.

Sister Snow was actively involved in the organization of the Primary Association. About the same time Sister Rogers was holding the first Primary meeting, Sister Snow was in Ogden laying the groundwork for the organization there. Upon her return to Salt Lake City, she reported to Relief Society women there about her activities with the Primary in the northern part of the state.

Over the next decade, the Primary Association was organized in almost every LDS settlement. During one trip through Southern Utah, Sister Snow and her second counselor in the Relief Society presidency, Zina Young, organized 35 Primaries.

From its beginning, Primary included songs, poetry and activities. The boys wore uniforms to the meetings. All the children met together at Primary for the first 10 years. After that, they were divided into age groups.

Sister Louie B. Felt was called as the first general president of the Primary in 1880, but the Relief Society continued to take the responsibility for organizing Primaries. Sister Felt and other general officers began taking more responsibility for Primary development after 1890.

Serving as Primary general president for 45 years, Sister Felt oversaw many developments in the organization. In 1902, publication of the *Children's Friend* magazine began. In 1913, the Primary began contributing to pediatric hospital care. That program was culminated in 1952 with the completion of the Primary Children's Hospital in Salt Lake City. Contributions from Primary children helped support the hospital.

Beginning in 1929 when the Primary took over more responsibility for the spiritual training of children, lessons were planned for three weeks of the month and an activity on the fourth week. The Cub Scout program became the responsibility of the Primary in 1952.

Primary meetings were held midweek until the Church instituted the consolidated meeting plan in 1980. Then it replaced junior Sunday School for providing Sunday religious instruction for children ages 3 to 11. The Primary meets for one hour and forty minutes of the meeting block, dividing the time between group meetings, classroom instruction and sharing time. Although women continued to serve exclusively in Primary presidencies, calls began going out to men to teach classes. Weekday activities continued on a quarterly basis.

Sources: *Sisters and Little Saints,* by Carol Cornwall Madsen and Susan Stake Oman; *Encyclopedia of Mormonism.*

PRIMARY GENERAL PRESIDENCY

**Anne G.
Wirthlin**
First Counselor

Patricia P. Pinegar
President

**Susan L.
Warner**
Second Counselor

President — Patricia Peterson Pinegar, Oct. 1, 1994 - present. Served as second counselor in the Young Women general presidency from April 4, 1992, until her call as Primary general president. She served on Primary general board, 1991-92. Born in Cedar City, Utah, to Laurence and Wavie Williams Peterson; attended BYU in general education; served with her husband when he was president of the Missionary Training Center in Provo, Utah, and when he was president of the England London South Mission; former stake and ward Primary president and teacher, ward Relief Society president and counselor and teacher, stake Young Women counselor and adviser, and ward Young Women president and adviser; married to Ed Pinegar, parents of eight children.

First Counselor — Anne Goalen Wirthlin, Oct. 1, 1994 - present. Member of the Young Women general board from 1993 until her call to the Primary general presidency. Served with her husband, David B. Wirthlin while he was president of the Germany Frankfurt Mission. Born in Salt Lake City, Utah, to Bernard Ivan and Hettie Le Royce Thomson Goalen. Former ward Relief Society and Primary president and counselor. Graduate of the University of Utah. She and her husband are parents of six children.

Second Counselor — Susan Lillywhite Warner, Oct. 1, 1994 - present. Member of the Primary general board from 1992 until her call to the Primary general presidency. Born in Salt Lake City to Justin Bryce and Alice Mitchell Lillywhite; former stake Primary president, ward Young Women president, Relief Society president. Graduate of BYU. Married C. Terry Warner, parents of 10 children.

HISTORICAL LISTING OF GENERAL PRESIDENCIES OF THE PRIMARY ASSOCIATION
(Presidents pictured)

President, Louie Bouton Felt, 19 Jun 1880 - 6 Oct 1925.

First Counselors, Matilda Morehouse W. Barratt — 19 Jun 1880 - Oct 1888, Lillie Tuckett Freeze — Oct 1888 - 8 Dec 1905, May Anderson — 29 Dec 1905 - 6 Oct 1925.

Second Counselors, Clare Cordelia Moses Cannon — 19 Jun 1880 - 4 Oct 1895, Josephine Richards West — 15 Dec 1896 - 24 Nov 1905, Clara Woodruff Beebe — 29 Dec 1906 - 6 Oct 1925.

President, May Anderson — 6 Oct 1925 - 11 Sep 1939.

First Counselors, Sadie Grant Pack — 6 Oct 1925 - 11 Sep 1929, Isabelle Salmon Ross — 11 Sep 1929 - 31 Dec 1939.

Second Counselors, Isabelle Salmon Ross — 6 Oct 1925 - 11 Sep 1929, Edna Harker Thomas — 11 Sep 1929 - 11 Dec 1933, Edith Hunter Lambert — 11 Dec 1933 - 31 Dec 1939.

President, May Green Hinckley — 1 Jan 1940 - 2 May 1943.

First Counselor, Adele Cannon Howells — 1 Jan 1940 - 2 May 1943.

Second Counselors, Janet Murdock Thompson — 1 Jan 1940 - May 1942, La-Vern Watts Parmley — May 1942 - 2 May 1943.

President, Adele Cannon Howells — 29 Jul 1943 - 14 Apr 1951.

First Counselor, La-Vern Watts Parmley — 20 Jul 1943 - 14 Apr 1951.

Second Counselor, Dessie Grant Boyle — 20 Jul 1943 - 14 Apr 1951.

President, LaVern Watts Parmley — 16 May 1951 - 5 Oct 1974.

First Counselors, Arta Matthews Hale — 16 May 1951 - 6 Apr 1962, Leone Watson Doxey — 6 Apr 1962 - 23 Oct 1969, Lucile Cardon Reading — 8 Jan 1970 - 6 Aug 1970,

Naomi Ward Randall — 4 Oct 1970 - 5 Oct 1974.

Second Counselors, Florence Holbrook Richards — 15 May 1951 - 11 Jun 1953, Leone Watson Doxey — 10 Sep 1953 - 6 Apr 1962, Eileen Robinson Dunyon — 6 Apr 1962 - 3 Jun 1963, Lucile Cardon Reading — 23 Jul 1963 - 8 Jan 1970, Florence Reece Lane — 8 Jan 1970 - 5 Oct 1974.

President, Naomi Maxfield Shumway — 5 Oct 1974 - 5 Apr 1980.

First Counselors, Sara Broadbent Paulsen — 5 Oct 1974 - 2 Apr 1977, Colleen Bushman Lemmon — 2 Apr 1977 - 5 Apr 1980.

Second Counselors, Colleen Bushman Lemmon — 5 Oct 1974 - 2 Apr 1977, Dorthea Christiansen Murdock — 2 Apr 1977 - 5 Apr 1980.

President, Dwan Jacobsen Young — 5 Apr 1980 - 2 Apr 1988.

First Counselor, Virginia Beesley Cannon — 5 Apr 1980 - 2 Apr 1988.

Second Counselor, Michaelene Packer Grassli — 5 Apr 1980 - 2 Apr 1988.

President, Michaelene Packer Grassli — 2 Apr 1988 - Oct. 1, 1994.

First Counselor, Betty Jo Nelson Jepsen — April 2, 1988 - Oct. 1, 1994.

Second Counselor, Ruth Broadbent Wright — April 2, 1988 - Oct. 1, 1994.

YOUNG WOMEN

President Brigham Young organized the Young Ladies Department of the Cooperative Retrenchment Association — predecessor to the Young Women program — on the evening of Nov. 28, 1869, in the parlor of the Lion House. He encouraged his older daughters, who were the charter members, to "retrench in your dress, in your tables, in your speech, wherein you have been guilty of silly, extravagant speeches and light-mindedness of thought. Retrench in everything that is bad and worthless, and improve in everything that is good and beautiful."

Thus, the Retrenchment Association was organized. Relief Society Gen. Pres. Eliza R. Snow supervised the association; Ella Young Empey was named as president.

News of the organization spread quickly. By the end of 1870, retrenchment associations had been established in several Mormon settlements. In addition, the organization had divided into senior and junior associations.

Not long after the creation of the Young Men's Mutual Improvement Association in 1875, President Young approved a name change to "Young Ladies' National Mutual Improvement Association" to correspond to the young men's organization. The two organizations began holding monthly meetings together. In 1904, the word "National" was dropped since the Young Ladies' organization had become international in scope. In 1934 the First Presidency approved the new name, "Young Women's Mutual Improvement Association."

Throughout the early years of the association's existence, the YLNMIA was directed through local ward efforts. The first stake board was organized in 1878 in the Salt Lake Stake, antedating the appointment of a general board. In 1880, Elmina S. Taylor was called as the first general president. She called as her counselors Margaret (Maggie) Y. Taylor and Martha (Mattie) Horne, with Louie Wells as secretary and Fanny Y. Thatcher as treasurer. That same year, Pres. Taylor presided over the first general conference of the YLNMIA.

Under the new general presidency's direction, the association encouraged the study of gospel principles, development of individual talents and service to those in need. General, stake and ward boards were subsequently appointed, lesson manuals were produced, and joint activities were established with the YMMIA. The *Young Woman's Journal* was inaugurated 1889 and soon began printing a series of lessons.

In 1888, the first annual June Conference for young women and young men was held. Leaders provided special training in physical activity, story-telling, and music and class instruction.

Four decades later, in 1929, a new summer camping program was announced at June Conference, and the *Young Woman's Journal* and *The Improvement Era* merged with the November issue. During the 1930s, MIA leaders gave new emphasis to music, dance and the performing arts, with an annual June Conference dance festival being held.

In the late 1940s and the 1950s, the First Presidency turned over to the YWMIA leaders a girls enrollment incentive program, previously administered by the Presiding Bishopric. It was designed to increase attendance at Church meetings.

In the early 1970s, President Harold B. Lee introduced a correlation program designed to integrate Church programs for youth. From this effort eventually came the Personal Progress program and the Young Womanhood Achievement Awards. During the 1980s, Sunday Young Women classes began meeting at the same time as priesthood meeting for Young Men.

During the tenure of general Pres. Ardeth G. Kapp, who served from 1984-1992, the Young Women motto, "Stand for Truth and Righteousness," was introduced, along with the Young Women logo, represented by a torch with the profile of the face of a young woman. The torch represents the light of Christ, inviting all to "come unto Christ." (D&C 20:59.)

During Pres. Kapp's administration, the Young Women theme and values were introduced. The values are faith, divine nature, individual worth, knowledge, choice and accountability, good works, and integrity.

As of end of 1993, 529,000 young women ages 12 to 17 in 151 different countries were enrolled in the Young Women program as Beehives, Mia Maids or Laurels.

Sources: *Encyclopedia of Mormonism*, vols. 3-4; *A Century of Sisterhood*; *History of the YWMIA*, by Marba C. Josephson; *Deseret News 1993-1994 Church Almanac*.

YOUNG WOMEN GENERAL PRESIDENCY

| **Virginia H. Pearce** | **Janette C. Hales** | **Bonnie D. Parkin** |
| **First Counselor** | **President** | **Second Counselor** |

President — Janette Callister Hales, April 4, 1992 - present. Born in Springville, Utah, to Thomas L. and Hannah Gudmundson Carrick Callister; received bachelor's degree in clothing and textiles from BYU; served as second counselor to Ardeth G. Kapp in Young Women general presidency March 31, 1990 to April 4, 1992; served on the Primary general board, 1988-90; former gospel doctrine teacher and ward Relief Society president; served in the Utah State House of Representatives; married the late Robert H. Hales, parents of five children.

First Counselor — Virginia Hinckley Pearce, April 4, 1992 - present. Born in Denver, Colo., to Gordon B. and Marjorie Pay Hinckley; received bachelor's degree in history from the University of Utah and master's degree in social work from the University of Utah; served on the Primary general board, 1988-92; former counselor in ward and stake Primary presidencies, gospel doctrine teacher, teacher in Primary, Relief Society and Young Women, and counselor in a ward Relief Society presidency; married to James R.M. Pearce, parents of six children.

Second Counselor — Bonnie Dansie Parkin, Oct. 1, 1994 - present. Served on the Relief Society general board from 1990 until called to the Young Women general presidency. Born in Murray, Utah, to Jesse H. and Ruth Butikofer Dansie. Former stake Young Women president's counselor, ward Relief Society and Primary president. Graduate of Utah State University. Married James L. Parkin, four children.

HISTORICAL LISTING OF GENERAL PRESIDENCIES OF YOUNG WOMEN'S MUTUAL IMPROVEMENT ASSOCIATION AND YOUNG WOMEN

(Presidents pictured)

President, Elmina Shepherd Taylor — 19 Jun 1880 - 6 Dec 1904.

First Counselors, Margaret Young Taylor — 19 Jun 1880 - 1887, Maria Young Dougall — 1887 - 6 Dec 1904.

Second Counselor, Martha Horne Tingey — 19 Jun 1880 - 6 Dec 1904.

President, Martha Horne Tingey — 5 Apr 1905 - 28 Mar 1929.

First Counselor, Ruth May Fox — 5 Apr 1905 - 28 Mar 1929.

Second Counselors, Mae Taylor Nystrom — 5 Apr 1905 - 15 Jul 1923, Lucy Grant Cannon, 15 Jul 1923 - 28 Mar 1929.

President, Ruth May Fox — 28 Mar 1929 - Oct 1937.

First Counselor, Lucy Grant Cannon — 28 Mar 1929 - Oct 1937.

Second Counselor, Clarissa A. Beesley — 30 Mar 1929 - Oct 1937.

President, Lucy Grant Cannon — Nov 1937 - 6 Apr 1948.

First Counselors, Helen Spencer Williams — Nov 1937 - 17 May 1944, Verna Wright Goddard — Jul 1944 - 6 Apr 1948.

Second Counselors, Verna Wright Goddard — Nov 1937 - Jul 1944, Lucy T. Anderson — 6 Jul 1944 - 6 Apr 1948.

President, Bertha Stone Reeder — 6 Apr 1948 - 30 Sep 1961.

First Counselor, Emily Higgs Bennett — 13 Jun 1948 - 30 Sep 1961.

Second Counselor, LaRue Carr Longden — 13 Jun 1948 - 30 Sep 1961.

President, Florence Smith Jacobsen — 30 Sep 1961 - 9 Nov 1972.

First Counselor, Margaret R. Jackson — 30 Sep 1961 - 9 Nov 1972.

Second Counselor, Dorothy Porter Holt — 30 Sep 1961 - 9 Nov 1972.

AARONIC PRIESTHOOD MIA (YOUNG WOMEN)

President, Ruth Hardy Funk — 9 Nov 1972 - 23 Jun 1974.

First Counselor, Hortense Hogan Child — 9 Nov 1972 - 23 Jun 1974.

Second Counselor, Ardeth Greene Kapp — 9 Nov 1972 - 23 Jun 1974.

President, Ruth Hardy Funk — 23 Jun 1974 - 12 Jul 1978.

First Counselor, Hortense Hogan Child — 23 Jun 1974 - 12 Jul 1978.

Second Counselor, Ardeth Greene Kapp — 23 Jun 1974 - 12 Jul 1978.

President, Elaine Anderson Cannon — 12 Jul 1978 - 7 Apr 1984.

First Counselor, Arlene Barlow Darger — 12 Jul 1978 - 7 Apr 1984.

Second Counselor, Norma Broadbent Smith — 12 Jul 1978 - 7 Apr 1984.

President, Ardeth Greene Kapp — 7 Apr 1984 - 4 Apr 1992.

First Counselors, Patricia Terry Holland — 11 May 1984 - 6 Apr 1986, Maurine Johnson Turley — 6 Apr 1986 - 4 Apr 1987, Jayne Broadbent Malan — 4 Apr 1987 - 4 Apr 1992.

Second Counselors, Maurine Johnson Turley — 11 May 1984 - 6 Apr 1986, Jayne Broadbent Malan — 6 Apr 1986 - 4 Apr 1987, Elaine Low Jack — 4 Apr 1987 - 31 Mar 1990, Janette Callister Hales — 31 Mar 1990 - 4 Apr 1992.

RELIEF SOCIETY

In 1842, a small group of women met at the home of Sarah M. Kimball in Navuoo, Ill., to organize a sewing society to aid Nauvoo Temple workmen. They sought the endorsement of the Prophet Joseph Smith, who praised their efforts but said the Lord had something better in mind for them. It would be an organization under the priesthood after the pattern of the priesthood. He organized the Female Relief Society on March 17, 1842. The Prophet said that the restored Church could not be perfect or complete without it. He charged members with the responsibility to save souls and taught them principles of the gospel. The women elected Emma Smith their president, and she selected two counselors.

From that original organization stemmed what is now the Relief Society, the official adult women's organization of the Church. Its motto, "Charity Never Faileth," states what has been the objective of society members from the first: to love and nurture one another and minister to the needs of Church members and others. The Female Relief Society of Nauvoo contributed to the Nauvoo Temple and supported moral reform. Members were primarily concerned with helping the poor. In July 1843, a visiting committee of four was appointed in each ward to assess needs and distribute necessities, the beginning of the visiting teaching effort that has been a part of Relief Society since then. By 1844, the society had 1,341 members.

The Female Relief Society of Nauvoo ceased to function after March 1844. The Prophet was martyred in June of that year.

Although women carried out charitable works and a few meetings were conducted at Winter Quarters, Neb., there was no formal Relief Society during the Saints' westward trek or for several years thereafter.

In February 1854, 16 women responded to an exhortation of President Brigham Young to form a society of females to make clothing for Indian women and children. This "Indian Relief Society" met until June, when President Young encouraged such organizations in individual wards. Many remained organized to assist the poor within their wards and help provide clothing and bedding for destitute handcart companies.

In 1866, President Young reorganized the Relief Society Churchwide, appointing Eliza R. Snow to assist bishops in establishing the organization in each ward.

By 1880 there was a local unit of the Relief Society in each of 300 wards, caring for the needy within its ward boundaries and using visiting teachers to collect and distribute donations. Ward Relief Societies managed their own finances, and many built their own meeting halls.

In line with the Church's move for self-sufficiency, the Relief Society sponsored in the late 1800s cooperative economic enterprises such as making and marketing homemade goods, raising silk, storing grain and financing the medical training of midwives and female doctors.

The Relief Society also promoted women's right to vote and helped organize and nurture the Young Ladies' Retrenchment Association (forerunner to the Young Women) and the Primary.

By the turn of the century, needs of women were changing, and the format of lessons was adapted and standardized to meet the needs. The *Relief Society Magazine,* introduced in 1915, contained lessons for each month on theological, cultural and homemaking topics. One week a month was spent on each topic, with time left over for charity projects and testimony bearing. The monthly format of rotating topics has remained since then, with the subject matter being varied.

Beginning in 1921, concern over high maternal and infant mortality led to the establishment of health clinics and two stake Relief Society maternity hospitals, one operated in the Snowflake (Arizona) Stake and another in the Cottonwood (Utah) Stake.

In 1944, visiting teachers ceased collecting charitable funds. Since 1921, the ward Relief Society president, under the direction of the bishop, has been responsible for assessing needs and distributing relief to the needy. Ward Relief Society presidents supervise other charitable work such as caring for the sick, called "compassionate service" to distinguish it from "welfare service."

In the latter 20th Century, Relief Society has become more fully coordinated under the larger Church structure. Reporting and financing systems, magazine and lesson materials and social services became the responsibility of priesthood leaders and Church departments. After September 1971, all LDS women were automatically included as members of the Relief Society.

In recent times, the Relief Society has promoted scholarly study of women's concerns by helping establish the Women's Research Center at BYU, has rallied members to contribute to the Monument to Women at Nauvoo, Ill., in 1978, and has celebrated its sesquicentennial in 1992. One aspect of this was starting a worldwide effort to improve literacy.

Sources: *Encyclopedia of Mormonism, Women of Covenant: The Story of Relief Society,* by Jill Mulvay Derr, Janath Russell Cannon, and Maureen Ursenbach Beecher, Deseret Book, 1992.

RELIEF SOCIETY GENERAL PRESIDENCY

Chieko N. Okazaki
First Counselor

Elaine L. Jack
President

Aileen H. Clyde
Second Counselor

President — Elaine Low Jack, March 31, 1990 - present. Born to Sterling O. and Lavina Anderson Low at Cardston, Alberta, Canada; attended University of Utah; former second counselor to Ardeth G. Kapp in the Young Women general presidency from April 4, 1987, to March 31, 1990; served on Relief Society general board from 1972 to 1984, former stake Relief Society president and ward and branch Young Women president; married Joseph E. Jack, parents of four sons.

First Counselor — Chieko Nishimura Okazaki, March 31, 1990 - present. Born to Kanenori and Hatsuko Nishi Nishimura at Kohala, Hawaii; bachelor's degree, University of Hawaii, master's degree in curriculum, University of Colorado; served on Primary general board, 1988 to 1990; Young Women's general board, 1960 to 1966, and 1971 to 1972; married Edward Y. Okazaki. He died March 20, 1992. Parents of two children.

Second Counselor — Aileen Hales Clyde, March 31, 1990 - present. Born in Springville, Utah, to G. Ray and M. Lesley Grooms Hales; received bachelor's degree in English from BYU, and did post-graduate work at BYU and the University of Utah; served on the Young Women general Board, 1977 to 1978; involved on many community advisory boards; regent, Utah System of Higher Education; married Hal M. Clyde, parents of three sons.

HISTORICAL LISTING OF GENERAL PRESIDENCIES
OF THE RELIEF SOCIETY
(Presidents pictured)

President, Emma Hale Smith — 17 Mar 1842 - 16 Mar 1844.

First Counselor, Sarah Marietta Kingsley Cleveland — 17 Mar 1842 - 16 Mar 1844.

Second Counselor, Elizabeth Ann Smith Whitney — 17 Mar 1842 - 16 Mar 1844.

President, Eliza Roxey Snow — 1866 - 5 Dec 1887.

First Counselor, Zina Diantha Huntington Young — 19 Jun 1880 - 8 Apr 1888.

Second Counselor, Elizabeth Ann Smith Whitney — 19 Jun 1880 - 15 Feb 1882.

President, Zina Diantha Huntington Young — 8 Apr 1888 - 28 Aug 1901.

First Counselor, Jane Snyder Richards — 11 Oct 1888 - 10 Nov 1901.

Second Counselor, Bathsheba Wilson Smith — 11 Oct 1888 - 10 Nov 1901.

President, Bathsheba Wilson Smith — 10 Nov 1901 - 20 Sep 1910.

First Counselor, Annie Taylor Hyde — 10 Nov 1901 - 2 Mar 1909.

Second Counselor, Ida Smoot Dusenberry, 10 Nov 1901 - 20 Sep 1910.

President, Emmeline Woodward B. Wells — 3 Oct 1910 - 2 Apr 1921.

First Counselor, Clarissa Smith Williams — 3 Oct 1910 - 2 Apr 1921.

Second Counselor, Julina Lambson Smith — 3 Oct 1910 - 2 Apr 1921.

President, Clarissa Smith Williams — 2 Apr 1921 - 7 Oct 1928.

First Counselor, Jennie Brimhall Knight — 2 Apr 1921 - 7 Oct 1928.

Second Counselor, Louise Yates Robison — 2 Apr 1921 - 7 Oct 1928.

President, Louise Yates Robison — 7 Oct 1928 - Dec 1939.

First Counselor, Amy Brown Lyman — 7 Oct 1928 - Dec 1939.

Second Counselors, Julia Alleman Child — 7 Oct 1928 - 23 Jan 1935, Kate Montgomery Barker — 3 Apr 1935 - 31 Dec 1939.

President, Amy Brown Lyman — 1 Jan 1940 - 6 Apr 1945.

First Counselor, Marcia Knowlton Howells — Apr 1940 - 6 Apr 1945.

Second Counselors, Donna Durrant Sorensen, Apr 1940 - 12 Oct 1942, Belle Smith Spafford, 12 Oct 1942 - 6 Apr 1945.

President, Belle Smith Spafford — 6 Apr 1945 - 3 Oct 1974.

First Counselor, Marianne Clark Sharp — 6 Apr 1945 - 3 Oct 1974.

Second Counselor, Gertrude Ryberg Garff

— 6 Apr 1945 - 30 Sep 1947, Velma Nebeker Simonsen — 3 Oct 1947 - 17 Dec 1956, Helen Woodruff Anderson — Jan 1957 - Aug 1958, Louise Wallace Madsen — Aug 1958 - 3 Oct 1974.

President, Barbara Bradshaw Smith — 3 Oct 1974 - 7 Apr 1984.

First Counselors, Janath Russell Cannon — 3 Oct 1974 - 28 Nov 1978, Marian Richards Boyer — 28 Nov 1978 - 7 Apr 1984.

Second Counselors, Marian Richards Boyer — 3 Oct 1974 - 28 Nov 1978, Shirley Wilkes Thomas — 28 Nov 1978 - 24 Jun 1983, Ann Stoddard Reese, 1 Oct 1983 - 7 Apr 1984.

President, Barbara Woodhead Winder — 7 Apr 1984 - 31 Mar 1990.

First Counselor, Joy Frewin Evans — 21 May 1984 - 31 Mar 1990.

Second Counselor, Joanne Bushman Doxey — 21 May 1984 - 31 Mar 1990.

WORLDWIDE
CHURCH

WORLDWIDE CHURCH
Areas of the World

Africa Area:
Membership, 77,000; Stakes, 10; Wards, 55; Missions, 12; Districts, 51 Branches, 340; Temples, 1; Headquarters, Johannesburg, South Africa.

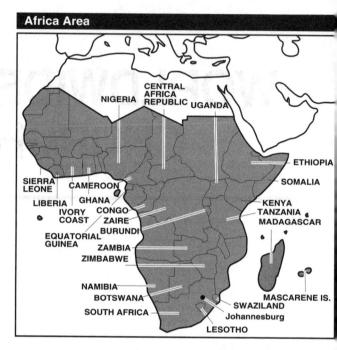

Asia Area:
Membership, 54,000; Stakes, 7; Wards, 43; Missions, 6; Districts, 17; Branches, 113; Temples, 1, (1 under construction); Headquarters, Hong Kong.

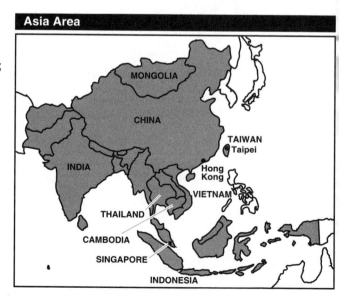

Asia North Area

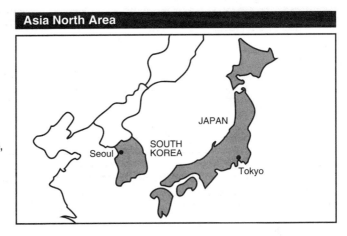

Asia North Area:
Membership, 167,000; Stakes, 41; Wards, 220; Missions, 14; Districts, 25; Branches, 227; Temples, 2; Headquarters, Tokyo, Japan.

Philippines / Micronesia Area

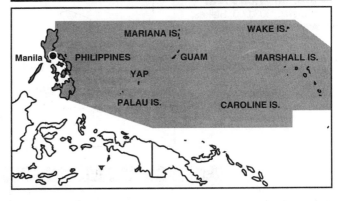

Philippines/ Micronesia Area:
Membership, 321,000; Stakes, 46; Wards, 276; Missions, 14; Districts, 92; Branches, 704; Temples, 1; Headquarters, Manila, Philippines.

Pacific Area

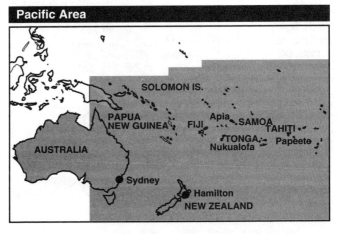

Pacific Area:
Membership, 297,000; Stakes, 61; Wards, 410; Missions, 13; Districts, 33; Branches, 370; Temples, 5; Headquarters, Sydney, Australia.

Mexico North Area

Mexico North Area: ; Membership, 341,000; Stakes, 60; Wards, 343; Missions, 10; Districts, 29; Branches, 303; Headquarters, Monterrey, Mexico.

Mexico South Area

Mexico South Area: Membership, 347,000; Stakes, 65; Wards, 437; Missions, 8; Districts, 18; Branches, 300; Temples, 1; Headquarters, Mexico City, Mexico.

Central America Area:
Membership, 303,000; Stakes, 51; Wards, 302; Missions, 11; Districts, 44; Branches, 444; Temples, 1; Headquarters, Guatemala City, Guatemala.

Central America Area

South America North Area:
Membership, 591,000; Stakes, 106; Wards, 654; Missions, 18; Districts, 84; Branches, 903; Temples, 1, 2 planned; Headquarters, Guayaquil, Ecuador.

South America North Area

Brazil Area

Brazil Area:
Membership, 474,000; Stakes, 104; Wards, 639; Missions, 19; Districts, 39; Branches, 474; Temples, 1; Headquarters, Sao Paulo, Brazil.

South America South Area

South America South Area:
Membership, 627,000; Stakes, 115; Wards, 651; Missions, 18; Districts, 84; Branches, 817; Temples, 2; Headquarters, Buenos Aires, Argentina.

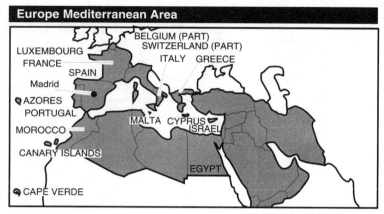

Europe Mediterranean Area

BELGIUM (PART)
SWITZERLAND (PART)
LUXEMBOURG
FRANCE
ITALY   GREECE
SPAIN
Madrid
AZORES
PORTUGAL
MALTA CYPRUS
MOROCCO
ISRAEL
CANARY ISLANDS
EGYPT
CAPE VERDE

Europe/Mediterranean Area: Membership, 110,000; Stakes, 20; Wards, 104; Missions, 18; Districts, 53; Branches, 436; Temples, 1 planned; Headquarters, Thoiry, France.

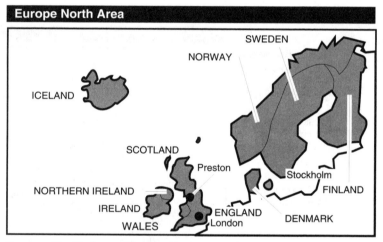

Europe North Area

SWEDEN
NORWAY
ICELAND
SCOTLAND
Preston
Stockholm
NORTHERN IRELAND
FINLAND
IRELAND
ENGLAND
DENMARK
WALES
London

Europe North Area: Membership, 184,000; Stakes, 48; Wards, 274; Missions, 12; Districts, 13; Branches, 207; Temples, 2, (1 planned); Headquarters, Solihull, England.

1. SLOVENIA
2. MACEDONIA
3. YUGOSLAVIA
4. CROATIA
5. BOSNIA
6. CZECH REPUBLIC
7. HUNGARY
8. SLOVAKIA

Europe Area: Membership, 61,000; Stakes, 21; Wards, 115; Missions, 21; Districts, 20; Branches, 279; Temples, 3; Headquarters, Frankfurt, Germany.

North America Northwest Area

North America Northwest Area:
Membership, 666,000; Stakes, 182; Wards, 1,310; Missions, 9; Districts, 5; Branches, 186; Temples, 4; Headquarters, Salt Lake City, Utah.

North America Southeast Area

North America Southeast Area:
Membership, 394,000; Stakes, 83; Wards, 548; Missions, 23; Districts, 22; Branches, 435; Temples, 2, (1 announced); Headquarters, Salt Lake City, Utah.

North America Northeast Area:
Membership, 396,000; Stakes, 102; Wards, 660; Missions, 24; Districts, 7; Branches, 396; Temples, 2, 1 planned; Headquarters, Salt Lake City, Utah.

North America Southwest Area:
Membership, 635,000; Stakes, 150; Wards, 1,060; Missions, 13; Branches, 273; Temples, 3; Headquarters, Salt Lake City, Utah.

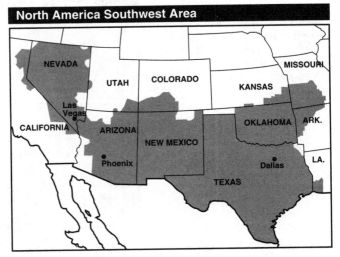

North America Central Area

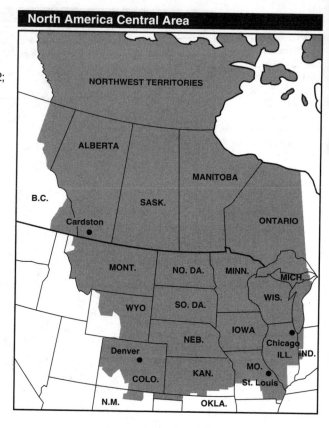

North America Central Area: Membership, 389,000; Stakes, 102; Wards, 705; Missions, 14; Districts, 11; Branches, 332; Temples, 3, (1 under construction); Headquarters, Salt Lake City, Utah.

North America West Area

North America West Area: Membership, 774,000; Stakes, 173; Wards, 1,272; Missions, 15; Branches, 193; Temples, 4; Headquarters, Salt Lake City, Utah.

Utah North Area:
Membership, 1,002,000; Stakes, 275; Wards, 1,982; Missions, 2; Branches, 71; Temples, 5; Headquarters, Salt Lake City, Utah.

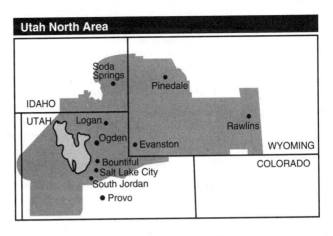

Utah South Area:
Membership, 478,000; Stakes, 146; Wards, 1,195; Missions, 1; Branches, 41; Temples, 3, (2 under construction); Headquarters, Salt Lake City, Utah.

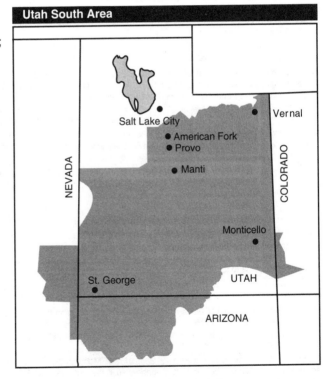

Editor's note: Information in this section has been gathered from a variety of sources and is believed to be the best available at the time of publication. Corrections, additional information and further country or state histories will be appreciated. Those with comments or information may write to: Church Almanac Histories, P.O. Box 1257, Salt Lake City, UT 84110.

UNITED STATES OF AMERICA

Year-end 1993: Est. population, 260 million; Members, 4,520,000; Stakes, 1,169; Wards, 8,433; Branches, 1,580; Districts, 16; Missions, 86; Temples, 27 (in use, under construction or announced); Percent LDS, 1.7, or one person in 58.

A few stakes and missions have headquarters in states other than that for which they are named. To simplify this listing, these stakes and missions are listed in the states for which they are named.

Numbers preceding stakes and missions are their chronological numbers assigned at the time of creation.
* Stake name changed 14 Jan 1974 or as indicated otherwise
† Original name
★ Transferred to

Alabama

Year-end 1993: Est. population, 4,226,000; Members, 24,000; Stakes, 6; Wards, 39; Branches, 32; Missions, 1; Percent LDS, 0.6 or one person in 176

Missionaries were reported to have preached on the Montgomery County courthouse steps Oct. 7, 1839, but concerted missionary efforts waited until 1842 and 1843 with the work of Elders James Brown and John U. Eldridge. Elder Brown organized branches in Tuscaloosa (the Cybry Branch) and Perry (Bogue-Chitto Branch) counties before Aug. 24, 1842. Elder Eldridge baptized his brother, wife and mother-in-law, probably in February or March of that year.

Other early missionaries included John Brown, Peter Haws and Hayden W. Church. Early missionaries frequently passed between Alabama and Mississippi in their work.

A typical experience was that of Elder John Brown, a 17-year-old missionary in ragged clothing, who visited an inn at Tuscumbria, Colbert County, on Aug. 27, 1843. When he asked for lodging as a preacher, he was thought to be a cotton picker. His host gathered a small group to be entertained at the expense of hearing a supposed cotton picker preach. After he began, however, "they were as motionless as statues of marble." None was baptized, but the young preacher was well-treated afterward.

Elder Brown later baptized a number of people in Tuscaloosa and Perry counties, and, according to some records, baptized some of the first African-Americans to join the Church, two men named Hagar and Jack, on Oct. 24, 1843.

In early 1844, three branches, reporting a combined membership of 123, attended a conference. Three months later, in April, seven branches reported a membership of 192, although this included some members from Mississippi.

Evidently most of the members immigrated to the West to join the body of the Saints and to avoid persecution. Some Alabama members were among the group of "Mississippi" Saints that emigrated under the leadership of John Brown and William Crosby in 1846.

Missionary work resumed in the South in 1876 with the creation of the Southern States Mission. However, persecution was widespread during the 1880s. As early as 1880, attempts were made to ask the governor of Alabama to force missionaries from the state. By 1894, the persecution subsided somewhat.

In 1898, John and James Edgar joined the Church in Andalusia, Ala., and that same year immigrated to Texas, where they later founded the LDS colony of Kelsey.

Early convert Olivia Tucker McCoy recalled missionaries coming to Magnolia in 1896, and in May of 1897 a conference was held in Magnolia with 36 elders and Southern States Mission Pres. John Morgan in attendance. Evicted from family property after their conversion, the McCoy family moved from Magnolia to another community and remained faithful.

A Sunday School was organized Aug. 22, 1911, in Montgomery. In the early days, converts were baptized in the Alabama River. In 1930, membership in the state was 2,516, with branches in Bradleyton and Lamison, and Sunday Schools in Bessemer, Birmingham, Camden, Clayton, Decatur, Dothan, Elmont, McCalla, Mobile, Pine Hill, Selma and Sneed.

Elder Theron W. Borup, district president, recalled that in the mid-1930s, Sunday School groups existed in Elkmont (which had a small chapel), Gadsen, Birmingham, McCalla and Montgomery. Branches were eventually organized from these Sunday Schools. In 1937 an east-west boundary was drawn through the

Alabama District and it was divided into the Alabama and North Alabama districts.

During this period, attitudes held by many people against the Church softened. In 1940, the Montgomery Branch staged a pioneer parade that attracted thousands.

Many LDS servicemen were stationed in the area as World War II proceeded, strengthening the branches. After the war, the branches began to grow. One prominent leader of the time was Stance H. Moore, president of the North Alabama District. A chapel was completed in 1955 in Montgomery, and the branch grew more rapidly after that. Alabama's first stake was created in Huntsville in 1968, the beginning of an influx of members brought by the military and the National Space and Aeronautics Administration. Membership in Alabama in 1974 was about 7,800, increasing to 14,000 in 1980 and to 20,000 in 1989, when the 150th anniversary of missionary work in Alabama was commemorated. One of the speakers at that commemoration was Chief Justice Ernest C. "Sonny" Hornsby of the Alabama Supreme Court.

Sources: *Encyclopedic History of the Church* by Andrew Jenson; *History of the Southern States Mission, 1831-1861,* by LaMar C. Barrett, a BYU thesis of July 1960; *Sesquicentennial Star,* history published by Montgomery Alabama Stake Oct. 7, 1989, courtesy Frank W. Riggs III, with interviews of Willie Lou Greene, and others; "Alabama: The northern Saints of a southern state," April 7, 1988, *Church News.*

Stakes — 6
(Listed alphabetically as of Oct. 1, 1994.)

No.	Name	Organized	First President
North America Southeast Area			
1362	Bessemer Alabama	12 Sep 1982	Robert Henry Shepherdson
678	Birmingham Alabama	2 Feb 1975	Fred M. Washburn
1588	Dothan Alabama	2 Mar 1986	Ned Philip Jenne
452	*Huntsville Alabama		
	†Alabama	3 Mar 1968	Raymond D. McCurdy
964	Mobile Alabama	8 Oct 1978	Dean Arthur Rains
717	Montgomery Alabama	2 Nov 1975	Gayle Dorwin Heckel

Mission — 1
(As of Oct. 1, 1994; shown with historical number. See MISSIONS.)

(166a) ALABAMA BIRMINGHAM MISSION
1560 Montgomery Highway, Suite 204
Birmingham, AL 35216
Phone: (205) 979-0686

Alaska

Year-end 1993: Est. population, 608,000; Members, 23,000; Stakes, 5; Wards, 32; Branches, 36; Missions, 1; Districts, 3; Percent LDS, 3.7, or one person in 26.

The first Latter-day Saints in Alaska, John Bigelow and Dr. Edward G. Cannon, were drawn by the gold rush of 1898. They arrived about the turn of the century. Little is known of Bigelow, but Dr. Cannon, a 79-year-old who had been converted in 1871, worked hard to establish the Church. He maintained a "tabernacle which he moved about on wheels from settlement to settlement" in the Seward Peninsula and Nome area.

On June 25, 1902, Dr. Cannon baptized a gold miner, K.N. Winnie, in the Bering Sea near Nome. Winnie reported in 1907 that they were holding gospel meetings and quite a number of people were interested. They taught Eskimos as well as miners and others. They worked together until Dr. Cannon's death in 1910, though they realized little success.

In 1913, a year after Alaska became a territory of the United States, the first two missionaries arrived in Juneau where they worked for a few weeks. The next missionaries arrived in Alaska in 1928 when Elders Heber J. Meeks, Alvin Englestead, James Judd, and Lowell T. Plowman came under the direction of Pres. William R. Sloan of the Northwestern States Mission.

The elders held 105 meetings and placed more than 1,300 copies of the Book of Mormon over the next year. They also dealt with a widespread rumor that the Church planned to colonize Alaska. Few people joined, however, and membership consisted only of a few scattered LDS homesteaders or fortune seekers.

The first branch was organized in Fairbanks on July 10, 1938, with Dr. Murray Shields as president. By 1941, membership in the territory reached 300. During the next 23 years, other branches were organized so that by 1961, membership was 3,051 with three branches in Anchorage, and additional branches in

Fairbanks, Palmer, and Juneau. The Anchorage Stake was created Aug. 13, 1961, with Orson P. Millett as president.

The Alaskan-Canadian Mission was created Jan. 1, 1961. In 1964, missionaries working among the native Americans introduced the gospel to many. A massive earthquake struck Alaska March 27, 1964, and among those killed were six members of the Valdez Branch.

As the area was rebuilt after the earthquake, the construction effort led to a building boom that brought additional members, and the stake grew along with the state. A new stake center was dedicated in Anchorage in 1966. In 1970, membership was 6,744. The Alaska Anchorage Mission was created in 1974.

Discovery of oil in the north accelerated growth. Construction of the trans-Alaska oil pipeline created a boom of membership that dropped after the construction project was completed. Special meetinghouses designed for the Arctic were built in many of the smaller branches under the leadership of mission Pres. Douglas T. Snarr in 1981. Membership in 1980 reached 14,414, and by 1990 it was 21,410. In the 1990s, members took part in community service projects that helped improve relationships for the Church.

Sources: *Encyclopedic History of the Church* by Andrew Jenson; *The History of the Mormons in Alaska,* by Barbara Jean Walther, *A Gathering of Saints in Alaska,* edited by Patricia B. Jasper and Beverly M. Blasongame; "The Saints in Anchorage Alaska," *Ensign,* November 1987; Alaskans: Determined Builders, Feb. 14, 1981, *Church News*; "Refuge facilities improved," *Church News* Dec. 18, 1993.

Stakes — 5
(Listed alphabetically as of Oct. 1, 1994.)

No.	Name	Organized	First President
North America Northwest Area			
331	*Anchorage Alaska †Alaska	13 Aug 1961	Orson P. Millett
962	Anchorage Alaska North	17 Sep 1978	Wesley R. Grover
1033	Fairbanks Alaska	27 May 1979	Dennis E. Cook
1507	Soldotna Alaska	9 Dec 1984	Merrill D. Briggs
1456	Wasilla Alaska	13 Nov 1983	Elbert Thomas Pettijohn

Mission — 1
(As of Oct. 1, 1994; shown with historical number. See MISSIONS.)

(114) ALASKA ANCHORAGE MISSION
201 Arctic Slope Ave., Suite 140
Anchorage, AK 99518-3031
Phone: (907) 344-4561

Arizona

Year-end 1993: Est. population, 3,999,000; Members, 256,000; Stakes, 62; Wards, 452; Branches, 55; Missions, 3; Temples, 1; Percent LDS, 6.4, or one person in 16.

The Mormon Battalion entered the area that is now Arizona in December 1847 and January 1848 during its famous march through the Southwest. As early as 1859, Jacob Hamblin did missionary work among the Navajos and Moquis Indians of the area. The first effort at colonization came in March 1873 when a group of Saints was sent from Utah to the Little Colorado River area under the direction of Horton D. Haight. Most returned to Utah but a few remained, including John L. Blythe. He and others established farms among the Indians at Moancopi. A second expedition under James S. Brown scouted the Little Colorado River preparing the way for a group that later colonized St. Joseph, Sunset, Obed and Brigham City. These settlers, who came in the spring of 1876, built a fort, dug canals and built dams and struggled to survive in the arid land. Most practiced the United Order. Settlers on the lower Little Colorado became discouraged after efforts failed to dam the unruly stream.

In 1876, Lot Smith and others established more colonies on the Little Colorado. A year later, Mormon colonizers settled in the Salt River Valley where Lehi and later Mesa were founded. Other colonies, such as Pima and Thatcher, were founded in Gila Valley in 1881. Eventually, some 34 Mormon colonies were started in Arizona.

The Little Colorado Stake was created in 1878, followed by the Maricopa and Saint Joseph stakes in 1882 and 1883, respectively.

Members overcame severe hardships in the early years. For example, in the colony of Woodruff, members built 17 successive dams after each previous one was washed out.

Over the years, members gained prominence and were involved in the progress of the state. They earned a good reputation for their industry and integrity. Colonies continued to grow. Pres. Jesse N. Smith of Snowflake helped locate the site of the Mormon colonies in Mexico. Arizona also became a place of refuge for the settlers of Mexico during the exodus of 1912.

The Arizona Temple was completed in 1923 and dedicated Oct. 23, 1927.

By 1930, Arizona had four stakes with 18,732 members. Two stakes were created in the 1930s, and another two in the 1940s; membership in 1940 was 25,272. In 1950, membership was 33,937, and during the decade and six more stakes were created. In 1960, membership had nearly doubled to 60,457; five stakes were created in the 1960s. Membership grew to 94,249 by 1970, and 21 new stakes were created in the 1970s. President Spencer W. Kimball, a long-time resident of Thatcher, Ariz., was president of the Church from 1973-1985.

To accommodate the increasing membership, the Arizona Temple was renovated and enlarged and, in 1975, became the first temple in the Church to be rededicated. A total of 205,248 members and non-members toured the renewed building during an open house held before its rededication. At that time, the temple district included 72 stakes, including 28 Spanish-speaking stakes.

The pageant "Jesus The Christ," started in 1938 and presented annually on the temple grounds, attracts about 80,000 people each year. Christmas lights on the Arizona Temple grounds also attracts many from the community.

By 1980, membership reached 171,880; and by 1990, 241,000. In the last few years, about two new stakes a year have been created in Arizona.

Sources: *Encyclopedic History of the Church* by Andrew Jenson; "Early History of Arizona," by Paul Updike, *The Pioneer*, Jan. 1981; *Heart Throbs of the West* by Kate B. Carter; "Mormons" in Arizona by Thomas Edwin Farrish, reprinted in the *Deseret News* Aug. 31, 1918.

Stakes — 62
(Listed alphabetically as of Oct. 1, 1994.)

No.	Name	Organized	First President
North America Southwest Area — 61			
1616	Apache Junction Arizona	16 Nov 1986	Charles Wray Squires
1666	Buckeye Arizona	13 Dec 1987	Charles Roy Rucker
888	Camp Verde Arizona	22 Jan 1978	John Edward Eagar
1819	Casa Grande Arizona	13 Oct 1991	Scott J. McEuen
988	Chandler Arizona	3 Dec 1978	Elone Evans Farnsworth
1513	Chandler Arizona Alma	24 Feb 1985	Martin H. Durrant
1773	Chinle Arizona	30 Sep 1990	Edwin I. Tano
963	Duncan Arizona	24 Sep 1978	Earl Adair Merrell
1627	Eagar Arizona	25 Jan 1987	Charles D. Martin
232	*Flagstaff Arizona		
	†Flagstaff	23 Sep 1956	Burton R. Smith
703	*Gilbert Arizona Greenfield 11 Oct 1981		
	†Gilbert Arizona	24 Aug 1975	Newell A. Barney
1295	Gilbert Arizona Stapley	11 Oct 1981	Wilburn James Brown
1661	Gilbert Arizona Val Vista	22 Nov 1987	Craig Allen Cardon
612	*Glendale Arizona		
	†Glendale	6 May 1973	Melvin L. Huber
1236	Glendale Arizona North	15 Feb 1981	Richard Johnson Barrett
650	Globe Arizona	16 Jun 1974	Bennie Joe Cecil
536	*Holbrook Arizona		
	†Holbrook	22 Nov 1970	Jay Barder Williams
1436	Kingman Arizona	21 Aug 1983	Louis George Sorensen
161	*Mesa Arizona		
	†Mesa	8 Dec 1946	L.M. Mecham Jr.
1265	Mesa Arizona Central	10 May 1981	Clayton H. Hakes
224	*Mesa Arizona East		
	*Mesa East 29 May 1970		
	†East Mesa	20 Nov 1955	Donald Ellsworth
1087	Mesa Arizona Kimball	25 Nov 1979	Allen Smith Farnsworth
1741	Mesa Arizona Kimball East	14 Jan 1990	Wayne D. Crismon
1026	Mesa Arizona Lehi	6 May 1979	Otto Stronach Shill Jr.
24	*Mesa Arizona Maricopa		
	†Maricopa	10 Dec 1882	Alexander F. MacDonald
1628	Mesa Arizona Mountain View	25 Jan 1987	James R. Adair

558	*Mesa Arizona North 15 Mar 1978		
	*Mesa Maricopa North		
	†Maricopa North	7 Nov 1971	Raymond L. Russell
1479	Mesa Arizona Pueblo	10 Jun 1984	E. Clark Huber
1904	Mesa Ariz Red Mountain	20 Sep 1992	James Joseph Humula
745	Mesa Arizona Salt River	15 Feb 1976	Elden S. Porter
362	*Mesa Arizona South		
	†Mesa South	18 Nov 1962	Stanley F. Turley
555	*Mesa Arizona West		
	†Mesa West	10 Oct 1971	Weymouth D. Pew
633	Page Arizona	10 Mar 1974	J Ballard Washburn
1061	Paradise Valley Arizona	9 Sep 1979	James David King
1631	Peoria Arizona	22 Feb 1987	Thomas G. Jones
121	*Phoenix Arizona		
	†Phoenix	27 Feb 1938	James Robert Price
1248	Phoenix Arizona Camelback	22 Mar 1981	Ernest Widtsoe Shumway
1233	Phoenix Arizona Deer Valley	8 Feb 1981	E. Wayne Pratt
212	*Phoenix Arizona East		
	*Phoenix East 29 May 1970		
	†East Phoenix	28 Feb 1954	Junius E. Driggs
253	*Phoenix Arizona North		
	†Phoenix North	19 Jan 1958	Rudger G. Smith
380	*Phoenix Arizona West		
	†Phoenix West	1 Sep 1963	Keith W. Hubbard
896	Phoenix Arizona West Maricopa 18 May 1978		
	†West Maricopa Arizona	5 Mar 1978	DeNelson Jones
1830	Pima Arizona	17 Nov 1991	Stephen Lavar John
517	*Prescott Arizona		
	†Prescott	7 Jun 1970	Edward A. Dalton
137	*Saint David Arizona		
	*Arizona South 29 May 1970		
	†Southern Arizona	2 Mar 1941	A.B. Ballantyne
31	*Saint Johns Arizona		
	†Saint Johns (Arizona, New Mexico)	23 Jul 1887	David K. Udall
120	*Safford Arizona		
	†Mount Graham (Ariz., N.M.)	20 Feb 1938	Spencer W. Kimball
364	*Scottsdale Arizona		
	†Scottsdale	9 Dec 1962	Junius E. Driggs
668	Show Low Arizona	24 Nov 1974	Elbert J. Lewis
1348	Sierra Vista Arizona	6 Jun 1982	C. Lavell Haymore
31a	*Snowflake Arizona		
	†Snowflake	18 Dec 1887	Jesse N. Smith
1212	Taylor Arizona	30 Nov 1980	Peter Delos Shumway
391	*Tempe Arizona		
	†Tempe	2 Feb 1964	George Isaac Dana
738	Tempe Arizona South	18 Jan 1976	Fred Dale Markham
1708	Tempe Arizona West	8 Jan 1989	Kent M. Christiansen
25	*Thatcher Arizona		
	†Saint Joseph	25 Feb 1883	Christopher Layton
238	*Tucson Arizona		
	†Tucson	2 Dec 1956	Leslie Odell Brewer
878	Tucson Arizona East	6 Nov 1977	Paul Eugene Dahl
477	*Tucson Arizona North		
	†Tucson North	2 Feb 1969	Don Hakan Peterson
1517	Tucson Arizona Rincon	3 Mar 1985	Ernest G. Blain
959	Winslow Arizona	17 Sep 1978	Thomas A. Whipple

North America West Area - 1

263	*Yuma Arizona		
	†Yuma (Arizona, California)	27 Apr 1958	Marion Turley

Discontinued

22	Eastern Arizona (Arizona, New Mexico)	29 Jun 1879	Jesse N. Smith
	18 Dec 1887 ★Saint Johns (31), Snowflake (31a)		
21	Little Colorado	27 Jan 1878	Lot Smith
	18 Dec 1887 ★Snowflake (31a)		

(As of Oct. 1, 1994; shown with historical number. See MISSIONS.)

(179b) ARIZONA PHOENIX MISSION
6265 North 82nd St.
Scottsdale, AZ 85250
Phone: (602) 951-8098

(231) ARIZONA TUCSON MISSION
1840 East River Road, #102
Tucson, AZ 85718
Phone: (602) 577-7076

(37) ARIZONA TEMPE MISSION
P.O. Box 27056
Tempe, AZ 85285-7056
Phone: (602) 838-0659

Arkansas

Year-end 1993: Est. population, 2,440,000; Members, 15,000; Stakes, 4; Wards, 25; Branches, 24; Missions, 1; Percent LDS, 0.6, or one person in 162.

Elders Wilford Woodruff and Henry Brown arrived as missionaries in Benton County, Ark., on Jan. 28, 1835. They held the first meeting Feb. 1, and preached to an attentive congregation. Later they were confronted by an apostate, a man who earlier endured severe persecution in Missouri but later turned bitterly against the Church. However, this man died suddenly and Elder Woodruff preached his funeral sermon. Afterward, Elder Woodruff baptized a "Brother and Sister Hubbel."

In 1838, Elder Abraham O. Smoot was called to a five-month mission to Arkansas where he preached frequently with varied results.

Elder Parley P. Pratt was murdered in the town of Van Buren, Ark., on May 13, 1857. He had just been acquitted by a court of charges pressed by the former husband of his wife Eleanor McLean Pratt. At the trial she testified that her former husband had frequently physically abused her. Disappointed with the verdict, the enraged accuser assassinated the apostle.

Little if any missionary success was realized until 1875 when Elders Henry G. Boyle and J.D.H. McAllister visited a member in Des Arc, Ark., and preached and "baptized a great many of the best citizens of the region," numbering from 80 to 90 people. In 1877, Des Arc Branch members moved a group of 27 families and 125 people to Utah by wagon train.

In 1897, Elder J.H. Peterson laboring in Arkansas reported being treated kindly while in Heber, Red River and Batesville. This changed attitude evidently paved the way for conversions in Marion and Faulkner counties about the turn of the century. Several pioneer members were baptized in March of 1900, including Benjamin Franklin Baker and his sister Emoline in Faulkner County, and Rowland William Perry and his family, as well as Mary Chapelle and Martha White in Marion County.

The Baker family established the nucleus of the Barney Branch, which was a headquarters for missionaries for many years.

Early members and missionaries faced persecution but kept the Church going. Some of these and other early converts migrated to the West but others stayed and reared LDS families. These families were very close and held most of their social activities together.

By 1930, membership in Arkansas was 944 with branches at Barney, El Dorado and Little Rock (Faulkner County). New buildings were erected for the Little Rock and El Dorado branches in 1952, the Pine Bluff Branch in 1954, and the Barney and Rolla branches in 1956.

The first Arkansas stake was created June 1, 1969, in Little Rock, with the Ft. Smith Stake created in 1978 and the Jacksonville Stake created in 1983. The Arkansas Little Rock Mission was created in 1975.

Membership in 1980 was 9,878 and in 1990, 13,753.

Sources: *Encyclopedic History of the Church* by Andrew Jenson; *History of the Southern States Mission*, a BYU thesis by LaMar C. Berrett, 1960; "History and Genealogy of the Early Mormon Church in Arkansas," by Emogene Tindall; "History of the Church in Marion County Arkansas," by Louise Perry Bird; *Juvenile Instructor*, 15:24; *Millennial Star*, 38:26, 59:15; Early Scenes in Church History; *Church News*, May 21, 1977; BYU Studies, 15:2.

Stakes — 4
(Listed alphabetically by area as of Oct. 1, 1994.)

No.	Name	Organized	First President
North America Southeast Area — 3			
1432	Jacksonville Arkansas	19 Jun 1983	Robert Michael McChesney

484	*Little Rock Arkansas		
	†Arkansas	1 Jun 1969	Dean C. Andrew
1807	Rogers Arkansas	11 Aug 1991	David Allen Bednar

North America Southwest Area — 1

| 911 | Fort Smith Arkansas | 30 Apr 1978 | Arthur Donald Browne |

Mission — 1
(As of Oct. 1, 1994; shown with historical number. See MISSIONS.)

(116) ARKANSAS LITTLE ROCK MISSION
University Tower, # 210
1123 South University Ave.
Little Rock, AR 72204-1690
Phone: (501) 664-3765

California

Year-end 1993: Est. population, 31,521,000; Members, 719,000; Stakes, 160; Wards, 1,169; Branches, 184; Missions, 14; Temples, 3; Percent LDS, 2.3, or one person in 43.

Immigrants on the way to the Great Basin by way of Cape Horn were the first Latter-day Saints to set foot in California, arriving in Yerba Buena (San Francisco) July 29 or 31, 1846. They built up the community and laid important foundations for what became San Francisco. Eventually, many of the members moved to Salt Lake City.

In January 1847, the Mormon Battalion arrived in San Diego and made similar if not more extensive contributions to that city, and then traveled to Los Angeles where they built a fort and raised the first American flag. Six battalion members were at Sutter's Mill Jan. 24, 1848, when gold was discovered. The attraction of gold to the Great Basin Saints was minimal, although the Church and various members did profit from its discovery.

In 1850 a Mormon colony, New Hope, was founded by Mormons who did not go to Utah. They were among California's first farmers, irrigating with a pole and bucket method. They built the first Mormon chapel in 1850. Apostle Parley P. Pratt presided over the California Mission at San Francisco from 1849-52.

The first outreach from Utah to California came in 1851 with the San Bernardino colonization effort, which was to provide a route to the coast and attract Latter-day Saints from northern California and immigrants. Apostles Charles C. Rich and Amasa M. Lyman took charge of the effort. The San Bernardino Stake was created July 6, 1851, but was discontinued by 1857. The faithful members in this colony were eventually outnumbered by less-committed members who created considerable dissension. When the troubled colony was dissolved by the Church at the advance of Johnston's army upon Salt Lake City in 1857, some 1,400 — fewer than half the total — returned to Utah to colonize other areas.

Little missionary work took place from 1857 to 1892. Elder John L. Dalton began work in San Francisco in 1892 and organized branches. Karl G. Maeser presided over the California Mission in 1894. Missionaries began work southward and the Los Angeles Branch was created Aug. 20, 1895. The Northern California and Southern California conferences were organized in 1896, and the Sacramento conference was added in 1898.

The land boom of the 1920s attracted many members. The Los Angeles Stake was created Jan. 21, 1923, and was divided just four years later. The Hollywood Stake was created in 1927, the same year the San Francisco Stake was formed. Membership in 1930 was 21,254.

After the 1920s, when the first three stakes were created, new stakes were added at a rapid pace. Eight were created in the 1930s, five in the 1940s and 30 in the 1950s.

During the 1930s, many members came to work in the wartime defense industry. Land for a temple was purchased in 1937 in Los Angeles and the temple was completed in 1956. A second temple in Oakland was dedicated in 1964. A third California temple was dedicated April 25, 1993, in San Diego.

Completion of the imposing Los Angeles Temple in 1956 seemed to mark the beginning of an era of Church members gaining a higher public profile. In the past few decades, Latter-day Saints throughout California have reached the highest levels of education, industry, military, medicine, entertainment, science and government.

In times of disasters, such as earthquakes, fires and floods, members have responded with organized volunteers and supplies for members and non-members alike. Members have taken leadership roles in moral issues, such as combatting pornography. They have also cooperated with other congregations in various inter-faith endeavors.

Missionary work has also prospered in the state, which has more missions than any other state. Many minority converts have been taught the gospel in their own language in California's major cities. With burgeoning population increases from Latin America, four Spanish-speaking stakes have been organized, two since 1992. Various Asian and Polynesian wards function as well, and a Tongan stake was created in San Francisco in 1992.

Membership reached 541,000 in 1980. From 1991 to 1993, because of an out-migration of members, membership dropped from 721,000 to 719,000.

Sources: *Encyclopedic History of the Church* by Andrew Jenson; "It Started in Yerba Buena," by Richard O. Cowan, *Instructor* June 1961; "The Church in Early California," by Albert L. Zobell, *Improvement Era*, May 1964; "The Rise and Decline of Mormon San Bernardino," by Edward Leo Lyman, *BYU Studies,* Fall 1989; *Encyclopedia of Mormonism,* edited by Daniel H. Ludlow; multiple sources in *Church News*; "Spanish spoken here," by Julie A. Dockstader, *Church News,* May 15, 1993.

Stakes — 159
(Listed alphabetically by area as of Oct. 1, 1994.)

No.	Name	Organized	First President
North America West Area — 158			
402	*Anaheim California		
	†Anaheim	14 Mar 1965	Max V. Eliason
1514	Anaheim California East	24 Feb 1985	William E. Perron
1042	Anderson California	10 Jun 1979	Richard Miller Ericson
1263	Antioch California	3 May 1981	Clifford Spence Munns
864	Arcadia California	9 Oct 1977	Cree-L Kofford
1032	Auburn California	27 May 1979	David Oliver Montague
186	*Bakersfield California		
	†Bakersfield	27 May 1951	E. Alan Pettit
944	Bakersfield California East	18 Jun 1978	William Horsley Davies
1622	Bakersfield California South	14 Dec 1986	Jack Ray Zimmerman
288	*Barstow California		
	†Mojave	16 Aug 1959	Sterling A. Johnson
750	Blythe California	14 Mar 1976	Jerry Dean Mortensen
763	Camarillo California	8 Aug 1976	Victor Glenn Johnson
309	*Carlsbad California		
	†Palomar	6 Nov 1960	Wallace F. Gray
1505	Carmichael California	25 Nov 1984	Marc Earl Hall
269	*Cerritos California		
	†Norwalk	26 Oct 1958	Lewis Milton Jones
656	Cerritos California West	8 Sep 1974	Kenneth Laurence Davis
565	*Chico California		
	†Chico	6 Feb 1972	Lloyd Johnson Cope
1072	Chino California	14 Oct 1979	Allen Clare Christensen
770	Chula Vista California	19 Sep 1976	Robert Eugene Floto
1150	Citrus Heights California	22 Jun 1980	James Barnes
378	*Concord California		
	†Concord	23 Jun 1963	Ted Eugene Madsen
983	Corona California	19 Nov 1978	Darvil David McBride
226	*Covina California		
	†Covina	26 Feb 1956	Elden L. Ord
502	*Cypress California		
	†Anaheim West	15 Feb 1970	Hugh J. Sorensen
229	*Danville California 19 Jun 1989		
	*Walnut Creek California		
	†Walnut Creek	26 Aug 1956	Emery R. Ranker
1151	Davis California	22 Jun 1980	Peter Glen Kenner
1740	Del Mar California	7 Jan 1990	Robert Geoffrey Dyer
279	*Downey California 18 Feb 1986		
	*Huntington Park California		
	†Huntington Park	19 Apr 1959	Clifford B. Wright
179	*East Los Angeles California (Spanish) 27 June 1993		
	East Los Angeles (California)	26 Feb 1950	Fauntleroy Hunsaker
	*Los Angeles California East		
	*Los Angeles East 29 May 1970		
261	*El Cajon California 30 Nov 1975		
	*San Diego California El Cajon		
	†San Diego East	20 Apr 1958	Cecil I. Burningham

1119	El Centro California	16 Mar 1980	Robert Lamoreaux
984	El Dorado California	19 Nov 1978	Harold George Sellers
588	*Escondido California		
	†Escondido	24 Sep 1972	Donald R. McArthur
1847	Escondido California South	9 Feb 1992	Louis L. Rothey
338	*Eureka California		
	†Redwood (California, Oregon)	22 Oct 1961	David DeBar Felshaw
428	Fair Oaks	12 Feb 1967	Harvey Stansell Greer
	*Fair Oaks California		
682	Fairfield California	16 Feb 1975	Byron Gale Wilson
1602	Fontana California	22 Jun 1986	Wayne Hall Bringhurst
425	*Fremont California		
	†Fremont	11 Dec 1966	Francis B. Winkel
1584	Fremont California South	12 Jan 1986	Jerry Valient Kirk
185	*Fresno California		
	†Fresno	20 May 1951	Alwyn C. Sessions
381	*Fresno California East		
	†Fresno East	15 Sep 1963	Melvin P. Leavitt
1463	Fresno California North	12 Feb 1984	Stephen L. Christensen
1464	Fresno California West	12 Feb 1984	Gary R. Fogg
707	Fullerton California	21 Sep 1975	Leon Tad Ballard
330	*Garden Grove California		
	†Garden Grove	25 Jun 1961	James Malan Hobbs
175	*Glendale California		
	†Glendale	4 Dec 1949	Edwin Smith Dibble
786	Glendora California	14 Nov 1976	William Marshall Raymond
107	*Gridley California		
	†Gridley	4 Nov 1934	John C. Todd
442	*Hacienda Heights California 15 Jan 1978		
	*El Monte California		
	†El Monte	17 Sep 1967	James Cyril Brown
948	Hanford California	6 Aug 1978	Gerald Leo Thompson
228a	*Hayward California		
	†Hayward	26 Aug 1956	Milton P. Ream
961	Hemet California	17 Sep 1978	Darrel D. Lee
1632	Hesperia California	22 Feb 1987	Larry Dale Skinner
1926	Highland California	14 Mar 1993	Dennis Alvin Barlow
420	*Huntington Beach California		
	†Huntington Beach	5 Jun 1966	Conway W. Nielsen
2802	Huntington Beach California North	16 Jan 1977	Wesley Charles Woodhouse
1477	Huntington Park California West	3 Jun 1984	Rafael Nestor Seminario
1633a	Irvine California	12 Apr 1987	Jack L. Rushton Jr.
1784	Jurupa California	9 Dec 1990	Lester C. Lauritzen
518	*La Crescenta California		
	†La Canada	7 Jun 1970	Robert C. Seamons
347	*La Verne California		
	†Pomona	21 Jan 1962	Vern R. Peel
1354	Laguna Niguel California	20 Jun 1982	Donald H. Sedgwick
794	Lancaster California	28 Nov 1976	Stephen N. Hull
1798	Lancaster California East	19 May 1991	John Milloy Martz
1654	Livermore California	13 Sep 1987	Willis Arthur Sandholtz
822	*Lodi California 3 May 1981		
	†Stockton California East	10 Apr 1977	Robert Graham Wade
1649	Lompoc California	23 Aug 1987	Billy Ray Williams
117	*Long Beach California		
	†Long Beach	3 May 1936	John W. Jones
177	*Long Beach California East		
	*Long Beach East 29 May 1970		
	†East Long Beach	12 Feb 1950	John C. Dalton
704	Los Altos California	24 Aug 1975	W. Kay Williams
98	*Los Angeles California		
	*Los Angeles 19 Nov 1939		
	†Hollywood	22 May 1927	George W. McCune
337	*Los Angeles California Canoga Park		
	†Canoga Park	8 Oct 1961	Collins E. Jones

129	*Inglewood California 21 Feb 1993		
	*Los Angeles California Inglewood		
	†Inglewood	26 Nov 1939	Alfred E. Rohner
231	*Los Angeles California North Hollywood		
	Burbank (California)	16 Sep 1956	James D. Pratt
	*North Hollywood California		
188	*Los Angeles California Santa Monica 14 Jan 1974		
	Santa Monica (California)	1 Jul 1951	E. Garrett Barlow
116	*Los Angeles California Van Nuys		
	*San Fernando 15 Oct 1939		
	†Pasadena	19 Apr 1936	David H. Cannon
1249	Manteca California	22 Mar 1981	David Leon Ward
156	*Menlo Park California		
	†Palo Alto	23 Jun 1946	Claude B. Petersen
659	Merced California	15 Sep 1974	Robert D. Rowan
826	Mission Viejo California	8 May 1977	Nolan C. Draney
399	*Modesto California		
	†Modesto	7 Jun 1964	Clifton A. Rooker
716	Modesto California North	26 Oct 1975	Charles Elwin Boice
258	*Monterey California		
	†Monterey Bay	2 Mar 1958	James N. Wallace Jr.
1656	Moreno Valley California	27 Sep 1987	David Lowell Briggs
831	Morgan Hill California	15 May 1977	Donald Russell Lundell
1693	Murrieta California	20 Mar 1988	Ronald Miguel Peterson
297	*Napa California		
	†Napa	17 Apr 1960	Harry S. Cargun
652	Newbury Park California	18 Aug 1974	Lavar M. Butler
453	*Newport Beach California		
	†Newport Beach	31 Mar 1968	Ferren L. Christensen
227a	*Oakland California		
	†Oakland-Berkeley	26 Aug 1956	O. Leslie Stone
1092	Ontario California	9 Dec 1979	Seth C. Baker
251a	*Orange California		
	†Santa Ana	8 Dec 1957	Karl C. Durham
441	Palm Springs	27 Aug 1967	Quinten Hunsaker
	*Palm Springs California		
459	*Palmdale California		
	†Antelope Valley	12 May 1968	Sterling A. Johnson
739	Palos Verdes California	18 Jan 1976	Merrill Bickmore
128	*Pasadena California		
	†Pasadena	1 Oct 1939	Bertram M. Jones
1608	Penasquitos California	21 Sep 1986	Michael Lee Jensen
215	*Placentia California		
	*Fullerton 14 Mar 1965		
	†Orange County	27 Jun 1954	John C. Dalton
675	Pleasanton California	8 Dec 1974	Dale Edwin Nielsen
1056	Poway California	26 Aug 1979	Paul B. Richardson
1648	Rancho Cucamonga California 13 Aug 1987		
	†Cucamonga California	28 Jun 1987	Steven Thomas Escher
319	*Redding California		
	†Redding	13 Dec 1960	Albert C. Peterson
938	*Redlands California 5 May 1987		
	†San Bernardino California East	4 Jun 1978	Donald L. Hansen
415	*Rialto California		
	†Rialto	20 Mar 1966	Wayne A. Reeves
521	*Ridgecrest California		
	†Mount Whitney	16 Aug 1970	AlDean Washburn
196	*Riverside California		
	†Mount Rubidoux	26 Oct 1952	Vern Robert Peel
430	*Riverside California West		
	†Arlington	23 Apr 1967	Clarence Leon Sirrine
1854	Rocklin California	19 Apr 1992	Jay Robert Jibson Jr.

515	*Roseville California		
	†Roseville	17 May 1970	S. Lloyd Hamilton
108	*Sacramento California		
	†Sacramento	4 Nov 1934	Mark W. Cram
1691	Sacramento California Antelope	6 Mar 1988	Roger William Mack
290	*Sacramento California East		
	†American River	6 Dec 1959	Austin G. Hunt
219	*Sacramento California North		
	*Sacramento North 30 Sep 1969		
	†North Sacramento	12 Dec 1954	Austin G. Hunt
1152	*Sacramento California Rancho Cordova 17 Sep 1985		
	†Sacramento California Cordova	22 Jun 1980	Richard W. Montgomery
487	Sacramento South (California)	15 Jun 1969	John Henry Huber
	*Sacramento California South 14 Jan 1974		
	*Elk Grove California 30 Sep 1993		
111	*San Bernardino California		
	†San Bernardino	3 Feb 1935	Albert Lyndon Larson
136	*San Diego California		
	†San Diego	9 Feb 1941	Wallace W. Johnson
736	San Diego California East	30 Nov 1975	Philip Alma Petersen
489	*San Diego California North		
	†San Diego North	22 Jun 1969	Ray Michael Brown
360	*San Diego California Sweetwater 30 Aug 1988		
	*Lemon Grove California 16 Aug 1983		
	*San Diego California South		
	†San Diego South	21 Oct 1962	Cecil I. Burningham
1915a	San Fernando California (Spanish)	6 Dec 1992	Jose Gerardo Lombardo
99	*San Francisco California		
	†San Francisco	10 Jul 1927	W. Aird Macdonald
1863	San Francisco California East	10 May 1992	Sione Fangu
1515	San Francisco California West	24 Feb 1985	Jeremiah I. Alip
202	*San Jose California		
	†San Jose	30 Nov 1952	Vernard L. Beckstrand
693	San Jose California East	4 May 1975	Leo E. Haney
450	*San Jose California South 14 Jan 1974		
	†San Jose South (California)	11 Feb 1968	DeBoyd L. Smith
329	*San Leandro California		
	†San Leandro	21 May 1961	Milton R. Ream
248	*San Luis Obispo California		
	†San Luis Obispo	22 Sep 1957	Arthur J. Godfrey
462	*San Rafael California		
	†Marin	23 Jun 1968	Weston L. Roe
787	Santa Ana California	14 Nov 1976	Wilbur Orion Jensen
1838	Santa Ana California South (Spanish)	5 Jan 1992	Renan Ramos Disner
184	*Santa Barbara California		
	†Santa Barbara	18 Mar 1951	Arthur J. Godfrey
642	*Santa Clarita California 2 Feb 1992		
	†Los Angeles California Santa Clarita	19 May 1974	Norman D. Stevensen
823	Santa Cruz California	24 Apr 1977	Edwin Reese Davis
1920	Santa Margarita California	17 Jan 1993	David Michael Daly
384	*Santa Maria California		
	†Santa Maria	20 Oct 1963	Clayton K. Call
181	*Santa Rosa California		
	†Santa Rosa	7 Jan 1951	J. LeRoy Murdock
1582	Santee California	8 Dec 1985	Robert Earl Harper
387	*Saratoga California		
	†San Jose West	10 Nov 1963	Louis W. Latimer
448	*Simi Valley California		
	†Simi	10 Dec 1967	John Lyman Ballif III
171	*Stockton California		
	†San Joaquin	25 Apr 1948	Wendell B. Mendenhall
1624	Thousand Oaks California	11 Jan 1987	Grant R. Brimhall
282	*Torrance California		
	†Torrance	3 May 1959	Roland Earl Gagon

220	*Torrance California North		
	†Redondo	29 May 1955	Leslie L. Prestwich
1591	Turlock California	23 Mar 1986	Robert Peebles Baker
877	Ukiah California	30 Oct 1977	Robert Vernon Knudsen
583	*Upland California		
	†Upland	13 Aug 1972	Frank E. Finlayson
1801	Vacaville California	26 May 1991	Edwin Gordon Wells Jr.
1845	Valencia California	2 Feb 1992	Reed E. Halladay
548	*Ventura California		
	†Ventura	30 May 1971	Joseph F. Chapman
1397	Victorville California	30 Jan 1983	Owen Dean Call
492	*Visalia California		
	†Visalia	24 Aug 1969	Alva D. Blackburn
967	Vista California	8 Oct 1978	Jack Robert Jones
281	*Walnut California 23 July 1985		
	*La Puente California		
	†West Covina	3 May 1959	Mark W. Smith
1587a	*Walnut Creek California 17 May 1992		
	†Walnut Creek California East	16 Feb 1986	Williams F. Matthews
280	*Whittier California		
	†Whittier	26 Apr 1959	John Collings
1079	Yuba City California	4 Nov 1979	Lowell R. Tingey
1969	Yucca Valley California	9 Jan 1994	Kipton Paul Madsen

North America Southwest Area — 1

| 1073 | Quincy California | 14 Oct 1979 | Floyd Eugene Warren |

Discontinued

159	Berkeley	13 Oct 1946	W. Glenn Harmon
	26 Aug 1956 ★Oakland-Berkeley (227a)		
806	Concord California East	23 Jan 1977	Vern W. Clark
	16 Feb 1986 ★Walnut Creek California East (1587)		
1107	Lawndale California	17 Feb 1980	Silvon Foster Engilman
	21 Feb 1993		
1683	Long Beach California North	31 Jan 1988	V. Jay Spongberg
	7 Nov 1993		
88	*Los Angeles South 29 May 1970		
	12 Aug 1973 ★Huntington Park (279)		
	*South Los Angeles 19 Nov 1939		
	†Los Angeles	21 Jan 1923	George W. McCune
817	Los Angeles California Granada Hills	13 Mar 1977	Clark Spendlove
	Discontinued 6 Dec 1992		
109	Oakland	2 Dec 1934	W. Aird Macdonald
	26 Aug 1956 ★Oakland-Berkeley (227a)		
230	Reseda (California)	16 Sep 1956	Hugh C. Smith
	*Los Angeles California Chatsworth 14 Jan 1974		
	6 Dec 1992		
247	*Pacifica California		
	21 Feb 1982 ★San Francisco California (99)		
	†San Mateo	15 Sep 1957	Melvin P. Pickering
4a	San Bernardino	6 Jul 1851	David Seely
	1857		
585	San Jose North (California)	20 Aug 1972	Lloyd M. Gustaveson
	*Santa Clara California 14 Jan 1974		
	10 May 1992		

Missions — 15
(As of Oct. 1, 1994; shown with historical number. See MISSIONS.)

(73a) CALIFORNIA ANAHEIM MISSION
501 N. Brookhurst #100
Anaheim, CA 92801
Phone: (714) 776-2725

(86) CALIFORNIA ARCADIA MISSION
170 West Duarte Road
Arcadia, CA 91007
Phone: (818) 446-8519

(37) CALIFORNIA SACRAMENTO MISSION
9480 Madison Ave. Suite 2
Orangeville, CA 95662
Phone: (916) 988-7037

(182) CALIFORNIA SAN BERNARDINO MISSION
8280 Utica Ave, #150
Rancho Cucamonga, CA 91730
Phone: (909) 466-1129

(283) CALIFORNIA CARLSBAD MISSION
785 Grand Ave. Suite 204
Carlsbad, CA 92008
Phone: (619)720-3430

(113) CALIFORNIA SAN DIEGO MISSION
3322 Sweetwater Springs Blvd., #203
Spring Valley, CA 91977-3142
Phone: (619) 660-8202

(118) CALIFORNIA FRESNO MISSION
2350 West Shaw Ave. # 123
Fresno, CA 93711
Phone: (209) 431-5510

(299) CALIFORNIA SAN FERNANDO
23504 Lyons Ave., Suite 107
Santa Clarita, CA 91321
Phone: (805) 288-1614

(5) CALIFORNIA LOS ANGELES MISSION
P.O. Box 24089
Los Angeles, CA 90024
Phone: (310) 474-2593

(158a) CALIFORNIA SAN JOSE MISSION
6489 Camden Ave., #107
San Jose, CA 95120-2898
Phone: (408) 268-9411

(85) CALIFORNIA OAKLAND MISSION
4945 Lincoln Way
Oakland, CA 94602
Phone: (510) 531-3880

(187a) CALIFORNIA SANTA ROSA MISSION
3510 Unocal Place, #302
Santa Rosa, CA 95403
Phone: (707) 579-9411

(235) CALIFORNIA RIVERSIDE MISSION
3233 Arlington Ave., Suite 107
Riverside, CA 92506
Phone: (714) 788-9690

(159) CALIFORNIA VENTURA MISSION
260 Maple Ct. #120
Ventura, CA 93003
Phone: (805) 644-1034

(284) CALIFORNIA ROSEVILLE
8331 Sierra College Blvd., #208
Roseville, CA 95661
Phone: (916) 791-7558

Colorado

Year-end 1993: Est. population, 3,635,000; Members, 95,000; Stakes, 25; Wards, 167; Branches, 35; Missions, 2; Temples, 1; Percent LDS, 2.6, or one person in 38.

In 1846, a group of 43 Saints in 19 wagons traveled to the West from Monroe County, Miss. They expected to meet Brigham Young's wagon train at the Platte River in the Iowa Territory, and accompany this train west. However, Brigham Young's pioneer train waited over a season after 500 men were enlisted in the Mormon Battalion. By the time the Mississippi company learned of this, they had reached western Nebraska. The Mississippians decided to winter at Fort Pueblo in Colorado in the upper Arkansas River Valley, where they arrived Aug. 7, 1846. During the following winter, three detachments of the Mormon Battalion, including wives and children of battalion members, and those who were ill, were sent to join the members in Pueblo.

By the end of winter in 1846, the colony had 275 people. It was soon disbanded as one party joined Brigham Young's company at Fort Laramie June 3, 1847. Others went east to bring back their families, and others joined later wagon trains going west. No remains of this settlement exist; its site is near the present-day town of Blende in metropolitan Pueblo.

In 1858, the S.M. Rooker family, traveling east from Utah, heard of a gold discovery and became the first settlers at Cherry Creek and the Platte River, which would later become Denver. As the city grew, a few members arrived, but the area was not under ecclesiastical leadership until the Colorado Mission was created Dec. 14, 1896. Presiding over the mission was Elder John W. Taylor of the Council of the Twelve. The first missionaries in the area were Elders John H. Broshard, Hebert A. White and William C. Clive. The Denver Branch was created Jan. 3, 1897, and a short time later, branches in Colorado Springs were organized.

In 1878, a group of 70 converts from the Southern States Mission, under the leadership of Elder James Z. Stewart, settled in Conejos County, Colo. They, and later immigrants under the direction of Church leaders from Utah, founded the communities of Manassa, Richfield and Sanford. In 1883, the San Luis Stake was created in the area.

In the summer of 1897, Bishop John I. Hart of Manassa was called to live in Pueblo and start a branch there among the handful of members. This branch was organized under the direction of Elder Taylor about mid-January, 1897.

Missionaries in this period generally found residents to be hospitable and baptized occasional converts. In 1909, missionaries campaigned against the growing number of saloons in the Denver. On Nov. 23, 1911, the Tabernacle Choir gave a concert in Denver, and another later in Colorado Springs. The Young Stake was created in the Montezuma and La Plata counties in 1913.

By 1930, the Denver, Pueblo, San Luis, and Western Colorado Districts, and the San Luis and Young stakes had a combined membership of 6,435 members.

A branch in Fort Collins started as LDS educators arrived to teach at Colorado State University in the 1930s.

The Denver Stake was organized in 1940. During World War II, a number of former missionaries served at military bases in the Denver area. Denver Stake Pres. Edward E. Drury and former mission Pres. Elbert R. Curtis (released at the start of the war) held a special service attended by more than 100 servicemen.

Membership continued to grow after the war, and many buildings were constructed. By 1950, membership was nearly 10,000, increasing to nearly 20,000 in 1960, nearly 40,000 in 1970, and 69,000 by 1980.

A temple to serve the LDS population in Colorado and nearby states was completed and dedicated in 1986. Membership began to emerge into public notice during the decade that the temple was dedicated. Released-time seminary was approved and seminary buildings were erected. Membership grew as jobs increased in areas of high technology and military. Agriculture continued to be a stable source of livelihood for many.

Indicative of the increasing profile of the Church, Colorado Gov. Roy Romer addressed a Church fireside in Willow Springs March 11, 1990. In August of 1993, many LDS volunteers assisted when Pope John Paul II of the Roman Catholic Church visited Denver.

Membership in 1990 reached 88,625.

Sources: *Encyclopedic History of the Church* by Andrew Jenson; "Colorado, Mormons and the Mexican War," by John F. Yurtinus, *Essays in Colorado History,* 1983, No. 1; "A Look at the History of the Church . . . in Pueblo, Colorado," by Gail McHardy; *Comprehensive History of the Church,* by B.H. Roberts; Pioneer Journeys, *Improvement Era,* July 1910, 802-810; "Mississippi Mormons," by Leonard Arrington, *Ensign,* June 1977; "Denver Saints Claim Spiritual Blessings," *Ensign,* November 1986; *Church News,* Oct. 7, 1944, Oct. 20, 1945, Feb. 9, 1974, June 4, 1977; Aug. 24, 1986; March 24, 1990; "LDS among volunteers for papal visit," by Twila Bird, *Church News,* Aug. 21, 1993.

Stakes — 25
(Listed alphabetically by area as of Oct. 1, 1994.)

No.	Name	Organized	First President
North America Central Area — 22			
1655	Arapahoe Colorado	27 Sep 1987	Lawry Evans Doxey
287	*Arvada Colorado		
	†Denver West	21 Jun 1959	Thomas L. Kimball
1318	Aurora Colorado	6 Dec 1981	Lawry Evans Doxey
595	*Boulder Colorado		
	†Boulder	28 Jan 1973	C. Rodney Claridge
301	*Colorado Springs Colorado		
	†Pikes Peak (Colorado, New Mexico)	11 Sep 1960	Ralph M. Gardner
1770	Colorado Springs Colorado East	26 Aug 1990	Jack Harmon Dunn
1134	Colorado Springs Colorado North	18 May 1980	Richard Larry Williams
1214	Columbine Colorado	7 Dec 1980	David M. Brown
132	*Denver Colorado		
	†Denver	30 Jun 1940	Douglas M. Todd Jr.
596	*Denver Colorado North		
	†Denver North	28 Jan 1973	Gus. F. Ranzenberger
470	*Fort Collins Colorado		
	†Fort Collins	1 Dec 1968	Raymond Price
1452	Golden Colorado	6 Nov 1983	John Marshall Simcox
223	*Grand Junction Colorado		
	†Grand Junction	16 Oct 1955	Loyal B. Cook
1415	Grand Junction Colorado West	24 Apr 1983	Andrew H. Christensen
1528	Greeley Colorado	28 Apr 1985	Gilbert I. Sandberg
394	*Lakewood Colorado		
	†Denver South	19 Apr 1964	R. Raymond Barnes
625	*Littleton Colorado		
	†Littleton	2 Sep 1973	Clinton L. Cutler
1778	Longmont Colorado	11 Nov 1990	Lynn Snarr Hutchings
320	Meeker Colorado		
	†Craig	15 Jan 1961	Loyal B. Cook

977	Montrose Colorado	5 Nov 1978	Robert M. Esplin
632	Pueblo Colorado	3 Mar 1974	Louis Edward Butler
1534	Willow Creek Colorado	19 May 1985	Robert K. Bills

North America Southwest Area — 3

1425	Alamosa Colorado	29 May 1983	Gary Reese Shawcroft
557	*Durango Colorado		
	†Mesa Verde	7 Nov 1971	Del A. Talley Sr.
26	*Manassa Colorado 31 May 1983		
	*La Jara Colorado		
	†San Luis (Colorado, New Mexico)	10 Jun 1883	Silas S. Smith

Missions — 2
(As of Oct. 1, 1994; shown with historical number. See MISSIONS.)

(286) COLORADO DENVER NORTH MISSION
11172 North Huron, Suite 21
Northglenn, CO 80234
Phone: (303) 252-7191

(17) COLORADO DENVER SOUTH MISSION
Box 2674
Littleton, CO 80161-2674
Phone: (303) 794-6457

Connecticut

Year-end 1993: Est. population, 3,281,000; Members, 10,000; Stakes, 2; Wards, 20; Branches, 6; Missions, 1; Temples, 1 announced; Percent LDS, 0.3, or one person in 363.

Elders Orson Hyde and Samuel H. Smith began missionary work in Connecticut in 1832 when they preached in the New England states. Evidently they did not have any converts in Connecticut. Other missionaries followed, including Elder Wilford Woodruff, a native of Farmington, Conn. He arranged to have a meeting with his family on July 1, 1838. Earlier on the day of the meeting, he wrote, "Distress overwhelmed the whole household, and all were tempted to reject the work." Later, he felt a dramatic change. "Filled with the power of God, I stood in the midst of the congregation and preached unto the people in great plainness the gospel of Jesus Christ." He afterward baptized his father, stepmother, sister and three others, and organized a small branch in Farmington.

The Eastern States Mission was created in 1839 and branches were established in Hartford and New Haven and other areas. Missionary work continued in the area until the 1850s when most members left the area, and any significant success waited until near the turn of the century. At that time missionaries throughout New England encountered prejudice and made little headway.

By 1930, branches existed in Hartford, New Haven, and Springfield. Membership was 198.

In 1932, missionaries reported "striving diligently" in Connecticut, and "large attendances" at each meeting of a conference held during the summer.

The New England Mission was created in 1937. On June 16, 1944, a meetinghouse at Bridgeport was dedicated at a branch conference. The chapel was converted from a home purchased two years earlier.

In 1952, the Hartford Branch meetinghouse was dedicated, the first meetinghouse to be erected in the New England Mission. Mission leaders began seeing growth in the 1950s and noted that membership increased following 1952, and doubled from 1955 to 1959. During this period, mission-wide youth conferences and annual Relief Society gatherings were well-attended by members.

The Hartford Stake was created in 1966 from the Connecticut Valley District, taking up most of the state and parts of western Massachusetts. The stake had a membership of nearly 3,000 with wards in Hartford, Manchester, New Haven, New London and Southington, and branches in Madison and Torrinton in Connecticut, as well as branches and wards in Massachusetts.

The Connecticut Hartford Mission was created in 1979. Membership in 1980 was 6,300.

On Oct. 3, 1992, President Gordon B. Hinckley, first counselor in the First Presidency, announced that a temple would be built in Hartford, Conn.

Sources: *Encyclopedic History of the Church* by Andrew Jenson; *Church News*, July 16, 1932; Sept. 3, 1938, July 22, 1944, Oct. 4, 1952, Sept. 24, 1966; June 11, 1977; Sept. 28, 1986; *Church* News, Oct. 10, 1992.

No.	Name	Organized	First President

North America Northeast Area

421	*Hartford Connecticut		
	†Hartford (Conn., Mass.)	18 Sep 1966	Hugh S. West
1288	New Haven Connecticut	30 Aug 1981	Steven Douglas Colson

Mission — 1
(As of Oct. 1, 1994; shown with historical number. See MISSIONS.)

(169) CONNECTICUT HARTFORD MISSION
P.O. Box 378
Bloomfield, CT 06002
Phone: (203) 242-2099

Delaware

Year-end 1993: Est. population, 708,000; Members, 3,300; Stakes, 1; Wards, 6; Branches, 2; Percent LDS: 0.5, or one person in 215.

Elder Jedediah M. Grant entered Delaware and began missionary work in 1837. Little record has been made of his progress, or other missionary work. However, Wilmington was an important rendezvous for missionaries of the Eastern States Mission. Its proximity to Philadelphia and its ocean frontage made it a likely route of passage for Church leaders.

In 1843, converts throughout the region were encouraged to gather with the Saints in Nauvoo. In the years that followed, many European converts sailed up the Delaware waterway to Philadelphia where they entered the United States.

On Feb. 4, 1901, Elder John E. Baird left Brooklyn, N.Y., to visit missionaries in eastern cities including those in Wilmington. On May 26, 1914, Elders Stanley A. Lawrence and Alphonso W. Taylor reported teaching a woman who had gained a testimony of the Book of Mormon. Two years later, on Nov. 7, 1916, two missionaries reported renting a hall in Wilmington where, beginning the next Sunday, meetings were to be held during the winter.

A missionary meeting was held Feb. 2, 1925, and in 1926, another meeting was held in a local hall with attendance of about 18 people. In 1931, missionaries broadcast their message over a local radio station. Lack of success resulted in missionaries being withdrawn until 1940 when Wilmington was re-opened.

Block teaching began in 1941 among some 16 LDS families. Meetings began May 4, and the Wilmington Branch was organized Sept. 28, 1941. The branch, with nine adults and 10 children, continued with little growth for the next decade. In 1950, some 63 attended a branch party at the home of the branch president. The Salisbury Branch was organized in 1953.

A new meetinghouse was completed and the first meeting was held in the building in 1960. That same year the Philadelphia Stake was created with a ward in Wilmington. Dover and Salisbury branches were included in the stake.

Activities increased with the new meetinghouse and by 1963 the ward boundaries were reduced. In December 1974, the Wilmington Delaware Stake was created. Membership in the state in 1974 was 1,350, increasing to 1,767 in 1980, and to 3,178 in 1990. By 1988, Wilmington was home of three large wards, and Dover, Salisbury and Elkton each had large wards. Branches were organized in Smyrna (one), and Cambridge (two). Many members and leaders work for the large chemical companies that have headquarters in Delaware.

Sources: *Encyclopedic History of the Church* by Andrew Jenson; *Journal History of the Eastern States Mission; The LDS Church in Delaware: A Book of Remembrance,* by Helen Candland Stark, published in Wilmington, Delaware, 1966; "Church grows larger in 2nd smallest state," by Kevin Stoker, *Church News,* Dec. 3, 1988.

Stake — 1
(As of Oct. 1, 1994.)

No.	Name	Organized	First President

North America Northeast Area

| 673 | Wilmington Delaware | 8 Dec 1974 | Rulon Edward Johnson Jr. |

District of Columbia

Year-end 1993: Est. population, 575,000; Members, 1,000; Stakes, 1; Wards, 1; Branches, 3; Missions, 2; Percent LDS, 0.2, or one person in 575.

The Prophet Joseph Smith, accompanied by Elias Higbee, visited the nation's capital in 1839 seeking redress of grievances suffered by the Saints in Missouri. As the coach in which they were riding approached the city, the horses began a runaway. The Prophet heroically saved his fellow passengers.

Joseph and Elias stayed in Washington for two weeks and called on President Martin Van Buren, who reportedly said, "Your cause is just, but I can do nothing for you."

The same year, Parley P. Pratt published an address setting forth the principles of the gospel and saw that a copy was presented to the President and each Cabinet member.

On Aug. 16, 1841, Samuel James was appointed to labor in Washington. Apostle John E. Page preached in Washington in 1843, baptizing one convert.

In 1843 Apostles Orson Hyde and Orson Pratt, and later joined by Apostles Heber C. Kimball, William Smith and Lyman Wight, presented the plight of the Saints to President John Tyler. Three years later Elder Jesse C. Little sought a government contract for the Church to haul freight to the West Coast. He instead won the opportunity for 500 men to join the Army and take part in a march through the Southwest. This was the genesis of the Mormon Battalion.

Elder Orson Pratt presided over the Saints in the Eastern States and served as a missionary in Washington D.C. He was later joined by Elder Jedediah M. Grant and together they met with Pres. Millard Fillmore. They published a magazine, *The Seer,* for about 18 months.

After arriving in the Great Basin, members requested a state government, but were granted territory status instead. In pursuing statehood, members from Utah paid occasional visits to Washington D.C. Some lived in Washington D.C. or nearby areas while serving as Utah's delegates to Congress. After the turn of the century, Elder Reed Smoot of the Council of the Twelve was elected to the Senate and, after four years of well-publicized hearings, was seated. His later powerful leadership in the Senate won many friends for the Church.

During the early years of Senator Smoot's term, a handful of members who lived in Washington met in his home. In June 1919, a branch was organized. By 1927, the branch was meeting in an auditorium. Some 150 attended services upstairs while activities, such as circuses and auto shows, went on below.

Later Latter-day Saint leaders, including J. Reuben Clark Jr., Marriner S. Eccles, Edgar Brossard, J. Willard Marriott and Ezra Taft Benson, made substantial contributions to the Church in the nation's capital.

In 1930 the Church began construction on a massive chapel built of imported Utah granite. The building was completed in 1933 and helped establish the Church's reputation as a permanent institution. By 1940, the Washington D.C. Stake was created with Ezra Taft Benson as president. President Benson later returned to the nation's capital as Secretary of Agriculture in the Eisenhower administration, 1953-60.

Membership in the region continued to grow as Latter-day Saints with important government jobs moved in. Additional stakes were created so that four covered the area of the original stake. In 1962, a site in suburban Kensington, Md., was purchased for a temple that was completed in 1974. The imposing temple immediately became a landmark for the Church in Washington. Within 15 years, the four stakes in the greater Washington D.C. area became 19 stakes and membership jumped from 21,000 to 63,000. However, within the boundaries of the actual District of Columbia, membership remained slight with fewer than 100 recorded in 1980 and 434 in 1990. In the 1990s, additional efforts were made in the inner city area, and new, small branches were created. Members participated in inter-faith food drives, using the resources of the Church cannery, and other inter-faith activities.

Each summer, ambassadors and members of the diplomatic community are invited to a western picnic at the J.W. Marriott ranch in nearby Virginia. In addition, the diplomats also attend lighting ceremonies at the Washington Temple.

Sources: *Encyclopedic History of the Church* by Andrew Jenson; "History of the Washington Branch," *Church News,* Nov. 4, 1933; "A Little Leavening," by Florian H. Thayn, *Brigham Young University Studies,* Spring 1981; "From Colony to Community; the Washington D.C. Saints," by Mary L. Bradford, *Ensign,* August 1974; "Membership Triples in Nation's Capital," *Church News,* Dec. 2, 1989; "Pioneer members recall rich memories," *Church News,* July 20, 1991; and Oct. 26, 1991, Oct. 23, 1993; Dec. 2, 1994 and Feb. 2, 1994.

Stake — 1

(As of Oct. 1, 1994. To simplify reference, the stake and missions in the Washington D.C. area that carry the name of Washington D.C. are listed in the District of Columbia rather than the state where the headquarters is located.)

No.	Name	Organized	First President

North America Northeast Area
131   *Washington D.C.
      †Washington (D.C., Pa., Md.)   30 Jun 1940   Ezra Taft Benson

Missions — 2
(As of Oct. 1, 1994; shown with historical number. See MISSIONS.)

(188b) WASHINGTON D.C. NORTH MISSION
904 Wind River Lane, #103
No. Potomac, VA 20878
Phone: (301) 926-7977

(54) WASHINGTON D.C. SOUTH MISSION
5631 Burke Centre Parkway, Suite H
Burke, VA 22015
Phone: (703) 250-0111

Florida

Year-end 1993: Est. population, 13,826,000; Members, 93,000; Stakes, 21; Wards, 144; Branches, 36; Missions, 4; Percent LDS, 0.7, or one person in 149.

Elders William Brown and Daniel Cathart were called to serve in Florida in April 1843, but no record exists of them doing so. Possibly the first missionary in Florida was Phineas Young, who reported placing copies of the Book of Mormon during a two-month mission from April to June in 1845 that reached into Florida. Missionary work evidently started before Nov. 1, 1895, when the Florida Conference was organized under the direction of Pres. Elias S. Kimball of the Southern States Mission. Fifteen missionaries were assigned to labor there.

Missionaries started a number of Sunday Schools, the first of which was at Coe Mills, Liberty County, in May 1895. By September 1897, 11 Sunday Schools had been organized. The first branch was created in Jefferson County in 1897. The Sanderson Branch, probably organized Jan. 3, 1898, was the site of a missionary conference in 1898. George P. Canova, a well-to-do landowner and chairman of the Baker County Commission, was the president of the branch. On June 5, 1898, following threats of violence, Pres. Canova was martyred as he returned home from a conference. Missionaries were also temporarily driven out of Tallahassee and Orlando but returned later. They found varying degrees of success in Key West, Sanford, Starke, Peoria, Kissimmee, St. Augustine, Tampa, St. Augustine, Duck Pond, Lake City and Middleburg.

In 1900, Elder William H. Boyle reported the branches in Florida to be "in apple pie order" and that missionaries traveling without purse or scrip were hospitably received. Growth came slowly, however. In 1906, a meetinghouse was dedicated in Jacksonville, and in 1907, another was completed in Oak Grove.

In 1906, Charles A. Callis, later mission president and a member of the Council of the Twelve, became president of the Florida Conference. By 1920 branches in Jacksonville, Sanderson and Tampa existed. By 1925, branches or Sunday Schools had been added in Miami, Oak Grove, Oldtown, Telogia, Westville, Springfield and St. Augustine. A larger meetinghouse was completed in Jacksonville in 1926. In 1930, the Florida District had 3,164 members in four branches and eight Sunday Schools. The West Florida District was created about this time, and branches or Sunday Schools increased. By 1935, the Florida District had 22 branches, and the West Florida District had another 13 branches.

Florida's first stake was created in Jacksonville Jan. 17, 1947, by Elder Charles A. Callis, who died there four days later. The new stake had 3,000 members in the Jacksonville, Springfield, Wesconnett, Lake City, Palatka, Axson, and Waycross wards. Called as president of the new stake was Alvin C. Chace, a grandson of early leader George P. Canova.

In 1950, the Church purchased a 300,000-acre area in Central Florida, which became Deseret Ranch.

Membership increased rapidly as members from the West moved into the state, drawn by a strong commerce and the aerospace industry. Additional converts were baptized. When the Florida Mission was created in 1960, four stakes had been organized. Membership in Florida in 1977 was 30,000, increasing to 54,674 in 1980, and to 82,413 in 1990. Creation of the first Spanish-speaking stake in the Southeast in Miami on Jan, 16, 1994, reflected the increase in membership among Latin Americans and immigrants.

In February of 1990, the First Presidency announced that a temple would be built in the Orlando area. Later, a scenic location in Windermere, five miles southeast of Orlando, was selected for the temple and ground was broken June 20, 1992. The temple was dedicated Oct. 9-11, 1992, by President Howard W. Hunter.

Sources: *Encyclopedic History of the Church* by Andrew Jenson; *History of the Southern States Mission,* a BYU thesis by LaMar C. Berrett, July 1960; A brief summation of the Growth of the Church . . . leading to the Florida Stake, by Stanley Clyde Johnson, 1986, unpublished; Church directories, 1919-1935; *Church News,* Jan. 25, 1947, Feb. 22, 1947, Dec. 1, 1956, Oct. 8, 1960, Sept, 14, 1963; March 6, 1976, July 2, 1977, and March 14, 1987; "The first Spanish-speaking stake in Southeast is created in Florida," by Kathleen Ryan, *Church News,* Feb. 19, 1994; *Church News,* May 28, 1994.

Stakes — 22
(Listed alphabetically as of Oct. 1, 1994.)

No.	Name	Organized	First President

North America Southeast Area

No.	Name	Organized	First President
1898	Brandon Florida	23 Aug 1992	James Franklin Henry
879	Cocoa Florida	13 Nov 1977	Cleavy Eugene Waters
530	*Fort Lauderdale Florida		
	†Fort Lauderdale	18 Oct 1970	Stanley C. Johnson
1472	Fort Myers Florida	13 May 1984	John M. Cyrocki
746	Gainesville Florida	29 Feb 1976	James R. Christianson
1842	*Homestead Florida 16 Jan 1994		
	†South Miami Florida	19 Jan 1992	Dean Michael Madsen
465	*Jacksonville Florida East		
	†Jacksonville	15 Sep 1968	Louis B. Vorwaller
1660	Jacksonville Florida North	15 Nov 1987	Robert Edwin Bone
163	*Jacksonville Florida West		
	†Florida (Florida, Georgia)	19 Jan 1947	Alvin C. Chace
1590	Lake City Florida	16 Mar 1986	Ernest Robert Peacock
1380	*Lake Mary Florida 27 Oct 1987		
	†Deland Florida	14 Nov 1982	Marvin Knowles
311	*Miami Florida		
	†Miami	13 Nov 1960	Paul R. Cheesman
257	*Orlando Florida		
	†Orlando	23 Feb 1958	W. Leonard Duggar
1900	Orlando Florida South	30 Aug 1992	Carl E. Reynolds Jr.
732	*Panama City Florida 4 Feb 1986		
	†Marianna Florida	16 Nov 1975	Riley Malone Peddie
486	*Pensacola Florida		
	†Pensacola	15 Jun 1969	S. Elroy Stapleton
1970	Pompano Beach Florida	16 Jan 1994	Richard Merlin Smith
651	Saint Petersburg Florida	18 Aug 1974	Bruce Earl Belnap
594	*Tallahassee Florida		
	†Tallahassee	21 Jan 1973	Jay Nicholas Lybbert
289	*Tampa Florida		
	†Tampa	25 Oct 1959	Edwin H. White
1190	*Stuart Florida 16 Jan 1994		
	†West Palm Beach Florida	12 Oct 1980	Donald Wayne Carson
1153	*Winter Haven Florida 10 Oct 1991		
	†Lakeland Florida	27 Jun 1980	Waymon E. Meadows

Missions — 4
(As of Oct. 1, 1994; shown with historical number. See MISSIONS.)

(178b) FLORIDA FT. LAUDERDALE MISSION
7951 SW 6th St., #110
Ft. Lauderdale, FL 33324
Phone: (305) 452-6960

(96) FLORIDA TALLAHASSEE MISSION
1535 Killearn Center Blvd., C-4
Tallahassee, FL 32308
Phone: (904) 893-4243

(197) FLORIDA JACKSONVILLE MISSION
8647 Baypine Road, #106
Jacksonville, FL 32256
Phone: (904) 636-0604

(139) FLORIDA TAMPA MISSION
13153 N. Dale Mabry, St. 109
Tampa, FL 33618
Phone: (813) 961-7400

Georgia

Year-end 1993: Est. population, 6,936,000; Members, 49,000; Stakes, 11; Wards, 76; Branches, 37; Missions, 2; Temples, 1; Percent LDS, 0.7, or one person in 142.

Elder John U. Eldredge opened missionary work in Georgia in 1843, though his service was brief. Other missionaries followed to preach and to campaign for Joseph Smith in his presidential bid. When the Prophet was martyred in 1844, the work waned, and was halted in 1846. Missionary work resumed in 1870 in the South, and in 1878 in Georgia. Southern States Mission headquarters were established in Rome, 60 miles north of Atlanta, in 1879. Pres. John Morgan wrote the pamphlet, *Plan of Salvation*, in Rome.

Success was realized in Rome and Axson, which was called "Little Utah," by local people. The Douglas Branch was called "Cumorah." One prominent convert, Judge Wyatt N. Williams, was baptized in Buchanan on April 25, 1879, and subsequently donated land and built a chapel in Haralson County at a place called "Mormon Springs" near his mill and cotton gin.

Missionaries were initially treated well upon their return to the South, but before long, their successes led to violent opposition. On July 21, 1879, Elder Joseph Standing was killed by a mob near Varnell's Station, Ga. His companion, Rudger Clawson, later a member of the Council of the Twelve, escaped serious injury. Mission leaders were unable to secure protection for missionaries, so Georgia was closed for a decade. In 1884, a small group of members from Georgia joined emigrants who went West by train from Chattanooga, Tenn. U.S. Census reports list 175 Mormons in Georgia in 1890.

Work resumed cautiously. In 1899, for example, convert Aldora Landrum Yarn was taught in a single meeting held after dark, then baptized. She did not see another missionary for three and a half years.

Disease and persecution slowed the work, the former taking a greater toll than the latter. In 1899, Ohio was added to the Southern States Mission at the request of Pres. Ben E. Rich, so he would have a place where ill missionaries could recover.

By 1908, some 6,800 converts had been baptized throughout the South during Pres. Rich's term. That year, a branch was organized and a meetinghouse constructed in Atlanta. It was replaced in 1915 with a larger building.

Pres. Charles A. Callis succeeded Pres. Rich. Pres. Callis embarked on a 25-year term that saw about 800 to 1,000 converts per year throughout the South. When then-Apostle Heber J. Grant visited Atlanta in 1911, he addressed an overflow congregation in a local Universalist church. He was favorably received.

In 1919, headquarters of the Southern States Mission was moved from Chattanooga, Tenn., to Atlanta, and a new meetinghouse was erected in that city in 1925.

Steady growth continued so that by 1930, the original Southern States Mission had some 50,000 members. The Georgia Conference, in northern Georgia, had 2,626 members in Atlanta, Augusta, Columbus, Macon and Savannah branches and in Cedar Crossing, Douglas, Empire, Glenwood, Milledgeville and Thomaston Sunday Schools. The South Georgia District had 1,686 members. The state membership was 4,311.

One of the prominent pioneer leaders in Atlanta was Homer Yarn. In 1916, he become the first local leader of a Sunday School in Atlanta. He became president of the Atlanta Branch in 1925. When the Georgia District was organized in 1937, Pres. Yarn was the first local district president. He served as mission president's counselor from 1939 to 1957.

LeGrand Richards, later a member of the Council of the Twelve, served as mission president from 1934-37, and wrote the outline for *A Marvelous Work and a Wonder* while in Atlanta.

In 1957, the Atlanta (later changed to Tucker) Stake was created, taking up the northern two-thirds of the state with 3,000 members with wards in Atlanta (2), Columbus, Macon and Empire, and branches in Buchanan, Athens, Givson, Milledgeville and Palmetto. Covering the rest of the state was the Georgia-Florida and South Georgia districts. Membership in Georgia in 1974 was 14,360, increasing in 1980 to 27,210 and in 1990 to 41,595.

In 1983, the Atlanta Temple was completed and dedicated, giving the South its first temple. Area headquarters in Atlanta include complete temporal and ecclesiastical distribution centers. From Atlanta, hurricane and flood relief has been shipped to many areas of disaster, including Hurricane Andrew devastation in 1992 and the Albany, Ga., flooding in 1994. At the latter, some 6,000 LDS volunteers from throughout the South turned out to assist homeowners. In the late 1980s and early 1990s, five branches were established in the central sections of Atlanta among minorities, including Asian and Hispanic people.

Sources: *Encyclopedic History of the Church* by Andrew Jenson; "William L. Nicholls to Preside Over New Altanta Stake," *Church News,* May 11, 1957; *History of the Southern States Mission* by LaMar C. Berrett, a BYU thesis July 1960; *A Brief History of the Southern States Mission for One Hundred Years 1830-1930,* by DeVon H. Nish, a BYU paper of 1966; Highlights of D. Homer Yarn, by David H. Yarn Jr.; "Georgia enters era of temples," by Gerry Avant, *Church News,* April 24, 1983; "Inner-city district gathers many of diverse cultures into 'gospel net,' by Mike Cannon, *Church News,* May 29, 1993; "6,000 ease aftermath of flooding," by Gerry Avant, *Church News,* July 30, 1994.

Stakes — 11
(Listed alphabetically as of Oct. 1, 1994.)

No.	Name	Organized	First President
North America Southeast Area			
889	*Augusta Georgia 21 Aug 1988		
	†West Columbia South Carolina	5 Feb 1978	George A. Huff Sr.

886	Columbus Georgia	15 Jan 1978	William F. Meadows Jr.
715	Douglas Georgia	26 Oct 1975	Roswald Mancil
921	*Jonesboro Georgia 29 Jan 1991		
	†Atlanta Georgia	14 May 1978	Warren Richard Jones
373	*Macon Georgia		
	†Macon (Georgia, Alabama)	10 Mar 1963	Rayford L. Henderson
1643	Marietta Georgia East	21 Jun 1987	Paul A. Snow
1208	*Powder Springs Georgia 10 Sep 1991		
	†Marietta Georgia	23 Nov 1980	William K. Farrar Jr.
640	*Roswell Georgia 21 Jun 1987		
	*Sandy Springs Georgia 1 Sep 1974		
	†Tucker Georgia	12 May 1974	Richard Parry Winder
916	Savannah Georgia	7 May 1978	Robert W. Cowart
1799	Sugar Hill Georgia	26 May 1991	Donald Arthur Cazier
241	*Tucker Georgia 1 Sep 1974		
	*Atlanta Georgia		
	†Atlanta (Georgia)	5 May 1957	William L. Nicholls

Missions — 2
(As of Oct. 1, 1994; shown with historical number. See MISSIONS.)

(8b) GEORGIA ATLANTA MISSION
1140 Hammond Drive , B-2100
Atlanta, GA 30328
Phone: (404) 551-9626

(239) GEORGIA MACON MISSION
5082 Forsyth Road, Units A & B
Macon, GA 31210-2107
Phone: (912) 471-9205

Hawaii

Year-end 1993: Est. population, 1,206,000; Members, 53,000; Stakes, 13; Wards, 103; Branches, 8; Missions, 1; Temples, 1; Percent LDS: 4.4, or one person in 23.

Sam Brannan and his party of Mormon immigrants aboard the ship *Brooklyn* stopped in Hawaii in 1846, en route to California and the Great Basin via Cape Horn.

Although missionaries had been called in 1843 to the Sandwich Islands, as the islands were then known, they worked instead at Tubuai, one of the southern islands of French Polynesia.

In 1850, gold-mining elders serving in northern California were called to open a mission in Polynesia. They landed in Honolulu Dec. 12, 1850, under the direction of Pres. Hiram Clark. On Feb. 10, 1851, Pres. Clark baptized a 16-year-old Hawaiian young man, the first convert in Hawaii. Other missionaries were not as successful and returned discouraged to the mainland. But Elders George Q. Cannon, James Keeler, William Farrer, Henry W. Bigler and James Hawkins remained and found ample converts. Elder Cannon baptized three well-educated Hawaiians, Jonathan Napela, Uaua and Kaleohano, who later became prominent missionaries for the Church.

On Aug. 6, 1851, the Kula Branch was organized in the village of Kealakou on the island of Maui. At a conference on Aug. 18, four more branches were organized and membership was 220. A small meeting-house was built in 1852 in Pulehu, on the island of Maui, which still stands. More missionaries arrived and by 1854, a colony and plantation were started at Lanai, a designated gathering place.

The Book of Mormon was published in Hawaiian in 1855. In 1857, missionaries were called home because of the so-called "Utah War."

In 1861 a self-appointed leader, Walter Murray Gibson, usurped Church leadership in the absence of missionaries. A recent convert called to a mission in the South Pacific, he took over the Church organization and property. Leading Hawaiian elders notified the Church of Gibson's unorthodox leadership and President Young sent Apostles Ezra T. Benson and Lorenzo Snow. They immediately excommunicated Gibson and reinstated many early members.

Defrauded of its property in Lanai, the Church purchased 6,000 acres at Laie, on the main island of Oahu, on Jan. 26, 1865, where a colony and sugar factory were started. Schools have been part of the colony since 1874.

Later, many of the Hawaiians wanted to gather to Utah to receive their temple blessings. So the Church purchased a ranch in Skull Valley, near Tooele, Utah, and the Hawaiian Saints founded the colony of Iosepa (Joseph) in 1889. By 1910 the colony was disbanded and the colonists returned to Hawaii.

The Church subsequently built a temple in the Laie settlement, dedicating the edifice Nov. 27, 1919.

In 1913, missionaries calculated that 22 percent of the Hawaiian population was LDS. Membership in Hawaii in 1920 was 11,078. By 1930, membership increased to 14,433, dropping to 9,789 in 1940 and, in

1950, following World War II, increasing to 11,855. By 1960, it increased to 18,327, and to 23,377 in 1970.

The Oahu Stake was created June 30, 1935, by Pres. Heber J. Grant. While there, the former missionary to Japan felt a need for a mission to the many Japanese in Hawaii. On Feb. 24, 1937, the Japanese Mission (later called the Central Pacific Mission) in Hawaii was organized. Over the next dozen years, nearly 700 Japanese-Americans were converted in this effort, including Elder Adney Y. Komatsu, who was called as a General Authority in 1975. Among the missionaries and converts were many of the leaders who helped open and continue missionary work in Japan after World War II. Hawaiian members also opened the door for missionary work in South Pacific islands.

The Church College of Hawaii opened Sept. 26, 1955. Many members from the South Pacific and Asia have been educated at the school, now called BYU-Hawaii. On Nov. 12, 1963, the Polynesian Cultural Center, a cluster of villages representing various South Pacific cultures, was opened. It quickly became one of Hawaii's top attractions. In recent years the center has been host to a number of heads of state, including those of China.

During times of disasters, such as floods and hurricanes, members have been quick to assist other members and non-members. When hurricane "Iniki" struck the islands in 1992, members donated thousands of boxes of relief supplies for those on the hard-hit island of Kaui.

In 1980, membership in Hawaii was 37,293, and in 1990, 50,726.

Sources: *Encyclopedic History of the Church* by Andrew Jenson; *Unto the Isles of the Sea,* by R. Lanier Britsch; *Guide to Mormon History Travel,* by William C. and Eloise Anderson; *Church News,* Sept. 19, 1992, Oct. 3, 1992.

Stakes — 13
(Listed alphabetically as of Oct. 1, 1994.)

No.	Name	Organized	First President
North America West Area			
807	*BYU-Hawaii 1st 22 Nov 1981		
	†BYU-Hawaii	23 Jan 1977	Eric B. Shumway
1313	BYU-Hawaii 2nd	22 Nov 1981	Herbert Kamaka Sproat
473	*Hilo Hawaii		
	†Hilo	15 Dec 1968	Rex Alton Cheney
222	*Honolulu Hawaii		
	†Honolulu (Hawaii, Guam)	28 Aug 1955	J. A. Quealy Jr.
348	*Honolulu Hawaii West		
	†Pearl Harbor (Hawaii)	4 Feb 1962	George Q. Cannon
729	Kahului Hawaii	9 Nov 1975	Evan Allan Larsen
560	*Kaneohe Hawaii		
	†Kaneohe (Hawaii)	21 Nov 1971	Robert H. Finlayson
851	Kauai Hawaii	24 Jul 1977	Garner Dalthum Wood
669	Kona Hawaii	24 Nov 1974	Haven J. Stringham
113	*Laie Hawaii		
	†Oahu	30 Jun 1935	Ralph E. Wooley
1395	Laie Hawaii North	16 Jan 1983	Willard Kaaihue Kekauoha
1103	Mililani Hawaii	3 Feb 1980	Kotaro Koizumi
566	*Waipahu Hawaii		
	†Pearl Harbor West (Hawaii)	20 Feb 1972	William E. Fuhrmann

Mission — 1
(As of Oct. 1, 1994; shown with historical number. See MISSIONS.)

(9) HAWAII HONOLULU MISSION
1500 S. Beretania St., Suite 410
Honolulu, HI 96826
Phone: (808) 942-0050

Idaho

Year-end 1993: Est. population, 1,107,000; Members, 316,000; Stakes, 97; Wards, 691; Branches, 38; Missions, 2; Temples, 2; Percent LDS, 28.5, or one person in 4.

On April 7, 1855, 26 men were called by Brigham Young to locate a settlement among the Bannock and Shoshone on the Salmon River. They arrived and established Fort Lemhi on June 15, 1855. However, problems with Indians led to the settlement's abandonment in 1858.

On April 14, 1860, a party of colonizers arrived at what is now Franklin, Idaho, in northern Cache Valley.

Preston Thomas became the first bishop in a ward created there in June. Franklin is both Idaho's oldest and the Church's oldest permanent settlement in Idaho. The settlers battled deep snows and extreme cold in the winter, but dug canals and began irrigating in the summer. Eventually, during the next 18 years, 16 settlements were founded in this region. They paved the way for the Oneida Stake, headquartered in Preston, near Franklin, to be created in 1884, Idaho's third.

Another colonization effort began over the mountains to the east when a party under Apostle Charles C. Rich explored Bear Lake Valley and established the settlement of Paris in the fall of 1863. About 110 people wintered there the first year. In 1864, 700 more settlers arrived and established the towns of Ovid, Liberty, Montpelier, Bloomington, St. Charles, Fish Haven and Bennington. Nine other settlements were established in the region within 13 years. The Bear Lake Stake, the first permanent stake outside Utah, was created June 20, 1869. Both Cache Valley and Bear Lake Valley were believed by the settlers to be in Utah until a survey in 1872.

In 1875, a third colonization movement came when LDS families settled in Oakley, Dayton, Elba and Almo in southcentral Idaho.

In the late 1870s, the Utah Northern Railroad line from Utah to Montana was completed. Many members were employed in the construction of the rail line. From their favorable reports of the Upper Snake River Valley, settlers soon began colonizing there, beginning in 1879. Under the leadership of Thomas E. Ricks, they established Rexburg in 1883 and 14 other colonies in Upper Snake River Valley, in Fremont and Bingham counties. Basic to their success was their expertise in irrigating. By 1910, more than 100 canals had been dug in the Upper Snake River Valley. The Bannock Stake, Idaho's second and headquartered in Rexburg, was organized in 1884.

Leaders encouraged members to continue to settle in Idaho. Many migrated to already established communities along the eastern side of Idaho, and on the western side in the Boise-Payette area. Most were farmers.

Members generally got along well with Indians and, in at least northern Cache and Bear Lake valleys, received permission from Indian leaders to settle. They preached the gospel to Native Americans, taught them agriculture, and shared their supplies with them. Shoshone Chief Washakie, the most prominent chief during the early colonization effort, was baptized by Amos Wright, an early Idaho missionary.

By 1890 when Idaho was given statehood, about one-fifth of the state was LDS. Some historians suggest that without the Mormon population, Idaho's land would have been annexed by adjoining states and it would never have become a state. Despite the contributions of Mormons, however, anti-Mormon sentiment grew during the last quarter of the 19th century.

Idaho Sen William E. Borah, though non-LDS, helped neutralize this anti-Mormon sentiment after the turn of the century. Mormon women led the statewide effort for women suffrage that was attained in 1896.

Membership in the "Gem State" was 29,421 in 1900, with seven stakes in existence. Membership increased to 79,887 by 1925, 1950, 137,250; 1975, 213,106; 1980, 272,670; and 1990, 296,782.

The Idaho Falls Temple was completed in 1945 and dedicated Sept. 23-25.

Following World War II, many members migrated to the Boise area where the first Boise stake had been created in 1913. Ezra Taft Benson was its president in 1938. Other area stakes were created following the war. The second temple in Idaho was built in Boise in 1984.

Born in Idaho were President Harold B. Lee, president of the Church from 1972-73, President Ezra Taft Benson, president of the Church from 1985 to 1994, and President Howard W. Hunter, president of the Church from June, 1994, to the present.

Sources: *Encyclopedic History of the Church*, by Andrew Jenson; *Treasures of Pioneer History,* Daughters of the Utah Pioneers, 1955; "Idaho vote spells 'finish' to old feud," by Arnold Irvine, *Church News*, Nov. 13, 1982; "Idaho — A shining Gem since 1855," by Golden A. Buchmiller, *Church News,* May 8, 1983; "Centennials preserving heritage," *Church News*, May 26, 1990; "Mormondom in Centennial Idaho," by Leonard J. Arrington, *This People,* Fall 1990; "First LDS Bishop in Idaho: A Pioneer for Gospel's Sake," by Elinor G. Hyde, *Church News*, Dec. 15, 1990; "Paris Tabernacle," by Dean Ward, published locally.

Stakes — 97
(Listed alphabetically by area as of Oct. 1, 1994.)

No.	Name	Organized	First President
North America Northwest Area — 88			
170	*American Falls Idaho		
	†American Falls	1 Feb 1948	George R. Woolley
1481	Arimo Idaho	17 Jun 1984	Douglas Sorensen
695	Ashton Idaho	18 May 1975	Horace E. Hess
52	*Blackfoot Idaho		
	†Blackfoot	31 Jan 1904	Elias S. Kimball

1391	Blackfoot Idaho East	12 Dec 1982	Franklin D. Transtrum
914	Blackfoot Idaho Northwest	30 Apr 1978	Reijo Laverne Marcum
214	*Blackfoot Idaho South		
	*Blackfoot South 1 Mar 1970		
	†South Blackfoot	20 Jun 1954	Lawrence T. Lambert
504	*Blackfoot Idaho West		
	†Blackfoot West	1 Mar 1970	Alan F. Larsen
66	*Boise Idaho		
	†Boise	3 Nov 1913	Heber Q. Hale
1460	Boise Idaho Central	5 Feb 1984	R. Clair Miles
1041	Boise Idaho East	10 Jun 1979	Cecil Frank Olsen
409	*Boise Idaho North		
	*Boise North Jan 1966		
	†North Boise	26 Sep 1965	L. Aldin Porter
701	Boise Idaho South	17 Aug 1975	Grant Ruel Ipsen
218	*Boise Idaho West		
	*Boise West 29 May 1970		
	†West Boise	7 Nov 1954	David Keith Ricks
1856	Boise State University	24 Apr 1992	Robert Reed Boren
77	*Burley Idaho		
	†Burley	27 Jul 1919	David R. Langlois
1421	Burley Idaho West	22 May 1983	Walter Ray Petersen
564	*Caldwell Idaho		
	†Caldwell	30 Jan 1972	Talmadge C. Blacker
1446	Caldwell Idaho North	9 Oct 1983	Gerald Leland Jensen
78	*Carey Idaho 31 Oct 1977		
	*Richfield Idaho		
	†Blaine	3 Aug 1919	William Lennox Adamson
960	*Chubbuck Idaho 8 Sep 1987		
	†Pocatello Idaho Chubbuck	17 Sep 1978	Errol Smith Phippen
359	*Coeur d'Alene Idaho		
	†Coeur d'Alene	14 Oct 1962	Gerald E. Browning
69	*Declo Idaho		
	*Cassia East 15 Jun 1969		
	†Raft River	27 Apr 1915	John A. Elison
50	*Driggs Idaho		
	†Teton (Wyoming, Idaho)	2 Sep 1901	Don Carlos Driggs
1840	Eagle Idaho	12 Jan 1992	Gary Wayne Walker
661	Emmett Idaho	22 Sep 1974	David Lee Morton
1147	Filer Idaho	15 Jun 1980	Karl E. Nelson
655	Firth Idaho	8 Sep 1974	Dale Lavar Christensen
36	*Idaho Falls Idaho		
	*Idaho Falls 16 Aug 1925		
	†Bingham	9 Jun 1895	James E. Steele
343	*Idaho Falls Idaho Ammon		
	†Ammon	26 Nov 1961	Harold W. Davis
825	Idaho Falls Idaho Ammon West	1 May 1977	Boyd Rencher Thomas
1448	Idaho Falls Idaho Central	16 Oct 1983	Paul Roger DeMordaunt
1665	Idaho Falls Idaho Eagle Rock	13 Dec 1987	Michael Dean Crapo
285	*Idaho Falls East 29 May 1970		
	†East Idaho Falls	7 Jun 1959	Charles P. Birzee
	*Idaho Falls Idaho East		
1149	Idaho Falls Idaho Lincoln	22 Jun 1980	Cleon Y. Olson
112	*Idaho Falls Idaho North		
	*Idaho Falls North 29 May 1970		
	†North Idaho Falls	12 May 1935	David Smith
157	*Idaho Falls Idaho South		
	*Idaho Falls South 29 May 1970		
	†South Idaho Falls	30 Jun 1946	Cecil E. Hart
602	*Idaho Falls Idaho West		
	†Idaho Falls West	4 Mar 1973	Terry L. Crapo
607	*Iona Idaho		
	†Iona	15 Apr 1973	Joseph Dudley Tucker
192	*Jerome Idaho		
	†Gooding	9 Mar 1952	Ross C. Lee

1015	Kimberly Idaho	15 Apr 1979	David LaVere Carter
268	*Lewiston Idaho		
	†Lewiston (Idaho, Wash.)	19 Oct 1958	Golden Romney
72	*McCammon Idaho 19 Feb 1983		
	*Arimo Idaho		
	†Portneuf	15 Aug 1915	George T. Hyde
1125	Menan Idaho	30 Mar 1980	Garth Victor Hall
580	*Meridian Idaho		
	†Meridian	11 Jun 1972	J. Richard Clarke
847	Meridian Idaho East	12 Jun 1977	Leonard E. Graham Jr.
1401	Meridian Idaho South	20 Feb 1983	Wenden Wayne Waite
79	*Moore Idaho		
	†Lost River	18 Aug 1919	William N. Patten
641	Mountain Home Idaho	19 May 1974	Kenneth Herbert Johns
125	*Nampa Idaho		
	†Nampa	27 Nov 1938	Peter E. Johnson
874	Nampa Idaho South	30 Oct 1977	Dean Ezra Beus
32	*Oakley Idaho		
	†Cassia (Idaho, Utah)	19 Nov 1887	Horton D. Haight
587	*Paul Idaho		
	†Minidoka West	24 Sep 1972	Keith C. Merrill Jr.
278	*Pocatello Idaho		
	†Pocatello	19 Apr 1959	Roland K. Hart
40	*Pocatello Idaho Alameda 17 Jun 1984		
	*Pocatello Idaho East		
	*Pocatello East 29 May 1970		
	*East Pocatello 19 Apr 1959		
	†Pocatello	7 Aug 1898	William C. Parkinson
1484	Pocatello Idaho Central	17 Jun 1984	Thomas William Ranstrom
971	*Pocatello Idaho East 17 Jun 1984		
	†Pocatello Idaho South	22 Oct 1978	John Burl McNabb
377	*Pocatello Idaho Highland 17 Jun 1984		
	*Pocatello Idaho Alameda		
	†Alameda	12 May 1963	Homer S. Satterfield
207	*Pocatello Idaho North		
	*Pocatello North 29 May 1970		
	†North Pocatello	21 Jun 1953	Jared O. Anderson
1444	Pocatello Idaho Tyhee	25 Sep 1983	Eugene Lester Hancock
406	*Pocatello Idaho University		
	†Idaho State University	9 May 1965	Robert E. Thompson
149	*Pocatello Idaho West		
	*Pocatello West 29 May 1970		
	†West Pocatello	6 May 1945	Twayne Austin
28	*Rexburg Idaho		
	*Rexburg 23 Jun 1935		
	*Fremont 6 Aug 1898		
	†Bannock	4 Feb 1884	Thomas E. Ricks
1369	Rexburg Idaho Center	24 Oct 1982	Ronald Curtis Martin
697	Rexburg Idaho East	1 Jun 1975	Keith Lester Peterson
153	*Rexburg Idaho North		
	*Rexburg North 29 May 1970		
	†North Rexburg	28 Oct 1945	Orval O. Mortensen
405	*Ricks College 1st 7 Nov 1989		
	*Rexburg Idaho College 1st		
	*Ricks College 1st 1 Jun 1969		
	†Ricks College	7 May 1965	J. Wendell Stucki
480	*Ricks College 2nd 7 Nov 1989		
	*Rexburg Idaho College 2nd		
	†Ricks College 2nd	27 Apr 1969	Loren Homer Grover
690	*Ricks College 3rd 7 Nov 1989		
	†Rexburg Idaho College 3rd	13 Apr 1975	Ray Wendell Rigby
1689	*Ricks College 4th 7 Nov 1989		

	†Rexburg Idaho College 4th	6 Mar 1988	Jay Lufkin Risenmay
1836	Ricks College 5th	8 Dec 1991	R. Brent Kinghorn
56	*Rigby Idaho		
	†Rigby	3 Feb 1908	Don Carlos Walker
158	*Rigby Idaho East		
	*Rigby East 29 May 1970		
	†East Rigby	7 Jul 1946	James E. Ririe
1140	Ririe Idaho	25 May 1980	Arlo J. Moss
606	*Roberts Idaho		
	†Jefferson	25 Mar 1973	Edwin Cutler Adamson
91	*Rupert Idaho		
	†Minidoka	11 May 1924	Richard C. May
1476	Rupert Idaho West	3 Jun 1984	Carl B. Garner
60	*Saint Anthony Idaho		
	†Yellowstone	10 Jan 1909	Daniel G. Miller
211	*Salmon Idaho		
	†Salmon River	18 Oct 1953	Earl Stokes
952	Sandpoint Idaho	20 Aug 1978	Richard William Goldsberry
67	*Shelley Idaho		
	†Shelley	16 Aug 1914	Joseph H. Dye
1180	Shelley Idaho South	14 Sep 1980	Kenneth P. Fielding
1129	Sugar City Idaho	4 May 1980	Ferron W. Sonderegger
76	*Twin Falls Idaho		
	†Twin Falls	26 Jul 1919	Lawrence Gomer Kirkman
490	*Twin Falls Idaho West		
	†Twin Falls West	17 Aug 1969	Joel A. Tate
1156	Ucon Idaho	29 Jun 1980	Joseph Dudley Tucker
126	*Weiser Idaho		
	†Weiser	27 Nov 1938	Scott B. Brown
1005	Wendell Idaho	25 Feb 1979	Orlo William Stevens

Utah North Area — 9

1419	*Franklin Idaho 17 Nov 1985		
	†Preston Idaho East	15 May 1983	Eudean Hawkins Gunnell
39	*Grace Idaho		
	†Bannock	25 Jul 1898	Lewis S. Pond
32a	*Malad Idaho		
	†Malad (Idaho, Utah)	12 Feb 1888	Oliver C. Hoskins
75	*Montpelier Idaho		
	†Montpelier (Idaho, Wyoming)	23 Dec 1917	Edward C. Rich
1020	Montpelier Idaho South	22 Apr 1979	Leonard H. Matthews
8a	*Paris Idaho		
	†Bear Lake (Idaho, Utah)	20 Jun 1869	David P. Kimball
29	*Preston Idaho North		
	†Oneida	1 Jun 1884	William D. Hendricks
81	*Preston Idaho South		
	†Franklin	6 Jun 1920	Samuel W. Parkinson
73	*Soda Springs Idaho		
	†Idaho	19 Nov 1916	Nelson J. Hogan

Discontinued

70	Curlew (Idaho, Utah)	17 May 1915	Jonathan C. Cutler
	11 Feb 1940 ★Malad (32), Pocatello (40)		
1273	Soda Springs Idaho North	31 May 1981	Cleston Murrie Godfrey
	27 Apr 1986 ★Montpelier Idaho (75), Soda Springs Idaho (73)		

Missions — 2
(As of Oct. 1, 1994; shown with historical number. See MISSIONS.)

(111) IDAHO BOISE MISSION
2710 Sunrise Rim Road, # 220
Boise, ID 83705
Phone: (208) 343-9883

(264) IDAHO POCATELLO MISSION
Horizon Plaza
1070 Hiline Road, #320
Pocatello, ID 83201
Phone: (208) 233-0130

Illinois

Year-end 1993: Est. population, 11,745,000; Members, 41,000; Stakes, 10; Wards, 74; Branches, 25; Missions, 2; Temples, 1; Percent LDS, 0.3, or one person in 286.

The first missionaries to Illinois were Oliver Cowdery, Parley P. Pratt, Peter Whitmer Jr., Richard Ziba Peterson and Frederick G. Williams, who visited in the fall of 1830 while on a mission to Native Americans. In 1834, Zion's Camp passed through southern Illinois, en route to Missouri. As a result of missionary work, a few branches were established in Illinois prior to 1839.

When the Saints were expelled from Missouri in 1839, they began to gather in Quincy, Springfield and other locations where they were generally received on friendly terms. One refugee, Israel Barlow, found his way to Commerce, Ill., where he laid the groundwork for the Church to purchase 660 acres of nearby property that later became Nauvoo. The city was platted and lots sold. As members poured in, the swampy land was drained and buildings erected. Converts from Canada and Europe arrived by thousands. Nauvoo grew to some 15,000 residents at its peak in 1845-46. It received a charter from the state of Illinois in 1840, and had a militia for self-defense. Members built music and cultural halls, as well as meeting halls for priesthood groups. Ten revelations of the Doctrine and Covenants were received in Illinois.

Joseph Smith planned or established in the area a network of 17 colonies, foreshadowing the colonization of the West by Brigham Young. Some of these that were founded or occupied by members included Ramus, Lima, Quincy, Mount Hope, Freedom, Geneva and Pleasant Vale.

In 1840 a site overlooking the city was selected for the Nauvoo Temple, which was completed in 1846. Proxy work for the dead began in Nauvoo, and temple endowments were first performed in 1842. The Relief Society was organized the same year.

In 1844, Joseph and Hyrum Smith were arrested and taken to jail in nearby Carthage, Ill., where they were martyred by a mob. Antagonism against the members increased, and they were expelled from Nauvoo by mobs in 1846. Members in the region left their homes, crossed the Mississippi River and traveled across Iowa to establish a temporary residence at Winter Quarters, Neb., some 300 miles away.

After the members left, the temple was destroyed by fire. The Church presence ended in Illinois for the time. After an interlude following the Saints' migration west, missionaries returned to Illinois in the 1870s. Illinois was included in the Northwestern States Mission, created in May 1878. Most converts from this mission migrated west. Mission headquarters were established in Chicago on July 20, 1889, and the name of the mission was changed to the Northern States Mission. By 1890, the mission extended into 22 states and Canada.

Following the conversions of Scandinavian settlers in Minnesota and other nearby states, Elder Christian D. Fjeldsted found success among the Scandinavians in Chicago from 1895-96.

A number of branches were created. By 1930, three conferences were organized: the Chicago, North Illinois and South Illinois. In Chicago, meetinghouses were built for the Logan Square and University branches. In 1930, state membership was 2,281. In 1933, when the World's Fair was held in Chicago, the Church's exhibit drew an estimated 10,000 people per day.

The first stake in Illinois since the Nauvoo era was organized in Chicago in 1936, followed in 1962 by the Illinois Stake (now Champaign).

In 1954, Dr. J. LeRoy Kimball purchased the Heber C. Kimball home in Nauvoo His efforts to restore the home were well-received. Nauvoo Restoration was started by the Church in 1962 and the Kimball home was included as part of Nauvoo Restoration Inc., with Dr. Kimball serving as the first president. The Church has since re-purchased some 1,000 acres and restored 25 of the buildings and cleared and erected a monument at the pioneer cemetery. A temple was completed in the Chicago suburb of Glenview in 1985, and an addition to the temple was dedicated in 1989. Membership in 1974 was about 18,000, increasing to 29,000 in 1980 and 38,000 in 1990. Membership in recent years has increased within Chicago's multiethnic neighborhoods.

Members were quick to respond to assist others in the 1993 Mississippi River flooding that damaged many areas in the state and resulted in the cancelation of the Nauvoo pageant. Attention of residents throughout the state was drawn to Carthage in June, 1994, when the Church commemorated the 150th anniversary of the martyrdom of the Prophet Joseph Smith and his brother, Hyrum.

Sources: *Encyclopedic History of the Church* by Andrew Jenson; "Spokes on the Wheel," by Donald Q. Cannon, *Ensign,* February 1986; "Harvest of Faith on Chicago's South Side," by Linda Hoffman Kimball, *Ensign,* February 1986; "He saved old Nauvoo from the ruin of time," *Church News,* Jan. 31, 1987; "Bittersweet memories of Ramus," by Calvin N. Smith and Joseph T. Woolley, *Church News,* Aug. 12, 1989; "A time to remember, honor, respect," by Dell Van Orden, *Church News,* July 2, 1994.

Stakes — 10
(Listed alphabetically by area as of Oct. 1, 1994.)

No.	Name	Organized	First President
North America Central Area			
1672	*Buffalo Grove Illinois 21 May 1991		
	†Long Grove Illinois	24 Jan 1988	William David Johnston
370	*Champaign Illinois		
	†Illinois	17 Feb 1963	Ross A. Kelly
646	Chicago Heights Illinois	2 Jun 1974	Robert E. Nichols
749	*O'Fallon Illinois 1 Jun 1993		
	†Fairview Heights Illinois	14 Mar 1976	John Odeen Anderson
368	*Naperville Illinois		
	†Chicago South (Illinois, Indiana)	3 Feb 1963	Lysle R. Cahoon
1000	Nauvoo Illinois	18 Feb 1979	Gene Lee Roy Mann
1163	Peoria Illinois	3 Aug 1980	Clive Edwin Ashton
1334	Rockford Illinois	11 Apr 1982	Brent L. Horsley
1094	Schaumburg Illinois	20 Jan 1980	Owen D. West Jr.
118	Wilmette Illinois		
	†Chicago (Ill., Ind., Wis.)	29 Nov 1936	William A. Matheson
Discontinued			
4	Crooked Creek [Ramus] 4 Dec 1841	4 Jul 1840	Joel Hills Johnson
8	Freedom 24 May 1841	27 Oct 1840	Henry W. Miller
9	Geneva 24 May 1841	1 Nov 1840	William Bosley
5	Lima 1845	22 Oct 1840	Isaac Morley
7	Mount Hope 24 May 1841	27 Oct 1840	Abel Lamb
2a	Nauvoo 1846	5 Oct 1839	William Marks
6	Quincy 24 May 1841	25 Oct 1840	Daniel Stanton
10	Springfield 24 May 1841	5 Nov 1840	Edwin P. Merriam

Missions — 2
(As of Oct. 1, 1994; shown with historical number. See MISSIONS.)

(9c) ILLINOIS CHICAGO MISSION
1319 Butterfield Road, # 522
Downers Grove, IL 60515
Phone: (708) 969-2145

(176a) ILLINOIS PEORIA MISSION
4700 North Sterling, # 100
Peoria, IL 61615
Phone: (309) 685-1116

Indiana

Year-end 1993: Est. population, 5,741,000; Members, 29,000; Stakes, 8; Wards, 54; Branches, 21; Missions, 1; Percent LDS, 0.5, or one person in 197.

Missionaries Samuel H. Smith and Reynolds Cahoon preached in the Indiana cities of Unionville, Madison and Vienna in the summer of 1831. Other missionaries came shortly after, including Parley P. and Orson Pratt. The first branches were organized in September, 1831, and the first conference was held Nov. 29, 1831. Joseph Smith spent four weeks in Greenville, Ind., in the spring of 1832.

In 1834, Zion's Camp crossed Indiana. Although trouble was predicted by their enemies, members of the group passed Indiana peacefully. In 1838, the Kirtland Camp, a group of seventies, also crossed Indiana. It is believed that a number of Indiana converts joined the Church in the early days.

In 1882, Indiana became part of the Northwestern States Mission. Among early converts after the turn of the century were Edward and Anna Faulting of Indianapolis, in whose home meetings were held until 1910. At that time, a home was rented and membership grew from 13 people to 10 families by 1913. The first branch was organized that year and the branch met in a hired hall. John L. Thomas was branch president. In 1920 a larger hall was rented which served until a meetinghouse was erected in 1927. This meetinghouse was dedicated by President Heber J. Grant.

In 1939, a second branch was organized in Indianapolis.

The Indianapolis Stake was created May 17, 1959, from the Central Indiana District. In the stake were two Indianapolis wards, and other wards in Bloomington, Columbus, Muncie, Purdue and Richmond, with branches in Kokomo, Anderson and Connersville, and a membership of 2,287.

The Great Lakes Mission, created in 1949 from the Northern States Mission, was changed to the Indiana Indianapolis Mission in 1974. That year, the state had 14,787 members, increasing to 20,738 in 1980, and to 26,169 in 1990.

Sources: *Encyclopedic History of the Church* by Andrew Jenson; *Church News,* May 23, 1959; Indianapolis Stake Center Dedication Program, Nov. 26, 1967; "Zions Camp, Across Swamplands," *Church News,* Sept. 5, 1970, and "Zions Camp, The First Prairie," *Church News,* Sept. 12, 1970; *Discovering Mormon Trails,* by Stanley B. Kimball, Deseret Book Co., 1979.

Stakes — 8
(Listed alphabetically as of Oct. 1, 1994.)

No.	Name	Organized	First President
North America Northeast Area			
1078	Bloomington Indiana	4 Nov 1979	Hollis Ralph Johnson
712	Evansville Indiana	19 Oct 1975	Frank R. Fults Jr.
352	*Fort Wayne Indiana		
	†Fort Wayne (Indiana, Ohio)	4 Mar 1962	Howard W. Thompson
283	*Indianapolis Indiana		
	†Indianapolis	17 May 1959	Phillip F. Low
624a	*Indianapolis Indiana North		
	†Indianapolis North	19 Aug 1973	David Val Glover
1417	Lafayette Indiana	15 May 1983	Koy Eldridge Miskin
1368	New Albany Indiana	24 Oct 1982	Henry Harvey Griffith
873	South Bend Indiana	30 Oct 1977	Kenneth Bryan Fugal

Mission — 1
(As of Oct. 1, 1994; shown with historical number. See MISSIONS.)

(46) INDIANA INDIANAPOLIS MISSION
P.O. Box 495
Carmel, IN 46032
Phone: (317) 844-3964

Iowa

Year-end 1993: Est. population, 2,815,000; Members, 13,000; Stakes, 3; Wards, 26; Branches, 12; Missions, 1; Percent LDS, 0.4, or one person in 216.

Following the expulsion of the Saints from Missouri in 1838, Iowa Gov. Robert Lucas expressed sympathy for their plight and offered them refuge. Although Joseph Smith instead chose to go to the site that later became Nauvoo in Illinois, members also entered and built up Lee County, Iowa, and resided in Montrose, Augusta, Keokuk and other areas. They founded Ambrosia and started a settlement named Zarahemla. A stake was organized in Lee County in 1839.

When the Saints were expelled from Nauvoo in 1846, the exiles crossed Iowa to found Winter Quarters, just across the Missouri River in Nebraska. On their westward trek they established Garden Grove and planted grain. Farther along, they again farmed at a place they called Mount Pisgah. Noah Rogers, returning from a mission in Tahiti, died and was buried there. Eventually 2,000 Saints lived in Mount Pisgah and members of the Mormon Battalion were recruited from among its residents in 1846. Mount Pisgah was disbanded in 1852, but Garden Grove remains as a farming community.

Members also lived in Council Bluffs, Iowa, across the river from Winter Quarters, Neb., and established some 70 temporary settlements. In 1848, Winter Quarters was abandoned when Indian officials protested. Members moved back to Iowa where they founded Kanesville, the name of which was changed in 1853 to Council Bluffs.

At Kanesville, Brigham Young became formal president of the Church on Dec. 7, 1847, and the same month sent the highly influential general epistle calling upon members all over the world to gather in Great Basin of the Rocky Mountains.

After 1848, Kanesville became an important staging area for thousands of Mormon and non-Mormon overland travelers.

An estimated 8,000 members lived in Iowa at this time. The settlements were vacated as pioneers moved west. In 1856-57, many handcart pioneers crossed the plains from what is now Iowa City, Iowa, where the railway ended. Of the 2,500 handcart pioneers who crossed the plains, 200 to 300 died on the trail. A marker was placed at the site in 1980, now part of the University of Iowa campus in Iowa City.

Missionary work began in Iowa in 1869 with Elders Israel Evans and Nymphus C. Murdock. A branch was reorganized in Keokuk in 1875, and Council Bluffs in 1878. Iowa was part of the Northwestern States Mission (changed to Northern States in 1889), organized in 1878.

In 1880, Elder B.H. Roberts began his missionary work in Iowa. On one occasion, he secured a school for preaching in West Fork, Iowa, and word spread in the community that three preachers would "tie the young Mormon with questions." Elder Roberts, though, nearly missed the appointment because of being stranded behind a washed-out bridge some distance away. He waded the stream, walked 10 miles and arrived to find a standing-room only crowd and three preachers. He spoke eloquently and no one contradicted him.

In 1887, mission headquarters were moved to Council Bluffs, where it remained until 1896, when it was transferred to Chicago. By 1930, Iowa included the Eastern and Western Iowa conferences with branches in Ames, Boone, Davenport and Sioux City. The Davenport Branch had a meetinghouse. Membership then was 560.

A stake was created in 1966 in Cedar Rapids with 2,000 members in the Cedar Falls, Cedar Rapids, Davenport, Iowa City and Rock Island wards and the Fayette, Muscatine, and Washington branches. Membership in the state in 1974 was 6,111. It increased to about 9,000 in 1980 and to 11,000 in 1990.

Appreciation for the contributions of the early members increased in the state as local members helped preserve early Mormon sites and the Mormon Trail during the late 1980s and 1990s.

Sources: *Encyclopedic History of the Church* by Andrew Jenson; "A meeting in Iowa," *Church News*, Nov. 24, 1973; "The LDS Legacy in Southwestern Iowa," by Gail Geo. Holmes, *Ensign*, Aug. 1988; "Handcart camp dedicated in Iowa as historic site," *Church News*, Aug. 9, 1980; "Middle Missouri Valley, 1846-1992," by Gail Geo. Holmes, *Church News* July 18, 1992.

Stakes — 3
(Listed alphabetically as of Oct. 1, 1994.)

No.	Name	Organized	First President
North America Central Area			
419	Cedar Rapids Iowa		
	†Cedar Rapids (Iowa, Illinois)	29 May 1966	Richard F. Hagland
902	Davenport Iowa	9 Apr 1978	James Earl Campbell
525	*Des Moines Iowa		
	†Des Moines	6 Sep 1970	Donald G. Woolley
	Discontinued		
3a	Iowa [Zarahemla]	5 Oct 1839	John Smith
	6 Jan 1842		

Mission — 1
(As of Oct. 1, 1994; shown with historical number. See MISSIONS.)

(140) IOWA DES MOINES MISSION
8515 Douglas Ave., #19
Des Moines, IA 50322
Phone: (515) 223-0797

Kansas

Year-end 1993: Est. population, 2,548,000; Members, 21,000; Stakes, 4; Wards, 35; Branches, 23; Districts, 1; Percent LDS, 0.8, or one person in 121.

In 1831, Oliver Cowdery and Parley Pratt taught Shawnee and Delaware Indians in what is now Kansas. In 1846, the Mormon Battalion was equipped for the longest infantry march in U.S. history at Fort Leavenworth, Kan. The immigration of 1854 passed through eastern Kansas. In 1855, what is now Atchison, Kan., was chosen as a layover site for immigrants who came up the Mississippi and Missouri rivers. They needed a more healthful place to disembark to avoid the ravages of cholera. A camp called Mormon Grove was established and more than 100 acres was cultivated and crops planted for future immigrants. The camp only lasted one summer, but fulfilled its purpose.

Missionary work in Kansas began anew in 1882 when Elders Joseph F. Doxford, Marcus L. Shepherd and James Mellor labored in Dickensen, Clay, Ottawa and Salina counties. In May 1882, they organized the Meridian Branch, located on the U.S. meridian that is a border between Dickinson and Salina counties. Ten converts from the branch immigrated to Utah. Others followed, but soon a mob ordered the missionaries to leave. In 1887, Pres. William M. Palmer of the Northern States Mission began laboring with "Bickertonites," a group that earlier splintered from the Church. His success led to the transfer of Kansas to the Northern States Mission from the Southern States Mission so the missionaries could continue their work.

In 1898, Kansas was transferred to the Indian Territory Mission. Among the earliest branches was one in Kansas City. By 1930, Kansas included branches in Blau, Kansas City, Leavenworth, St. John, Topeka and Wichita, with a membership of 2,063.

The Kansas City Stake (with headquarters in Missouri) was organized in Oct. 21, 1956, and it included, in Kansas, the Kansas City 1st and 2nd wards, the Topeka Ward and the Leavenworth, Hiawatha and Lawrence branches. The first stake headquartered in Kansas was in Wichita, organized June 24, 1962.

In 1974, Kansas received its first institute building, an historic estate across from Kansas State University. In that year, membership reached 8,134. In 1980, membership grew to 12,246 members; and in 1990, to 18,169 members.

Sources: *Encyclopedic History of the Church* by Andrew Jenson; "Martin V. Witbeck, Former Utahn, Called to Preside Over New Unit," *Church News,* Oct. 27, 1956; "Estate Home Now Building for Institute," *Church News,* Sept. 7, 1974; "Mormon Grove," by Dean L. May, *Church News,* Aug. 20, 1977.

Stakes — 4
(Listed alphabetically as of Oct. 1, 1994.)

No.	Name	Organized	First President
North America Central Area			
1610	Olathe Kansas	19 Oct 1986	Clifton D. Boyack Jr.
1696	Salina Kansas	29 May 1988	Thomas R. Coleman
747	Topeka Kansas	29 Feb 1976	Vahl W. Bodily
355	*Wichita Kansas		
	†Wichita (Kansas, Oklahoma)	24 Jun 1962	Lee R. Meador

Kentucky

Year-end 1993: Est. population, 3,820,000; Members, 19,000; Stakes, 3; Wards, 30; Branches, 30; Missions, 1; Percent LDS, 0.5, or one person in 201.

The first missionaries known to have visited Kentucky were Samuel H. Smith and Reynolds Cahoon. Coming from Kirtland, Ohio, they passed through the northern part of the state in late June 1831 on their way to Missouri. However, it is unlikely they preached. About the same time, the Prophet Joseph Smith and several of the brethren, traveling by steamer on the Ohio River, stopped at Louisville for three days. Because of his pattern of frequent preaching, it is likely that he was the first missionary to preach in Kentucky, though no record of converts exists. The Prophet also stopped in Louisville in 1832.

After this beginning, missionary work was done in Ballards, Carlisle, McCracken, Graves, Calloway, Jefferson, Boone, Kenton, and Campbell counties, and a few branches were started. The first was in Licking River, started before May 1834 by Robert Gulbertson, a convert from Indiana. In April 1835, Elders Wilford Woodruff and Warren Parrish crossed into Kentucky. From July 1835 on, Elder Woodruff labored alone. In Kentucky and Tennessee, they found that several branches had been formed by earlier missionaries in the region. A typical diary entry indicated that they "preached on the gospel of Jesus Christ, the authenticity of the Book of Mormon and the scattering and gathering of the House of Israel."

In 1835, James Emmett and Peter Dustin baptized 22 people including Benjamin and David Lewis. Benjamin Lewis was killed at Haun's Mill in 1838.

The first conference of the Church was conducted Feb. 26, 1836, at the home of Lewis Clapp in Calloway County, Ky.

The first company of Kentucky Saints gathering to Zion left for Missouri in September 1836. This started what became a 50-year movement of the Saints from the Southern States area. Missionary work continued until the end of 1839, then began again in 1842. In July of 1843, Brigham Young and Wilford Woodruff visited Kentucky on a missionary swing through the east. Converts were still being baptized a year later when the Prophet Joseph Smith was martyred and the missionaries were called back to Illinois.

Church growth was very slow as the Saints left the Southern States through the late 1800s to gather in the West. In 1868, Jessee W. Crosby Jr. and Owen Dix worked in Kentucky "with some success."

However, post-Civil War circumstances in the South were difficult. Persecution dogged missionaries and members through the 1880s, but by mid-1890s, toleration improved for them. By 1900, some 1,170 members lived in the state. Kentucky was placed briefly in the Middle States Mission in 1903.

The history of the Lebanon Branch is typical of the growth of the Church in Kentucky. In 1907, Elder M. P.

Stinson and Elder Kossnth Dyal, two traveling missionaries, visited the tiny community of Jonah, Ky., several miles east of Lebanon, and baptized Alfred Crews and his wife, Fannie. In late 1908 or early 1909, the Jonah Fork Branch of the Kentucky Conference was organized. There is no record of a branch president, but one of the first Church buildings in Kentucky was completed and dedicated at Jonah in 1910.

With the advent of the automobile and improved roads, Bradfordsville, six miles west of Jonah and seven or eight miles south of Lebanon, became the gathering place for Saints in the surrounding communities. Meetings were held in homes and outdoors into the 1920s and 1930s, as missionary activity in the region continued. One annual tradition was a July 4th fish fry, attended by up to 200 people, including many non-members of the Church. Fiddle and banjo music would accompany the meal, which was followed by "preaching" by the elders.

Membership in the state in 1930 was 2,879 in the Kentucky and East Kentucky districts, with a total of six branches with meetinghouses: Grant's Leek, Kentenia, Martin, Owingsville, Louisville and Larkin.

In 1971, the Louisville Stake was formed with wards in Fort Knox, Louisville (three), and New Albany, and branches in Lebanon, Salem, and Sulphur Well.

Membership in the state in 1980 was 13,956. In 1990, Dan Kelly was elected state senator, the the first LDS member to be elected to a state office. Membership in Kentucky in 1990 was 17,000.

Sources: *Encyclopedic History of the Church* by Andrew Jenson; *History of the Southern States Mission,* a BYU thesis by LaMar C. Berrett, July 1960; *Church News,* Jan 30, 1971; "His first fruits," by Ronald G. Watt, *Church News,* Aug. 27, 1977; and *Church News,* "My Old Kentucky Home," by Mike Cannon, Feb. 22, 1992.

Stakes — 3
(Listed alphabetically by area as of Oct. 1, 1994.)

No.	Name	Organized	First President
North America Northeast Area — 2			
571	*Lexington Kentucky		
	†Lexington	23 Apr 1972	Philip M. Moody
540	*Louisville Kentucky		
	†Louisville	17 Jan 1971	Henry H. Griffith
North America Southeast Area — 1			
926	Hopkinsville Kentucky	21 May 1978	Robert Laurence Fears

Mission — 1
(As of Oct. 1, 1994; shown with historical number. See MISSIONS.)

(29) KENTUCKY LOUISVILLE MISSION
P.O. Box 4247, Baxter Ave. Station
Louisville, KY 40204
Phone: (502) 451-3010

Louisiana

Year-end 1993: Est. population, 4,315,000; Members, 23,000; Stakes, 7; Wards, 37; Branches, 28; Missions, 1; Percent LDS, 0.5, or one person in 187.

Elder Parley P. Pratt considered going to New Orleans in 1837, hoping to establish a mission there, but felt impressed to instead remain in New York. In 1841, Joseph Smith received a letter from Elam Luddington (later the first missionary to Thailand) and Eli G. Terrill of New Orleans who indicated they had a group of members and requested an elder to assist them. "Send us Peter, or an Apostle to preach unto us Jesus," they wrote, and enclosed $10 to help defray expenses. They may have been among a group from the sailing ship *Isaac Newton,* the first to carry Saints to New Orleans, which arrived from London on Dec. 21, 1840.

Elder Harrison Sagers was sent, arriving in New Orleans on March 28, 1841. Elder Sagers preached to large crowds and was troubled by mobs, but was defended on one occasion by a group of courageous women who circled him in defense. He baptized several people and ordained Terrill an elder.

In November of 1841, New Orleans became the principal port of arrival for members, 17,463 of whom emigrated from Europe via New Orleans to the gathering place of the Saints before their migration west. Most disembarked from their sailing vessel, took passage on a river steamer and traveled up the Mississippi River to Nauvoo, St. Louis or other river ports to begin their westward trek. A branch functioned in New Orleans from 1844 until 1855, when New York became the port of arrival for the Church immigrants.

Missionaries returned to Louisiana in 1896 as part of the Southern States Mission. Elder Joseph A.

Cornwall arrived in Louisiana on Sept. 10, laboring on the Red River in North Louisiana with little results. In 1897, he and his companions baptized their first converts. The Red Rock Branch was organized in 1898. That year, 24 missionaries labored in Louisiana. A sawmill owner, John R. Jones, befriended the missionaries and protected them from opposition. Alexander Colman Wagley, first president of the Red Rock Branch, was baptized Sept. 4, 1898. By June 16, 1899, Elder David A. Broadbent, president of the Louisiana District from 1898 to 1899, reported that 110 people had been baptized. Pres. Wagley and missionaries were held hostage by mobs but were unharmed. When a mob threatened a missionary under the medical care of Jane Holt Clark, a midwife, she confronted the mob with a shotgun and said, "I brought a good many of you into the world and I can take you out again just as easily." The mob left.

In 1915, a wagon train of members from Pride, La., traveled to Corleyville where they settled and erected a meetinghouse in 1920. Other prominent branches were the Hardytown and Many branches. The Many Branch, which eventually absorbed the Hardytown Branch, was organized in 1933 and a meetinghouse was built in 1942.

Missionaries labored in New Orleans for 20 years before a branch was organized. Howard and Marian Bennion arrived in Louisiana in the 1920s and a branch was organized in their apartment in 1924. By 1926 the branch began meeting in a public hall. The branch faltered in the early 1930s, but members joined missionaries, and contacting through radio, newspapers and street meetings, helped the branch grow. Some 100 people celebrated the branch's centennial in 1944. In 1948, the branch had grown to 300 members, due in part to an influx of LDS servicemen who came during World War II. A meetinghouse was begun in January 1951 and dedicated about two years later. That same year meetinghouses were dedicated in Hammond, Williamson and Lake Charles, and an addition on the Many Branch was dedicated.

The New Orleans Stake was created in 1955. In 1964, a new stake center was completed. Membership within the former branch area in 1973 was about 2,500.

President Spencer W. Kimball visited Baton Rouge in 1977 and addressed 12,000 people from the surrounding regions. Membership in Louisiana in 1980 was about 16,000, increasing to 22,000 in 1990.

Elder L. Lionel Kendrick of the First Quorum of the Seventy is a native of Louisiana, and was a professor of health education at the time of his calling in 1988.

Sources: *Encyclopedic History of the Church* by Andrew Jenson; "Boats on the Mississippi are still reminder of part of LDS History," by J Malan Heslop, *Church News,* Dec. 24, 1977; "From Red Rock to Denham Springs," by Carol Ann Wagley Burnham, *Ensign,* April 1983; Branch Notes 100th Anniversary, *Church News,* Jan. 22, 1944; and *Church News:* Dec. 6, 1952; Jan. 20, 1973; Sept. 13, 1975; Sept. 3, 1977; and May 21, 1977.

Stakes — 7
(Listed alphabetically as of Oct. 1, 1994.)

No.	Name	Organized	First President
North America Southeast Area			
954	Alexandria Louisiana	27 Aug 1978	Jeffie Jackson Horn
476	*Baton Rouge Louisiana		
	†Baton Rouge	26 Jan 1969	Harmon Cutler
1254	Denham Springs Louisiana	19 Apr 1981	Stephen H. Cutler
1550	Monroe Louisiana	18 Aug 1985	John Robert Falk
221	*New Orleans Louisiana		
	†New Orleans	19 Jun 1955	Clive M. Larson
254	*Shreveport Louisiana		
	†Shreveport (Louisiana, Texas)	26 Jan 1958	J. Milton Belisle
1575	Slidell Louisiana	17 Nov 1985	Joseph T. Kuchin

Mission — 1
(As of Oct. 1, 1994; shown with historical number. See MISSIONS.)

(31) LOUISIANA BATON ROUGE MISSION
12025 Justice Ave.
Baton Rouge, LA 70816
Phone: (504) 293-6060

Maine

Year-end 1993: Est. population, 1,244,000; Members, 7,500; Stakes, 2; Wards, 16; Branches, 8; Percent LDS, 0.6, or one person in 166.

On Sept. 19, 1832, two years after the Church was organized, Elders Orson Hyde and Samuel H. Smith crossed the Piscataqua River in a canoe to Maine. They went from door to door in search of converts, soon starting a branch in Saco, York County. One of their first converts was Timothy Smith, baptized about Oct. 31, 1832. Other missionaries followed. In 1833, additional branches were organized, including one in York County that included converts from a mass conversion of 30. The Maine Conference was created in 1835 with about 317 members.

In 1837, Elder Wilford Woodruff and Jonathan H. Hale found missionary success on the Fox Islands, where several branches were organized among some 100 converts. The converts gathered to Nauvoo a short time later.

Little missionary work was done in Maine after the martyrdom of Joseph Smith in 1844. In 1850, Brigham Young requested all the Saints in Maine to go to the West. In 1855, Elder E.B. Tripp found converts in the town of Mexico, Maine, and organized a branch that remained until 1869. Little activity occurred until after the turn of the century.

In 1904, missionaries began work in Portland. Work proceeded very slowly. The Maine Conference was reorganized in 1909, and missionaries found "practically a new field for missionary work." They visited homes near Litchfield in 1908, and met Percy E. and Annie Louise Rowe Lane. Five years later, on July 4, 1913, missionaries baptized Sister Lane and her daughter, Mildred, and the rest of the family afterward. Missionaries started a Sunday School in their home.

After 1925, when Maine was placed in the Canadian Mission, the northern part of the state was visited more often by missionaries. Bangor became a Church center for missionary work. Some 275 people, including eight converts, attended a conference in Bangor on Oct. 14, 1930.

Scattered branches continued into the 1950s before significant growth occurred. The first building was dedicated in 1957 in Portland. Another was dedicated in Bangor the same year. The Maine Stake was created in 1968 with 2,208 members. Members from the West added to the membership. In 1974, membership was 3,851; in 1980 it was 4,664, and in 1990, 7,253.

Sources: *Encyclopedic History of the Church* by Andrew Jenson; "A Partial History of Litchfield," by Percy E. Lane, unpublished; "Wilford Woodruff's Mission to Maine," by Donald Q. Cannon, *Improvement Era*, September, 1970; "Old Mormon Palmyra and New England," by Richard Neitzel Holsapfel and T. Jeffery Cottle; *The Narrative of the Saints in Maine from 1831 to the 1990s*, an unpublished manuscript by Paul Edward Damron.

Stakes — 2
(Listed alphabetically as of Oct. 1, 1994.)

No.	Name	Organized	First President
North America Northeast Area			
461	*Augusta Maine		
	†Maine	23 Jun 1968	Olie W. Ross
1595	Bangor Maine	20 Apr 1986	Paul Herald Risk II

Maryland

Year-end 1993: Est. population, 5,015,000; Members, 29,000; Stakes, 7; Wards, 51; Branches, 15; Missions, 1; Temples, 1; Percent LDS, 0.5, or one person in 173.

Elders Jedediah M. Grant, Erastus Snow, William Bosley and John F. Wakefield began missionary work in Maryland in the summer of 1837. Elders Snow and Bosley worked in Washington County between May and October and organized a branch. Elder Snow reported preaching in Greencastle and engaging in a formal debate that lasted 10 hours in Leitersburgh, Washington County, with a Campbellite minister. He afterward baptized 11 people. He also baptized seven people in Leitersburgh. In 1838, Elder Benjamin Winchester preached in the same vicinity, traveling with Elder Snow. On this journey, Elder Snow baptized an 89-year-old man after cutting through ice 18 inches thick.

An LDS newspaper, the *Mormon Expositor,* began in 1842 in Baltimore but was discontinued. Elders Heber C. Kimball and Lyman Wight traveled to Baltimore in 1844 where they received information about the martyrdom of the Prophet Joseph Smith.

After the exodus west and the gathering of the Saints, little work was done in Maryland until the turn of the century. The Maryland Conference was reorganized June 30, 1899, with Charles A. Hardy as president. At that time, mission leadership wanted to increase the conference size, so they requested an additional four Virginia counties from the Southern States Mission. Southern States Mission Pres. Ben E. Rich humorously agreed to yield the Virginia counties on the condition that they would take six, not four.

By 1900, the conference included the Pratt and Mount Savage branches, but in 1905, the Maryland Conference was absorbed into the Eastern Pennsylvania Conference. That year a tiny group of members in Baltimore organized a Book of Mormon class that lasted several years. Sunday Schools were organized in Baltimore in 1907 and reorganized in 1917.

Missionary work picked up in 1915 as work proceeded in Havre de Grace, Baltimore, Frederick and Salisbury. In 1918, street meetings in Baltimore brought interest. Work in Annapolis began in 1920. Branch meetings in Washington and Baltimore, presided over by missionaries, and Sunday Schools and Relief Societies in other areas, were held in rented halls. One small frame meetinghouse in Capitol Heights accommodated a membership of mostly Westerners — students or those with government jobs.

The Washington Stake was created June 30, 1940, with Ezra Taft Benson as president. This stake included parts of Maryland where the first Maryland stake was later created in 1970.

A site for the showcase Washington Temple was selected in Kensington, Md., in 1962. The temple was dedicated in 1974 and has become a prominent landmark in the region. The temple grounds have become a popular place for national leaders and diplomats to visit on special occasions, such as during the Christmas season. At the 15th anniversary of the temple in 1988, it was noted that membership around the nation's capital had increased by some 200 percent since the temple's construction, and numbered some 63,000 members in 19 stakes.

Maryland membership in 1980 was 17,617.

Sources: *Encyclopedic History of the Church* by Andrew Jenson; *History of the Southern States Mission,* by LaMar C. Berrett, a BYU thesis, July 1960; Mission and ward histories; *Church News,* Sept. 19, 1970, Sept. 14, 1974, and Sept. 17, 1977.

Stakes — 7
(Listed alphabetically as of Oct. 1, 1994.)

No.	Name	Organized	First President
North America Northeast Area			
1429	*Annapolis Maryland 13 Nov 1988		
	†Columbia Maryland	12 Jun 1983	Stephen P. Shipley
674	Baltimore Maryland	8 Dec 1974	Kyle W. Petersen
1825	Columbia Maryland	10 Nov 1991	Cecil Brent Bargeron
1390	Frederick Maryland	12 Dec 1982	Earl J. Wahlquist
1566	Seneca Maryland	27 Oct 1985	David Warne Ferrel
526	*Silver Spring Maryland		
	†Chesapeake (Maryland)	13 Sep 1970	June B. Thayn
1051	Suitland Maryland	19 Aug 1979	Thomas Bailey Kerr

Mission — 1
(As of Oct. 1, 1994; shown with historical number. See MISSIONS.)

(298) MARYLAND BALTIMORE MISSION
4785 Dorsey Hall Drive, Suite 105
Ellicott City, MD 21042
Phone: (410) 715-0875

Massachusetts

Year-end 1993: Est. population, 6,025,000; Members, 15,000; Stakes, 3; Wards, 26; Branches, 13; Missions, 1; Percent LDS, 0.2, or one person in 334.

The first missionaries in Massachusetts are believed to be Elders Orson Hyde and Samuel H. Smith, who arrived in Boston June 22, 1832. They baptized four people and, by the end of the year, had organized two branches. These branches were short-lived, however.

In 1838, Brigham Young and his brother Joseph baptized 17 people in Boston as they preached the gospel. The Eastern States Mission was created under John P. Greene in 1839 (Greene was the reverend who received a copy of the Book of Mormon during Samuel H. Smith's first missionary journey in New York in 1830). By February 1843 some 14 branches in the Boston area had been organized. Joseph Smith and others visited Boston in December 1839. They were en route to Washington D.C. seeking redress for the unjustices in Missouri.

In 1843, Elder George J. Adams preached nightly to an enthusiastic audience of some 1,200 in Charlestown. Later, eight members of the Council of the Twelve attended a Boston conference as part of an effort they were making to press missionary work forward in New England. Their work ended after the martyrdom of Joseph Smith in 1844. A year later the Boston Branch had some 300-400 members. In 1849, Mission Pres. William Appleby led a company of 79 members to St. Louis and on to the Great Basin. Many died of cholera.

Work slowed in 1850, and stopped in 1857 when all missionaries were called to Utah during the so-called "Utah War." Until 1893, most of New England, including Massachusetts, saw little progress in the development of the Church.

The Eastern States Mission reopened in 1893 and missionaries sought out old members. After a year, membership numbered 96. Despite emphasis on public relations, missionaries encountered substantial hostilities. Highly publicized U.S. Senate hearings on Apostle and Senator-elect Reed Smoot fanned anti-LDS sentiments. Police often refused to allow missionaries to conduct open-air meetings. President Joseph F. Smith addressed a large gathering at Deacon's Hall in Boston in 1905 on a return trip from dedicating a monument at Joseph Smith's birthplace in Vermont.

A Mutual Improvement Association was started in Boston on Jan. 5, 1908, and a branch in Lynn, Mass., was started in 1910. The Church began to grow about 1917 but the onset of World War I halted efforts.

After the war, more missionaries resumed labor in Massachusetts and the membership began to increase. On April 18, 1930, missionaries took part in a radio broadcast. At that time, membership in the Massachusetts District numbered about 356. Longtime member Naomi B. Cranney recalled that membership in the 1930s included only about 10 permanent families in the area. Returned missionaries who were students at Harvard University provided great strength, she said. The Great Depression and World War II again slowed growth. But the war also brought couples from Utah to work at the Massachusetts Institute of Technology in Cambridge. In 1947, missionaries were sent to rural areas, where they found some success.

The first meetinghouses were completed in the early 1950s. An exceptional piece of Church property was the Longfellow estate in Cambridge, Mass., that was purchased by Elder Levi Edgar Young. It later became headquarters for the New England Mission. A meetinghouse was dedicated on this site in 1956.

When Pres. Truman G. Madsen began serving in 1962, missionaries baptized about 1,000 per year for two years. The same year the Church purchased the shortwave radio station, WRUL, to beam Church-related information to Europe, Africa, and Latin America.

In 1963, some 2,200 members met in a conference in Boston, the largest LDS gathering in New England history.

The Boston Stake, the first in New England, was created in 1962. It included parts of New Hampshire and Rhode Island. During the 1960s, a number of meetinghouses were erected with beneficial effects on membership. Members enjoyed a higher profile during the next years with improved relations with government and educational figures. Additional stakes were created in Massachusetts in Hingham in 1981 and in Springfield in 1987. Membership in 1974 was 5,628, increasing to 8,174 in 1980, and 13,931 in 1990.

Sources: "Yankee Saints: The Church in New England in the Twentieth Century," by Richard O. Cowan, *Regional Studies in Latter-day Saint History,* New England; Highlights in the History of The Church of Jesus Christ of Latter-day Saints, a paper by J.D. Williams, Cambridge Branch.

Stakes — 3
(Listed alphabetically as of Oct. 1, 1994.)

No.	Name	Organized	First President
North America Northeast Area			
354	*Boston Massachusetts		
	†Boston (Mass., N.H., R.I.)	20 May 1962	Wilbur W. Cox
1287	Hingham Massachusetts	30 Aug 1981	Brent W. Lambert
1646	Springfield Massachusetts	28 Jun 1987	David O. Sutton

Mission — 1
(As of Oct. 1, 1994; shown with historical number. See MISSIONS.)

(35) MASSACHUSETTS BOSTON MISSION
4 Longfellow Park
Cambridge, MA 02138-4895
Phone: (617) 868-0630

Michigan

Year-end 1993: Est. population, 10,001,000; Members, 30,000; Stakes, 8; Wards, 51; Branches, 31; Missions, 2; Districts, 1; Percent LDS, 0.3, or one person in 333.

Visiting her relatives in Pontiac, Lucy Mack Smith arrived in Michigan in the spring of 1831. With her was her niece, Almira Mack of Pontiac, who had been baptized in New York in 1830. They visited Lucy Mack Smith's brother, Col. Stephen Mack, considered the founder of Pontiac.

Preaching in Pontiac, she warned one unfriendly pastor that one third of his flock would soon be members, including the deacon. Upon her return to Kirtland, Ohio, the Prophet Joseph Smith sent Jared Carter and Joseph Wood to Pontiac where they arrived Jan. 7, 1833, and baptized 22 people from the pastor's congregation, including the deacon, Samuel Bent.

In 1834, Joseph Smith visited Pontiac with his father and Hyrum, the three witnesses to the Book of Mormon, Frederick G. Williams and Robert Orton. Missionary work continued in Michigan, although no records exist of how many were converted because converts often soon gathered with the body of the Church.

Parley P. and Orson Pratt visited Detroit in the fall of 1839 where they preached to crowded houses. Parley published a pamphlet, *History of the Late Persecution by the State of Missouri upon the Mormons.*

Elder Mephibosheth Serrine was a leader of the Church in southeastern Michigan, and the early 1840s saw branches in Oakland, Lapeer, Wayne, Livingston, Washtenaw and Lenawee counties. Converts from Jared Cater's efforts of 1833 continued to spread the gospel to most of western Michigan. On Jan. 12, 1844, Elder Serrine reported that in the previous six months, more than 100 converts had left to gather in Nauvoo. Visiting Church authorities created more branches in June 1844. The martyrdom of Joseph and Hyrum Smith on June 27 ended the early period of Church advancement. Many members accepted the leadership of Brigham Young and joined the westward movement. Apostate James J. Strang claimed to be the successor of the Prophet. He was denounced by leaders but attracted a group who later settled on Beaver Island in Lake Michigan before disbanding. Other splinter groups resided in Michigan as well.

In 1876, William M. Palmer served a mission in Michigan. He soon organized several branches despite serious persecution. The Northwestern States Mission was organized in 1878 with Cyrus H. Wheelock as president. Faithful converts migrated steadily to Utah. In 1889, the Northern States Mission was organized and included Michigan. After the turn of the century, the first branch in Michigan was created by German E. Ellsworth in Detroit on April 21, 1915. By 1930, membership in the East Michigan and West Michigan districts, created that year, had a combined membership of 972.

The first meetinghouse in Detroit was erected and dedicated in December 1928. In 1939, 25 missionaries who had been recalled from foreign areas because of World War II formed a chorus that performed public concerts. By 1945, some 7,183 members resided in branches in Detroit (3), Ann Arbor, Battle Creek, Grand Rapids, Jackson, Muskegon, Flint, Lansing, Pontiac, and Saginaw. Michigan's first stake was created Nov. 9, 1952, in Detroit, with later-to-be Michigan Gov. George W. Romney as president. Additional stakes were created in 1962 (Lansing), 1969, (Dearborn) and 1979 (Kalamazoo).

The Great Lakes Mission was created in 1949, and the Indiana-Michigan Mission in 1970. In 1973, the Michigan Mission (changed later to Michigan Lansing) was created. In 1980, Michigan had a membership of 22,607, and in 1990, 28,245.

Sources: *The Michigan Mormons,* written and compiled by Hilda Faulkner Browne; "The Saints Come to Michigan," by John and Audrey Cumming, *Michigan History,* March 1965; The Mormon Era in Detroit, by John Cumming, *Detroit Historical Society Bulletin,* March 1968; *Encyclopedic History of the Church* by Andrew Jenson; "LDS influence felt in much of Michigan history," by Frank C. Davis, *Church News,* Nov. 15, 1980, and Dec. 11, 1983.

Stakes — 8
(Listed alphabetically as of Oct. 1, 1994.)

No.	Name	Organized	First President
North America Northeast Area			
854	Ann Arbor Michigan	14 Aug 1977	Duane Marvin Laws
197	*Bloomfield Hills Michigan		
	†Detroit (Michigan, Ohio, Canada)	9 Nov 1952	George W. Romney
940	Grand Blanc Michigan	11 Jun 1978	Trent Pickett Kitley
684	Grand Rapids Michigan	2 Mar 1975	Glenn Goodwin
1091	Kalamazoo Michigan	9 Dec 1979	Donald Lee Lykins
349	*Lansing Michigan		
	†Lansing	18 Feb 1962	Sylvan H. Wittwer
469	*Midland Michigan		
	†Mid-Michigan	1 Dec 1968	E. Richard Packham
474	*Westland Michigan 14 Aug 1978		
	*Dearborn Michigan		
	†Dearborn (Michigan)	12 Jan 1969	Carl S. Hawkins

Missions — 2
(As of Oct. 1, 1994; shown with historical number. See MISSIONS.)

(164) MICHIGAN DETROIT MISSION
33505 State St., #101
Farmington, MI 48335
Phone: (313) 478-8588

(104) MICHIGAN LANSING MISSION
1400 Abbott, #460
East Lansing, MI 48823
Phone: (517) 351-3430

Minnesota

Year-end 1993: Est. population, 4,537,000; Members, 18,000; Stakes, 5; Wards, 33; Branches, 16; Missions, 1; Percent LDS, 0.4, or one person in 252.

In 1854, a Mormon elder, Ralph Joung, "preached at Spring Grove," according to a Minnesota county newspaper.

In 1857, missionaries baptized Minnesota settler Robert Pope and his wife, Sarah Leduc Pope, along with Edwin Theodore Pope and his wife, whose name was not recorded, in Morristown in southern Minnesota. These converts soon "gathered" to Utah.

The next missionary to Minnesota was Elder Silas Hoyt, who labored in Minnesota in September 1868. In 1870, Ariah C. Brower and Eli Whipple worked in Minnesota and adjoining states. They were received with enthusiasm, but gained few converts. In 1875 Elder Bengt P. Wulffenstein, who spoke Swedish, German and Danish, began a systematic and successful effort to teach the many Scandinavians who had settled in Minnesota.

In 1875 Elder Wulffenstein organized Minnesota's first branch, a small group of converts in Freeborn County. By 1877, five more branches were organized, and in February 1882, mission history records indicate that Minnesota had 74 members. The town of Monticello became a center for the work as Deborah Houghton Riggs, the wife of its founder, Ashley C. Riggs, joined the Church.

Work in Minnesota was incorporated into the Northwestern States Mission in 1878, when nine missionaries served in this state. The missionaries located Mormons or those who had heard the gospel preached in their homeland. Missionaries were often the target of eggs, stones and threats as they made arduous journeys across the sparsely populated region. With few exceptions, their efforts were rewarded only with a handful of converts. During this period, several small companies of members immigrated to Utah from Minnesota, the largest being a party of 70 from Monticello.

In 1886, some 227 members belonged to the Minnesota Conference, then including Wisconsin, the Dakotas and Iowa.

Missionary work halted from 1891 until 1896. However, following the Manifesto of 1890, public opinion began to improve as people began to understand the Mormons had been maligned. In 1899, a conference was attended by Apostle Heber J. Grant. By the turn of the century most Minnesota converts had left for Zion. The handful of members who remained worked as a very small minority to build a Mormon presence.

Minnesota Conference headquarters were established in Minneapolis in 1900. A Sunday School was organized May 20, 1900, in Minneapolis. Another was organized in St. Paul on Aug. 5. The Sunday Schools were combined in 1902, and the new unit had an average attendance of 50. Mission Pres. German E. Ellsworth served from 1904-1919, and under his leadership the mission made steady progress. More Sunday Schools were started, and branches organized and divided. The first Church-owned building in Minnesota was purchased May 9, 1914, for the St. Paul Branch, and a baptismal font installed in its basement was used for baptismal services for converts from the entire state.

By 1919, membership had increased to 4,000 in 30 branches, and possibly hundreds of others migrating west. A large meetinghouse was erected and dedicated in 1924. By 1930, there were three districts in the state: the North, South and Lake districts. Over the next 20 years, many branches were established. The Minnesota Stake was organized Nov. 29, 1960, with six wards and five branches, and a membership of 2,600. By 1970, its membership had reached 4,800. The Minnesota-Manitoba Mission was created in 1970, and the Minnesota-Wisconsin Mission in 1973. When the Minnesota Stake was changed to the Minneapolis Minnesota Stake in 1974, it had 4,936 members. In 1976, the St. Paul Stake was created, and the same year the Minnesota Minneapolis Mission was created. Membership in 1980 was 11,755, and in 1990, 16,741.

Sources: *Encyclopedic History of the Church* by Andrew Jenson; *Minnesota Mormons*, a History of the Minneapolis Minnesota Stake, by Fayone B. Willes; The Church in Minnesota, unpublished, no author listed; Mormon Missionaries and Minnesota Scandinavians, by Kenneth O. Bjork, *Minnesota History*, published by the Minnesota Historical Society; *Church News*, Dec. 3, 1960.

Stakes — 5
(Listed alphabetically as of Oct. 1, 1994.)

No.	Name	Organized	First President
North America Central Area			
1562	Anoka Minnesota	20 Oct 1985	Lyle T Cottle
317	*Minneapolis Minnesota		
	†Minnesota (Minnesota, Wisconsin)	29 Nov 1960	Delbert F. Wright

1939	Duluth Minnesota	9 May 1993	John G. Hancock
910	Rochester Minnesota	30 Apr 1978	Lee McNeal Johnson
744	Saint Paul Minnesota	15 Feb 1976	Thomas Albert Holt

Mission — 1
(As of Oct. 1, 1994; shown with historical number. See MISSIONS.)

(26a) MINNESOTA MINNEAPOLIS MISSION
5931 West 96th St.
Bloomington, MN 55438
Phone: (612) 835-7788

Mississippi

Year-end 1993: Est. population, 2,665,000; Members, 15,000; Stakes, 4; Wards, 25; Branches, 16; Missions, 1; Percent LDS, 0.5, or one person in 178.

Missionary work in Mississippi evidently began when Elder John D. Hunter and Benjamin L. Clapp arrived in Tishomingo County in 1839. They baptized 13 people in Tishomingo County. In 1840, Elder Norvel M. Head said he visited a branch in the same county. Elders Daniel Tyler and R. D. Sheldon began work in Copiah, Miss., and baptized five people in 1841. A group of between 80 and 90 members in 40 wagons, escaping persecution, arrived in Nauvoo from Mississippi in April 1842. A small branch was organized in Monroe County in 1843, where other converts, including plantation owner James M. Flake were converted and baptized by Elder Clapp. Several branches were created and membership continued to increase.

In 1846, a company of emigrants left Monroe County expecting to join the main body of Saints in the Rocky Mountains. Instead, they became the first group of Mormons to cross the plains, wintering with fur trappers in Pueblo, Colo., that year. These members made significant contributions. They were the first to establish a religious colony in the West since the Spanish priests of 1769. They later founded the second colony in Utah at Cottonwood (once called the Mississippi Ward) and Holladay (named after a Mississippi-an), helped found San Bernardino, Calif., and years later, other colonies along the Little Colorado in Arizona. (Snowflake, Ariz., was originally named Snow Flake after Erastus Snow and James M. Flake.) African-American servants of these members — Green Flake, Oscar and Mark — were in the first group that entered the Salt Lake Valley. One of the children of these early pioneers from Mississippi was Alice Rowan, who taught school in Riverside, Calif., among the first African-American women to teach at a public school in the nation.

Missionary work was said to continue in Mississippi until the Civil War. It resumed in 1870s. In 1880, enemies of the Church tried but failed to enlist the governor of Mississippi in forcing missionaries to leave the state.

A colony of African-American converts may have created a township in 1891 called Republican Square near the Mississippi Gulf Coast, but all traces of this community subsequently vanished.

Persecution increased and missionaries were often abused. Elder Alma P. Richards was murdered in 1888, though a Church investigation committee concluded the motive likely was robbery, not religious persecution.

The U.S. Census listed 123 members in Mississippi in 1890. By 1906, that number had increased to 1,018.

A meetinghouse in Quitman, Miss., was completed in 1908, and the branch had 11 members but grew in 10 years to 30 members.

By 1930, the Mississippi Conference had a membership of 2,170 in the Darburn and Red Star branches and Bay St. Louis, Meadville, Raytown, Red Hill, Sarah and Smithville Sunday Schools. New buildings were completed for the Senatobia, McNeill and Jackson branches in 1943, and for Biloxi in 1954.

The first two stakes in Mississippi were created in 1965. The first, Jackson, had a membership of 2,245 members in two Jackson wards, Meridian, Natchez, Columbus, Vicksburg and Red Star wards and the Greenville Branch. The second in Biloxi included 2,515 members in the Biloxi, Columbia, Gulfport, Hattiesburg, Liberty, and Pascagoula wards and the Bayou La Croix, Darbun, Laurel, McNiel, Sant Hill and Seminary branches.

Membership grew slowly, reaching 6,527 in 1970 and 10,403 in 1980 and 13,000 in 1990.

Sources: *Encyclopedic History of the Church* by Andrew Jenson; "Anniversary Noted for Old Backwoods Chapel," *Church News*, Aug. 9, 1958; *History of the Southern States Mission 1831-1861*, by LaMar C. Berrett, a BYU thesis, July 1960; "Gulf States Get New Stake, *Church News*," May 8, 1965 and July 3, 1965; *A Brief History of the Southern States Mission for One Hundred Years, 1830-1930*, by DeVon H. Nish, a BYU paper, August 1966; "Orthodoxy Versus Nonconformity: The Mormon Experience in Tennessee and Mississippi, 1875-1905," a University of Chicago paper by Mary Elizabeth Stovall, March 1976; "Mississippi Mormons," by Leonard Arrington, *Ensign*, June 1977.

Stakes — 4
(Listed alphabetically as of Oct. 1, 1994.)

No.	Name	Organized	First President
North America Southeast Area			
1364	Gulfport Mississippi	10 Oct 1982	John Sibbald Scott II
408	*Hattiesburg Mississippi		
	†Hattiesburg	27 Jun 1965	Edwin White
404	*Jackson Mississippi		
	†Jackson	2 May 1965	Neil J. Ferrell
1801	Tupelo Mississippi	9 June 1991	Thomas Evan Nebeker

Mission — 1
(As of Oct. 1, 1994; shown with historical number. See MISSIONS.)

(171) MISSISSIPPI JACKSON MISSION
5200 Keele St.
Jackson, MS 39206
Phone: (601) 362-1518

Missouri

Year-end 1993: Est. population, 5,262,000; Members, 40,000; Stakes, 10; Wards, 72; Branches, 31; Missions, 2; Temples, 1 under construction; Percent LDS, 0.8, or one person in 132.

Oliver Cowdery, Parley P. Pratt and Frederick G. Williams arrived in Missouri on Jan. 13, 1831, and preached to Delaware and Shawnee Indians in the adjacent Indian Territory. Indian agents soon asked them to leave. The same year, Joseph Smith received a revelation indicating that Independence, Jackson County, Mo., was to be the "New Jerusalem," and gathering site for the Saints.

This revelation led to an immediate influx of members, some of whom were ill-prepared for settling and less obedient to Church instructions. This influx laid the groundwork for what became, in essence, a battle for turf between old settlers and Mormon colonists with their strikingly different economic, political, and spiritual values. By June 1833, 1,200 members in 12 branches lived in Jackson County. On July 30, 1833, nearly 500 Missourians ordered Mormons from Jackson County. Church leaders tried to seek protection through the courts but failed. Mormons seeking to defend themselves were disarmed, and mobs drove them out.

In 1834, Joseph Smith and group of 150-200 armed men, called Zion's Camp, arrived to protect the members. A violent storm prevented the confrontation and undoubtedly preserved the group that was subsequently disbanded at the Prophet's direction.

The Jackson County LDS refugees found safety in adjacent Clay County for two years and then, amid new adversity, moved to western, uninhabited Caldwell and Daviess counties. By 1838, Far West, the principal settlement in Daviess County, became Church headquarters and had more than 100 homes, hotels, a printing house and a school. Joseph F. Smith, president of the Church from 1901-18, was born in Far West in 1838.

It was revealed to Joseph Smith that Adam-ondi-Ahman, in Daviess County, was where Adam had lived, and a temple site was dedicated at the location and cornerstones placed on July 4, 1838. Twenty revelations of the Doctrine and Covenants were received in Missouri.

Apostasy fueled internal problems in 1838. Several prominent leaders were excommunicated, and unwise rhetoric against them incited Missourians again against the Church.

Violence erupted on Aug. 6, 1838, when Mormons were prevented from voting at Gallatin, Mo., on Aug. 6. Mob raids began and Mormons organized, armed themselves, and fought against the attacks as their county charter allowed. Apostle David W. Patten, who was in line to be president of the Church after Joseph Smith, was killed Oct. 25. Hearing exaggerated reports of Mormon armies, Missouri Gov. Lilburn W. Boggs, who refused to aid the Mormons or quell violence, signed the infamous order on Oct. 26 to drive out or exterminate the Mormons. Seventeen men and boys were killed at Haun's Mill on Oct. 30 by the unauthorized Livingston County Militia. On Oct. 31, Joseph Smith was arrested and the next day sentenced to death. Brig. Gen. A.W. Doniphan refused to carry out the order. On Nov. 2, the militia plundered Far West and drove out the Saints. The 12,000-15,000 LDS refugees in Missouri settled on the Mississippi River in Illinois where they established Nauvoo.

During this period, members found shelter in the more tolerant city of St. Louis, where citizens once raised funds for their aid. In 1844, a branch was started in St. Louis by LDS refugees. Shiploads of LDS immigrants used St. Louis as a port of debarkation. After the exodus from Nauvoo in 1846, more members came to St. Louis. By 1849, a district was formed with 3,000-4,000 members. The St. Louis Stake was organized in 1854. Immigrants earned money and helped build the city as they awaited overland passage. Many pioneer supplies were imported to Utah through St. Louis. The so-called "Utah War" of 1857 brought the end of the St. Louis Stake when Brigham Young called all members to Utah.

With the members gone, little missionary work occurred in Missouri until later in the century. The state became part of the Northern States Mission and in 1900 was transferred to the Southwestern States Mission, which became the Central States Mission in 1904. A branch in St. Louis was reorganized in 1898, and the Church entered an exhibit in the 1904 World's Fair at St. Louis. In 1915, Elder Spencer W. Kimball became president of the district and helped purchase a meetinghouse.

Mission headquarters moved to Independence in 1907. A meetinghouse was erected in 1913 in Independence.

By 1930, eight branches functioned at Independence, Joplin, Kansas City, St. Louis, Sedalia, St. Joseph, Springfield and Webb City.

The first modern stake in Missouri was the Kansas City (Missouri) Stake, created in Oct. 21, 1956, and it included one Kansas City war, the Independence Ward, Liberty Ward, St. Joseph Ward, Rock Hill Branch, and Albany and Chillicothe Sunday Schools.

The St. Louis Stake was organized in June 1, 1958, and additional stakes followed in the 1970s. On June 25, 1976, Gov. Christopher S. Bond signed an executive order rescinding the extermination order issued in 1838 by Gov. Lilburn W. Boggs.

The Missouri St. Louis Mission was created in 1977. Membership in Missouri in 1974 was 13,796, in 1980, 25,243 and in 1990, 35,084. On Dec. 29, 1990, the First Presidency announced plans for a temple in St. Louis.

As the temple was constructed, community leaders enthusiastically supported the effort. The temple's location at the intersection of two major freeways has raised awareness of the Church.

In Independence, local members have taken part in inter-faith activities. The visit of the Tabernacle Choir in 1992, performing in the RLDS Church's Auditorium, helped solidify friendships as well.

Sources: *Encyclopedic History of the Church* by Andrew Jenson; "Martin V. Witbeck, Former Utahn, Called to Preside over New Unit," *Church News*, Oct. 27, 1956; *Encyclopedia of Mormonism*, edited by Daniel H. Ludlow; "Missouri's Impact on the Church," by Max H Parkin, *Ensign*, April 1979; "Saints in Independence," by Janet Brigham, *Ensign*, June 1979; "The Saints in Saint Louis," by Violet Kimball, *Ensign*, March 1988; "Missouri Past Forgotten, Church gains," by Hal Knight, *Church News*, Oct. 20, 1979; "Growth continues in river port where Church thrived in 1850s," by John L. Hart, *Church News*, Jan. 20, 1990; *Church News*, Nov. 6, 1993; *Church News*, Jan. 8, 1994.

Stakes — 10
(Listed alphabetically by area as of Oct. 1, 1994.)

No.	Name	Organized	First President
North America Central Area — 8			
1563	Cape Girardeau Missouri	20 Oct 1985	David E. Payne
511	*Columbia Missouri †Columbia	19 Apr 1970	Samuel D. Richards
544	*Independence Missouri †Independence	25 Mar 1971	Melvin James Bennion
234	*Kansas City Missouri †Kansas City (Missouri, Kansas)	21 Oct 1956	Martin V. Witbeck
1071	Liberty Missouri	14 Oct 1979	Dell Earl Johnsen
265	Saint Louis (Missouri, Illinois) *Saint Louis Missouri	1 Jun 1958	Roy W. Oscarson
1634	Saint Louis Missouri North	15 Mar 1987	Neal C. Lewis
1118	Saint Louis Missouri South	16 Mar 1980	Verner Lorenzo Stromberg Jr.
North America Southwest Area — 2			
859	Joplin Missouri	28 Aug 1977	Kenneth Rae Martin
610	*Springfield Missouri †Ozark	29 Apr 1973	Carroll S. Claybrook
Discontinued			
2	Clay-Caldwell	3 Jul 1834	David Whitmer
3	Adam-Ondi-Ahman	28 Jun 1838	John Smith
6a	Saint Louis	4 Nov 1854	Milo Andrus

(14b) MISSOURI INDEPENDENCE MISSION
517 West Walnut,
Independence, MO 64050
Phone: (816) 252-6050

(153) MISSOURI ST. LOUIS MISSION
745 Craig Road, #306
Creve Coeur, MO 63141
Phone: (314) 872-8510

Montana

Year-end 1993: Est. population, 844,000; Members, 37,000; Stakes, 10; Wards, 61; Branches, 36; Missions, 1; Districts, 1; Percent LDS, 4.4, or one person in 23.

The Church's Fort Lemhi settlement on the Salmon River in Idaho lasted only from 1855 to 1858, but it familiarized various members with the trail to Montana that became an important trading route, known as the Montana Trail, for members following the Montana gold rush of the 1860s.

A Mormon, E.W. Van Etten, traded with Flathead Indians in the late 1850s, and a Mormon woman, Minnie Miller, wife of Henry G. Miller, was the first white woman to live in western Montana. When Col. Albert Sydney Johnston's army approached Utah in 1857, some members left Utah and moved to Montana.

After the gold discovery and subsequent gold rush, Mormon freighters hauled food and goods along the Montana Trail for substantial profit. The overland railway was completed in 1869 and afterward a Utah company was formed by Mormon leaders that constructed a narrow gauge railway from Ogden, Utah, to Butte, and the Northern Pacific Railway at Garrison, Mont., in 1884.

Although some members came to Montana in the gold rush and stayed, no Church units were organized. Evidently, all of these members fell away. In 1896, the Montana Mission was organized and efforts were made to find those members who had moved to Montana earlier. However, Church leaders did not encourage members to go to Montana to live.

Phineus Tempest was called as president of the mission. He soon organized a branch in Lima. On Oct. 27, 1897, Pres. Tempest's successor, Franklin S. Bramwell, and three missionaries met with Montana Gov. John E. Rickards and received the promise of religious freedom. Four converts were baptized near Gregson Springs on March 31, 1897. A meeting of 75 people was held in Anaconda, and a gathering of 300 met in Butte later that spring. The mission was dissolved into the Northwestern States Mission in 1898, after 71 converts had been baptized and the way paved for the establishment of the Church.

By 1930, Church organization had grown to 10 branches and a membership of 1,181 with meeting-houses in Anaconda, Butte, Allendale, Dillon, Great Falls and Sun River. Membership increased to 5,210 in 1940 and 6,416 in 1950.

Montana's first stake was created in Butte on June 28, 1953, and the first wards were created in Butte, Anaconda, Dillon, Bozeman, and Helena. Stake population was about 3,500.

Stakes were also created June 16, 1957, in Great Falls and Missoula. The Great Falls Stake had about 2,500 members and the Missoula Stake had 3,085 members. At that time, Montana had 14,223 members. That number increased to 23,890 in 1960. In 1980, membership was 30,784 and in 1990, 34,401.

Sources: *Mormonism in Montana,* theses in 1969 at Montana State University by Don Cornelius; *Encyclopedic History of the Church,* by Andrew Jenson.

Stakes — 10
(Listed alphabetically as of Oct. 1, 1994.)

No.	Name	Organized	First President
North America Central Area			
369	*Billings Montana		
	†Billings (Montana, Wyoming)	10 Feb 1963	Howard C. Anderson
849	Billings Montana East	12 Jun 1977	Wynn J. Ferrell
1066	Bozeman Montana	16 Sep 1979	Frank Wilbert Call
208	*Butte Montana		
	†Butte	28 Jun 1953	Edgar T. Henderson
244	*Great Falls Montana		
	†Great Falls	16 Jun 1957	Victor Bowen
976	Great Falls Montana East	5 Nov 1978	Howard Merle Hennebry
464	*Helena Montana		
	†Helena	8 Sep 1968	Ronald Rex Dalley
535	*Kalispell Montana		
	†Kalispell	20 Nov 1970	Roy K. Deming

243	*Missoula Montana		
	†Missoula	16 Jun 1957	Grant K. Patten
1074	Stevensville Montana	21 Oct 1979	Robert H. Sangster

Mission — 1

(As of Oct. 1, 1994; shown with historical number. See MISSIONS.)

(43a) MONTANA BILLINGS MISSION
1848 Rimrock Road
Billings, MT 59102
Phone: (406) 245-6146

Nebraska

Year-end 1993: Est. population, 1,593,000; Members, 14,000; Stakes, 4; Wards, 24; Branches, 20; Missions, 1; Percent LDS, 0.9, or one person in 114.

After the Saints were driven from Nauvoo, Ill., in February 1846, they carefully skirted the entire state of Missouri and traveled 300 miles before establishing a headquarters in Indian country west of the Missouri River. They negotiated with the Indians and then built the city of Winter Quarters. Eventually, some 1,000 homes were constructed for a population of 11,800. Though most of the homes were log cabins and dugouts, the city was as carefully laid out as the many Mormon colonies later founded.

The Saints created a city government, schools, ferries, bridges, developed trades — especially those to make and outfit wagons — established a mail service, and took time for dances and concerts. Many trades were plied en route to Winter Quarters. A stockade and water-powered grist mill were added later. Crops were planted.

Before the lead company had crossed the river into Nebraska, however, the mustering of 500 men for the Mormon Battalion was completed. The departure of 500 able men led to the advance company of pioneers waiting an extra year in Winter Quarters to prepare for the great overland journey.

It was from Winter Quarters that the first pioneer train under Brigham Young left on April 5, 1847. Nine other trains followed that year.

When Brigham Young returned from Utah in October, he received word that the Indian agent wanted the members off the Indian territory. So in the spring of 1848 the remaining members crossed back over the Missouri River and founded Kanesville in Iowa. They left Winter Quarters as a ghost settlement, which was burned in a prairie fire in the 1850s.

In 1854, the Florence Land Company, which included some Mormons, was organized to occupy the old Winter Quarters site, and from 1856 to 1864 Florence became an important Mormon pioneer staging area. An estimated 60,000 Mormon pioneers crossed the plains before the transcontinental railroad was completed in 1869. Many were outfitted in Florence, including the famous handcart companies of 1856-60. Today, Florence is part of greater Omaha. Only the pioneer cemetery and a gristmill remain from the Winter Quarters era.

While preparing to go west, Mormon travelers traded labor for food and helped establish Council Bluffs, Glenwood, Macedonia, Honey Creek and about 50 other towns. In the 1850s, Brigham Young hoped to establish settlements along the trail and started Genoa, or the "Nebraska Mission," in May 1857. Several other colonies were started. The so-called "Utah War" led to the migration west of most of these settlers, although those in Genoa remained until Indian agents forced them from the land in 1859.

Missionary work evidently started again in Nebraska in 1877 when Ferdinand F. Hintze and Anders Frandsen baptized 11 people and created a branch in Fremont, Dodge County.

The area was included in the Northwestern States Mission (later the Northern States Mission) until it became part of the Colorado Mission (later Western States Mission) in 1900. At this time the Omaha and Lincoln branches had been organized. A conference of missionaries was held April 21, 1901, for those laboring in Nebraska. In 1916, about 40 people attended a Sunday School in Lincoln. In 1921, a conference numbering from 75 to 200 was "the largest ever held by missionaries of this conference." Some 23 people were baptized under the direction of Elder Amasa Lyman. Progress was also made in Columbus, despite some opposition.

In 1930, the first meetinghouse had been erected, and districts functioned in East and West Nebraska with a total of 1,052 members. Nebraska's first stake was organized in Omaha, called Winter Quarters, on Dec. 11, 1960, with the Omaha 1st and 2nd wards, Bellevue and Lincoln wards in Nebraska. The Fremont, Grand Island, Kearney and Hastings branches were included in the stake. Membership in Nebraska in 1980 was 8,406, increasing in 1990 to 13,089, probably more than the number who ever lived at Winter Quarters at any one time. Members in Nebraska have continued to educate their communities on the significance of historical sites. Through education, community awareness of the contributions of the early members has improved.

Sources: *Liahona, The Elder's Journal,* June 21, 1921; *Encyclopedic History of the Church* by Andrew Jenson; "Winter Quarters, Nebraska," by E. Widtsoe Shumway, *Nebraska History,* June, 1954; "Proposed New Stake has Historic Setting," *Church News,* Dec. 10, 1960 and Dec. 17, 1960; "After Winter Quarters and Council Bluffs: The Mormons in Nebraska Territory, 1854-1867," by Michael W. Homer, *Nebraska History,* Winter 1984; "Mormons, Nebraska, and the Way West," by A. R. Mortensen, *Nebraska History,* December 1965; *Mormons at the Missouri,* 1846-1852," by Richard E. Bennett, University of Oklahoma Press, 1987; "Reflections on Winter Quarters," by Gail Geo. Holmes, unpublished; "Seven-year epic flowed along Missouri River with tragedy, triumph," by Gail Geo. Holmes, *Church News,* July 18, 1992.

Stakes — 4
(Listed alphabetically as of Oct. 1, 1994.)

No.	Name	Organized	First President
North America Central Area			
1803	Kearney Nebraska	16 Jun 1991	Arthur Haymore Taylor
663	*Lincoln Nebraska 2 Nov 1986		
	†Bellevue Nebraska	27 Oct 1974	Leonard Leroy Gregory
318	*Omaha Nebraska		
	†Winter Quarters (Nebraska, Iowa)	11 Dec 1960	William D. Hardy
1614	Papillion Nebraska	2 Nov 1986	Wayne Leon Mangelson

Missions — 2
(As of Oct. 1, 1994; shown with historical number. See MISSIONS.)

(289) NEBRASKA OMAHA MISSION
11904 Arbor Street, Suite 201
Omaha, NE 68144
Phone: (402) 691-0882

Nevada

Year-end 1993: Est. population, 1,425,000; Members, 117,000; Stakes, 26; Wards, 196; Branches, 28; Missions, 1; Temples, 1; Percent LDS, 8.2, or one person in 12.

Samuel Brannan and his party became the first Latter-day Saints to set foot in Nevada as they crossed from the West Coast to Utah in the spring of 1847 to report the arrival by ship of the Brannan party in San Francisco.

Three years later, after the discovery of gold in California, 13 members joined 65 non-LDS overlanders and crossed Nevada from Utah toward California. Seven men dropped out of the party near what is now Genoa, and founded a trading post. These men included Abner Blackburn, a former member of the Mormon Battalion who had found a little gold near the area on an earlier trip through. They traded profitably during the summer but sold out and returned to Utah. A year later, John Reece came with others and provisions in 13 wagons and established a trading post that became known as Mormon Station, located two miles south of the original trading post. The Reece station became a profitable trading post and site of Nevada's first colony, Genoa. Member and non-member settlers soon followed. Apostle Orson Hyde became president of the Carson Valley Stake, organized in 1856. Elder Hyde hoped to maintain the station for the assistance of immigrants coming via the West Coast, and did much to establish it. The LDS presence in the promising colony ended and the stake was dissolved when the settlers were recalled at the approach of Johnston's army to Salt Lake City.

In 1855, the same time colonists were sent to Genoa, a group of 30 men was sent to establish an Indian mission at the Meadows in southern Nevada at what is now Las Vegas. The party, under the direction of William Bringhurst, arrived June 15, 1855, and soon built a fort. They found farming difficult in the hot region, but discovered a lead mine and made friendships with the many Indians who lived nearby and on the Muddy River, a fertile area in a valley to the northwest.

Another mission was sent to mine the lead, which was partly silver, and years later became a prosperous silver mine. This metal, melted into bullets by the settlers, was the basis for a legend that Mormons used silver bullets. Both missions were recalled at the advance of Johnston's army. The abandoned fort was then named Fort Baker and served as an uninhabited but strategic outpost during the Civil War. It later became a ranch headquarters and foundation for Las Vegas, Nevada's largest city.

On May 6, 1864, colonists from St. George under the direction of Francis C. Lee arrived at what is now Panaca, a site earlier considered an alternative Church place of settlement should the Saints be driven from Salt Lake City by Johnston's army. The Lee party made a prosperous settlement, the oldest continuous Mormon colony in the state. In December 1864, Anson Call and a group established Call's landing on the Colorado River, about 12 miles above the present Hoover Dam. This settlement briefly became an important inland dock for boats that navigated the Colorado River from the Pacific Ocean with goods for Utah settlers and the U.S. Army in Arizona. The settlement continued until 1867.

The Muddy River area north of Las Vegas, known to the Church ever since the Bringhurst mission to the Meadows in 1855, was settled, beginning May 22, 1865, under the direction of Joseph Warren Foote. The long growing season and fertile land helped the settlers survive the difficulties of that frontier. Several colonies began but were eventually abandoned when the land became part of Nevada, and Nevada officials demanded back taxes. The area was re-settled in the 1880s and the Overton Branch was reorganized in 1883. Overton became headquarters of Nevada's first permanent stake, the Moapa Stake, in 1912. In 1877, Bunkerville was founded when families practiced the United Order for a time.

In 1897, the government offered the Church 15,000 acres in the White Pine area in remuneration for Church livestock that the government confiscated and lost following the 1882 Edmunds Act. Here, the present-day communities of Lund and Preston were founded.

Completion of the railroad from Salt Lake to Los Angeles in 1905 began steady growth in Nevada. The first Sunday School in Las Vegas was organized by Newell Leavitt in 1914 and became a ward in 1925. In the 1920s many Utahns moved to Nevada in search of better economic conditions. Membership in the state increased from 2,328 in 1920, to 5,319 in 1930 and to 9,139 by 1940.

Construction of the Hoover Dam in the 1940s brought an influx of people, and that same decade gaming, was legalized in 1931, was widely promoted. Members did not support the move, but, as a minority, avoided confrontation. The Las Vegas Stake was created in 1954, and now half (13) of Nevada's stakes are in the Las Vegas metropolitan area.

Substantial membership also grew in the Humboldt (Elko) and Ely areas, though these communities were not originally founded by Mormons. Eastern Nevada reflects a great deal of Utah culture. Members have increasingly greater strength today in this area where colonization efforts failed during Brigham Young's day. Members also gathered in western Nevada in Reno and nearby Sparks. Growth in "the Silver State" has been steady. The Las Vegas Nevada Temple was dedicated in 1989 as "an oasis of peace and light." On Nov. 14, 1993, a regional welfare complex was dedicated near the site of the original fort. The new facilities comprised 9,000 square feet of area for services to help care for the growing southern Nevada membership.

Nevada membership in 1950 was 14,223; in 1960, 23,890; in 1970, 44,282; in 1980, 71,462; and in 1990, 110,060.

Sources: *Encyclopedic History of the Church* by Andrew Jenson; "The Mormons in Nevada: an Historical Portrait," by Leonard J. Arrington, *Las Vegas Sun*; *The Old Fort,* compiled by the Daughters of the Utah Pioneers; History of the Las Vegas First Ward, compiled by Marion B. Earl; "Panaca: Mormon Outpost Among Mining Camps, The Afterlife of St. Mary's County; or, Utah's Penumbra in Eastern Nevada," by James W. Hulse, *Utah Historical Quarterly,* Vol. 55, (1987); "Regional Welfare Center with multiple facilities dedicated in Las Vegas," by Ashley Hall, *Church News,* Nov. 20, 1993.

Stakes — 27
(Listed alphabetically as of Oct. 1, 1994.)

No.	Name	Organized	First President
North America Southeast Area			
906	Carson City Nevada	9 Apr 1978	Edgar Gilbert Carlson
143	*Elko Nevada		
	†Humboldt	31 May 1942	Rodney S. Williams
96	*Ely Nevada		
	†Nevada	19 Sep 1926	Carl K. Conrad
500	*Fallon Nevada		
	†Fallon	18 Jan 1970	G. Verl Hendrix
1650	Fallon Nevada South	30 Aug 1987	Robert Floyd Weed
228	Henderson Nevada Lake Mead 2 Mar 1993		
	*Henderson Nevada		
	†Lake Mead (Nevada, Arizona, Calif.)	19 Aug 1956	James I. Gibson
605	*Henderson Nevada Black Mountain 10 Mar 1992		
	*Henderson Nevada West		
	†Lake Mead West	11 Mar 1973	Joseph Dee Reese
216	*Las Vegas Nevada		
	†Las Vegas	10 Oct 1954	Thomas Gay Meyers
451	*Las Vegas Nevada Central		
	†Las Vegas Central	18 Feb 1968	Samuel M. Davis
915	Las Vegas Nevada East	30 Apr 1978	Kendall E. Jones
1519	Las Vegas Nevada Green Valley	3 Mar 1985	Roger Lee Hunt

1542	Las Vegas Nevada Lakes	23 Jun 1985	Dennis E. Simmons
1775	Las Vegas Nevada Lone Mountain	4 Nov 1990	Scott Keith Higginson
1406	*Las Vegas Meadows 4 Nov 1990		
	†Las Vegas Nevada West	20 Mar 1983	Terry Dale Rogers
401	*Las Vegas Nevada Paradise 30 Apr 1978		
	*Las Vegas Nevada East		
	†Las Vegas East	24 Jan 1965	Rulon A. Earl
855	Las Vegas Nevada Redrock	14 Aug 1977	E. LeGrande Bindrup
1776	Las Vegas Nevada Sandstone	4 Nov 1990	Keith R. Edwards
509	*Las Vegas Nevada South		
	†Las Vegas South	29 Mar 1970	Erval L. Bindrup
1576	Las Vegas Nevada Sunrise	17 Nov 1985	Norman Wellington Gates
1777	Las Vegas Nevada Warm Springs	4 Nov 1990	Roger Lee Hunt
64	*Logandale Nevada		
	†Moapa	9 Jun 1912	Willard L. Jones
1974	Mesquite Nevada	13 Feb 1994	Elwin J. Whipple
308	*North Las Vegas Nevada		
	†Las Vegas North	6 Nov 1960	William L. Taylor
135	*Reno Nevada		
	†Reno (Nevada, California)	9 Feb 1941	Nathan T. Hurst
635	Reno Nevada North	24 Mar 1974	Wilford Darrell Foote
339	*Sparks Nevada		
	†Reno North (Nevada, California)	22 Oct 1961	Vern Waldo
1296	Winnemucca Nevada	11 Oct 1981	Kenneth H. Lords
	Discontinued		
7a	Carson Valley	4 Oct 1856	Orson Hyde
	1858		

Mission — 1
(As of Oct. 1, 1994; shown with historical number. See MISSIONS.)

(127) NEVADA LAS VEGAS MISSION
3910 Pecos-McLeod, Suite B-140
Las Vegas, NV 89121-4304
Phone: (702) 435-0025

New Hampshire

Year-end 1993: Est. population, 1,133,000; Members, 6,400; Stakes, 3; Wards, 12; Branches, 5; Missions, 1; Percent LDS, 0.6, or one person in 177.

Elders Orson Pratt and Lyman E. Johnson arrived in New Hampshire in 1832. During their 26-day stay they baptized 20 people in Bath, N.H., among whom were Hazen Aldrich and Amasa M. Lyman. Later that year Elders Orson Hyde and Samuel H. Smith preached and baptized others. A branch of 15 members was created in July 1833, at Dalton, Coos County. Other branches were created in New Rowley and Lyman, Grafton County. The latter was organized in 1835 by Erastus Snow, then 17 years old. A conference held in Nashua, N.H. on Dec. 15, 1840, was attended by 55 people.

In 1841, Zadock Parker wrote that the Grafton County Branch continued to meet and that he baptized 13 more people. Some 20-30 members continued to meet in the Gilsum Branch. Eli P. Maginn wrote that he could not "fill from one to twenty of the calls for preaching; there is the greatest excitement in the country."

The Petersborough Branch was created, and by 1843, it had 115 members. Most of the members "removed" to the West following the martyrdom of the Prophet Joseph Smith. In 1856, Solomon Mack headed the membership in New Hampshire. This state was part of the Eastern States Mission, but little work was done during the next few years. The mission was discontinued from 1869 to 1893, when New Hampshire was placed in the New England Conference. The New Hampshire Conference was created in 1909, combined with Maine, 1913-1925, with Vermont, 1925-1928, and in 1928, included in the Canadian Mission. In 1930, the New Hampshire District was headquartered at Nashua, evidently under the direction of a missionary. A branch was organized in Nashua by September 1937, the date of the creation of the New England Mission, but later dissolved. A branch in Concord was created in 1945. In 1951, Sunday Schools were held in Keene and Portsmouth.

Additional branches and Sunday schools were subsequently organized. In 1970, the Merrimack (Nashua) Stake was created with wards in Keene, Laconia, Manchester, Portsmouth and Concord, with two wards and a branch in Massachusetts and a branch in Maine.

Wards and branches continued to be organized. A branch in Petersborough was formed in 1980. The

New Hampshire Manchester Mission was created in 1987. Membership in New Hampshire in 1980 was 4,237, increasing to 6,383 in 1990.

Sources: *Encyclopedic History of the Church* by Andrew Jenson; Church directories, 1920-1980; "4 new stakes are organized," *Church News*, April 4, 1970; "The gospel net," *Church News*, Nov. 19, 1977; "She helped nurture fledgling Church during life of service," by J Malan Heslop, *Church News*, Jan. 23, 1993.

Stakes — 3
(Listed alphabetically as of Oct. 1, 1994.)

No.	Name	Organized	First President
North America Northeast Area			
1289	Concord New Hampshire	6 Sep 1981	John Tucker Hills
1290	*Exeter New Hampshire		
	†Portland Maine	6 Sep 1981	J. Barton Seymour
507	*Nashua New Hampshire 9 May 1980		
	*Manchester New Hampshire		
	†Merrimack	22 Mar 1970	William A. Fresh

Mission — 1
(As of Oct. 1, 1994; shown with historical number. See MISSIONS.)

(195) NEW HAMPSHIRE MANCHESTER
Bedford Farms, Bldg. 6
Bedford, NH 03110-6532
Phone: (603) 622-0429

New Jersey

Year-end 1993: Est. population, 7,931,000; Members, 17,000; Stakes, 4; Wards, 26; Branches, 18 Missions, 1; Percent LDS, 0.2, or one person in 467.

The first missionaries to work in New Jersey were Elders Orson Pratt and Lyman E. Johnson, who arrived in the state in 1832. In 1837, Elders Parley P. Pratt, Benjamin Winchester and Jedediah M. Grant preached and converted people in New Jersey. Elder Winchester preached in Toms River, Ocean County, and baptized 11. By 1840, the branch had 90 members. Several missionaries labored in New Jersey during the next few years. At a conference in New York on Oct. 19, 1842, branches were represented from Patterson, Lodi Print Works, Wacake, Newark and Mead's Basin in New Jersey. Converts often joined the westward movement. For example, William Smith arrived in Illinois from New Jersey on April 22, 1844, with a group of 40 or 50.

Other branches were organized so that by 1848, 21 dotted the New Jersey map. After the exodus from Nauvoo, missionary work slowed. Branches in Toms Corner and Hornerstown existed in 1857. Many others had "gathered" previously.

Little work was performed until well after the trek West. In 1879, B.F. Cummings reported meeting some "old-time Saints" in Perth Amboy, N. J., whom he tried to inspire with the spirit of gathering. Ten members from there migrated to Utah in 1896.

In the 1920s, Ernest L. Wilkinson, who later became president of Brigham Young University, was among the presidents of the Newark Branch. A branch also functioned in Metuchen in the 1930s with Robert H. Daines as branch president. When the New Jersey Stake was created in 1960, it included the Montclair, North Jersey and Short Hills wards and the New Brunswick, Trenton, Monmouth and Lakehurst branches.

By 1974 membership reached 6,799. By 1980, membership was 10,512 in three stakes, and in 1990, reached 16,000. The New Jersey Morristown Mission was created in 1987. Local and state dignitaries took part in the Church's sesquicentennial in New Jersey, which was celebrated in 1988.

Sources: Eastern States Mission history; *Deseret News*, Jan. 7, 1879, and Jan. 8, 1896; *Encyclopedic History of the Church,* by Andrew Jenson; "New Stake Created By Division of New York," *Church News*, March 5, 1960; "Neighborliness: Daines Style," by Orson Scott Card, *Ensign*, April 1977; "New Jersey Church members celebrate 150 years," *Church News*, Sept. 17, 1988,

Stakes — 4
(Listed alphabetically as of Oct. 1, 1994.)

No.	Name	Organized	First President
North America Northeast Area			
1252	Caldwell New Jersey	12 Apr 1981	Weldon Courtney McGregor
1084	*Cherry Hill New Jersey 23 Sep 1986		
	†Pitman New Jersey	18 Nov 1979	Victor Warren Hammond

429	*East Brunswick New Jersey		
	†New Jersey Central (N.J., Penn.)	26 Mar 1967	Robert H. Daines
292	*Morristown New Jersey 26 Feb 1976		
	*Caldwell New Jersey		
	†New Jersey	28 Feb 1960	George H. Mortimer

Mission — 1
(As of Oct. 1, 1994; shown with historical number. See MISSIONS.)

(202) NEW JERSEY MORRISTOWN MISSION
2 Ridgedale Ave., #210
Cedar Knolls, NJ 07927-1100
Phone: (201) 326-9494

New Mexico

Year-end 1993: Est. population, 1,632,000; Members, 51,000; Stakes, 12; Wards, 81; Branches, 31; Missions, 1; Percent LDS, 3.1, or one person in 32.

In 1831, just one year after the organization of the Church, Oliver Cowdery preached to Indians in Missouri and, from that experience, reported to Joseph Smith of a civilized "Navashoes" (Navajo) tribe living 300 miles west of Santa Fe. Leaders once discussed sending a delegation to Santa Fe in 1844 to begin exploration for a possible colonization site. In 1846, the Mormon Battalion crossed what is now New Mexico during its historic march to the Pacific Coast from Fort Leavenworth, Kan. The first part of the battalion arrived in Santa Fe Oct. 9, 1846. At Santa Fe, the battalion sent a detachment of sick to winter in Colorado.

Missionary work among the Indians perhaps began as early as the 1860s when Jacob Hamblin and James S. Brown may have traveled to New Mexico in their labors. Missionaries called to Mexico in 1875 included Ammon M. Tenney and Robert H. Smith. Elders Tenney and Smith found success while laboring among the Zuni Indians on the Little Colorado River in New Mexico, baptizing more than 100. In 1876, a colony was established among the converts. It succeeded until smallpox decimated the Indian converts. Two years later, at an adjacent site, LDS settlers founded what is now Ramah. In 1878, the settlement of Burnham (originally called Fruitland) was founded, followed in 1883 by the community of Luna. The settlers at Luna had clear title to their land, but had trouble with a cattle baron who claimed the area. The San Juan Stake, organized from settlers of the Utah "Hole-in-the-Rock" expedition of 1879-1880, included members in the New Mexico settlements of Kirtland and Waterflow. During this period, settlers were troubled by outlaws. A severe drought from 1900-1904 seriously affected settlers, but eliminated the outlaws.

Nearly all of the Mormon settlements in New Mexico absorbed some refugees from the Mormon colonies in Mexico during the Mexican Revolution of 1912. Other refugees founded the town of Virden, near the Mexican border.

The Young Stake was created in 1912. Other units in New Mexico were made wards and were included in Arizona and Utah stakes. By 1930, membership in the state was 1,643.

The Albuquerque Stake was created in 1957. Membership increased during the 1960s and 1970s. The New Mexico Albuquerque Mission was organized in 1975.

In the 1980s, H. Vern Payne, president of the Santa Fe New Mexico Stake, served as chief justice of the New Mexico Supreme Court. A number of LDS scientists worked at the U.S. research facility at Los Alamos.

Membership in the state in 1980 was 36,881, and in 1990, 48,000. Members have learned to interact with patience and understanding in a state where three cultures meld — Indian, Hispanic and Anglo.

Sources: *Encyclopedic History of the Church* by Andrew Jenson; "New Mexico and the Mormons," by Robert Thomas Devitt, *Southwest Heritage*, Vol. 6, Spring 1976; *Do You Remember Luna? 100 Years of Pioneer History*, published by the Luna Ward, Adobe Press, 1983; *Church News*, July 24, 1983.

Stakes — 12
(Listed alphabetically as of Oct. 1, 1994.)

No.	Name	Organized	First President
North America Southwest Area			
250	*Albuquerque New Mexico		
	†Albuquerque	27 Oct 1957	William J. Wilson
422	*Albuquerque New Mexico East		
	†Albuquerque East	25 Sep 1966	George Van Lemmon

1353	Albuquerque New Mexico South	20 Jun 1982	Ivan Gary Waddoups
742	*Bloomfield New Mexico 19 Sep 1982		
	†Farmington New Mexico East	1 Feb 1976	Marlo L. Webb
63	*Farmington New Mexico		
	†Young (New Mexico, Colorado)	21 May 1912	David Halls
687	Gallup New Mexico	16 Mar 1975	Donald C. Tanner
1298	Grants New Mexico	18 Oct 1981	Elbert Leon Roundy
1363	Kirtland New Mexico	19 Sep 1982	John Scot Fishburn
654	Las Cruces New Mexico	25 Aug 1974	Harold A. Daw
816	Roswell New Mexico	13 Mar 1977	J. Allen Levie
1219	Santa Fe New Mexico	4 Jan 1981	H. Vern Payne
1409	Silver City New Mexico	17 Apr 1983	Hal Butler Keeler

Mission — 1
(As of Oct. 1, 1994; shown with historical number. See MISSIONS.)

(128) NEW MEXICO ALBUQUERQUE MISSION
6100 Seagull Lane, N.E., #109
Albuquerque, NM 87109
Phone: (505) 888-0225

New York

Year-end 1993: Est. population, 18,252,000; Members, 44,000; Stakes, 9; Wards, 57; Branches, 50; Missions, 3; Districts, 2; Percent LDS, 0.2, or one person in 414.

In 1820, Joseph Smith received "the glorious vision which marked the ushering in of the Dispensation of the Fullness of Times" in a grove of trees near Palmyra, N.Y. Later, sacred records were received from the Hill Cumorah and were translated in Pennsylvania and Fayette, N.Y., into the Book of Mormon, published by Egbert Grandin at Palmyra in early 1830. On April 6, 1830, the Church was organized at the home of Peter Whitmer Sr. at Fayette, with some 50 people and six official members present. Samuel H. Smith began a missionary journey in late June. By year's end, membership increased to more than 100 with members from Colesville to Canandaigua. Many moved in 1831 to Kirtland, Ohio.

Twenty-five revelations of the Doctrine and Covenants were received in New York.

Among successful later missionaries were Martin and Emer Harris, who baptized 100 people in Chenango Point, N.Y., in 1832. During the next few years, missionaries organized several branches as well as the Freedom and Black River conferences. In July 1837, Parley P. Pratt was the first missionary to preach in New York City, and he organized a branch there. Branches were also organized in Long Island and Brooklyn. While there, he published his *Voice of Warning* pamphlet. In 1839, John P. Greene became the first president of the Eastern States Mission, headquartered in New York City.

A group of LDS emigrants, some 41 people, arrived from England on the ship *Britannia* July 20, 1840, the first of an estimated 50,000 to arrive between 1840 and 1890.

A newspaper, *The Prophet,* began publication in 1844 in New York. On Feb. 4, 1846, Samuel Brannan headed a company of Saints aboard the sailing ship *Brooklyn* that sailed from New York harbor to California. They also carried the press to California that was formerly used to print *The Prophet*. *The Mormon*, a weekly newspaper, was printed by John Taylor in 1855. Afterwards, because of the so-called "Utah War" most missionaries were withdrawn from New York. The Civil War also hindered work; little progress was realized until the 1880s. By 1890, the New York Conference was organized. New York was returned to the Eastern States Mission in 1893, when in January, Elder Job Pingree was set apart to re-open work in New York City. Headquarters at the time were established in Brooklyn. By 1900, the mission had a total membership of 975 in eight conferences within three states and Canada. When the radio came into use in the 1920s, missionaries were quick to take advantage of the new media to promote the gospel cause. By 1930, branches had been organized in Albany, Brooklyn, Erie, Hudson, Rochester and Susquehanna (including parts of Pennsylvania). By that time, the Church had purchased the Sacred Grove and the Hill Cumorah.

The first Book of Mormon pageant was produced in 1928, a forerunner to the present pageant, "America's Witness for Christ" that has attracted as many as 100,000 people during its seven-night run.

The New York Stake was created in 1934. The stake took part in Church events, including a special exhibit on the centennial of the coming of Elijah in 1936 and observance of the centennial of the sailing ship *Brooklyn* in 1946. LDS servicemen and leaders of businesses headquartered in New York helped strengthen the stake.

In 1964, the Church's pavilion at the World's Fair pioneered media technology and drew a large response to the specially made film,"Man's Search for Happiness." This paved the way for future use of technology in spreading the gospel message.

Membership in New York in 1974 reached 17,000. In 1980, the sesquicentennial of the Church was held jointly in Fayette, N.Y., and Salt Lake City, Utah, as President Spencer W. Kimball spoke to the Church in conference by satellite from the rebuilt Peter Whitmer cabin at the site where the Church was organized.

Membership in New York in 1980 was 26,000, increasing to nearly 40,000 in 1990.

Sources: *Encyclopedic History of the Church,* by Andrew Jenson; *Church News,* May 16, 1936; and Jan. 19, 1946; "The Church in New York City," by William Woolf, *Improvement Era,* December 1938; *Palmyra — a Bicentennial Celebration,* edited by Betty Troskosky, published by Historic Palmyra Inc., 1989; "LDS history unfolded in New York and Ohio," *Church News,* Jan. 7, 1989; "Legacy of the Mormon Pavilion," by Brent L. Top, *Ensign,* October 1989.

Stakes — 9
(Listed alphabetically as of Oct. 1, 1994.)

No.	Name	Organized	First President
North America Northeast Area			
485	*Albany New York		
	†Hudson River	8 Jun 1969	Thomas Lorin Hicken
657	Buffalo New York	15 Sep 1974	Ronald Glen Vincent
110	*New York New York		
	†New York (N.Y., Connecticut)	9 Dec 1934	Fred G. Taylor
483	*Owego New York 9 Oct 1990		
	*Ithaca New York		
	†Susquehanna	25 May 1969	Harold R. Capener
439	*Plainview New York		
	†Long Island	20 Aug 1967	Gordon E. Crandall
346	*Rochester New York		
	†Cumorah	21 Jan 1962	Bryant W. Rossiter
1543	Rochester New York Palmyra	30 Jun 1985	Kay R. Whitmore
711	Syracuse New York	19 Oct 1975	George Dale Weight
909	*Yorktown New York 28 Aug 1978		
	†Kitchiwan New York	30 Apr 1978	Victor B. Jex
Discontinued			
1574	New York New York East	17 Nov 1985	Mark Eliot Butler
	19 May 1991		

Missions — 4
As of Oct. 1, 1994; shown with historical number. See MISSIONS.)

(290) NEW YORK NEW YORK NORTH MISSION
700 White Plains Road, Suite 34
Scarsdale, NY 10583
Phone: (914) 722-4105

(77) NEW YORK ROCHESTER MISSION
P.O. Box 92580
Rochester, NY 14692
Phone: (716) 248-8570

(2) NEW YORK NEW YORK SOUTH MISSION
55 Northern Blvd., #206
Great Neck, NY 11021
Phone: (516) 365-6023

(299) NEW YORK UTICA
P.O. Box 220
New Hartford, NY 13413
Phone: (315) 733-4580

North Carolina

Year-end 1993: Est. population, 7,051,000; Members, 48,000; Stakes, 12; Wards, 74; Branches, 34; Missions, 2; Percent LDS: 0.7, or one person in 147.

Evidently the first missionary to enter North Carolina was Jedediah M. Grant. On May 18, 1838, he reported that he had preached for six months in Stokes, Surrey and Rockingham counties in North Carolina and baptized four people. In 1840, two additional missionaries joined Elder Grant, and they soon baptized another six or eight people. Missionaries also began work in other parts of the state. Writing in 1844, Elder John Eldridge said meetings he held "caused the greatest stirs imaginable. . . . I never thought that one poor mortal could make such a stir." He mentioned "some" baptisms, and also located earlier converts, whom he encouraged to gather to Zion.

Elder Grant wrote in 1845 that before he left North Carolina, he had organized a conference of 200 members in seven branches, and 150 more had joined since he left.

Following the exodus of the main body of the Church from Nauvoo, Ill., in 1846, little work was done for some time in North Carolina. In 1868, a Southern convert, Elder Henry G. Boyle, wrote that he'd held 40 public meetings, baptized 30 members and organized the Surrey County Branch. This branch (soon changed to Pilot Mountain) was dissolved following migration to the West in 1870.

The Southern States Mission was created in 1875 and the Pilot Mountain Branch was reorganized 1876. The Mount Airy Branch was organized July 28, 1879, and the Burke County Branch followed in 1885. Continuation of these branches was sporadic as converts migrated to the West. Membership in 1894 was 128, with 35 immigrating to the West during the previous three years. Some 1,000 members from surrounding areas attended a conference held in Bradford Cross Roads on Nov. 21, 1894. After 1895, members were encouraged to remain in North Carolina.

Anti-Mormon sentiment was strong, but the majority of citizens remained above mob actions. In 1906, however, a newly completed meetinghouse on Harker's Island was burned and missionaries driven out by a mob. The meetinghouse was replaced in 1936 and the island's members remained faithful.

Occasional mobs gathered in various other locations, but after the turn of the century, public attitudes generally improved and missionaries were offered more freedom to preach.

Over the next 30 years, many local leaders presided over branches and Sunday Schools, forming a strong base of experience. In 1921 Andrew Jenson, visiting as Church historian, reported three branches and 15 Sunday Schools in North Carolina. Meetinghouses were built in Mount Airy, Hampstad, Union Ridge, Wilmington, Goldsboro and Gilreath by 1930. Membership in the state then was 2,725.

North Carolina was divided into the East and West districts in 1935. James L. Bennett Sr. was the first local member to be district president, sustained on March 26, 1939. The Central District was created July 11, 1948. A large building program was started in 1947 and 16 buildings were subsequently added.

In 1961, the North Carolina Stake was created from the East District, and the Central District was organized into the Greensboro Stake the next month.

Membership in the state in 1980 was 29,512, and in 1990, 45,960. North Carolina members were among many from Southern states to respond to storm-caused disasters in the South in the 1990s.

Sources: *Encyclopedic History of the Church* by Andrew Jenson; *History of The Church of Jesus Christ of Latter-day Saints in North Carolina,* by Wallace R. Draughon; Members provide outpouring of help," *Church News,* Sept. 12, 1992; "Fierce storm claims lives of 3," *Church News,* March 20, 1993.

Stakes — 12
(Listed alphabetically as of Oct. 1, 1994.)

No.	Name	Organized	First President
North America Southeast Area			
1086	Asheville North Carolina	25 Nov 1979	Luther Andrew Goad
1606	Charlotte North Carolina Central	21 Sep 1986	Kenneth Larson
591	*Charlotte North Carolina South	21 Sep 1986	
	†Charlotte	19 Nov 1972	Byron Cole Williams
	*Charlotte North Carolina		
1637	Durham North Carolina	3 May 1987	James L. Bennett Jr.
698	Fayetteville North Carolina	8 Jun 1975	Leland Reid Fillmore
1344	Goldsboro North Carolina	30 May 1982	James William Dixon
335	*Greensboro North Carolina		
	†Greensboro	13 Sep 1961	Eugene A. Gulledge
1371	Hickory North Carolina	31 Oct 1982	Gordon M. Thornton
332	*Kinston North Carolina		
	†North Carolina	27 Aug 1961	Cecil E. Reese
363	*Raleigh North Carolina		
	†Raleigh	9 Dec 1962	William V. Bartholomew
574	*Wilmington North Carolina		
	†Wilmington	21 May 1972	Dean Bevin Powell Jr.
881	*Winston-Salem North Carolina	25 Nov 1979	
	†Statesville North Carolina	20 Nov 1977	Michael Stephen Bullock

Missions — 2
(As of Oct. 1, 1994; shown with historical number. See MISSIONS.)

(105) NORTH CAROLINA CHARLOTTE MISSION
6407 Idlewild, #533
Charlotte, NC 28212
Phone: (704) 563-1560

(186) NORTH CAROLINA RALEIGH MISSION
6508 Falls of Neuse, #100
Raleigh, NC 27615-6845
Phone: (919) 876-2091

North Dakota

Year-end 1993: Est. population, 639,000; Members, 4,800; Stakes, 1; Wards, 3; Branches, 12; Districts, 1; Percent LDS, 0.7, or one person in 133.

Missionary work in the Dakotas began in 1883, but the first recorded work in North Dakota occurred in 1885 when four elders labored from house to house across the scattered farmland. The missionaries made friends in the "northern part, [in] Johnstown [Grand Forks County] especially. . . . The Elders are bound to leave those paths through the winter season, so as not to be exposed to the cold, which is a drawback to the Mission." In 1885, it was reported that there were three members in the Dakotas.

South and North Dakota were organized into separate conferences on July 5, 1898, and Charles A. Haacke was appointed president of the North Dakota Conference. "The Lord has seen fit to carry the Gospel to this northern state," a report in the *Deseret News* noted. Two pairs of missionaries started in Fairmont, N.D., but found little success so they planned to go north. Before leaving they held a prayer meeting in a grove of box elder trees near the train station. Afterward, one pair of elders traveled to Wahpeton and one to Fargo. In Fargo, missionaries were warned by the mayor that he would do everything he could to obstruct them. Local newspapers were more accommodating, however, and published favorable reports of the missionaries. In 1899, the missionaries transferred to South Dakota "as very little good was being done in North Dakota."

In 1900, North Dakota was taken from the Central States Mission and placed in the Colorado Mission (changed in 1907 to the Western States Mission). After the turn of the century, a convert from Montana named Sitting Eagle moved to North Dakota and explained the gospel to many people. Chief Moses White Horse corresponded with the missionaries and received a copy of the Book of Mormon. When Elders Lewis Roberts and Russell Woolf first visited Shell Village in the summer of 1914, they taught 108 Indians and baptized seven converts. Within a few years the Sully Lake Branch, under Indian leadership, included 40 members from the Fort Berthold Reservation. This unit comprised the majority of membership in the state for many years.

In 1919, a meetinghouse was completed in Sully Lake, and by 1930, a second meetinghouse had been completed in Grand Forks. Membership in 1930 was 145. In 1943, member Dorothy Hanks recalled that the Fargo Branch consisted of five to 10 people attending meetings in the basement of the YMCA building.

After 1950, the Church organizations began to increase with converts and members moving in. Buildings were erected and leaders began traveling more to nurture small branches. In the 1970s, more professionals moved in and continued strengthening the branches.

Church history was made Aug. 7, 1977, when the Fargo North Dakota Stake was created. With its creation, every state in the union had a stake within its boundaries. The new stake had a population of 2,000 with four wards and seven branches. Church membership in 1980, was 3,495 and in 1990, 4,570. In the late 1980s and 1990s, the Church became better known as members took part in many service projects in their communities.

Sources: *Church News*, Aug. 13, 1977, Dec. 24, 1977; March 11, 1989; *Encyclopedic History of the Church* by Andrew Jenson; *Deseret News*, 57:273; Northern States Mission history.

Stake — 1
(As of Oct. 1, 1994.)

No.	Name	Organized	First President
North America Central Area			
852	Fargo North Dakota	7 Aug 1977	John R. Price

Ohio

Year-end 1993: Est. population, 11,135,000; Members, 40,000; Stakes, 11; Wards, 68; Branches, 31; Missions, 2; Districts, 1; Percent LDS, 0.3, or one person in 287.

One month after Parley P. Pratt was baptized in New York on Sept. 1, 1830, he began his first missionary journey. In the company of Oliver Cowdery, Peter Whitmer Jr. and Richard Ziba Peterson, he returned to Ohio, where he previously homesteaded, on a mission to the Native Americans. Before they reached the Native Americans, however, they taught the gospel to Sidney Rigdon, who was then a preacher, and to his congregation in Painesville, near Kirtland. Within a week, a nucleus for the Church was established in Kirtland. In a few weeks they had baptized 127 people including Rigdon and Frederick G. Williams. Later the missionaries preached to Wyandot Indians in Sandusky, Ohio, and to Delaware Indians in Missouri.

In 1831, Joseph Smith was instructed by revelation to go to Ohio. He made the trip in February, and met

Newel K. Whitney at the Gilbert and Whitney store in Kirtland. He and his wife, Emma, lived with Whitney for a time. Members soon gathered to Kirtland, and in June, Joseph received the revelation naming Missouri as the gathering place. From 1831 to 1838, Kirtland was headquarters of the Church with the first stake in the Church created there in 1834. Some 46 revelations were received in the Whitney store, and an additional 16 at the nearby John Johnson farm. In all, 65 revelations of the Doctrine and Covenants were received in Ohio. Numerous visions were received here, and priesthood keys restored. The Quorum of the Twelve was restored here, as was the First Quorum of the Seventy. Newspapers were started, and missionaries sent to other areas in the United States, Canada and Great Britain. Lorenzo Snow, president of the Church from 1898 to 1901, was born in Ohio in 1814.

Construction of the Kirtland Temple began June 5, 1833, and it was dedicated March 27, 1836. In its prime, Kirtland had some 3,200 members. The Saints left Kirtland and surrounding areas for Missouri, mostly completing the exodus in 1838. Apostle Lyman Wight returned to Kirtland in 1842 and re-baptized some 200 members. The temple was acquired in the late 1800s by the Reorganized Church of Jesus Christ of Latter Day Saints and opened for tours.

Ohio was part of the Northern States Mission until 1899, when it was included in the Southern States Mission as a place were ill missionaries could come to recover. In 1926, it was returned to the Northern States Mission.

In 1930, Ohio had two conferences with branches in Akron, Cincinnati, Dayton, Middleton, Portsmouth and Toledo. The Cincinnati and Dayton branches had meetinghouses. Membership was 899.

In 1949, Ohio became part of the Great Lakes Mission. The Ohio Mission was created in 1967.

In 1954, a branch meetinghouse was dedicated in Cleveland by President David O. McKay. Work prospered in Cincinnati, Columbus and Cleveland where stakes were organized in 1958, 1961 and 1963, respectively.

Full-time missionaries returned to Kirtland in 1977, the same year the Kirtland Ward of the Cleveland Ohio Stake was created. In 1979, the Church acquired the Newel K. Whitney store, and it has since become a well-visited historic site.

In 1980, membership in the state reached 28,000, and in 1990, 38,000.

Sources: *Encyclopedic History of the Church* by Andrew Jenson; "Kirtland: The Crucial Years," by Milton V. Backman Jr., *Ensign*, January 1979; "Kirtland Today," by Janet Brigham, *Ensign*, February 1979; "Kirtland stirs once again as Church grows in Ohio," by Hal Knight, *Church News*, Sept. 22, 1979; *Ohio History*, by Joseph H. Young, unpublished manuscript, Dec. 21, 1979; *Church News*, Nov. 29, 1958, Nov. 3, 1979, March 18, 1979 and Jan. 7, 1989.

Stakes — 11
(Listed alphabetically as of Oct. 1, 1994)

No.	Name	Organized	First President
North America Northeast Area			
696	Akron Ohio	25 May 1975	Carmen J. Libutti
270	*Cincinnati Ohio		
	†Cincinnati (Ohio, Kentucky)	23 Nov 1958	Thomas Blair Evans
1523	Cincinnati Ohio North	17 Mar 1985	William B. Wallis
336	*Cleveland Ohio		
	†Cleveland (Ohio, Pennsylvania)	20 Sep 1961	E. Doyle Robison
351	*Columbus Ohio		
	†Columbus	25 Feb 1962	James L. Mortensen
793	Columbus Ohio East	28 Nov 1976	Paul Frank Eastman
1609	Columbus Ohio North	19 Oct 1986	D. Richard McFerson
516	*Dayton Ohio		
	†Dayton	24 May 1970	Joseph M. McPhie
1029	Dayton Ohio East	27 May 1979	Melvin Edwin Gourdin
1447	Kirtland Ohio	16 Oct 1983	Zane F. Lee
1204	Toledo Ohio	2 Nov 1980	Ronald Rufus Burke
Discontinued			
1	Kirtland	17 Feb 1834	Joseph Smith Jr.
	24 May 1841		

Missions — 2
(As of Oct. 1, 1994; shown with historical number. See MISSIONS.)

(154) OHIO CLEVELAND MISSION
24600 Center Ridge Road, #450
Westlake, OH 44145
Phone: (216) 871-0937

(77a) OHIO COLUMBUS MISSION
P.O. Box 20130
Columbus, OH 43220
Phone: (614) 451-6183

Oklahoma

Year-end 1993: Est. population, 3,273,000; Members, 29,000; Stakes, 7; Wards, 42; Branches, 28; Missions, 2; Percent LDS, 0.9, or one person in 113.

In the late 1840s, George Miller, a former bishop who delayed going to the West, traveled from Winter Quarters to visit his son in Texas. He and two other members with him, Joseph Kilting and Richard Hewitt, found construction work available in the Cherokee Nation. They arrived in Tahlequah on July 9, 1847, and began to build houses. They also began to teach others about the Church but antagonism forced Miller to leave in December. Hewitt and Kilting remained to work.

In 1855 Orson Spencer and James McGaw visited Indian Territory from St. Louis, Mo., and on April 8, 1855, five more missionaries were sent from Salt Lake City and four from St. Louis. The Indian Territory Mission was created and placed under the leadership of Henry W. Miller on June 26, 1855. The missionaries met and re-converted followers of Lyman Wight. One of these was Jacob Croft, who had met missionaries earlier and started for Utah, but met another apostate group that told them untruths about conditions in Utah. The discouraged Croft party had then settled in Indian Territory and built a gristmill.

As early as July, the missionaries preached to some 400 Indians, and the Cherokee Branch was started at Croft's Spavinaw Creek mill. This became mission headquarters. Croft later led a party of 56, including other former followers of Wight and some re-converted "Strangites," to Utah.

Later in the year missionaries were sent from St. Louis to southern portions of the Cherokee Nations. In 1856, the Princess Creek Branch was organized. The Lehi and Nephi branches were organized in 1858.

Illness was a problem in this mission for many years. At least four missionaries died from the effects of serving in Indian Territory, including Orson Spencer. Many suffered the effects of malaria afterward.

In 1858 and 1859 the remaining groups immigrated to Utah and by 1860 all the missionaries but John A. Richards, who had married an Indian wife, returned to Utah. The Civil War destroyed what was left of the Church. Members and leaders were scattered.

When Elders Matthew Dalton and John Hubbard returned in 1877 they found John Richards was still faithful, and they received hospitality from him. Elder Hubbard died later that year and work stopped until 1883 when the next missionaries, Elder Dalton and Elder George Teasdale, came. Tracts in the Cherokee language were printed. Plagued with ill health, these missionaries persevered and found converts in Arkansas.

Andrew Kimball, the father of President Spencer W. Kimball, presided over the mission in 1885. Although he contracted malaria, he was assisted by John Richards and later by additional full-time missionaries. In 1892, the first meetinghouse was erected in Manard, Cherokee County. Another was erected at Massey, Choctaw Nation.

Converts during this period whose descendants became stalwarts in the local branches included the families of former minister John W. Davis, Simon Peter Hubler, William Edward Roberts, and George Washington Aaron, to name a few.

In 1904, the mission became the Central States Mission. By 1921, a branch was established at Gore, Okla., with 113 members but was later dissolved. A Sunday School began in Bartlesville in 1924. Membership increased but many converts went West. By 1930, membership throughout the mission numbered 10,804.

Membership began to increase in the 1950s, and in 1960 a stake was created in Tulsa. Included in the stake were parts of Kansas, Arkansas, and Oklahoma with a membership of about 2,000. The Oklahoma City Stake was organized in the fall of the same year with James A. Cullimore as president, who later served as an Assistant to the Twelve and a member of the First Quorum of the Seventy. Other stakes followed in 1970, 1977, 1978, and three in the 1980s. Membership in 1974 was 10,105 and in 1980, 20,819 and in 1990, 26,596.

Sources: *A History of the Church of Jesus Christ of Latter-day Saints in Eastern Oklahoma, from Oklahoma and Indian Territories to 1980* by Lynette K. Bingham, Bonnie Lee Blamires, Clara Laster and Lenet Read, published by the Tulsa Oklahoma Stake; *Mormon Indian Missions — 1855* a BYU thesis by Wesley R. Law, 1959; "The Cherokee Nation," by A.W. Miller, *Millennial Star*, Oct. 6, 1855, p. 637.

Stakes — 7
(Listed alphabetically as of Oct. 1, 1994.)

No.	Name	Organized	First President
North America Southeast Area			
777	Lawton Oklahoma	31 Oct 1976	Ralph E. Siebach
531	*Norman Oklahoma		

	†Oklahoma South	18 Oct 1970	H. Aldridge Gillespie
305	*Oklahoma City Oklahoma		
	†Oklahoma	23 Oct 1960	James A. Cullimore
1381	Oklahoma City Oklahoma South	14 Nov 1982	Lawrence Andrew Jackson
1277	Stillwater Oklahoma	14 Jun 1981	C. Jay Murray
298	*Tulsa Oklahoma		
	†Tulsa (Okla., Ark., Kan.)	1 May 1960	Robert N. Sears
912	Tulsa Oklahoma East	30 Apr 1978	Raleigh L. Huntsman

Discontinued

1418	Muskogee Oklahoma	15 May 1983	Samuel J. Hughes
	11 Aug 1991		

Missions — 2
(As of Oct. 1, 1994; shown with historical number. See MISSIONS.)

(248) OKLAHOMA OKLAHOMA CITY MISSION
1236 SW 89th St. Suite C
Oklahoma City, OK 73139
Phone: (405) 691-8690

(88) OKLAHOMA TULSA MISSION
5215 East 71st St., #300
Tulsa, OK 74136
Phone: (918) 496-0056

Oregon

Year-end 1993: Est. population, 3,061,000; Members, 121,000; Stakes, 34; Wards, 218; Branches, 36; Missions, 2; Temples, 1; Percent LDS, 4.0, or one person in 25.

In 1838, Joseph Smith visited Washington D.C. where, on one occasion, Henry Clay, "the great compromiser" suggested the Prophet take the Mormons to Oregon Territory. The Prophet did not take the suggestion seriously. Oregon, however, was one of several locations considered for possible settlement after difficulties in Illinois in the early 1840s. At the time, Oregon was claimed by both Great Britain and the United States. Saints in both Great Britain and America offered to settle there with their government's support, but both offers were declined.

As early as Sept. 25, 1850, Elder R. Boyd Stewart, who lived in a settlement on the Sacramento River in California, was called to serve in Oregon. Additional missionaries served in 1854 and later, but were called back with their converts at the onset of the so-called "Utah War" in 1857. The exodus to Utah began March 6, 1858.

After Oregon became a state in 1858, a more favorable attitude toward members developed. During the 1860s, Mormons found work as loggers in Oregon. A few settled, but any significant Mormon presence did not occur until 1887 when LDS businessmen from Utah, David Eccles and Charles Nibley (joined in 1889 by John Stoddard), built a lumber mill on North Powder River and persuaded several hundred LDS families to migrate to Oregon. The Baker Branch was organized in 1893.

The Northwestern States Mission was organized for the second time July 26, 1897, under the direction of George C. Parkinson. Early convert Jens Christensen (James) Westergaard became the first branch president in Portland after his baptism in 1898.

Around the turn of the century, another LDS movement into Oregon occurred when ranches in eastern Oregon were purchased and divided into sugar beet farms. The Eccles partnership supported this migration effort. By June 9, 1901, enough members had migrated that the Union Stake was created. Two years later, the five original wards had increased to 12 "all in excellent working order." Completion of the Oregon Shortline Railroad led more members to migrate to the Northwest.

Both World War I and World War II defense industry efforts led to more members moving to Oregon. In 1929, a meetinghouse was completed in Portland. By 1930, membership of the state was 3,226, with wards at Baker, Imbler, LaGrande (two), Mt. Glen and Union, and branches in Bend, Eugene, Klamath Falls, Medford, Portland, Hood River and Salem.

Members continued to move in and another stake was organized in Portland in 1938. Many members also moved into Oregon in the post-war boom and additional stakes were created.

In 1961 or earlier, the Church purchased property near Portland for eventual use for a junior college in Portland. However, the site was later chosen for the location of the Portland Oregon Temple, which was dedicated in 1989. More than 300,000 people toured the temple during its open house.

One evidence of the growing LDS population in the state was a dance festival held in July 1989 in which some 10,000 youth participated.

Members continued to support missionary work, and in 1990, the Oregon Eugene Mission was created. Membership in 1980 was 94,093, increasing to 113,774 in 1990.

Sources: *Encyclopedic History of the Church* by Andrew Jenson; *Mormon Migration to Oregon's Grande*

Ronde Valley: A Portent of Future Mormon Expansion, by Kenneth Gerald Dull, master's theses, Utah State University, 1981; "Enterprising beet farmers," by Bruce D. Blumell, *Church News,* Jan. 14, 1978; *Church News,* July 22, 1989, Jan. 27, 1990; *History of the Church in the Pacific Northwest,* by Leonard J. Arrington, Task Papers in LDS History, No. 18.

Stakes — 34
(Listed alphabetically by area as of Oct. 1, 1994.)

No.	Name	Organized	First President

North America Northwest Area

No.	Name	Organized	First President
386	*Beaverton Oregon		
	†Portland West (Oregon)	10 Nov 1963	C. Carlile Carlson
472	*Bend Oregon		
	†Bend	15 Dec 1968	Norman K. Whitney
1373	Cedar Mill Oregon	31 Oct 1982	Edgar Lee Stone
1325a	Central Point Oregon	7 Mar 1982	Michael T. Robinson
493	*Coos Bay Oregon		
	†Oregon West	12 Sep 1969	Edward Harold Sypher
385	*Corvallis Oregon		
	†Corvallis	3 Nov 1963	Hugh F. Webb
1171	*Dallas Oregon 25 Sep 1990		
	†Salem Oregon East	24 Aug 1980	William Paul Hyde
191	*Eugene Oregon		
	†Willamette	2 Dec 1951	Ralph B. Lake
1410	Eugene Oregon Santa Clara	17 Apr 1983	Terrel B. Williams
767	Eugene Oregon West	12 Sep 1976	Robert W. Hill
779	Grants Pass Oregon	31 Oct 1976	Darwin Jay Wright
643	Gresham Oregon	26 May 1974	Wilford Smith Stevenson Jr.
1365	Gresham Oregon South	10 Oct 1982	Max B. Holbrook
1200	Hermiston Oregon	26 Oct 1980	Allen D. Alder
710	Hillsboro Oregon	12 Oct 1975	H. Keith Buhler
743	*Keizer Oregon 4 Apr 1984		
	*Salem Oregon Keizer 25 Oct 1981		
	†Salem Oregon North	8 Feb 1976	Jay Gerald Nelson
205	*Klamath Falls Oregon		
	†Klamath (Oregon, California)	22 Mar 1953	Carroll William Smith
49	*La Grande Oregon		
	†Union	9 Jun 1901	Franklin S. Bramwell
1469	Lake Oswego Oregon	29 Apr 1984	Thomas Dean Cottle
1102	Lebanon Oregon	3 Feb 1980	Henry Boyd Walthuis
1300	McMinnville Oregon	25 Oct 1981	Thomas Babb III
400	*Medford Oregon		
	†Medford (Oregon, California)	23 Aug 1964	Dennis R. Hassell
999	Milwaukie Oregon	11 Feb 1979	Thomas Dean Cottle
176	*Nyssa Oregon		
	†Nyssa (Oregon, Idaho)	8 Jan 1950	Arvel L. Child
1504	Ontario Oregon	18 Nov 1984	Reed Neils Dame
563	*Oregon City Oregon		
	†Oregon City	16 Jan 1972	James Hayward Bean
123	*Portland Oregon		
	†Portland	26 Jun 1938	Monte L. Bean
190	*Portland Oregon East		
	†Columbia River (Ore., Wash.)	2 Dec 1951	R. Spencer Papworth
1852	Ranier Oregon	8 Mar 1992	Marion Royal Johnstun
1239	*Redmond Oregon 18 Feb 1986		
	†Prineville Oregon	1 Mar 1981	Heber D. Perrett
830	Roseburg Oregon	15 May 1977	Gary Richards Lowe
321	*Salem Oregon		
	†Salem	22 Jan 1961	Hugh F. Webb
850	The Dalles Oregon	26 Jun 1977	Wayne B. Bush
1895	Tualatin Oregon	16 Aug 1992	Paul Walker Roberts

(249) OREGON EUGENE MISSION
1142 Willagillespie Rd., #2
Eugene, OR 97401
Phone: (503) 342-2344

(18) OREGON PORTLAND MISSION
13635 N.W. Cornell Rd., #100
Portland, OR 97229
Phone: (503) 643-1696

Pennsylvania

Year-end 1993: Est. population, 12,073,000; Members, 32,000; Stakes, 9; Wards, 60; Branches, 42; Missions, 3; Districts, 2; Percent LDS, 0.3, or one person in 377.

Joseph Smith moved to Harmony, Pa., in December 1827, and first lived in the home of Isaac Hale, his father-in-law. A few weeks later, he moved a small cabin to an adjacent farm where he eventually translated most of the Book of Mormon. His scribes were himself, his wife Emma, Martin Harris, Oliver Cowdery and David Whitmer. At the nearby Susquehanna River, he and Oliver Cowdery were ordained to the Aaronic Priesthood May 15, 1829. The ordinance of baptism was then first performed in this dispensation as Oliver Cowdery baptized Joseph Smith. Later the Melchizedek Priesthood was restored, and 15 of the revelations in the Doctrine and Covenants were received in Harmony. The first infant son of Joseph and Emma is buried at this site. The farm was purchased by the Church Feb. 7, 1947, and a historical marker has been erected.

After the Church was formally organized in 1830, Orson Hyde, Samuel H. Smith, and a number of others began missionary work. A branch was organized in Columbia, Bradford County, by 1831. Another was created in Pittsburgh in 1832, and in 1833, in Springfield and Elk Creek. A total of 12 branches were created in the 1830s, although these branches were of short duration as members gathered to Ohio, or later Missouri and Illinois with the body of the Saints.

Among the most prominent branches was in Philadelphia, created in 1839 after initial efforts by Elders Jedediah M. Grant, Joshua Grant and Benjamin Winchester, and sustained efforts by Elders Samuel and Lewis James.

Converts from Philadelphia included Edward Hunter, a wealthy landowner, who later became Presiding Bishop of the Church, and John Neff, a well-to-do businessman. Both contributed generously of their means to sustain the members during their later privations brought about by persecution. By 1840, more than 200 members belonged to the branch and 8 to 10 were baptized weekly.

From 1839 to 1846, missionary work in the Church was focused mostly in the cities of Philadelphia, Boston and New York.

Following the martyrdom of Joseph Smith in 1844, Sidney Rigdon and James J. Strang claimed leadership of the Church and established apostate groups from among Church members who had not "gathered," including those in Pennsylvania. However, many were later reclaimed. Apostate leader William Bickerton drew away members in western Pennsylvania who became known as the Bickertonites.

On March 26, 1850, Gen. Thomas L. Kane delivered a landmark address, "History of the Persecutions of the Latter-day Saints" to the Historical Society of Pennsylvania. During the 1850s, the city was a port of entry for many LDS immigrants.

Missionary work continued sporadically. The Redstone and New England (later called Wilson) branches were organized in May 1886. The Northwestern States Mission (which at the time included the Eastern states) was created in 1878, becoming the Northern States Mission in 1889. Pennsylvania was transferred to the Eastern States Mission in 1897, and the East and West Pennsylvania districts were created.

By 1930, the East District included one branch in Philadelphia with 284 members, and a branch in Pittsburgh, which had its own meetinghouse, and another in Wilson, with a total of 510 members in the West District.

During World War II membership increased and additional branches were created. For example, missionaries arrived in Lancaster, near Harrisburg, in 1941. Their first converts were Lester D. Ross and his wife, Mary Eleanor. A branch was organized in 1943, with 10-14 members. As it grew, its members often moved to the West. After a 10-year fund drive the branch purchased property and a small meetinghouse was eventually completed. In 1970, this branch became a ward when the Gettysburg Stake was created.

The Philadelphia Stake was created Oct. 16, 1960, with 2,000 members in Pennsylvania in Philadelphia, Valley Forge and Wyncote wards, and the in Allentown, Chester and Reading branches.

The Pittsburgh Stake was created May 11, 1969, with 2,258 members in four wards in Pittsburgh, and others in Beaver Valley, Butler, Punxsutawney and Washington, and branches in Greensburg and Monongahela.

In 1970, the Pennsylvania (now Pennsylvania Harrisburg) Mission was created. The Pennsylvania Philadelphia Mission was created in July 1, 1977. Membership in Pennsylvania in 1980 was 22,211, increasing to 28,976 in 1990.

Sources: *Encyclopedic History of the Church* by Andrew Jenson; *A Study of the Origins of the Church in the States of New York and Pennsylvania, 1816-1831*, a BYU dissertation by Larry C. Porter, August 1971; *Church News*, Oct. 22, 1960, May 17, 1969, Nov. 30, 1986; *Missionary Activities and Church Organizations in Pennsylvania, 1840-1840*, a BYU thesis by V. Alan Curtis, 1976; "The Hospitable Squire," by William Hartley, *Church News*, Jan. 21, 1978; *The Church in Pennsylvania, (1830-1854)*, a East Stroudsburg State College thesis by Paul Zilch Rosenbaum, December 1982; Neff History, unpublished; Interview with Lester D. Ross by Julie Dockstader, *Church News*, Oct. 19, 1991.

Stakes — 9
(Listed alphabetically as of Oct. 1, 1994.)

No.	Name	Organized	First President
North America Northeast Area			
946	*Altoona Pennsylvania 31 Oct 1982		
	†State College Pennsylvania	23 Jul 1978	Robert Armstrong Wood Sr.
1592	Erie Pennsylvania	23 Mar 1986	Philip Dale Baker
1047	Harrisburg Pennsylvania	12 Aug 1979	Charles A. Cooper
304	*Philadelphia Pennsylvania		
	†Philadelphia (Penn., Del., Md., N.J.)	16 Oct 1960	Bryant F. West
481	*Pittsburgh Pennsylvania		
	†Pittsburgh	11 May 1969	William P. Cook
985	*Pittsburg Pennsylvania North 18 Feb 1992		
	†Pittsburgh Pennsylvania East	26 Nov 1978	Garth Harrison Ladle
1372	Reading Pennsylvania	31 Oct 1982	Hugh G. Daubek
1044	Scranton Pennsylvania	2 Aug 1979	Frederick Adelman Alderks
510	*York Pennsylvania 12 Aug 1979		
	*Gettysburg Pennsylvania		
	†Gettysburg (Pennsylvania)	19 Apr 1970	Laurence L. Yager

Missions — 3
(As of Oct. 1, 1994; shown with historical number. See MISSIONS.)

(91a) PENNSYLVANIA HARRISBURG MISSION
3607 Rosemont Ave.
Camp Hill, PA 17011-6998
Phone: (717) 761-3611

(129) PENNSYLVANIA PITTSBURGH MISSION
2589 Washington Road, Suite 410
Pittsburgh, PA 15241
Phone: (412) 831-7557

(156) PENNSYLVANIA PHILADELPHIA MISSION
300 West State St., St. 107
Media, PA 19063
Phone: (610) 565-1150

Rhode Island

Year-end 1993: Est. population, 1,001,000; Members, 2,000; Stakes, 1; Wards, 5; Branches, 1; Percent LDS: 0.2, or one person in 558

Elders Orson Hyde and Samuel H. Smith arrived in Rhode Island on July 13, 1832, baptizing their first convert on July 18. They baptized another person before persecutors drove them from the state a few days afterward.

Four years later, records note the existence of a Rhode Island branch represented by Brigham Young at a conference in Newry, Maine. The Newport Branch was organized by 1844 with 21 members.

Elder John Druce worked as an engraver and missionary in Pawtucket, R.I., in 1846, where he also preached and baptized many converts into the Church. A branch was organized June 7, 1857, in Providence, but discontinued as the members moved to the West. Druce immigrated to the West in 1861, but returned in 1876 to resume his missionary work.

In 1873, Elder Henry G. Bywater organized another branch in Providence with 25 members, and predicted many would soon emigrate. In 1876, Elder Erastus Snow wrote that he and Elder Benjamin F. Cummings met with the Saints in Pawtucket who were on their way to the Great Basin from England. A year later, Elder Cummings preached to an attentive audience in a school house in Pawtucket. In 1896, Elder Joseph A. Anderson reported illness after sleeping outside in the rain for some 12 days as he traveled in

Rhode Island without purse or scrip. A conference of the Eastern States Mission was held March 22, 1899, in Providence and received favorable publicity in the *Providence Journal* and the *Telegram*. Missionaries also reported that residents treated them kindly.

The Providence Branch was organized in 1905, and by 1917 increased to about 20 people. Membership in the nation's smallest state continued to accrue gradually. In 1938, a private library was purchased for the Providence Branch, which was remodeled into a meetinghouse by the members. The facility was dedicated by Elder John A. Widtsoe of the Council of the Twelve on June 14, 1944. The branch was often decimated when members moved to the West to be closer to the Church. However, the branch was bolstered by converts introduced to the Church by LDS servicemen stationed at nearby military bases. The library meetinghouse was sold and another site purchased in 1960. A new building was dedicated in 1966.

The Providence Stake was created March 20, 1977, the 49th state to receive its first stake. Rhode Island wards in the stake included those in Newport and Providence, and the Davisville Branch. Also in the stake were two wards and two branches in Massachusetts and two wards in Connecticut. Membership in Rhode Island in 1974 was 799, increasing to 1,052 in 1980, and 1,701 in 1990.

Sources: *Encyclopedic History of the Church* by Andrew Jenson; Journal History of the Church, Aug. 14, 1836, Oct. 22, 1843, July 30, 1844, March 10, 1873, March 13, 1876, Feb. 5, 1977; *Deseret News,* March 31, 1877, July 12, 1877, Oct. 9, 1878, Aug 11, 1896, April 1, 1899, Dec. 3, 1932; *Church News,* March 31, 1945, March 26, 1977, and "Missionary Printer," by Ronald G. Watt, *Church News,* Jan. 28, 1978.

Stake — 1
(As of Oct. 1, 1994.)

No.	Name	Organized	First President
North America Northeast Area			
818	*Providence Rhode Island	20 Mar 1977	Morgan W. Lewis Jr.

South Carolina

Year-end 1993: Est. population, 3,692,000; Members, 24,000; Stakes, 4; Wards, 38; Branches, 14; Missions, 1; Percent LDS, 0.7, or one person in 154.

While missionary work in the Southern States began as early as 1831, the first member in South Carolina is believed to be Emmanual Masters Murphy, who was baptized in Tennessee in 1836. When Elder Lysander M. Davis arrived in South Carolina about the first of November in 1839, he found the Murphys had people prepared for baptism. Seven of these were baptized.

Opposition arose and Elder Davis was briefly jailed, but progress continued with additional conversions. Murphy reportedly later visited Joseph Smith in Carthage Jail shortly before the Prophet's martyrdom. The Prophet reminded him of the prophecy that soon war would begin in South Carolina, and exhorted Murphy to warn the people of his home state.

Elder Abraham O. Smoot preached in Charleston, and upstate in 1841, but failed to gain any converts. However, an "unknown missionary" traveled to Charleston earlier that year and baptized three ministers and eight others. Another missionary, Elder John Eldredge preached in South Carolina in 1842-43.

The next missionary activity in the state began in the 1870s. The South Carolina Conference was organized in July 1882. Among the earliest branches were at King's Mountain (1882), Gaffney (1883), and among the Catawba Indian community (1885). Conference headquarters were established at the plantation of John Black, a man who remained unbaptized in order to provide refuge to the Church. Many converts, including Indians, moved onto his plantation to escape persecution. The Catawbas also shielded missionaries from persecutors. Most of the Catawbas joined the Church and remained faithful.

Stalwart missionaries braved such adversities as floggings, jailings, disease (12 missionaries died from illness from 1895-1900 in the Southern States Mission), frequent exposure to the elements, walking hundreds of miles, often missing meals, and other privations. But they continued to find converts and organize branches. From 1880 to 1888, 2,238 converts were baptized throughout the South, and 1,169 converts immigrated to Utah.

Mission leaders of the 1880s and later included Henry G. Boyle, John Morgan, William Spry, J. Golden Kimball, Elias S. Kimball and Benjamin E. Rich. Later, Ephraim H. Nye, Charles A. Callis and LeGrand Richards were prominent leaders.

In the 1890s, progress and persecution continued. Mobs often gathered to punish and banish missionaries. But the members and missionaries persevered. Branches were organized in Society Hill, Columbia, Charleston and Fairfield, to name a few. About 350 members attended a conference in Society Hill in 1897. However, as converts migrated to the West, branches dwindled and some were reorganized later with new converts.

At the turn of the century, membership in the state was 1,200. That membership increased to 3,343 in 1930. The conference included six branches (four with meetinghouses,) and 10 Sunday Schools. In the 1930s, mission president LeGrand Richards introduced "systematic teaching," a forerunner of today's missionary discussions. By 1937, membership in the entire mission had increased to 18,000.

South Carolina's first stake was created in Columbia in 1947. It included the entire state with wards in Columbia, Greenville, Charleston, Gaffney, Hartsville, Ridgeway and Spartanburg, and branches in Augusta (Ga.), Sumter, Society Hill, Winnsboro and Darlington. Membership totaled about 1,900 members.

Additional stakes were added in 1963, 1968, and 1972. Church membership in South Carolina in 1974 was 10,775, increasing to 17,012 in 1980, and 23,731 in 1990. Following natural disasters from storms that occurred in the South in the 1990s, South Carolina members were among those who helped provide relief.

Sources: *Encyclopedic History of the Church* by Andrew Jenson; *Columbia South Carolina Stake Fortieth Anniversary,* Oct. 19, 1947 to 1987, compiled under direction of stake Pres. Gary L. Fish; *History of the Southern States Mission 1831-1861* a BYU thesis by LaMar C. Berrett, July 1960; *Brief History of the Southern States Mission for One Hundred Years, 1830-1930* by DeVon H. Nish, a BYU paper of August 1966; "Stake Birthday Notes Growth of Church in South Carolina," *Church News,* Dec. 9, 1972, *Southern States Mission and the Administration of Ben E. Rich, 1898-1908,* A thesis for BYU by Ted S. Anderson, April 1976; "Persecutor converted," by Richard L. Jensen, *Church News,* Feb. 4, 1978; "Members provide outpouring of help," *Church News*, Sept. 12, 1992; "Fierce storm claims lives of 3," *Church News,* March 20, 1993.

Stakes — 4
(Listed alphabetically as of Oct. 1, 1994.)

No.	Name	Organized	First President
North America Southeast Area			
584	*Charleston South Carolina		
	†Charleston	20 Aug 1972	Fred Ittner Harley
169	*Columbia South Carolina		
	†South Carolina (S.C., Georgia)	19 Oct 1947	W. Wallace McBride
454	*Florence South Carolina 5 Feb 1978		
	*Columbia South Carolina East		
	†South Carolina East (South Carolina)	21 Apr 1968	Clyde Elmer Black Sr.
366	*Greenville South Carolina		
	*Greenville 19 Nov 1972		
	†South Carolina West (S.C., N.C.)	27 Jan 1963	Ivan A. Larsen

Mission — 1
(As of Oct. 1, 1994; shown with historical number. See MISSIONS.)

(130) SOUTH CAROLINA COLUMBIA MISSION
1345 Garner Lane, #307
Columbia, SC 29210
Phone: (803) 798-8855

South Dakota

Year-end 1993: Est. population, 720,000; Members, 8,100; Stakes, 2; Wards, 10; Branches, 28; Missions, 1; Districts, 3; Percent LDS, 1.1, or one person in 89.

In the 1840s, Church leaders seeking a refuge in the West considered various locations for settlement. One of these locations was the Indian country of the Dakotas. An area was chosen in 1845 for settlement by a group of volunteer colonizers under maverick leader James Emmett. The group, which evidently communicated en route with Brigham Young but did not have his full approval, penetrated deep into South Dakota's Indian country and established a settlement at Fort Vermillion on the Missouri River. They arrived at the fort June 17, 1845, and immediately began building cabins and planting crops. They preached to the Sioux Indians and befriended them, but the threat of attack was constant. The colony was nearly attacked when Emmett unwisely interfered in a horse-trading deal between the Indians and traders and an argument ensued.

Emmett, who had lost some favor with Church leaders after the death of Joseph Smith, returned to Nauvoo the summer of 1845 and sought to regain favor with the Church. He was accepted in full fellowship, but on his return to Fort Vermillion, he was accompanied by two other leaders, Henry G. Sherwood and John S. Fullmer, who rebaptized the settlers. In the spring of 1846, the group received word from Brigham Young to join the Saints in the westward trek. The settlement was abandoned as most members complied with President Young's directions.

Missionary work in South Dakota began May 3, 1883, when, at a conference in Kirkhaven, Minn., Charles N. Nielsen and N.L. Lund were appointed to "open the Gospel door in the states of Dakota." Elder Nielsen arrived at Big Stone, Dakota Territory, on June 5, staying only one day. In 1885, the Dakota Conference membership was listed at "four souls," including two elders from Utah. The same year, Elder Soren Christiansen reported that he received both hospitality and threats backed up by guns as he traveled in Dakota. Missionaries reported in 1887 that Dakota was a "worn-out" territory. Missionary work continued in 1888, and in 1898, missionaries from North Dakota were transferred to the Southern Dakota Conference. The Dakotas were placed in the Colorado Mission in 1900. The mission name was changed to Western States Mission in 1907. Missionary work continued with another organization of the South Dakota Conference in 1925, and a re-opening in 1931.

The South Dakota Conference was organized for western South Dakota and a Sunday School was organized in Sioux Falls on Aug. 17, 1930, and made a branch June 19, 1949. Another branch existed in Gettysburg. By 1950, Sunday Schools were organized at Mitchell, Aberdeen, Brookings, Ft. Thompson, and Huron. That same year ground was broken for a meetinghouse in Sioux Falls. The North Central States Mission, which included the western half of the state, was changed to the Dakota-Manitoba Mission in 1970. This mission had 230 missionaries and about 800 members. In 1974, its name was changed to the South Dakota Rapid City Mission. A number of meetinghouses were completed in the 1970s. The Rapid City South Dakota Stake was created in 1973. Membership in South Dakota in 1980 was 6,121, which grew to 7,657 in 1990.

Sources: *Encyclopedic History of the Church* by Andrew Jenson; The Church in South Dakota, no author listed; *Church News,* July 8, 1944, "An Early Mormon Settlement in South Dakota," by Gerald E. Jones, *South Dakota State Historical Society Quarterly,* Spring of 1971; "Mormon Renegade: James Emmett at the Vermillion, 1846," by Richard E. Bennett, *South Dakota History,* Fall of 1985.

Stakes — 2
(Listed alphabetically as of Oct. 1, 1994.)

No.	Name	Organized	First President
North America Central Area			
592	*Rapid City South Dakota		
	†Rapid City	10 Dec 1972	Briant LeRoy Davis
1085	Sioux Falls South Dakota	18 Nov 1979	Russell Lloyd Harward

Mission — 1
(As of Oct. 1, 1994; shown with historical number. See MISSIONS.)

(78) SOUTH DAKOTA RAPID CITY MISSION
2525 West Main, Suite 311
Rapid City, SD 57702
Phone: (605) 348-1520

Tennessee

Year-end 1993: Est. population, 5,147,000; Members, 25,000; Stakes, 8; Wards, 43; Branches, 20; Missions, 2; Percent LDS, 0.5, or one person in 206.

Apostle David W. Patten and Elder Warren Parrish arrived in Tennessee shortly before Oct. 11, 1834, when they preached at a large Campbellite meeting and baptized seven. Another 24 were baptized later. A small branch was organized by the end of the year. Missionary efforts took place in Henry, Benton and Humphreys counties. In 1835, Elder Parrish worked alone after Elder Patten returned to Kirtland, Ohio. Elder Parrish continued to baptize converts and was unable to fill all the requests for preaching. One of his converts was Abraham O. Smoot, who later became a prominent Church leader in Salt Lake City.

On March 27, 1835, Wilford Woodruff, then a priest, came to assist Elder Parrish. He arrived at a tavern covered with mud, and identified himself as a preacher. In jest, the innkeeper urged him to preach and gathered 500 people to hear him. Elder Woodruff told the rowdy congregation individually of "their wicked deeds and the reward they would obtain." One by one, the people left until he was alone. During the next three months, he and Elder Parrish baptized 20 converts.

When Elder Parrish was called as a seventy in July 1835, he ordained Elder Woodruff an elder and placed him in charge of the work in Tennessee. At that time, membership in the district was 86 members in six branches (one in Kentucky). Elder Woodruff continued the work, reporting at year's end that he had traveled 3,248 miles, baptized 43 people, three of whom were Campbellite preachers and had three mobs rise against him. Mob activity temporarily forced missionaries from Benton County in 1836. However, work progressed well, and by 1839, 12 branches existed in Tennessee. Work continued though 1844 as missionaries promoted Joseph Smith's short-lived candidacy for president of the United States.

By 1846, missionaries had preached in 26 counties in Tennessee. Following the exodus to the West, little work was done in Tennessee. Missionaries visited the state in 1857 to call the Saints to gather in the West.

In 1870, Elder Hayden Church resumed missionary work in Tennessee. The Southern States Mission was formally organized in 1875 with headquarters in Nashville, which were moved to Chattanooga in 1882 and remained there until 1919, when Atlanta, Ga., became mission headquarters.

Elder Henry G. Boyle had established a branch at Shady Grove, Tenn., in 1875. Mob activity increased significantly in 1879. Some converts in the South left their homes and immigrated to the West in 1883. In 1884, members were fired upon in separate incidents. The worst massacre of Church members in the South occurred on Aug. 10, 1884, when mobbers shot to death Elders William S. Berry and John H. Gibbs, and local members Martin Condor and John Riley during Church services near Cane Creek, Lewis County, Tenn. Mission Pres. B.H. Roberts heroically donned a disguise, traveled to the tense area and retrieved the bodies of the slain missionaries. During this period, missionaries faced down many mobs and sometimes suffered violence. Occasionally, non-members courageously defended the missionaries. In 1888, a group of 177 Saints left Chattanooga for Colorado and Utah.

By the 1890s, public opinion became more tolerant. U.S. Census records list 136 members in Tennessee in 1890. By 1906, membership had increased to 841.

The oldest existing meetinghouse in the Southeast was dedicated in Northcutts Cove in 1909. By 1919, branches were listed in Chattanooga and Memphis.

By 1930, some 2,832 members lived in the Middle and East Tennessee districts in the Chattanooga, Memphis and Nashville branches, and Sunday Schools in Brighton, Pope, Short Creek, Silver Point and Turkey Creek.

On April 18, 1965, the Memphis Stake was created with two wards in Memphis and another in Jackson, plus wards in Mississippi and Arkansas.

The Tennessee Nashville Mission was created in 1975. Membership in Tennessee in 1980 was 15,839, increasing to 23,007 in 1990.

Sources: Southern States Mission directories, 1919-1935; *Encyclopedic History of the Church* by Andrew Jenson; *History of the Southern States Mission,* a BYU thesis by LaMar C. Berrett, July 1960; *Orthodoxy Versus Nonconformity: The Mormon Experience in Tennessee and Mississippi, 1875-1905,* a University of Chicago paper by Mary Elizabeth Stovall, March 12, 1976; *Church News,* April 24, 1965, March 22, 1975, Nov. 9, 1986, and "Chattanooga: LDS in Tennessee build on a firm foundation," by R. Scott Lloyd, *Church News,* May 25, 1991.

Stakes — 9
(Listed alphabetically as of Oct. 1, 1994.)

No.	Name	Organized	First President
North America Southeast Area			
927	Chattanooga Tennessee	21 May 1978	Earl Eugene Callens Jr.
1089	Franklin Tennessee	2 Dec 1979	Buryl Gene McClurg
1093	Kingsport Tennessee	13 Jan 1980	William Keith Clay
581	*Knoxville Tennessee		
	†Knoxville	25 Jun 1972	Eugene H. Perkins
1991	McKinney Texas	11 Sep 1994	Robert C. Packard
1810	McMinnville Tennessee	18 Aug 1991	Gary Wayne Bradford
403	*Memphis Tennessee		
	†Memphis (Tenn., Mo., Ark., Miss.)	18 Apr 1965	Richard Stoddard
1179	Memphis Tennessee North	14 Sep 1980	Edward Victor Martin
537	*Nashville Tennessee		
	†Nashville	6 Dec 1970	Robert N. Brady

Missions — 2
(As of Oct. 1, 1994; shown with historical number. See MISSIONS.)

(294) TENNESSEE KNOXVILLE MISSION
P.O. Box 22730
Knoxville, TN 37933-0730
Phone: (615) 671-3466

(131) TENNESSEE NASHVILLE MISSION
P.O. Box 1287
Brentwood, TN 37024-1287
Phone: (615) 373-1836

Texas

Year-end 1993: Est. population, 18,279,000; Members, 170,000; Stakes, 38; Wards, 273; Branches, 110; Missions, 6; Temples, 1; Percent LDS, 0.9, or one person in 108.

The Church's first missionary to Texas was William C. Steffey in 1843. In 1844, Joseph Smith considered Texas as an alternate location for the Saints should they be driven from Illinois. The Church negotiated with Sam Houston and considered purchasing a large tract of land in western Texas. However, the martyrdom of Joseph Smith cut short these tentative plans. Lyman Wight, an apostle who lost faith after the martyrdom, proceeded on his own to lead a colony of 100 people into central Texas, leaving Nauvoo March 25, 1845, and arriving in the spring of 1846. Although he was excommunicated in 1848, Wight and his followers pioneered in five counties in Texas and generally left a good reputation for Mormons in the area.

Among the first successful missionaries to Texas was Preston Thomas who visited the Wight colonies in 1849 and baptized some of them back into the Church. He also baptized his brother, Daniel. Preston Thomas led the first company of Texas converts to Salt Lake City in April 1853. He served six missions to Texas and led several companies to Utah.

In 1853, Thomas A. Martindale and James McGaw labored in Harris, Grimes and Montgomery counties. Two years later, Elder Benjamin L. Clapp labored in Freestone County. The Texas Conference was organized Dec. 25, 1855. Work also went forward in Washington, Milam, McLennan and Ellis counties. From 1854 to 1857, several hundred converts immigrated to Utah. Many privations accompanied some of these immigrants. For example, Edward Wallace and Wilmirth Greer East, converts from Port Sullivan, Texas, lost four of their six young children as well as her father and brother from cholera on an 1855 trek to the West.

While records of missionary work after this period are scarce, some 276 members in Texas were on Church records after the Civil War ended. However, harsh attitudes against the members existed for many years and little growth was realized. Elder J. Golden Kimball entered the mission field in 1892, and in 1897, he reported that public opinion was by then more favorable toward the Church. The Texas Conference was reorganized June 17, 1893, and membership began a slow but steady increase. The Texas Conference was divided into several conferences in 1898, and local leaders were called.

On Dec. 31, 1898, John and James Edgar purchased property that eventually became the Mormon colony of Kelsey, where 300 members lived. In 1906, the settlements at Kelsey, Poynor and Williamson, and Spurger were the largest places of LDS worship, and membership throughout the state reached 1,000. Missionaries began tracting the areas, though some were overwhelmed by the 1901 oil boom in Beaumont that brought in thousands of people.

Until 1917, members in Houston met in rented halls while branches at Williamson and Josey built their own meetinghouses. By 1930, the state had 14 branches and an additional 11 independent Sunday Schools with a total membership of 3,837. A non-member donated her home to the Houston Branch and it was remodeled and dedicated in 1933.

For about the next 20 years, membership in Texas continued to grow slowly and local members assumed more and more leadership roles. During World War II they instituted "home missions."

The El Paso Stake was created Sept. 21, 1952, and in 1953, stakes were organized in Houston and Dallas. The San Antonio Stake was created in 1958.

Growth of the Church in Texas continued and by 1977, membership totaled more than 50,000. The Dallas Texas Temple was completed in 1984 and dedicated Oct. 19-24. The temple district at the time included 46 stakes and 120,000 members in Texas and nearby states. In 1990, membership in Texas was 154,000. On Oct. 14, 1993, Richard A. Searfoss of League City, Texas, became the first Latter-day Saint to pilot a flight of a space shuttle.

Sources: *Encyclopedic History of the Church* by Andrew Jenson; Church in Texas, by Ruby Denton; *A History of the Mormon Church in Texas 1843-1906*, by Bonnie Means Durning, a master's theses for East Texas State College; *The Houston First Ward: From Stopover to Ward in One Hundred and Ten Years*, by Robert C. Petersen, a BYU paper, 1971; "Mormon Grove Trail beset with travails," by Chris Miasnik, *Church News*, July 24, 1993; "Shuttle pilot fulfilling childhood dream," by Julie A. Dockstader, *Church News*, Sept. 18, 1993.

Stakes — 39
(Listed alphabetically as of Oct. 1, 1994.)

No.	Name	Organized	First President
North America Southwest Area			
1262	Abilene Texas	3 May 1981	William E. Seegmiller
1272	Amarillo Texas	31 May 1981	Donald Eugene Pinnell
1594	Arlington Texas	13 Apr 1986	Richard S. Pickering
626	Austin Texas	14 Oct 1973	Amos Luther Wright
1835	Austin Texas Oak Hills	1 Dec 1991	Gary Scott Robinson
1818	Bay City Texas	13 Oct 1991	Joseph Nathanial Cannon Jr.

333	*Beaumont Texas		
	†Beaumont (Texas, Louisiana)	3 Sep 1961	Alden C. Stout
1076	*College Station Texas 10 Oct 1989		
	†Conroe Texas	28 Oct 1979	Nylen Lee Allphin Jr.
398	*Corpus Christi Texas		
	†Corpus Christi	31 May 1964	Clarence Cottam
1451	Cypress Texas	6 Nov 1983	Bruce A. Nelson
210	*Dallas Texas		
	†Dallas	18 Oct 1953	Ervin W. Atkerson
828	Dallas Texas East	15 May 1977	Arthur Eugene Gabriel
1860	Denton Texas	3 May 1992	James Boyd Martino
194	*El Paso Texas		
	†El Paso (Texas, New Mexico)	21 Sep 1952	Edward V. Turley Sr.
1359	El Paso Texas Mount Franklin	29 Aug 1982	Gerald Merrell Pratt
443	*Fort Worth Texas		
	†Fort Worth (Texas)	24 Sep 1967	John Kelly Jr.
843	Friendswood Texas	29 May 1977	Newell Kenneth Hill
1394	Gilmer Texas	16 Jan 1983	Von Webber Freeman
1247	Harlingen Texas	22 Mar 1981	Leonard Moore
209	*Houston Texas		
	†Houston (Texas, Louisiana)	11 Oct 1953	Jack Byron Trunnell
456	*Houston Texas East		
	†Houston East (Texas)	5 May 1968	Martell A. Belnap
733	Houston Texas North	16 Nov 1975	Harold Elison DeLaMare
1211	Houston Texas South	30 Nov 1980	Leo C. Smith
784	*Hurst Texas 12 Apr 1981		
	†Fort Worth Texas North	14 Nov 1976	Richard W. Ragsdale
1834	Katy Texas	1 Dec 1991	Collins Wise Steward
986	Killeen Texas	26 Nov 1978	Stephen Brian Hutchings
1337	Kingwood Texas	18 Apr 1982	Robert Lee Ezell
1253	Lewisville Texas	12 Apr 1981	Richard W. Ragsdale
496	*Longview Texas		
	†Texas East	9 Nov 1969	Gerald C.F. Knackstedt
446	*Lubbock Texas		
	†Texas North	26 Nov 1967	Franklin S. Gonzalez
692	McAllen Texas	4 May 1975	Daniel Birch Larsen
1991	McKinney Texas	11 Sep 1994	Robert C. Packard
471	*Odessa Texas		
	†Texas West	15 Dec 1968	Roland Lamar Hamblin
1360	Orange Texas	29 Aug 1982	Bernard E. Packard
616	*Plano Texas 12 Apr 1981		
	*Dallas Texas North		
	†Dallas North	27 May 1973	Ivan Leslie Hobson Jr.
1396	Richardson Texas	30 Jan 1983	Larry Wayne Gibbons
252	*San Antonio Texas		
	†San Antonio	19 Jan 1958	Roland C. Bremer
758	San Antonio Texas East	30 May 1976	Archie M. Brugger
1426	San Antonio Texas West	5 Jun 1983	Jan M. Sterneckert

Missions — 6
(As of Oct. 1, 1994; shown with historical number. See MISSIONS.)

(60) TEXAS DALLAS MISSION
13747 Montfort Drive, #120
Dallas, TX 75240-4454
Phone: (214) 239-5621

(189) TEXAS FORT WORTH MISSION
1331 Airport Freeway, #305
Euless, TX 76040
Phone: (817) 354-7444

(142) TEXAS HOUSTON MISSION
16333 Hafer Road
Houston, TX 77090
Phone: (713) 440-6770

(254) TEXAS HOUSTON EAST MISSION
820 So. Friendswood Drive, #100
Friendswood, TX 77546
Phone: (713) 992-1001

(224) TEXAS MCALLEN MISSION
3825 North 10th St., Suite E
McAllen, TX 78501
Phone: (210) 664-0273

(233) TEXAS SAN ANTONIO MISSION
84 N.E. Loop 410 #152
San Antonio, TX 78216-5860
Phone: (210) 349-3268

Utah

Year-end 1993: Est. population, 1,887,000; Members, 1,425,000; Stakes, 405; Wards, 3,046; Branches, 104; Missions, 3; Temples, 10 in use, announced or under construction; Percent LDS, 76, or one person in 1.3.

On Aug. 6, 1842, Joseph Smith prophesied that the Saints would be driven to the Rocky Mountains and there "become a mighty people."

The Saints were driven from Nauvoo, Ill., in 1846, and traveled as far as Winter Quarters, Neb., that year.

On April 5, 1847, some 148 people, in a party led by Brigham Young, began their emigration from Winter Quarters. Of this group, Orson Pratt and Erastus Snow were the first to enter the Great Basin, arriving July 21, 1847, followed by the advance party, and on the 24th by the rest of the group and Brigham Young. The Saints found a habitable but unsettled place where they hoped to live in peace. They planted crops and explored, and on July 28, Brigham Young selected the site where the Salt Lake Temple now stands. Within a month, the city had been surveyed, 80 acres of land planted, 29 log houses built, nearby valleys explored, a bowry built, an adobe fort constructed, Indians befriended, and trade shops started.

Other companies of pioneers followed, starting a flood of immigration into the Great Basin that continued until the turn of the century and afterward. About 4,500 people were in the valley before the harsh winter of 1848. Many subsisted on roots of sego lillies and boiled rawhide.

On Sept. 26, 1847, Perregrine Sessions arrived in what is now Bountiful and established a colony. Nearby Farmington was founded the same year by Hector C. Haight. In 1848, Captain James Brown of the Mormon Battalion purchased the land rights of early settler Miles Goodyear and built Brown's Fort in what is now Ogden. Centerville was established in 1848, and many Salt Lake-area colonies, such as East Millcreek and Sugar House, were started the same year. Provo was founded in 1849, along with Kaysville, Granger, Tooele and the central Utah community of Manti. By 1850, Iron City in southern Utah and 28 other colonies had been started. That year, Salt Lake City had a population of more than 11,000 people and the essentials of a successful commerce.

Before the turn of the century, up to 500 settlements had been founded within the state and in the adjoining states of Idaho, Nevada, California, Arizona, New Mexico, Colorado and Wyoming. Many of the first settlers were members from the Nauvoo period — either American or British immigrants. Later colonies were made up of emigrants from Scandinavia, Europe, and a variety of lands such as Australia, India, South Africa and even Hawaii. At least 236 parties or companies of pioneers crossed the plains for Utah, in independent companies, with wagon freighters, handcart companies, and various Church companies. Many were assisted by the Church's Perpetual Emigration Fund. An estimated 60,000 Mormons crossed the plains as pioneers. Of these, some 3,000 people crossed with handcart companies in 1856-60. Two companies, however, the late-starting Willie and Martin companies of 1856, met with tragedy in Wyoming with an unseasonably early winter, and 200 died from exposure and starvation. The majority of the people in these two handcart companies, some 875, were rescued through heroic personal effort of the Saints in Utah.

Members generally got along well with the Indians, and the most prominent local leader, Ute Chief Walker, was friendly and was baptized in 1850, though he led a brief resistance movement in 1853. Members traded with Indians and shared food with them, and the Indians helped members survive. Indian farms were established in the 1850s, but troubles between the Mormons and the government discouraged most of the Indians.

In 1857, responding to false reports of insurrection, President James Buchanan sent an army under General Albert Sidney Johnston to put down the rebellion and install a new governor in Utah. In Utah, members considered it another act of persecution (see New York, Ohio, Missouri and Illinois histories) and prepared to protect themselves. If attacked, the Saints would not fight but would burn their homes to the ground, leaving their persecutors nothing but "scorched earth," said Brigham Young. However, partly through intercession of friends of the Church, particularly Col. Thomas L. Kane, war was averted and Johnston's army passed peacefully through Salt Lake City. At the height of the war-time hysteria, a group of 120 Missouri immigrants passing through southern Utah who had provoked the Indians were killed by Indians and settlers at Mountain Meadows.

Difficulties between federal appointees and citizens continued until Utah was granted statehood in 1896. A major obstacle to statehood was the practice of plural marriage, which ended with the Manifesto issued by President Wilford Woodruff on Sept. 24, 1890.

On Feb. 14, 1853, ground was broken for the granite, six-spired temple in Salt Lake City. The edifice was constructed of stone quarried 20 miles away. The stone was hauled from the quarry by ox-drawn wagons until 1869 when the railroad was completed. Dedicated in 1892, this temple with its gilded statue of an angel and trumpet (Rev. 14:6) on the top spire has become the most recognized worldwide symbol of the

Church. Before the completion of the Salt Lake Temple, three other temples in the state were built and dedicated. Three other temples were erected and dedicated in the 1970s and 1980s. The Bountiful Utah Temple will be dedicated in 1995.

The companion building to the temple, the Tabernacle on Temple Square, was built from 1863-67 and dedicated in 1875. It is among largest timber-roofed buildings in the world and from its impressive interior emanates the weekly broadcast of the Tabernacle Choir, the longest continuous broadcast program in the United States.

During the pioneer period and shortly after the turn of the century, many of the larger outlying communities also erected tabernacles, ornate meetinghouses built for large gatherings. Many of these stand today as outstanding examples of pioneer craftsmanship.

Completion of the overland railroad in 1869 brought many changes, including more extensive mining interests. The state's population, which reached 40,273 in 1860, jumped to 210,779 in 1890. By 1900, the population was 276,749, and Utah had 27 stakes. The number of stakes increased by 12 by 1910, eight by 1920, 15 by 1930, 14 by 1940.

Throughout this period, the Church's stakes shifted from being predominantly in Utah to being about half in Utah. In 1950 Utah gained 28 new stakes and 46 were created elsewhere. By 1992, about one stake in five was in Utah.

Converts from other nations and states continued to migrate to Utah. Many non-members also came to the state. Utah officially became a mission field with its own headquarters in 1975 when the Utah Salt Lake City Mission was organized. Previously, missionaries worked in Utah under the leadership of missions headquartered in other states. The mission proved to be successful and has been divided twice. Utah's three missions, according to mission leaders, are among the most successful in the United States.

Temple Square in Salt Lake City is visited annually by nearly 5 million people and ranks among the top tourist attractions in the nation.

Over the years, the Utah membership supplied the Church with many missionaries and leaders, and has taken a pivotal role in supporting the expansion of the Church.

On Oct. 3, 1992, President Gordon B. Hinckley, first counselor in the First Presidency, announced that a second temple would be built in Utah County, Utah's ninth. Later it was announced that the temple would be located in American Fork and named the Mt. Timpanogos Utah Temple. On Feb. 13, 1994, the First Presidency announced that the Uintah Tabernacle in Vernal, Utah, would be renovated for a temple, the 10th in Utah and the first to come from an existing, renovated building.

Sources: *Utah's Heritage,* by S. George Ellsworth; *Utah's History,* Richard D. Poll, general editor, BYU Press; *Pioneer Companies that Crossed the Plains,* by Melvin S. Bashore; *Encyclopedic History of the Church* by Andrew Jenson; *Deseret News 1991-1992 Church Almanac;* multiple sources in *Church News.*

Stakes — 405
(Listed alphabetically by area as of Oct. 1, 1994.)

No.	Name	Organized	First President
Utah North Area — 258			
664	Bennion Utah	27 Oct 1974	John Labrum
1459	Bennion Utah East	29 Jan 1984	Jack L. Green
875	Bennion Utah West	30 Oct 1977	Glenn A. Weight
1482	*Bennion Heights Utah 28 Aug 1988		
	†Bennion Utah Central	17 Jun 1984	Glen Alvin Weight
918	Benson Utah	7 May 1978	Dale Morgan Rindlisbacher
1521	Bluffdale Utah	10 Mar 1985	Michael Van Jeppson
193	*Bountiful Utah		
	†Bountiful	23 Mar 1952	Thomas Amby Briggs
539	*Bountiful Utah Central		
	†Bountiful Center	10 Jan 1971	Steven S. Davis
383	*Bountiful Utah East		
	†Bountiful East	29 Sep 1963	Rendell N. Mabey
546	*Bountiful Utah Heights		
	†Bountiful Heights	16 May 1971	Jesse Earl Godfrey
1127	Bountiful Utah Mueller Park	27 Apr 1980	Duane Bowring Welling
260	*Bountiful Utah North		
	†Bountiful North	20 Apr 1958	Henry E. Peterson
1206	Bountiful Utah North Canyon	9 Nov 1980	Robert Heiner Garff
71	*Bountiful Utah Orchard		
	South Davis	20 Jun 1915	James H. Robinson
	*Davis South 29 May 1970		

262	*Bountiful Utah South		
	†Bountiful South	20 Apr 1958	Ward C. Holbrook
1269	Bountiful Utah Stone Creek	24 May 1981	Richard Scott Lemon
501	*Bountiful Utah Val Verda		
	†Val Verda	25 Jan 1970	Milton W. Russon
382	*Brigham City Utah		
	†Brigham City	22 Sep 1963	Lawrence C. Taylor
148	*Brigham City Utah Box Elder		
	*Box Elder 30 Aug 1959		
	†South Box Elder	12 Nov 1944	Abel S. Rich
147a	*Brigham City Utah North		
	*Box Elder North 29 May 1970		
	†North Box Elder	12 Nov 1944	John P. Lillywhite
375	*Brigham City Utah South		
	*Box Elder South 29 May 1970		
	†South Box Elder	28 Apr 1963	LeGrande Tea
1242	Brigham City Utah West	8 Mar 1981	Lowell Sherratt Jr.
575	*Centerville Utah		
	†Centerville	21 May 1972	Joseph A. Kjar
1798	Centerville Utah Canyon View	12 May 1991	Bruce Garrett Pitt
1335	Centerville Utah North	11 Apr 1982	Richard Crockett Edgley
903	Centerville Utah South	9 Apr 1978	Robert A. Trump
277	*Clearfield Utah		
	†Clearfield	12 Apr 1959	George Smith Haslam
966	Clearfield Utah North	8 Oct 1978	Alfred Clyde Van Wagenen
728	Clinton Utah	9 Nov 1975	Albert DeMar Mitchell
1467	Clinton Utah North	15 Apr 1984	Jay Barr Snelgrove
18	*Coalville Utah		
	†Summit	9 Jul 1877	William W. Cluff
142	*Draper Utah		
	†Mount Jordan	3 May 1942	Stanley A. Rasmussen
1319	*Draper Utah Eastridge 25 Aug 1991		
	†Draper Utah North	6 Dec 1981	Richard D. Alsop
152	*Farmington Utah		
	†Davis	14 Oct 1945	Leroy H. Duncan
1342	Farmington Utah North	16 May 1982	Richard J. White
1769	Farmington Utah Oakridge	19 Aug 1990	Jerry L. King
1750	Farmington Utah South	13 May 1990	John Leon Sorenson
1531	Fielding Utah	12 May 1985	Mark H. Jensen
1568	Fruit Heights Utah	27 Oct 1985	Newell John Law
59	*Garland Utah		
	†Bear River	11 Oct 1908	Milton H. Welling
147	*Grantsville Utah		
	†Grantsville	16 Jan 1944	Paul E. Wrathall
1069	Grantsville Utah West	23 Sep 1979	Don Henning Johnson
1494	Harrisville Utah	23 Sep 1984	Robert Lynn Nielsen
141	*Hooper Utah		
	†Lakeview	22 Mar 1942	John Child
924	Huntsville Utah	14 May 1978	Marlin Keith Jensen
1559	Hyde Park Utah	22 Sep 1985	Vincent Eugene Erickson
46	*Hyrum Utah		
	†Hyrum	30 Apr 1901	William C. Parkinson
1046	Hyrum Utah North	5 Aug 1979	J. Spencer Ward
106	*Kamas Utah		
	*Summit South 29 May 1970		
	†South Summit	8 Jul 1934	Zach J. Oblad
1635	Kanesville Utah	19 Apr 1987	Roland B. Hadley
350	*Kaysville Utah		
	†Kaysville	18 Feb 1962	Alan B. Blood
1027	Kaysville Utah Crestwood	13 May 1979	Wallace Eldean Holliday
568	*Kaysville Utah East		
	†Kaysville East	27 Feb 1972	Lawrence E. Welling
1010	Kaysville Utah South	11 Mar 1979	Newell John Law

255	*Kearns Utah		
	†Kearns	2 Feb 1958	Merrill A. Nelson
1055	Kearns Utah Central	26 Aug 1979	Garth D. Mecham
990	Kearns Utah East	10 Dec 1978	Earl M. Monson
256	*Kearns Utah North		
	†Kearns North	2 Feb 1958	Volma W. Heaton
653	Kearns Utah South	25 Aug 1974	Garth D. Mecham
1462	Kearns Utah West	12 Feb 1984	Rodney W. Bushman
1258	Kearns Utah Western Hills	26 Apr 1981	Clarence Myron White
203	*Layton Utah		
	†Layton	25 Jan 1953	I. Haven Barlow
449	*Layton Utah East		
	†Layton East	4 Feb 1968	Robert F. Bitner
957	Layton Utah Holmes Creek	3 Sep 1978	K. Roger Bean
1529	Layton Utah North	5 May 1985	Lorin Winslow Hurst Jr.
1657	Layton Utah Northridge	11 Oct 1987	Samuel Clair Bankhead
1629	Layton Utah South	8 Feb 1987	William C. Barney Jr.
1948	Layton Utah Valley View	27 June 1993	Floyd Stenquist
858	Layton Utah West	21 Aug 1977	William C. Barney Jr.
80	*Logan Utah		
	†Logan	4 Jun 1920	Oliver H. Budge
13	*Logan Utah Cache		
	†Cache	21 May 1877	Moses Thatcher
1422	Logan Utah Cache West	22 May 1983	Miles Peter Jensen
1241	Logan Utah Central	8 Mar 1981	Thad August Carlson
164	*Logan Utah East		
	*Cache East 29 May 1970		
	†East Cache	2 Feb 1947	J. Howard Maughan
160	*Logan Utah Mount Logan		
	†Mount Logan	17 Nov 1946	A. George Raymond
1347	Logan Utah South	6 Jun 1982	Ronald Skeen Peterson
259	*Logan Utah University 1st		
	†Utah State University	13 Apr 1958	Reed Bullen
427	*Logan Utah University 2nd		
	†Utah State University 2nd	12 Feb 1967	Reynold K. Watkins
785	Logan Utah University 3rd	14 Nov 1976	LaGrande C. Larsen
1719	Logan Utah University 4th	7 May 1989	Russell Miles Warren
90	*Magna Utah		
	†Oquirrh	3 Jun 1923	George A. Little
1013	Magna Utah Central	8 Apr 1979	Charles Robert Canfield
410	*Magna Utah East		
	†Oquirrh East	17 Oct 1965	William B. Martin
1510	Magna Utah South	20 Jan 1985	Hendrick Dorenbosch
246	*Midvale Utah		
	†Midvale	30 Jun 1957	Reed H. Beckstead
457	*Midvale Utah East		
	*Midvale East 29 May 1970		
	†East Midvale	5 May 1968	R. Kent King
1561	Midvale Utah North	13 Oct 1985	Grant Leon Pullan
96a	*Midvale Utah Union Fort		
	*Midvale Utah Fort Union		
	*Fort Union 17 Jun 1973		
	*Jordan East 29 May 1970		
	†East Jordan	8 May 1927	Heber J. Burgon
16	*Morgan Utah		
	†Morgan	1 Jul 1877	Willard G. Smith
1240	Morgan Utah North	8 Mar 1981	Robert Warner Poll
183	*Murray Utah		
	†Murray	11 Feb 1951	Oral J. Wilkinson
543	*Murray Utah Little Cottonwood 8 Jan 1989		
	*Murray Utah East		
	†Little Cottonwood	21 Feb 1971	James S. McCloy
1009	Murray Utah North	11 Mar 1979	John Mace Johnson
1849	Murray Utah Parkway	1 Mar 1992	Dan Alan Anderson
240	*Murray Utah South		

	†Murray South	28 Apr 1957	Donald W. Challis
468	*Murray Utah West		
	†Murray West	24 Nov 1968	Robert H.M. Killpack
528	*North Logan Utah		
	†Cache North	11 Oct 1970	Charles L. Hyde
146	*North Ogden Utah		
	†Ben Lomond	21 Nov 1943	William Arthur Budge
956	North Ogden Utah Ben Lomond	27 Aug 1978	Calvin J. Heiner
1804	North Ogden Utah Coldwater	23 June 1991	Eugene Jensen Low
1016	North Salt Lake Utah	15 Apr 1979	Clare Anderson Jones
57	*Ogden Utah		
	†Ogden	19 Jul 1908	Thomas B. Evans
998	Ogden Utah Burch Creek	4 Feb 1979	James Kirk Moyes
1133	Ogden Utah Canyon View	18 May 1980	Luan Holly Ferrin
199	*Ogden Utah East		
	*Ogden East 29 May 1970		
	†East Ogden	23 Nov 1952	Scott B. Price
198	*Ogden Utah Lorin Farr		
	†Lorin Farr	16 Nov 1952	Elton W. Wardle
140	*Ogden Utah Mound Fort 23 Sep 1984		
	*Ogden Utah Farr West		
	†Farr West	18 Jan 1942	Wilmer J. Maw
1157	Ogden Utah Mount Lewis	29 Jun 1980	Kenneth J. Alford
87	*Ogden Utah Mount Ogden		
	†Mount Ogden	21 May 1922	Robert I. Burton
314	*Ogden Utah North		
	†Ben Lomond South	20 Nov 1960	Robert M. Yorgason
201	*Ogden Utah Riverdale		
	†Riverdale	30 Nov 1952	Rudolph L. VanKampen
798	Ogden Utah Terrace View	12 Dec 1976	Leo Neeley Harris
520a	*Ogden Utah Weber		
	†Weber	16 Aug 1970	Nathan C. Tanner
272	*Ogden Utah Weber Heights		
	†Weber Heights	30 Nov 1958	Keith W. Wilcox
58	*Ogden Utah Weber North		
	*Weber North 29 May 1970		
	†North Weber	19 Jul 1908	James Wotherspoon
1191	*Ogden Utah West 23 Nov 1993		
	†Ogden Utah Weber South	12 Oct 1980	Allan T. Clarke
1520	Park City Utah	10 Mar 1985	B. Douglas Glad
876	Plain City Utah	30 Oct 1977	Kent W. Calvert
559	*Pleasant View Utah		
	†Ben Lomond West	21 Nov 1971	Jay Herbert Rhees
561	*Providence Utah		
	†Providence	12 Dec 1971	Asa L. Beecher
1351	Providence Utah South	13 Jun 1982	Lanny J. Nalder
47	*Richmond Utah		
	†Benson	1 May 1901	William H. Lewis
303	*Riverton Utah		
	†Riverton	18 Sep 1960	J. Harold Berrett
1067	Riverton Utah North	23 Sep 1979	Keith LeRoy Bergstrom
1843	Riverton Utah Summerhill	19 Jan 1992	L. Chad Campbell
328	*Roy Utah		
	†Roy	26 Mar 1961	Henry Adolph Matis
1485	Roy Utah Central	24 Jun 1984	Mark Lee Angus
438	*Roy Utah North		
	†Roy North	11 Jun 1967	Walter D. Bingham
1673	Roy Utah South	24 Jan 1988	Alonzo C Heiner
942	Roy Utah West	11 Jun 1978	Lewis R. Child
1a	Salt Lake	3 Oct 1847	John Smith
576	*Salt Lake Big Cottonwood		
	†Big Cottonwood	28 May 1972	Robert B. Barker
115	*Salt Lake Bonneville		
	†Bonneville	27 Oct 1935	Joseph L. Wirthlin

603	*Salt Lake Brighton		
	†Butler South	4 Mar 1973	Alvin Don Nydegger
361	*Salt Lake Butler		
	†Butler	18 Nov 1962	James C. Taylor
418	*Salt Lake Butler West		
	†Butler West	8 May 1966	Sherman M. Crump
204	*Salt Lake Cannon		
	†Cannon	1 Mar 1953	Fred H. Peck
237	*Salt Lake Canyon Rim		
	†Canyon Rim	28 Oct 1956	Verl F. Scott
291	*Salt Lake Central		
	†University West	7 Feb 1960	Lemonte Peterson
133	*Salt Lake Cottonwood		
	*Cottonwood 11 Feb 1951		
	†Big Cottonwood	20 Oct 1940	Irvin T. Nelson
936	Salt Lake Cottonwood Heights	28 May 1978	R. Gordon Porter
1607	Salt Lake Eagle Gate	21 Sep 1986	W. Herbert Klopfer
150	*Salt Lake East Millcreek		
	†East Millcreek	17 Jun 1945	L.B. Gunderson
996	Salt Lake East Millcreek North	28 Jan 1979	Joel R. Garrett
129a	*Salt Lake Emigration		
	†Emigration	10 Mar 1940	George A. Christensen
55	*Salt Lake Ensign		
	†Ensign	1 Apr 1904	Richard W. Young
249	*Salt Lake Foothill		
	†Monument Park West	29 Sep 1957	Frank Carl Berg
266	*Salt Lake Granger		
	†Granger	8 Jun 1958	Wm. Grant Bangerter
491	*Salt Lake Granger East		
	†Granger East	24 Aug 1969	David D. Lingard
324	*Salt Lake Granger North		
	†Granger North	26 Feb 1961	Frankland J. Kennard
764	Salt Lake Granger South	22 Aug 1976	Gordon Ward Evans
497	*Salt Lake Granger West		
	†Granger West	4 Jan 1970	Dwayne T. Johnson
42	*Salt Lake Granite		
	†Granite	28 Jan 1900	Frank Y. Taylor
1457	Salt Lake Granite Park	4 Dec 1983	Robert T. Fitt
92	*Salt Lake Grant		
	†Grant	25 May 1924	Joseph J. Daynes
114	*Salt Lake Highland		
	†Highland	8 Sep 1935	Marvin O. Ashton
154	*Salt Lake Hillside		
	†Hillside	13 Jan 1946	Casper Hugh Parker
227	*Salt Lake Holladay		
	†Holladay	18 Mar 1956	G. Carlos Smith Jr.
891	Salt Lake Holladay North	12 Feb 1978	John A. Larsen
460	*Salt Lake Holladay South		
	†Holladay South	16 Jun 1968	Marvin L. Pugh
390	*Salt Lake Hunter		
	†Hunter	5 Jan 1964	E. Verne Breeze
982	Salt Lake Hunter Central	19 Nov 1978	Evans Thomas Doxey
1533	Salt Lake Hunter Copperhill	12 May 1985	Stanley Martin Kimball
839	Salt Lake Hunter East	22 May 1977	Merrill Dimick
1539	Salt Lake Hunter South	9 Jun 1985	Morris L. Terry
582	*Salt Lake Hunter West		
	†Hunter West	13 Aug 1972	Evans Thomas Doxey
863	Salt Lake Jordan	9 Oct 1977	Robert Bennion Arnold
162	*Salt Lake Jordan North		
	*Jordan North 29 May 1970		
	†North Jordan	12 Jan 1947	John B. Hill
53	*Salt Lake Liberty		
	†Liberty	26 Feb 1904	Hugh J. Cannon

68	*Salt Lake Millcreek		
	*Millcreek 11 Feb 1951		
	†Cottonwood	29 Nov 1914	Uriah G. Miller
187	*Salt Lake Monument Park		
	†Monument Park	24 Jun 1951	George L. Nelson
1832	Salt Lake Monument Park North	24 Nov 1991	B. Lloyd Poelman
2393	*Salt Lake Mount Olympus		
	†Mount Olympus	12 Apr 1964	Orin R. Woodbury
904	Salt Lake Mount Olympus North	9 Apr 1978	William Schaubel Partridge
267	*Salt Lake Olympus		
	†Olympus	29 Jun 1958	Heber E. Peterson
145	*Salt Lake Park		
	†Park	24 Oct 1943	J. Percy Goddard
273	*Salt Lake Parleys		
	†Parleys	7 Dec 1958	Walter J. Eldredge Jr.
54	*Salt Lake Pioneer		
	†Pioneer	24 Mar 1904	William McLachlan
130	*Salt Lake Riverside		
	†Riverside	24 Mar 1940	John B. Matheson
222a	*Salt Lake Rose Park		
	†Rose Park	9 Oct 1955	Joseph F. Steenblik
412	*Salt Lake Rose Park North		
	†Rose Park North	28 Nov 1965	Joseph L. Lundstrom
345	*Salt Lake South Cottonwood		
	†South Cottonwood	10 Dec 1961	James S. McCloy
144	*Salt Lake Sugar House		
	†Sugar House	16 May 1943	Thomas M. Wheeler
178	*Salt Lake University 1st		
	*University 1st 30 Apr 1967		
	†University	12 Feb 1950	J. Quayle Ward
433	*Salt Lake University 2nd		
	†University 2nd	30 Apr 1967	Oscar W. McConkie Jr.
1488	Salt Lake University 3rd	19 Aug 1984	James Stuart Jardine
1857	Salt Lake University 4th	26 Apr 1992	John C. Pingree
1934	Salt Lake University 5th	18 Apr 1993	Kem C. Gardner
236	*Salt Lake Valley View		
	†Valley View	28 Oct 1956	Lamont B. Gundersen
1928	Salt Lake Utah (Tongan)	28 Mar 1993	Pita Masaku Kinikini
1111	Salt Lake Wasatch	24 Feb 1980	Richard G. Peterson
105	*Salt Lake Wells		
	†Wells	31 Dec 1933	Thomas E. Towler
182	*Salt Lake Wilford		
	†Wilford	11 Feb 1951	George Z. Aposhian
274	*Salt Lake Winder		
	†Winder	25 Jan 1959	M. Elmer Christensen
706	Salt Lake Winder West	21 Sep 1975	Wayne O. Ursenbach
276	*Sandy Utah		
	†Sandy	12 Apr 1959	Stanley A. Rasmussen
1489	Sandy Utah Alta View	19 Aug 1984	G. Scott Dean
611	*Sandy Utah Canyon View 31 Jul 1990		
	*Sandy Utah North		
	†Sandy North (Utah)	29 Apr 1973	Eugene D. Tenney
955	Sandy Utah Central	27 Aug 1978	Charles Alma Jones
968	Sandy Utah Cottonwood Creek	15 Oct 1978	John Robert Ruppel
627	*Sandy Utah Crescent		
	†Crescent Utah	21 Oct 1973	Allen Eugene Hilton
1110	Sandy Utah Crescent North	24 Feb 1980	Gerald Leigh Gunnell
1639	Sandy Utah Crescent Park	17 May 1987	Brad Jensen Sheppard
981	Sandy Utah Crescent South	19 Nov 1978	Marlin Alma Fairborn
775	Sandy Utah Crescent West	24 Oct 1976	John Burton Anderson
365	*Sandy Utah East		
	†Sandy East	13 Jan 1963	Orren J. Greenwood
972	Sandy Utah Granite	22 Oct 1978	William Stanley Bush
1367	Sandy Utah Granite South	17 Oct 1982	Charles Winston Dahquist II
1612	Sandy Utah Granite View	26 Oct 1986	Alan Snelgrove Layton

1812	Sandy Utah Hidden Valley	25 Aug 1991	Mark James Pendleton
811	Sandy Utah Hillcrest	13 Feb 1977	Arnold Christensen
1278	*Sandy Utah Midvalley 9 Oct 1988		
	†Midvale Utah Fort Union South	14 Jun 1981	Kenneth William Kraudy
579	*Sandy Utah West		
	†Sandy West	11 Jun 1972	Reed Neff Brown
623	*Sandy Utah Willow Creek		
	†Willow Creek	17 Jun 1973	Wayne E. Saunders
119	*Smithfield Utah		
	†Smithfield	9 Jan 1938	Alfred W. Chambers
1384	Smithfield Utah North	21 Nov 1982	W. Noble Erickson
482	*South Jordan Utah		
	*South Jordan 30 Nov 1970		
	*Jordan South 29 May 1970		
	†South Jordan	18 May 1969	Theron B. Hutchings
1192	*South Jordan Utah Glenmoor 19 Sep 1993		
	†South Jordan Utah West	12 Oct 1980	Calvin George Osborne
1956	South Jordan Utah Parkway	19 Sept 1993	Roger Glen Christensen
1491	*South Jordan Utah River 18 Dec 1900		
	†South Jordan Utah East	9 Sep 1984	Charles Elmo Turner
139	*South Ogden Utah		
	†South Ogden	7 Dec 1941	William J. Critchlow
138	*South Salt Lake 31 May 1979		
	*Salt Lake South		
	†South Salt Lake	2 Sep 1941	Axel J. Andresen
1705	South Weber Utah	27 Nov 1988	LeRoy Horace Poll
424	*Sunset Utah		
	†Sunset	11 Dec 1966	John L. Nicholas
70a	*Syracuse Utah		
	*Davis North 29 May 1970		
	†North Davis	20 Jun 1915	Henry H. Blood
1858	Syracuse Utah South	26 Apr 1992	Wesley Miller White
217	*Taylorsville Utah		
	†Taylorsville	10 Oct 1954	Wayne Charles Player
598	*Taylorsville Utah Central		
	†Taylorsville Central	4 Feb 1973	Richard A. Barker
629	Taylorsville Utah North	28 Oct 1973	LeVere Elihu Brady
1473	Taylorsville Utah North Central	13 May 1984	Floyd Keith Rupp
1461	Taylorsville Utah South	5 Feb 1984	Clinton D. Topham
809	*Taylorsville Utah Valley Park 4 Dec 1988		
	†Taylorsville Utah West Central	6 Feb 1977	Floyd Keith Rupp
411	*Taylorsville Utah West		
	†Taylorsville West	31 Oct 1965	Richard A. Barker
15	*Tooele Utah		
	†Tooele	24 Jun 1877	Francis M. Lyman
206	*Tooele Utah North		
	*Tooele North 29 May 1970		
	†North Tooele	29 Mar 1953	Orland T. Barrus
928	Tooele Utah South	21 May 1978	Joel James Dunn
173	*Tremonton Utah		
	*Bear River South 29 May 1970		
	†South Bear River	1 May 1949	Clifton G.M. Kerr
1004	Tremonton Utah South	25 Feb 1979	Boyd Lee Cullimore
371	*Washington Terrace Utah		
	†Washington Terrace	24 Feb 1963	Ernest B. Wheeler
458	Weber State University Stake 21 Aug 1990		
	*Ogden Utah College		
	†Weber State College	12 May 1968	E. LaMar Buckner
1043	Wellsville Utah	17 Jun 1979	Donald Joseph Jeppesen Jr.
578	*West Bountiful Utah 9 Oct 1984		
	*Bountiful Utah West		
	†Bountiful West	11 Jun 1972	Clarence D. Samuelson
97	*West Jordan Utah		
	†West Jordan	8 May 1927	Joseph M. Holt

1511	*West Jordan Utah Bingham Creek 29 Nov 1988		
	†West Jordan Utah Southeast	27 Jan 1985	Frederick James Haydock
1099	West Jordan Utah Central	27 Jan 1980	M. Curtis Jewkes
735	West Jordan Utah East	30 Nov 1975	Dale P. Bateman
929	*West Jordan Utah Heritage 9 Oct 1990		
	†West Jordan Utah West	21 May 1978	Robert B. Rowley
614	*West Jordan Utah Mountain View 21 Feb 1989		
	*West Jordan Utah South		
	†Jordan River	20 May 1973	Max Curtis Jewkes
1311	West Jordan Utah Oquirrh	22 Nov 1981	Johannes Gerald Erkelens
1686	West Jordan Utah Prairie	7 Feb 1988	J. Kim Christensen
1443	West Jordan Utah River	18 Sep 1983	Dennis Arthur Hope
1509	West Jordan Utah Welby	20 Jan 1985	Russell Jean Abney
1512	*West Jordan Utah Westbrook 16 May 1989		
	†West Jordan Utah North	3 Feb 1985	Henry Keonaona Chai II
1128	West Point Utah	27 Apr 1980	Vern L. Thurgood
636	*West Valley Utah 17 Jan 1989		
	†Salt Lake Granger Central	31 Mar 1974	Norman H. Bangerter
1506	Willard Utah	25 Nov 1984	Robert Kent Lund
498	*Woods Cross Utah		
	†Woods Cross	4 Jan 1970	D. Hatch Howard
1333	Woods Cross Utah East	21 Mar 1982	Wayne A. Beers

Discontinued

20	Box Elder	19 Aug 1877	Oliver G. Snow
	12 Nov 1944 ★North Box Elder (147), South Box Elder (148)		
14	Davis	17 Jun 1877	William R. Smith
	20 Jun 1915 ★North Davis (70), South Davis (71)		
41	Jordan	21 Jan 1900	Orrin P. Miller
	8 May 1927 ★East Jordan (96), West Jordan (97)		
275	*Salt Lake Granite Park		
	31 May 1979 ★South Salt Lake (138)		
	†Granite Park	22 Feb 1959	Rolf Christiansen
155	*Salt Lake Temple View		
	24 June 1979 ★Salt Lake Wells (105), Salt Lake Liberty (53)		
	*Temple View 14 Apr 1946		
	†Temple	13 Jan 1946	Adiel F. Stewart
2b	Weber	26 Jan 1851	Lorin Farr
	14 Jun 1970 ★Mount Ogden (87)		

Utah South Area — 147

44	*Alpine Utah		
	†Alpine	13 Jan 1901	Stephen L. Chipman
1526	Altamont Utah	21 Apr 1985	Everett Dee Roberts
376	*American Fork Utah		
	†American Fork	12 May 1963	Stanley D. Roberts
1022	American Fork Utah East	29 Apr 1979	Dale Orville Gunther
624	*American Fork Utah North		
	†American Fork North	17 Jun 1973	Leland Forbes Priday
1218	American Fork Utah West	14 Dec 1980	Brent Lindsay Milne
7b	*Beaver Utah		
	†Beaver	12 Mar 1869	John R. Murdock
897	Blanding Utah	5 Mar 1978	Fred Eugene Halliday
1283	Blanding Utah West	12 Jul 1981	Preston Gardner Nielson
1690	Bloomington Utah	6 Mar 1988	Steven Howard Peterson
1623	Bloomington Hills Utah	4 Jan 1987	James Grey Larkin
225	*Brigham Young University 1st		
	†Brigham Young University	8 Jan 1956	Antone K. Romney
295	Brigham Young University 2nd	17 Apr 1960	Bryan W. Belnap
296	Brigham Young University 3rd	17 Apr 1960	William Noble Waite
395	Brigham Young University 4th	3 May 1964	William R. Siddoway
396	Brigham Young University 5th	3 May 1964	A. Harold Goodman
397	Brigham Young University 6th	3 May 1964	Wayne B. Hales
431	Brigham Young University 7th	30 Apr 1967	Dean A. Peterson
432	Brigham Young University 8th	30 Apr 1967	David H. Yarn
478	Brigham Young University 9th	27 Apr 1969	Carl D. Jones

479	Brigham Young University 10th	27 Apr 1969	Ivan J. Barrett
688	Brigham Young University 11th	13 Apr 1975	Gregory E. Austin
689	Brigham Young University 12th	13 Apr 1975	Charles Verl Clark
973	Brigham Young University 13th	29 Oct 1978	Leo Preston Vernon
974	Brigham Young University 14th	29 Oct 1978	Curtis Nicholas VanAlfen
1605	Brigham Young University 15th	31 Aug 1986	H. Donl Peterson
1688	Brigham Young University 16th	21 Feb 1988	Donald J Butler
1722	Brigham Young University 17th	21 May 1989	Stanley Armond Taylor
1889	Brigham Young University 18th	28 Jun 1992	Clark D. Webb Jr.
23	*Castle Dale Utah		
	†Emery	Aug 1880	Christen G. Larsen
172	*Cedar City Utah		
	†Cedar	2 May 1948	David L. Sargent
901	Cedar City Utah North	19 Mar 1978	Robert L. Blattner
316	*Cedar City Utah West		
	†Cedar West	27 Nov 1960	Franklin D. Day
65	*Delta Utah		
	†Deseret	11 Aug 1912	Alonzo A. Hinckley
1068	Delta Utah West	23 Sep 1979	Glen Wilford Swalberg
62	*Duchesne Utah		
	†Duchesne	14 Sep 1910	William H. Smart
1564	Enoch Utah	20 Oct 1985	Robert Louis Blattner
134	*Enterprise Utah		
	†Uvada (Utah, Nevada)	15 Dec 1940	David J. Ronnow
1524	Ephraim Utah	24 Mar 1985	Joseph C. Nielsen
83	*Escalante Utah		
	†Garfield	29 Aug 1920	Charles E. Rowan Jr.
1336	Ferron Utah	11 Apr 1982	Jerry D Mangum
6b	*Fillmore Utah		
	†Millard	9 Mar 1869	Thomas Callister
89	*Gunnison Utah		
	†Gunnison	6 May 1923	Allen E. Park
19	*Heber City Utah		
	†Wasatch	15 Jul 1877	Abraham Hatch
649	Heber City Utah East	16 Jun 1974	Robert F. Clyde
1170	Helper Utah	24 Aug 1980	Robert E. Olsen
1167	Highland Utah	10 Aug 1980	Merlin B. Larson
1827	Highland Utah East	10 Nov 1991	Stephen Mark Studdert
871	Huntington Utah	23 Oct 1977	Ira Wallace Hatch
104	*Hurricane Utah		
	†Zion Park	8 Dec 1929	Claudius Hirschi
106	*Kamas Utah		
	*Summit South 29 May 1970		
	†South Summit	8 Jul 1934	Zach J. Oblad
11	*Kanab Utah		
	†Kanab (Utah, Arizona)	18 Apr 1877	L. John Nuttall
1638	*Kanab Utah Kaibab 20 Aug 1991		
	†Kanab Utah South	3 May 1987	Nils G. Bayles
1294	*La Verkin Utah 30 Nov 1984		
	†Hurricane Utah North	11 Oct 1981	Floyd Leon Lewis
100	*Lehi Utah		
	†Lehi	1 Jul 1928	Anchor C. Schow
637	Lehi Utah North	5 May 1974	Francis Russell Hakes
1416	Lehi Utah West	8 May 1983	Boyd Sabey Stewart
1392	Lindon Utah	12 Dec 1982	Noel Thomas Greenwood
34	*Loa Utah		
	†Wayne	27 May 1893	Willis E. Robison
43	*Manti Utah		
	*Sanpete South 29 May 1970		
	†South Sanpete	9 Dec 1900	Canute Peterson
714	Mapleton Utah	19 Oct 1975	Jay M. Smith Jr.
1407	Midway Utah	27 Mar 1983	Wayne Watkins Probst
553	*Moab Utah		
	†Moab	19 Sep 1971	Leland D. Teeples

85	*Monroe Utah		
	*Sevier South 29 May 1970		
	†South Sevier	30 Jan 1921	John E. Magleby
27	*Monticello Utah		
	†San Juan (Utah, Colorado)	23 Sep 1883	Platte D. Lyman
102	*Moroni Utah		
	†Moroni	16 Jun 1929	James Louis Nielsen
42a	*Mount Pleasant Utah		
	*Sanpete North 29 May 1970		
	†North Sanpete	9 Dec 1900	Christian N. Lund
5b	*Nephi Utah		
	*Juab 1871		
	†Nephi	20 Sep 1868	Jacob G. Bigler
1538	Nephi Utah North	9 Jun 1985	James Randy McKnight
166	Orem Utah		
	†Orem	13 Apr 1947	Walter R. Holdaway
1668	Orem Utah Aspen	10 Jan 1988	Ross Steve Wolfley
1518	*Orem Utah Canyon View 1 Mar 1988		
	†Orem Utah Northeast	3 Mar 1985	Jerry C. Washburn
271	*Orem Utah Cherry Hill 15 Apr 1988		
	*Orem Utah Sharon West		
	*Sharon West 29 May 1970		
	†West Sharon	30 Nov 1958	Clyde M. Lunceford
751	Orem Utah East	21 Mar 1976	Mirl Blake Hymas
251	*Orem Utah Geneva Heights 5 Apr 1988		
	*Orem Utah West		
	†Orem West	3 Nov 1957	Edward C. Bunker
1581	*Orem Utah Hillcrest 27 Nov 1988		
	†Orem Utah Sharon South	1 Dec 1985	Wynn Howard Hemmert
867	*Orem Utah Lakeridge 1 Mar 1988		
	†Orem Utah South Central	16 Oct 1977	Gordon Max Thomas
1184	Orem Utah Lakeview	28 Sep 1980	Merrill Gappmayer
533	*Orem Utah North		
	†Orem North	1 Nov 1970	Eli Karl Clayson
1682	Orem Utah Northridge	31 Jan 1988	Larry V. Perkins
1176	Orem Utah Park	7 Sep 1980	Richard S. Johns
103	*Orem Utah Sharon		
	†Sharon	15 Sep 1929	Arthur V. Watkins
812	*Orem Utah Sharon Park 20 Dec 1988		
	†Orem Utah Central	13 Feb 1977	Clifton M. Pyne
1490	Orem Utah College	26 Aug 1984	Charles E. Peterson
	Orem Utah Student 8 Jan 1991		
862	*Orem Utah Suncrest 1 Mar 1988		
	†Utah West Central	18 Sep 1977	James Edwin Mangum
554	*Orem Utah Sunset Heights 19 Apr 1988		
	*Orem Utah South		
	†Orem South	19 Sep 1971	Richard P. Shumway
1048	Orem Utah Timpview	12 Aug 1979	Carl Crawford
905	Orem Utah Windsor	9 Apr 1978	Dennis LeRoy Hill
12	*Panguitch Utah		
	†Panguitch	23 Apr 1877	James Henrie
5a	*Parowan Utah		
	†Parowan	May 1852	John C.L. Smith
45	*Payson Utah		
	†Nebo	13 Jan 1901	Jonathan S. Page Jr.
634	Payson Utah East	24 Mar 1974	David R. Mangelson
1297	Payson Utah South	18 Oct 1981	Joe Lynn Spencer
1310	Payson Utah West	22 Nov 1981	Gerald M. Finch
529	*Pleasant Grove Utah		
	†Pleasant Grove	11 Oct 1970	Leon R. Walker
894	Pleasant Grove Utah East	26 Feb 1978	Evan Mack Palmer
1958	Pleasant Grove Utah Grove Creek	24 Oct 1993	David Wesley Dickerson
1124	Pleasant Grove Utah Manila	23 Mar 1980	Grant Kay Fugal
101	*Pleasant Grove Utah Timpanogos		
	†Timpanogos	1 Jul 1928	Wilford W. Warnick

61	*Price Utah		
	†Carbon	8 May 1910	Gustave A. Iverson
151	*Price Utah North		
	*Carbon North 29 May 1970		
	†North Carbon	24 Jun 1945	Cecil Broadbent
127	*Provo Utah		
	†Provo	19 Feb 1939	Charles E. Rowan Jr.
1437	Provo Utah Bonneville	28 Aug 1983	Norman Dean Anderson
3b	*Provo Utah Central		
	*Utah 1855		
	†Provo	19 Mar 1851	Isaac Higbee
165	*Provo Utah East		
	*Provo East 29 May 1970		
	†East Provo	13 Apr 1947	Charles E. Rowan
541	*Provo Utah Edgemont		
	†Edgemont	17 Jan 1971	Richard A. Call
1692	Provo Utah Edgemont North	20 Mar 1988	Clayton S. Huber
899	Provo Utah Edgemont South	19 Mar 1978	Keith Hale Hoopes
1209	Provo Utah Grandview	23 Nov 1980	Laren R. Robison
547	*Provo Utah North		
	†Provo North	30 May 1971	Wayne Alvin Mineer
821	Provo Utah Oak Hills	10 Apr 1977	John R. Christiansen
200	*Provo Utah Sharon East		
	*Sharon East 29 May 1970		
	†East Sharon	23 Nov 1952	Henry D. Taylor
1090	Provo Utah South	2 Dec 1979	Moorlan Wayne Snow
1424	Provo Utah Sunset	29 May 1983	Glen Howard Snyder
167	*Provo Utah West		
	*Utah West 29 May 1970		
	†West Utah	4 May 1947	J. Earl Lewis
10a	*Richfield Utah		
	†Sevier	24 May 1874	Joseph A. Young
848	Richfield Utah East	12 Jun 1977	Warren T. Harward
82	*Roosevelt Utah		
	†Roosevelt	26 Jun 1920	William H. Smart
1458	Roosevelt Utah East	11 Dec 1983	Earl V. Allred
685	Roosevelt Utah West	2 Mar 1975	Alvin Leonard Bellon
9a	*St. George Utah		
	†Saint George (Utah, Arizona)	7 Nov 1869	Joseph W. Young
759	St. George Utah College	30 May 1976	Peter A. Nyberg
1814	St. George Utah Dixie Downs	25 Aug 1991	Thomas Randy Judd
322	*St. George Utah East		
	†St. George East	5 Feb 1961	Rudger C. Atkin
1813	St. George Utah Green Valley	25 Aug 1991	La Rell David Muir
1625	*St. George Utah Pine View 12 Dec 1989		
	†Washington Utah West	18 Jan 1987	H. Carlyle Stirling
895	St. George Utah West	5 Mar 1978	Dale Gubler
686	*Salem Utah 8 Dec 1976		
	†Spanish Fork Utah Salem	9 Mar 1975	Kent Blaine Hansen
84	*Salina Utah		
	*Sevier North 29 May 1970		
	†North Sevier	30 Jan 1921	Moroni Lazenby
1361	Santa Clara Utah	29 Aug 1982	Dale Gubler
74	*Santaquin Utah		
	*Santaquin-Tintic 2 Apr 1939		
	†Tintic	22 Apr 1917	Erastus Franklin Birch
1525	Snow College Utah	24 Mar 1985	Allen P. Jacobson
413	*Southern Utah University 13 Dec 1990		
	*Cedar City Utah College		
	*Southern Utah State College 12 Oct 1969		
	†College of Southern Utah	6 Jan 1966	Robert B. White Jr.
233	*Spanish Fork Utah		
	†Spanish Fork	30 Sep 1956	Joseph Y. Toronto
94	*Spanish Fork Utah Palmyra		
	†Palmyra	23 Nov 1924	Henry A. Gardner

1115	Spanish Fork Utah South	9 Mar 1980	Wilbur Angus Stephenson
900	Spanish Fork Utah West	19 Mar 1978	Clair O. Anderson
235	*Springville Utah		
	†Springville	21 Oct 1956	Leo A. Crandall
1483	Springville Utah Hobble Creek	17 Jun 1984	Donald Blaine Hadley
93	*Springville Utah Kolob		
	†Kolob	23 Nov 1924	George R. Maycock
705	*Springville Utah Spring Creek 21 Jun 1988		
	†Springville Utah North	31 Aug 1975	F. Calvin Packard
239	*Vernal Utah Ashley		
	†Ashley	2 Dec 1956	William Budge Wallis
1434	Vernal Utah Glines	19 Jun 1983	Gayle F. McKeachnie
913	Vernal Utah Maeser	30 Apr 1978	Venil P. Johnson
30	*Vernal Utah Uintah 10 Jun 1986		
	*Vernal Utah		
	†Uintah	11 Jul 1886	Samuel R. Bennion
991	Washington Utah	7 Jan 1979	Lorel Wynn Turek
1193	Wellington Utah	12 Oct 1980	Charles V. Bradshaw

Discontinued

122	Moon Lake	24 Apr 1938	Edwin L. Murphy
	10 Nov 1957 ★Duchesne (62)		
17	Sanpete	4 Jul 1877	Canute Peterson
	9 Dec 1900 ★North Sanpete (42), South Sanpete (43)		

Missions — 3
(As of Oct. 1, 1994; shown with historical number. See MISSIONS.)

(132) UTAH OGDEN MISSION
2133 Washington Blvd.
Ogden, UT 84401
Phone: (801) 392-9325

(187) UTAH SALT LAKE CITY MISSION
7938 South 3500 East, #4
Salt Lake City, UT 84121
Phone: (801) 942-7983

(222) UTAH PROVO MISSION
2500 N. University Ave., #100
Provo, UT 84604
Phone: (801) 377-1490

MISSIONARY TRAINING CENTER
2005 North 900 East
Provo, UT 84604
Phone: (801) 378-2602

Vermont

Year-end 1993: Est. population, 579,000; Members, 3,200; Stakes, 1; Wards, 6; Branches, 5; Percent LDS, 0.5, or one person in 181.

The Prophet Joseph Smith was born in Sharon, Vt., on Dec. 23, 1805. Other prominent leaders born in this state include Oliver Cowdery, Brigham Young, Heber C. Kimball and Erastus Snow. In all, about a dozen of the early Church leaders were born in Vermont.

Jared Carter arrived in Benson, Rutland County, Vt., about Oct. 25, 1831, and after preaching, baptized 27 converts. Most of these members, and those baptized later, remained faithful, migrating to the West in 1833.

Elders Orson Pratt and Lyman E. Johnson supposedly preached in Vermont in early 1832. Other missionaries followed. By 1835, branches were organized in St. Johnsbury, Danville, Charleston, Andover, and Benson. Additional branches were organized in Irasburg in 1836, Addison in 1840, and Woodstock in 1843. Elders Erastus Snow and William Hyde were laboring in Woodstock in 1844 when they heard of the martyrdom.

Members of these branches dispersed in large numbers to join the westward movement, and missionary work did not resume until many years later. Membership in the mostly rural state, which is the third least populated in the United States, has remained sparse. On Dec. 23, 1905, at the centennial of Joseph Smith's birth, a 100-ton granite shaft 50 feet 10 inches tall was dedicated. Community members supported the construction and the dedication was well-attended. Some 30,000 people visit the marker and its attendant historic site facility each year. The monument was a frequent site for missionary conferences in the early years.

The Eastern States Mission, reopened in 1893, maintained responsibility for Vermont until the state was transferred to the Canadian Mission in 1927. The Vermont Conference was organized in 1909, though no branches were organized. In 1916, 30 people attended a conference at Barre. The Morrisville Branch existed by 1924. In 1930, a small branch functioned at Burlington, organized in 1927 or after. Responsibility for the state was placed with the New England Mission when it was created in 1937. Its first conference was held at the Joseph Smith monument in July, 1938 with 60 missionaries in attendance. Beginning in 1987, lights were placed around the Joseph Smith Monument during the Christmas season, attracting thousands of visitors. About 70,000 visitors, including those at Christmas, come to the site annually.

The Montpelier Vermont Stake, where the bulk of the state's LDS membership resides today, was created April 11, 1976, with a membership of 2,116 members. (Two of its wards were in New Hampshire.) In 1980, statewide membership was 2,196. It increased to 2,758 in 1990.

Church membership today is almost entirely converts and a large percentage of them are natives of Vermont.

Sources: "Proceedings at the dedication of the Joseph Smith Memorial Monument," distributed at the dedication Dec. 23, 1905; *Encyclopedic History of the Church* by Andrew Jenson; "The Benson Exodus of 1833: "Gospel Brothers," by James L. Kimball, *Church News*, March 11, 1978; Mormon Converts and the Westward Movement," by Erik Barnouw, Summer, 1986, *Vermont Journal History;* "Yankee Saints: The Church in New England during the Twentieth Century," by Richard O. Cowan, 1988, "Members reflect spirit of pioneers in state rich in Church history," by Sheridan R. Sheffield, *Church News,* Dec. 21, 1991; *Regional Studies in Latter-day Saint History,* BYU; *Church News,* Dec. 18, 1993.

Stake — 1
(Listed alphabetically as of Oct. 1, 1994.)

No.	Name	Organized	First President
North America Northeast Area			
753	Montpelier Vermont	11 Apr 1976	C. Lynn Fife

Virginia

Year-end 1993: Est. population, 6,638,000; Members, 59,000; Stakes, 15; Wards, 93; Branches, 31; Missions, 1; Districts, 0; Percent LDS, 0.9, or one person in 113.

Elder Jedediah M. Grant preached in Patrick County, Va., from 1837 to 1838, establishing a small branch there. In 1838, Elder George A. Smith preached in Montgomery County and realized some success. Francis Gladden Bishop labored in various locations in Virginia from 1838-39 and baptized many converts. Other missionaries also worked in Wythe and Nelson counties.

Elder Grant returned to Virginia in 1840 and preached successfully in Smyth, Washington and Tazewell counties. He was in high demand as a preacher and had three invitations for every one he could fill. He frequently read Joseph Smith's prophecy of the Civil War. His listeners gave him a horse, clothing and funds to assist him in preaching in more locations.

In 1841, Elder Grant's companion, his brother Joshua, reported a membership of 80 in the state, including a branch of 25 in Rich Valley, Smythe County. After the Grant brothers left in 1842, Elder R.H. Kinnamon traveled to nine counties and baptized more than 100 persons. Prominent Southern States missionary and mission president, Henry G. Boyle, was among those converted from Tazewell County. He preached in his home state in 1844-45 and baptized a number of converts.

Work progressed well until the martyrdom of the Prophet Joseph Smith, when some elders returned to Nauvoo. Membership at the time was probably in excess of 350. Most of these faithful early members migrated west.

Missionary work resumed with some success in 1870. In 1879, when Elders Mathias F. Cowley and Frank A. Benson preached in Tazewell, Bland and Smythe counties, they baptized a few children and grandchildren of those who first heard the gospel preached by Elder Grant. Some of these people recalled the prophecy of the Civil War that was fulfilled 20 years after it was given.

In 1886, the Virginia Conference was divided and the West Virginia Conference created. The state was briefly placed in the Middle States Mission from 1902 until 1903 when it was returned to the Southern States Mission.

By 1919, branches existed in Danville, Petersburg, Portsmouth and Richmond. In 1929, the state was transferred to the East Central States Mission. In 1930, the Virginia Conference had a membership of 2,267 in the Danville, Norfolk, Richmond and Roanoke branches and Sunday Schools in Mt. Lake, Petersburg, Portsmouth, Scholfield, Vinton and Oilville. The Virginia East District was created in 1944. The Virginia Stake was created June 30, 1957, with about 1,600 members in the Dutch Gap, Petersburg, Newport News, Norfolk, Richmond, and Portsmouth wards, and the Franklin Branch in Virginia. Missionary work and an influx of members involved in military and industrial fields accounted for the recent growth of the district. Growth also came as members assumed roles in governmental agencies headquartered in Washington D.C.

Membership in 1972 was 22,000, increasing to 35,485 in 1980 and to 55,367 in 1990.

Sources: *Encyclopedic History of the Church* by Andrew Jenson; Southern States Mission, manuscript history; *Church News,* July 6, 1957; *History of the Southern States Mission,* a BYU thesis by LaMar C. Barrett, July 1960; and "Church blossoms where history's roots run deep," by Mike Cannon, *Church News,* April 21, 1990.

Stakes — 15
(Listed alphabetically as of Oct. 1, 1994.)

No.	Name	Organized	First President
North America Northeast Area			
512	*Annandale Virginia		
	†Mount Vernon	26 Apr 1970	Allen Claire Rozsa
1671	Chesapeake Virginia	17 Jan 1988	Joseph Craig Merrell
740	Fairfax Virginia	1 Feb 1976	Ed Mordue Hayward
1198	Fredericksburg Virginia	26 Oct 1980	Douglas Lynn Marker
1325	McLean Virginia	14 Feb 1982	Earl John Roueche
1583	Mount Vernon Virginia	5 Jan 1986	Keith Alan Gulledge
922	*New River Virginia 24 Oct 1989		
	†Bluefield Virginia	14 May 1978	Norman Perry Tyler Jr.
846	Newport News Virginia	12 Jun 1977	Kirk Thomas Waldron
392	*Norfolk Virginia		
	†Norfolk (Virginia, North Carolina)	12 Apr 1964	Walter H. Hick
372	*Oakton Virginia		
	†Potomac (Virginia, D.C., Md.)	3 Mar 1963	Miller F. Shurtleff
245	*Richmond Virginia		
	†Virginia (Va., N. C.)	30 Jun 1957	Cashell Donahoe Sr.
1450	Richmond Virginia Chesterfield	30 Oct 1983	John Leonard Ruckart Jr.
499	*Roanoke Virginia		
	†Roanoke	11 Jan 1970	Russell B. Maddock
934	*Waynesboro Virginia 16 Dec 1982		
	†Charlottesville Virginia	28 May 1978	Wilford John Teerlink
837	Winchester Virginia	22 May 1977	Harold S. Harrison

Mission — 1
(As of Oct. 1, 1994; shown with historical number. See MISSIONS. Washington D.C. missions, though headquarters are located in Virginia, are listed under District of Columbia.)

(42) VIRGINIA RICHMOND MISSION
9327 Midlothian Tpk, # 1-B
Richmond, VA 23235
Phone: (804) 330-9630

Washington

Year-end 1993: Est. population, 5,343,000; Members, 203,000; Stakes, 50; Wards, 385; Branches, 45; Missions, 3; Temples, 1; Percent LDS, 3.8, or one person in 26.

In 1854, four missionaries serving in California, Elders John Hughes, Clark Faben, Alfred Bybee and Silas Harris, were sent to labor in the Washington and Oregon territories. One of these, Elder Hughes, converted enough people to start at branch on the Lewis River.

One early convert who remained in Washington despite persecution was was Louisa A. Johns Bozarth. She was faithful throughout her life. When she died in 1911, animosity against the Church was still so pronounced that her grave was dedicated secretly at night.

Many Mormons worked on the construction of the Northern Pacific Oregon Short Line railroads in the 1880s and a few later moved into the Northwest.

In 1886, a mission was organized under the direction of George C. Parkinson, president of the Oneida Stake in southeastern Idaho. He wanted to search for the members of his stake who had moved into Washington, Oregon and Montana. The first full-time missionaries were active in Spokane by 1896. A second Northwestern States Mission was created in that city July 26, 1897. (The first Northwestern States Mission, created in 1878, had its headquarters in Chicago, Ill.)

A meeting held in a Church facility in Colfax, Wash., on Jan. 3, 1898, had an attendance of 65 people. Missionaries began working in Walla Walla on Jan. 17, 1898.

A year later, an Eastern Washington Conference was held with one elder and 20 members in attendance. On Sept. 9, 1906, a Sunday School was organized in Spokane, and a branch was organized on March 12, 1916. The branch obtained a meetinghouse in 1920. In Seattle, a Sunday School was started in 1915, and a branch organized Sept. 12, 1920. A building for this branch was purchased in 1927. Many people joined the Church, and many members moved in. Many came to work in defense industries.

In 1930, membership was 1,855 in eight branches, with chapels in Everett, Spokane, Seattle and Olympia. World War II brought an influx of members to Washington to take part in the war effort. The Seattle Stake was created July 31, 1938. Membership in the state reached 5,000 in 1940.

The completion of the Grand Coulee Dam on the Columbia River in the early 1940s opened the way for additional farming in the Columbia River Basin, and many members flocked to the state. Membership increased to 11,000 by 1960. Growth continued, and by 1970, membership doubled at 67,203. Membership reached 138,00 in 1980. The Seattle Temple was dedicated that year. By 1990, membership reached 189,000. In 1992, Washington became the fifth state in the United States with at least 50 stakes.

Sources: *Encyclopedic History of the Church* by Andrew Jenson; *Latter-day Saints in the Great Northwest,* by J. Arthur Horne, published by Graphic Arts Press, Seattle, Wash.; *History of the Church in the Pacific Northwest,* by Leonard J. Arrington, Task papers in LDS History, No. 18.

Stakes — 50
(Listed alphabetically as of Oct. 1, 1994.)

No.	Name	Organized	First President
North America Northwest Area			
1388	Auburn Washington	28 Nov 1982	Alan Warner Bolles
388	*Bellevue Washington		
	†Seattle East	1 Dec 1963	Raymond W. Eldredge
1266	Bellingham Washington	10 May 1981	Eugene Clifford Hatch
1312	Bothell Washington	22 Nov 1981	Arnold R. Parrott
299	*Bremerton Washington		
	†Puget Sound	19 Jun 1960	Herbert S. Anderson
958	Centralia Washington	10 Sep 1978	Frank Edward Berrett
1299	Colville Washington	18 Oct 1981	Garnett Russell Port
1438	Elma Washington	28 Aug 1983	Lou Elwin Green
1148	Ephrata Washington	15 Jun 1980	Robert A. Hammond
532	*Everett Washington		
	†Cascade South	25 Oct 1970	Wesley K. Duce
883	Federal Way Washington	20 Nov 1977	Jack Lynn Smith
776	Kennewick Washington	24 Oct 1976	Elton Elias Hunt
1374	Kennewick Washington East	31 Oct 1982	Donald LeRoy Brunson
1495	Kent Washington	14 Oct 1984	Owen Edvin Jensen
1855	Kirkland Washington	19 Apr 1992	Peter Gideon Condie
1565	Lakewood Washington	20 Oct 1985	James Rolland Ely
599	*Longview Washington		
	†Columbia River West	4 Feb 1973	Walter Lee Robinson
925	Lynnwood Washington	14 May 1978	Robert C. Barnard
1251	Marysville Washington	29 Mar 1981	Verle George Call
213	*Moses Lake Washington		
	†Grand Coulee	18 Apr 1954	Elmo J. Bergeson
379	*Mount Vernon Washington		
	†Cascade	30 Jun 1963	Robert E. Jones
440	*Olympia Washington		
	†Olympia	27 Aug 1967	Herbert S. Anderson
1049	Othello Washington	12 Aug 1979	Jay L. Christensen
437	*Pasco Washington		
	†Pasco (Washington, Oregon)	21 May 1967	David K. Barber
1848	Port Angeles Washington	23 Feb 1992	Richard Ernest Shaw
638	Pullman Washington	5 May 1974	John Leo Schwendiman
542	*Puyallup Washington		
	†Mount Rainier	17 Jan 1971	Owen H. Dickson
1389	Puyallup Washington South	28 Nov 1982	Dennis Tripp Sampson
844	Redmond Washington	29 May 1977	Arnold R. Parrott
514	*Renton Washington		
	†Renton	3 May 1970	Harris A. Mortensen
1244	Renton Washington North	15 Mar 1981	Denzel Nolan Wiser
180	*Richland Washington		
	†Richland (Washington, Oregon)	25 Jun 1950	James V. Thompson

124	*Seattle Washington		
	†Seattle	31 Jul 1938	Alex Brown
242	*Seattle Washington North		
	*Seattle North 29 May 1970		
	†North Seattle	19 May 1957	Wilford H. Payne
1496	Seattle Washington Shoreline	14 Oct 1984	Brent Isaac Nash
1023	*Selah Washington 31 Aug 1982		
	†Yakima Washington North	29 Apr 1979	Robert Atwood Hague
1057	Silverdale Washington	26 Aug 1979	David Junior Jones
1890	Snohomish Washington	28 Jun 1992	Craig L. Morrison
168	*Spokane Washington		
	†Spokane	29 Jun 1947	Albert I. Morgan
556	*Spokane Washington East		
	†Spokane East	17 Oct 1971	James B. Cox
992	Spokane Washington North	7 Jan 1979	Dwaine E. Nelson
1841	Spokane Washington West	12 Jan 1992	Elroy C. McDermott
195	*Tacoma Washington		
	†Tacoma	28 Sep 1952	Elvin E. Evans
1052	Tacoma Washington South	19 Aug 1979	James Rolland Ely
389	*Vancouver Washington		
	*Columbia River North 29 May 1970		
	†North Columbia	1 Dec 1963	Wallace V. Teuscher
1570	Vancouver Washington North	3 Nov 1985	Bruce A. Schreiner
979	Vancouver Washington West	5 Nov 1978	Earl Clifford Jorgensen
1011	Walla Walla Washington	11 Mar 1979	David L. Hafen
426	*Wenatchee Washington 7 Dec 1978		
	*Quincy Washington		
	†Grand Coulee North	29 Jan 1967	Leslie H. Boyce
284	*Yakima Washington		
	†Yakima	24 May 1959	F. Edgar Johnson

Missions — 3
(As of Oct. 1, 1994; shown with historical number. See MISSIONS.)

(78a) WASHINGTON SEATTLE MISSION
13353 Bel-Red Road, Suite 3
Bellevue, WA 98005
Phone: (206) 641-5050

(255) WASHINGTON TACOMA MISSION
4007 D Bridgeport Way W., Suite D
Tacoma, WA 98466-4330
Phone: (206) 566-5480

(166) WASHINGTON SPOKANE MISSION
P.O. Box 14808
Spokane, WA 99214-0808
Phone: (509) 924-8932

West Virginia

Year-end 1993: Est. population, 1,824,000; Members, 11,000; Stakes, 3; Wards, 16; Branches, 18; Missions, 1; Percent LDS, 0.6, or one person in 166.

Missionaries entered what is now West Virginia in 1832 when Luke S. Johnson and William W. M'Lellin preached in Cabell County, which lies just over the Ohio River from Ohio on the western tip of the state. The Prophet Joseph Smith visited Wheeling on April 4, 1832, and purchased paper for the Church's press that was then in Jackson County, Mo. The paper was used to publish the *Book of Commandments*, which was later mostly scattered by a mob. That same year, Elder Amasa M. Lyman and an Elder Johnson baptized 40 converts. In 1836, Elders Lorenzo D. Barnes and Samuel James baptized enough converts to start a branch in Shinnston, Harrison County. In 1837, some 1,200 (mostly non-members) attended a meeting there. Elder George A. Smith taught a grammar school at or near Shinnston, which had 75 members.

One convert was Bathsheba Wilson Bigler Smith, sister of Jacob G. Bigler and later the wife of Apostle George A. Smith, who was baptized Aug. 21, 1837, along with a number of other family members including parents, brothers and sisters. "The spirit of gathering with the Saints in Missouri came upon me, . . ." she wrote in her autobiography. "About this time my father sold his farm in West Virginia and we started for Far West." She later served as Relief Society general president.

Others felt the same spirit and emigrated to the West with the Saints, and the branches were discontinued.

Missionary work didn't resume until 1881 when Elder John E. Carlisle and Elder Joseph L. Townsend toured in McDowell County and baptized three adults.

Laboring in Logan County in June 1884, Elders Andrew W. Spence and an Elder Vickers were served with a warrant for suspicion of being part of a band of robbers. The pair opened their satchels and not only convinced the officers that they were innocent, but also distributed tracts that opened the way for the missionaries to teach at the courthouse. From this opening, a branch of 26 people was organized. The West Virginia Conference was organized Sept. 18, 1886. A year later, missionaries from the Northern States Mission searched out and taught "Bickertonites" (see Pennsylvania history) but failed to make any headway among them. In 1889, a local newspaper wrote of the "serious" success of the missionaries among other residents in the Wheeling area.

West Virginia was placed in the Eastern States Mission in 1897. It became part of the Middle States Mission in 1902, but was soon after reunited with the Eastern States Mission.

In 1906, Elder George D. Ward and a companion completed a small chapel for the Franklin Branch. One of the early converts in this branch was William Perry Hartman, and three branches later developed from his family's influence.

The West Virginia Conference was divided and the West Virginia North and South conferences were created. In 1930, the North conference had 888 members and the South conference 1,397 members, for a statewide total of 2,285.

The membership built up gradually and the first stake was created in 1970 in Charleston, comprised of the West Virginia South District with a membership of 3,966. Units in West Virginia included the Asheland, Charleston, Charleston 2nd, Huntington and Parkersburg wards and the Beckley, Logan, Portsmouth, Ripley, Point Pleasant and Webster Spring branches. Additional stakes were created in 1979 and 1982. Membership in West Virginia in 1974 was 9,149, growing to 9,734 in 1980, and 10,000 in 1990.

Sources: *Encyclopedic History of the Church* by Andrew Jenson; *Autobiography,* Bathsheba Wilson Bigler Smith; Southern States, Eastern States and Northern States Missions' histories; *Church News,* Sept. 5, 1970; West Virginia and Mormonism's Rarest Book, by Lisle G. Brown, *West Virginia History,* January/April 1978, Vol. 39; "Bell-snickeled' builders," by Richard L. Jensen, *Church News,* April 1, 1978; "West Virginia," by Mike Cannon, *Church News,* Oct. 2, 1989.

Stakes — 3
(Listed alphabetically as of Oct. 1, 1994.)

No.	Name	Organized	First President
North America Northeast Area			
522	*Charleston West Virginia		
	†West Virginia (W. Va., Ky.)	23 Aug 1970	David L. Atkinson
1025	Fairmont West Virginia	6 May 1979	David Glen Williams
1375	Huntington West Virginia	7 Nov 1982	Grant Earl Jenson

Mission — 1
(As of Oct. 1, 1994; shown with historical number. See MISSIONS.)

(188) WEST VIRGINIA CHARLESTON MISSION
405 Capitol St., #406
Charleston, WV 25301-1727
Phone: (304) 342-8332

Wisconsin

Year-end 1993: Est. population, 5,055,000; Members, 15,000; Stakes, 3; Wards, 22; Branches, 23; Missions, 1; Districts, 1; Percent LDS, 0.3, or one person in 337.

Settlement of the Saints in Wisconsin was suggested as early as 1836 at a citizens meeting in Liberty County, Mo. The suggestion was not acted upon, however.

Missionary work in Wisconsin began in 1841. In that year, Elder Elisha H. Groves opened a small branch in Vienna, Dane County. William O. Clark also baptized 17 people at Mineral Point, Lafayette County. Amasa Lyman also labored in Wisconsin that year.

After Nauvoo, Ill., was settled, a group of 14 members was sent in 1841 to obtain lumber from the pine forests along Black River in Wisconsin Territory, some 600 miles to the north. Workers in this "pinery expedition" floated logs to Nauvoo for the temple and other buildings. By 1843, the camp at Black River had more than 150 people and was a settlement. But members learned then that they were on Indian territory. Bishop George Miller met with Menominee Indian Chief Oshkosh and reached an agreement to pay for the wood. He also preached to the Indians.

After the 1847 exodus from Nauvoo, little work was done in Wisconsin until the Northwestern States Mission was organized in 1878. Cyrus H. Wheelock, laboring in Fond du Lac, Wis., in 1877, was called to organize the mission. Some converts likely were gained over the next decade who migrated to Utah, but work proceeded slowly in the early 1890s with few or no missionaries serving. The Milwaukee District was organized in 1896, and the Milwaukee Branch on April 16, 1899. Christopher Leonard Rueckert, a former missionary in Wisconsin, was assigned by the Church to return to the city with his family and head the new branch.

On March 23, 1907, a chapel was dedicated for the branch. The branch was later divided. By 1930, membership in the state was 932 in the Eleva, La Crosse, Milwaukee and Racine branches. When the Chicago (Illinois) Stake was organized in 1936, the Milwaukee Ward was created and included in the stake. This ward was divided in 1958. The Milwaukee Stake was created in 1963, and a stake center dedicated in 1967. Membership in 1974 was more than 6,000. In 1980, Wisconsin had 9,855 members, and in 1990, 13,159 members.

Sources: *Encyclopedic History of the Church* by Andrew Jenson; "Brief History of the Milwaukee Stake," published at the dedication of the Milwaukee Stake Center, Aug. 27, 1967; "The Pinery Expedition," by Jill Mulvay Derr, *Church News,* April 8, 1978; "Minnesota Mormons," by Fayone B. Willes, published by the Minnesota Stake, 1990.

Stakes — 3
(Listed alphabetically as of Oct. 1, 1994.)

No.	Name	Organized	First President
North America Central Area			
1597	Appleton Wisconsin	11 May 1986	Nevin Richard Limburg
702	*Madison Wisconsin 11 Apr 1982		
	†Beloit Wisconsin	24 Aug 1975	Arval Lewis Erikson
367	*Milwaukee Wisconsin		
	†Milwaukee	3 Feb 1963	DeWitt C. Smith

Mission — 1
(As of Oct. 1, 1994; shown with historical number. See MISSIONS, p. 286.)

(167) WISCONSIN MILWAUKEE MISSION
5651 Broad St.
Greendale, WI 53129-1889
Phone: (414) 421-7506

Wyoming

Year-end 1993: Est. population, 474,000; Members, 54,000; Stakes, 16; Wards, 118; Branches, 14; Percent LDS, 11.5, or one person in 9.

In 1846, a group of Mississippi converts came West hoping to join the Saints en route to the Great Basin. However, they stopped a few miles below Fort Laramie in July 1846. There, they learned that the Saints had waited a year at Winter Quarters, Neb., so the Mississippians decided to winter in Colorado. Some of these Mississippi members joined Brigham Young's pioneer wagon train, which entered Wyoming May 31, 1847, near Fort Laramie. The Mississippi group included members of the Mormon Battalion sick detachments as well. On June 28, the combined company under Brigham Young met mountainman Jim Bridger, who gave them a generally optimistic appraisal of the Great Basin area.

Most later emigrant companies crossed Wyoming without incident, but the Willie and Martin Handcart companies of 1857 were trapped in snows before reaching South Pass, Wyo., and about 200 of the 1,075 in the companies died. The rest were saved by rescue parties from Utah.

Fort Supply was erected near Fort Bridger and a colony started in 1853. It provided supplies for wagon companies coming from the East. This flourishing colony was abandoned and burned at the advance of Johnston's army in 1856. Fort Bridger, which the Church had purchased in 1855, was partially burned at the same time. The army subsequently camped at Fort Bridger before a peaceful settlement was reached in Utah the following summer.

In 1877, seeking areas to colonize, Moses Thatcher and William Preston came to western Wyoming, then know as Salt River Valley. Thatcher re-named the area Star Valley. Brigham Young visited the area the following year and dedicated it as a gathering place. The first settlers from Bear Lake Valley, Idaho, stayed the winter of 1879-80 near what is now Auburn. In the 1880s, the colonies of Grover, Afton, Freedom, Smoot, Thayne, Bedford, and Fairview were established. Others followed. Star Valley today remains primarily LDS and has two stakes.

The Big Horn Basin was settled in 1900 after a request for settlers by Wyoming Gov. DeForrest Richards to President Lorenzo Snow. The first settlement of Burlington was founded by LDS settlers from Uintah County, Utah, and organized under Apostle Abraham O. Woodruff. Also founded near the turn of the century were the settlements of Byron, Cowley, Lowell, and others after the turn of the century. The settlers dug a 37-mile canal to provide irrigation water only to find that irrigation lifted underground alkali to the surface. Settlers persevered, however, and the problem abated. The Big Horn Basin presently has three stakes.

In 1930, about 12,000 members lived in Wyoming. Most lived in the western part of the state, but members began moving into other areas as well. By 1980, membership in Wyoming reached 47,314, increasing to 51,692 in 1990.

During the observance of Wyoming's state centennial in 1990, the LDS heritage of the state, including the Mormon Trail, were included in commemorations.

In 1992, the Riverton Wyoming Stake erected three monuments in memory of the Willie and Martin handcart pioneer companies. The monuments were dedicated Aug. 15, 1992, by President Gordon B. Hinckley of the First Presidency. Later purchased by the Church was the site surrounding a monument at the mouth of Sweetwater Canyon where 21 people perished in one night, and was dedicated in 1994 by President Hinckley.

Sources: *Encyclopedic History of the Church* by Andrew Jenson; "Star Valley and its Communities," by Lee Roland Call, Afton, Wyo., *Star Valley Independent,* 1970; *Lovell, Our Pioneer Heritage,* by Rosa Vida Bischoff Black; "Fort Supply: Brigham Young's Green River Experiment," by Frederick R. Gowans and Eugene E. Campbell, BYU, 1976; *Wyoming Place Names,* by Mae Urbanek, Mountain Press Publishing Co., 1988; *Church News,* May 26, 1990, Dec. 15, 1990, Dec. 22, 1990; "Mormon Settlers helped make Wyoming a state," *Church News,* May 26, 1990; " 'Second rescue' of handcart pioneers," by Dell Van Orden, *Church News,* Aug. 22, 1992; "Project stands as reminder of legacy," by Julie A. Dockstader, *Church News*, July, 30, 1994.

Stakes — 16
(Listed alphabetically by area as of Oct. 1, 1994.)

No.	Name	Organized	First President
North America Central Area — 8			
357	*Casper Wyoming		
	†Casper	14 Oct 1962	W. Reed Green
286	*Cheyenne Wyoming		
	†Cheyenne (Wyoming, Colorado)	21 Jun 1959	Archie R. Boyack
593	*Cody Wyoming		
	†Cody	7 Jan 1973	Parley J. Livingston
1158	Gillette Wyoming	29 Jun 1980	Marion A. Dalene
1420	Laramie Wyoming	15 May 1983	Philip Munro Hoyt
48	*Lovell Wyoming		
	†Big Horn	26 May 1901	Byron Sessions
358	*Riverton Wyoming		
	†Wind River	14 Oct 1962	J. Rex Kocherhans
1194	Worland Wyoming	12 Oct 1980	David Harris Asay
Utah North Area — 8			
33	*Afton Wyoming		
	†Star Valley	14 Aug 1892	George Osmond
38	*Evanston Wyoming		
	†Woodruff (Wyoming, Utah)	5 Jun 1898	John M. Baxter
1493	Evanston Wyoming South	23 Sep 1984	Harold Sidney Stock
660	Green River Wyoming	22 Sep 1974	Ronald Clyde Walker
708	Kemmerer Wyoming	12 Oct 1975	Merrill R. Anderson
790	Lyman Wyoming	21 Nov 1976	Ronald C. Walker
95	*Rock Springs Wyoming		
	†Lyman (Wyoming, Utah)	18 Jul 1926	H. Melvin Rollins
975	Thayne Wyoming	29 Oct 1978	Marlow C. Bateman

WORLDWIDE CHURCH

U.S. territories or possessions are listed by their own name in this section. Other territories are listed under the name of the administrating country.

Numbers preceeding stakes and missions are their chronological numbers assigned at the time of creation.

* Name changed 14 Jan 1974 unless indicated otherwise

† Original name

★ Transferred to

ALBANIA

Year-end 1993: Est. population, 3,333,000; Members, 100; Branches, 3; Europe Area; Switzerland Zurich Mission.

Albania is a small mountainous country in southeastern Europe's Balkan Peninsula where the Albanian- and Greeek-speaking people are 70 percent Sunni Moslem, with 20 percent Orthodox and 10 percent Roman Catholic.

Elder Hans B. Ringger of the Seventy and president of the Europe Area, accompanied by Pres. Kenneth D. Reber, president of the Austria Vienna Mission, visited Albania in 1991. In June 1992, four full-time missionaries arrived in Albania: Elders Matthew Wirthlin, Mark Slabaugh, Paul McAlister and Jonathan Jarvis. In addition, Elder George Niedens and Sister Nancy Niedens were transferred from Austria to assist in agriculture.

On May 17-20, 1992, Elder Dallin H. Oaks of the Council of the Twelve participated in a major international consultation on religious liberty and ethnic rights. Held in Budapest, Hungary, the consultation brought together 72 participants to discuss problems and share ideas pertaining to church-state issues in east central European nations that were once part of the communist bloc, particularly Albania, Bulgaria, Czechoslovakia, Hungary, Latvia, Poland, Romania, Croatia, Slovenia and Russia. The consultation helped emphasize religious freedom in many countries.

Elder Oaks visited Albania in April 1993, and spoke to a gathering of 78 people, including 55 Albanian members.

Sources: "Seeking to enthrone religious liberty," *Church News,* June 22, 1992; *Church News,* June 12, 1993.

AMERICAN SAMOA

Year-end 1993: Est. population, 47,100; Members, 12,000; Stakes, 2; Wards, 19; Branches, 4; Percent LDS, 25, or one in 4; Samoa Apia Mission.

Located in the south Pacific Ocean, American Samoa is a U.S. territory. The people are Protestant, 50 percent; LDS, 25 percent; and Roman Catholic, 20 percent.

In 1863, two missionaries from Hawaii arrived in Samoa. The two, Kimo Pelia and Samuela Manoa, however, had been sent by an unauthorized leader, Walter Murray Gibson, excommunicated by the Church. The pair labored faithfully for nearly 20 years without the knowledge or support of the Church. They baptized a few people on Tutuila, which is now American Samoa. Later, after Elder Joseph H. Dean and his wife, Florence, arrived in Samoa in 1888, missionaries were again sent to Tutuila. The first branch was started in Pago Pago on May 27, 1893, and before the turn of the century, 11 branches had been organized on the island.

On April 27, 1900, the U.S. flag was raised over Tutuila and conflict between the German and U.S. governments that had hindered missionary work was largely resolved.

On Nov. 26, 1906, a Relief Society was founded at Mapusaga with Malia as president, and 14 members enrolled. Malia later served a full-time mission in Tonga. A Primary was organized May 24, 1908. An LDS village with a school and a supporting plantation, was founded at Mapusaga May 10, 1903.

In 1938, the Boy Scout organization was started at Mapusaga.

Missionaries were recalled in 1940 prior to World War II because of troubled conditions, and local members assumed more leadership. After the war, the work quickened considerably. The Pago Pago Stake was created in 1969.

In 1989, F. Eni Hunkin Jr., former lieutenant governor of American Samoa, was elected as a non-voting member of 101st U.S. Congress, the first Samoan LDS member to do so.

During hurricanes in February 1990 and December 1991, members suffered considerable losses but local units responded well in dealing with the devastation. Membership in 1990 was 7,500.

Sources: *Encyclopedic History of the Church* by Andrew Jenson; *Unto the Isles of the Sea,* by R. Lanier Britsch; *Samoa Apia Mission History, 1888-1983*, published by R. Carl Harris, president of the Samoa Apia Mission; *Church News,* Feb. 25, 1989; *Church News,* Feb. 17, 1990; *Church News,* Dec. 21, 1991; "Church responds swiftly to Samoa disaster," *Church News,* Dec. 28, 1991;

Stakes — 3
(Listed alphabetically as of Oct. 1, 1994.)

No.	Name	Organized	First President
Pacific Area			
488	*Pago Pago Samoa		
	†Pago Pago	15 Jun 1969	Patrick Peters
1972	Pago Pago Samoa Central	6 Feb 1994	Beaver T. Ho Ching
1169	Pago Pago Samoa West	24 Aug 1980	William T. Geleai

ANTIGUA AND BARBUDA

Year-end 1993: Est. population, 101,000; Members, fewer than 100; Branches, 1; North America Southeast Area; West Indies Mission.

These eastern Caribbean islands are a constitutional monarchy with a British type of parliament. The population speaks English and is mostly members of the Church of England.

Missionary work began in St. John's, Antigua, on May 19, 1984, when President Kenneth Zabriskie of the West Indies Mission visited the governor of Antigua and received permission to station missionaries on the island.

The first missionaries, Elder Ralph and Sister Aileen Tate arrived on July 28, 1984, under the direction of Pres. Zabriskie. They were followed in late August by Elders Gill W. Halford, Jay R. Schroeder, Carl Read and Russell T. Hansen. The first baptism was Evelyn Shaw, on Sept. 15, 1984. On Dec. 2, Ezzard Weston received the Aaronic Priesthood, the first to receive it on Antigua.

Elder Rex B. Blake, serving with his wife, Ruth, was the first president of the St. John's Branch, which was organized Jan. 6, 1985, in a rented conference room of a bank.

Sources: Journal of Pres. Kenneth L. Zabriskie and his wife, LeOra; interview with Rex and Ruth Blake; *Church News*, Dec. 11, 1993; Unpublished St. John's Branch history.

ARGENTINA

Year-end 1993: Est. population, 33,515,000; Members, 205,000; Stakes, 34; Wards, 194; Branches, 431; Missions, 10; Districts, 54; Temples, 1; Percent LDS, .60, or one person in 164.

Located in southern South America, the Republic of Argentina has a Spanish-speaking population that is about 92 percent Roman Catholic.

Church members Wilhelm Friedrichs and Emil Hoppe and their families emigrated from Germany to Argentina about 1923. Brother Friedrichs was particularly missionary-minded and began announcing gospel messages in local newspapers. He also sent letters to the First Presidency requesting missionaries.

In response, Elder Melvin J. Ballard of the Council of the Twelve and Elders Rulon S. Wells (German speaking) and Rey L. Pratt (Spanish speaking), were sent to Argentina, arriving in Buenos Aires Dec. 6, 1925. On Dec. 13, they baptized six persons who had been taught by Brother Friedrichs: Anna and Jacob Kullick and their adoptive daughter, Herta; Ernst and Maria Biebersdorf and their daughter, Maria. On Dec. 25, Elder Ballard dedicated South America for the preaching of the gospel. He later prophesied that "the work will go forth slowly just as the oak grows from an acorn. . . . [But] the South American Mission will become a power in the Church."

Reinhold Stoof, the first mission president, arrived in 1926 to preside over the South American Mission. The mission was divided into the Brazilian and Argentine missions in 1936. A decade later, after a slowing of activity during World War II, membership in Argentina was 800. Branches had been established ranging up to 500 miles south of Buenos Aires and 700 miles to the north and west.

The Argentine Mission was divided in 1962, and additional missions have been created since then, including two in 1990. The Buenos Aires Stake was organized in Nov. 20, 1966, with Angel Abrea, now a member of the First Quorum of the Seventy, as stake president. By 1978, membership had reached about 40,000 members. A temple was announced for Argentina in 1980, and dedicated Jan. 17, 1986.

Buenos Aires was designated presidency headquarters of the South America South Area in 1984. Three new missions in 1990 — Mendoza, Resistencia, and Trelew, and the Buenos Aires West in 1992, reflect the continuing growth in Argentina. Membership in 1990 was 171,000.

Sources: *Encyclopedic History of the Church* by Andrew Jenson; *From Acorn to Oak Tree,* by Frederick S. Williams and Frederick G. Williams; *LDS Beginnings in South America, A Look at Argentina,* BYU paper by Denise H. Williams; *50 Anos de la Iglesia in Argentina — Cronologia,* by Nestor Curbelo, seminary system, 1986.

Stakes — 36
(Listed alphabetically as of Oct. 1, 1994.)

No.	Name	Organized	First President
South America South Area			
1097	Bahia Blanca Argentina	23 Jan 1980	Daniel Humberto Fucci
920	Buenos Aires Argentina Banfield	14 May 1978	Heber Omar Diaz
1992	Buenos Aires Argentina Belgrano	18 Sep 1994	Nestor Esteban Curbelo
1143	Buenos Aires Argentina Castelar	8 Jun 1980	Jorge H. Michalek
423	*Buenos Aires Argentina East		
	†Buenos Aires	20 Nov 1966	Angel Abrea
1797	Buenos Aires Argentina Ezeiza	12 May 1991	Carlos Ernesto Aguero
1178	Buenos Aires Argentina Litoral	12 Sep 1980	Jorge Fernandez
950	Buenos Aires Argentina Merlo	13 Aug 1978	Enrique Alfredo Ibarra
1824	Buenos Aires Argentina Monte Grande	10 Nov 1991	Hugo Vicente Riccinti
1405	Buenos Aires Argentina Moreno	20 Mar 1983	Carlos Domingo Marapodi
995	Buenos Aires Argentina North	28 Jan 1979	Tomas Federico Lindheimer
1946	Buenos Aires Argentina Sarmiento	27 Jun 1993	Carlos Antonio Moure
639	Buenos Aires Argentina West	12 May 1974	May Hugo Angel Catron
1975	Comodoro Rivadavia Argentina	20 Feb 1994	Jorge EstebanDetlefsen
569	*Cordoba Argentina		
	†Cordoba	28 Feb 1972	Arturo Palmieri
1021	Cordoba Argentina North	29 Apr 1979	Juan Aldo L.
1959a	Cordoba Argentina Sierras	7 Nov 1993	Roberto Jose Echegaray
1951	Florencio Varela Argentina	22 Aug 1993	Jorge Luis del Castillo
1036	Godoy Cruz Argentina	6 Jun 1979	Salvador Molt'o
1978	Guaymallen Argentina	17 Apr 1994	Angel Licursi
1642	Jujuy Argentina	7 Jun 1987	Pedro Horacio Velazquez
1207	La Plata Argentina	23 Nov 1980	Hector Alejandro Olaiz
997	Mar del Plata Argentina	31 Jan 1979	Hector Luis Catron
570	*Mendoza Argentina		
	†Mendoza	1 Mar 1972	Mario A. Rastelli
1918	Neuquen Argentina	20 Dec 1992	Ruben Sabatino Tidei
1902	Posadas Argentina	20 Sep 1992	Manuel Aristides Franco
694	Quilmes Argentina	15 May 1975	Hugo Nestor Salvioli
1237	Resistencia Argentina	17 Feb 1981	Leopoldo Oscar Fuentes
636a	Rosario Argentina	5 May 1974	Hugo Ruben Gazzoni
1177	Rosario Argentina North	10 Sep 1980	Daniel Arnoldo Moreno
1260	Salta Argentina	29 Apr 1981	Victor Hugo Machado
1871	San Juan Argentina Nuevo Cuyo	24 May 1992	Jorge Eduardo Chacon
1001	San Nicolas Argentina	22 Feb 1979	Deolindo Antonio Resek
1161	Santa Fe Argentina	20 Jul 1980	Raimundo Eduardo Rippstein
1945	Santiago Del Estero Argentina	20 Jun 1993	Jose Badami
1727	Trelew Argentina	11 Jun 1989	Oscar Daniel Filipponi
1095	Tucuman Argentina	21 Jan 1980	Ronaldo Juan Walker

Discontinued

1250	Parana Argentina	29 Mar 1981	Carlos Arturo Sosa
	15 Apr 1990		
1096	San Juan Argentina	22 Jan 1980	Ricardo N. Ontiveros
	30 Jul 1989 ★Argentina Cordoba Mission		

Missions — 10
(As of Oct. 1, 1994; shown with historical number. See MISSIONS.)

(180) ARGENTINA BAHIA BLANCA MISSION   (228) ARGENTINA MENDOZA MISSION

Casilla de Correo 70
8000 Bahia Blanca, Buenos Aires
Argentina
Phone: (011-54-91) 36-492

(32) ARGENTINA BUENOS AIRES NO. MISSION
Ituzaingo 355, C.C. 46
1642 San Isidro
Buenos Aires, Argentina
Phone: (011-54-1) 743-2450

(112) ARGENTINA BUENOS AIRES SO. MISSION
Bonpland 2349
1425 Capital
Buenos Aires, Argentina
Phone: (011-54-1) 292-4380

(269) ARGENTINA BUENOS AIRES W. MISSION
Bonpland No. 2349/55
1425 Capital Federal
Buenos Aires, Argentina
Phone: (011-54-1) 772-7010

(73) ARGENTINA CORDOBA MISSION
Casilla de Correo 17 - Suc. 9
(5009) Cordoba
Argentina
Phone: (011-54-543) 20699

Casilla de Correo 631
5500 Mendoza
Argentina
Phone: (011-54-61) 38-02-12

(230) ARGENTINA NEUQUEN MISSION
Casilla de Correo #321
8300 Neuquen, Neuquen
Argentina
Phone: (011-54-99) 32413

(229) ARGENTINA RESISTENCIA MISSION
Casilla de Correo 1
3500 Resistencia - CHACO
Argentina
Phone: (011-54-722) 31722

(100) ARGENTINA ROSARIO MISSION
Casilla de Correo 341
2000 Rosario, Santa Fe
Argentina
Phone: (011-54-41) 564827

(206) ARGENTINA SALTA MISSION
Casillo de Correo 429
(4400) Salta
Argentina
Phone: (011-54-87) 31-06-68

ARMENIA

Year-end 1993: Est. population, 11,306,000; Members, fewer than 100; Europe Area.

Missionaries worked among Armenian people in Turkey and Syria as early as the 1880s. However, units established among the Armenians were discontinued following unsettled conditions in 1909. Some converts immigrated to the United States.

In modern times, the Church provided assistance in Armenia following the devastating earthquake of 1988 that killed 55,000 people and left half a million people homeless.

The Church and LDS industrialist Jon Huntsman worked together to help provide housing. Huntsman's company built a factory to build cement panels for homes. In response, Armenia donated property where the Church built a multipurpose building for the factory workers.

In 1992, Utah farmers donated tons of milk for Armenian children.

Sources: *Church News,* April 28, 1981, July 4, 1981, July 6, 1991, Sept. 28, 1991, April 2, 1992.

AUSTRALIA

Year-end 1993: Est. population, 17,807,000; Members, 82,000; Stakes, 18; Wards, 118; Branches, 104; Missions, 6; Districts, 16; Temples, 1; Percent LDS, 0.5, or one LDS in 217.

Southeast of the Indian Ocean and in the southwest South Pacific, the island-continent of Australia is a democratic federal state in the British commonwealth. Australia's population speaks English, and is Anglican, 26 percent; other Protestant, 25 percent; and Roman Catholic, 25 percent.

In 1840, William Barratt was called at age 17 from England to serve as a missionary in Australia. He found circumstances difficult, but evidence suggested that he baptized converts, including Robert Beauchamp, who later became an influential mission president in Australia. Historians believe Barratt was unable to contact the Saints in England or the United States after the martyrdom of Joseph Smith, and so married and remained in Australia until his death in 1891. The next missionary was Andrew Anderson, a Scottish immigrant to Australia who had been baptized by Orson Pratt in Scotland and given license to preach before sailing to Australia. He and his family arrived in 1841. He found converts and by the end of 1844, organized a branch in the private township of Montefiores, some 220 miles northwest of Sydney. Elder James Wall also served and baptized converts about this time, but information about his work is largely unknown.

Missionaries from Utah, Elders John Murdock and Charles Wandell, arrived in Sydney Oct. 30, 1851, which became mission headquarters. They published tracts, began preaching, and found a few converts among a people very distracted by a gold rush. A year later, 47 members were in the mission when Elder Murdock left because of ill health. On April 6, 1853, Elder Wandell left with a company of Saints. A few days later, another 10 missionaries arrived under the direction of Elder Augustus Farnham to continue the work. More branches were established but emigrations of converts continued, and at least two voyages involved serious mishaps. Among the emigrants in 1856 was Joseph Ridges, who carried with him the first of the Tabernacle organs.

Work continued in the 1860s and 1870s with a great emphasis on immigrating to Utah. During one period, mission headquarters were moved to New Zealand and little work was done in Australia. On Jan. 1, 1898, the Australasian Mission was divided, forming a mission in Australia and a mission in New Zealand, and work resumed. At the time, membership was about 200.

The first LDS meetinghouse built in Australia was completed in Brisbane in 1904, and other meeting-houses followed. Emigrating members continually depleted numbers and upset the Australian government who in 1918 forbade "emigration propaganda."

The Church grew slowly, and the lack of buildings was a serious hindrance. In 1920, membership was about 1,000, and in 1940, 2,000. World War II particularly slowed the work. However, activity resumed in 1950-55, as President David O. McKay visited in 1955 and authorized building of many more meeting-houses. The mission was divided in 1955, with a second mission in Melbourne. The new meetinghouses proved the base for further growth. Membership reached 7,071 in 1960, 25,063 in 1970, and 40,000 in 1980.

Australia's first stake was organized in Sydney March 27, 1960, with Dell C. Hunt as president. Additional missions were created in 1958 (Adelaide), 1973 (Brisbane) and 1975 (Perth). The Sydney Australia Temple was dedicated Sept. 20, 1984. Membership in 1990 was 76,000.

Members in Brisbane helped computerize government genealogy records in 1992, and Australia's sixth mission was created that year in Sydney. Elder Robert E. Sackley, who served in the Second Quorum of the Seventy from 1989 until his death in 1993, was a native of Australia. In the 1993 brush fires that burned 1.5 million acres, members responded with food for firefighters and stranded motorists. In 1994, a group of 40 aborigine members gathered to do temple work and enjoy their culture.

Sources: *History of the Church,* Vol. 4, p. 154; *Encyclopedic History of the Church* by Andrew Jenson; *Unto the Islands of the Sea,* by R. Lanier Britsch; *Church News,* Feb. 12, 1955, Dec. 27, 1958, Oct. 28, 1967, July 29, 1978; "The Church in Australia," by Garry P. Mitchell, *Ensign* February 1976, pp.13-19; "Australia Today: And Now the Harvest," by Michael Otterson, *Ensign,* October 1986; "Pioneering in the Gospel," by Marjorie A. Newton, *Ensign,* October 1986; *Church News,* Aug. 15, 1992; *Church News,* Nov. 29, 1992; *Church News,* Feb. 27, 1993; *Church News,* Jan. 15, 1994; "Aborigines gather for temple work," *Church News,* Feb. 5, 1994; *Church News,* March 26, 1994.

Stakes — 19
(Listed alphabetically as of Oct. 1, 1994.)

No.	Name	Organized	First President
Pacific Area			
414	*Adelaide Australia Marion 6 Jan 1982		
	*Adelaide Australia Payneham 23 Apr 1978		
	*Adelaide Australia		
	†Adelaide	23 Feb 1966	Dudley Russell Tredrea
907	Adelaide Australia Modbury	23 Apr 1978	Douglas E. Hann
306	*Brisbane Australia		
	†Brisbane	23 Oct 1960	William E. Waters
1684	Brisbane Australia North	7 Feb 1988	Douglas Walter Hill
892	Brisbane Australia South	19 Feb 1978	John D. Jeffrey
860	Hobart Australia	14 Sep 1977	John Douglas Jury
1279	*Ipswich Australia 6 May 1986		
	†Brisbane Australia West	21 Jun 1981	John D. Jeffrey
551	*Melbourne Australia Dandenong 18 Mar 1986		
	*Melbourne Australia Moorabbin		
	†Melbourne South	22 Aug 1971	Bruce James Opie
1175	*Melbourne Australia Deer Park 18 Mar 1986		
	†Melbourne Australia Fairfield West	7 Sep 1980	Edward Anderson
307	*Melbourne Australia Fairfield		
	†Melbourne	30 Oct 1960	Boyd C. Bott
1617	Melbourne Australia Waverly	7 Dec 1986	Ian Frank Davenport
1106	*Newcastle Australia 15 Jul 1986		
	†Sydney Australia Newcastle	15 Feb 1980	Peter R. Barr
447	*Perth Australia Dianella 6 Jul 1980		

	*Perth Australia		
	†Perth	28 Nov 1967	Donald W. Cummings
1159	Perth Australia Southern River	6 Jul 1980	Roy B. Webb
1988	Sydney Australia Campbelltown	28 Aug 1994	Ma'a Ma'a Jr.
293	*Sydney Australia Greenwich		
	†Sydney	27 Mar 1960	Dell C. Hunt
1105	Sydney Australia Hebersham	15 Feb 1980	Peter J. Moir
435	*Sydney Australia Mortdale 2 Jun 1992		
	*Mortdale Australia 31 Mar 1992		
	*Sydney Australia Mortdale 15 Feb 1980		
	*Sydney Australia South		
	†Sydney South	14 May 1967	John Daniel Parker
495	*Sydney Australia Parramatta 2 Jun 1992		
	*Parramatta Australia 31 Mar 1992		
	*Sydney Australia Parramatta 15 Feb 1980		
	*Parramatta Australia 14 Jan 1974		
	†Parramatta (Australia)	2 Nov 1969	Stanley Owen Gray

Missions — 6

(As of Oct. 1, 1994; shown with historical number. See MISSIONS.)

(82) AUSTRALIA ADELAIDE MISSION
P.O. Box 97
Marden, South Australia 5070
Australia
Phone: 011-61-8 332-2588

(106) AUSTRALIA BRISBANE MISSION
P.O. Box 348
Hamilton, Brisbane 4007
Queensland, Australia
Phone: 011-61-7 268-7077

(43c) AUSTRALIA MELBOURNE MISSION
1216 Old Burke Road
North Balwyn 3104, Victoria
Australia
Phone: 011-61-3 819-7000

(117) AUSTRALIA PERTH MISSION
P.O. Box 185
Tuart Hill, Western Australia 6060
Australia
Phone: 011-61-9 275-7177

(278) AUSTRALIA SYDNEY NORTH MISSION
P.O. Box 60
Epping, N.S.W. 2121
Australia
011-61-2 869-0022

(10) AUSTRALIA SYDNEY SOUTH MISSION
P.O. Box 905
Crows Nest, N.S.W. 2065
Australia
Phone: 011-61-2 438-3733

AUSTRIA

Year-end 1993: Est. population, 7,908,000; Members, 3,900; Stakes, 1; Wards, 7; Branches, 13; Missions, 1; Percent LDS, 0.05, or one person in 2,027.

Austria, which is 98 percent German-speaking, is in south-central Europe. Some 85 percent of the people in the parliamentary democracy are Roman Catholic.

Elder Orson Pratt of the Council of the Twelve and Elder William W. Ritter arrived in Austria on Jan. 18, 1865, but were soon banished. The first Austrian convert was Joseph A. Oheim, baptized Jan. 22, 1870, in Munich, Germany. The first convert baptized in Austria was Paul Haslinger, on Nov. 25, 1883. In 1883, Elders Thomas Biesinger and Paul E. B. Hammer arrived, and baptized a few converts. These elders were also expelled. By 1901 a branch was established in the Haag am Hausruck. A second branch was established in Vienna in 1909. Government restrictions then stopped work for a time.

The Church began to grow at the end of World War I when religious freedom was allowed. Missionaries were withdrawn during World War II and local members carried on. Missionary work began again in 1946 when Elder Ezra Taft Benson, then of the Council of the Twelve and president of the European Mission, established the Austrian District of the Swiss Austrian Mission. The Austrian government officially recognized the Church in 1955. In 1965, the centennial of the Church in Austria was celebrated, and by 1972, there were 2,675 members in Austria. By 1979, there were 2,756 members. President Benson presided on April 20, 1980, at the creation of the Vienna Austria Stake, with Johann A. Wondra, former Vienna District president, as its first president.

In the late 1980s and 1990s, the Austria mission supervised developing areas in Eastern Europe. During the subsequent difficult economic times for various countries, including the conflict in the former country of Yugoslavia, members donated food and clothing for relief. In October 1992, members began receiving general conference live via satellite. Membership in 1990 was 3,700.

Sources: *Encyclopedic History of the Church* by Andrew Jenson; Austria gains 1st new stake," *Church News*, May 3, 1980; "Humanitarian relief in Europe," *Church News,* Feb. 29, 1992; *Church News,* Oct. 3, 1992.

Stake — 1
(As of Oct. 1, 1994)

No.	Name	Organized	First President
Europe Area			
1126	Vienna Austria	20 Apr 1980	Johann Anton Wondra

Mission — 1
(As of Oct. 1, 1994; shown with historical number. See MISSIONS.)

(53) AUSTRIA VIENNA MISSION
Fuerfanggasse 4
A-1190 Vienna,
Austria
Phone: (011-43-1) 37-32-57

BAHAMAS

Year-end 1993: Est. population, 302,000; Members, 300; Districts, 2; Branches, 2; Percent LDS, 0.1, or one person in 1,006; North America Southeast Area; West Indies Mission.

A Caribbean commonwealth, the Bahamas is made up of nearly 800 islands and has a population that speaks English. They are Baptist, 29 percent; Anglican, 23 percent; and Roman Catholic, 22 percent.

Two LDS families, Larry and Marge McCombs and Albert and Karen Ballard, moved to Nassau in the summer of 1979. Missionaries arrived in December of that year but were refused visas and were asked to leave, which they did the following May. Alexandre Paul, consul general from Haiti to the Bahamas, and his wife were baptized Jan. 6, 1980. Some 48 investigators and members attended the first branch conference Sept. 12, 1981. A missionary couple, Dr. Thomas E. and Donna Bauman, arrived Dec. 11, 1982. A number of members from the Bahamas have served full-time missions. Full-time missionaries returned in March 1985.

A new meetinghouse was dedicated May 8, 1988, and within a few weeks the Soldiers Road and Nassau branches began to outgrow the building. The Soldiers Road Branch is made up of French Creole-speaking Haitians. In 1992, a collection of LDS books was donated to the College of the Bahamas library.

Sources: Personal journal, Margery McCombs; *Church News,* April 22, 1984, Nov. 9, 1986, March 19, 1988, June 18, 1988; *Church News,* Dec. 5, 1992.

BANGLADESH

Year-end 1993: Est. population, 114,000,000; Members, fewer than 100; Branches, 1; Asia Area.

Located on the northern coast of the Bay of Bengal, the People's Republic of Bangladesh is a parliamentary republic and member of the commonwealth of nations. Its people are Islam, 83 percent and Hindi, 16 percent.

Among the first members here were Kenneth and Beatrice Nielsen, an LDS couple working for the Canadian government in 1985. A year or two later, the Nielsens' former cook, Bono Barua and his family, were baptized, the first converts in the country. Also baptized was Roseline Gomes, a young woman who later became the first of her nationality to serve a full-time mission. She left her homeland at age 19 to live in Canada with Church members who had lived in Bangladesh.

Sources: "Welcome mat is out in several countries," by Sheridan R. Sheffield, *Church News,* Oct. 23, 1993; *Church News,* May 15, 1993.

BARBADOS

Year-end 1993: Est. population, 301,000; Members, 400; Branches, 4; Districts, 4; Percent LDS, 0.17, or one LDS in 604; North America Southeast Area; West Indies Mission.

A Caribbean independent sovereign state of Great Britain, English-speaking Barbados is made up of one island and a population where some 70 percent are Anglican.

Among the first LDS in Barbados were John and Norman Namie, who served as presidents of the Black Rock and Christ Church branches. The island was in the Puerto Rico San Juan Mission and transferred to the West Indies Mission when that mission was created in 1983. In 1994, headquarters of the West Indies

Mission were transferred from Barbadoes to Tobago.

The Christ Church Branch was created Oct. 20, 1979, and the Black Rock Branch was organized Aug. 24, 1983.

BELARUS

Year-end 1993: Est. population, 10,300,000; Members, fewer than 100; Branches, 2; Europe Area; Ukraine Kiev Mission.

Formerly Byelorussia (also spelled Belorussia) or White Russia, Belarus is a hilly lowland with forests, rivers and lakes. It is bordered by Latvia, Lithuania, Ukraine, Russia and Poland. Its people speak Belarusian and are mostly Russian Orthodox.

Belarus is part of the Ukraine Kiev Mission, which was created July 1, 1991. The country was visited by Church leaders in May 1993. Two branches in Minsk, the Minsk Pushkinsky and the Minsk Tsentralny, were created in January 1994.

Sources: *Church News* articles.

BELGIUM

Year-end 1993: Est. population, 10,110,000; Members, 5,600; Stakes, 1; Wards, 8; Branches, 18; Missions, 1; Percent LDS, 0.05, or one person in 1,867.

Located in northwest Europe on the North Sea, Belgium is a parliamentary democracy under a constitutional monarch. Its population speaks Flemish, 55 percent, French, 33 percent and minority languages. About 75 percent of the population is Roman Catholic.

A Hungarian converted in Turkey, Mischa Markow, is believed to be the first member to have come to Belgium. Markow, baptized in Turkey in 1887, visited Antwerp in 1888. He preached to a family named Esselman, and baptized the mother, Henreite, and her oldest son, Frederick, on Oct. 17, 1888. Four other members of the family were baptized later.

Three missionaries from the Swiss and German Mission were then sent, and within two months they had baptized 80 people and organized branches in Liege, Brussels and Antwerp. In 1891, Belgium became part of the Netherlands Mission.

Opposition was manifest in 1896 when a mob estimated at nearly 500 people threatened to kill Elder John Ripplinger in Liege. The mob stormed the home where he was staying, but was dispersed by police. However, he remained in the city and eventually baptized some 10 people.

Several branches were transferred to the French Mission in 1924, with the Flemish-speaking branches remaining in the Netherlands Mission.

Work stopped during World War I, and by 1930, just a few scattered members remained in the country. Members in six branches remained active during World War II, during the German occupation of Belgium. However, when the Flemish section of Belgium was re-opened in January 1948, by the Netherlands Mission, there were no known members in Antwerp. Work progressed slowly, and in 1963 the Franco-Belgian Mission was organized. Ten years later, there were some 3,500 members in three districts in Belgium. The Belgium Antwerp Mission (232) was organized in 1975, discontinued in 1982, and reorganized in 1990 and discontinued again in 1994.

Membership in 1990 was 4,900. Elder Charles Didier of the Seventy is a native of Ixelles, Belgium.

Sources: *Encyclopedic History of the Church* by Andrew Jenson; *Ensign,* August 1973; *Church News* Oct. 22, 1977; "Anti-LDS Boomerang," by William Hartley, *Church News,* Aug. 12, 1978; "Missionary to the Balkans: Mischa Markow," by William Hale Kehr, *Ensign,* June 1980; *Church News,* Jan. 10, 1981.

Stake — 1
(As of Oct. 1, 1994.)

No.	Name	Organized	First President
Europe Mediterranean Area			
813	Brussels Belgium	20 Feb 1977	Joseph Scheen

Mission — 1
(As of Oct. 1, 1994; shown with historical number. See MISSIONS.)

(76) BELGIUM BRUSSELS MISSION
87, Blvd. Brand Wilcox
B-1040 Bruxelles, Belgium
Phone: (011-32-2) 736-99-33

BELIZE

Year-end 1993: Est. population, 203,000; Members, 1,400; Districts, 3; Branches, 8; Percent LDS, 0.7, or one person in 145; Central America Area; Guatemala Guatemala City North Mission.

Located on the eastern coast of Central America, Belize formerly was known as British Honduras; a parliamentary government with a population that speaks English, Spanish and Creole. They are Roman Catholic, 60 percent; Protestant, 40 percent.

Missionary work opened in Belize on May 5, 1980, when President Samuel Flores of the Honduras Tegucigalpa Mission and Elder Robert Henke arrived. The first Church meeting was held May 11, 1980. Missionary work proceeded systematically. By 1987, some 1,000 members made up the Belize District, with seven branches. On July 1, 1990, the Honduras Tegucigalpa Mission was divided, and Belize was placed in the new Honduras San Pedro Sula Mission.

Elder Russell M. Nelson of the Council of the Twelve visited and dedicated a meetinghouse in December 1992, at which some 289 members attended.

Sources: Honduras Tegucigalpa Mission history; *Church News,* Feb. 16, 1990; *Church News,* Dec. 19, 1992.

BERMUDA

Year-end 1993: Est. population, 61,000; Members, fewer than 100; Districts, 1; Branches, 1; North America Southeast Area; New York New York Mission.

Bermuda consists of 360 small coral islands, 20 of which are inhabited, located 580 miles east of North Carolina. Most of the residents of the United Kingdom dependency are Protestant.

Church members serving in the Air Force and Navy and their families created the first LDS presence in Bermuda. On July 16, 1953, a group of servicemen's wives organized a Relief Society, which was brought under the Eastern States Mission on Oct. 11, 1956. Sacrament meetings and Sunday School were held beginning Oct. 8, 1961, among the military personnel.

Arthur L. McMullin and his wife, Melba, arrived April 19, 1966, and received permission to proselyte on May 3, 1966. On May 31, Elders Kenneth R. French and Curt S. Call arrived and began tracting and proselyting. The Bermuda Branch, which had about 50 in attendance, was organized June 25, 1966, by mission Pres. W. Jay Eldredge. This branch was made part of the New York New York Mission in 1974.

Native Bermudans began to join the branch in the 1980s. Vernon Every, converted in 1982, became the first Bermudan priesthood holder, and the first called to the branch presidency in 1985. In 1993, Bermuda was placed in the New York New York South Mission.

Sources: *Church News,* Dec. 14, 1957; Bermuda Branch manuscript history; "Bermuda Branch sprouts in gentle island climate," by Heidi Waldrop, *Church News,* Aug. 25, 1985; *Church News* March 13, 1993.

BOLIVIA

Year-end 1993: Est. population, 8,021,000; Members, 78,000; Stakes, 12; Wards, 75; Districts, 10; Branches, 104; Missions, 2; Percent LDS, 1.0, or one person in 102.

Bolivia, located in central South America, is a republic with a population that speaks Spanish, Quechua, and Aymara. Some 95 percent are Roman Catholic.

Three LDS families who lived in Bolivia in 1963 — Duane Wilcox and Dube Thomas in La Paz, and Norval Jesperson in Cochabamba — helped the Church gain legal status. On Nov. 24, 1964, missionaries arrived from the Andes Mission. They baptized Victor Walter Vallejos at Cochabamba just before Christmas in 1964. In two years, branches had been opened in Oruro and Santa Cruz. In 1968, the Church had about 350 members, among whom was the first Bolivian to serve a mission, Desiderio Arce Cano, who left a singing career in Argentina to serve in his native land. He was called April 25, 1967.

By 1977, membership in Bolivia numbered 9,700. Church education, including seminary, helped prepare many young people for leadership positions. The Andes South Mission was organized in 1966, later named the Bolivia La Paz Mission. In 1977, the Bolivia Santa Cruz Mission was organized, and has since been re-named the Bolivia Cochabamba Mission. Some 4,373 members attended an area conference in La Paz on March 3, 1977. President Kimball also met with the head of state, President Hugo Bonzer Suarez.

The Santa Cruz Bolivia Stake, the first stake in Bolivia, was organized Jan. 14, 1979, with Noriharu Ishigaki Haraguichi as president.

In recent years, a number of Church-sponsored humanitarian projects have improved the health of members and non-members in various rural areas. Membership in 1990 was 64,000.

Sources: *Improvement Era*, January 1965; "Bolivia," *Ensign*, February 1977; "Love, respect and emotion end area conference series," by Dell Van Orden, *Church News*, March 12, 1977; *Church News*, Jan. 27, 1979, Feb. 24, 1990, May 26, 1990, June 8, 1991.

Stakes — 13
(Listed alphabetically as of Oct. 1, 1994.)

No.	Name	Organized	First President
South America North Area			
1465	Cochabamba Bolivia Cobija	19 Feb 1984	Guillermo Rivero Paz Soldan
1062	*Cochabamba Bolivia Universidad 19 Feb 1984		
	†Cochabamba Bolivia	11 Sep 1979	Carlos L. Pedraja
1940	Cochabamba Bolivia Los Alamos	16 May 1993	Jose Ruben Rivero Zeballos
1831	El Alto Bolivia	24 Nov 1991	Edmundo Chavez Vasquez
1227	*El Alto Bolivia Satelite 6 Mar 1992		
	†La Paz Bolivia El Alto	18 Jan 1981	Victor Hugo Saravia R.
1112	*La Paz Bolivia Constitucion 18 Jan 1981		
	†La Paz Bolivia West	24 Feb 1980	Victor Hugo Saravia R.
1007	*La Paz Bolivia Miraflores 18 Jan 1981		
	†La Paz Bolivia	11 Mar 1979	Jorge Leano
1670	La Paz Bolivia Sopocachi	17 Jan 1988	Eduardo Gabarret I.
1213	Oruro Bolivia	1 Dec 1980	J. Adrian Velasco C.
993	*Santa Cruz Bolivia Canoto 15 Feb 1981		
	†Santa Cruz Bolivia	14 Jan 1979	Noriharu Ishigaki Haraguichi
1782	Santa Cruz Bolivia Equipetrol	2 Dec 1990	Antonio Rolando Oyola
1235	Santa Cruz Bolivia Paraiso	15 Feb 1981	Erwin Birnbaumer
1981	Santa Cruz Bolivia Piray	19 June 1994	Rolando A. Oyola Suarez

Missions — 2
(As of Oct. 1, 1994; shown with historical number. See MISSIONS.)

(150) BOLIVIA COCHABAMBA MISSION
Casilla de Correo 1375
Cochabamba
Bolivia
Phone: 011-591 411-7207

(75a) BOLIVIA LA PAZ MISSION
20 de Octubre 2550
Casilla 4789
La Paz, Bolivia
Phone: 011-591-2 327-062

BOTSWANA

Year-end 1993: Est. population, 1,420,000; Members, 300; Districts, 1; Branches, 3; Africa Area; South Africa Johannesburg Mission.

Located north of South Africa, Botswana is a parliamentary democracy with a population that speaks English and Setswana. The majority follow indigenous beliefs, and 15 percent are Christian.

Missionary work in Botswana began in 1990 with the arrival in Gabarone of Pres. R.J. Snow of the South Africa Johannesburg Mission, followed by occasional visits by Elder Karl and Sister Marjorie Jenkins. The first missionaries assigned to Botswana were Elder Bruce Midgley and his wife, Patricia, who established a group in Gabarone on June 24, with Elder Midgley as the presiding elder.

Members living in Botswana at the time included two returned missionaries, who had become Peace Corps workers, Patricia Lutz of Levittown, Pa., in Molepolole, and Javotte Pickering of Enterprise, Utah, stationed in Kang. The Maurice Mzwinila and Anthony Mogare families, who had joined the Church while studying in the United States, were later located through a newspaper article.

In September 1990, a baptismal service was held. Among the converts was Kwasi Agyare Dwomoh, an architect from Ghana working for the Botswana government. When the Church registration was filed in August 1991 and the first branch was organized, Brother Dwomoh was called as its first president. By March 1992, the fast-growing branch was ready to be divided into two branches, and Brother Dwomoh was called as the first district president in Botswana. He also was the first member in Botswana to receive his endowments at the Johannesburg South Africa Temple.

By August 1992, membership had grown to 160, with a number of baptisms planned for the city of Lobatse. A third unit was added to the district in 1992. .

Sources: Correspondence from Pres. R.J. and Sister Marilyn M. Snow; "Missionary work begins in Botswana," by Elder Darwin and Sister Maureen Cook, *Church News,* Sept. 15, 1990; "Four nations in central, southern Africa," by Mary Mostert and Gerry Avant, *Church News*, Sept. 26, 1992.

BRAZIL

Year-end 1993: Est. population, 152,000,000; Members, 474,000; Stakes, 104; Wards, 639; Branches, 474; Missions, 19; Districts, 39; Temples, 1; Percent LDS, 0.3, or one LDS in 320.

Brazil, a federal republic, covers almost half the continent of South America, and has a population that speaks Portuguese and is 89 percent Roman Catholic.

The first Church members in Brazil were German immigrants, Augusta Kuhlmann Lippelt and her four children. Her husband, Roberto, was baptized several years later. They arrived in Brazil in 1923. The first missionaries were Elders William Fred Heinz and Emil A.J. Schindler, accompanied by Pres. Rheinold Stoof of the South American Mission in Buenos Aires, Argentina. Pres. Stoof first visited Brazil in 1927, and returned with the elders to begin proselyting among German-speaking people in September 1928. Bertha Sell and her children, Theodore, Alice, Seigfried and Adell, were the first converts, baptized April 14, 1929. The first Church-owned meetinghouse in South America was dedicated Oct. 25, 1931, in Joinville.

A mission was created and headquartered in Brazil on May 25, 1935. At first, missionaries taught only in German. However, the Book of Mormon was translated into Portuguese in 1937, and missionaries began teaching in Portuguese a year later. By 1940, there were still fewer than 200 members in the country. Missionary work progressed very slowly during World War II. More than a decade later, in 1957, the Church had reached about 1,000 members.

In the next decade, however, the work began to accelerate. By 1959, membership was 3,700. The Sao Paulo Stake, the first in Brazil, was organized in 1966 with Walter Spat as president. Ten years later, Brazil had 10 stakes, and a temple had been announced for Sao Paulo. President Spencer W. Kimball attended a cornerstone ceremony for the temple March 9, 1977, at which 3,000 people attended. President Marion G. Romney of the First Presidency performed the ceremonial mortaring of the cornerstone.

The Sao Paulo Temple was dedicated Oct. 30, 1978, by President Spencer W. Kimball. The Brazil Area was created in August 1987.

On Feb. 2, 1986, Brazil became the third country outside the United States to have 50 stakes. With the creation of the Sao Leopoldo Stake in Dec. 5, 1993, Brazil reached 100 stakes, the second country out of the United States to do so. Elder Helio A. Camargo was the first Brazilian to serve as a General Authority. Brazilian Elders Helvecio Martins and Claudio R.M. Costa of the Seventy are currently serving in the Second Quorum of the Seventy. Membership in 1990 was 368,000.

In October 1993, construction began on Brazil's missionary training center, the Church's second largest. With 22 missions in 1994, Brazil has the largest number of missions outside the United States.

Sources: *From Acorn to Oak Tree,* by Frederick S. Williams and Frederick G. Williams; *Deseret News,* Nov. 14, 1935; "Brazil, A new frontier for the Restored Gospel," by Rulon S. Howels, *Improvement Era,* May 1936 and September 1938; "Brazilian Missions," *Improvement Era,* May 1963; "Sao Paulo Temple cornerstone laid by President Romney," by Dell Van Orden, *Church News,* March 19, 1977; "Gospel story in Brazil begun by German Family," by Jason Souza Garcia, *Church News,* May 31, 1980; *Church News*, Sept. 18, 1993; *Church News*, Feb. 19, 1994.

Stakes — 107
(Listed alphabetically as of Oct. 1, 1994.)

No.	Name	Organized	First President
Brazil Area			
1292	Alegrete Brazil	20 Sep 1981	Waldomiro Siegfried Radtke
1851	Aracaju Brazil	8 Mar 1992	Manuel Durval Andrade Neto
1886	Aracatuba Brazil	14 June 1992	Paulo Henrique Itinose
970	Araraquara Brazil	22 Oct 1978	Marcio Rodrigues Galhardo
1959	Bage Brazil	31 Oct 1993	Cecer Ronaldo Loureiro Dutra
1893	Bauru Brazil	2 Aug 1992	Lazaro Beteto
1837	Belem Brazil	29 Dec 1991	Luiz Carlos Silva De Franca
1234	*Belo Horizonte Brazil 6 Mar 1990		
	*Belo Horizonte Brazil De Siao 10 Jan 1989		
	†Belo Horizonte Brazil	15 Feb 1981	Ernani Teixeira
1963a	Belo Horizonte Brazil West	12 Dec 1993	Rodrigo de Lima e Myrrha
1189	Brasilia Brazil	12 Oct 1980	Daniel Alberta da Gloria

1393	*Brasilia Brazil Alvorada 22 Mar 1983		
	†Alvorada Brazil	9 Jan 1983	Manoel Francisco Clavery G.
1984	Camaragibe Brazil	24 Jul 1994	Altair Roque da Silva
1442	Campina Grande Brazil	18 Sep 1983	Jose Francisco Barbosa
621	*Campinas Brazil		
	†Campinas	9 Jun 1973	Nelson de Genaro
1586	Campinas Brazil Castelo	2 Feb 1986	S. Lourenco de Oliveira
1897	Campinas Brazil Flamboyant	23 Aug 1992	Luiz Antonio Cairo
1805	Campo Grande Brazil	30 Jun 1991	Ricardo Kasimerczak
1962	Canoas Brazil	5 Dec 1993	Raul Anibal Proenca Krieger
1963	Caxias Do Sul Brazil	5 Dec 1993	Alvacir Luiz Siedschlag
1942	Contagem Brazil	6 June 1993	Evandro Chevitarese Parada
552	*Curitiba Brazil		
	†Curitiba	12 Sep 1971	Jason Garcia Souza
1302	Curitiba Brazil Bacacheri	1 Nov 1981	Casemiro Antunes Gomes
1243	*Curitiba Brazil Boqueirao 14 Mar 1989		
	†Curitiba Brazil East	15 Mar 1981	Francisco Reguim
1468	Curitiba Brazil Iguacu	29 Apr 1984	Waldemar de Lima
1974a	Curitiba Brazil Novo Mundo	29 Feb 1994	Valdemiro Skraba
893	*Curitiba Brazil Portao 14 Mar 1989		
	†Curitiba Brazil South	26 Feb 1978	Albina Bruno Schmeil
1569	Florianopolis Brazil	3 Nov 1985	Cesar A. Seiguer Milder
1284	Fortaleza Brazil	19 Jul 1981	Orville Wayne Day Jr.
1828	Fortaleza Brazil Bom Sucesso	17 Nov 1991	Manoel A. De Carvalho Filho
1935	Fortaleza Brazil Ceara	2 May 1993	Jose Vieira de Matos Filho
1454	Fortaleza Brazil Montese	13 Nov 1983	Fernando J. Duarte D.
1578	Fortaleza Brazil West	24 Nov 1985	Antenor Silva Junior
1952	Franca Brazil	5 Sep 1993	Donizete Pugliesi Braz
1641	Goiania Brazil	24 May 1987	Antonio Casado Rodriguez
1891	*Jaboatao Brazil Dos Guararapes 15 May 1994		
	†Recife Brazil Jaboatao	26 Jul 1992	Jose Antonia da Silva
1979	Jaboatao Brazil Litoral	15 May 1994	Domingos Savio Linhares
1185	Joao Pessoa Brazil	2 Oct 1980	Jose Francisco Barbosa
1896	Joao Pessoa Brazil Rangel	23 Aug 1992	
1338	Joinville Brazil	21 Apr 1982	Heins Dorival Halter
1833	Jundiai Brazil	1 Dec 1991	Domingos Fatobene Jr.
1821	Livramento Brazil	27 Oct 1991	Clademir Elton Trage
1080	Londrina Brazil	11 Nov 1979	Carlos Roberto Moeller
1322	Maceio Brazil	21 Jan 1982	Abelardo Rodrigues Camara
1923	Maceio Brazil Litoral	7 Feb 1993	Gilberto C. da Silva Moraes
1700	Manaus Brazil	16 Oct 1988	Eduardo A. Soares C.
1941	Manaus Brazil Rio Negro	30 May 1993	Divino Presenca
1449	Marilia Brazil	23 Oct 1983	Wilson de Souza Novelli
1964	Monte Cristo Brazil	19 Dec 1993	Adelson de Paula Parrella
1894	Natal Brazil	16 Aug 1992	Ricardo Gueiros
987	Novo Hamburgo Brazil	3 Dec 1978	Paulo R. Grahl
1282	Olinda Brazil	12 Jul 1981	Reinhold Kraft
1932	Osasco Brazil	18 Apr 1993	Marcos Anthony Aidu Kaitis
1604	Passo Fundo Brazil	10 Aug 1986	Helio Rodrigues Severo
1658	Pelotas Brazil	18 Oct 1987	Marco Antonio Rais
1377	Petropolis Brazil	14 Nov 1982	Antonio Jose Mendoza
1182	*Ponta Grossa Brazil Parana 7 Apr 1992		
	†Ponta Grossa Parana Brazil	22 Sep 1980	Silvina Mendes de Jesus
601	*Porto Alegre Brazil		
	†Porto Alegre	13 Feb 1973	Miguell Sorrentino
1858	Porto Alegre Brazil Moinhos De Vento	3 May 1992	Claudio Weihert
1256	Porto Alegre Brazil North	21 Apr 1981	Silvio Geschwasdtner
1793	Porto Alegre Brazil Partenon	5 May 1991	Ulisses Pereira Filho
1201	Recife Brazil	31 Oct 1980	Iraja Bandeira Soares
1332	Recife Brazil Boa Viagem 26 Jul 1992		
	Boa Viagem Brazil	21 Mar 1982	Iraga Bandeira Soares
1811	Recife Brazil Jardim Sao Paulo 10 May 1994		
	Recife Brazil Southwest	25 Aug 1991	Herbert Otto Homolka
1916a	Ribeiro Pires Brazil	13 Dec 1992	Guilherme Tell Peixoto

1645	Ribeirao Preto Brazil	28 Jun 1987	Moises Barreiro Damasceno
1888	Ribeirao Preto Brazil Centro	21 Jun 1992	Augusto Martinez Perez
1953	Ribeirao Preto Brazil Ipiranga	5 Sep 1993	Jose Alberto Borges da Silva
1954	Ribeirao Preto Brazil Quintino	5 Sep 1993	Euclides Jose Maggio
1135	Rio Claro Brazil	21 May 1980	Marcio Rodriques Galhardo
589	*Rio de Janeiro Brazil		
	†Rio de Janeiro	22 Oct 1972	Veledmar Cury
1028	Rio de Janeiro Brazil Andarai	20 May 1979	Nelson Gennari
1378	Rio de Janeiro Brazil Madureira	14 Nov 1982	Atilio Pinto Maio
769	Rio de Janeiro Brazil Niteroi	19 Sep 1976	Joao Eduardo Kemeny
1862	Salvador Brazil	10 May 1992	Carlos Shunji Obata
1934a	Salvador Brazil North	2 May 1993	Sandro Silva Quatel
1922	Santa Maria Brazil	31 Jan 1993	Aires Luciano
1136	Santo Andre Brazil	23 May 1980	Ademar Leal
620	*Santos Brazil		
	†Santos	8 Jun 1973	Jose Gonzalez Lopes
523	*Sao Bernardo Brazil 23 May 1980		
	*Sao Paulo Brazil South		
	†Sao Paulo South	6 Sep 1970	Saul Messias de Oliveira
1909a	Sao Carlos Brazil	15 Nov 1992	Justino Carlos Atchiza Peres
1965	Sao Jose Brazil	19 Dec 1993	Jose Jorge Cordeiro Campos
1917	Sao Jose Do Rio Preto Brazil	13 Dec 1992	Guilherme Tell Peixoto
1516	Sao Jose Dos Campos Brazil	3 Mar 1985	Eric Brito Correa
1961	Sao Leopoldo Brazil	5 Dec 1993	Valmir Severo Dutra
417	*Sao Paulo Brazil		
	†Sao Paulo	1 May 1966	Walter Spat
1846	Sao Paulo Brazil Campo Limpo	9 Feb 1992	Dejanir Hadleck de Castro
1868	Sao Paulo Brazil Guarulhos	24 May 1992	Gilmar Silva Diasta
1536	Sao Paulo Brazil Interlagos	26 May 1985	Walter Guedes de Queiroz
1137	Sao Paulo Brazil Ipiranga	25 May 1980	Demar Staniscia
1869	Sao Paulo Brazil Itaquera	24 May 1992	Vanderlei Zanchetta
1870	Sao Paulo Brazil Mogi Das Cruzes	24 May 1992	Gilberto Vicente da Silva
815	Sao Paulo Brazil North	20 Feb 1977	Jorge Flavio de Moraes
467	*Sao Paulo Brazil Penha 24 May 1992		
	*Sao Paulo Brazil East		
	†Sao Paulo East	24 Nov 1968	Helio da Rocha Camargo
1138	Sao Paulo Brazil Perdizes	25 May 1980	Oswaldo Silva Camargo
1913	Sao Paulo Brazil Piratininga	6 Dec 1992	Luiz Carlos Coronetti
1082	Sao Paulo Brazil Santo Amaro	12 Nov 1979	Wilson Sanchez Netto
1823	Sao Paulo Brazil Sao Miguel Paulista	10 Nov 1991	Gilberto Vicente Da Silva
1441	Sao Paulo Brazil Taboao	18 Sep 1983	Octavio Baptists de Carvalho
1921	Sao Paulo Brazil Vila Sabrina	24 Jan 1993	Jose Olimpio Fabrizio
622	*Sao Paulo Brazil West		
	†Sao Paulo West	10 Jun 1973	Jose Benjamin Puerta
1291	Sao Vincente Brazil	20 Sep 1981	Vicente Verta Jr.
989	Sorocaba Brazil	10 Dec 1978	Nelson de Genaro
1892	Sorocaba Brazil Barcelona	26 Jul 1992	Mauro Junot De Maria
1960a	Teresina Brazil	28 Nov 1993	Alexandre J. Gomes da Cruz
1966	Tubarao Brazil	19 Dec 1993	Gelson Januario
1912	Uruguaiana Brazil	29 Nov 1992	Saul E. Seiguer Milder
1630	Vitoria Brazil	15 Feb 1987	Pedro J. da Cruz Penha

Discontinued

1030	Curitiba Brazil North	27 May 1979	Alfredo Heliton de Lemos
	30 Apr 1989 ★Curitiba Brazil Iguacu (No. 1468)		

Missions — 22

(As of Oct. 1, 1994; shown with historical number. See MISSIONS.)

(296) BRAZIL BELEM MISSION
Avenida Nazare
532 Salas 412/414/416 4th Floor
Belem, Brazil
Phone: 011-55-91 223-7316

(167a) BRAZIL RECIFE MISSION
Caixa Postal 1620 - Centro
50.001 Recife - PE
Brazil
Phone: 011-55-81 231-6496

(213) BRAZIL BELO HORIZONTE EAST MISSION
Rua Sao Paulo, 1781, 10 Andar
Edif. 17 de Maio, Sala 1001
30170 Belo Horizonte - MG, Brazil
Phone: 011-55-31 335-7553

(297) BRAZIL BELO HORIZONTE WEST MISSION
Rua Sao Paulo, 1781, 10 Andar
Edificia 17 de Maio, Sala 1001
30170 Belo Horizonte - MG
Brazil
Phone: 011-55-31 335-7553

(185a) BRAZIL BRASILIA MISSION
SEPS EQ 714/914 - Bl. A Sala 110
70.390 Brasilia - DF
Brazil
Phone: 011-55-61 245-5399

(190) BRAZIL CAMPINAS MISSION
Caixa Postal 1814
CEP 13001-970 Campinas - SP
Brazil
Phone: 011-55-192 33-53-66

(181) BRAZIL CURITIBA MISSION
Caixa Postal 9501
80613-991 Curitiba - Parana
Brazil
Phone: 011-55-41 345-1010

(281) BRAZIL FLORIANAPOLIS MISSION
Caixa Postal: 361
CEP: 88010-970
Florianapolis - SC
Brazil
Phone: 011-55-482 22-8350

(200) BRAZIL FORTALEZA MISSION
Rua Barao de Aracati, No. 1145
Aldeota, Fortaleza 60 115-081
Brazil
Phone: 011-55-85 221-1335

(233) BRAZIL MANAUS MISSION
Caixa Postal No 3461
Alvorada I
69042-010 Manaus, AM
Brazil
Phone: 011-55-92 238-5433

(256) BRAZIL PORTO ALEGRE NORTH MISSION
Caixa Postal 4008 - Azenha
Porto Alegre - RS
90630-970 Brazil
Phone: 011-55-51 223-5744

(48) BRAZIL PORTO ALEGRE SOUTH MISSION
Caixa Postal 4089
Porto Alegre - RS
90631-730 Brazil
Phone: 011-55-51 223-0288

(282) BRAZIL RECIFE SOUTH MISSION
Rua General Joaquim Inacio, 414
Sala 1202
50070-270 Recife - OE, Brazil
Phone: 011-55-81 222-3658

(279) BRAZIL RIBEIRAO PRETO MISSION
Caixa Postal 388
14001.970 Ribeirao Preto - SP
Brazil
Phone: 011-55-16 636-7253

(80) BRAZIL RIO DE JANEIRO MISSION
Av. das Americas, 1155, salas 502/502
(Barra Space Center) - Barra da Tijuca
Rio de Janeiro - RJ, Brazil 22631-000
Phone: 011-55-21 439-9243

(280) BRAZIL RIO DE JANEIRO NORTH MISSION
Rua da Gloria
344 - Sala - 904 - Gloria
202410180 Rio de Janeiro - RJ, Brazil
Phone: 011-55-21 252-7495

(234) BRAZIL SALVADOR MISSION
Caixa Postal 7384
CEP 41810 Salvador, Bahia
Brazil
Phone: 011-55-71 358-7345

(298) BRAZIL SALVADOR SOUTH MISSION
Edificio Empresarial Delta
Av. Antonio Carlos Guinaeaes, 3247
Salvador
Brazil
Phone: 011-55-71 247-2111

(102) BRAZIL SAO PAULO EAST MISSION
Caixa Postal 15674
03316-990 Tatuape
Sao Paulo, SP, Brazil
Phone: 011-55-11 264-5185

(102) BRAZIL SAO PAULO INTERLAGOS MISSION
Rua Comendador Elias Zarzur, 311
Santo Amaro
04736-000 Sao Paulo - SP
Brazil
Phone: 011-55-11 522-3677

(101) BRAZIL SAO PAULO NORTH MISSION
Caixa Postal 26095
05599 Sao Paulo - SP
Brazil
Phone: 011-55-11 211-5920

(102) BRAZIL SAO PAULO SOUTH MISSION
Caixa Postal 46031
04046-970 Sao Paulo - SP
Brazil
Phone: 011-55-11 579-5278

BULGARIA

Year-end 1993: Est. population, 9,045,000; Members, 700; Branches, 10; Missions, 1; Districts, 1; Europe Area.

Located on the eastern Balkan peninsula on the Black Sea, Bulgaria has a population that speaks Bulgarian, Turkish and Greek, and they have an Orthodox background in religion.

Mischa Markow, prominent early missionary to the Balkans, visited Bulgaria in about 1900 when he registered with the police and received permission to preach. Soon he was challenged by a Protestant minister, which had the effect of bringing in many more curious people. He preached to many, but was soon banished by the police.

The first missionaries to Bulgaria in recent times were two couples and two sisters, who arrived Sept. 10, 1990. The first missionary couples were Elder Delbert and Sister Marilyn Fowler who taught English in the town of Pravets, and Elder Morris and Sister Annetta Mower who served in Sofia. Sisters Judy Gubler and Rose Marie Daigle were the first sister missionaries. They taught English in the city of Smolyan. The first elders arrived Nov. 13, 1990, from the Austria Vienna East Mission. The elders also took part in charitable endeavors.

Elder Russell M. Nelson of the Council of the Twelve and Elder Hans B. Ringger of the Seventy visited government officials Feb. 13, 1990. Following their visit, the Bulgaria Sofia Mission was created July 1, 1991, at which time there were about 50 members, mostly in Sofia. President of the mission was Kiril P. Kiriakov, 68, of Manassas, Va., a native of Bulgaria.

Missionaries were also brought from Yugoslavia because they spoke Serbo-Croatian, a language similar to Bulgarian, which helped them overcome the language barrier. The Lamanite Generation from BYU toured the country in 1991.

Sources: "Missionary to the Balkans, Mischa Markow," by William Hale Kehr, *Ensign*, June 1980; *Church News*, May 18, 1991.

Mission — 1
(As of Oct. 1, 1994; shown with historical number. See MISSIONS.)

(259) BULGARIA SOFIA MISSION
Blvd. Tsar Boris III No. 94
1612 Sofia, Bulgaria
Phone: (011 359-2) 492-11-04

BURUNDI

Year-end 1993: Est. population, 5,807,000; Members, fewer than 100; Branches, 1; Africa Area; Zaire Kinshasa Mission.

About the size of Maryland, Burundi is a republic bordered by Tanzania, Zaire and Rwanda. Its people speak Kirundi and French, the official language, and are 62 percent Roman Catholic, 5 percent Protestant and 32 percent indigenous beliefs.

The Church established a branch in the capital city of this East Central African country following its adoption of a new constitution in 1992. After its first six months of organization, the Bujumbura Branch in Burundi continues to flourish with 36 members, and four full-time missionaries.

The first branch president, Pres. Egide Nzojibwami, was set apart by Elder J Ballard Washburn of the Africa Area presidency and a member of the Seventy, on Nov. 27, 1992. The first branch meeting was held two days later with 39 in attendance. Pres. Homer M. LeBaron of the Zaire Kinshasa Mission and his wife, Aleene, met with the Nzojibwami family and arranged for the organization. Pres. Nzojibwami and his wife, Beatrice, were baptized in Liege, Belgium, in 1984 while pursuing studies in that country. He was dean of the school of Geological Engineering at the University of Burundi.

Soon after the branch was organized, missionaries from the Ivory Coast Abidjan Mission (formerly Cameroon Yaounde Mission) arrived and began teaching the pool of investigators. These missionaries were Elders Francois Boue, Felix Gnamba, Aime Cesar Kipre and Bassin Kouhon.

Source: *Church News*, Aug. 21, 1993.

CAMBODIA

Year-end 1993: Est. population, 9,000,000; Members, fewer than 100; Asia Area.

Many Cambodian refugees in the United States joined the Church in the 1970s following the Vietnam War. Cambodian branches are established in a number of metropolitan centers in other countries.

On March 4, 1994, the government of Cambodia granted legal recognition to the Church. Missionary couples serving there do not proselyte but perform Christian service work. The announcement of the legal recognition was made by President Gordon B. Hinckley, first counselor in the First Presidency, on March 6, 1994.

Source: *Church News*, March 12, 1994.

CAMEROON

Year-end 1993: Est. population, 11,900,000; Members, fewer than 100; Branches, 1; Africa Area; Ivory Coast Abidjan Mission.

Located on the western coast of Africa on the Gulf of Guinea, Cameroon is a republic where the people speak tribal languages, including Bamileke and Fulani. The people follow Animist, Christian and Moslem beliefs.

A few members lived in Cameroon representing various health organizations in the 1980s and earlier. Cameroon Pres. Paul Biya approved the Church's request for legal recognition on Sept. 9, 1993. At the time, two missionary couples, Elder Gerard and Sister Georgette Gagne of Montreal, Quebec, and Elder Ken and Sister Bea Nielsen from Calgary, Alberta, were serving in the French-speaking country. Up to the time the government granted recognition, about 30 people had been baptized, and another 60 investigators were attending Sunday meetings. Since then, 30 more have been baptized and Sunday attendance averages about 100 per week.

The Cameroon Yaounde Mission was created on July 1, 1992, with Robert L. Mercer as its first president. The mission headquarters were moved to Abidjan, Ivory Coast, on May 18, 1993, which is also French speaking.

Sources: *Church News*, Feb. 2, 1992; *Church News*, Jan. 22, 1994.

CANADA

Year-end 1993: Est. population, 27,888,000; Members, 138,000; Stakes, 37; Wards, 256; Branches, 154; Missions, 7; Districts, 8; Temples, 2; Percent LDS, 0.5, or one person in 202.

At the northern end of North America, Canada is a confederation with a parliamentary democracy and a population speaking English and French, and is Roman Catholic, 46 percent; and Protestant, 41 percent.

ALBERTA

Year-end 1993: Est. population, 2,607,000; Members, 58,000; Stakes, 17; Wards, 129; Branches, 42; Missions, 1; Districts, 1; Temples, 1; Percent LDS, 2.20, or one person in 45.

Mormon railway crews from northern Utah helped lay track for the Canadian Pacific Railway as early as 1883 and were familiar with southern Alberta. They evidently readily supported later colonization efforts. In 1886, Charles O. Card, president of the Cache Valley Stake in Logan, Utah, explored southern Alberta, seeking a location to colonize in Canada. In March 1887, he left with a small advance party, arrived at Lee's Creek on June 3, and started a settlement that later became Cardston. The Cardston Ward was organized in 1888. Others welcomed the opportunity for land away from the burgeoning population of the Great Basin. Soon settled were Mountain View and Aetna (1890); Beazer (1891); Leavitt (1893); Kimball (1897); Caldwell, Taylorville, Magrath and Stirling, (1898); and after the turn of the century, Woolford, Welling, Orton, Raymond, Barnwell, Welling, Taber, Frankburg, Glenwood and Hill Spring.

Completion of some 115 miles of irrigation canal by 1900, contracted to the Church by C.A. McGrath, and considerable investment from Utahn Jesse Knight in starting a sugar beet industry facilitated development of the prairie.

The Alberta Stake was created in 1895, the Taylor Stake in 1903 and the Lethbridge Stake in 1921. By 1914, more than 10,000 members lived in the vicinity. In 1913, ground was broken for the Alberta Temple, which was dedicated in 1923. In 1920, membership was 8,896, increasing to 10,067 in 1930.

The Edmonton Branch began in 1933. Headquarters of the Western Canadian Mission was established in Edmonton in September 1941. In 1951, the first meetinghouse in Edmonton was dedicated. Membership in 1940 was 11,343, and in 1950, 14,583.

Members began dispersing to population centers, including Calgary, Alberta, the province of British Columbia, and to eastern Canada, where they continue to provide stability and leadership. The Calgary Stake was created in 1953. Over the next decades membership increased in 1960 to 19,985, and in 1970, 27,989. In 1981, membership in Alberta was 41,444, increasing to 56,000 in 1990. Nathan Eldon Tanner, who served as first counselor in the First Presidency, was a resident of Canada at the time of his calling as a General Authority. Current General Authorities from Alberta are Elders Ted E. Brewerton, Alexander B. Morrison and Lowell D. Wood. In addition, Relief Society Gen. Pres. Elaine Jack was born in Alberta.

Sources: *Encyclopedic History of the Church* by Andrew Jenson; *A History of the Mormon Church in Canada*, compiled and published by the Lethbridge Stake in 1968; "Canada," by Richard E. Bennett, *Ensign*, September 1988; "The Alberta Settlements, 1887-1925," chapters by Brigham Y. Card and Leonard Arrington, *The Mormon Presence in Canada*, published by the University of Alberta Press, 1990.

Stakes — 17
(Listed alphabetically as of Oct. 1, 1994.)

No.	Name	Organized	First President
North America Central Area			
211a	*Calgary Alberta		
	†Calgary	15 Nov 1953	N. Eldon Tanner

1924	Calgary Alberta East	14 Feb 1993	Geoffrey Bryan Grunewald
416	*Calgary Alberta North		
	†Calgary North	17 Apr 1966	Gerald E. Melchin
1101	Calgary Alberta South	3 Feb 1980	Clarence Lee Robertson
1031	Calgary Alberta West	27 May 1979	Lynn Albert Rosenvall
35	*Cardston Alberta		
	†Alberta	9 Jun 1895	Charles O. Card
1455	Cardston Alberta West	13 Nov 1983	Brent L. Nielson
655	*Edmonton Alberta Bonnie Doon 6 Nov 1983		
	†Edmonton Alberta East	3 Nov 1974	Bryant L. Stringham
1453	Edmonton Alberta Millwoods	6 Nov 1983	Kenneth Orland Higginbotham
312	*Edmonton Alberta Riverbend 6 Nov 1983		
	*Edmonton Alberta		
	†Edmonton	15 Nov 1960	Leroy Rollins
1560	Fort Macleod Alberta	29 Sep 1985	Heber James Beazer
189	*Lethbridge Alberta		
	*Lethbridge 15 Nov 1953		
	*East Lethbridge	28 Oct 1951	Grant G. Woolley
667	Lethbridge Alberta East	24 Nov 1974	Bryce C. Stringham
1199	Magrath Alberta	26 Oct 1980	James Dickson Bridge
51	*Raymond Alberta		
	†Taylor	30 Aug 1903	Heber S. Allen
1350	Red Deer Alberta	13 Jun 1982	Dennis William Guenther
302	*Taber Alberta		
	†Taber	11 Sep 1960	Ray B. Evenson

Discontinued

86   Lethbridge   10 Nov 1921   Hugh B. Brown
15 Nov 1953 ★Calgary (No. 211a), Lethbridge (No. 189)

Mission — 1
(As of Oct. 1, 1994; shown with historical number. See MISSIONS.)

(36a) CANADA CALGARY MISSION
6940 Fisher Road S.E., #122
Calgary, Alberta T2H 0W3
Canada
Phone: (403) 252-1141

BRITISH COLUMBIA

Year-end 1993: Est. population, 3,390,000; Members, 25,000; Stakes, 6; Wards, 42; Branches, 33; Missions, 1; Districts, 2; Percent LDS, 0.7, or one person in 136.

Vancouver Island was one of several locations Brigham Young considered as a western settlement site for the Saints. In a letter to the members published Nov. 1, 1845, he mentioned the island as "one of many good locations for settlement on the Pacific." The letter sparked a petition by the members in England to Queen Victoria to support them in settling the island. However, the petition was ignored, and no LDS immigrants settled on the island until 1875. That year William Francis and Maria Judson Copley and their three children settled at Shawigan. For the next 15 years they were the only members here. The first convert on the island was Anthony Maitland Stenhouse, a member of the legislative assembly of British Columbia who chose to resign from the assembly and be baptized in 1887. He became a vigorous defender of the faith, living in Cardston, Alberta, and eventually returning to his homeland of Great Britain.

On March 15, 1902, most of British Columbia was placed in the Northwestern States Mission. On May 13, 1903, seven missionaries, led by mission Pres. Nephi Pratt, arrived. The Victoria Conference was organized the next day. Their first converts were unbaptized members of the Copley family. By 1918 membership on the island was 21. A Sunday School was organized on Vancouver Island but later dissolved when several families moved away. It was resumed in 1937.

World War II brought members to the island, and a branch was started in Victoria. A second group began meeting in Nanaimo in 1946. Missionaries arrived following the war, and additional branches were started. Membership over the years has increased. In 1920, British Columbia had 200 members, growing to 584 in 1930 and 455 in 1940.

Work in Vancouver City on the mainland began in 1904 when Pres. Pratt visited and located an LDS family, that of Edward Neill. A conference with 12 in attendance was held in 1909 and a branch was organized in Feb. 12, 1911. By 1925 the branch had a chapel. The branch was made a ward and included in the new Seattle Stake in 1938. The Vancouver District of the new Western Canadian Mission was created in 1948. From then on, the area grew significantly as members moved in and more converts joined the Church. Membership in the province grew to 1,582 in 1950, 4,104 in 1960, and 10,123 in 1970.

On Nov. 21, 1960, the Vancouver Stake was created with wards in Vancouver (two), North Shore, New Westminister, Fleetwood, Richmond, White Rock, Langley and Chilliwack. A new stake center was started in 1966.

Membership in Vancouver has grown increasingly international. Membership in British Columbia in 1981 was 15,494. Membership reached 24,000 in 1990.

Sources: *A History of the Mormon Church in Canada,* compiled and published by the Lethbridge Stake in 1968; "The Church of Jesus Christ of Latter-day Saints and Vancouver Island: The Establishment and Growth of the Mormon Community," by Robert J. McCue, *BC Studies,* Summer 1979; "No One Is an Island," by Giles H. Florence Jr., *Ensign,* August 1990.

Stakes — 7
(Listed alphabetically as of Oct. 1, 1994.)

No.	Name	Organized	First President
North America Northwest Area			
1980	Abbottsford British Columbia	12 Jun 1994	Andrew Howard Rattray
994	Cranbrook British Columbia	14 Jan 1979	Brian James Erickson
1905	Prince George British Columbia	26 Sep 1992	A. Brice Gurney
315	*Vancouver British Columbia		
	†Vancouver	21 Nov 1960	Ernest E. Jensen
1014	Vancouver British Columbia South	8 Apr 1979	Richard Bulpitt
709	Vernon British Columbia	12 Oct 1975	James Ronald Burnham
679	Victoria British Columbia	9 Feb 1975	Howard Lowell Biddulph

Mission — 1
(As of Oct. 1, 1994; shown with historical number. See MISSIONS.)

(58) CANADA VANCOUVER MISSION
P.O. Box 149
Point Roberts, WA 98281
Phone: (604) 271-3585

MANITOBA

Year-end 1993: Est. population, 1,105,000; Members, 3,800; Stakes, 1; Wards, 5; Branches, 6; Missions, 1; Percent LDS, 0.34, or one person in 290.

A request from John Sherman, a member who lived in Souris, Manitoba, to Pres. Charles O. Card of the Canadian Mission led to missionaries coming to Manitoba. Elder Niels Hansen supervised six other missionaries who were called in 1896 and who arrived in Manitoba in 1897 and made progress in spreading the gospel. Soon another dozen elders arrived to help. Several converts immigrated to Alberta. In 1899, Manitoba was placed in the Northern States Mission. A conference organized in 1901 was later discontinued but re-opened in 1906. That year, missionaries vigorously sold copies of the Book of Mormon, with eight missionaries selling 308 copies. A year later their efforts bore fruit, and five in the province were baptized. Many of the converts later moved to LDS centers in other areas.

In 1910, the Winnipeg Sunday School was organized with 37 members. The branch was organized in 1922.

Membership in the district in 1930 was 197, including the Winnipeg and Bergland, Ontario, branches. The Brandon Branch was created in 1955, and a second branch in Winnipeg was created in 1961. Other branches were organized in Portage La Prairie (for U.S. Air Force personnel in 1951), Kenora, (1955), Thompson (a nickle mining center, in 1963), Dauphin (a Sunday School in 1957). Membership in the province in 1966 was 1,368.

The Canada Winnipeg Mission was created in 1976 with about 4,200 members in four districts, including those in Saskatchewan and western Ontario. The Winnipeg Manitoba Stake was created Nov. 12, 1978. A new stake center was dedicated in 1988, and stake membership reached 2,500. Membership in Manitoba in 1981 was 2,136. Membership in 1990 was 3,700.

Sources: *Encyclopedic History of the Church* by Andrew Jenson; Northern States Mission, manuscript history, 1899-1908; *A History of the Church of Jesus Christ of Latter-day Saints in Canada, 1830-1963,* a BYU dissertation by Melvin S. Tagg, May 1963; *A History of the Mormon Church in Canada,* compiled by the Lethbridge Stake, 1968; "North Star Harvest," by Carol Cornwall Madsen, *Church News,* May 13, 1978; "Thompson Saints Sink Roots in Manitoba Soil," by Bruce Northcott, *Ensign,* August 1986; "In Winnipeg: An Exciting Time to be a Member," by Raman Job, *Ensign,* May 1989.

No.	Name	Organized	First President

North America Central Area

980	Winnipeg Manitoba	12 Nov 1978	Lorne Leslie Clapson

Mission — 1
(As of Oct. 1, 1994; shown with historical number. See MISSIONS.)

(136) CANADA WINNIPEG MISSION
1661 Portage Avenue, #306
Winnipeg, Manitoba R3J 3T7
Phone: (204) 775-0466

NEW BRUNSWICK

Year-end 1993: Est. population, 729,700; Members, 2,100; Stakes, 1; Wards, 5; Branches, 3; Percent LDS, 0.3, or one person in 347; Canada Halifax Mission.

Missionary work in the Maritime provinces began in 1833 when Lyman E. Johnson and James Heriot began proselyting in Nova Scotia and New Brunswick. Elder Johnson preached in Saint John, New Brunswick, in the spring of 1836 and later in Sackville, where he baptized 18 people and organized the first branch in the Maritimes.

Among those baptized in Sackville was Marriner W. Merrill, who later preached extensively in Canada and eventually become a member of the Council of the Twelve.

In 1920, a branch was organized in Saint John, New Brunswick. The branch was discontinued and reorganized and has been continuous since 1948. A meetinghouse was completed in 1954. The Fredericton Branch was organized in 1940, later discontinued and started again in 1957, and completed a meetinghouse in 1963. The Moncton Branch, created in 1966, includes the Sackville area where the first branch of the Church in the Maritimes was created. Membership in this branch reached 160 in 1974. The Saint John New Brunswick Stake was created in 1988. Growth of the Church in the Maritimes has fluctuated over time, but the work of missionaries and members has pushed efforts along in the 1990s. Membership in 1990 was 2,100.

Sources: *Encyclopedic History of the Church,* by Andrew Jenson; *A History of the Mormon Church in Canada,* published in 1968 by the Lethbridge Alberta Stake under the direction of Dr. Melvin S. Tagg; "Portrait of a New Mission," by Jack E. Jarrard, *Church News,* Sept. 22, 1973; "The Saints in Canada's Maritime Provinces," by Eleanor Knowles, *Ensign,* June 1974; and "LDS in Canada — Growth through faithfulness," *Church News,* Oct. 23, 1983; "Maritime provinces," by Sheridan R. Sheffield, *Church News,* Oct. 24, 1992.

Stake — 1
(As of Oct. 1, 1994.)

No.	Name	Organized	First President

North America Northeast Area

1698	Saint John New Brunswick	26 Jun 1988	Blaine E. Hatt

NEWFOUNDLAND

Year-end 1993: Est. population, 574,700; Members, 600; Branches, 4; Percent LDS, 0.08, or one person in 956; North America Northeast Area; Canada Halifax Mission.

The St. John's Branch in Newfoundland was created Feb. 7, 1957, and in 10 years grew to 92 members. Other branches in the province include Cornerbook and Gander.

About half of the converts in this area are immigrants, often from eastern European countries. Retention of converts in the area is extremely high. Unemployment and economic difficulties are challenges that hamper growth.

Sources: *Encyclopedic History of the Church,* by Andrew Jenson; *A History of the Mormon Church in Canada,* published in 1968 by the Lethbridge Alberta Stake under the direction of Dr. Melvin S. Tagg; "Portrait of a New Mission," by Jack E. Jarrard, *Church News,* Sept. 22, 1973; "The Saints in Canada's Maritime Provinces," by Eleanor Knowles, *Ensign,* June 1974; and "LDS in Canada — Growth through faithfulness," *Church News,* Oct. 23, 1983; "Maritime provinces," by Sheridan R. Sheffield, *Church News,* Oct. 24, 1992.

NOVA SCOTIA

Year-end 1993: Est. population, 910,000; Members, 4,000; Stakes, 1; Wards, 6; Branches, 9; Missions, 1; Percent LDS, 0.3, or one person in 324.

Lyman E. Johnson and James Heriot began proselyting in the Maritime Provinces in 1833 when they arrived in Nova Scotia and New Brunswick. Two missionaries were sent to Nova Scotia by Joseph Smith in 1843. A conference there was attended by 18 members under district Pres. Robert Dixon. The Halifax Branch was created Nov. 14, 1843, and smaller branches began in Preston, Popes Harbour, and Onslow.

In 1845, John Sherry, a member from Nova Scotia, preached in Prince Edward Island. Branches were organized at Beddeque and Charlottetown. Persecution followed the members and most left for the West by 1855. One group of 50, most of the Halifax Branch, traveled with their branch president, John A. Jost, aboard the ship *Barque Halifax,* which left May 12, 1855, and took them the first leg of their journey around Cape Horn to San Francisco to the West. This exodus ended organized branches in the Maritimes until work resumed under the Canadian Mission in 1920. Membership in the area after this time was often depleted when converts moved to be closer to the established Church.

After missionary work resumed, missionaries presided over groups in Halifax, Windsor, and New Glasgow in Nova Scotia. The Halifax Branch in Nova Scotia was organized in July 1947 by mission Pres. S. Dilworth Young. In 1974, the Halifax and Dartmouth branches numbered about 750. A meetinghouse was started in 1958 and completed in 1959.

In 1959, converts were baptized in Bridgewater, Nova Scotia. The branch, created in 1961, grew to 135 in 1967. A meetinghouse was completed in 1966. A branch in Sydney was created in 1958. Membership in Nova Scotia is among the most rapidly growing in Canada. With 250 members in 1972, it increased more than 800 percent in 10 years, reaching 2,331. The Dartmouth Nova Scotia Stake was created in 1985. The Dartmouth/Halifax area in Nova Scotia continues to serve as the center of Church activity in the Maritimes, and is among the fastest growing in Canada. The youth continue to be an active part of the membership and associate with other LDS youth in stake activities. Membership in Nova Scotia in 1990 was 3,800.

Sources: *Encyclopedic History of the Church,* by Andrew Jenson; *A History of the Mormon Church in Canada,* published in 1968 by the Lethbridge Alberta Stake under the direction of Dr. Melvin S. Tagg; "Portrait of a New Mission," by Jack E. Jarrard, *Church News,* Sept. 22, 1973; "The Saints in Canada's Maritime Provinces," by Eleanor Knowles, *Ensign,* June 1974; and "LDS in Canada — Growth through faithfulness," *Church News,* Oct. 23, 1983; "Maritime provinces," by Sheridan R. Sheffield, *Church News,* Oct. 24, 1992.

Stake — 1
(As of Oct. 1, 1994.)

No.	Name	Organized	First President
North America Northeast Area			
1530	Dartmouth Nova Scotia	12 May 1985	Terry Lee Livingstone

Mission — 1
(As of Oct. 1, 1994; shown with historical number. See MISSIONS.)

(107) CANADA HALIFAX MISSION
202 Brownlow Ave., Unit F, Bldg F
Dartmouth, Nova Scotia B3B 1T5
Canada
Phone: (902) 468-5728

ONTARIO

Year-end 1993: Est. population, 10,377,000; Members, 32,000; Stakes, 8; Wards, 53; Branches, 31; Missions, 2; Districts, 2; Temples, 1; Percent LDS, 0.3, or one person in 324.

The first Mormons to enter Canada were Hiram Page and Oliver Cowdery, who crossed the border from New York in the winter of 1829-30, before the Church was organized, seeking ways to finance the publication of the Book of Mormon. In 1830, Phinehas Young traveled to Earnestown. Though unbaptized, he preached about the Book of Mormon.

Joseph Smith Sr. and Don Carlos Smith entered Canada briefly in September 1830, visiting a few villages north of the St. Lawrence River. Early in June 1832, Phinehas Young returned to Canada, this time as an ordained elder in the company of five others. Before the last of these missionaries had left Canada, four branches had been organized. Other missionaries soon followed, including Joseph Smith, who visited in October 1833 and again in July 1837. Two of the most successful missionaries were John E. Page and

Parley P. Pratt. Elder Page baptized almost a thousand converts. Elder Pratt brought in such future Church leaders as John Taylor, who later became president of the Church; and Isaac Russell, John Snider, John Goodson and Joseph Fielding. These four opened the highly successful work in Great Britain. Missionaries organized a district in Toronto that was placed under the direction of John Taylor.

Between 1830 and 1850, an estimated 2,500 Canadians, mostly from Ontario, joined the Church. Most of these who remained faithful gathered with the Saints in the Great Basin in the West. By 1861, the Ontario census lists only 74 members.

Little work progressed in eastern Canada until the Canadian Mission was organized in 1919, with conferences in Toronto and Ottawa. That same year, branches were organized in Toronto and Hamilton. Another was organized in Kitchener in 1923. The Ottawa Branch was created in July 1926. The St. Catherine's Branch was organized in 1933. The Oshawa Branch began in 1947 after functioning off and on as a Sunday School since 1944. Other units were created after 1950. Membership in all of eastern Canada reached 1,974 in 1950.

The first meetinghouse in eastern Canada was dedicated in Toronto in 1939, and the first eastern stake was organized in 1960 in Toronto, while Pres. Thomas S. Monson, now second counselor in the First Presidency, was mission president. The Toronto Temple was announced April 7, 1984, and dedicated Aug. 25-27, 1990. On July 1, 1993, Toronto's second mission was created. Missionaries may potentially work with people from upwards of 100 nations who come in hopes of immigrating. From Toronto, efforts to increase the profile of the Church through media led to a television series in 1994 during prime time across Canada. Membership in 1981 was 16,138, and in 1990, 28,00.

Sources: *Encyclopedic History of the Church* by Andrew Jenson; *A History of the Mormon Church in Canada*, compiled and published by the Lethbridge Stake, 1968; "Canada: From Struggling Seed, The Church Has Risen to Branching Maple," by Richard E. Bennett, *Ensign*, September 1988; "Toronto, A Growing Light in the East," by Richard Robertson, *Ensign*, September 1988; "Plucking not Planting," by Richard E. Bennett, *The Mormon Presence in Canada*, published by the University of Alberta Press, 1990; " 'Our treasure,' a new temple is dedicated," and "Past legacy builds today's faith," both by Dell Van Orden, *Church News*, Sept. 1, 1990; *Church News*, March 13, 1993; "Church begins series on TV across Canada," by William B. Smart, *Church News*, Feb. 5, 1994.

Stakes — 8
(Listed alphabetically as of Oct. 1, 1994.)

No.	Name	Organized	First President
North America Northeast Area			
1222	Brampton Ontario	11 Jan 1981	Cecil Malcolm Warner
524	*Hamilton Ontario		
	†Niagara	6 Sep 1970	Eldon C. Olsen
1600	Kitchener Ontario	22 Jun 1986	Graeme K. Hingston
752	London Ontario	11 Apr 1976	Harold Crookell
1907	Mississauga Ontario	18 Oct 1992	Lawrence R. Fuller
761	*Oshawa Ontario 22 Jun 1986		
	†Toronto Ontario East	13 Jun 1976	John Bruce Smith
796	Ottawa Ontario	12 Dec 1976	Boyden E. Lee
300	*Toronto Ontario		
	†Toronto	14 Aug 1960	William M. Davies

Missions — 2
(As of Oct. 1, 1994; shown with historical number. See MISSIONS.)

(285) CANADA TORONTO EAST MISSION
2025 Sheppard Avenue East, Suite 2300
Willowdale, Ontario M2J 1V7
Canada
Phone: (416) 490-6869

(23a) CANADA TORONTO WEST MISSION
338 Queen Street East, Suite 214
Brampton, Ontario
Canada
Phone: (905) 452-7484

PRINCE EDWARD ISLAND

Year-end 1993: Est. population, 131,000; Members, 300; Branches, 3; Percent LDS, 0.21, or one person in 437; North America Northeast Area; Canada Halifax Mission.

The first missionary to preach in the province was John Sherry, coming to Prince Edward Island in 1845. Branches were organized in Bedeque and Charlottetown, but were disbanded in 1850 when all members immigrated to Utah.

The first modern presence of the Church in Prince Edward Island came in 1964 when Ralph and Gerda

Waugh, converts from New York, returned to the land of Brother's Waugh's birth. They contacted another member and began holding Sunday School.

Elder Boyd K. Packer, then an Assistant to the Twelve, was president of the New England Mission at the time, which included Prince Edward Island. Elder Packer visited the Waugh home with missionaries in July 1966. About two weeks later full-time missionaries were transferred to the island and missionaries have been here since then.

Brother Waugh was called as the first branch president of the Summerside Branch on Dec. 21, 1969. In 1974 the branch was divided and the Charlottetown Branch was formed.

The Church continued to grow on the island, and in 1982 the Prince Edward Island District was formed. Excavation also began in Summerside on construction of the island's first meetinghouse. The building was completed on June 18, 1983. A second meetinghouse in Charlottetown was started in 1983 and completed on July 14, 1984. The Montague Branch was formed in November 1985 and a meetinghouse was completed in June 1988. The three branches became part of the Saint John New Brunswick Stake on June 26, 1988.

One of the most popular tourist locations in the Maritimes, this area is home to the smallest number of members of any province in Canada. Membership in Prince Edward Island in 1990 was 300.

Sources: *A History of the Mormon Church in Canada,* published in 1968 by the Lethbridge Alberta Stake under the direction of Dr. Melvin S. Tagg; "The Saints in Canada's Maritime Provinces," by Eleanor Knowles, *Ensign,* June 1974; Prince Edward Island: Members find peace in 'little land' where 'you find your soul,' " by Sheridan R. Sheffield, *Church News,* July 10, 1993.

QUEBEC

Year-end 1993: Est. population, 6,987,000; Members, 7,400; Stakes, 2; Wards, 11; Branches, 10; Missions, 1; Districts, 1; Percent LDS, 0.1, or one person in 944.

Early missionaries in the 1830s frequently traveled through but found little success in Lower Canada, as the province of Quebec was then called. They found proselyting difficult among its largely French-speaking people. In 1836, however, Hazen Aldrich and Winslow Farr labored in Stanstead County and baptized a number of people. Twenty-three of these emigrated July 20, 1837. Converts also came from the community of Eardley, north of Ottawa. After the 1840s, missionary work experienced an interlude until the next century.

The Canadian Mission was organized in 1919. By 1930, an English-speaking branch began meeting in Montreal. A meetinghouse for this branch was purchased from another faith in 1942 and served the branch until the late 1970s.

The Ottawa-Montreal District was created in 1953 as part of the Canadian Mission. The same year a mission district was created in Quebec. In 1961, then-Mission Pres. Thomas S. Monson sent six French-speaking missionaries into the area around Quebec. The missionaries found converts and established a base that attracted LDS French-speaking immigrants. From this effort, missionaries entered Quebec City where a branch was started in 1969. The Quebec (later changed to the Canada Montreal) Mission was created in 1972, and by 1974, a French-speaking district was created. By 1987, membership among the French-speaking people was 2,753, some 65 percent of the total membership in the province. These converts tended to stay in Quebec where their roots were instead of moving to the West as did many of their English-speaking counterparts.

The Tung Fong Branch was created in 1975 for the many Chinese people in the Montreal area.

The Montreal Quebec Stake, considered the first French-speaking stake in North America, was created in 1978. A high councilor was Kitchner Young, one of the first French-speaking missionaries. A stake center for this stake was completed, following an open house, in 1993.

In addition, French-speaking members from Quebec have made contributions as missionaries in French-speaking countries in West Africa and other developing nations of the world.

The Quebec District consists of the Quebec (1969), Alma (1984), Chicoutimi (1976) and Rimouksi (1979) branches. In 1975, membership in this district was 977 members.

In 1980, the English-speaking Montreal Mt. Royale Quebec Stake was created. Membership in Quebec reached 3,246 in 1981. In 1990, membership was 6,800.

Sources: *Encyclopedic History of the Church* by Andrew Jenson; *The Mormon Church in Canada,* compiled and published by the Lethbridge Stake, 1968; "History of the Church in Quebec and Ontario," *Culture for Missionaries,* Missionary Training Center, 1977; "Converts in Quebec," *Church News,* by Maureen Ursenbach Beecher, June 24, 1978; *Church News,* July 8, 1978; "Canada, From Struggling Seed, the Church has Risen to Branching Maple," by Richard E. Bennett, *Ensign,* September 1988; "Canadian Mormon Identity and the French Fact," by Dean R. Louder, in *The Mormon Presence in Canada,* published by the University of Alberta Press, 1990; *Church News,* June 5, 1993.

Stakes — 2

(Listed alphabetically as of Oct. 1, 1994.)

No.	Name	Organized	First President
North America Northeast Area			
943	Montreal Quebec	18 Jun 1978	Gerard C. Pelchat
1160	Montreal Quebec Mount Royal	6 Jul 1980	Ian Gillespie Wilson

Mission — 1

(As of Oct. 1, 1994; shown with historical number. See MISSIONS.)

(99a) CANADA MONTREAL MISSION
1320 Blv. Graham, Suite 310
Ville Mont-Royal, Quebec H3P 3C8
Canada
Phone: (514) 731-0612

SASKATCHEWAN

Year-end 1993: Est. population, 993,000; Members, 4,400; Stakes, 1; Wards, 5; Branches, 11; Districts, 1; Percent LDS, 0.5, or one person in 226; Canada Winnipeg Mission.

In the early 1920s, G. Gordon Whyte of Moose Jaw encountered a copy of the Book of Mormon, accepted it as truth and requested baptism. He was baptized Aug. 17, 1923, in Moose Jaw and later lived in Regina. His membership was kept in the Raymond 1st Ward, under Bishop John G. Allred. That same year, Bishop Allred, who later was to serve as president of the North Central States Mission from 1925-29, and Brother Whyte held a street meeting in Regina where they placed 16 copies of the Book of Mormon.

The first missionaries in Saskatchewan were Elders Leo E. Nielsen and John A. Ward in Saskatoon and Reuben T. Reynolds and Raymond L. Allen in Regina, who arrived in 1925. The North Saskatchewan and South Saskatchewan conferences were organized Aug. 6 of that year.

Missionaries found progress slow, but a Sunday School was organized May 8, 1927, in Saskatchewan which became a branch on May 27, 1934, under Pres. Whyte. The north and south conferences were combined by 1930 and had a membership of 145. A meetinghouse was dedicated for the Regina Branch in 1939.

In 1934, LDS farmers in southern Alberta, and their non-LDS neighbors, donated two boxcars of vegetables and food to 200 families in Saskatchewan suffering form the effects of a severe drought. Among them were 20 families in the Regina Branch.

Saskatchewan became part of the Western Canadian Mission Dec. 6, 1942, and a mission home was purchased in Saskatchewan on Dec. 9. At that time, the district had 173 members including 79 in the Regina Branch.

During this time, Brother Whyte continued to do missionary work among various Indians on nearby reserves. An Indian seminary program began in 1965 with 45 Lamanite children on the Piapot, Carry-the-Kettle and Cowesses reserves east of Regina.

In 1949, the Saskatoon Branch functioned for a short time with no actual membership as members had moved away and investigators held positions. Later missionary work and baptisms led to the normalization of the branch.

By 1961, branches in Regina (May 27, 1934), Moose Jaw (a Sunday School functioned from 1929 until a branch was organized in 1945), Saskatoon (1944), Swift Current (1952), Prince Albert (1959) and Silver Park (re-named Melfort; organized in 1947), were included in the Saskatchewan District, with a total of about 600 members. On Sept. 3, the district was divided into the North and South districts. The Yorktown and Carry-the-Kettle branches were organized in 1966.

The Saskatoon Saskatchewan Stake was created Nov. 5, 1978, combining two districts, with 2,101 members. At that time, Saskatoon and Regina had two wards each. Membership in Saskatchewan in 1980 was 2,857, increasing to 4,200 in 1990.

Sources: *Encyclopedic History of the Church* by Andrew Jenson; *Liahona,* Oct. 20, 1925, p. 182; North Central States Manuscript History, 1925-40; *History of the Western Canadian Mission,* by Wilbur Gordon Hackney, a BYU Thesis, May 17, 1950; *A History of the Mormon Church in Canada,* compiled and published by the Lethbridge Stake, 1968; "The Christian Way," by Carol Cornwall Madsen, *Church News* July 1, 1978; *Church News,* Feb. 10, 1945, Feb. 2, 1949, July 5, 1950, Nov. 18, 1978, Oct. 23, 1983.

No.	Name	Organized	First President

North America Central Area

978   Saskatoon Saskatchewan   5 Nov 1978   Noel W. Burt

NORTHWEST TERRITORIES

Year-end 1993: Est. population, 60,000; Members, 100; Branches, 1; Percent LDS, 0.1, or one person in 600; North America Central Area; Canada Calgary Mission.

The Yellowknife Branch in the Northwest Territories covers half a million square miles and is called the largest branch in area in the Church. Half the members live in Yellowknife and half are scattered in the communities of Hay River, Fort Smith, Coppermine, Inuvik, Rankin Inlet and Iqaluit. Members occasionally travel hundreds of miles to meet for socials and meetings.

Sources: *A History of the Mormon Church in Canada,* published in 1968 by the Lethbridge Alberta Stake under the direction of Dr. Melvin S. Tagg; "Northern Hospitality," by Ronald G. Watt, *Church News,* July 8, 1978; "Largest Branch in the World," *Ensign,* September 1988.

YUKON TERRITORY

Year-end 1993: Est. population, 29,000; Members, 100; Branches, 1; Percent LDS, 0.3, or one person in 290; North America Northwest Area; Alaska Anchorage Mission.

A branch was created in Whitehorse, Yukon Territories, on Oct. 15, 1963, and meetings were held in rented quarters with a mostly 100 percent attendance of the 35 members. The branch now has a meetinghouse.

A highlight in branch history came in 1968 when Apostle LeGrand Richards visited and witnessed the baptism of four people. His was the first known visit of a General Authority to the branch.

Sources: *A History of the Mormon Church in Canada,* published in 1968 by the Lethbridge Alberta Stake.

CAPE VERDE

Year-end 1993: Est. population, 350,000; Members, 2,000; Districts, 3; Branches, 13; Percent LDS, 0.6; or one LDS in 175; Europe Mediterranean Area; Portugal Lisbon South Mission.

The Republic of Cape Verde is made up of 10 main islands, 400 miles west of Senegal off the African coast. The people, who are mostly Roman Catholics influenced by indigenous beliefs, speak Portuguese and Criuolo.

Spain Canary Islands Mission Pres. Marion K. Hamblin opened the Cape Verde area by visiting the islands in November 1988 and sending Elders Christopher Lee and Ken Margetts there a short time later to create the Praia/Lajes Branch on Cape Verde. The ambassador of Cape Verde attended the lighting ceremony of the Washington Temple in 1993. In September 1994, Elder Dallin H. Oaks visited the islands and made courtesy visits to the president of the republic, Antonio Mascarenhas, and Paia mayor Jacinto Santos.

At that time, Pres. Robert Coleman of the Portugal Lisbon South Mission said that by September 1994, some 50 members from Cape Verde had been called to serve full-time missions.

Sources: Spain Canary Islands Mission; *Church News,* Dec. 7, 1991; *Church News,* Dec. 11, 1993; *Church News,* Sept. 24, 1994.

CENTRAL AFRICA REPUBLIC

Year-end 1993: Est. population, 3,130,000; Members, fewer than 100; Branches, 2; Africa Area; Ivory Coast Abidjan Mission.

Located in Central Africa along the northern border of Zaire, the Central Africa Republic is a republic with a population that speaks French and local dialects. The population is Protestant, 25 percent; Catholic, 25 percent; traditional, 24 percent; and other beliefs.

The first known member living in Central Africa Republic was Carol Forrest of the U.S. Peace Corps, a returned missionary and one of the medical personnel, who arrived in June 1991. She shared the gospel with many of her associates and in September 1991 was set apart as a district missionary. Elder J Ballard Washburn of the Seventy and a counselor in the Africa Area presidency visited Sister Forrest and a group of investigators in September 1992.

Traveling with Elder Washburn was Pres. Robert L. Mercer of the Cameroon Yaounde Mission. On Sept. 19, 1992, 20 converts were baptized and two branches organized. Celestin N'Gakondou was called as president of the Bangui 1st Branch, and Gaspard Lapet was called to preside over the Bangui 2nd Branch.

A French couple, Elder and Sister Frutina, arrived in January of 1993.

Sources: "Medical officer ministers to souls," by Mary Mostert, *Church News,* Dec. 5, 1992; Correspondence from the Ivory Coast Abidjan Mission, March 1994.

CHILE

Year-end 1993: Est. population, 13,513,000; Members, 345,000; Stakes, 67; Wards, 391; Branches, 246; Missions, 6; Districts, 16; Temples, 1; Percent LDS, 2.6, or one person in 39.

On the west coast of South America, the Republic of Chile has a Spanish-speaking population that is 89 percent Roman Catholic.

Parley P. Pratt, his wife, Phebe, and Elder Rufus C. Allen traveled to Chile, arriving Nov. 8, 1851, but remained only five months. Their inability to speak the language and their meager funds, along with continuing civil turbulence in the country proved insurmountable obstacles. The next LDS presence began with LDS families living in Santiago in the early 1950s. President David O. McKay visited the William Fotheringham family, residents of Santiago, on Feb. 8, 1954. On May 26, 1956, Chile became part of the Argentine Mission. At that time, Elders Joseph Bentley and Verle Allred crossed the Andes from Argentina and arrived in Chile June 23, 1956, beginning missionary work in Chile. They stayed with the Fotheringhams and on July 5, the first branch was organized. A few months later they baptized Ricardo and Perla Garcia and others on Nov. 2, 1956. Six more branches were created by 1959.

Growth in Chile has been rapid. When Elder Spencer W. Kimball, then of the Council of the Twelve, visited in 1959, the country had about 450 members. In October of that year, 45 more were added, a 10 percent increase in one month. The Chile Mission was organized Oct. 8, 1961, with 1,100 members. When the first stake was organized 11 years later with Carlos A. Cifuentes as president, membership had grown to more than 20,000 members.

On Feb. 27, 1977, President Spencer W. Kimball visited Santiago and addressed nearly 7,000 members. At the same gathering, Elder Bruce R. McConkie of the Council of the Twelve predicted that in the future, the Church would become the most powerful influence in the nation. President Kimball returned to Chile May 30, 1981, to break ground for a temple, attended by 6,000 people who waited in the rain for several hours.

The temple was completed in 1983, and dedicated on Sept. 15. At that time, the country had 140,400 members in 27 stakes. Chile became the fourth country in the world to reach 50 stakes on Oct. 29, 1988. Chile has strong local leadership, a high percentage of local missionaries and a number of local mission and temple presidents.

Chile's first General Authority was Elder Eduardo Ayala of the Seventy. Membership in 1990 was 298,000. At the commemoration of the 10th anniversary of the temple in 1994, it was noted that membership and stakes had doubled during the decade.

Sources: *Encyclopedic History of the Church* by Andrew Jenson; "Chile," by Steven J. Iverson, *New Era,* February 1977; "Love, respect and emotion end area conference series," by Dell Van Orden, *Church News,* March 12, 1977; *Los Mormones in Chile,* by Rodolfo Acevedo Acevedo, published in Santiago, Chile, 1989; *Church News,* Sept. 25, 1993.

Stakes — 68
(Listed alphabetically as of Oct. 1, 1994.)

No.	Name	Organized	First President
South America South Area			
1499	Achupallas Chile	28 Oct 1984	Luis Alino Pereira P.
1075	Andalien Chile	28 Oct 1979	Pedro E. Arias
1165	Antofagasta Chile	10 Aug 1980	Octavio Araya Y.
1955	Antofagasta Chile Portada	5 Sep 1993	Miguel A. Gonzalez Romero
1100	Arica Chile	29 Jan 1980	Jose Ulloa C.
1598	Arica Chile El Morro	18 May 1986	Sergio Alberto Funes
1522	Calama Chile	17 Mar 1985	Ivan Gonzalez Castillo
1501	Caliche Chile	4 Nov 1984	Ricardo Manuel Palma F.
1398	Chillan Chile	13 Feb 1983	Sergio Rios S.
808	Concepcion Chile	30 Jan 1977	Claudio Signorelli G.

1929	Copiapo Chile	11 Apr 1993	Sergio Orlando Mora Oviedo
1960b	Conquimbo Chile	5 Dec 1993	Marco Oyarzun Vera
1264	Curico Chile	10 May 1981	Jose Luis Ferreira P.
1931	El Belloto Chile	11 Apr 1993	Hugo L. Garrido Gonzalez
1146	*Hualpen Chile 26 Jul 1988		
	†Talcahuano Chile Hualpen	15 Jun 1980	Fernando Aguilar
1621	Iquique Chile	14 Dec 1986	Nelson C. Mondaca I.
1702	La Serena Chile	23 Oct 1988	Ricardo Thomas Rubina
1694	Linares Chile	24 Apr 1988	Alberto Ariosto Alveal V.
1949	Los Andes Chile	4 Jul 1993	Vicente E. Zuniga Figueroa
1599	Los Angeles Chile	1 Jun 1986	Mario Carlos Escobar
1950	Melipilla Chile	18 Jul 1993	Natanael Toro Navarrete
1967	Miraflores Chile	19 Dec 1993	Jorge Bernardo Toro
1267	Osorno Chile	17 May 1981	Raul Hernan Paredes P.
1976	Ovalle Chile	20 Feb 1994	Wilson B. Nunez Castillo
1268	Penco Chile	24 May 1981	Abel Poblete Flores
1339	Puerto Montt Chile	25 Apr 1982	Juan Carlos Lopez L.
1478	Punta Arenas Chile	10 Jun 1984	Luis Elqueda C.
1275	Quillota Chile	7 Jun 1981	Maximo Ananias Iribarren I.
791	Quilpue Chile	28 Nov 1976	Eduardo Lamartine A.
1285	Rancagua Chile	26 Aug 1981	Hector Verdugo Radrigan
1930	Rancagua Chile Tupahue	11 Apr 1993	Juan Carlos Fredes Duran
1731	San Antonio Chile	2 Jul 1989	Sergio Enrique Gonzalez S.
1703	San Fernando Chile	30 Oct 1988	Jose Luis Ferreira P.
1286	San Pedro Chile	30 Aug 1981	Juan Cuevas I.
1960	Santiago Chile Cerro Navia	7 Nov 1993	Juan David Huaiguinir Castro
1038	Santiago Chile Cinco de Abril	10 Jun 1979	Poblibio Gonzalez Gutierrez
1077	Santiago Chile Conchali	4 Nov 1979	Juan Castro Duque
1216	Santiago Chile El Bosque	14 Dec 1980	Eduardo Ayala Aburto
1933	Santiago Chile Gran Avenida	18 Apr 1993	Andres Maja Basaez
1024	Santiago Chile Independencia	6 May 1979	Wilfredo Lopez G.
1902	Santiago Chile Javiera Carrera	20 Sep 1992	Patricio LaTorre Orellana
672	*Santiago Chile La Cisterna 18 Apr 1976		
	†Santiago Chile South	8 Dec 1974	Eduardo Ayala
1039	Santiago Chile La Florida	10 Jun 1979	Carlos G. Zuniga Campusano
1899	Santiago Chile La Granja	30 Aug 1992	Arturo del Carmen Jorquera M.
1402	Santiago Chile Las Condes	12 Mar 1983	E. Gustavo Flores Carrasco
1947	Santiago Chile La Reina	27 June 1993	Santiago Vicente Vera Barrera
1915	Santiago Chile Maipu	6 Dec 1992	Julio Cesar Valdivia Marin
792	Santiago Chile Nunoa	28 Nov 1976	Gustavo Alberto Barrios C.
1919	Santiago Chile O'Higgins	20 Dec 1992	Victor A. Cifuentes Droguett
1320	Penaflor Chile 18 Jul 1993		
	*Santiago Chile Penaflor 10 Apr 1990		
	Penaflor Chile	10 Dec 1981	Sergio Venegas Pacheo
1403	Santiago Chile Pudahuel	13 Mar 1983	Enrique Espinoza
1548	Santiago Chile Puente Alto	18 Aug 1985	Jorge A. Pedrero Martinez
1205	*Santiago Chile Quilicura 13 Dec 1988		
	†Santiago Chile Huechuraba	9 Nov 1980	Juan Humberto Body B.
590	*Santiago Chile Quinta Normal 10 Jan 1980		
	*Santiago Chile Providencia 18 Apr 1976		
	*Santiago Chile		
	†Santiago (Chile)	19 Nov 1972	Carlos A. Cifuentes
1492	Santiago Chile Renca	16 Sep 1984	Eduardo Cabezas O.
754	Santiago Chile Republica	18 Apr 1976	Julio Jaramillo
1003	Santiago Chile San Bernardo	25 Feb 1979	Hugo Balmaceda
1549	Santiago Chile San Miguel	18 Aug 1985	Hector G. Carvajal Arenas
1927	Santiago Chile Vicuna Mackenna	21 Mar 1993	Jorge Andres Pedrero Martinez
1379	*Santiago Chile Zapadores 13 Dec 1988		
	†Santiago Chile Las Canteras	14 Nov 1982	Juan Castro Duque
1083	Talca Chile	17 Nov 1979	Emilio Diaz
866	Talcahuano Chile	16 Oct 1977	Claudio Daniel Signorelli G.
1245	Temuco Chile	18 Mar 1981	Eleazar F. Magnere D.
1667	Valdivia Chile	10 Jan 1988	Armando Ambrosio Linco P.

882	Valparaiso Chile	20 Nov 1977	Abel Correa Lopez
1230	Valparaiso Chile South	1 Feb 1981	Juan Rios R.
1037	Villa Alemana Chile	8 Jun 1979	Eduardo Adrian LaMartine
671	Vina del Mar Chile	5 Dec 1974	Jose Leyton

Missions — 6
(As of Oct. 1, 1994; shown with historical number. See MISSIONS.)

(214) CHILE ANTOFAGASTA MISSION
Casilla 704
Antofagasta
Chile
Phone: (011-56-55) 22-28-41

(119) CHILE CONCEPCION MISSION
Casilla 2210
Concepcion, Chile
Phone: (011-56-41) 229-641

(151) CHILE OSORNO MISSION
Casilla 7-0
Osorno, Chile
Phone: (011-56-64) 23-76-26

(148) CHILE SANTIAGO NORTH MISSION
Casilla 172
Santiago 29, Providencia
Chile
Phone: (011-56-2) 223-6466

(67) CHILE SANTIAGO SOUTH MISSION
Casilla 137, Providencia
Santiago 29, Chile
Phone: (011-56-2) 223-5366

(168) CHILE VINA DEL MAR MISSION
Casilla 24-D
Vina del Mar, Chile
Phone: (011-56-32) 976-080

CHINA

Year-end 1993: Est. population, 1,178,500,000; Members, fewer than 100; Branches, 2; Asia Area.

Encompassing most of east Asia, the People's Republic of China has a population that speaks Mandarin Chinese, Yue, Wu Minbei, Minnan and Xiang. Population inlcudes atheists, and traditional Confucians, Buddhists and Taoists.

In 1853, Hosea Stout, James Lewis and Chapman Duncan were called to teach the gospel to the Chinese. They arrived in Hong Kong April 27, 1853, and stayed only four months, finding access to the country impossible. They may have baptized one convert.

On a world tour, Elder David O. McKay, then of the Council of the Twelve, visited China in January 1921.

In more recent times, annual visits by BYU performing groups beginning in 1979 have led to warmer relations. The Chinese ambassador, Chai Zemin, visited Church headquarters Jan. 9-11, 1981. His visit was followed by a visit to the Polynesian Cultural Center by Premier Zhao Ziyang Jan. 7, 1984. President Li Xiannian visited the cultural center July 31, 1985.

Further exchanges were made as Elder Russell M. Nelson of the Council of the Twelve was named an honorary professor in 1985 by a Chinese medical college in appreciation for his earlier work in China.

As cultural exchanges continued, a few expatriate LDS families began living in China. For these families and Chinese people who joined the Church while living abroad, branches were established in Beijing and Shanghai.

Elder Nelson and Elder Dallin H. Oaks of the Council of the Twelve continued discussions with Chinese leaders in the late 1980s.

A group of high-ranking Chinese educators visited Elder Oaks in his office in the Church Administration Building Nov. 10, 1989, and received a set of LDS books that will be placed in their institutions' libraries. On Feb. 21, 1990, on behalf of the First Presidency, Elder Nelson presented to the Chinese ambassador to the United States a check for $25,000 to help in reconstruction efforts after a major earthquake caused extensive damage in China.

While in Beijing Jan. 19-23, 1990, Elder Dallin H. Oaks was invited by the Chinese Academy of Social Sciences to deliver an hour-and-a-half lecture about the Church.

David Hsiao Hsin Chen, a professor at BYU-Hawaii who was born and raised in China, was sustained as the first traveling elder in China at the Beijing Branch Jan. 21, 1990, by Beijing Branch Pres. Timothy Stratford. Elder Chen's responsibility is to go to China several times a year to train LDS Chinese leaders and to oversee the Church's membership in China.

Most of the LDS members in China are foreign teachers, foreign businessmen or diplomats and their families, and Chinese members who have returned to their homeland after having studied or worked in North America, Europe or other parts of the world. There is no proselyting in the People's Republic of China.

Sources: *Encyclopedic History of the Church* by Andrew Jenson; *Church News*, Jan. 17, 1981, Jan. 15, 1984, Nov. 18, 1989, Feb. 3, 1990.

COLOMBIA

Year-end 1993: Est. population, 34,900,000; Members, 98,000; Stakes, 13; Wards, 85; Branches, 177; Missions, 4; Districts, 21; Temples, 1 planned; Percent LDS, 0.3, or one person in 356.

Located in the northwest corner of South America, Colombia is a republic with a Spanish-speaking population that is predominantly Roman Catholic.

In early 1966, some 45 members, mostly North Americans, were meeting in branches in Bogota and Cali. Elders Randall Harmsen and Jerry Broome of the Andes Mission were assigned to Bogota in May of that year. Among the first converts was Antonio Vela. Aura Ivars was the first convert in Cali. The Colombia-Venezuela Mission was created in 1968, and by 1971, 27 branches had been established in 10 cities, and the Venezuela Mission was divided from Colombia, where the mission headquarters were in Bogota. In 1975, the Colombia Cali Mission was created. President Spencer W. Kimball visited Colombia and addressed a gathering of 4,600 at an area conference on March 5, 1977.

Seminaries and institutes were begun in 1972, and by 1976, 900 students were taking part in the educational programs, and membership reached 6,178. By 1986, membership mushroomed to 45,800.

A temple was announced for Colombia on April 7, 1984, and a site for the temple was announced in 1988. Ground was broken for the Bogota Colombia Temple on June 26, 1993, by Elder William R. Bradford of the Seventy, but construction has been delayed pending government approvals.

In September 1988, internal political difficulties led to a withdrawing of North American missionaries. Despite these problems, missionary work continued to progress. The Colombia Barranquilla Mission was formed in 1988, in a city where the first stake was created in 1985. Since then, three other stakes have been created in Barranquilla. Membership in Colombia in 1990 was 83,000. The first General Authority from Colombia was Julio Davila, who was called to the Second Quorum of the Seventy in 1991. He was president of the first stake in Colombia.

Sources: "Church in Colombia moving ahead," by Jack E. Jarrard, *Church News* Feb. 1, 1969; "The Saints in Colombia," by Colleen J. Heninger, *Ensign*, October, 1976; "Colombia," *Ensign*, February 1977; "Love, respect and emotion end area conference series," by Dell Van Orden, *Church News,* March 12, 1977; *Church News,* Oct. 23, 1976, March 19, 1988.

Stakes — 13
(Listed alphabetically as of Oct. 1, 1994.)

No.	Name	Organized	First President
South America North Area			
1878	Barranquilla Colombia Cevillar	31 May 1992	Carlos M. Lopez Mangones
1537	*Barranquilla Colombia El Carmen 30 May 1992		
	†Barranquilla Colombia	30 May 1985	Libardo Rodriguez
1879	Barranquilla Colombia Hipodromo	31 May 1992	Donaldo Antonio Osorio Perez
1880	Barranquilla Colombia Paraiso	31 May 1992	Jose Peralbo Aparicio
805	Bogota Colombia	23 Jan 1977	Julio E. Davila P.
1113	Bogota Colombia Ciudad Jardin	2 Mar 1980	Miguel Oswaldo Porras
1659	Bogota Colombia El Dorado	18 Oct 1987	Humberto Lopez S.
1008	Bogota Colombia Kennedy	11 Mar 1979	Miguel A. Vargas
1308	Bucaramanga Colombia	22 Nov 1981	Horacio Julio Insignarez
937	Cali Colombia	4 Jun 1978	Luis Alfonso Rios
1054	Cali Colombia Americas	24 Aug 1979	Libber A. Montoya O.
1697	Medellin Colombia	5 Jun 1988	Arnold Porras Martinez
1968	Pereira Colombia	19 Dec 1993	Jose Luis Gonzalez

Missions — 4
(As of Oct. 1, 1994; shown with historical number. See MISSIONS.)

(215) COLOMBIA BARRANQUILLA MISSION
Calle 82 No. 55-20, Apt 2
A.A. 50710
Barranquilla - Atlantico
Colombia
Phone: (011-57-58) 56-22-16

(270) COLOMBIA BOGOTA SOUTH MISSION
Calle 72 No. 10-07 Oficina 1001
A.A. 77604
Santafe de Bogota 2
D.C. Colombia
Phone: (011-57-1) 210-4693

(79a) COLOMBIA BOGOTA NORTH MISSION
Apartado Aereo 90746
Bogota 8, D.E.
Colombia
Phone: (011-57-1) 210-1396

(120) COLOMBIA CALI MISSION
Apartado Aereo 4892
Cali, Valle
Colombia
Phone: (011-57-23) 67-18-16

CONGO

Year-end 1993: Est. population, 2,424,000; Members, 800; Branches, 5; Districts, 1; Africa Area; Ghana Accra Mission.

Congo is a West African republic, where the people speak French and Kongo. A slight majority of the population is Christian but many follow traditional beliefs.

Congo granted the Church formal recognition Dec. 23, 1991. Missionaries were subsequently assigned to Congo from the Zaire Kinshasa Mission. Branches have been established in the capital city of Brazzaville.

For a period in 1992, missionaries to the Congo were withdrawn because of political turmoil.

Source: *Church News,* Dec. 28, 1991; *Church News,* Dec. 18, 1993.

COOK ISLANDS (RAROTONGA)

Year-end 1993: Est. population, 18,000; Members, 800; Districts, 1; Branches, 6; Percent LDS, 4.44, or one person in 22; Pacific Area; New Zealand Auckland Mission.

Located in the South Pacific, about 400 miles southwest of French Polynesia, the Cook Islands are self-governing, and 75 percent of the population are Protestants. The islands maintain close ties with New Zealand.

The first missionaries arrived in 1899, but failed to gain converts. Elder Osborne J.P. Widtsoe and a companion, Elder Mervin Davis, arrived in Rarotonga May 23, 1899, becoming the first LDS missionaries in the Cook Islands. During World War II, Matthew Cowley, then president of the New Zealand Mission, assigned Fritz Kruger, a New Zealand baker who owned a business at Avarua, Rarotonga, to help establish the Church on the Cook Islands. He and his family subsequently moved to Rarotonga, and their first convert was Samuel Glassie and his family.

In 1947, a couple, Elder and Sister Trevor Hamon, and later Elders Donlon DeLaMar and John L. Sorenson, were sent to Avarua. By 1949, 160 Cook Islanders had joined the Church.

During the next decades, the Cook Islands were transferred to several missions in an attempt to maintain better communication with the remote location. The islands were part of the Samoan Mission (1954), New Zealand North Mission (1966), Fiji Mission (1971), and the Tahiti Papeete Mission (1975). The Islands are now part of the New Zealand Auckland Mission.

President David O. McKay visited in 1955. A Rarotonga Mission was created Nov. 20, 1960, but later became part of the New Zealand Mission. In the early 1960s, the Book of Mormon was translated into Cook Island Maori. In 1979, there were 718 members in 10 branches in the Cook Islands.

President Spencer W. Kimball visited Rarotonga in February 1981 during a trip to the South Pacific, and held a short service with members there in an airport hangar.

In 1990, the government issued a series of stamps featuring the first missionaries to the Cook Islands of various denominations. The LDS stamp featured a painting of Elder Widtsoe in the foreground and a drawing of an LDS meetinghouse in the background.

Sources: *Unto the Islands of the Sea,* by R. Lanier Britsch; "New day dawns for temples in Pacific," by Dell Van Orden, *Church News,* Feb. 28, 1981; "Island stamp honors LDS elder," *Church News*, June 23, 1990; interview with Fritz Kruger; *Church News,* Feb. 28, 1991, Aug. 29, 1992.

COSTA RICA

Year-end 1993: Est. population, 3,330,000; Members, 22,000; Stakes, 4; Wards, 20; Branches, 45; Missions, 1; Districts, 6; Percent LDS, 0.7, or one LDS in 151.

A Central American democratic republic, Costa Rica has a population that speaks Spanish, and is 95 percent Roman Catholic.

Pres. Arwell L. Pierce of the Mexican Mission was authorized by the First Presidency to add Costa Rica to the Mexican Mission on July 8, 1946. He visited the country on Sept. 12, 1946, staying at the home of a member, H. Clark Fails.

Elders Robert B. Miller and David D. Lingard arrived in Costa Rica about Sept. 10, 1946. They presented the president of the republic with a copy of the Book of Mormon. The missionaries left to avoid being in the nation during a revolution in 1948, but Elder Lingard and Elder Jack M. Farnsworth returned in 1949 and enjoyed a Pioneer Day celebration of the members on July 24. The first conference was held in Costa Rica

June 7, 1950, and about 70 attended. A branch was organized Aug. 25, 1950. Property for a meetinghouse was purchased in 1951.

General Authorities visited several times in the 1950s as the Church grew slowly. The Central American Mission was organized from the Mexican Mission Nov. 16, 1952. When the Guatemala-El Salvador Mission was created in 1965, it included Costa Rica. The first district conference was held in August 1968, with 296 people in attendance. The Costa Rica Mission was organized June 20, 1974.

The San Jose Costa Rica Stake was created Jan. 20, 1977, with Manuel Najera Guzman as president, and a month later an area conference was held in San Jose. At that time, there were 3,800 members in the country. By 1986, Costa Rica had 7,100 members. Eight years later, by 1994, this number had tripled, to 22,000.

Sources: San Jose Branch *manuscript history;* Address by Pres. Manuel Najera at San Jose, Costa Rica, area conference Feb. 23, 1977.

Stakes — 4
(Listed alphabetically as of Oct. 1, 1994.)

No.	Name	Organized	First President
Central America Area			
1783	San Jose Costa Rica Alajuela	9 Dec 1990	Milton Perez Ruiz
1826	San Jose Costa Rica La Paz	10 Nov 1991	Max Enrique Urena Fallas
917	San Jose Costa Rica La Sabana	7 May 1978	Jorge Arturo Solano Castillo
803	*San Jose Costa Rica Los Yoses 10 Nov 1991		
	†San Jose Costa Rica	20 Jan 1977	Manuel Najera G.

Mission — 1
(As of Oct. 1, 1994; shown with historical number. See MISSIONS.)

(43b) COSTA RICA SAN JOSE MISSION
Apartado Postal 2339-1000
San Jose, Costa Rica
Phone: (011-506) 234-1940

CROATIA

Year-end 1993: Est. Population, 4,400,000; Members, 100; Branches, 3; Districts, 1; Europe/Mediterranean Area; Austria Vienna Mission.

Located on the Balkan Peninsula in southeast Europe, Croatia is a republic made up of what was a northern internal division of Yugoslavia.

Mischa Markow, a Hungarian who had immigrated to Salt Lake City, Utah, arrived as a missionary in Yugoslavia in May 1899. He was banished to Hungary a month later because government authorities objected to his preaching.

Some 70 years passed before members returned. By the early 1970s, a few Latter-day Saints were living in Yugoslavia, some of whom had joined the Church while working or studying abroad. Their first testimony meeting was held in Zadar Sept. 11, 1972.

In early 1975, Neil D. Schaerrer, president of the Austria Vienna Mission, established the Church as a legal entity in Yugoslavia and organized a branch in Zadar. He met with members in Zadar and Zagreb during the following months.

Among those who joined the Church while studying abroad was Kresimir Cosic, a BYU basketball star who returned to play on and coach the Yugoslavia Olympic team. He served as president of the Yugoslavia District. Following the dissolution of Yugoslavia, he persuaded the United States to send a representative to Croatia, and he was appointed deputy ambassador to the United States from Croatia in 1992.

Humanitarian relief was provided Croatia by the Church and Church members in the United States and Europe, including food, clothing, blankets and medical supplies.

Sources: Yugoslavia, manuscript history; "Missionary to the Balkans, Mischa Markow," by William Hale Kehr, *Ensign,* June 1980; Zagreb Branch history, published by the branch at dedication of meetinghouse, Oct. 30, 1985; "Tears of joy," by Richard L. Jensen, *Church News,* Dec. 8, 1979; "Yugoslavia's bright future," *Church News,* March 2, 1986; *Church News,* Sept. 26, 1992.

CYPRUS

Year-end 1993: Est. population, 733,000; Members, fewer than 100; Branches, 1; Europe/Mediterranean Area; Greece Athens Mission.

Located in the Mediterranean Sea off the Turkish coast, the republic has groups speaking Greek and Turkish and following the Greek Orthodox and Moslem religions.

The Cyprus LDS group was organized in 1962 among member families living in Cyprus on government service. The group, also called the Nicosia Branch, was dissolved in 1969, reorganized in 1971, temporarily dissolved in 1980 and later reorganized. The members are part of an English-speaking community residing in Cyprus, and they occasionally meet with other religious denominations for interdenominational meetings.

CZECH REPUBLIC

Year-end 1993: Est. population, 10,300,000; Members, 1,000; Branches, 13; Missions, 1; Districts, 2; Europe Area.

In east-central Europe, the Czech Republic's people speak Czech and Slovak, both of which are official languages. Some 65 percent of the population is Roman Catholic.

Elder Thomas Biesinger, the first missionary to enter what was then Czechoslovakia, arrived in 1884. However, he was imprisoned and banished following a trial. After his release and before his departure, he baptized and confirmed Anthon Just, one of his previous investigators and a witness at his trial, on June 21, 1884.

After Elder Biesinger left, the work awaited his return in 1928, at the age of 84. On his second attempt, he obtained legal permission for the Church. The Czechoslovakia Mission was organized July 24, 1929, by Elder John A. Widtsoe, president of the European Mission. Arthur Gaeth, one of the elders in the German-Austrian Mission, was chosen to preside over the new mission. At that time, there were seven members in the nation. Among them were Franziska Brodil, a widow whose two daughters, Frances and Jane, were baptized in Czechoslovakia in 1921.

Lectures on the Church were delivered over radio, and at a cultural fair in 1931 missionaries handed out more than 150,000 tracts. The Book of Mormon was translated in 1933, and additional materials were later translated and published. A shortage of missionaries during the Great Depression slowed the work. With the approach of World War II, missionaries were recalled from the country. The mission was left under the direction of a young convert, Josef Roubicek. During the war, Pres. Roubicek kept the Saints together, added 28 members, and published a mission circular letter. Missionary work resumed in 1946 and continued until April 6, 1950, when the mission was closed. Roubicek immigrated to America in 1949.

The Czechoslovakia District was organized Feb. 3, 1982. Local missionaries began having success after about 1985. After the democratization of the nation in 1989-90, the first full-time missionaries arrived in 1990. About that time, the Church applied for recognition. According to President Thomas S. Monson, second counselor in the First Presidency, "The government leaders had said to us, 'Don't send an American, a German or a Swiss. Send us a Czech.'" Acknowledging Church leadership during the prohibition of religion was tantamount to imprisonment. Pres. Jiri Snederfler, Czechoslovakia district president, answered the call and faced this risk as he applied to the government for recognition.

Pres. Snedefler met in Prague on Feb. 6, 1990, with Deputy Prime Minister Josef Hromadka, and recognition that was first granted to the Church in 1928 was officially renewed on Feb. 21, 1990. The Czechoslovakia Prague Mission was reorganized July 1, 1990, from a division of the Austria Vienna East Mission, with Richard W. Winder as president. He had served a mission in Czechoslovakia 40 years earlier. By 1990, there were more than 200 members. The Tabernacle Choir performed in Prague in 1991. In 1993, Czech broadcasters visited Salt Lake City and broadcast a nationwide feature on the Church.

Sources: *Encyclopedic History of the Church,* by Andrew Jenson; *Church News,* Feb. 22, 1936, Feb. 29, 1936, March 7, 1936, March 14, 1936; Feb. 14, 1951, March 3, 1990; "A Missionary's Two Months in Jail," by William G. Hartley, *New Era,* November 1982; "Prayed for a mission," by Davis Bitton, *Church News,* Oct. 28, 1978, Swiss Mission history, May 8, 1968; "Czech broadcasters see Church close-up," by R. Scott Lloyd, *Church News,* May 22, 1993; Correspondence from Kahlile Mehr, Dec. 29, 1992.

Mission — 1
(As of Oct. 1, 1994; shown with historical number. See MISSIONS.)

(236) CZECH REPUBLIC PRAGUE MISSION
Milady Horakove 85/95
170 00 Praha 7
Czech Republic
Phone: (011-42-2) 329 314

DENMARK

Year-end 1993: Est. population, 5,200,000; Members, 4,400; Stakes, 2; Wards, 12; Branches, 11; Missions, 1; Percent LDS, 0.09, or one person in 1,155.

Located in northern Europe on the Baltic Sea, Denmark is a constitutional monarchy with a population that speaks Danish, and 90 percent of whom are Evangelical Lutherans.

Elder Erastus Snow was called in October 1849 to open the work in Scandinavia. He and Elders John E. Forsgren and George P. Dykes traveled to Denmark, arriving in Copenhagen June 14, 1850. Another member, Peter O. Hansen, had arrived about a month earlier.

The first baptism took place Aug. 12, 1850, and within two months, the elders had established the headquarters of the mission in Copenhagen and baptized 15 people. The first branch was organized Sept. 15 in Copenhagen. Elder Dykes opened a second branch in Aalborg Nov. 25, 1850.

Work continued to progress as the elders pushed into every corner of Denmark, but heavy persecution was waged against members. In Aalborg in 1851, a mob vandalized the hall where the Saints were meeting. Soon, conferences (districts) were established in eight areas to accommodate the multiplying branches. The first converts to emigrate left Jan. 31, 1852. Of about 26,000 people who were converted during this early period, 13,984 converts immigrated to the United States by 1930.

The Danish Mission was organized April 1, 1920. Convert baptisms varied from 50 to 200 a year between 1966 and 1974. In 1971, the Church membership in Denmark consisted of about 4,193 people in three districts. Although members were limited in number, they took part in home seminary, served missions and attended the Swiss Temple after it was dedicated in 1955.

The Copenhagen Denmark Stake, the first in the country, was organized June 16, 1974, with Johan H. Benthin as president. In 1983, membership totaled 4,097, and in 1990, 4,200.

Sources: *Encyclopedic History of the Church* by Andrew Jenson; *History of the Danish Mission, 1850-1964,* a BYU thesis by Marius A. Christensen, March 1966.

GREENLAND

Year-end 1993: Population, 54,000; Members, fewer than 100; North America Northeast Area.

This very large island, slightly larger than Mexico, in the North Atlantic between Canada and Iceland is a province of Denmark under home rule. Greenland has a parliamentary government with a population that speaks Danish and Greenlandic, and most are members of the Evangelic Lutheran Church.

A branch of LDS servicemen was organized in 1953 and functioned for at least five years. The branch was discontinued in 1989, but a military group continues to meet at Thule Air Base.

Sources: *Church News,* April 19, 1958, Jan. 9, 1960.

Stakes — 2
(Listed alphabetically as of Oct. 1, 1994.)

No.	Name	Organized	First President
Europe Area			
945	Aarhus Denmark	2 Jul 1978	Knud Bent Andersen
648	Copenhagen Denmark	16 Jun 1974	Johan Helge Benthin

Mission — 1
(As of Oct. 1, 1994; shown with historical number. See MISSIONS.)

(23b) DENMARK COPENHAGEN MISSION
Tornerosevej 127 B
2730 Herlev, Denmark
Phone: (011-45) 42-84-39-99

DOMINICAN REPUBLIC

Year-end 1993: Est. population, 7,680,000; Members, 47,000; Stakes, 7; Wards, 43; Branches, 82; Missions; 3; Districts, 9; Percent LDS, 0.6, or one LDS in 163.

An island in the West Indies, Dominican Republic is about the size of Vermont and New Hampshire combined, but has nearly five times their combined populations. The Dominican Republic is a representative democracy. Its population speaks Spanish, and is mostly Roman Catholic.

The Eddie and Mercedes Amparo family arrived in the Dominican Republic on June 9, 1978, the day the revelation was announced that allowed all worthy men to hold the priesthood. They and another newly arrived family, John and Nancy Rappleye, began doing missionary work. An associate of the Amparos, Rodolfo Bodden, was the first convert, baptized in August 1978. Among the first missionaries were John A. and Ada Davis of Provo, Utah. The Dominican Republic Santo Domingo Mission was organized Jan. 1, 1981. At that time, membership was at 2,500. A highlight came March 8-9, 1981, when President Spencer W. Kimball visited.

Membership increases have been rapid. In 1979, 354 people were baptized. By 1986, membership reached 11,000. The Santo Domingo Dominican Republic Stake was organized March, 23, 1986. A second mission was organized in Santiago on July 1, 1987, when the country's membership was about 13,000. A second stake was organized Oct. 16, 1988, and a third on Nov. 5, 1989. Membership in 1990 was 31,000. In 1992, the Dominican members received satellite transmissions of general conference.

The first temple in the Caribbean was announced for Santo Domingo, Dominican Republic by President Gordon B. Hinckley of the First Presidency on Dec. 4, 1993.

Sources: *Church News,* Dec. 6, 1980; March 21, 1981; Dominican Growth: From Zero to Thousands since 1978, *Ensign,* January 1987; "2 families bring gospel to a nation," by William B. Smart, *Church News,* July 11, 1981; *Church News,* Aug. 25, 1985; July 15, 1989; Jan 26, 1986; Rendering Service to Others, an address by Pres. Spencer W. Kimball, *Ensign,* May 1981; Conversion account of Eric Olivero delivered May 26, 1991, and conference report by Elder Stan Bradshaw, and "Dominican Republic, a Second Decade for Dominican Saints," by Elizabeth and Jed VanDenBerghe, *Ensign,* October 1990; *Church News,* Dec. 4, 1993.

Stakes — 7
(Listed alphabetically as of Oct. 1, 1994.)

No.	Name	Organized	First President
North America Southeast Area			
1800	San Francisco de Macoris Dominican Republic	26 May 1991	Eric Edison Olivero P.
1701	Santo Domingo Dominican Republic Geronimo 18 Oct 1992		
	San Geronimo Dominican Republic	16 Oct 1988	Victor Alejandro Navarro M.
1786	Santiago Dominican Republic	17 Feb 1991	Ramon Matias Lantigua
1593	Santo Domingo Dominican Republic	23 Mar 1986	Jose Delio Ceveno
1906	Santo Domingo Dominican Republic Independencia	18 Oct 1992	Felix Sequi-Martinez
1735a	*Santo Domingo Dominican Republic Oriental 2 Feb 1992		
	*Oriental Dominican Republic 29 Oct 1991		
	*Santo Domingo Dominican Republic Oriental 24 Sep 1991		
	†Santo Domingo Dominican Republic East	5 Nov 1989	Pedro Arturo Abreu C.
1844	Santo Domingo Dominican Republic Ozama	2 Feb 1992	Jose Andres Taveras Arias

Missions — 3
(As of Oct. 1, 1994; shown with historical number. See MISSIONS.)

(196) DOMINICAN REPUBLIC
SANTIAGO MISSION
Apartado 1240
Santiago
Dominican Republic
Phone: (809) 575-1145

(188a) DOMINICAN REPUBLIC
SANTO DOMINGO WEST MISSION
Apt. #30103, Ensanche La Fe
Santo Domingo
Dominican Republic
Phone: (809) 562-6969

(259) DOMINICAN REPUBLIC SANTO DOMINGO EAST
Apartado #20579 Gazcue
Santo Domingo
Dominican Republic
Phone: (809) 687-9085

ECUADOR

Year-end 1993: Est. population, 10,350,000; Members, 115,000; Stakes, 17; Wards, 99; Branches, 149; Missions, 3; Districts, 12; Temples, 1 planned; Percent LDS, 1.10, or one LDS in 90.

Located on the equator on the Pacific Coast side of South America, the Republic of Ecuador is divided into three zones by two ranges of Andes mountains. Its Spanish- and Quechua-speaking population is 95 percent Roman Catholic.

A letter from Elder Spencer W. Kimball, then of the Council of the Twelve, received by Pres. J. Averil Jesperson of the Andes Mission in Lima, Peru, on Sept. 22, 1965, suggested opening missionary work in Ecuador. Elders Craig Carpenter, Bryant R. Gold, Lindon Robinson and Paul O. Allen were sent to Quito two weeks later, and on Oct. 9, Elder Kimball visited Quito. Work progressed rapidly, and when the Ecuador Mission, with headquarters in Quito, was created Aug. 1, 1970, membership was 1,000.

Some of the first proselyting was done among the Otavalo Indians near Quito, among whom the first all-Lamanite stake in South America was organized in 1981.

Others in Ecuador eagerly accepted the gospel. By the end of 1975, membership had tripled to 3,226. Ecuador's first stake was organized in Guayaquil June 11, 1978, under the direction of Pres. Lorenzo A. Garaycoa, and a second mission was organized in Guayaquil, on July 1, 1978. Membership at the beginning of 1979 was 19,000.

A temple was announced for Guayaquil by President Gordon B. Hinckley on March 31, 1982. As of Oct. 1, 1994, construction of the temple was pending government approvals. Despite the delay, however, members continued to prepare family names for temple work. The headquarters for the South America North Area was moved from Lima, Peru, to Quito, Ecuador, in 1989. Membership in 1986 reached 43,000, and in 1991, 92,000.

Sources: *The Improvement Era,* May 1966; Ecuador, *Ensign,* February 1977; "Language no barrier," *Church News,* Nov. 11, 1978; "Tip your Panama hat, this is Ecuador," by Gerry Avant, *Church News,* Feb. 14, 1981; *Church News,* July 8, 1978; "In the Andes, Lehi's children grow strong in the gospel," by Elayne Wells, *Church News,* Feb. 17, 1990; Church News, June 25, 1994.

Stakes — 17
(Listed alphabetically as of Oct. 1, 1994.)

No.	Name	Organized	First President
South America North Area			
1882	Duran Ecuador North	31 May 1992	Mark Roy Kent
1883	Duran Ecuador South	31 May 1992	Jimmy Winston Olvera
1808	Guayaquil Ecuador Centenario	18 Aug 1991	Luis Guillermo Granja G.
1716a	Guayaquil Ecuador Central	30 Apr 1989	Gonzalo Eduardo Alvarado R.
1809	Guayaquil Ecuador East	18 Aug 1991	Jimmy Winston Olvera C.
1916	Guayaquil Ecuador Huancavilca	6 Dec 1992	Jose Eladio Paredes Garcia
1117	*Guayaquil Ecuador North 22 Mar 1987		
	†Guayaquil Ecuador Febres Cordero	16 Mar 1980	Douglas Alarcon Arboleda
1006	*Guayaquil Ecuador South 22 Mar 1987		
	Guayaquil Ecuador Centenario	4 Mar 1979	Vincente de la Cuadra S.
939	*Guayaquil Ecuador West 22 Mar 1987		
	†Guayaquil Ecuador	11 Jun 1978	Lorenzo A. Garaycoa
1853	Machala Ecuador	22 Mar 1992	Manuel Andres Galan Pereira
1796	Milagro Ecuador	5 May 1991	Alberto W. Guillen Fuentes
1316	Otavalo Ecuador	6 Dec 1981	Luis Alfonso Morales C.
1224	Portoviejo Ecuador	13 Jan 1981	Jorge Vicente Salazar H.
1259	Quevedo Ecuador	27 Apr 1981	Pedro Jose Cantos J.
1053	*Quito Ecuador Colon 15 Jan 1981		
	†Quito Ecuador	22 Aug 1979	Ernesto Franco
1839	Quito Ecuador Inaquito	12 Jan 1992	Horacio Araya Olivares
1225	Quito Ecuador Santa Ana	15 Jan 1981	Cesar Hugh Cacuango C.

Discontinued

1116	Guayaquil Ecuador Duran	16 Mar 1980	Lorenzo Augusto Garaycoa
	22 Mar 1987 ★Guayaquil Ecuador West (No. 939), Guayaquil Ecuador South (No. 1006), Guayaquil Ecuador North (No. 1117)			
1221	Guayaquil Ecuador Kennedy	11 Jan 1981	Fausto Montalvan Morla
	22 Mar 1987 ★Guayaquil Ecuador West (939), Guayaquil Ecuador South (No. 1006), Guayaquil Ecuador North (No. 1117)			

Missions — 3
(As of Oct. 1, 1994; shown with historical number. See MISSIONS.)

(261) ECUADOR GUAYAQUIL NORTH MISSION
Casilla 8757
Guayaquil,
Ecuador
Phone: (011-593-4) 289-570

(160) ECUADOR GUAYAQUIL SOUTH MISSION
Masion
Casilla 8750
Guayaquil, Ecuador
Phone: 011-593-4 289-408

EGYPT

Year-end 1993: Est. population, 58,300,000; Members, fewer than 100; Branches, 1; District 1; Europe Mediterranean Area.

Located in the northeast corner of Africa, the republic has a population that speaks Arabic and English, and is 94 percent Sunni Moslem.

The Cairo Branch functioned from 1971-74 as part of the Switzerland Mission. In 1974, two students arrived in Cairo for intensive study of Arabic, Dilworth B. Parkinson and John Sharp, met with Carol Azeltine, a teacher at an international school in suburban Digla, and began holding LDS meetings in the garden area of the American University in downtown Cairo.

From 1974 to 1987, the branch was in the International Mission until the mission was dissolved and the branch was placed in the Austria Vienna East Mission. Membership of the branch is made up of about 100 expatriates, most of whom are in the country on U.S. or other government service projects, or for BYU's ongoing archaeology studies. The members met in each other's homes until 1982, when a villa was rented in Maadi. On Feb. 1, 1985, the branch began meeting in a larger, two-story villa in the same community. They hold outings in historic places and ways, such as camel rides and boating on the Nile.

Beginning in 1980, a continual string of couples has come to Egypt specifically to serve as special Church representatives, who make friends for the Church but do not proselyte.

Among those who helped make significant contributions in Egypt in recent years are members who have worked with: mechanization for small farms, modern drip irrigation methods, various farm production projects, dental service projects, medical technology training, and a significant on-going BYU archaeology excavation performed under the direction of Dr. C. Wilfred Griggs.

Sources: *Church News,* Nov. 26, 1988; "Benson Institute improves lives," *Church News,* Nov. 18, 1989; "Branch in land of pyramids is 'home away from home' " By Edwin O. Haroldsen, *Church News,* June 12, 1993.

EL SALVADOR

Year-end 1993: Est. population, 5,250,000; Members, 50,000; Stakes, 10; Wards, 56; Branches, 56; Missions, 2; Districts, 1; Percent LDS, 1.0, or one person in 105.

El Salvador, in Central America, is a republic with a Spanish- and some Nahuatl-speaking population of mostly Roman Catholics.

On Aug. 20, 1948, Pres. Arwell L. Pierce of the Mexican Mission visited El Salvador and explored the possibility of proselyting. On May 26, 1949, he assigned Elders Glenn Whipple Skousen and Omer Farnsworth to go to El Salvador and open the work. A conference was held at San Salvador on Feb. 16, 1951, attended by Elder Albert E. Bowen of the Council of the Twelve, at which 63 people were present. A short time later, on March 2, 1951, Ana Villasenor became the first person baptized in the country. Elder Vance Whipple performed the baptism at Apulo Beach at Lake Ilopango. Eleven others were baptized at the same time.

The country was transferred from the Mexican Mission on Nov. 16, 1952, when the new Central America Mission was created. The San Salvador District was organized in January 1965, and was soon followed by the Guatemala-El Salvador Mission. Membership then numbered 4,200. On June 3, 1973, the district was organized into the San Salvador Stake, which had a membership of 5,600. President of the stake was former district president Mario Edmundo Scheel. The El Salvador San Salvador Mission was organized July 1, 1976, at which time the nation had 4,745 members. Ten years later in 1986, membership had climbed to 15,100, and the number of stakes increased to six. The nation reached self-sufficiency in local missionaries in 1989. In 1990, the El Salvador San Salvador East Mission was created and membership was 38,000.

Sources: *El Salvador San Salvador Mission history,* year ending Dec. 31, 1976; *El Salvador District Manuscript History*; *Church News*, Feb. 3, 1990.

(Listed alphabetically as of Oct. 1, 1994.)

No.	Name	Organized	First President
Central America Area			
1817	Ahuachapan El Salvador	22 Sep 1991	Juan Antonio Merlos V.
1223	San Miguel El Salvador	11 Jan 1981	Carlos Antonio Hernandez
618	*San Salvador El Salvador		
	†San Salvador (El Salvador)	3 Jun 1973	Mario Edmundo Scheel
1035	San Salvador El Salvador Cuzcatlan	3 Jun 1979	Franklin Henriquez Melgar
741	*San Salvador El Salvador Ilopango 3 Jun 1979		
	†San Salvador El Salvador East	1 Feb 1976	Alfonso Octavio Diaz
1745a	San Salvador El Salvador Los Heroes	8 Apr 1990	Cristobal A. Hernandez
1744	San Salvador El Salvador Soyopango	8 Apr 1990	Rene Francisco Esquivel G.
1217	Santa Ana El Salvador Modelo	14 Dec 1980	Jorge Alberta Benitez M.
1088	*Santa Ana El Salvador El Molino 14 Dec 1980		
	†Santa Ana El Salvador	2 Dec 1979	Elmer Barrientos
1816	Sonsonate El Salvador	22 Sep 1991	Rolando Arturo Rosales H.

Missions — 2
(As of Oct. 1, 1994; shown with historical number. See MISSIONS)

(137a) EL SALVADOR SAN
SALVADOR EAST MISSION
Apartado Postal #3362
San Salvador
El Salvador
Phone: (011-503) 26-12-15

(181a) EL SALVADOR SAN
SALVADOR WEST MISSION
Apartado Postal 367
San Salvador
El Salvador
Phone: (011-503) 23-56-54

ENGLAND
(See United Kingdom)

EQUATORIAL GUINEA

Year-end 1993: Est. population, 360,000; Members, fewer than 100; Africa Area; Ivory Coast Abidjan Mission.

Located near the equator on the west coast of Africa, Equatorial Guinea is a unitary republic with a population that is mostly Roman Catholic.

Equatorial Guinea was included in the Ivory Coast Abidjan Mission when it was created Feb. 1, 1992.

ESTONIA

Year-end 1993: Est. population, 1,600,000; Members, 200; Branches, 2; Europe Area; Latvia Riga Mission.

The first contacts in recent times in what was the Soviet Union were established by Finnish members who worked in Tallinn, Estonia. Among these were Valtteri Rotsa and Enn Lembit, who were baptized in Helsinki, Finland.

LDS Finnish businessman Pekka Uusituba, who was visiting in Estonia, taught the gospel to a group of 10 investigators at Lembit's home in November 1989. The first Estonians baptized in Estonia were Alari Allik, Eva Reisalu, Jaana Lass and Kristi Lass, on Dec. 17, 1989. Later, Jaanus Silla from Tallin, was baptized Jan. 6, 1990. He was the first missionary from Estonia, and was called to the Utah Salt Lake City Mission. At that time, the branch had an attendance of some 50 people.

Branches established in Estonia have had good progress. In May 1991, the Estonian and Russina branches (both in Tallinn) had 130 members. Humanitarian relief was supplied members in Estonia from Europe and the United States during 1990-92. During the summer of 1993, BYU's Young ambassadors toured Estonia and other Eastern European countries, helping raise the Church's profile.

In July 1993, Estonia was placed in the newly created Latvia Riga Mission.

Sources: Interview and records of Elder Jaanus Silla; correspondence from Mission Pres. Gary L. Browning; correspondence from Kahlile Mehr, Dec. 29, 1992; "Y. troupe tours Russia, Baltic states," *Church News,* July 17, 1993; "Growth of Church in 'that vast empire' " by Gary L. Browning, *Church News,* Nov. 6, 1993; *Church News,* March 6, 1993.

ETHIOPIA

Year-end 1993: Est. population, 56,700,000; Members, fewer than 100; Branches, 1; Africa Area; Kenya Nairobi Mission.

In east central Africa, Ethiopia has a population that speaks Amharic, English, Orominga, and Tigrigna and who are primarily Ethiopian Orthodox, Islam and animist (a belief of conscious life within objects).

The first members in Ethiopia were expatriates attached to embassies who held Church meetings in homes in Addis Ababa. In March 1985, Elders M. Russell Ballard and Glenn L. Pace visited Addis Ababa with LDS relief supplies. They held a sacrament meeting in the home of Harry Hadlock, an expatriate airline consultant, on March 17, 1985. The Church donated some $2.8 million for famine relief and irrigation development in Ethiopia and neighboring countries, such as Sudan.

After the Kenya Nairobi Mission was created in 1991, Robert DeWitt, serving with the American embassy, and his wife arrived and stayed for two years. The first official meeting was held in the DeWitt home in August 1992 with Brother Dewitt presiding. The Church was legally registered Sept. 16, 1993, in Addis Ababa. The first missionaries were Elder Eugene and Sister Ruth Hilton, who arrived Feb. 28, 1993. The first convert was Dereje Ketsahu, baptized April 16, 1993. The Addis Ababa Branch was created Jan. 5, 1994.

The first Ethiopian branch president was Girma Denisa, who was baptized while attending Ricks College in 1973.

Source: Correspondence from Larry K. Brown, president of the Kenya Nairobi Mission, April 12, 1994.

FIJI

Year-end 1993: Est. population, 808,000; Members, 9,500; Stakes, 1; Wards, 5; Branches, 20; Missions, 1; Districts, 2; Percent LDS, 1.20, or one LDS in 85.

Located in western South Pacific, the republic of Fiji has a population speaking English, Hindustani and Fijian. The archipelago has 322 islands, of which 106 are inhabited.

In the 1950s, LDS Tongan and Samoan families, including Cecil B. Smith and Mele Vea Ashley and their families, held Church meetings in Suva, Fiji. When the first missionaries, Elders Boyd L. Harris and Sheldon L. Abbott, arrived, they began working with this group and organized the Suva Branch Sept. 5, 1954.

Work proceeded slowly. Missionaries were limited by the multiple languages spoken in Fiji, and by restrictions of only two missionary visas at a time. In January 1955, President David O. McKay had a airplane layover in Suva, and he met the missionaries and attended services at the Smith home. Twenty-eight people attended that day. He urged missionaries to proceed, and to purchase property for a meetinghouse. The meetinghouse that was later built was a nearly normal-sized stake center, anticipating future growth. Fiji was placed in the Tonga Mission on Jan. 15, 1958, and 93 people attended the conference that day. Later in 1958, 300 attended dedicatory services for the new meetinghouse. About that time, the quota of missionaries was increased by six. Gideon Dolo was the first Fijian to serve a mission, leaving in February 1959.

Growth continued in the 1960s. In 1966, 150 attended district conferences in Suva. Three years later, the attendance at conference reached 500, and the district was divided. The Fiji Mission was created July 23, 1971. In 1972, mission Pres. Eb L. Davis expanded the mission into several new areas. By 1972, the meetinghouse was filled with Fijians, Indians, Rotumans, Tongans, Samoans, New Zealanders, Australians, Europeans, and Americans.

Educational efforts were also strengthened. In 1969, a Church school was held in the meetinghouse, and in 1973, it had more than 100 students. In 1975, the LDS Fiji Technical College was opened. By 1984, 372 students were enrolled at the college.

The Suva Fiji Stake was organized June 12, 1983, with Inosi Naga as president. At year-end 1983, membership in Fiji was 2,722. By 1990, membership was 8,592. Latter-day Saints are among a number of prominent industry and company leaders. Membership is also increasing among the various minorities of the island.

Sources: *Unto the Isles of the Sea,* by R. Lanier Britsch; *Church News,* Sept. 14, 1991; "Fiji: Church gaining prominence in isle cultures," *Church News,* Nov. 2, 1991.

No.	Name	Organized	First President

Pacific Area

| 1428 | Suva Fiji | 12 Jun 1983 | Inosi Naga |

Mission — 1
(As of Oct. 1, 1994; shown with historical number. See MISSIONS.)

(99) FIJI SUVA MISSION
GPO Box 215
Suva, Fiji Islands
Phone: (011-679) 314-277

FINLAND

Year-end 1993: Est. population, 5,100,000; Members, 4,400; Stakes, 2; Wards, 11; Branches, 17; Missions, 1; Districts, 3; Percent LDS, 0.09, or one LDS in 1,159.

Located in northern Europe, the Republic of Finland has a population that speaks Finnish and Swedish, and 90 percent are Lutherans.

The first Latter-day Saints in Finland were Finnish emigrants who had been baptized in Sweden in the early 1870s. The first missionaries were Swedish brothers Carl A. and John E. Sundstrom. They preached in Vaasa and found converts in 1876. During the first decade in Finland, the missionaries worked among Swedish-speaking Finns, and by 1886 had baptized 25 people. Because Finnish law forbade "getting up and preaching," missionaries learned to preach while sitting.

In 1903, Elder Francis M. Lyman of the Council of the Twelve visited Finland.

Efforts were made to establish branches in several areas, but the branches were not permanent. When Anders and Lovis Stromberg were converted in Larsmo, a permanent branch eventually grew up around them. Membership in the country was 35 in 1930. As late as 1941, all Church members in Finland had their records in Larsmo.

In 1946, seven missionaries from Sweden were sent to Finland, the first being Mark E. Anderson. In 1947, Henry A. Matis, an American with Finnish roots, was called as president of the Finnish Mission. Membership in Finland was 129 when he arrived. During the seven years that he served, the Church gained legal status (July 1, 1948), began microfilming Finnish church records (December 1948-November 1955), and translated and published the Book of Mormon (December 1954). Missionaries taught English, played basketball and did everything they could to raise the Church's profile.

After 1954, local Finnish members served missions. A building program was started and more people were converted. By 1957, membership was 904. The first of many successful temple trips to Switzerland was made in June 1960.

The Helsinki Stake was organized Oct. 16, 1977, with Kari Haikkola as president. At that time there were 3,642 members. Ten years later, it had increased to 4,100.

Finnish members were the first to introduce the gospel to Estonia and parts of Russia (see Estonia history). The Helsinki East Mission was created in 1990 to serve members in Leningrad and other areas in the Soviet Union. It was discontinued with the creation of the Russia missions in 1991, although Finnish leaders were among those called to serve in Russia. Membership in 1990 was 4,200.

Sources: *Ensign*, May 1973; "A man worth the wait," by John L. Hart, *Church News,* Nov. 14, 1987; *Church News,* Nov. 16, 1991; *Church News,* Feb. 15, 1992; "Finland."

Stakes — 2
(Listed alphabetically as of Oct. 1, 1994.)

No.	Name	Organized	First President

Europe North Area

| 865 | Helsinki Finland | 16 Oct 1977 | Kari Juhani Aslak Haikkola |
| 1408 | Tampere Finland | 17 Apr 1983 | Kari Juhani Aslak Haikkola |

Mission — 1
(As of Oct. 1, 1994; shown with historical number. See MISSIONS.)

(41) FINLAND HELSINKI MISSION
Neitsytpolku 3 A 4
00140 Helsinki, Finland
Phone: (011-358-0) 626-110

FRANCE

Year-end 1993: Est. population, 57,700,000; Members, 25,000; Stakes, 7; Wards, 34; Branches, 72; Missions, 3; Districts, 6; Percent LDS, 0.04, or one LDS in 2,308.

In western Europe, France has a population that speaks French, and includes minorities who speak Breton, Alsatian, German, Flemish, Italian, Basque and Catalan. The population of France is mostly Roman Catholic.

A Welsh member named William Howells arrived in Le Havre, France, in July 1849, and on July 30, 1849, baptized Augustus Saint d'Anna. After a short detour to the Island of Jersey, Howells returned to France and baptized a man named Pebble, and a young woman, Anna Browse. The Boulogne-sur-Mer Branch with six members, was organized April 5, 1850. On June 18, Apostle John Taylor and Elder Curtis E. Boulton arrived. The party traveled to Paris, and on Dec. 8, 1850, a branch of eight members was organized in that city. The Book of Mormon was translated and published in French in January 1852. By July 24, 1853, nine branches had been organized, with 337 members including 289 from the Channel Islands.

Government restrictions by French Emperor Louis Napoleon prohibited gathering of any more than 20 people, making it difficult for missionaries to hold meetings. Louis Bertrand, a member of the original branch in Paris, published a periodical and tried to extend missionary work. In 1859, Pres. Bertrand was called to preside over the mission but in 1864, the work in France was closed. The work re-opened in 1912 when the French Mission was reorganized. Sixty-two converts joined that year, but World War I halted the work until 1923 when the French Mission was re-established. In 1924, the first year of mission activity, some 200 converts joined. By 1930, there were two meetinghouses in the French Mission (both were in the Belgian sector of the French Mission) and missionaries were working in 33 cities in the two countries.

Missionaries worked hard to build the Church's image and some helped by singing in groups while others played on successful basketball teams. During World War II, a local leader, Leon Fargier, conducted the affairs of the Church. After World War II, missionary work resumed. The Tabernacle Choir visited in 1955. In 1959, membership reached 1,909 members. The first meetinghouse in France was constructed in Nantes in 1962. In 1974, 29 French members were serving full-time missions. The Paris France Stake, the first stake in France, was created Nov. 16, 1975, with Gerard Giraud-Carrier as president. At that time, membership in the nation was about 10,000. A decade later, it had grown to 16,500 in three stakes.

The France Bordeaux Mission was created in 1989, and the France Marseille Mission was created in July 1, 1991. On Aug. 15, 1992, the Europe Mediterranean Area was created and headquarters were established in Thoiry, France.

Sources: "Moments in History," *Church News*, July 31, 1971; "Church in Europe," *Ensign*, August, 1973; "Church's Second Generation Growth is Strong in France," by J Malan Heslop, *Church News*, Dec. 1, 1973; *Church News* Feb., 25, 1989; "His Faith Wouldn't Go Underground," by Alain Marie, *Ensign*, September 1991; *Church News*, Sept. 7, 1991.

Stakes — 7
(Listed alphabetically as of Oct. 1, 1994.)

No.	Name	Organized	First President
Europe/Mediterranean Area			
1867	Bordeaux France	24 May 1992	Jacquie Simonet
1669	Lille France	17 Jan 1988	Dominique Degrave
1772	Lyon France	9 Sep 1990	Pierre-Marie Brenders
1413	Nancy France	24 Apr 1983	John Keith Bishop
1130	Nice France	14 May 1980	Joseph Michel Paya
731	Paris France	16 Nov 1975	Gerard Giraud-Carrier
1850	Paris France East	8 Mar 1992	Dominique Calmels

Missions — 3
(As of Oct. 1, 1994; shown with historical number. See MISSIONS.)

(221a) FRANCE BORDEAUX MISSION
67 Rue Furtado
33800 Bordeaux
France
Phone: (11-33-56) 91-78-11

(262) FRANCE MARSEILLE MISSION
48, Ave Robert Schumann
F-13090 Aix-en-Provence,
France
Phone: (011-33-42) 26-88-63

(6) FRANCE PARIS MISSION
23, rue Du Onze Novembre
F-78110 Le Vesinet
France
Phone: (011-33-1) 3976-5588

FRENCH GUIANA

Year-end 1993: Est. population, 135,000; Members, 100; Branches, 2; North America Southeast Area; West Indies Mission.

French Guiana is an overseas department of France located in northern South America. Charles Fortin, a native of French Guiana, was baptized in France and returned to his homeland. Rosiette Fauvette, also baptized in France, returned to French Guiana July 8, 1981, and sacrament meetings with the two were held at Brother Fortin's home in Cayenne. Brother Fortin introduced the Church to many people before his death in April 1986. By then several other members were attending services including Gerard Charpentier, who later became branch president. Meetings were then held in the home of the Masinski family until January 1987 when the metings were moved to Sister Fauvette's home in Kourou, which had a special room added for the meetings.

Elder Charles Didier of the Seventy visited on March 4, 1988, and organized a group. On Nov. 5, 1988, Serge and Christie Bonnoit of France became the first converts in French Guiana. On June 26, 1989, the Kourou Branch was divided and the Cayenne Branch created. On July 1, 1989, Michaela Papo, the first native Guyanaise convert, was baptized.

The first missionary couple was Elder Wilbur and Sister Jacqueline Wortham, followed in November 1989 by Elder A. Edward and Sister Louise P. Schmidt. The newly organized branch in Cayenne had about 23 members in 1989.

Source: "History of the Church in French Guiana," supplied by Pres. Elden L. Wood, 1994; Interview with Elder A. Edward and Louise P. Schmidt.

FRENCH POLYNESIA
(Tahiti)

Year-end 1993: Est. population, 202,000; Members, 13,000; Stakes, 4; Wards, 25; Branches, 31; Missions, 1; Districts, 2; Temples, 1; Percent LDS, 6.4, or one person in 16.

Located in the South Pacific midway between South America and Australia, the French Polynesia archipelago is a French overseas territory. Tahiti's population speaks French and Tahitian. Most of the French Polynesians are Protestants.

Elders Benjamin F. Grouard, Addison Pratt, Noah Rogers and Knowlton F. Hanks were sent by Joseph Smith to the Pacific Islands. They boarded the whaling ship *Timoleon* Oct. 10, 1843, and sailed around the Cape of Good Hope. During the voyage, Elder Hanks died of tuberculosis and was buried at sea. When the ship reached Tubuai, an island about 500 miles south of Tahiti, on April 30, 1844, Elder Pratt disembarked and remained to preach. He is considered the first missionary to a foreign language area in modern Church history. He baptized many people and established a branch.

Elders Grouard and Rogers went on to Tahiti, where initially they found proselyting difficult. Elder Rogers returned to the United States, while Elder Grouard visited the Tuamotu Islands and was successful, though at great personal sacrifice and effort. He was later joined by Elder Pratt, and their converts numbered in the hundreds. Elder Pratt returned to United States in 1848, and came back with his family in 1850. This promising start for the Church was halted when French government restrictions led to the mission being closed in May 1852.

Work was re-opened in 1892, with Elders Joseph W. Damron and William A. Seegmiller, who found most of the early members had fallen away. They started branches again among those who had remained stalwart, and built meetinghouses that helped speed the work.

Completion of the New Zealand Temple in 1958 was a blessing for the Tahitian Saints, who proved to be faithful attenders.

On May 23, 1963, in the worst-recorded sea disaster for Latter-day Saints in the South Pacific, 15 members of the Maupiti Branch, about 160 miles northwest of Tahiti, lost their lives when the boat in which they were returning from a meetinghouse dedication cracked up on the Maupiti reef. Elder Gordon B. Hinckley, then of the Council of the Twelve, visited the bereaved branch members to offer solace and comfort.

In 1991, a group of members from the Maupiti Branch, many of them aged, made their first trip to the temple.

In 1964, the Church constructed an elementary school in Tahiti, and in 1972 the Tahiti Stake was organized. The Papeete Tahiti Temple was dedicated Oct. 27, 1983. Tahiti's second stake was created in 1982, and its third stake in 1990.

In 1991, Saints in Takaroa in the Tuamotu islands observed the 100th anniversary of a meetinghouse built by early members, the oldest meetinghouse in the South Pacific. The imposing building took 20 years to complete and has withstood tropical storms. On Jan 6, 1991, the Takaroa Branch was divided, with a total membership of more than 300. Some of the members are descendants of those converted in the 19th century.

In 1994, members celebrated the 150th anniversary of the missionaries arriving in their islands. Closer relations with other religions resulted as Elder Russell M. Nelson of the Council of the Twelve was formally introduced to the territory's president and full cabinet. President Gaston Flosse and other top government leaders attended several events.

Sources: *Encyclopedic History of the Church,* by Andrew Jenson; *Histoire de l'Eglise Mormone en Polynesie Francaise de 1844 a 1982,* by Yves R. Perrin; "A bright new future dawns for Polynesian atoll and 100-year-old meetinghouse," by Kathleen C. Perrin, *Church News,* Feb. 2, 1991; "Temple Blessings broaden view of paradise," by Kathleen C. Perrin, *Church News,* Aug. 24, 1991; "150th year of Church in Tahiti," by Kathleen C. Perrin, *Church News,* May 7, 1994; "LDS note 150 years in French Polynesia," by John L. Hart, *Church News* May 14, 1994; "Sesquicentennial: 'Spiritual feast,' " by John L. Hart, *Church News,* May 21, 1994.

Stakes — 4
(Listed alphabetically as of Oct. 1, 1994.)

No.	Name	Organized	First President
Pacific Area			
1747	Paea Tahiti	15 Apr 1990	Jean Alexis Tefan
573	*Papeete Tahiti		
	†Tahiti	14 May 1972	Raituia Tehina Tapu
1355	Pirae Tahiti	20 Jun 1982	Lysis G. Terooatea
1962a	Uturoa Tahiti Raiatea	5 Dec 1993	Michel Just Doucet

Mission — 1
(As of Oct. 1, 1994; shown with historical number. See MISSIONS.)

(3) TAHITI PAPEETE MISSION
B.P. 93
Papeete, Tahiti
French Polynesia
Phone: (011-689) 50-55-21

MARTINIQUE AND GUADELOUPE

Year-end 1993: Est. population, 800,000; Members, fewer than 100; Branches, 2; North America Southeast Area; West Indies Mission.

The Caribbean Islands of Martinique and Guadeloupe are departments (states) of France. Guadeloupe has a population of 400,000. Martinique is the northernmost of the windward islands and has a population of 400,000. Martinique and Guadeloupe each have one branch with fewer than 100 members.

Andre Condoris, a young man baptized in France while serving in the military, returned to his homeland Aug. 9, 1980. He encouraged Mission Pres. Kenneth Zabriskie to send missionaries. French-speaking Elders Mark Richards, Stan Jones and David Simons were transferred from missions in Paris, France, and Brussels, Belgium, to open the work in Martinique and Guadeloupe. Joell Joseph-Agathe, a young woman baptized in France, returned to Martinique and also welcomed missionaries to the country. They arrived May 4, 1984, and held the first meeting May 6. The branch first met in Case Pilote, then Ducos and then in Chateau Boef. The branch now meets in Lamentin.

By 1985, five converts had been baptized. By 1994, the branch in Martinique had 80 members. Among the first converts in Guadeloupe were the Claire Dinane family, who soon moved to the the small island of St. Martin.

Source: Journal of Pres. Kenneth and Sister LeOra Zabriskie; "A religion, the Mormons," by Albert Albicy, *France-Antilles,* Jan. 27, 1994, courtesy Pres. J. Richard Toolson.

NEW CALEDONIA

Year-end 1993: Est. population, 200,000; Members, 1,000; Branches, 5; Districts, 1; Percent LDS, 0.5, or one in 200; Pacific Area; Fiji Suva Mission.

An overseas territory of France, New Caledonia is a group of islands in the South Pacific.

Church activity in New Caledonia began in the 1950s as a few Tahitian members migrated to work in a nickel smelter. They were organized into the Noumea Branch on Oct. 21, 1961. However, visas for missionaries were not obtained until 1967. On July 15, 1968, the first two missionaries arrived, Harold and Jeannine Richards, and their daughter, Jacquelina.

In June 1975, administration over the island group was transferred to the Fiji Suva Mission, and more progress was realized. The Noumea Branch was divided, and the small meetinghouse was enlarged. In July 1978, the Tontouta Branch was organized. In 1990, there were 382 members in New Caledonia.

Source: *Unto the Islands of the Sea,* by R. Lanier Britsch.

ST. MARTIN

Year-end 1993: Est. population, 4,500; Members, fewer than 100; Branches, 1; North America Southeast Area.

The island of St. Martin in the Caribbean, with 20 square miles, was part of the France Toulouse Mission when the St. Martin Branch was organized Jan. 9, 1979. The mission was discontinued a short time later, and work resumed under the West Indies Mission in 1983. Elders Thad Ariens and Victor Quarty began working in St. Martin, the administration of which is is divided between two governments, French and Dutch. The Claire Dinane family, which was baptized on Guadeloupe, moved to St. Martin and helped re-open the St. Martin Branch on Jan. 31, 1984.

Source: *Manuscript history of France Toulouse Mission.*

REUNION

Year-end 1993: Est. population, 575,000; Members, 500; Districts, 1; Branches, 4; Percent LDS, 0.09, or one LDS in 1,150; Africa Area; South Africa Durban Mission.

A volcanic Island in the Indian Ocean, Reunion is a department of France.

Missionary work began in Reunion in 1979 under the direction of the International Mission. In 1986, the islands were transferred to the South Africa Johannesburg Mission. Among the first members in Reunion were Alain and Danielle Chion-Hock, converted in France. On Nov. 4, 1979, Chion-Hock baptized his sister, Rose Tahi Soui Tchong, the first convert on Reunion.

Elder Joseph T. Edmunds and his wife, Ruth, were the first modern missionaries on the islands. They were joined by Elder Theo and Sister Nita Verhaarens. The first branch was established on Dec, 30, 1979. The Mascarene Islands Mission was created July 1, 1988, at which time there were 400 members on the islands with three branches in Reunion and two on the nearby island of Mauritius, which is included in the same district. Headquarters of the mission was transferred to Durban, South Africa, in January 1992.

Sources: *Church News,* Sept. 21, 1986, Feb. 7, 1987, Oct. 24, 1987, March 19, 1988, Nov. 5, 1987, Dec. 17, 1988; "Tropical Isles receive best news as mission opens," by Allen W. Palmer, *Church News,* Nov. 5, 1988; "At Home on the Island of Mauritius," by Lori Palmer, *Ensign,* March, 1991, February 1986, March 1989.

GABON

Year-end 1993: Est. population, 1,110,000; Members, fewer than 100; Africa Area; Ivory Coast Abidjan Mission.

Gabon is a republic on the Atlantic coast of west central Africa where the people speak French and Bantu dialects, and follow tribal beliefs, although some are Christians. Some 100,000 expatriate Europeans, as well as Africans, live in Gabon, including about 18,000 of French ancestry.

Jerome Obounou-Mbogo, first counselor in the Embassy of Gabon, traveled to Utah and had a favorable visit with Elder Neal A. Maxwell of the Council of the Twelve and Elder Richard P. Lindsay of the Seventy in their offices as part of his visit Aug. 4-6, 1990. The Church received permission enter the country in 1992.

Jean Mickouma, a member of the Church from Gabon, accompanied Obounou to Salt Lake City, Utah.

Mickouma joined the Church several years previous while working in Washington D.C.

Gabon was included in the Cameroon Yaounde Mission that was created on Feb. 1, 1992, and later transferred to the Ivory Coast Abidjan Mission.

Sources: *Church News*, Aug. 25, 1990.

GERMANY

Year-end 1993: Est. population, 81,100,000; Members, 36,000; Stakes, 15; Wards, 85; Branches, 92; Missions, 6; Districts, 1; Temples, 2; Percent LDS, 0.04, or one LDS in 2,253.

A central European nation divided following World War II and reunited in October 1990, Germany is composed of Catholics, 45 percent, and Protestants, 44 percent.

The first Latter-day Saint into Germany was James Howard, a British convert working in Germany in 1840. He tried to preach but was unsuccessful. Elder Orson Hyde spent 10 months in Germany in 1841-42, but was unsuccessful in preaching, although he did study German and introduce the language to the Prophet Joseph Smith. He saw translation of a tract into German completed.

Another missionary, Johan Greenig, is often credited with having established the first German branch, in Darmstadt, Germany, in 1843.

In 1849, apostles and other missionaries were sent to Scandinavia, Italy and France. Each of these mission efforts also reached into Germany. George P. Dykes, assigned to the Scandinavian Mission, went to Schleswig-Holstein, which was at that time under Danish rule, and may have baptized the first two German converts on Sept. 15, 1851. Elder John Taylor, assigned to France, went to Hamburg in October 1851, where he joined Elder Dykes and supervised translation of the Book of Mormon into German.

Daniel Carn was called by Brigham Young to be the first mission president in Germany. Pres. Carn arrived in Hamburg April 3, 1852. By Aug. 1, he had baptized 12 and organized the Hamburg Branch. Pres. Carn was exiled but continued to supervise the German Saints, and strengthened Danish branches as well. Five additional missionaries from the United States arrived, but within four months went to England, discouraged by constantly being called before the police.

The first converts to emigrate left Germany Aug. 13, 1852. In 1854, apostates and police halted missionary work as the missionaries were imprisoned and exiled. Most of the local faithful converts emigrated and the branch was dissolved.

A prominent convert of this period from Dresden was Karl G. Maeser, who was attracted to the Church by an anti-Mormon tract. He as taught by Elder William Budge, a native of Scotland who later became president of the Logan Temple. On Oct. 21, 1855, the Dresden Branch was established with Maeser as president. The branch lasted until 1857, when opposition led to the emigration of most members of the branch, including its president.

Southern Germany's first branch was organized in Karlsruhe in 1860, under the direction of the Swiss-German Mission. During the next seven years, missionaries were halted by rigid law and frequently prevented from effective proselyting. The faltering mission was boosted in 1867 by the return as a missionary of Karl G. Maeser. More than 600 people joined the Church in the next three years. However, for the next decades, work proceeded slowly amid opposition. As the Church seemed poised for progress, World War I began. Nearly 200 missionaries left some 60 branches in Switzerland and Germany. Despite the war, most branches remained intact. By 1925, the German Mission was divided, leaving 6,125 members in the German-Austrian Mission, and 5,305 members in the Swiss-German Mission.

On Sept. 16, 1938, the First Presidency ordered missionaries to be evacuated from Germany. During World War II, more than 600 German Saints were killed, 2,500 were missing, and 80 percent were homeless.

Relief efforts by the Church, supervised by Elder Ezra Taft Benson, then of the Council of the Twelve, and neighboring members including the Dutch, helped sustain German members during the difficult post-war period. Missionaries returned in 1947. In the next 20 years, five stakes were organized, three missions created, and European headquarters were established for the Church in Frankfurt.

Membership in Germany in 1975 was 13,829. In 1985, it had increased to 29,900. A temple in Frankfurt was announced in 1981, and was dedicated Aug. 28, 1987. Following the publicity of the dedication and an increased missionary effort, missionary work increased in the late 1980s. The Germany Duesseldorf Mission, started in 1961 but dissolved in 1982, was re-organized in July 1990.

The German Democratic Republic, which existed following World War II until reunification in 1990, was the home of many faithful members cut off from the rest of the Church. These members continued in faithfulness despite many difficult problems, strengthening each other through fellowship. "The war cost us everything," said one. "But there was something they couldn't take — our testimonies."

Among the leaders to visit in the 1960s was Elder Thomas S. Monson, then of the Council of the Twelve, who promised the Saints they would eventually have every blessing of members elsewhere. A patriarch was ordained, and plans for a meetinghouse were made and completed. Later, following prayers and fasting of the members, government relations improved and German Democratic Republic leaders gave permission for a temple to be built in Freiberg. After the temple was completed, 89,789 people toured the public open house. It was dedicated June 29, 1985. Government approval was later given for missionary work to begin. On March 30, 1989, foreign missionaries arrived in the country, and on May 28, 1989, missionaries from the German Democratic Republic entered the Missionary Training Center to begin foreign missions.

The Berlin Wall separating East and West Berlin for 28 years fell Nov. 9, 1989, and the two Germanys were reunified on Oct. 3, 1990. When American military personnel were withdrawn in 1993, overall membership was reduced. In October of that year, the first offical broadcast of general conference to Germany was completed.

Elder F. Enzio Busche of the First Quorum of the Seventy was called as a General Authority on Oct. 1, 1977, and Elder Dieter Uchtdorf was sustained to the Second Quorum of the Seventy on April 2, 1994.

Sources: *Encyclopedic History of the Church,* by Andrew Jenson; *Mormonism in Germany,* by Gilbert W. Scharffs, Deseret Book, 1970; "Memories of West German Evacuation," by J. Richard Barnes, unpublished; interview with Emil Fetzer; correspondence from Tim T. Brosnahan Jr., June 15, 1985; multiple newspaper sources, 1989-91; *Church News,* Oct. 2, 1993 and April 9, 1994.

Stakes — 14
(Listed alphabetically as of Oct. 1, 1994.)

No.	Name	Organized	First President
Europe Area			
334	*Berlin Germany		
	†Berlin	10 Sep 1961	Rudi Seehagen
768	Dortmund Germany	19 Sep 1976	Klaus Fritz K. Hasse
1358	*Dresden Germany 21 Oct 1990		
	†Freiberg German Democratic Republic	29 Aug 1982	Frank Herbert Apel
577	*Duesseldorf Germany		Frerich Jakob Emil Goerts
	†Duesseldorf	4 Jun 1972	
766	Frankfurt Germany	12 Sep 1976	Magnus R. Meiser
342	*Hamburg Germany		
	†Hamburg	12 Nov 1961	Michael Panitsch
845	Hannover Germany	12 Jun 1977	Michael Schulze
	Hanover Germany 25 Jan 1993		
466	*Kaiserslautern Germany Servicemen		
	†Servicemen Stake Europe (W. Germany)	30 Oct 1968	Herbert B. Spencer
1475	*Leipzig Germany 21 Oct 1990		
	†Leipzig German Democratic Republic	3 Jun 1984	Hermann M. Schutze
1324	Mannheim Germany	7 Feb 1982	Baldur H.H. Stoltenberg
870	Munich Germany	23 Oct 1977	August Schubert
1305	*New Muenster Germany 9 Apr 1985		
	†Hamburg Germany North	8 Nov 1981	Karl-Heinz Danklefsen
1651	Nuremberg Germany Servicemen	6 Sep 1987	Jon Paul Baker
340	*Stuttgart Germany		
	†Stuttgart	26 Oct 1961	Hermann Moessner

Discontinued

No.	Name	Organized	First President
824	Frankfurt Germany Servicemen	1 May 1977	Kenneth Alvin Nessen
	20 Feb 1994		
765	Stuttgart Germany Servicemen	12 Sep 1976	Gary K. Spencer
	15 Nov 1992		

Missions — 6
(As of Oct. 1, 1994; shown with historical number. See MISSIONS.)

(263) GERMANY BERLIN MISSION
P.S.F. 480-418
12254 Berlin 48
Federal Republic of Germany
Phone: (011-49-30) 773-8359

(36) GERMANY HAMBURG MISSION
Rugenbarg 7A
22549 Hamburg
Federal Republic of Germany
Phone: (011-49-40) 804-027

(240) GERMANY DUESSELDORF MISSION
Morsenbroicherweg 184 A
40470 Duesseldorf 30
Federal Republic of Germany
Phone: (011-49-211) 611-042

(35a) GERMANY FRANKFURT MISSION
Arndtstrasse 18
60325 Frankfurt/Main 1
Federal Republic of Germany
Phone: (011-49-69) 74-77-74

(225) GERMANY LEIPZIG MISSION
Springerstrasse 16
04105 Leipzig
Federal Republic of Germany
Phone: (011-49-341) 5646 723

(49) GERMANY MUNICH MISSION
Boschetsrieder Str. 10a
81379 Munich
Federal Republic of Germany
Phone: (011-40-89) 724-2044

GHANA

Year-end 1993: Est. population, 16,500,000; Members, 12,000; Stakes, 2; Wards, 13; Branches, 33; Missions, 1; Districts, 4; Percent LDS, 0.01, or one person in 1,375.

With an authoritarian government, Ghana is located on the south central west coast of Africa and has a population of Christian, 52 percent, traditional, 30 percent and Moslem, 13 percent.

In the 1950s, various pamphlets about the Church found their way to Ghana which were read by Ghanaians, believed and used as the basis to start their own LDS congregations. Ghanaians also learned of the Church as they visited other countries. Pricilla Sampson-Davis, for example, received a copy of the Book of Mormon from missionaries during a visit to the Netherlands in 1963, from which she gained a testimony. In 1964, Joseph W.B. Johnson gained a testimony of the Book of Mormon and began organizing congregations. As early as 1960, President David O. McKay attempted to have leaders visit these sincere, but unauthorized, congregations, but the leaders were unable to obtain visas.

In August of 1978, just two months after the revelation on the priesthood, Merrill Bateman and Edwin Q. "Ted" Cannon were sent by the Church to West Africa on a fact-finding trip and on Nov. 8, 1978, Elder Cannon, with his wife, Janath, and Rendell N. and Rachel Mabey arrived in Nigeria as Church representatives. They entered Ghana in 1978. They met and baptized Sister Sampson-Davis shortly after their arrival. Johnson and many of his congregations were baptized. A building program began in 1979.

Within a year, more than 400 people had been baptized, and branches organized. By 1981, seven branches functioned in Ghana. The first president of the mission, Pres. Bryan Espenschied, and his successsor, Pres. Sylvester Cooper, saw that all converts were taught the gospel in their own language, and trained in leadership skills.

One of the early converts was Dr. Emmanuel Abu Kissi, a physician who established a clinic supported by friends of the Church. A number of humanitarian projects were completed by the Church in Ghana in the 1980s.

Growth continued and by 1983, the number of branches increased to 28. The Africa West Mission was organized July 1, 1980, and the Ghana Accra Mission July 1, 1985. By 1987, membership reached 5,500.

On June 14, 1989, the Ghana government expelled the missionaries and banned the Church. Members were permitted to hold services in the privacy of their homes, however. On Dec. 1, 1990, the government permitted Church activities to resume. (Sacrament meetings resumed Dec. 9. By year-end 1990, membership was more than 9,000.) The government announcement expressed satisfaction that the Church teaches members to be obedient to government laws, and promotes racial harmony.

Sources: *Church News*, Dec. 22, 1979, Sept. 30, 1984, Oct. 17, 1987, June 24, 1989, Dec. 8, 1990; "Nigeria and Ghana," by Janet Brigham, *Ensign*, February 1980; "Pioneers in Africa," by E. Dale LeBaron; *Church News*, Sept. 21, 1991 and Oct. 23, 1994.

Stakes — 2
(Listed alphabetically as of Oct. 1, 1994.)

No.	Name	Organized	First President
Africa Area			
1791	Accra Ghana	21 Apr 1991	Emmanuel Ohene Opare
1792	Cape Coast Ghana	21 Apr 1991	Kweku Prah Ghartey

Mission — 1
(As of Oct. 1, 1994; shown with historical number. See MISSIONS.)

GHANA ACCRA MISSION
P.O. Box 2585 Main
Accra, Ghana
Phone: (011-233-21) 222531

GREECE

Year-end 1993: Est. population, 10,500,000; Members, 200; Missions, 1; Districts, 1; Branches, 7; Europe/Mediterranean Area.

Located on the southern end of the Balkan Peninsula in southeast Europe, Greece is a presidential parliamentary republic. About 98 percent of the Greek-speaking population belongs to the Greek Orthodox Church.

A letter to Church leaders requesting more information from Rigas Profantis, a printer in Athens, led missionaries to Greece about the turn of the century. He and a friend, Nicholas Malavetis, had started a search for truth in 1895 that led them to write to Church headquarters in Salt Lake City, Utah. Pres. Ferdinand F. Hintze of the Turkish Mission visited the pair in April 1899, and taught them about the Church. In 1905, Profantis wrote requesting baptism, and noted that he had translated a pamphlet into Greek, and that three other people were awaiting baptism as well. They were baptized Oct. 22, 1905, by J. Wilford Booth of the Near East Mission.

The group continued until 1909 or 1910, after which missionaries were withdrawn.

Little activity by the Church in Greece occurred until the 1950s. The Church donated wheat seed to Greece for humanitarian purposes in November 1947. In Salt Lake City in the 1950s, LDS Greek-Americans formed the Hellenic Latter-day Saint Society to retain their heritage and maintain ties with their homeland.

The Athens Branch was created in 1965 and reorganized in 1967 at a conference presided over by Pres. Rendell N. Mabey of the Swiss Mission. Many of those in attendance were expatriates stationed with the military in Greece.

A number of diplomatic exchanges were made during the next decades, including a visit in Greece by President Ezra Taft Benson in 1979, and a visit to Salt Lake City Oct. 14, 1980, by the Greek ambassador to the United States, John A. Tzounis.

The Greece Athens Mission was created from a division of the Austria Vienna East Mission on July 1, 1990. On Feb. 9, 1992, the Thessaloniki Branch was created with 32 in attendance, including 12 non-LDS investigators.

Sources: Swiss Mission manuscript history; *Church News*, March 3, 1990, March 3, 1991, May 18, 1991; "Branch begins in historic city," *Church News*, May 9, 1992.

Mission — 1
(As of Oct. 1, 1994; shown with historical number. See MISSIONS.)

(241) GREECE ATHENS MISSION
Papadiamanti Street 4
Paleo Psychiko 15452
Athens, Greece
Phone: (011-30-1) 685-5267

GRENADA

Year-end 1993: Est. population, 101,000; Members, fewer than 100; Branches, 1; North America Southeast Area; West Indies Mission.

Composed of three Caribbean mountainous islands, Grenada is an independent state with a parliamentary democracy. Its population is Roman Catholic, 64 percent, and Anglican, 22 percent.

Although LDS members lived in Grenada attending medical school, little permanent missionary work started until after the 1983 coup and subsequent invasion of Grenada by U.S. and United Nations forces. Under the direction of Pres. Kenneth L. Zabriskie of the West Indies Mission, Elders Robert W. Hoffmaster and Leonard G. Gill arrived in Grenada in May 1985. They met with a medical student, Tom Nuttal, and his wife, Julie, and their children. A branch was established in St. George on Sept. 3, 1985.

Sources: *Church News*, Nov. 20, 1983, Nov. 6, 1983; Kenneth and LeOra Zabriskie journals.

GUAM
(See also MICRONESIA)

Year-end 1993: Est. population, 136,000; Members, 1,200; Branches, 4; Missions, 1; Districts, 1; Percent LDS, .73, or one LDS in 136; Philippines/Micronesia Area.

The largest of the Mariana islands in the South Pacific, the self-governing U.S. territory of Guam has a population that is mostly Roman Catholic.

The first LDS members on Guam probably came as members of the armed forces during World War II. Guam branches of from 50 to 300 servicemen began functioning in 1944, acting under the Far East Mission. In 1945, four groups were organized on the island. On one occasion, they dedicated the graves of fallen LDS servicemen.

In 1951, fund-raising events by the members raised enough money to purchase land and two quonset huts, which they used for a chapel and classrooms. The facilities were dedicated in 1953 and Guam became a dependent branch of the Oahu Hawaii Stake.

In 1952, Ethel T. Kurihara, a native of Guam, became the first local Relief Society president.

Elders Danny Gallego and Paul Ray arrived on Aug. 25, 1955, and served for a year and a half.

As more LDS military personnel arrived, land for another meetinghouse was purchased. A new meeting-house in Barrigada was dedicated March 10, 1970, and the Guam Branch became a ward. Open houses were frequently held, but few joined the Church. In May 1976, the Guam Ward was divided. The first Chamorro couple to join, Don Calvo and his wife, Maria, were baptized in May 1977. The Agat Branch was created in 1978. And in 1979, Herbert J. Leddy, the first missionary of Chamorro lineage, was called to the Tennessee Nashville Mission.

The Micronesia Guam Mission was created April 1, 1980. In June, the Guam District was created with four branches.

In 1989, selections of the Book of Mormon were translated into Chamorro, and the same year, Herbert J. Leddy became the first Chamorro member to be called as district president. Membership in 1990 was 1,400.

Sources: "A Brief History of the Micronesia-Guam Mission, 1980-1990," published by the Micronesia Guam Mission, 1990; *Unto the Islands of the Sea*, by R. Lanier Britsch.

Mission — 1
(As of Oct. 1, 1994; shown with historical number. See MISSIONS.)

(178) MICRONESIA GUAM MISSION
P.O. Box 21749 GMF
Barrigada, GU 96921
Phone: 011-671 734-3526

GUATEMALA

Year-end 1993: Est. population, 10,010,000; Members, 140,000; Stakes, 24; Wards, 151; Branches, 187; Missions 4; Districts, 18; Temples, 1; Percent LDS, 1.40, or one LDS in 72.

The northernmost isthmus country in Central America, the Republic of Guatemala has people who speak Spanish and various Indian dialects, and are mostly Roman Catholics.

John F. O'Donnal from the Mormon colonies in Mexico moved to Central America in 1942 as an agricultural adviser of the U.S. government. He paved the way for the arrival of the first missionaries in 1947. Pres. A. L. Pierce of the Mexican Mission assigned Elders Seth G. Mattice, Earl E. Hansen, Robert B. Miller and David D. Lingard, who arrived in Guatemala on Sept. 4, 1947. They held a sacrament meeting, and with the assistance of Brother O'Donnal, visited several government leaders. A year later, on Aug. 12, Brother O'Donnal was set apart as district president. Some 66 people attended the first meeting in a rented building on Aug. 22, 1948. On Nov. 13, 1948, Pres. O'Donnal baptized his wife, Carmen, the first convert in Guatemala.

In Nov. 16, 1952, Elder Spencer W. Kimball, then of the Council of the Twelve, visited and organized the Central American Mission. By 1956, three branches with a membership of about 250 had been established. The Guatemala-El Salvador Mission was created Aug. 1, 1965.

When the Church received official recognition in November 1966, there were 10,000 members. On May 21, 1967, the Guatemala City Stake was organized with Udine Falabella as president. The stake was divided in 1972, and the mission was divided in 1976, creating separate missions in Guatemala and El Salvador. By 1977, the mission had been divided again with the creation of the Guatemala Quetzaltenango Mission, with John F. O'Donnal as president. Four stakes had been established and membership was more than 17,000. A temple was announced for Guatemala in 1981, and completed and dedicated Dec. 14-16, 1984. Called as president of the temple was John F. O'Donnal. At that time, membership was 40,000 in eight stakes and 13 districts. A third mission, the Guatemala City North, was created Jan. 1, 1988. The fourth, Guatemala Central, was created July 1, 1993. Membership in 1990 was 125,000.

On April 1, 1989, Elder Carlos H. Amado, former temple committee chairman, was called to the Second Quorum of the Seventy, becoming the first Guatemalan General Authority. A tragedy occurred Nov. 22, 1993, when a mission president and counselor, Jose Jimenez and Julio Afre, died in a plane crash.

On Jan. 22, 1994, Elder Boyd K. Packer of the Council of the Twelve dedicated a new 36,400-square-foot missionary training center in Guatemala City.

Sources: Guatemala Branch manuscript history; *Encyclopedic History of the Church,* by Andrew Jenson; Guatemala City conference report, Feb. 21, 22, 1977; *Church News,* Jan. 13, 1979, Nov. 10, 1966, Sept. 10, 1966, Aug. 20, 1966, June 30, 1985, Nov. 27, 1993, Feb. 12, 1994.

Stakes — 25
(Listed alphabetically as of Oct. 1, 1994.)

No.	Name	Organized	First President
Central America Area			
1611	*Chimaltenango Guatemala 22 Mar 1988		
	†Guatemala City Guat. Chimaltenango	26 Oct 1986	Mario Salazar Moran
1738	Coatepeque Guatemala	10 Dec 1989	Ricardo Rolando Morales
1681	*Escuintla Guatemala 3 Apr 1990		
	†Guatemala City Guatemala Escuintla	31 Jan 1988	Enrique Leveron L.
436	*Guatemala City Guatemala		
	†Guatemala City	21 May 1967	Udine Falabella
1618	Guatemala City Guatemala Atlantico	7 Dec 1986	Luis Alvarez Ovando
1619	Guatemala City Guatemala Central	7 Dec 1986	Armando G. Diaz L.
1768	Guatemala City Guatemala El Molino	19 Aug 1990	Jose Julio Aguilar
1620	Guatemala City Guatemala Florida	7 Dec 1986	Miguel A. Gomez L.
1704	Guatemala City Guatemala La Laguna	27 Nov 1988	Carlos Estrado Mouna M.
778	Guatemala City Guatemala Las Victorias	31 Oct 1976	Carlos Enrique Soto D.
1040	Guatemala City Guatemala Mariscal	10 Jun 1979	Samuel Ramirez Abrego
1745	Guatemala City Guatemala Milagro	15 Apr 1990	Victor Manuel Canenguez P.
1733	Guatemala City Guatemala Nimajuyu	9 Jul 1989	Rene Humberto Oliva L.
699	*Guatemala City Guatemala Utatlan 31 Oct 1976		
	†Guatemala City Guatemala West	8 Jun 1975	Mario Antonio Lopez
1706	Huehuetenango Guatemala	4 Dec 1988	Edgar Leonardo Fuentes P.
1982	Huehuetenango Guatemala Calvario	19 June 1994	Victor M. Rodas Corado
1937	Jalapa Guatemala	9 May 1993	Luis Daniel Aragon Aquino
1938	Malacatan Guatemala	9 May 1993	Edilzar Joel Barrios Rodriguez
1737	Mazatenango Guatemala	10 Dec 1989	Mario Antonio de Leon S.
713	Quetzaltenango Guatemala	19 Oct 1975	Jorge Herminio Perez C.
1497	Quetzaltenango Guatemala West	24 Oct 1984	Amilcar Raul Robles A.
1168	Retalhuleu Guatemala	17 Aug 1980	Manuel Efrain Barrios F.
1955a	San Felipe Guatemala	19 Sep 1993	Mario A. Monterroso Gonzalez
1498	San Marcos Guatemala	24 Oct 1984	Abraham Raymundo Juarez C.
1785	Villa Nueva Guatemla	27 Jan 1991	Luis Gomez Garcia

Missions — 4
(As of Oct. 1, 1994; shown with historical number. See MISSIONS.)

(287) GUATEMALA GUATEMALA CITY
CENTRAL MISSION
Avenida La Reforma 8 - 60,Zona9
Edificio Galerias Reforma 5to, Nivec
Guatemala City, Guatemala
Phone: (011-502-2) 31-86-17

(205a) GUATEMALA GUATEMALA CITY
NORTH MISSION
Apartado Postal 332-A
Guatemala City, Guatemala
Phone: (011-502) 31-86-67

(76a) GUATEMALA GUATEMALA CITY
SOUTH MISSION
Apartado Postal 340-A
Guatemala City, Guatemala
Phone: (011-502-2) 31-86-11

(152) GUATEMALA QUETZALTENANGO
MISSION
Apartado Postal 206
Quetzaltenango, Guatemala 09001
Phone: (011-502-9) 61-6736

GUYANA

Year-end 1993: Est. population, 800,000; Members, 300; Branches, 1; North America Southeast Area; West Indies Mission.

On the northern coast of South America, Guyana is a republic in the United Kingdom commonwealth of nations. Its population speaks English and Amerindian dialects, and is Christian, 57 percent; and Hindu, 37 percent.

Elder Benjamin Hudson and his wife, Ruth, entered Guyana Aug. 19, 1988, and held a sacrament meeting in September 1988. Among those who attended was the Majid Abdulla family, which had been baptized previously in Canada. The first convert was Indra Sukhdeo, baptized Oct. 23, 1988, by Brother Abdulla.

The Church gained recognition in February 1989, and a small branch in Georgetown was organized in March with about 23 in attendance.

In February 1990, Elder M. Russell Ballard of the Council of the Twelve visited the branch, and, along with missionary couples Carvel G. and Lois N. Jackson and Joseph W. and Florence B. Allen, attended services with 45 members and investigators.

Kenrick Latchmansingh was called as the first local branch president in 1990.

On Sept. 15, 1992, President Desmond Hoyte, Guyana's head of state, was a special guest at a luncheon hosted by Elder Stephen D. Nadauld of the Seventy and a member of the North America Southeast Area presidency, and Pres. J. Richard Toolson of the Trinidad Tobago Mission.

Sources: History, personal histories, other information submitted by Joseph and Florence Allen, Benjamin and Ruth Hudson, and Carvel and Lois Jackson; "Taking root in 'Land of Waters,' *Church News,* May 18, 1991; *Church News,* Nov. 7, 1992.

HAITI

Year-end 1993: Est. population, 6,560,000; Members, 5,000; Branches, 18; Mission, 1; Districts, 2; Percent LDS, 0.1, or one person in 1,312; North America Southeast Area.

On the west side of Hispaniola Island in the West Indies, Haiti has a people who speak French and Creole. Eighty percent are Roman Catholic and 10 percent are Protestant; voodoo is influential.

The first LDS member in Haiti was Alexandre Mourra, who traveled to Florida from his home to be taught and baptized by the missionaries on June 30, 1977. Earlier, he had read a pamphlet and the Book of Mormon in Haiti.

On July 2, 1978, 22 Haitians were baptized in Hatte-Maree, near Port-au-Prince. In September of that year, J. Frederick Templeman of the Canadian embassy arrived. He and Alexandre Mourra worked to start the first branch, which was created in October 1980 in Port-au-Prince.

Missionary work opened in Haiti in May 1980, under the direction of Pres. Glen E. Stringham of the West Indies Mission. In 1982, 12 missionaries were serving in Haiti.

A branch was created in Petion-ville on March 31, 1981, with Alexandre Mourra as president, and divided in 1982. At that time, the Haiti District was created, and four missionaries were sent to open the city of Cap Hatien. Called as president was Ludner Armand. Missionaries had more referrals than they could teach. In August 1981, Fritzner Joseph, called to Puerto Rico, was the first Haitian to serve a full-time mission. In 1992, he was called as the first Haitain mission president, serving in the Haiti mission.

Selections of the Book of Mormon were translated into Haitian Creole in 1983, and that year, Haitian convert Luckner Huggins translated several hymns into Creole. Year-end membership was 485. The Haitian mission was created Aug. 4, 1984. By 1986, membership reached 1,500, and by 1988 it was 2,200. At a Port-au-Prince District conference in May 1989, 1,200 of the total 3,000 members attended district conference, and 49 men were ordained elders. Due to troubled internal conditions, foreign missionaries were removed from Haiti on Oct. 25, 1991. Haitian members rejoiced with the announcement of a temple in Dominican Republic, a more accessible location.

Sources: *Church News,* June 10, 1989, April 22, 1984, July 10, 1983, May 22, 1983, Nov. 29, 1980; Kenneth and LeOra Zabriskie journals; "Haitian Saints See Hope in Gospel," by Elizabeth and Jed VandenBerge, *Ensign,* March 1991; correspondence from Margene Stringham, Oct. 9, 1991; correspondence from Dr. Michael T. Johnson, Feb. 16, 1993; *Church News,* June 27, 1992 and March 26, 1994.

Mission — 1
(As of Oct. 1, 1994; shown with historical number. See MISSIONS.)

(180a) HAITI PORT-AU-PRINCE MISSION
Boite Postale 15319
Petion-ville,
Port-au-Prince, Haiti, F.W.I.
Phone: (011-509) 46-4482

HONDURAS

Year-end 1993: Est. population, 5,650,000; Members, 53,000; Stakes, 9; Wards, 53; Branches, 56; Missions, 2; Districts, 6; Percent LDS, 0.9 or one LDS in 106.

In Central America between Nicaragua and Guatemala, Honduras has a population that speaks Spanish and Indian dialects, and most are Roman Catholic.

Elders Spencer W. Kimball and Marion G. Romney, then of the Council of the Twelve, were instrumental in promoting missionary work in Central America. Early in the 1950s, they visited and left a tract and a copy of the Book of Mormon with a hotel waiter, who was later baptized. Missionary work in Honduras began Dec. 10, 1952, a month after the Central America Mission was opened in Guatemala City, Guatemala. Elders James T. Thorup and George W. Allen, the first two missionaries in Honduras, baptized Jose Ortega, Alicia Castanado, Corina de Bustamonte, Mario A. de Chotria and Carmen B. Corina on March 21, 1953. They organized a branch in Tegucigalpa March 22, 1953. Missionaries opened San Pedro Sula on Oct. 4, 1954, and a branch was organized there in 1955. The San Pedro Sula District was organized June 4, 1961.

The first stake in Honduras was created April 10, 1977. The Honduras Mission was created Jan. 1, 1980, with 6,300 members in the country.

By the end of 1987, membership had increased to 23,000. The mission was divided July 1, 1990, and the country's ninth stake was created in September 1990. Membership in 1990 was 43,000.

Sources: *Church News*: Sept. 28, 1974, April 23, 1977, Oct. 27, 1979, July 20, 1986, Nov. 30, 1986, Oct. 3, 1987, April 16, 1988, Feb. 3, 1990; *Ensign*, August 1977, June 1990; Honduras Tegucigalpa manuscript history.

Stakes — 10
(Listed alphabetically as of Oct. 1, 1994.)

No.	Name	Organized	First President
Central America Area			
1383	Comayaguela Honduras	21 Nov 1982	Jorge Alberto Sierra B.
1990	Comayaguela Honduras Torocagua	4 Sep 1994	Luis Gustavo Duarte Fonseca
1757	El Merendon Honduras	17 Jun 1990	Jose Francisco Funes R.
1647	La Ceiba Honduras	28 Jun 1987	Luis Alfredo Salazar V.
1601	La Lima Honduras	22 Jun 1986	Rodolfo Arguello A.
820	San Pedro Sula Honduras	10 Apr 1977	Samuel Ben-Zion Ventura
1709	Tegucigalpa Honduras Guaymuras	29 Jan 1989	Armando Antonio Sierra
947	Tegucigalpa Honduras	30 Jul 1978	Jose Miguel Dominguez C.
1771	Toncontin Honduras	2 Sep 1990	Ricardo Valladares B.
1732	Valle de Sula Honduras	2 Jul 1989	Solomon Jaar Welchez

Missions — 2
(As of Oct. 1, 1994; shown with historical number. See MISSIONS.)

(242) HONDURAS SAN PEDRO SULA MISSION
Apartado Postal 1970
San Pedro Sula, Honduras
Phone: (011-504) 53-4890

(177) HONDURAS TEGUCIGALPA MISSION
Apartado Postal 556
Tegucigalpa, Honduras
Phone: (011-504) 36-66-23

HONG KONG

Year-end 1993: Est. population, 5,800,000; Members, 18,000; Stakes, 4; Wards, 24; Branches, 8; Missions, 1; Temples, 1 under construction; Percent LDS, 0.3, or one LDS in 322.

At the mouth of the Canton River on the southern coast of mainland China, Hong Kong is a British Crown Colony acquired in 1841, which reverts to China in 1997. Its people speak Cantonese and English, and are mostly Buddhists and Taoists, although small groups of Christians, Hindus and Jews also live in Hong Kong.

In 1852, Hosea Stout, James Lewis and Chapman Duncan were called to teach the gospel to the Chinese. They arrived in Hong Kong April 27, 1853. They stayed only four months, finding access to the country impossible. They may have baptized one convert.

On a world tour, Elder David O. McKay visited China in 1921. However, because of internal problems in China, a mission was not opened in Hong Kong until 1949. Hilton A. Robertson was president of the new China Mission.

The first two missionaries, H. Grant Heaton and William K. Paalani, arrived Feb. 25, 1950, and later their ranks increased to eight. Three converts were baptized Dec. 31, 1950. Soon, an average of 30 people attended weekly meetings. Work in Hong Kong was interrupted by the Korean War and did not reopen until 1955, when Grant Heaton returned as mission president of the new Southern Far East Mission. Leaders emphasized language training and translation. By November of that year, two branches were opened. On April 26, 1956, 11 converts were baptized.

Four years later, there were 91 full-time foreign and 12 full-time local missionaries serving, with eight branches and a membership of about 1,700.

Membership grew to 3,000 over the next five years, but continuing emigration took a heavy toll on both membership and leadership. A district was established in 1965. That same year, the Book of Mormon was printed in Chinese, and work began to increase. The first meetinghouse was completed in 1966. In 1971, the Hong Kong Mission served exclusively in the area. Area conferences were held in 1975 and 1980. The Hong Kong Stake was organized April 25, 1976. The stake had a membership of 3,410. Membership remained at that number for about five years, but by 1986 had jumped to 12,200 members in four stakes.

On Oct. 3, 1992, President Gordon B. Hinckley, first counselor in the First Presidency, announced that a temple would be built in Hong Kong. Ground was broken for the temple on Jan. 22, 1994, by Elder John K. Carmack of the Seventy, Asia Area president. The site was the former mission home in Kowloon Tong on the Kowloon Peninsula.

Sources: *The Church Encounters Asia,* by Spencer J. Palmer, Deseret Book, 1970; Hong Kong, Pearl of the Orient, by Jay A. Parry, *Ensign,* August 1975; *Church News,* May 15, 1976; Culture for Missionaries, Taiwan, Hong Kong, Missionary Training Center, 1980; "Saints throng to area meetings in the Far East," by Dell Van Orden, *Church News,* Nov. 1, 1980; "Pearls of the Orient," by Kellene Ricks, *Ensign,* September 1991; *Church News,* Feb. 5, 1994.

Stakes — 5
(Listed alphabetically as of Oct. 1, 1994.)

No.	Name	Organized	First President
Asia Area			
756	*Hong Kong Island 29 May 1980		
	†Hong Kong	25 Apr 1976	Shiu-Tat Sheldon Poon
1141	*Hong Kong Kowloon 11 Nov 1984		
	†Kowloon Hong Kong	29 May 1980	Patrick Chung-hei Wong
1502	Hong Kong Kowloon North	11 Nov 1984	Fu Man Yau
1977	Hong Kong Kowloon West	20 Mar 1994	Poon Yin Sang Peter
1503	Hong Kong New Territories	11 Nov 1984	Johnson Ma

Mission — 1
(As of Oct. 1, 1994; shown with historical number. See MISSIONS.)

(44a) HONG KONG MISSION
#7 Castle Road
Central, Hong Kong
Hong Kong
Phone: (011-852) 857-1098

HUNGARY

Year-end 1993: Est. population, 10,300,000; Members: 1,400; Branches, 18; Missions, 1; Districts, 2; Percent LDS, 0.01, or one in 7,357; Europe Area.

In east central Europe, Hungary's population speaks Hungarian (Magyar), and is Roman Catholic, 67 percent; and Protestant, 25 percent.

The first missionary effort into Hungary was made by Elders Thomas Biesinger and Paul E.B. Hammer in Vienna, in what was then in the dual sovereignty of Austria-Hungary. Elder Biesinger labored in Prague, but was eventually banished from the country.

Mischa Markow, a native of Hungary who was converted near Constantinople in 1887, preached the gospel in Belgium, Hungary, Romania, Bulgaria, Germany, Turkey, Russia and Serbia, which later became part of Yugoslavia. He visited Hungary the year of his baptism to preach to his parents, but they were not converted. He immigrated to America, and returned as a missionary in about May 1899 and preached in Serbia until banished to Hungary three months later. In about July 1899, he was banished from Hungary after being imprisoned in solitary confinement. He went to Temesvar, Hungary, Sept. 3, 1900. He and his companion, Elder Hyrum Lau, were soon ordered to surrender their passports. In the few days afterward, while they could legally remain in the country, they worked feverishly, and the day before they were banished they baptized 12 people and ordained leaders to watch over a branch of 31 people.

Missionaries worked among German-speaking Hungarians in 1908, and the Church received legal recognition in 1911. However, missionary work among Hungarian-speaking people was not successful, and the area was closed by March 10, 1913.

The Book of Mormon was translated into Hungarian in 1933, but selections were not published until 1979.

In modern times, the Church received legal recognition from Hungary on June 24, 1988. A fireside on that day was attended by Elder Russell M. Nelson of the Council of the Twelve, as well as a congregation of 85 people. Two converts were baptized the next day. The first meetinghouse in Hungary was dedicated Oct. 17, 1989, by President Thomas S. Monson, second counselor in the First Presidency.

Yuri and Ludmilla Terebenin and their daughter Anna of Leningrad, then in the Soviet Union, heard about the Church during a trip to Budapest, Hungary, where they were baptized on July 1, 1989. They were were among the first converts in Russia. One of Lithuania's first converts, Irute Meskiene of Vilnius, also heard the gospel preached in Szeged, Hungary, and she was baptized in Hungary.

The Hungary Budapest Mission was created from the Austria Vienna East Mission on June 1, 1990. At the time there were some 75 members in one district. The Tabernacle Choir performed in Budapest in 1991 to an enthusiastic audience.

In 1992, the Hungary-based Democracy After Communism Foundation helped sponsor a major international consultation on religious liberty and ethnic rights for eastern European nations May 17-20, which was attended by Elder Dallin H. Oaks of the Council of the Twelve.

Sources: *Millennial Star,* March 13, 1913; "Hungary — Then and Now," by Kahlile Mehr, *Ensign,* June 1990; German and Swiss mission manuscript histories; *Church News,* May 30, 1992, June 27, 1992.

Mission — 1
(As of Oct. 1, 1994; shown with historical number. See MISSIONS.)

(243) HUNGARY BUDAPEST MISSION
H-1029 II Ker.
Kinizsi Pal Utca 37
Budapest, Hungary
Phone: (011-36-1) 176-5174

ICELAND

Year-end 1993: Est. population, 300,000; Members, 200; Branches, 3; Districts, 1; Percent LDS, 0.10, or one person in 999; Europe North Area; Denmark Copenhagen Mission.

Located between Scandinavia and Greenland, the constitutional Republic of Iceland has a people who speak Icelandic and who are 95 percent Evangelical Lutheran.

Converted in Denmark while learning trades, Thorarinn Thorason and Gudmund Gudmundson of Iceland were baptized in 1851. They returned to Iceland that year and began preaching on Westmann Island. A number believed, and Benedikt Hanson and his wife were among the first baptized by Thorason. Unfortunately, Thorason drowned a short time later and Gudmundson, who had been ordained a teacher, was not authorized to baptize. He continued his work, but not until 1853 did other missionaries receive permission to enter and assist him. Missionaries and members endured severe persecution. Johan P. Lorentzen arrived and ordained Gudmundson an elder, baptized several more converts and organized a branch June 19, 1853. Soon after, nearly all the members immigrated to America.

In 1873, Elders Magnus Bjarnason and Loptur Johnson of the Scandinavian Mission returned to Westmann Island and baptized a few more converts and re-organized a branch. In 1874, 11 converts immigrated to America. Missionary work continued in 1875 with the return of Samuel Bjarnason and Thordar Dedikson. In 1879, a pamphlet was translated, printed in Denmark, and distributed in Iceland. Small emigrating companies left Iceland throughout the early 1880s. Many of the Icelandic members settled in Spanish Fork, Utah. An Icelandic Mission was organized for a short time, from about 1894 until after 1900. Proselyting in Iceland was discontinued in 1914.

Missionary work, under the direction of the Denmark Copenhagen Mission, resumed in Iceland in 1975, building on the efforts of LDS servicemen who had been stationed in Iceland. A branch was organized on a military base at Keflavik with 130 servicemen and their families. Byron and Melva Geslison, with their twin sons, returned missionaries David and Daniel, were called from Utah to re-open the work. In two years, some 40 Icelanders were baptized and a branch was organized at Reykjavik Aug. 8, 1976, with about 10 members. A year later, it had grown to 40 members. A meetinghouse was dedicated in 1981 by Elder David B. Haight of the Council of the Twelve.

Missionary work has proceeded slowly. The Book of Mormon was translated into Icelandic in 1980, and the other standard works followed. By 1986, membership had reached 180.

Sources: *Encyclopedic History of the Church* by Andrew Jenson; Denmark Mission manuscript history, "Fire and Ice," by Flint J. Stephens, *The New Era,* December 1981; correspondence from D.B. Timmins; "Gospel touches remote Iceland," by Tod Harris, *Church News,* Aug. 6, 1994.

INDIA

Year-end 1993: Est. population, 904,000,000; Members, 1,300; Missions, 1; Districts, 4; Branches, 14; Asia Area.

Occupying the Indian subcontinent in south Asia, India is a federal republic with a population that speaks 16 languages including the official Hindi and associate official English, and is Hindu, 83 percent; Moslem, 11 percent; Christian, 3 percent; and Sikh, 2 percent.

Church members Benjamin Richey and George Barber, British sailors converted in 1849, visited Calcutta, India, in 1850 and shared their testimonies. They were followed in 1851 by Elder Joseph Richards, who also preached in Calcutta. He baptized James Patrick Meik, Mary Ann Meik, Matthew McCune and Maurice White, and set them apart as missionaries. Soon after, White was appointed to preside over the branch, and he baptized Anna, a native. The little branch was depleted by emigration, but additional missionaries arrived and baptized a few more people, and a small meetinghouse was built.

In 1853, additional missionaries took the gospel message to Madras, Bombay, Rangoon, Karatchi, Poona and other areas, and several small branches were established.

However, when these missionaries returned to Utah in 1858, some of the converts also emigrated. Although other missionaries and conversions followed, the India Mission was not considered a successful one. At least one branch existed through 1903. Missionaries were not successful in learning the Hundustani, Tamil, Telugu or other native languages.

In 1954, S. Paul Thiruthuvadoss, an accountant for a cement company in Coimbatore in southern India, found an LDS tract, and through it found the Church. He was not baptized until Feb. 7, 1965, when missionaries from the Southern Far East Mission visited. His baptism was performed by mission Pres. Jay A. Quealy Jr., grandson of early India convert Matthew McCune.

Thiruthuvadoss held schools for underprivileged children, and shared the message of the gospel with many people. In 1967, Pres. G. Garlos Smith of the Singapore Mission visited and baptized 24 of the people prepared by Thiruthuvadoss. Converts have been added to the branch constantly since that time. As of 1980, the Coimbatore branch had 225 members and regular services are conducted in Tamil.

In Delhi, northern India, Baldwin Das was baptized by Charles Redford in 1968, and was joined by the Roshan Juriel family. In 1972, Maureen Das was the first to serve a mission from India. In 1981, government regulations allowed a missionary couple, Horace and Edna Hayes, to establish a branch. A visit by the BYU Young Ambassadors in 1983, and the arrival of LDS families involved in diplomatic service strengthened the branch. Later, the branch was divided for Indian and American members. By 1987, a congregation of 50 met in the Indian branch with all the auxiliaries functioning.

In 1977, Edwin and Elsie Dharmaraju of Hyderabad, India, living in Samoa, were converted to the Church. They received permission to return to India and teach the gospel to their family. They arrived in December 1978, and on Dec. 27, 18 members of their family were baptized. A branch was organized with Victor David as president. In 1981, the Dharmarajus delivered a 700-page manuscript to the Church, the Book of Mormon translated into Telegu by her father, the Rev. P. Sreenivasam.

This translation of the Book of Mormon was printed in 1982, as was another full translation in Hindi, and translated selections of the Book of Mormon in Tamil. In the 1980s, the Church microfilmed genealogical records in India. In December 1992, Elaine L. Jack, Relief Society general president, visited branches in Bangalore and reported that members met in homes three times a month and at a rented building on the fourth Sunday.

The India Bangalore Mission was created Jan. 1, 1993, with Gucharan Singh Gill as president. About 30 missionaries from India and other countries serve in the mission, including couples and elders. At that time, in January 1993, India had 1,150 members and 13 branches.

Sources: *Encyclopedic History of the Church,* by Andrew Jenson; Church History in North India, report by Baldwin Das and Douglas Rose, August 1987; Testimony of S. Paul Thiruthuvadoss; *The Church in Asia,* by J. Spencer Palmer, Deseret Book, 1970; "India fills genealogy link," by William B. Smart, *Church News,* Jan. 9, 1988; *Church News,* Dec. 19, 1992; "Asia Area: Welcome mat is out in several countries," by Sheridan R. Sheffield, *Church News,* June 19, 1993.

(277) INDIA BANGALORE MISSION
780, 8th Cross, 11th Main
Indira Nagar, 2nd Stage
Bangalore 560 038
India
Phone: (011-91-80) 559-3823

INDONESIA

Year-end 1993: Est. population, 189,000,000; Members, 4,600; Branches, 18; Districts, 3; Asia Area; Singapore Mission.

An archipelago of more than 13,500 islands, including Java, one of the world's most densely populated areas, Indonesia is a republic whose population speaks Bahasa Indonesian (the official language), Javanese and up to 100 other Austronesian languages.

Six missionaries entered Indonesia on Jan. 5, 1970, and began work on Jan. 20. The Jakarta Branch was organized Feb. 15, 1970, and first converts were baptized March 29, 1970. Door-to-door tracting was halted by the government in April 1970, but it resumed in May after the Church was granted clearance on April 20. The Church was officially recognized Aug. 11, 1970.

During the next few years, branches were organized throughout Java, where the work was performed. The Indonesia Jakarta Mission was organized July 1, 1975. By 1977, when the Book of Mormon was published in Indonesian, membership reached 1,200 and local missionaries carried on the work.

However, difficulties with missionary visas and government limitations continued to restrict missionaries. Indonesia's difficult internal religious conflicts and activities by others against missionary work made progress difficult.

On Aug. 1, 1978, the government issued restrictions on proselyting.

The mission was discontinued Jan. 1, 1981. In 1982, some 30 local missionaries maintained efforts and were finding success. An Indonesian, Effian Kadarusman, was called as mission president and the mission was reopened July 1, 1985. He served through 1988. A new mission home was dedicated July 24, 1988, but all foreign missionaries were restricted from the country on Nov. 26, 1988, and the Indonesia Mission was consolidated with Singapore Mission on July 1, 1989.

In 1993, Dr. Dean and Sister Elan Belnap entered Indonesia to work with the medical school in Jakarta, and help with the local branches. Their service helped raise the Church's profile.

Highly illustrated cloth batiks created by Indonesian members regularly contributed to art displays at the Museum of Church History and Art in the 1990s.

Sources: *Spreading the Gospel in Indonesia: Organizational Obstacles and Opportunities,* a university paper by Garth N. Jones, Winter 1982; *Church News*, Aug. 3, 1991; "Asia Area: Welcome mat is out in several countries," by Sheridan R. Sheffield, *Church News*, June 19, 1993; *Church News,* June 19, 1993.

IRELAND

Year-end 1993: Est. population, 3,600,000; Members, 2,200; Branches, 12; Missions, 1; Districts, 2; Percent LDS, 0.06, or one LDS in 1,636; Europe North Area.

The island of Ireland lies in the Atlantic Ocean, west of Great Britain. It is a parliamentary republic where English is the dominant language, but Irish (Gaelic) is also spoken. The population is Roman Catholic, 95 percent, and Anglican, 3 percent.

The first missionary to Ireland was Reuben Hedlock, who arrived in Belfast in May 1840, but stayed only three days before sailing to Paisley. He was followed on July 28 by Apostle John Taylor, who was accompanied by James McGuffie and William Black, a native Irishman. A non-member Irishman, Thomas Tait (or Tate), also accompanied them. More than 600 people heard Elder Taylor preach that evening in Newry. On July 31, as the party walked between towns and arrived at a lake called Loughbrickland, Tait was baptized, becoming Ireland's first convert.

Two months later, Elder Theodore Curtis arrived in Ireland and established a branch of 35 in Hillsborough. A second branch, organized in Crawfordsburn, had 22 members by July 21, 1841.

In 1842, many of the 71 members in Ireland emigrated. Membership declined over the next years, despite renewed efforts in 1843. The 1845-47 famine prompted the emigration of most of the remaining 51 members.

Early missionaries remarked that proselyting was slowed by opposition, particularly that of landholders who threatened sharecroppers with expulsion if they welcomed LDS missionaries. However, historians believe that a good number of the British converts during the 1840s and '50s were expatriated Irish.

In the early 1850s, missionaries established a few branches, but in 1853 most missionaries left for America. Another group arrived in 1854, found new converts and saw membership increase from some 20 to 210 in 1855, and to nearly 300 in 1856. However, the 1857 "Utah War" led to the recall of the missionaries and the branches were unsupervised for four years. Missionary work was discontinued in 1867.

In 1884, a few native Irish members were called as missionaries in their homeland. They found some success despite opposition and established a branch in Belfast that by the end of 1884 had 50 members. Political unrest prompted most of the converts to emigrate. By 1900, about 90 had left Ireland for Utah.

However, a branch grew up in Dublin after 1900, made up of Germans. By 1920, there were about 225 members in the Belfast Conference (District) and 60 in and around Dublin.

The Emerald Isle was divided in 1949, amid continued unrest, into an independent Ireland and Northern Ireland, which remained under the British government.

As part of the 150th anniversary of the Church in the British Isles in 1987, markers were dedicated at the site of the first baptism and at the birthplace in Dublin of Elder Charles A. Callis of the Council of the Twelve, a former missionary in Ireland. Membership in 1990 was 1,800.

Indicative of the strength of the Church, Pres. Van F. Dunn noted in 1994 that seven missionaries from Ireland were serving at the same time in the England London South Mission.

Sources: *Encyclopedic History of the Church* by Andrew Jenson; "Emerald Isle Hosts Beauty, Friendliness," by Gerry Avant, *Church News*, Feb. 25, 1978; "The Saints in Ireland," by Orson Scott Card, *Ensign*, February 1978; *Church News*, July 6, 1974, Dec. 1, 1985; "Markers tell where history was made," by Dell Van Orden and Gerry Avant, *Church News*, Aug. 1, 1987, and *Church News*, Aug. 8, 1987; *Church News*, Aug. 27, 1994.

Mission — 1
(As of Oct. 1, 1994 shown with historical number. See MISSIONS.)

(70) IRELAND DUBLIN MISSION
The Willows, Finglas Road
Glasnevin, Dublin 11, Ireland
Phone: (011-353-18) 306899

ITALY

Year-end 1993: Est. population, 57,800,000; Members, 16,000; Stakes, 2; Wards, 10; Branches, 93; Missions, 4; Districts, 10; Percent LDS, 0.03, or one person in 3,612.

In southern Europe jutting into the Mediterranean Sea, the boot-shaped Republic of Italy has a population that speaks Italian, and is nearly all Roman Catholic.

The first missionaries in Italy were Elders Lorenzo Snow of the Council of the Twelve, Joseph Toronto and Thomas B.H. Stenhouse. They arrived in Genoa, Italy, on June 25, 1850. They traveled to the Piedmont Valley to work among a group of Protestants of French origin called the Waldenses. They were joined there by Elder Jabez Woodard.

On Oct. 27, 1850, Elder Snow baptized Jean Antoine Box at La Tour. Other baptisms followed and three branches of the Church were organized in Angrogne, St. Germain and St. Bartholomew, all in Piedmont. Tracts were published in the French language for the Waldenses. The Book of Mormon was published in 1852. By 1855, 50 members had immigrated to America and membership was 64.

Proselyting outside the Piedmont Valley was very difficult, due to a great deal of anti-Mormon activity. Missionaries labored with little success in Italy, departing for Switzerland in 1857. Elder Daniel B. Hill Richards tried to re-open the work in 1900, but was refused legal permission.

In 1965, the Church was given legal status and missionary work resumed. The first modern convert of Italy was Leopoldo Larcher, who later served as the first Italian mission president and as regional representative. On Aug. 2, 1966, the Italian Mission was re-established.

By that time, there were two Italian branches and seven combined servicemen and Italian branches, and a membership of 66. By 1978, membership had increased to 7,271, and the nation had four missions. Italy's first stake was created June 7, 1981, in Milan, under the direction of Pres. Mario Vaira.

Local missionaries and leaders contributed to increased growth in the 1980s. By mid-1985, membership increased to 12,000. Membership in 1990 was 14,000.

A milestone was reached May 12, 1993, when Italy formally granted legal status to the Church for the first time. The application to have the Italian government officially recognize the Church was filed four to five years earlier, underwent several reviews and an investigation, and was signed by Italy's president, Oscar Luigi Scalfaro, on Feb. 22, 1993. Italy law does not require legal status for proselyting.

On Dec. 19, 1993, a group of 50 missionaries was invited to sing on Vatican Radio from St. Peter's Basilica at the Vatican.

Sources: *Millennial Star,* Dec. 15, 1850; *Encyclopedic History of the Church,* by Andrew Jenson; *The Scriptural Allegory,* by Dr. Daniel B. Richards, Magazine Publishing Company, Salt Lake City, Utah, April 1931; *History of the French Mission of the Church, 1850-1960,* by Gary Ray Chard, master's thesis at Utah State University, 1965; *Church News,* June 12, 1993; *Church News,* Jan. 15, 1994.

Stakes — 2
(Listed alphabetically as of Oct. 1, 1994)

No.	Name	Organized	First President
Europe Mediterranean Area			
1274	Milan Italy	7 Jun 1981	Mario Vaira
1556	Venice Italy	15 Sep 1985	Claudio E. Luttmann

Missions — 4
(As of Oct. 1, 1994 shown with historical number. See MISSIONS.)

(158) ITALY CATANIA MISSION
Via Corsaro 84 (Parco Inglese)
95030 S. Agata Li Battiati (Ct.), Italy
Phone: (011-39-95) 411009

(244) ITALY PADOVA MISSION
Via Caldonazzo #10
35030 Selvazzano Dentro (PD), Italy
Phone: (011-39-49) 805-5629

(98) ITALY MILAN MISSION
Via Pavoni, 1/3
20052 Monza (MI), Italy
Phone: (011-39-39) 230-1019

(7) ITALY ROME MISSION
C.P. 11/282
I-00141 Rome, Italy
Phone: (011-39-6) 827-2708

IVORY COAST

Year-end 1993: Est. population, 11,526,000; Members, 1,500; Missions, 1; Districts, 2; Branches, 12; Africa Area.

Located on the Gulf of Guinea on the west coast of Africa next to Ghana, Ivory Coast has a population that speaks tribal languages and French, and belong to tribal religions and Islam.

Isolated LDS families lived in Ivory Coast in the 1970s and earlier, including Bernar and Cherry Silver and Terry and Bobby Broadhead.

Lucien Yapi Affoue and his wife, Agathe, joined the Church in 1980 in Lyon, France, where he was a student. They were sealed in the Swiss Temple and served in the Bordeaux Branch. They returned to Abidjan on March 1984, and eventually helped establish four branches. They were joined by Philippe Assard and his wife, Anelise Noetzel Assard, and their two children in 1986. There were 16 members in the country in 1987.

In 1988, the Church donated $60,000 to Rotary International for polio vaccinations of children in Ivory Coast.

The Affoue family moved to Bouake, where another branch was established on Oct. 4, 1988. The Abidjan Branch was created on June 1, 1989.

The first missionaries to Ivory Coast were Elder Barnard Stewart Silver and his wife, Cherry, who arrived in April 1988. Elder Robert M. and Sister Lola Walker arrived in April 1989, and introduced the gospel to some 100 members. A U.S. expatriate, Douglas Arnold, was called as the first district president in October 1989.

The first district conference was held March 10-11, 1990, in Abidjan with about 200 people from the branches of Abidjan and Boauke. At the time, local records indicated a membership of 350. Two missionary couples from the Ghana Accra Mission continued baptizing about 30-35 a month. The Plateau Dokui Branch, Ivory Coast's fourth, was organized at the conference. At the time, 35 men held the Melchizedek Priesthood.

The Church received legal recognition on April 19, 1991.

Eighteen local elders were called to serve in the mission in December 1991. In June 30, 1992, Ivory Coast was transferred from the Ghana Accra Mission to the Cameroon Yaounde Mission. Mission Pres.

Robert L. Mercer moved the Cameroon Yaounde Mission headquarters to Ivory Coast and this became the Ivory Coast Abidjan Mission on May 1993.

The mission concentrated its resources in the Abidjan area to establish a center of the Church here for French-speaking Africa.

In 1993, Mayor Alan Dawson of Midrand, South Africa, a Church member, initiated a sister city partnership with Yamoussoukro, Ivory Coast.

Sources: "When a Woman Is Alone," by Cherry Silver, *Ensign*, June 1978; *Church News*, Oct. 17, 1987, June 25, 1988, June 10, 1989, April 28, 1990; Correspondence from Chirley Roundy Arnold, April 19-23, 1991; *Church News*, Dec. 4, 1993; correspondence from the Ivory Coast Abidjan Mission, March 1994.

Mission — 1

(271) IVORY COAST ABIDJAN MISSION
06BP1077
Abidjan 06, Ivory Coast
Phone: 011-225 412933

JAMAICA

Year-end 1993: Est. population, 2,243,000; Members, 3,000; Districts, 2; Branches, 14; Missions, 1; Percent LDS, 0.1, or one LDS in 747; North America Southeast Area.

Located in the West Indies, south of Cuba, Jamaica is an independent state where English and Jamaican Creole are spoken, and 70 percent of the people are Protestants.

The first LDS elder on Jamaica was Harrison Sager, who preached here briefly in 1841. Twelve years later, Elders James Brown, Aaron F. Farr, Alfred B. Lambson, Darwin Richardson and Elijah Thomas returned to preach, but found a great deal of antagonism and stayed only six weeks.

In modern times, two LDS families, the John L. Whitfields and Jay P. Bills families, began holding meetings in Mandeville, and the Mandeville Branch was created March 22, 1970. One of the first converts was Victor Nugent and his family, baptized Jan. 20, 1974. As new converts, the Nugents remained faithful when the branch's priesthood leaders moved away. They introduced the gospel to soccer star Errol Tucker and his family, who helped them maintain the branch. Full-time missionaries began work again in Jamaica in November 1978, under the direction of Pres. Richard L. Millett of the Florida Ft. Lauderdale Mission. By 1983, membership had increased to 300, and by 1985, to 520.

The first Jamaican branch president was Joseph Hamilton. Vaughn and Mary Soffe microfilmed the statistical records of Jamaica in 1982. Seminary began in Jamaica in the mid-1980s and by 1989, 141 students were taking seminary. Membership in 1990 was 1,900.

Sources: *Millennial Star*, April 2, 1853; *Encyclopedic History of the Church*, by Andrew Jenson; "A Trusted Friend," by Ronald W. Walker, *Church News*, March 17, 1979; Kenneth and LeOra Zabriskie journals; "Jamaicans nurture new gospel tradition," by Wanda Kenton Smith, *Church News*, Jan. 29, 1984; *Church News*, Aug. 28, 1976; Nov. 29, 1980, April 22, 1984, Nov. 24, 1985, May 27, 1989.

CAYMAN ISLANDS

In September 1985, missionaries from the West Indies Mission opened work in the Grand Cayman Islands, located in the Caribbean Sea some 400 miles south of Florida. One branch with fewer than 100 members is organized here. It was created on Nov. 25, 1981.

Mission — 1
(As of Oct. 1, 1994; shown with historical number. See MISSIONS.)

JAMAICA KINGSTON MISSION
Box 2316
Kingston 8, Jamaica, West Indies
Phone: (809) 924-0116

JAPAN

Year-end 1993: Est. population, 124,450,000; Members, 103,000; Stakes, 25; Wards, 132; Branches, 157; Missions, 10; Districts, 21; Temples, 1; Percent LDS, 0.1, or one person in 1,208.

Off the eastern coast of Asia, Japan is a parliamentary democracy with people who are primarily Buddhists and Shintoists.

The history of the Church in Japan dates back to the turn of the century when Elder Heber J. Grant of the

Council of the Twelve, and missionaries Horace S. Ensign, Louis A. Kelsch and Alma O. Taylor arrived in the country Aug. 12, 1901.

Under Elder Grant's direction, the first Church mission was established in Asia with headquarters in Tokyo. The first baptism came March 8, 1902, when Elder Grant baptized Hijime Nakazawa, a former Shinto priest, in Tokyo Bay. A second baptism came on March 10, 1902, when Saburo Kikuchi was baptized.

Elder Taylor began translating the Book of Mormon into Japanese in 1904, and continued that work for 5½ years, while he served as president of the Japanese Mission. The book was printed in October 1909.

Missionary work came to a halt in 1924 when President Heber J. Grant, then president of the Church, closed the mission to await a more "favorable time," which came following World War II. Fujiya Nara was one of the converts who saw the missionaries off, later being appointed a presiding elder over the small group that remained. He visited them and published a newsletter, Shuro (Palm). In 1926 the MIA was organized. The Japan Mission was re-opened in 1937 with headquarters in Honolulu, Hawaii. Hilton Robertson was named president. Then in 1947, Edward L. Clissold was called to preside over the Japan Mission and in 1948 was given permission to return to Japan to do missionary work. He found a group of about 50 meeting with Brother Nara each Sunday. The first five missionaries arrived in June that year.

During the time the mission was closed, LDS servicemen had prepared the way for proselyting by baptizing Tatsui Sato on July 7, 1946. His wife, Chiyo, and son, Yasuo, were also baptized. One serviceman, Boyd K. Packer, later of the Council of the Twelve, baptized Sister Sato. This was the first baptism of local members in Japan in more than 20 years and was the beginning of a new era for the Church in the Far East.

Sato re-translated the Book of Mormon, the Doctrine and Covenants, the Pearl of Great Price, and other important works. Work went forward, and the Japanese Mission was divided in July 1955 to form the Northern Far East Mission and the Southern Far East missions.

The first Mormon meetinghouse in Asia, housing the Tokyo North Branch, was dedicated by Elder Gordon B. Hinckley, then of the Council of the Twelve, on April 26, 1964.

Adney Y. Komatsu was called as mission president in 1965, the first mission president of Japanese ancestry. Ten years later, in April 1975, he was called to be a General Authority, also the first of Japanese ancestry. The first General Authority from Japan was Elder Yoshihiko Kikichi, who was called to the First Quorum of the Seventy in 1977.

The first stake of the Church in Asia, the Tokyo Stake, was organized on March 15, 1970, with Kenji Tanaka as president.

The Japan Nagoya Mission was formed from the Japan Mission and the Japan Central Mission in 1973.

Building of the Tokyo Temple was announced in August 1975 and dedicated on Oct. 27, 1980. Since that time, 11 stakes have been created, and progress has continued on that island. The Japan Okinawa Mission was created in 1985. In 1991, the Asia North Area was created and the area offices were established in Tokyo.

Sources: *Encyclopedic History of the Church,* by Andrew Jenson; *A History of the Church in Japan from 1948 to 1980,* by Terry G. Nelson, a BYU thesis August 1986; "Kyoto, the cultural center of Japan," by Sheridan Sheffield, *Church News,* June 22, 1991; "Growth reflected in Asia areas," by Sheridan Sheffield, *Church News,* Nov. 16, 1991; "The Blossoming of the Church in Japan," by R. Lanier Britsch, *Ensign,* October, 1992; "Fujiya Nara, Twice a Pioneer," by Yukikon Konn, *Ensign,* April 1993.

Stakes — 25
(Listed alphabetically as of Oct. 1, 1994.)

No.	Name	Organized	First President
Asia North Area			
1901	Abiko Japan	13 Sep 1992	Shigejiro Akamatsu
1018	Fukuoka Japan	20 Apr 1979	Yoshizawa Toshiro
1271	Hiroshima Japan	31 May 1981	Satoshi Nishihara
1120	Kobe Japan	19 Mar 1980	Keiichi Mizuno
1874	*Kyoto Japan 25 Apr 1993		
	†Kyoto Japan North	31 May 1992	Kaatsuichiro Fukuyama
1197	Machida Japan	26 Oct 1980	Koichi Aoyagi
919	Nagoya Japan	10 May 1978	Masaru Tsuchida
1203	Nagoya Japan West	2 Nov 1980	Take Shi Nakamura
1195	Naha Okinawa Japan	23 Oct 1980	Kensei Nagamine
1404	Okayama Japan	20 Mar 1983	Akira Watanabe
586	*Osaka Japan		
	†Osaka (Japan)	12 Sep 1972	Noboru Kamio

1873	Osaka Japan East	31 May 1992	Ryochi Tanaka
872	Osaka Japan North	30 Oct 1977	Noboru Kamio
1328	Osaka Japan Sakai	17 Mar 1982	Hiroshi Takayoshi
949	Sapporo Japan	13 Aug 1978	Geiji Katanuma
1154	Sapporo Japan West	29 Jun 1980	Bin Kikuchi
1202	Sendai Japan	2 Nov 1980	Shigenori Funayama
1255	Shizuoka Japan	21 Apr 1981	Tadachika Seno
1164	Takasaki Japan	10 Aug 1980	Masataka Kitamura
505	*Tokyo Japan		
	†Tokyo	15 Mar 1970	Kenji Tanaka
1121	Tokyo Japan East	23 Mar 1980	Ryotaro Kanzaki
869	Tokyo Japan North	23 Oct 1977	Ryo Okamoto
1270	Tokyo Japan South	30 May 1981	Kazutoshi Ono
1329	Tokyo Japan West	21 Mar 1982	Koichi Aoyagi
662	Yokohama Japan	27 Oct 1974	Hitoshi Kashikura

Discontinued

1875	Kyoto Japan South	31 May 1992	Kenichiro Kimura
	25 Apr 1993		
1257	Takamatsu Japan	23 Apr 1981	Takejiro Kanzaki
	2 June 1991		

Missions — 10
(As of Oct. 1, 1994; shown with historical number. See MISSIONS.)

(91) JAPAN FUKUOKA MISSION
46 Josui-machi, Hirao, Chuo-ku
Fukuoka, 810
Japan
Phone: (011-81-92) 522-0386

(83) JAPAN KOBE MISSION
6-28 4-Chome, Shinohara Honmachi
Nada Ku, Kobe, T 657
Japan
Phone: (011-81-78) 881-2712

(108) JAPAN NAGOYA MISSION
1-304 Itakadai
Meito-ku Nagoya-shi T 465, Japan
Phone: (011-81-52) 773-0755

(144) JAPAN OKAYAMA MISSION
87-4 Kokufuichiba
Okayama-Shi, Okayama-Ken 703, Japan
Phone: (011-81-862) 75-4833

(245) JAPAN OKINAWA MISSION
Ginowan-shi, Nodake 3-4-9
Okinawa 901-22, Japan
Phone: (011-81-98) 893-6955

(185) JAPAN OSAKA MISSION
Osaka Fu, Hirakata Shi
Asahigaoka-Cho 15-12, T 573
Japan
Phone: (011-81-720) 46-5551

(90) JAPAN SAPPORO MISSION
Sapporo-Shi Chuo-ku
Kita 2 Jo Nishi 24 Chome 1-25
064, Japan
Phone: (011-81-11) 643-6411

(109a) JAPAN SENDAI MISSION
Yagiyama Minami 3 Chome 1-5
Taihaku-Ku Sendai-Shi 982 Japan
Phone: (011-81-222) 45-8851

(82a) JAPAN TOKYO NORTH MISSION
4-25-12 Nishi Ochiai
Shinjuku-ku, Tokyo 161, Japan
Phone: (011-81-33) 952-6802

(162) JAPAN TOKYO SOUTH MISSION
1-7-7 Kichijoji-Higashi Machi
Musashino-shi, Tokyo T 180, Japan
Phone: (011-81-422) 21 2619

KENYA

Year-end 1993: Est. population, 28,000,000; Members, 1,400; Missions, 1; Districts, 2; Branches, 11; Africa Area.

American USAID employees and their families serving in Kenya in the 1970s held Church services in their own homes. The first African converts in Kenya were baptized Oct. 21, 1979, Elizaphan Osaka and his wife, Ebisiba, and their two oldest children, Margaret and Jairo. Brother Osaka, a former minister, was ordained a priest the same day.

The first missionaries were Elder Farrell and Sister Blanch McGhie of Palo Alto, Calif., who arrived Sept. 6, 1980. They realized considerable success.

The Kenya District, with two branches in Nairobi and Kiboko, was created May 10, 1981. The first Kenyan called as a full-time missionary was Benson Kasue, who served in the Los Angeles, Calif., area from 1983-85.

In 1988, the Church donated funds that were collected on special fasts to bring water to 15 Kenyan villages, located 100 miles from Nairobi. The water systems were installed by 1989. The first branch was organized in Nairobi March 15, 1989.

The Church received official recognition in Kenya in Feb. 25, 1991, following a visit to Kenya by Judge Clifford Wallace of San Diego, Calif., a member who made the request to proper authorities. The Kenya Nairobi Mission, which includes Kenya, Uganda, and Tanzania, was created in July 1991. In February 1992, more than 200 members and investigators from five branches attended a district conference in Nairobi, in the Parklands Branch meetinghouse. The meeting was conducted by district Pres. Joseph Sitati. Pres. Sitati, a convert since 1985, and his wife, Gladys, and their children were the first Kenyans to go through the temple. More than 30 missionaries served during the first year of the mission.

In 1992, the Church provided food staples to Somalian and Kenyan refugees affected by severe drought conditions. On Oct. 21, 1992, a six-acre plot of Church land was planted under the direction of LDS agronomist Joel K. Ransom, and the self-help project expanded later to members' own property and saw vital crops harvested.

By 1994, four districts had been created and large congregations attended many of the meetings. The first meetinghouse was completed in July 1994 for the Langata Branch in Nairobi.

Sources: *Church News,* March 18, 1989, March 23, 1991, April 25, 1992, Sept. 26, 1992 and Nov. 21, 1992; Journals and correspondence of Kirk P. Lovenbury, 10 June 1993; correspondence from Pres. Larry K. Brown, Kenya Nairobi Mission, April 12, 1994.

Mission — 1
(As of Oct. 1, 1994; shown with historical number. See MISSIONS.)

(265) KENYA NAIROBI MISSION
P.O. Box 39634
Nairobi, Kenya
Phone: (011-254-2) 740-444

KIRIBATI

Year-end 1993: Est. population, 70,000; Members, 4,600; Districts, 1; Branches, 17; Percent LDS, 6.5, or one LDS in 15; Pacific Area; Fiji Suva Mission.

Made up of 36 Micronesian islands in the mid-Pacific where the equator and international dateline meet, Kiribati is a republic that became independent in 1979. The islands' population speaks Gilbertese and English. About half of the population is Protestant and half, Roman Catholic.

The Church was introduced to Kiribati when Waitea Abiuta, a school teacher and headmaster of a school, asked to have graduates from his school attend Liahona High School in Tonga. Fijian mission Pres. Eb L. Davis visited Kiribati in September 1972, and approved 12 students to come to the Church school. Students were converted at the high school and began serving as missionaries in Kiribati on Oct. 19, 1975.

Among those who joined the Church were Waitea Abuita and several of the staff and students of the school. However, when opposition to the Church rose, enrollment at the school declined. In August 1976, Grant and Pat Howlett, LDS educators at Liahona High, were called to teach at the Kiribati school. Through their efforts, enrollment increased and government relations improved. Later, the Church took over the school and renamed it Moroni Community School, and other teachers arrived from Tonga as enrollment continued to increase. In 1984, the student body reached 240, and has remained at that number.

In 1982, a new meetinghouse was completed, and Buren Ratieta, Gilbertese branch president, held services in February of that year. Among the 250 who attended the dedicatory services was the president of the Kiribati Republic, Ieremia T. Tabai. He said government leaders at first feared the Church would divide the people, but when he saw the great social contribution the Church made, he became happy to cooperate with the Church.

Since that time, missionary work has expanded to more distant islands in Kiribati. Selections of the Book of Mormon were translated into Gilbertese in 1988.

In the fall of 1993, a group of first-time basketball players from Moroni High School, the age of U.S. high school sophomores and juniors, won the championship of Kiribati in their division. They also defeated the 20-30-year-olds division champions. Membership in 1990 was 2,300.

In 1994, Teatao Teanaki, president of the Republic, was the main speaker at the graduation ceremony at Moroni High School.

Sources: *Unto the Isles of the Sea,* by R. Lanier Britsch; interviews with various missionaries; *Church News,* Oct. 23, 1993; *Church News,* Feb. 5, 1994.

KOREA

Year-end 1993: Est. population, 44,619,000; Members, 65,000; Stakes, 16; Wards, 88; Branches, 70; Missions, 4; Districts, 4; Temples, 1; Percent LDS, 0.15, or one LDS in 686.

In northern east Asia, the Republic of Korea, or South Korea, has a population that speaks Korean, and principally follows Buddhism, Confucianism and Christianity.

LDS servicemen performed the first missionary work during the Korean War in 1951. Among the first Korean members was Ho Jik Kim, converted while earning a doctorate in the United States. Kim became an influential leader in the Korean government and paved the way for missionaries to enter Korea. His children, Tai Whan and Young Sook, were among the first four baptized on Aug. 3, 1952. His unfortunate death following a stroke in 1959 ended an impressive period of Church service.

The first missionaries, Elders Richard L. Detton and Don G. Powell, arrived in Korea in 1954. At that time, membership in Korea was 64. The missionaries learned to speak Korean and taught many young students.

The Korean Mission was created on July 8, 1962, with Gail C. Carr, one of the early missionaries to Korea, as president. The new mission had seven branches, in Seoul, Pusan and Taegu. By 1964, membership had reached 1,800. The Book of Mormon was printed in Korean in 1967. By 1968, significant increases in membership began to develop. From 1974 to 1977, a girls choir in an orphanage operated by LDS member Whang Keun-Ok was promoted on national media, increasing the percent of those who recognized the name of the Church from 10 to 70 percent. The first stake was created in Seoul on March 8, 1973, with Ho Nam Rhee as president. He later served as mission president. Membership increased to 9,000 in 1975, and by 1983, it had reached 28,795. Membership in Korea in 1990 was 59,000, increasing to 62,000 the next year.

A temple was announced for Seoul, Korea, on April 1, 1981, and was dedicated Dec. 14, 1985. Following the temple's dedication, many of the Korean members did the temple work for their ancestors.

When the 1988 Olympic games were held in Korea, the BYU Folk Dancers performed at opening ceremonies, viewed by an estimated audience of 1 billion worldwide.

Elder In Sang Han, called to the Second Quorum of the Seventy on June 1, 1991, was the first Korean General Authority.

In 1992, a record of the testimonies of the early Korean converts was published by Spencer J. and Shirley Palmer, the first of its kind in the Church.

Sources: *History of the Church in Korea,* by John D. Nash; *The Church Encounters Asia,* by Spencer J. Palmer, Deseret Book, 1970; *Ensign,* November 1985; *Church News,* Oct. 1, 1988;*Church News,* Feb. 5, 1992; "Whang Keun-Ok: Caring for Korea's Children," by Shirleen Meek Saunders, *Ensign,* October 1993.

Stakes — 16
(Listed alphabetically as of Oct. 1, 1994.)

No.	Name	Organized	First President
Asia North Area			
1865	Anyang Korea	24 May 1992	Young Hwan Lee
1385	*Chong Ju Korea 23 Sep 1986		
	†Seoul Korea Chong Ju	28 Nov 1982	Chung Yul Hwang
1435	*Tae Gu Korea 29 Jun 1993		
	*Dae Gu Korea 3 Dec 1990		
	†Daegu Korea	24 Jun 1983	Chan Tae Kwon
1306	Inchon Korea	12 Nov 1981	Chea Huo
1596a	Jeon Ju Korea	27 Apr 1986	Ju In Pak
1196	Kwang Ju Korea	25 Oct 1980	Bjong Kyu Pak
1059	Pusan Korea	6 Sep 1979	Chaewhan Chang
1382	Pusan Korea West	20 Nov 1982	Gil Whe Do
604	*Seoul Korea		
	†Seoul	8 Mar 1973	Ho Nam Rhee
1412	Seoul Korea Dong Dae Mun	24 Apr 1983	Son Awunf Ju
1017	Seoul Korea East	18 Apr 1979	Won Yong Ko
1386	Seoul Korea Kang Seo	28 Nov 1982	Do Hwan Lee
1060	Seoul Korea North	9 Sep 1979	Moo Kwang Hong
834	Seoul Korea West	22 May 1977	Chang Sun Kim
1387	Seoul Korea Yong Dong	28 Nov 1982	Jae Am Park
1866	Suwon Korea	24 May 1992	Yong Hwan Lee

(As of Oct. 1, 1994; shown with historical number. See MISSIONS.)

(124) KOREA PUSAN MISSION
Tongnae P.O. Box 73
Pusan 607-600, Korea
Phone: (011-82-51) 552-7011

(170) KOREA SEOUL WEST MISSION
Songpa P.O. Box 31
Seoul, 138-600, Korea
Phone: (011-82-2) 409-4164

(71) KOREA SEOUL MISSION
Gwang Hwa Moon, KPO 210
Seoul 110-602, Korea
Phone: (011-82-2) 734-3653

(191) KOREA TAEJON MISSION
Taejon P.O. Box 38
Taejon, 300-600, Korea
Phone (011-82-42) 628-1482

LATVIA

Year-end 1993: Est. population: 2,700,000; Missions, 1; Members, fewer than 100; Europe Area.

Latvia is a republic on the eastern shore of the Baltic Sea.

Mischa Markow, a Hungarian who had previously pioneered missionary work in Serbia, Hungary, Romania and Bulgaria, was the first to preach in Latvia. Elder Markow registered with the district court and then preached to Germans in Riga, Latvia, on Oct. 9, 1903, and three families requested baptism. However, when he was summoned to court, he chose to comply with earlier instructions from Pres. Francis M. Lyman of the European Mission: leave the country if he were summoned to court.

In modern times, Elder Dallin H. Oaks of the Council of the Twelve addressed Latvian and other leaders at a major international consultation on religious liberty and ethnic rights held in Budapest, Hungary, May 17-20, 1992.

The first modern missionaries to Latvia were Elders Matthew H. Lyman and Michael G. Van Patten, who opened the work in Riga on June 17, 1992. Two weeks later, a missionary couple arrived, Elder Boris A. and Sister Liselotte Schiel. The first convert in Latvia, Gunars Kavals, was baptized July 25, 1992.

In March 1993, Latvia was visited by Elder James E. Faust of the Council of the Twelve, and at that time, some 40 Latvian members comprised the membership of Church in this land.

The Latvia Riga Mission was created July 1, 1993, and included Latvia, Lithuania and Estonia.

Source: "Missionary to the Balkans: Mischa Markow" by William Hale Kehr, *Ensign,* June 1980; *Church News,* Nov. 16, 1991, June 27, 1992; *Church News,* March 6, 1993 and June 12, 1993.

Mission — 1

(285) LATVIA RIGA MISSION
Poste Restante
LV 1050 Riga Latvia
Phone: 011-371-2 287-916

LESOTHO

Year-end 1993: Est. population, 2,000,000; Members, 300; Branches, 1; Africa Area; South Africa Johannesburg Mission.

Completely surrounded by South Africa, Lesotho is a mountainous kingdom where the people speak English and Sesotho, and are primarily Roman Catholic, 38 percent; and Protestant, 42 percent.

Scattered LDS families from the United States lived in Lesotho during the 1980s. In July 1988 at a meeting attended by 15 people, the Maseru Branch was organized by Pres. R. J. Snow of the South Africa Johannesburg Mission at the home of expatriate Garry Dell and Mary Massey. Brother Massey was called as president. John and Elaine Scott later moved to Lesotho from Swaziland. The Church was registered July 6, 1989, and the first missionaries, Elders Marc Modersitzki of Bancroft, Idaho, and Bradley Saunderson of Durban, South Africa, entered in September. They baptized Paul Khobutle and Lawrence van Tonder Dec. 17 of that year. As the branch grew, facilities were rented in a local school. A home was purchased to be remodeled into a meetinghouse and the first meeting in it was held Jan. 2, 1994.

A seminary program functioned in country as early as 1991. On July 31, 1993, six converts traveled to the Johannesburg South Africa Temple. The first full-time missionary from Lesotho was Patrick Molapo, 23, who began serving in the Durban mission Dec. 21, 1993.

A second branch was created July 4, 1993, at Mazenod, which functioned for a short time before being disbanded because facilities for meeting were not available.

Sources: Correspondence from R.J. Snow; *Church News,* Dec. 12, 1989, March 10, 1990, Dec. 15, 1990, Jan. 26, 1991, April 25, 1992; Lesotho Historical Information, by Peter Daubney, May 1994.

LIBERIA

Year-end 1993: Population, 2,544,000; Members: 1,400; Districts, 1; Branches 7; Africa Area; Ivory Coast Abidjan Mission.

On the southwest coast of West Africa, the republic has a marshy coastline that gives way to low mountains and plateaus; the interior is forested. It is 20 percent Moslem, 20 percent percent Christian and 60 percent traditional beliefs.

Among the early Church members in Liberia were Joan Raily, baptized in New Jersey in 1986, and expatriates Steven P. and Barbara Wolf, who were in Liberia on a military assignment. Meetings were held in their home in 1986. A year earlier, Thomas Peihopa of New Zealand began teaching a Sunday School class for Joe Jawloh, a school principal in New Kru Town. Peihopa brought some 80 investigators to a social in the Wolf's home. Bihise "Biz" Kajunju and his family, converts from Zaire, also joined the group.

Missionary couples opened missionary work in Liberia in 1987. Among the early couples were J. Duffy and Jacelyn Palmer, who arrived July 3, 1987, and Philander and Juanita Smartt. The first convert was John Tarsnoh, baptized Aug. 22, 1987. The missionaries baptized 47 people in Aug. 27, 1987, in a lagoon. The New Kru Town and Congo Town branches were organized that day. On Feb. 21, 1988, Joseph Forkpah became the first Liberian branch president. The Liberia Monrovia Mission was created March 1, 1988, when missionary couples were working with some 133 members in Congo Town and New Kru Town.

Under the direction of Pres. Miles Cunningham, a handful of newly converted young men served full-time missions in 1990. At the beginning of 1990, the mission had one district and 8 branches.

The mission was closed in April 1991 because of a civil war that started Dec. 24, 1989. Missionaries from Liberia were transferred to Freetown, Sierra Leone, on May 8, 1990. David A. Tarr, then first counselor in the Monrovia District, was left in charge. During that time, about 400 members remained, another 400 fled to neighboring countries and another 400 were unaccounted for. Since the war began to abate, some of the members have returned. While conditions remained unsettled, no missionaries were assigned to Liberia.

In 1992, a second outbreak of serious hostilities occurred. Members started regrouping in 1991, however, and by the spring of 1993, seven of the eight branches had been reorganized.

A number of young men have been called on missions from Monrovia, including six from the Congo Town Branch, to serve in the Ghana Accra Mission. Nineteen young men were called as missionaries from the district from Jan. 23-Feb. 6, 1994.

Sources: Interview with Miles Cunningham, correspondence from James C. Palmer, Bill K. Jarkloh, June, 1994, and information from David A. Tarr.

LITHUANIA

Year-end 1993: Est. Population, 3,7500,000; Members, fewer than 100; Europe Area; Latvia Riga Mission.

Lithuania is a republic on the eastern shore of the Baltic Sea. Several expatriates have joined the Church and live in various countries.

One of the first converts in modern Lithuania was Irute Meskiene of Vilnius. She heard the gospel preached in Szeged, Hungary, and was baptized in 1988 in Hungary. Robert and Ruth Rees, retired literature and music teachers, respectively, were called to Lithuania as missionaries in October 1992.

BYU's Young Ambassadors performed in Lithuania and stayed three nights with host families from the Neamanus Folk Ensemble in Kaunas.

In late 1993 and 1994, Lithuanian media presented Church-produced programs and also focused on missionaries and their work.

Source: *Church News,* June 12, 1993, and July 17, 1994; correspondence from Elder Robert A. Rees and Gabriele Sirtle, May 2, 1994.

LUXEMBOURG

Year-end 1993: Est. population, 371,000; Members, 100; Branches, 1; Europe/Mediterranean Area; Belgium Brussels Mission.

Located in western Europe, the Grand Duchy of Luxembourg's population speaks French, German, and Luxembourger. The people are 97 percent Roman Catholic.

On Nov. 19, 1963, Elders Hyrum M. Smith and Gerald E. Malmrose of the Franco-Belgian Mission went into the city of Luxembourg to help new missionaries there get started in their labors. They were there four days and left several missionaries to continue the work.

A branch was formed in the mid-1960s, and in 1965 Sunday meetings were conducted in the Hotel Kons. Attendance varied from one to three members and six missionaries. The branch remained small and struggled until it was discontinued in 1971.

The city and country of Luxembourg became part of the newly created Belgium Brussels Mission June 20, 1974, and continues as part of that mission today.

Missionary work in Luxembourg has been slow, but shows recent signs of picking up. In late 1989 more than 1,000 people from 23 countries attended a nine-day exhibition titled "The Origin of Man" at the Luxembourg municipal hall. The event was hosted by area Church members and full-time missionaries. Of the 1,000 guests, nearly 200 signed the visitors book, leading to the placement of 190 copies of the Book of Mormon. In about June 1994, Luxembourg became part of the newly created Metz France District, which was divided from the Nancy France Stake.

Sources: *Church News*, Jan. 6, 1990; Belgian Mission manuscript history; *Church News,* July 9, 1994.

MADAGASCAR

Year-end 1993: Est. population, 13,400,000; Members, 100; Districts, 1; Branches, 1; Africa Area; South Africa Durban Mission.

Located in the Indian Ocean off Mozambique, Madagascar is the world's fourth largest island. Its population speaks Malagasy and French, and 52 percent follow traditional beliefs, while 41 percent are Christian and 7 percent are Islam.

The first member in Madagascar was Razanapanala Rameandricso, who was baptized in Bordeaux, France, in about 1986. He returned to Madagascar in 1989 and began teaching the gospel to a small group of people in his home. He contacted Pres. Girard Giraud-Carrier of the Mascarene Islands Mission, who visited. The first five converts were baptized upon his visit, near the end of 1990.

The first missionaries to Madagascar were Elder Fred L. and Sister Eileen Forsgren, who arrived March 3, 1991. The Antananarivo Branch was organized in February 1991 in a restaurant in Antananarivo. When the second couple, Elder Marvyn and Sister LaVeeta Hogenson, arrived in May 1991, the branch had 33 members. During their stay, the Church continued to grow. They completed their mission in September of 1992 and there were more than 130 attending meetings.

The first young full-time missionaries, Elders Jason Tarbet and Jeffry Gifford, arrived Sept. 25, 1992. The Hogensons returned for a second mission, and served from December 1993 to August 1994. During that period, seminary was started and the auxiliaries functioned.

The Church received legal status in Madagascar on July 13, 1993. At the end of August, 1994, membership was at 375.

Source: Journal of Eileen Forsgren, interview with LaVeeta Hogensen and journal of Elder Jason Tarbet.

MALAYSIA

Year-end 1993: Est. population, 17,205,000; Members, 500; Districts, 1; Branches, 5; Asia Area; Singapore Mission.

On the southeast tip of Asia and the northern half of the island of Borneo, Malaysia is a federal parliamentary democracy with a constitutional monarch. Its people speak Malay, Chinese, English and Indian languages, and practice primarily Moslem, Hindu, Buddhist, Confucian, Taoist and local religions.

The first missionaries to Malaysia came to the city of Solo in Central Java on June 27, 1972. After only a few weeks, they had more than 100 people in attendance at their English classes and were also teaching English on radio, but proselyting was limited due to government regulations.

When the Singapore Mission opened in 1974, with Malaysia a part of the mission, missionaries were rotated in and out of the country on 30-day tourist visas to comply with the law of the land.

Elder and Sister Werner Kiepe of Salt Lake City, Utah, special representatives of the International Mission, were sent to Malaysia shortly after the government granted the Church a recognition status in 1977. They helped acquire the first property owned by the Church in Malaysia in a suburb of Kuala Lumpur, the capital of Malaysia. Church membership was small, with many members being Americans and Australians temporarily working in the country, as well as some Chinese members living in the country.

A milestone was reached when two native Malaysian elders were called to serve as missionaries in

1981 in the Singapore Mission. A district was organized in Malaysia.

In 1986, the seminary and institute program was established with groups of young people attending in Pinang, Ipoh and Kuala Lumpur.

On Oct. 20, 1990, King Syed Putra Jamallai, the rajah of Perlis state in Malaysia, was honored during a visit at the Polynesian Cultural Center in Laie, Hawaii.

Elder Halvor P. Hansen, serving in the Singapore Mission with his wife, Colleen, presented a set of the Encyclopedia of Mormonism books to the National Library of Malaysia in 1993.

Elder Monte J. Brough of the Seventy, then Asia Area president, reported in 1993 that while proselyting is not allowed, members and leaders are very devoted to the Church.

Sources: *The Church Encounters Asia,* by Spencer J. Palmer, Deseret Book, 1970; *Church News,* May 23, 1981; Aug. 14, 1982; Dec. 9, 1984; March 10, 1985; "Specific Prayers led him to specific answers," by Gerry Avant, *Church News,* Jan. 20, 1985; *Church News,* May 11, 1986, Nov. 3, 1990; *Church News,* Aug. 21, 1993; "Welcome mat is out in several countries," by Sheridan R. Sheffield, *Church News,* June 19, 1993.

MALTA

Year-end 1993: Est. population, 400,000; Members, fewer than 100; Branches, 1; Europe/Mediterranean Area; Italy Catania Mission.

Located in the Mediterranean Sea, Malta is a republic with a population that speaks Maltese and English, and is mostly Roman Catholic. For the third time in recent history, the gospel is being taught in Malta.

When Apostle Lorenzo Snow was in charge of missionary work in Italy in the early 1850s, he saw the island as a possible jumping off point for carrying the gospel to other countries in the region.

After a visit to Malta in 1852, he left Elders Jabez Woodard and Thomas Obray in charge of missionary efforts here. Between 1852 and 1856, some proselyting progress was made, and a branch of about 25 people came into existence. But there was intense opposition to the work, and when the Crimean War scattered most of the British military personnel who had joined the Church, missionary efforts on the island ceased.

More than a century later, in 1979, a second effort on Malta was undertaken when the Italy Catania Mission sent Elders Victor Bonnici (of Maltese descent) and Paul Anderson to the island. They had good contacts among the island's nearly 350,000 inhabitants, but because of visa problems were unable to stay long enough to establish a branch.

Then in early 1988, Elder Rodger and Sister Helen Gunn were sent as a missionary couple to Malta. Assisted by two elders from the mission, they baptized several Maltese people, established a branch and sponsored cultural evenings and a family history seminar.

The branch, under early convert Pres. Emanuel d'Emanuele, meets in an old villa near Naxxar. Another milestone in 1993 came when the Malta Branch held its first branch conference, presided over by Pres. G. Robert Dewitt of the Italy Catania Mission.

Sources: *Encyclopedic History of the Church,* by Andrew Jenson; *Church News,* Jan. 12, 1974; "Soldier converts," by Ronald W. Walker, *Church News,* April 21, 1979; "A Valiant Little Band: LDS Soldiers in the Crimean War," by Wilford Hill LeCheminant, *Ensign,* January 1981; *A History of the Discontinued Mediterranean Missions of the Church,* by Ralph L. Cottrell Jr., a BYU masters thesis, 1983; *Church News,* Dec. 3, 1993.

MARSHALL ISLANDS

Year-end 1993: Est. population, 52,000; Members, 2,200; Districts, 2; Branches, 7; Percent LDS, 4.2, or one person in 24; Philippines/Micronesia Area; Micronesia Guam Mission.

Made up of two atoll chains in the South Pacific, the Marshall Islands are a republic.

MAJURO

Elders William Wardel and Steven Cooper arrived in Majuro Feb. 3, 1977, and they baptized Misao Lokeijak, who had been introduced to the Church in Hawaii. By the end of 1977, there were 27 converts on the island. The Laura Branch was created May 11, 1978, with Misao Lokeijak as president. By the end of 1979, there were 177 members. Meetinghouses for the Laura and Rita branches were started in September 1984 and dedicated Jan. 13 and 14, 1986, respectively. By 1987, Majuro had a district with five branches. By 1990, Majuro had 1,100 members.

In May 1992, BYU and the Republic of Marshall Islands agreed to have BYU give special training for government administrators and teachers.

KAWJALEIN/EBEYE

The Kwajalein Island Branch in the Marshall Islands was organized in 1978, made up entirely of U.S. citizens serving in the military or as Civil Service personnel. Missionaries opened the island of Ebeye on May 16, 1989, and Elders Kepiloni Foliaki and Michael Steele baptized Mary Kekuhuna on Jun 11, 1989.

ARNO AND MILI

Arno and Mili, located at the eastern end of Micronesia, some 2,200 miles west of Hawaii, are part of the 28-island Marshall group. With the addition of branches in Arno and Mili, the Church now has four branches in the Marshall Islands and three Church-owned meetinghouses.

Source: *Brief History of the Micronesia-Guam Mission,* published by the Micronesia Guam Mission, 1990, Lewis V. Nord, president,

MAURITIUS

Year-end 1993: Est. population, 1,100,000; Members, 200; Branches, 2; Africa Area; South Africa Durban Mission.

East of Madagascar in the Indian Ocean, Mauritius is a subtropical island with a parliamentary democracy, composed of an English, French, Creole, Hindi, Urdu, Hakka and Bojpoori speaking population that is 51 percent Hindu, 30 percent Christian and 16 percent Moslem.

Elder George Kershaw, an LDS settler in South Africa, served two months in Mauritius in 1856. His only known converts were an army private and seven of eight members of the crew of the ship he arrived on.

In modern times, missionary work began in the Mascarenes in 1979 under the direction of the International Mission. In 1986, the islands were transferred to the South Africa Johannesburg Mission.

Elder Joseph T. Edmunds and his wife, Ruth, and Elder Theo and Sister Nita Verhaarens visited the island briefly. The first branch was established on Feb. 25, 1982, by Elder Preston and Sister Isabelle Gledhill, the first full-time missionaries on the island. The Mascarene Islands Mission was created July 1, 1988, at which time there were 400 members on the islands in three branches in Reunion and two in Mauritius. Headquarters of the mission was transferred to Durban, South Africa, in January 1992.

Sources: *Church News,* Sept. 21, 1986, Feb. 7, 1987, Oct. 24, 1987, Nov. 5, 1987, March 19, 1988, Dec. 17, 1988; "Tropical Isles receive best news as mission opens," by Allen W. Palmer, *Church News,* Nov. 5, 1988; "At Home on the Island of Mauritius," by Lori Palmer, *Ensign,* March, 1991.

MEXICO

Year-end 1993: Est. population, 90,000,000; Members, 688,000; Stakes, 125; Wards, 780; Branches, 603; Missions, 18; Districts, 47; Temples, 1; Percent LDS, 0.8, or one LDS in 130.

In southern North America, Mexico is a federal republic with a Spanish-speaking population that is 97 percent Roman Catholic.

In 1875, a party of six was called by Brigham Young to take materials, translated into Spanish by convert Meliton Trejo from Salt Lake City to Mexico. On the way, they preached to Indians and gave a favorable colonization report that led to the founding of Mesa, Ariz.

Rebuffed at first in Mexico in 1876, the missionaries divided into two groups. The first, Daniel W. Jones and Ammon N. Tenney, traveled to Chihuahua, where they were well-received. There, they scouted settlement sites and mailed pamphlets containing translated sections of the Book of Mormon to 500 influential leaders throughout Mexico. They found many listeners among the mountain villages and Indians, but did not baptize. The second group of missionaries attempted to preach to the fierce Yaqui Indians and were nearly killed.

In 1876, Helaman Pratt and Meliton Trejo traveled to Hermosillo, Sonora, where they baptized the first five members in Mexico, and returned home.

Dr. Plotino C. Rhodakanaty of Mexico City received a tract from the original Jones expedition and began corresponding with Meliton Trejo. Rhodakanaty claimed a group of 20 believers and asked for missionaries to baptize them. Apostle Moses Thatcher and Elders Trejo and James Z. Stewart were sent to Mexico City, where on Nov. 20, 1879, they baptized Rhodakanaty and Silviano Arteaga, organized a branch and placed Rhodakanaty over it. By 1880, more literature had been translated. Political difficulties in Utah and changing moods in Mexico resulted in less success in Mexico City. Missionaries left Mexico City, and found converts in the small rural town of Ozumba. Additional missionaries arrived, and despite setbacks, the work moved forward in Ozumba and the surrounding villages near Mount Popocateptl.

In 1885, a group of nearly 400 colonists from Utah arrived at the northern Mexico Casas Grandes River and acquired property. Mexico's first stake was created in Colonia Juarez in 1895. In 1887, members from central Mexico arrived at the colonies but found circumstances difficult and returned to their homes. By 1912, more than 4,000 members had settled in Chihuahua and Sonora.

In 1901 Ammon M. Tenney became president of the Mexican Mission. Visiting village branches in central Mexico, he found early converts still faithful. Branches were re-organized and by 1911, membership in the region reached 1,000.

The Mexican Revolution halted much of the Church's progress, as colonists in the north left Mexico in the 1912 exodus to avoid the conflict, and members in central Mexico were left without leaders and were abused by conflicting armies. Two local leaders, Rafael Monroy and Vicente Morales, were executed because of their faithfulness to the Church.

When Rey L. Pratt returned to central Mexico in November 1917, he found the members had remained faithful despite extreme hardship. Work again progressed, but in 1926 all foreign clerics were expelled from Mexico. Local Mexican leaders again maintained stability and expanded the work, calling six local missionaries in 1930. In 1936, however, a group called the Third Convention broke away from the Church for a period, but was re-united under the leadership of mission Pres. Arwell Pierce. In 1946 Church President George Albert Smith visited the members. Membership then was more than 5,300.

During the next two decades membership increased as local leaders were called to more leadership positions, and the missionary zeal of the Mexican members was manifest.

On June 10, 1956, the mission was divided. On Dec. 3, 1961, the Mexico Stake was created, with Harold Brown as president. He was shortly succeeded by pioneer member Agricol Lozano. Membership then was about 25,000.

Church schools were established in 1959; the capstone of these was the large preparatory school, Benemerito, which was established in 1963. This flagship of the Church in Mexico helped the Church advance in leadership and reputation.

Membership began to expand rapidly. By 1972, it reached 100,000. On April 3, 1976, a temple was announced for Mexico City and the completed temple was dedicated Dec. 2-4, 1983. At that time, membership in Mexico was conservatively placed about 240,000. Mexico was the first country outside the United States to reach 100 stakes. When the 100th stake was created at Tecalco in 1989, membership in Mexico was estimated to be more than half a million. In 1992, Mexico made Church history when it became the first nation outside the United States to be divided into two areas, Mexico North and Mexico South.

Elder Waldo Call of the Seventy, called in 1985 from the original Mexican colonies, was the first Mexican General Authority. He was followed in 1989 by Elder Horacio Tenorio, the first of Mexican ancestry to be called. Elder Jorge A. Rojas Ornales was called in 1991, and Elder Lino Alvarez was called in 1992.

An historic moment came June 29, 1993, when Mexican government formally registered the Church, allowing it to own property. The recognition was granted at a rarely held ceremony presided over by Patrocinio Gonzalez Garrido, Secretary of Government. Instrumental in gaining the recognition was Agricol Lozano H., the Church's legal counsel, who bore his testimony at the ceremony. The effort was under the direction of Elders F. Burton Howard and Angel Abrea of the Seventy, presidents of the Mexico North and Mexico South areas. They were supervised by Elder Russell M. Nelson of the Council of the Twelve, who worked under the direction of the First Presidency on the project.

The recognition was granted just six days after the Church filed its application on June 23. In filing its application, Church representatives presented more than 25 encyclopedia-sized volumes containing the history of the Church, particularly in Mexico.

Sources: *Historia Del Mormonismo en Mexico,* by Agricol Lozano; Tecalco history, unpublished history by "Ixta" and "Popo" wards; extensive selections from journals, publications and histories courtesy Gerry R. Flake; multiple other published and unpublished papers and books and *Church News* articles; "Mexico formally registers Church," *Church News* July 17, 1993.

Stakes — 128
(Listed alphabetically by area as of Oct. 1, 1994.)

No.	Name	Organized	First President
Mexico North Area — 60			
1640	Aguascalientes Mexico	17 May 1987	Jose Luis Rios A.
941	Celaya Mexico	11 Jun 1978	Armando Gaona
782	Chihuahua Mexico	13 Nov 1976	Gustavo Ulises Cortez S.

No.	Unit	Date	President
1633	*Chihuahua Mexico Chuviscar 14 Nov 1989	1 Mar 1987	Humberto Enrique Serna G.
	†Chihuahua Mexico East		
1736a	Chihuahua Mexico Tecnologico	26 Nov 1989	Arturo Galindo Rubalcava
1109	Ciudad Juarez Mexico East	24 Feb 1980	Armando Arzate Saldana
1699	Ciudad Juarez Mexico North	9 Oct 1988	Luis Carlos Gomez M.
783	*Ciudad Juarez Mexico South 9 Oct 1988		
	†Ciudad Juarez Mexico	14 Nov 1976	Sergio Armando de la Mora M.
1301	*Ciudad Mante Mexico 25 Jan 1982		
	†Mante Mexico	1 Nov 1981	Humberto Noriega F.
772	Ciudad Obregon Mexico	10 Oct 1976	Jorge Mendez I.
1712	Ciudad Obregon Mexico Nainari	19 Feb 1989	Jesus Angulo Montoya
1500	Ciudad Obregon Mexico Yaqui	28 Oct 1984	Jorge Mendez Ibarra
797	Ciudad Victoria Mexico	12 Dec 1976	Jesus Martinez T.
1742	Colonia Dublan Mexico	25 Feb 1990	Carl L. Call
37	*Colonia Juarez Mexico		
	†Juarez	9 Dec 1895	Anthony W. Ivins
838	Culiacan Mexico	22 May 1977	Federico Fragoza Diaz
1710	Culiacan Mexico Humaya	12 Feb 1989	Jose Exaltacion Astorga E.
1644	Culiacan Mexico Tamazula	21 Jun 1987	Rosario Lobo
1707	Delicias Mexico	18 Dec 1988	Sergio Trejo L.
1228	Durango Mexico	21 Jan 1981	Ernesto Padilla Lozano
1761	*Ensenada Mexico 8 Aug 1990		
	†Tijuana Mexico Ensenada	24 Jun 1990	Jose Pedroza A.
935	Gomez Palacio Mexico	28 May 1978	Ruben Martinez A.
1749	Gomez Palacio Mexico La Laguna	6 May 1990	Magdaleno Sanchez S.
1183	Guadalajara Mexico Independencia	27 Sep 1980	Felipe Covarrubias S.
1753	Guadalajara Mexico Reforma	3 Jun 1990	Jose Saavedra T.
683	*Guadalajara Mexico Union 28 Sep 1980		
	†Guadalajara Mexico	23 Feb 1975	Emilio Garcia L.
1779	Guaymas Mexico	18 Nov 1990	Ruben A. Palestino
771	Hermosillo Mexico	8 Oct 1976	Hector Ceballos L.
1636	Hermosillo Mexico Pitic	26 Apr 1987	Carlos Pineda O.
1232	*Irapuato Mexico 24 Mar 1992		
	†Leon Mexico	8 Feb 1981	Armando Gaona J.
1734b	*La Paz Mexico 30 Jan 1990		
	†Finisterra Mexico	10 Sep 1989	Antonio Aguilar V.
1139	Los Mochis Mexico	25 May 1980	Victor Manuel Soto
1714	Los Mochis Mexico El Fuerte	5 Mar 1989	Ezequiel Fernando Ramirez Q.
795	Madero Mexico	11 Dec 1976	Gabriel Raymundo Saldivar F.
1131	Matamoros Mexico	18 May 1980	Luciano Ramirez
1718	Mazatlan Mexico	7 May 1989	Jose Alberto Holcombe I.
819	Mexicali Mexico	20 Mar 1977	Eduardo Del Rio P.
1626	Mexicali Mexico Los Pinos	18 Jan 1987	Jose de Jesus Ruelas U.
644	Monclova Mexico	26 May 1974	Francisco Aragon Garza
774	Monterrey Mexico Anahuac	17 Oct 1976	Lehi Gracia L.
572	*Monterrey Mexico Libertad 17 Oct 1976		
	*Monterrey Mexico East		
	†Monterrey East	7 May 1972	Jose Humberto Gonzalez
1765	Monterrey Mexico Los Angeles	22 Jul 1990	Carlos Charles Plata
508	*Monterrey Mexico Mitras 8 Jun 1980		
	*Monterrey Mexico		
	†Monterrey	22 Mar 1970	Guillermo G. Garza
1114	Monterrey Mexico Moderna	9 Mar 1980	Mauro Garcia Herrera
1144	Monterrey Mexico Morelos	8 Jun 1980	Carlos R. Merino D.
908	Monterrey Mexico Paraiso	23 Apr 1978	Alfredo Gallegos L.
773	Monterrey Mexico Roma	16 Oct 1976	Jose Humberto Gonzalez G.
1615	Monterrey Mexico Valle Verde	2 Nov 1986	Jose F. Torres M.
857	Piedras Negras Mexico	21 Aug 1977	Fidencio Guzman Lugo
1132	Reynosa Mexico	18 May 1980	Noe Flores Silva
1767	Saltillo Mexico Miravalle	12 Aug 1990	Edmundo Rodriguez Pena
1155	Saltillo Mexico Republica	29 Jun 1980	Roberto Teodoro Guzman R.
1231	San Luis Potosi Mexico	1 Feb 1981	Guillermo G. Soubervielle R.
567	*Tampico Mexico		
	†Tampico	27 Feb 1972	Guillermo Garmendia
757	Tijuana Mexico	23 May 1976	Carlos Mendez S.

1587	*Tijuana Mexico La Mesa 15 Apr 1986		
	†La Mesa Mexico	9 Feb 1986	Angel Luevano Cordova
781	Torreon Mexico	12 Nov 1976	David Limon Miranda
1532	Torreon Mexico Jardin	12 May 1985	Rafael Leon Miranda
1736	Torreon Mexico Reforma	15 Oct 1989	Miguel Angel Rivera C.
628	*Valle Hermosa Mexico		
	†Valle Hermosa	28 Oct 1973	Benjamin Morales

Mexico South Area — 68

1735	Acapulco Mexico	24 Sep 1989	Francisco Javier Torres G.
1971	Atlixco Mexico	16 Jan 1994	Hector Garcia Ceballos
1474	Campeche Mexico	27 May 1984	Gabriel Francisco Ramos G.
722	Chalco Mexico	9 Nov 1975	Ruben Valenzuela G.
1822	Chetumal Mexico	27 Oct 1991	Raul Gaspar Rodriguez F.
1043a	Coatzacoalcos Mexico	1 Jul 1979	Raymundo Madris Carbajal
1766	Coatzacoalcos Mexico Puerto	29 Jul 1990	Raul Munoz Z.
721	Cuautla Mexico	9 Nov 1975	Juan Angel Alvaradejo
1983	Cuautla Mexico Aguahedionda	19 Jun 1994	Luis F. Rodriguez Trejo
1427	Cuernavaca Mexico	5 Jun 1983	Sergio Rojas Espinoza
1589	Jalapa Mexico	2 Mar 1986	Jorge Sanchez
1764	Juchitan Mexico	22 Jul 1990	Gerardo Castellanos A.
804	Merida Mexico	22 Jan 1977	Abel R. Ordaz R.
1728	Merida Mexico Centro	11 Jun 1989	Joaquin Eduardo Carrillo V.
1754	Merida Mexico Itzimna	10 Jun 1990	Mauro Jose Luis Gil P.
923	Merida Mexico Lakin	14 May 1978	Benigno Pena Pech
1603	Mexico City Mexico Anahuac	29 Jun 1986	Luis Manuel Angel B.
617	*Mexico City Mexico Aragon		
	†Mexico City Aragon	27 May 1973	Agricol Lozano H.
658	Mexico City Mexico Arbolillo	15 Sep 1974	Guillermo Torres
1317	Mexico City Mexico Azteca	6 Dec 1981	Juan Alberta Ramos B.
719	Mexico City Mexico Camarones	8 Nov 1975	Jorge Rojas O.
1357	Mexico City Mexico Chapultepec	27 Jun 1982	Jose Ismael Ruiz G.
716a	Mexico City Mexico Churubusco	8 Nov 1975	Juan Casanova C.
1752	Mexico City Mexico Cuautepec	20 May 1990	Salvador Aguirre Osorio
1763	Mexico City Mexico Cuautitlan	8 Jul 1990	Victor M. Cardenas L.
1759	Mexico City Mexico Culturas	17 Jun 1990	Octavio Saul Morales A.
1663	Mexico City Mexico Ecatepec	6 Dec 1987	Juan Manuel Rodriguez C.
718	Mexico City Mexico Ermita	8 Nov 1975	Aurelio Valdespino O.
723	Mexico City Mexico Industrial	9 Nov 1975	Juan Roberto Alva
1070	Mexico City Mexico Iztapalapa	14 Oct 1979	Aurelio Valdespino
1760	Mexico City Mexico La Perla	24 Jun 1990	Pedro Espinosa C.
965	Mexico City Mexico Linda Vista	8 Oct 1978	Fernando R. Dorantes T.
726	Mexico City Mexico Moctezuma	9 Nov 1975	Filiberto Ledezma M.
727	Mexico City Mexico Netzahualcoyotl	9 Nov 1975	Jaime Garay M.
1433	Mexico City Mexico Oriental	19 Jun 1983	Felipe Gerardo Ramirez N.
717a	Mexico City Mexico Tacubaya	8 Nov 1975	Roman Gomez I.
720	*Mexico City Mexico Tlalnepantla 10 Oct 1978		
	†Mexico City Mexico Satelite	9 Nov 1975	Horacio Tenorio O.
1356	Mexico City Mexico Tlalpan	27 Jun 1982	Jose Alberto Rasales G.
1579	Mexico City Mexico Valle Dorado	28 Nov 1985	Arturo Lopez G.
1980	Mexico City Mexico Vergel	15 May 1994	Ernesto Rosas Vazquez
724	Mexico City Mexico Villa de las Flores	9 Nov 1975	Juan Manuel Cedeno R.
715a	Mexico City Mexico Zarahemla	8 Nov 1975	Bonaerges Rubalcava E.
829	Minatitlan Mexico	15 May 1977	Ignacio Cruz S.
1280	Oaxaca Mexico	21 Jun 1981	M. Ociel Bengoa Vargas
1685	Oaxaca Mexico Monte Alban	7 Feb 1988	Valentin Cruz B.
801	Orizaba Mexico	16 Jan 1977	Humberto Sanchez R.
1466	*Pachuca Mexico 13 Nov 1990		
	†Mexico City Mexico Pachuca	18 Mar 1984	Alejandro Chavez Rodriguez
1716	Papantla Mexico	23 Apr 1989	Antonio Casino C.
730	Poza Rica Mexico	13 Nov 1975	Jose Luis Pichardo M.
799	Poza Rica Mexico Palmas	15 Jan 1977	Angel Valle G.
1293	Puebla Mexico Fuertes	11 Oct 1981	Francisco Pineda Salazar
680	Puebla Mexico La Paz	16 Feb 1975	Santiago Mejia M.
1758	Puebla Mexico Nealtican	17 Jun 1990	Marcelino Osorio P.

898	Puebla Mexico Popocateptl	12 Mar 1978	Zeferino Tlatelpa
681	Puebla Mexico Valsequillo	16 Feb 1975	Ramiro Goana M.
951	Tapachula Mexico	20 Aug 1978	Jorge David Arrevilla M.
1762	Tapachula Mexico Izapa	8 Jul 1990	Guillermo Sanchez R.
1730	Tecalco Mexico	25 Jun 1989	Felipe Hernandez L.
1829	Toluca Mexico	17 Nov 1991	Gilberto Lopez D'Antin
725	Tula Mexico	9 Nov 1975	Silvino Mera U.
1943	Tuxtepec Mexico	6 June 1993	Marcelo Valis Medina
1174	Tuxtla Gutierrez Mexico	31 Aug 1980	Enrique Sanchez Casillas
1653	Valle del Mezquital Mexico	13 Sep 1987	Joel Gandara Salazar
700	Veracruz Mexico	15 Jun 1975	Leon Lopez Alavez
1751	Veracruz Mexico Mocambo	20 May 1990	Fernando Lagunez V.
800	Veracruz Mexico Reforma	16 Jan 1977	Leon Lopez A.
1166	Villahermosa Mexico	10 Aug 1980	Jose Luis Madrigal N.
1746	*Villahermosa Mexico Gaviotas 5 Oct 1993		
	†Villahermosa Mexico Las Gaviotas	15 Apr 1990	Joaquin Gonzalez L.

Discontinued

344 †Mexico City   May 1967
8 Nov 1975 ★Mexico City Mexico Churubusco (No. 716a), Mexico City Mexico
Tacubaya (No. 717a), Mexico City Mexico Ermita (No. 718), Mexico City
Mexico Chapultepec (No. 1357)
*Mexico City Mexico
†Mexico   3 Dec 1961   Harold Brown

534 †Mexico City East   15 Nov 1970   Agricol Lozano
8 Nov 1975 ★Chalco Mexico (No. 722), Mexico City Mexico Villa de las
Flores (No. 724), Mexico City Mexico Moctezuma (No. 726), Mexico City
Mexico Netzahualcoyotl (No. 727)
*Mexico City Mexico East

434 †Mexico City North   7 May 1967   Agricol Lozano
8 Nov 1975 ★Tampico Mexico (No. 567), Mexico City Mexico Camarones
(No. 719), Mexico City Mexico Satelite (No. 720)
*Mexico City Mexico North

Missions — 18
(As of Oct. 1, 1994; shown with historical number. See MISSIONS.)

(208) MEXICO CHIHUAHUA MISSION
Sucursal "3" de Correos
Apartado Postal 3-41
Chihuahua, Chihuahua
C.P 31250 Mexico
Phone: (011-52-14) 13-77-76

(125) MEXICO GUADALAJARA MISSION
Apartado Postal 22-3
C.P. 44290
Guadalajara, Jalisco
Mexico
Phone: (011-52-36) 51-49-15

(56) MEXICO HERMOSILLO MISSION
Apartado Postal 557
Hermosillo, Sonora, C.P. 83000
Mexico
Phone: (011-52-62) 14-15-02

(222a) MEXICO LEON MISSION
Apartado Postal 1-1125
Leon, Guanajuato
3700 Mexico
Phone: (011-52-47) 12-67-07

(201) MEXICO MAZATLAN MISSION
A.P. 531
Rio Culiacan #49, Fracc. Tellerias
Mazatlan, Sinaloa
Mexico C. P. 82000
Phone: (011-52-69) 850616

(126) MEXICO MERIDA MISSION
Apartado Postal #26 y 27 Sucursal C
97000, Merida, Yucatan,
Mexico
Phone: (011-52-99) 24-51-08

(193) MEXICO MEXICO CITY EAST MISSION
Fuente de Medusa #26
Lomas de Tecamachalco
C.P. 53950 Edo. de Mexico
Mexico
Phone: (011-52-5) 751-8656

(163) MEXICO MEXICO CITY NORTH MISSION
Fuente del Rey #55
Tecamachalco, Edo. de Mexico
C.P. 53970 Mexico
Phone: 011-52-5 251-1709

(20) MEXICO MEXICO CITY SOUTH MISSION
Monte Caucaso 1110
Lomas de Chapultepec
Mexico D.F., C.P. 11000
Mexico
Phone: 011-52-5 540-3797

(45) MEXICO MONTERREY NORTH MISSION
Calle Cerralvo # 134
Colonia Libertad
Cd. Guadalupe, Nuevo Leon
Mexico
Phone: 011-52-83 79-68-58

(276) MEXICO MONTERREY SOUTH MISSION
Calle Chiapas #2202
Colonia Roma Sur
Monterrey, Nuevo Leon, 64700
Mexico
Phone: 011-52-8 358-1044

(217) MEXICO PUEBLA MISSION
Calle 25 Sur #907
Col. La Paz
Puebla, Puebla 72160,
Mexico
Phone: 011-52-22 49-88-07

(247) MEXICO TIJUANA MISSION
Apartado Postal 3379
Tijuana, B.C.N. 22000
Mexico C.P. 27000
Phone: (011-52-66) 85-72-78

(209) MEXICO TUXTLA-GUTIERREZ MISSION
Apartado 278
Tuxtla Guitierrez, Chiapas
Mexico C.P. 29000
Phone: 011-52-961 2-14-41

(246) MEXICO OAXACA MISSION
Huerta de los Olivos #100
Fracc. Trinidad de las Huertas
C.P. 68 120, Oaxaca, Oaxaca,
Mexico
Phone: (011-52-951) 4 20 17

(218) MEXICO TAMPICO MISSION
Apartado Postal 241
Cd. Madero, Tamaulipas
A.P. 89460
Mexico
Phone: 011-52-12 16-65-50

(81) MEXICO TORREON MISSION
Apartado Postal 792
Torreon, Coahuila
Mexico
Phone: (011-52-17) 12-33-92

(75) MEXICO VERACRUZ MISSION
Apartado Postal 103
Veracruz, Veracruz C.P. 91700
Mexico
Phone: (011-52-29) 31-35-66

MICRONESIA

Year-end 1993: Est. population, 101,000; Members, 2,400; Districts, 5; Branches, 20; Percent LDS, 2.3, or one LDS in 42; Philippines/Micronesia Area; Micronesia Guam Mission.

Extending along the 1,800-mile Caroline Islands archipelago, the Federated States of Micronesia has a culturally diverse population that speaks eight island dialects.

CHUUK

In Chuuk (Truk), two missionaries, Elders Dan Baldwin and Torlik Tima arrived, July 7, 1977. They baptized T. M. Conrad Mailo and his wife, Nisor Cerly David, on Oct. 22, 1977. The first Trukese missionary was Happiness Ichin, the second convert on the island. By 1980, membership reached 170, and on May 31, 1981, the Truk-Pohnpei District was created. A meetinghouse was dedicated April 24, 1983. By 1990, the district had been divided, and two meetinghouses dedicated.

A visit to Micronesia by Michaelene P. Grassli, Primary general president, and Virginia H. Pearce, board member, in June 1991, included stops in Chuuk, Pohnpei, Kosrae, and Kwajalein.

KOSRAE

Work in Kosrae began in March 1985, but missionaries found little success. They worked hard to break down public opinion against the Church. The first Kosrean, Isidro Abraham, was baptized April 26, 1986. By October 1989 when a branch conference was held at Lela, 72 people attended. Kosrae became a district on March 14, 1990. The first seminary graduation took place on Aug. 1, 1990. Ground was broken for the Malem meetinghouse on Dec. 21, 1989, and the completed facility dedicated Dec. 3, 1992. The Lelu meetinghouse was dedicated in January 1993.

POHNPEI

Pohnpei Island was opened to missionary work on Oct. 23, 1976, when Elders George L. Mortensen and Aldric Porter arrived. The first baptism on the island, however, didn't occur until Feb. 7, 1981. Missionary work progressed steadily and the Pohnpei District was created Nov. 22, 1985. In 1990, membership was 464. In late 1993, 18 young women in the Pohnpei District held their first camp on the island of Madolenihmn.

YAP

The Church came to Yap in 1977, with Charles Keliikipi, under contract to organize a police department on the island, assigned to organize the Church here. The first missionaries, Elders David S. Ige and Douglas Andrews, came that year as well. The first convert was baptized in March 1978, and afterwards, several families came into the Church. The first missionary couple was Elder and Sister Stewart, who arrived Aug. 2, 1979. A meetinghouse was completed Jan. 13, 1981. By 1990, membership on the island was 150. The first seminary graduation on Yap was held Aug. 16, 1990.

Sources: *Church News,* Jan 9, 1952; *Unto the Isles of the Sea,* by R. Lanier Britsch; *Church News,* March 4, 1989; *Brief History of the Micronesia-Guam Mission,* published by the Micronesia Guam Mission, 1990, Lewis V. Nord, president; "Visit to area reveals growing gospel roots," by Sheridan R. Sheffield, *Church News,* June 22, 1991; *Church News,* Nov. 13, 1993.

MONGOLIA

Year-end 1993: Est. population, 2,310,000; Members, fewer than 100; Branches, 1; Asia Area.

In east central Asia between Russia and China, Mongolia is a socialist country with a population that speaks Mongolian, and traditionally follows Lama Buddhist beliefs.

Elder Monte J. Brough of the Asia Area presidency met with top government officials and the directors of five universities in May and August 1992. Afterward, six missionary couples were sent to assist the country's higher education program and to teach others about the Church. The first couples arrived Sept. 16, 1992, and lived in Ulaanbaatar, which is home to half the population of Mongolia. Elder Kenneth H. Beesley, former president of LDS Business College, and his wife, Donna, headed the couples. The first sacrament meeting was held Sept. 20, 1992, in Elder and Sister Beesley's apartment. The Ulaanbaatar Branch was organized in 1993. The first converts were Lamjav Purevsuren and Tsendkhuu Bat-Ulzii, baptized Feb. 6, 1993.

The first six missionary couples to arrive included the Beesleys, Royce P. and Mary Jane Flandro, Richard G. and Anna M. Harper, Stanley B. and Marjorie Smith, C. DuWayne and Alice C. Schmidt, and Gary and Barbara L. Carlson. The first full-time elders were Bart Jay Birch, Duane Lee Blanchard, Brett Andrew Hansen, Jared K. Meier, Curtis Dee Mortensen, and Bradley Jay Pierson.

A foundation representing the Church was legally registered Jan. 17, 1994, and efforts continue to have the Church fully recognized.

As of March 1, 1994, attendance at the branch averaged between 85 and 110. There were 53 local members, including 16 missionaries. Local members served in the branch presidency, Relief Society presidency and 24 other branch positions. Among the early converts were: a professor at Mongolian University of Art, editor of an English-language newspaper, a veterinarian, a physician, and a computer operator.

Source: *Church News,* Sept. 19, 1992; correspondence from Elder Kenneth H. Beesley to Asia Area presidency, Feb. 24, 1994.

NAMIBIA

Year-end 1993: Est. population, 1,600,000; Members, fewer than 100; Branches, 1; Africa Area; South Africa Cape Town Mission.

The Republic of Namibia in Southern Africa became an independent nation March 21, 1990, and has a population that speaks Afrikaans, English, and indigenous languages. Namibians are Lutheran, 50 percent, and other Christian, 30 percent.

A few weeks before Namibia gained its independence, four elders and one couple began proselyting in Windhoek. At the time there were fewer than 20 members in the entire country.

Converts were steadily added to the Windhoek and Rehoboth branches, and about 100 people attended each branch as of October 1991.

Leaders report that the branches frequently have more people attending than are on the record books. A Scouting program was organized in Windhoek that provides wholesome activities for the young men. Relief Society sisters took part in an educational program for less-fortunate women during a service project in 1992-93.

Sources: "Gospel springs forth in harsh desert land of new Africa nation," by Mark Newman and Greg Hagen, *Church News,* Oct. 5, 1991; "Four nations in central, southern Africa," by Mary Mostert and Gerry Avant, *Church News* Sept. 26, 1992.

NETHERLANDS

Year-end 1993: Est. population, 15,200,000; Members, 7,000; Stakes, 3; Wards, 13; Branches, 21; Missions, 1; Percent LDS, 0.05, or one LDS in 2,171.

In northwest Europe on the North Sea, The Netherlands is a constitutional monarchy with a Dutch-speaking population that is 36 percent Roman Catholic and 19 percent Dutch Reformed.

The Church's presence in The Netherlands goes to 1841, when Elder Orson Hyde, while on a missionary journey to Jerusalem, spent more than a week in Rotterdam and Amsterdam, explaining the gospel to Jewish rabbis.

The first missionaries assigned to labor in The Netherlands arrived Aug. 5, 1861. By May 10, 1862, they had baptized 14 people in Amsterdam, and organized the first branch here.

For the first three years, the area was part of the Swiss-German Mission. The Netherlands Mission was established Nov. 1, 1864. The mission also serves the Flemish speaking northern half of Belgium.

For many years, the Church was not allowed to own property in The Netherlands, and it remains difficult to obtain permits to purchase land for meetinghouses. Official recognition of the Church was received in August 1955, after nearly 20 years of petitioning. This was considered a major breakthrough, since legal recognition gives the Church the right to hold property, exemption from taxation on Church properties and a certain degree of stature.

In the first 100 years of the Church in The Netherlands, some 4,500 missionaries served here, and more than 14,000 people were baptized. A large percentage of those converts immigrated to the United States.

In recent years, however, with temples more accessible, few members have emigrated, and today there are many second-, third- and even fourth-generation members in the wards and branches. The first non-English-speaking stake in the Church was organized in The Hague in 1961, with Johan Paul Jongkees as president. Elder Jacob de Jager, an emeritus member of the Seventy, was the first General Authority born in Holland.

More than 2,000 people attended the first regional conference held in the Netherlands in June 1984.

In 1990, Church members organized a food drive among members and non-members that resulted in the shipment to Romania of 12 large truckloads of food. LDS member Jeane Henny Kirschbaum received a royal golden medal of honor from the burgomaster of Heemstede in 1993 for her community service.

Sources: *Encyclopedic History of the Church,* by Andrew Jenson; *Church News,* March 11 and 25, 1961; *History of the Netherlands Mission 1861-1966,* by Keith C. Warner, a BYU thesis, August 1967; "Netherlands," *Ensign,* August, 1973; *Church News,* June 24, 1984, March 17, 1990; *Church News,* Nov. 20, 1993.

Stakes — 3
(Listed alphabetically as of Oct. 1, 1994.)

No.	Name	Organized	First President
Europe Area			
1720	Apeldoorn Netherlands	14 May 1989	Max Henning Van Der Put
326	*The Hague Netherlands 12 Aug 1976		
	*The Hague Holland		
	†Holland	12 Mar 1961	Johan Paul Jongkees
933	Utrecht Netherlands	28 May 1978	Eugene M. Engelbert

Mission — 1
(As of Oct. 1, 1994; shown with historical number. See MISSIONS.)

(8a) NETHERLANDS AMSTERDAM MISSION
Noordse Bosje 16
1211 BG Hilversum, Netherlands
Phone: (011-31-35) 248346

NETHERLANDS ANTILLES

Year-end 1993: Est. population, 200,000; Fewer than 100; Branches, 3; North America Southeast Area; West Indies Mission.

Made up of two groups of islands in the Caribbean, the Netherlands Antilles are considered part of The Netherlands. Work was opened and closed on Curacao in 1978-79 by the Venezuela Caracas Mission. However, a branch was created on Curacao Oct. 31, 1979. The branch was divided in April 1987, but rejoined in January 1988. A meetinghouse was dedicated in August 1988.

Sources: Venezuela Caracas Mission manuscript history; "Book of Mormon now in 80 Languages," *Ensign,* March 1988; *Church News,* April 2, 1988.

ARUBA

Year-end 1993: Est. population, 64,000; Members, fewer than 100; Branches, 1; North America Southeast Area; West Indies Mission.

An autonomous member of The Netherlands, Aruba lies 18 miles off the coast of Venezuela. A branch was organized on Aruba Aug. 13, 1986, and missionaries were sent in January 1987. Selections of the Book of Mormon were translated into Papiamento in 1987, and coupled with activity by missionaries, brought a successful re-activation effort.

Sources: Venezuela Caracas Mission manuscript history; "Book of Mormon now in 80 Languages," *Ensign*, March 1988; *Church News*, April 2, 1988.

ST. MAARTEN

Year-end 1993: Est. population, 4,500; Members, fewer than 100; Branches, 1; North America Southeast Area; West Indies Mission.

The Island of St. Maarten in the Caribbean, with 20 square miles and a estimated population of 4,500, was part of the France Toulouse Mission when the St. Maarten Branch was organized Jan. 9, 1979. The mission was discontinued and work resumed with the West Indies Mission. Elders Thad Ariens and Victor Quarty began working in St. Maarten, the administration of which is divided between the Dutch and French governments. The Claire Dinane family, which was baptized on Guadeloupe, moved to St. Maarten and helped re-open the St. Maarten Branch on Jan. 31, 1984.

Source: *Manuscript History of the France Toulouse Mission.*

NEW ZEALAND

Year-end 1993: Est. population, 3,440,000; Members, 80,000; Stakes, 16; Wards, 108; Branches, 76; Missions, 2; Districts, 5; Temples, 1; Percent LDS, 2.3, or one LDS in 43.

Located in the South Pacific in the Tasman Sea, New Zealand has a parliamentary government. Its English-speaking population is Anglican, 29 percent; Presbyterian, 18 percent; and Roman Catholic, 15 percent.

Augustus Farnham, president of the Australian Mission, accompanied by William Cooke, arrived in New Zealand Oct. 27, 1854, and preached with little success in Auckland and Nelson for two months. Elder Cooke then remained alone and in March 1855, baptized 10 people, and organized a branch at Karori in April. A few other missionaries followed, and a handful of converts immigrated to Utah. Persecution arose, and in 1871 the New Zealand parliament briefly considered the "Mormon invasion."

At first missionary work centered among Europeans. At the end of 1880, seven branches had been established with 133 members. However, at this time President Joseph F. Smith of the First Presidency instructed missionaries to concentrate on the indigenous Maori people.

Mission Pres. William F. Bromley subsequently assigned Elders Alma Greenwood and Ira N. Hinckley Jr. to teach Maoris in the southern tip of the North Island.

Prior to the arrival of the missionaries to the Maoris, at least five Maori leaders, some of whom were Tohungas or spiritual leaders while others were tribal wise men, had told of a "true religion" that would come. Because many beliefs of the Maoris and missionaries were similar, a number of Maoris were converted. The first conversions came in the Waikato region, but others soon followed. The first Maori baptized was Ngataki, on Oct. 18, 1881.

By the end of 1884, membership included 265 Europeans and 811 Maoris. Membership among the Maoris increased to nearly 4,000 in 79 branches by the turn of the century, an almost all-Maori membership.

The Book of Mormon was translated into Maori in April 1889. The New Zealand Mission was created Jan. 1, 1898. In 1907, the First Presidency authorized a secondary school to add to the primary educational program that was previously established. The Maori Agricultural College was completed in 1913. It operated until 1931, when it was damaged beyond repair by an earthquake. Elder Matthew Cowley of the Council of the Twelve made many contributions to the Church as he served as missionary, mission president and supervising General Authority of New Zealand.

By the mid-1930s, the Church had grown to 8,600. After World War II ended, the Church expanded beyond its primarily Maori membership, as many of European ancestry joined.

In 1948, Elder Cowley announced plans for a new school, and in February 1955, the First Presidency announced plans for a temple. Both facilities were largely constructed by labor missionaries. Dedicated in 1958 were the newly built temple on April 20, and the Church College of New Zealand on April 26. The first stake in New Zealand was created in Auckland May 18 of the same year. Membership at the time was 17,000 but grew to 26,000 in the next eight years. In 1968-70, the seminary program was established. Some 12,000 members attended an area conference in 1976 at which President Spencer W. Kimball spoke.

In 1987, Elder Douglas J. Martin, a former stake president from Hamilton, was called to the Second Quorum of the Seventy. Membership in 1990 was 76,000.

Sources: *Zion in New Zealand* by Brian W. Hunt; *Encyclopedic History of the Church* by Andrew Jenson; Origin of the Maori People in New Zealand, by Stewart Meha; *Church News*, Jan. 18, 1964, p. 6; *Church News*, May 9, 1936, p. 1; The Church in New Zealand, by Mervyn Dykes, *Ensign*, February 1976.

Stakes — 17
(Listed alphabetically as of Oct. 1, 1994.)

No.	Name	Organized	First President
Pacific Area			
630	Auckland New Zealand Harbour	4 Nov 1973	Kenneth M. Palmer
1304	Auckland New Zealand Henderson	8 Nov 1981	Alan Robert Patterson
861	Auckland New Zealand Manukau	18 Sep 1977	Oscar Westerlund
455	*Auckland New Zealand Manurewa †Auckland South	5 May 1968	Geoffrey R. Garlick
264	*Auckland New Zealand Mount Roskill †Auckland	18 May 1958	George R. Biesinger
1973	Auckland New Zealand Panmure	13 Feb 1994	Stephen Aubrey Keung
1664	Auckland New Zealand Tamaki	13 Dec 1987	Clark W. Palmerston Larkins
953	Christchurch New Zealand	27 Aug 1978	Bardia Pine Taiapa
1104	Gisborne New Zealand	14 Feb 1980	William Pakimana Taurima
310	*Hamilton New Zealand †Hamilton	13 Nov 1960	Wendell H. Wiser
313	*Hastings New Zealand †Hawkes Bay	20 Nov 1960	Joseph Alvin Higbee
475	*Kaikohe New Zealand †New Zealand North (New Zealand)	19 Jan 1969	Stanley J. Hay
1012	Palmerston North New Zealand	18 Mar 1979	James Dunlop
884	Rotorua New Zealand	27 Nov 1977	Paul Robert Thomas
445	*Temple View New Zealand †Hamilton South	19 Nov 1967	Harry S. Peckham
853	Upper Hutt New Zealand	14 Aug 1977	Trevor A. Beatson
407	*Wellington New Zealand †Wellington	12 May 1965	Keith A. Harrison

Missions — 2
(As of Oct. 1, 1994; shown with historical number. See MISSIONS.)

(20) NEW ZEALAND AUCKLAND MISSION
P.O. Box 33-840
Takapuna, Auckland, 9
New Zealand
Phone: (011-64-9) 489-5102

(143) NEW ZEALAND WELLINGTON MISSION
P.O. Box 50448
Porirua,
New Zealand
Phone: (011-64-4) 237-0722

NICARAGUA

Year-end 1993: Est. population, 4,110,000; Members, 13,000; Missions, 1; Districts, 8; Branches, 59; Percent LDS, 0.3, or one LDS in 316; Central America Area.

Located in Central America, the Republic of Nicaragua has a Spanish-speaking population that is 95 percent Roman Catholic.

Elder Spencer W. Kimball, then of the Council of the Twelve, promoted work in Central America that led to the opening of the Central America Mission in 1952. Two missionaries from that mission, Elders Manuel Arias and Archie R. Mortensen, entered Nicaragua in 1953. They encountered difficulties at first, but on April 11, 1954, baptized Jose D. Guzman. Other conversions followed. The Nicaraguan District was organized in 1959. The Managua Stake was organized March 22, 1981, with Jose R. Armando Garcia A. as president, but it was discontinued on Oct. 15, 1989.

Missionary work was interrupted in September 1978, as internal conflicts and a civil war led to missionaries being withdrawn. Work continued under local missionaries, and full-time work resumed in the late 1980s. During the periods when few outside leaders entered the country, the local members continued faithfully. In the summer of 1987, members of the Managua Stake received government permission and traveled by bus to the Guatemala City Temple for their temple work.

When the Nicaragua Managua Mission was organized Oct. 15, 1989, following normalization of the government, membership was 3,453. By December 1990, membership had increased to 8,000 members. The members had 100 percent home teaching in the last three months of 1990, and 800 men were ordained to the Melchizedek Priesthood, reported Elder Ted E. Brewerton of the Seventy, area president.

Sources: "LDS Scene," *Ensign*, November, 1978; "Church Continues to Progress in Nicaragua," *Ensign*, February 1979; "A Prayer Answered," by William Hale Kehr, *Church News* May 19, 1979;"Nicaraguans eager to learn, improve lives through gospel," by Gerry Avant, *Church News*, Nov. 22, 1980; "Church Denies Charges in Nicaragua," *Ensign*, October 1982; "Work is booming as members eagerly share their testimonies with friends," *Church News*, Feb. 16, 1991.

Stakes — 0

No.	Name	Organized	First President
		Discontinued	
1246	Managua Nicaragua	22 Mar 1981	Jose R. Armando Garcia A.
	15 Oct 1989 ★Nicaragua Managua Mission		

Mission — 1
(As of Oct. 1, 1994; shown with historical number. See MISSIONS.)

(227) NICARAGUA MANAGUA MISSION
Apartado Postal 3527
Managua, Nicaragua
Phone: (011-505-2) 66-19-50

NIGERIA

Year-end 1993: Est. population, 95,100,000; Members, 22,000; Stakes, 3; Wards, 17; Branches, 109; Missions, 4; Districts, 15; Percent LDS, 0.02, or one LDS in 4,322.

On the west coast of Africa bordering the Gulf of Guinea, the Federal Republic of Nigeria has a military government with a population that speaks English, Hausa, Yoruba and Ibo. The population of the northern half is Moslem, and 40 percent of the southern half is Christian.

The restored gospel took root spontaneously in Nigeria two decades before it was formally preached in that country. From the late 1950s on, some Nigerians learned about the Church through magazine articles and acquired Church literature.

Groups of people began meeting unofficially in the Church's name, and through the years some of them wrote to Church headquarters requesting missionaries. Glen G. Fisher, returning from serving as president of the South Africa Mission, visited Nigeria in 1960 and reported that the groups were sincere, and recommended sending missionaries. However, attempts to send missionaries were thwarted because visas were unavailable.

The historic revelation on the priesthood, announced June 9, 1978, was the catalyst for the start of missionary work in Nigeria. In November of that year, two couples — Elder and Sister Rendell N. Mabey and Elder and Sister Edwin Q. Cannon Jr. — were sent to Nigeria and Ghana as special representatives of the Church's International Mission. They searched out and taught the gospel to people who had been meeting in the Church's name and praying for the coming of Church representatives. The first baptized was Anthony Obinna, one of those who had waited many years for the coming of the missionaries. By early 1980, more than 1,700 converts were baptized in the two countries.

The Africa West Mission was organized July 1, 1980. The name was changed to Nigeria Lagos Mission July 1, 1985.

Less than 10 years after the Church's establishment in Nigeria, membership approached 10,000 in 1987. Twin milestones occurred in 1988, with the creation of the Aba Nigeria Stake May 15, under the direction of Elder Neal A. Maxwell of the Council of the Twelve, and the division July 1 of the Nigeria Lagos Mission to create the Nigeria Aba Mission. The Jos and Ilorin missions, with Nigerian mission presidents Ato Kwamina Dadson and John Agbonkonkon Ehanire, respectively, were organized July 1, 1992. In the local branches, self-help was emphasized.

By 1994, Nigeria had three stakes and 12 districts.

Sources: Swiss Mission manuscript history; Nigeria and Ghana, by Janet Brigham, *Ensign*, February 1980; *Brother to Brother,* by Rendell N. Mabey and Gordon T. Allred, Bookcraft, 1984; "Nigeria marks twin milestones," *Church News*, May 21, 1988; *All Are Alike unto God,* edited by E. Dale LeBaron, Bookcraft, 1990.

Stakes — 3
(Listed alphabetically as of Oct. 1, 1994.)

No.	Name	Organized	First President
Africa Area			
1695	Aba Nigeria	15 May 1988	David William Eka
1957	Benin City Nigeria	24 Oct 1993	Alexander Afamefuna Odume
1781	Port Harcourt Nigeria	25 Nov 1990	Ephriam Sobere Etete

Missions — 4
(As of Oct. 1, 1994; shown with historical number. See MISSIONS.)

(221) NIGERIA ABA MISSION
19 Brass Street
P.O. Box 3636
Aba, Abia State,
Nigeria
Phone: 011-234-82 225-360

(275) NIGERIA ENUGU MISSION
Plot No. 638, Riakos Village
Liberty Dam, Layout
P.O. Box 7751
Jos, Plateau State, Nigeria
Phone: 011-234-73 52543

(274) NIGERIA IBADAN MISSION
Box 5902
No. 9 Plantation Road
Ilorin, Nigeria
Phone: (011-234-31) 220-677

(179) NIGERIA LAGOS MISSION
P.O. Box 9028
Ikeja, Lagos State,
Nigeria
Phone: (011-234-1) 966-192

NIUE

Year-end 1993: Est. population, 1,751; Members, 300; Districts, 1; Branches, 3; Percent LDS, 17, or one LDS in 6; Pacific Area; New Zealand Auckland Mission.

Niue, located in the South Pacific about 300 miles south of the Samoan Islands, is a self-governing island under New Zealand protection. Most residents speak Niuean, and belong to the London Missionary Society religion. The island has a minus-6 percent growth rate.

The first LDS members in Niue were Fritz Bunge-Kruger and his family, who arrived in 1952 to do missionary work. He traveled about the island and showed movies, and then, with the contacts he made, started a home Sunday School. It soon grew to an attendance of 80. They moved to a local dance hall for meetings and on May 29, 1952, a Mutual Improvement Association was organized. The following August, 26 converts were baptized by Elder Thayne Christensen. Other baptismal services followed, and a total of 65 were baptized the first year. Because of persecution during open air meetings, activities were held quietly at first, but at times entire villages attended. The first Niuean missionary was Sionemologa Tagavaitau.

On Feb. 12, 1955, work commenced on the Alofi Chapel with a handful of members raising money, and doing much of the building by hand. They were assisted by labor missionaries. The building was completed in 1958. Additional Church buildings were erected later.

About a third or more of the Niuean members have moved to New Zealand. Devastating hurricanes hit the island in 1959, 1960 and 1990. Many homes were leveled. Members in Niue, particularly the youth, have often distinguished themselves in island competitions.

Sources: *History of the Church in Niue* by Sister Relva R. Price, May 1973; *Unto the Islands of the Sea,* by R. Lanier Britsch; correspondence from Adelia Shumway from Niue Island, Aug. 24, 1990; and interview with Fritz Kruger, 1991; *Church News,* Aug. 29, 1992.

NORTHERN IRELAND
(See United Kingdom)

NORTHERN MARIANA ISLANDS

Year-end 1993: Est. population, 20,000; Members, 400; Branches, 2; Percent LDS, 0.92, or one person in 108; Philippines/Micronesia Area; Micronesia Guam Mission.

The Northern Mariana Islands are a commonwealth administered by the United States. It population is primarily of Chamorro people.

SAIPAN

Among the first members to Saipan were American servicemen in 1944, including L. Tom Perry, later a member of the Council of the Twelve. Missionary work in Saipan began in the early 1970s, but was stopped because of local hostility. In February 1975, Elders Jeff Frame and Callis Carlton began full-time missionary work. One of the first group meetings on the island was held July 24, 1975.

LDS member Alfred "Mustang" Gonzalez became construction manager of the new airport, arriving July 16, 1975, and brought his family the following October. They brought a small vacant quonset hut that had been abandoned in the jungle, and used it for a meetinghouse. After this building was too small, meetings were held in the elders' kitchen and living room. Sunday School classes were held outside under the coconut trees. A small building was completed in 1983. Brad T. Nago and his wife, Jean, were converts in Saipan, baptized Jan. 24, 1976, and became president of Saipan's Chalan Laulau Branch after the Gonzales family returned to Hawaii. At the time the Micronesia Guam Mission was created in 1980, the Saipan Branch had 85 members.

ROTA — TINIAN

Elders Stephen Jones and Kamealoha Kaniho were assigned to open Rota, an island in the Northern Marianas, for proselyting on Sept. 5, 1986. Work was opened on Tinian Aug. 14, 1992, by Elder James Adamson and an Elder McCune.

Source: *Brief History of the Micronesia-Guam Mission,* published by the Micronesia Guam Mission, 1990, Lewis V. Nord, president; Unpublished "History of the Chalan Laulau Branch of the Guam Micronesia Mission."

NORWAY

Year-end 1993: Est. population, 4,300,000; Members, 4,000; Stakes, 1; Wards, 7; Branches, 16; Missions, 1; Districts, 3; Percent LDS, 0.1, or one LDS in 1,075.

In western Scandinavia on the Norwegian Sea, the kingdom of Norway is a hereditary constitutional monarchy. Its people speak Norwegian and Lappish and 94 percent are Evangelical Lutheran.

Missionary work in Norway grew out of the effort in Denmark. Hans F. Petersen, one of the first converts in Denmark, was sent as a missionary to Norway in September 1851. Other elders followed, and the first baptisms took place at Osterrisor on Nov. 26, 1851. A branch was organized there July 16, 1852, and another in Frederikstad July 25, 1852.

Church units in Norway were part of the Scandinavian Mission until 1905, when the Danish-Norwegian Mission was organized. Norway was separated from Denmark into a mission of its own in 1920.

In the early days, many missionaries in Norway were arrested and imprisoned because of their preaching.

By 1930, 8,555 baptisms had been performed in Norway, with about 3,500 converts immigrating to Zion. Members remained under local leadership during World War II, and some missionary work was done. The war's damage left the nation very poor, and many Church members immigrated to the United States after the war.

Until 1950, members and missionaries in Norway used the Danish translation of the Book of Mormon. That year, a Norwegian translation was published, and Norwegian translations of the Doctrine and Covenants and the Pearl of Great Price followed in 1954 and 1955, respectively.

The Oslo Norway Stake was created on May 22, 1977, with Osvald Bjareng as its first president. Elder John A. Widtsoe of the Council of the Twelve was born in Norway.

In the 1980s, member-missionary work proceeded. Pres. Stein Pedersen called 30 stake missionaries to assist missionaries of the Norway Oslo Mission. Membership in 1990 was 3,700.

At the same time, stake public affairs director Rigmor Heistoe helped improved relationships between university professors and the Church. In 1988, Elder Russell M. Nelson of the Council of the Twelve presented Kjell Eliassen, Norwegian ambassador to the United States, with a book containing his family history.

In the 1990s, work also progressed in the Tromso District, made up of four small branches: Tromso, Alta/Hammerfest, Bodo and Harstad/Narvik, headquartered in the largest city in the part of Norway above the Arctic Circle.

Sources: *Encyclopedic History of the Church* by Andrew Jenson; "Norway Saints Note Anniversary," *Church News,* July 1950; "Beyond the Arctic Circle," by Elder Dennis Mead, *Church News,* Jan. 17, 1959; *The Mormon Migration from Norway,* a University of Utah thesis by Helge Slejaas, August 1972; "Norway," *Ensign,* July 1974; "First Stakes for Norway. . ." *Church News,* June 11, 1977; "Norway — Land of the Blue Fjords," *Relief Society Courses of Study,* 1979-80; *Church News,* Jan. 16, 1988; "Field is white' in

Norway's Arctic region," by R. Scott Lloyd, *Church News,* March 16, 1991; "Inner peace can come during time of war," by John Floisand, *Church News,* Feb. 26, 1994.

Stake — 1
(As of Oct. 1, 1994.)

No.	Name	Organized	First President
Europe North Area			
835	Oslo Norway	22 May 1977	Osvald Bjareng

Mission — 1
(As of Oct. 1, 1994; shown with historical number. See MISSIONS.)

(24) NORWAY OSLO MISSION
Baerumsveien 373
Postboks 145
1346 Gjettum, Norway
Phone: 11-47-67 56-84-80

PANAMA

Year-end 1993: Est. population, 2,510,000; Members, 23,000; Stakes, 4; Wards, 22; Branches, 36; Missions, 1; Districts, 2; Percent LDS, 0.9, or one LDS in 109.

Located in southern Central America, the Republic of Panama has a population that speaks Spanish and some English. The country is 93 percent Roman Catholic.

The first members in Panama were LDS servicemen associated with the Panama Canal. In 1941, the first branch in Panama was organized for the military personnel. The branch reached a membership of 100 in its first year. Because the Panamanian government did not recognize the Church until 1965, missionary work was limited. In 1961, Elder Marion G. Romney, then of the Council of the Twelve, presented a copy of the Book of Mormon to the president of the republic, Roberto F. Chiari. In 1965, the Church was officially recognized and proselyting began in Panama and in the nearby San Blas Islands.

Word of the Church spread to the San Blas Islands, located just off the coast and considered part of Panama, when various San Blas Indians heard of the Church while visiting the Canal Zone. In 1965, mission Pres. Ted E. Brewerton visited San Blas and started full-time missionary work. Because the people there had traditions that corresponded closely with Book of Mormon events, many joined the Church. The first meetinghouse, completed in April 1970, was built on the island of Ustopo. The Panama Stake was created Nov. 11, 1979, with Nelson L. Altamirano as president.

The Panama Panama City Mission was created July 1, 1989. At the time, some 10,400 members lived in Panama. Most North American missionaries were withdrawn from the country in 1988, but local leaders and missionaries continued the work.

Cuna Indians from the San Blas Islands have regularly contributed outstanding molas, or fabric paintings, to the Church's international art competitions.

Sources: "Elder Romney sets busy schedule in Canal Zone," *Church News*, Dec. 2, 1961; "San Blas Indians," by Ronald K. Esplin, *Church News*, June 2, 1979; "Panama gains first stake from Costa Rica mission," *Church News*, April 25, 1970, Dec. 22, 1979; "New Missions," *Church News*, Feb. 25, 1989 and *Church News* Aug. 8, 1993.

Stakes — 4
(Listed alphabetically as of Oct. 1, 1994.)

No.	Name	Organized	First President
Central America Area			
1734	Bella Vista Panama 25 Jan 1993		
	Bellavista Panama	23 Jul 1989	Gustavo Brandaris Vergara
1634a	David Panama	19 Apr 1987	Manuel Salvador Arauz
1081	Panama City Panama	11 Nov 1979	Nelson Altamirano Lopez
1596	San Miguelito Panama	20 Apr 1986	Domingo Estribi

Missions — 1
(As of Oct. 1, 1994; shown with historical number. See MISSIONS.)

(226) PANAMA PANAMA CITY MISSION
Apdo 55-0036
Paitilla, Panama
Phone: (011-507) 23-02-19

PAPUA NEW GUINEA

Year-end 1993: Est. population, 3,910,000; Members, 3,300; Missions, 1; Districts, 2; Branches, 16; Percent LDS, 0.08, or one LDS in 1,184; Pacific Area.

On the eastern half of the island of New Guinea in the Coral Sea and spreading across hundreds of smaller islands, Papua New Guinea is a parliamentary democracy. Its population speaks up to 700 village languages. They are 63 percent Protestant and 31 percent Roman Catholic.

Members visited Papua New Guinea long before the first missionaries arrived in 1980. The Port Moresby Branch was organized Oct. 10, 1979, with Athol Pike as branch president. Attending were mostly expatriates of Australia. Elder L. Douglas and Sister Eva Johnson of the Australia Brisbane Mission arrived Aug. 15, 1980. On Oct. 19, 1980, Maria Biai, Komara Nana, Sarah Nana and Rhoda Baka were baptized. Some 63 investigators attended services the following Sunday. Elder Douglas and Sister Nita Campbell succeeded the Johnsons, and during their service, property was obtained for a mission home and meetinghouse. Membership at that time had grown to 280. By October 1982, membership had reached 475 in three branches. Many of those converted had heard of the Church by word of mouth and contacted the missionaries to learn more.

By 1983, five branches had been organized under the direction of mission Pres. Dennis D. Flake. A meetinghouse was completed in 1984. Also that year, two Papuans, Elders George Mauhi and Robert Goisisi, were called as full-time missionaries.

Despite opposition, membership continued to increase. By March 1987, there were 1,450 members in nine branches. As the Church grew, more and more contacts were made in remote villages where many were interested in learning about the gospel. For example, residents of the Daru Village asked for missionaries, who arrived in July, 1990. Just three months later, the Daru Branch had 160 members. During this short time, two full-time missionaries, Elders Brian Mott of Washington and Benjamin Lish of Ohio, were involved in the conversion of approximately 100 of the new branch members.

District Pres. Vabia Rome, one of the early converts, led some 138 Papuans to the Sydney Australia Temple in late 1991.

The Papua New Guinea Port Moresby Mission was created Feb. 13, 1992, and includes the Solomon Islands. The Relief Society continues to make contributions to the branches. Some sisters have learned to read the scriptures through the Relief Society's gospel literacy effort. And in a Relief Society service project in the 1990s, sisters in the Popondetta Branch, completed a service project of donating bandages for the hospital in their city.

Sources: Manuscript History of Church in Papua New Guinea; *Unto the Islands of the Sea,* by R. Lanier Britsch; "Light and Truth pouring into nation 10 years following Church's arrival," by Carol West, *Church News,* Sept. 16, 1989; *Church News,* Feb. 2, 1992; "Literacy opened 'whole new world' for her," *Church News,* Feb. 6, 1993; *Church News,* May 15, 1993.

Mission — 1
(As of Oct. 1, 1994; shown with historical number. See MISSIONS.)

(275) PAPUA NEW GUINEA PORT MORESBY
P.O. Box 6947
Boroko, N.C.D.
Papua New Guinea
Phone: (011-675) 25-2191

PARAGUAY

Year-end 1993: Est. population, 4,210,000; Members, 16,000; Stakes, 3; Wards, 15; Branches, 60; Missions, 1; Districts, 6; Percent LDS, 0.4, or one person in 263.

The Republic of Paraguay in central South America has a population that speaks Spanish and Guarani. They are 87 percent Roman Catholic.

Among the first Latter-day Saints to visit Paraguay was Frederick S. Williams, president of the Argentine Mission, who came in 1939. Samuel J. Skousen, a former missionary in Argentina working for the U.S. government in Rio de Janeiro and later in Asuncion, Paraguay, introduced the gospel to Carlos Alberto Rodriguez and his wife, Mafalda. Rodriguez was baptized in Asuncion Aug. 21, 1948, and his wife, awaiting the birth of their baby, followed Jan. 15, 1949. A branch with Brother Skousen as president was organized in Asuncion on July 26, 1948. The first missionaries arrived Jan. 9, 1950. Their efforts proceeded slowly, but by 1951 two branches had been organized. Their first baptism was Clara Ans de Krisch.

The Paraguay Mission was organized July 1, 1977, with a membership of 2,063, and the first stake was organized Feb. 25, 1979, with Carlos Ramon Espinola as president. Membership then was about 2,900.

An interesting development occurred in 1980 when a colony of 200 Nivacle Indians, who returned to their ancestral homeland in the Gran Chaco, joined the Church. The colony, under its own leadership for 10 years, continued to progress into the 1990s.

The Church in the population center continued to progress, indicated by the creation of the Asuncion Paraguay North Stake in late 1992. Membership in 1990 was 12,000.

Sources: *From Acorn to Oak Tree,* by Frederick S. Williams and Frederick G. Williams; "The Church in Uruguay and Paraguay," *Ensign,* Feburary 1975; "Unexpected Welcome," by William Slaughter, *Church News,* June 9, 1979; *Church News,* Nov. 27, 1983; "Chulupi colony, Mistolar, thrives deep in interior," by Nestor Curbelo, *Church News,* June 2, 1990; *Church News,* Jan. 2, 1993.

Stakes — 3
(Listed alphabetically as of Oct. 1, 1994.)

No.	Name	Organized	First President
South America South Area			
1002	Asuncion Paraguay	25 Feb 1979	Carlos Ramon Espinola
1911	Asuncion Paraguay North	22 Nov 1992	Gregorio Figueredo Servian
1142	Fernando de la Mora Paraguay	1 Jun 1980	Guillermo M. Riveros A.

Mission — 1
(As of Oct. 1, 1994; shown with historical number. See MISSIONS.)

(155) PARAGUAY ASUNCION MISSION
Casilla de Correo 818
Asuncion, Paraguay
Phone: (011-595-21) 601-392

PERU

Year-end 1993: Est. population, 22,910,000; Members, 234,000; Stakes, 52; Wards, 328; Branches, 349; Missions, 6; Districts, 30; Temples, 1; Percent LDS, 1.0, or one LDS in 97.

Located on the Pacific Coast side of South America, Peru is a constitutional republic with a population that speaks Spanish, Quechua and Aymara. Some 90 percent are Roman Catholic.

Prior to 1956, LDS families living in Peru held group meetings, but no organized missionary work was done. A copper mine owned by a member in Salt Lake City, Utah, Alfred W. McCune, also brought a few members to Peru. On Jan. 1, 1956, Frederick S. Williams, a former mission president in Argentina and Uruguay, and his family moved to Peru and contacted Church headquarters for permission to organize a branch and begin missionary work. A branch was organized July 8, 1956, by Elder Henry D. Moyle, then of the Council of the Twelve. Elders Darwin Thomas, Edward T. Hall, Donald L. Hokanson and Shirrel M. Plowman arrived Aug. 7, 1956, and began proselyting. A building for branch meetings was purchased Nov. 30. At the first branch conference held Feb. 24, 1957, 44 attended, 22 of whom were investigators. Missionaries were sent to Arequipa later in the year. The Andes Mission, headquartered in Lima, was established Nov. 1, 1959. At the time, there were five branches and 300 members.

The mission was divided Oct. 1, 1961. After the division, the Chile and Andes missions (comprising Bolivia and Peru) each had 12 branches and more than 2,000 members. The number of members in Peru increased to 6,391 in 1965. When the first stake was organized in Lima on Feb. 22, 1970, membership in Peru was 10,771. Called as president was Roberto Vidal, an early convert. That same year, the mission was divided, and renamed the Peru Mission.

Growth continued as local leaders assumed priesthood leadership, and by 1977 there were 17,000 members. At an area conference presided over by President Spencer W. Kimball held in Lima Feb. 26-27, 1977, 7,900 attended. Four years later in 1981, President Kimball announced a temple for Lima, which was completed and dedicated Jan. 10-12, 1986.

On Jan. 30-31, 1988, just 32 years after missionary work started in Peru, seven stakes in Lima were created in one weekend by Elder M. Russell Ballard of the Council of the Twelve, and Lima became the city with the second largest number of stakes of any metropolitan area outside the United States.

In July, 1993, Peru's sixth mission was created, the Peru Chiclayo, which includes the highland Andes, where many of Lamanite descent live, and land bordering Ecuador. Seven additional stakes were created from October 1992 to October 1994. A seventh mission in Peru was created July 1, 1994.

Sources: Andes Mission manuscript history; Peru, *Ensign,* February 1977; *From Acorn to Oak Tree,* by Frederick S. Williams and Frederick G. Williams; *Church News,* Jan. 19, 1986; "Resourceful people of Lima making Church 'blossom'," by Lee Warnick, *Church News,* Feb. 6, 1988.

No.	Name	Organized	First President
South America North Area			
1815	Arequipa Peru Central	15 Sep 1991	Cesar Leoncio Gamarra G.
1540	Arequipa Peru Manuel Prado	20 Jun 1985	Efrain Jorge Rodriguez M.
1985	Arequipa Peru Selva Alegre	24 Jul 1994	Elias A. Rebaza Rado
1108	*Arequipa Peru Umacollo 20 Jun 1985		
	†Arequipa Peru	21 Feb 1980	Victor H. Gamero
1743	Canto Grande Peru	18 Mar 1990	Augusto Ordinalo S.
1145	Chiclayo Peru	8 Jun 1980	Jorge Humberto del Carpio M.
1567	Chiclayo Peru Central	27 Oct 1985	Franklin D. Orroyo S.
1820	Chiclayo Peru North	20 Oct 1991	Javier Delgado Torres
1122	Chimbote Peru	23 Mar 1980	Carlos Santos Lopez O.
1790	Chimbote Peru South	17 Mar 1991	Julio Arturo Leiva P.
1860	Chincha Peru	8 May 1992	Alfonso Eduardo Ormeno Villa
1527	Cuzco Peru	28 Apr 1985	Jose U. Coacalla
1910	Cuzco Peru Inti Raymi	15 Nov 1992	Miguel A. Vallenas Frisancho
1725	Huacho Peru	4 Jun 1989	Carlos Manuel Zapata P.
1471	Huancayo Peru	6 May 1984	Moises Sanchez T.
1756	Huanuco Peru	17 Jun 1990	Raul Rodriguez S.
1739	Ica Peru	17 Dec 1989	Alexander Alfonso Nunez T.
1162	Iquitos Peru	3 Aug 1980	Carlos Rojas Romero
1864	Iquitos Peru Punchana	23 May 1992	Alfonso Frederico Rojas R.
1541	Iquitos Peru Sachachorro	23 Jun 1985	Jorge Diaz Suarez
1924a	Lima Peru Bayovar	7 Mar 1993	Augusto R. Ordinola Salva
1063	Lima Peru Callao	16 Sep 1979	Manuel Paredes
1743	*Lima Peru Canto Grande 7 Mar 1993		
	†Canto Grande Peru	18 Mar 1990	Augusto Ordinalo S.
789	Lima Peru Central	21 Nov 1976	Oscar H. Aguayo U.
1679	Lima Peru Chorrillos	31 Jan 1988	Israel Antonio Gonzalez B.
1794	Lima Peru Chosica	5 May 1991	Ricardo Enrique Lazo T.
1675	Lima Peru Comas	31 Jan 1988	Grover Pinto R.
1680	Lima Peru El Olivar	31 Jan 1988	Antero Miguel Sanchez M.
788	Lima Peru Lamanita	21 Nov 1976	Rafael de la Cruz
1677	Lima Peru Las Flores	31 Jan 1988	Miguel Fernando Rojas A.
1674	Lima Peru Las Palmeras	31 Jan 1988	Albina Isidro Chagua C.
503	*Lima Peru Limatambo 21 Nov 1976		
	*Lima Peru		
	†Lima	22 Feb 1970	Roberto Vidal
670	*Lima Peru Magdelena 21 Nov 1976		
	†Lima Peru West	1 Dec 1974	Manuel Paredes L.
1678	Lima Peru Maranga	31 Jan 1988	Benedicto S. Pacheco M.
1486	Lima Peru Palao	1 Jul 1984	Rene Loli
1439	Lima Peru San Felipe	11 Sep 1983	Mauro Luis Artica Q.
1064	Lima Peru San Juan	16 Sep 1979	Jorge Salazar
1440	Lima Peru San Luis	11 Sep 1983	Philippe J. Kradolfer
1065	Lima Peru San Martin	16 Sep 1979	Rene Loli
1795	Lima Peru Tahuantinsuyo	5 May 1991	Albino Isidro Chagua C.
1553	Lima Peru Villa Maria	25 Aug 1985	Juan Maguina Colquis
1881	Lima Peru Villa Salvador	31 May 1992	Victor Nicolas Anicama
1676	Lima Peru Vitarte	31 Jan 1988	Luis E. Stiglich S.
1734a	Mantaro Peru	30 Jul 1989	Manuel Moises Sanchez T.
1925	Pisco Peru	13 Mar 1993	Marcelo P. Munante Salguero
1400	Piura Peru	16 Feb 1983	Pedro Puertas Rojas
1755	Piura Peru Castilla	17 Jun 1990	Oscar Alfredo Galvez C.
1961a	Pucallpa Peru	5 Dec 1993	Ferrando Vela Lopez
1872	Puno Peru	28 May 1992	Adan Bravo Mathens
1399	Tacna Peru	13 Feb 1983	Abraham La Torre Parades
1914	Tacna Peru Arias Araguez	6 Dec 1992	Derliz Guzman Tejadi
1802	Trujillo Peru East	16 Jun 1991	Raymundo Aponte Garcia
1987	*Trujillo Peru Central	14 Aug 1994	Pedro Gerardo Rodriguez H.

1887	*Peru North 19 Aug 1984		
	†Trujillo Peru	22 Jan 1978	Teofilo Puertas Vega
1487	Trujillo Peru Palermo	12 Aug 1984	Jose Neyra

Missions — 7
(As of Oct. 1, 1994; shown with historical number. See MISSIONS.)

(165) PERU AREQUIPA MISSION
Casilla 1884, Arequipa,
Peru
Phone: (011-51-54) 22-34-63

(291) PERU CHICLAYO MISSION
Los Manzanos 127
Urbanizacion Santa Victoria
Chiclayo, Peru
Phone: 011-51-74 237-407

(302) PERU LIMA CENTRAL MISSION
Av. Arequipa 660, Piso 1
Lima, Peru
Phone: 011-51-14 33-87-98

(210) PERU LIMA EAST MISSION
Apartado 14-0196
Lima 14, Peru
Phone: (011-51-14) 33-15-66

(149) PERU LIMA NORTH MISSION
Casilla de Correo 11-0123
Lima 11, Peru
Phone: (011-51-14) 33 15 96

(50) PERU LIMA SOUTH MISSION
Casilla de Correo 14-0293
Lima 14, Peru
Phone: 011-51-14 33-59-82

(184a) PERU TRUJILLO MISSION
Casilla 10
Urbanizacion California
Trujillo, Peru
Phone: (011-51-44) 25-41-74

PHILIPPINES

Year-end 1993: Est. population, 64,660,000; Members, 314,000; Stakes, 46; Wards, 276; Branches, 667; Missions, 13; Districts, 83; Temples, 1; Percent LDS, 0.5, or one LDS in 205.

An archipelago off the southeast coast of Asia, the Republic of the Philippines has a population that speaks Tagalog and English. They are Roman Catholic, 83 percent; Protestant, 9 percent; and Moslem, 5 percent.

The Church was introduced in the Philippines during the Spanish-American War in 1898. Two artillery batteries from Utah were sent to the Philippines, and Willard Call and George Seaman were set apart as missionaries, making them the first Mormon elders to preach the gospel among the people of the Philippine islands.

There was no missionary activity in the Philippines until the end of World War II, when Maxine Grimm, wife of a U.S. Army colonel, serving in the American Red Cross in the Philippines, introduced the gospel to Aniceta Pabilona Fajardo, the first Filipino to join the Church in the islands. Sister Fajardo was baptized in 1945. Dean Franklin Clair, a U.S. Army medic, was another LDS pioneer in the Philippines when he married Filipina Leona H. Seno.

The Church experienced a growth spurt in the area in 1953 during the Korean War when the Luzon Servicemen's District was organized.

On April 28, 1961, Elder Gordon B. Hinckley, then of the Council of the Twelve, met with a small group of local servicemen, American residents, Filipino members and their families at the American War Memorial Cemetery to offer a prayer for the islands and open the islands for missionary work. The first missionaries, Elders Ray Goodson, Harry Murray, Kent Lowe and Nestor Ledesma, arrived in Manila on June 5, 1961.

The first two to be baptized by the missionaries were Jose Gutierez Sr. and Lino Brocka. By the end of 1961, there had been eight baptisms.

In 1967, the Philippine Mission was organized with Paul S. Rose as president. Two years later the Church had spread to eight major islands of the country and the mission had the highest number of baptisms in the Church.

The Philippines Mission was divided into two missions in 1974, creating the Philippines Manila Mission, under the leadership of Pres. Raymond L. Goodson, and the Philippines Cebu City Mission, under the direction of Pres. Carl D. Jones. In the next 12 years, seven more missions were created.

In recent years, missionaries have baptized Filipinos at the rate of a stake a month during peak periods.

The Manila Missionary Training Center was established in 1983 to train missionaries, and in September 1984 the Manila Philippines Temple was dedicated. At that time, membership was 76,000.

In 1987, the Philippines/Micronesia Area was created with headquarters in Manila. Nine new missions were created in the Philippines between 1986-92.

During 1990-91, members experienced volcanic eruptions, earthquakes, flooding and conflicts between insurgent and government forces. Church relief efforts were sent to help in the recovery of the natural disasters. Membership has continued to grow, reaching 237,000 in 1990.

The first Filipino General Authority, Elder Augusto A. Lim, was called to the Second Quorum of the Seventy June 6, 1992. The Church became more prominent as Christmas lights on the temple grounds attracted more people, and its youth become involved in more service projects.

Sources: "The Philippines," *The Improvement Era,* March 1964; *History of the Church in the Philippines,* compiled by the Luzon District, 1965; "Philippines: the Land of Joyous Service," *Ensign,* August 1975; "Missionaries in Khaki," by Carol Cornwall Madsen, *Church News,* June 23, 1979; "Gospel flourishes in soil of Filipino faith," by Francis M. Orquiola, *Ensign,* September, 1984; "Dateline Philippines," *Tambuli,* April 1991; *Church News,* Dec. 25, 1993.

Stakes — 46
(Listed alphabetically as of Oct. 1, 1994.)

No.	Name	Organized	First President
Philippines/Micronesia Area			
1226	Angeles Philippines	18 Jan 1981	Orlando D. Aquilar
1281	Bacolod Philippines	5 Jul 1981	Remus G. Villarete
1323	Bacolod Philippines North	7 Feb 1982	Rufino Alvarez Villaneuva Jr.
1573	Baguio Philippines	17 Nov 1985	Carlos F. Chavez
1806	Balanga Philippines	7 Jul 1991	Torbio Nuguid Santos
1788	Binalbagan Philippines	3 Mar 1991	Jose Vicente Pioquinto
1711	Butuan Philippines	19 Feb 1989	Henry Ferrer Acebedo
1340	Cabanatuan Philippines	9 May 1982	Arsenio A. Pacaduan
1884	Cabuyao Philippines	7 June 1992	Tomas S. Merdegia Jr.
1572	Cadiz Philippines	10 Nov 1985	Carmelino M. Cawit
1535	Cagayan De Oro Philippines	26 May 1985	Loreto Balanta Libid
1748	Cagayan de Oro Philippines East	6 May 1990	Danilo D. De La Vega
1238	Caloocan Philippines	22 Feb 1981	Godofredo Hilario Esguerra
1807	Camiling Philippines	14 Jul 1991	Celso Arenzana Nicolas
1545	*Cavite Philippines 24 Oct 1989		
	†Makiling Philippines	18 Aug 1985	Jose Trinidad Aguilar
1220	Cebu City Philippines	11 Jan 1981	Jacob Torres Lopez
1229	Dagupan Philippines	25 Jan 1981	Bernardo G. Reamon
1307	Davao Philippines	15 Nov 1981	George S. Lavarino
1544	Davao Philippines Buhangin	18 Aug 1985	Patrick Hartford M. Clair
1876	Digos Philippines	31 May 1992	Paul Farinas Bunoan
1908	Iligan Philippines	18 Oct 1992	William C. Garife
1508	Iloilo Philippines	20 Jan 1985	Hannibal Delgado D.
1877	Kidapawan Philippines	31 May 1992	Rodolfo Bergado Estrella
1547	La Carlota Philippines	18 Aug 1985	Antonio V. Custodio
1715	Laoag Philippines	23 Apr 1989	Jose Miguel Tumaneng
1555	Las Pinas Philippines	15 Sep 1985	Delfin T. Justiniano
1551	Legaspi Philippines	19 Aug 1985	Jose P. Leveriza
1557	Lingayen Philippines	22 Sep 1985	Oberlito R. Cantillo
841	Makati Philippines	29 May 1977	Ruben Moscaira Lancanienta
1726	Malolos Philippines	11 Jun 1989	Rogelio C. Coronel
1735b	Mandaue Philippines	19 Nov 1989	Cesar Abina Perez Jr.
613	*Manila Philippines		
	†Manila	20 May 1973	Augusto Alandy Lim
1210	Marikina Philippines	30 Nov 1980	Augusto Alandy Lim
1546	Naga Philippines	18 Aug 1985	Avelino S. Babia Sr.
1713	Olongapo Philippines	5 Mar 1989	Richard Noboru Kivabu
1309	Paranaque Philippines	22 Nov 1981	Ruben M. Lacanienta
1554	Pasig Philippines	15 Sep 1985	Macario Molina Yasona Jr.
842	Quezon City Philippines	29 May 1977	Augusto Alandy Lim
1789	San Fabian Philippines	17 Mar 1991	Loreto D. Querimit
1315	San Fernando Philippines La Union	6 Dec 1981	Angel B. Salanga Jr.
1552	San Pablo Philippines	20 Aug 1985	Cleofas S. Canoy
1875	Santa Cruz Philippines	31 May 1992	Rolando Pramis Nueva
1330	*Talisay Philippines 10 Aug 1989		
	†Cebu City Philippines South	21 Mar 1982	Bienvenido Pangilinan Flores

1321	Tarlac Philippines	13 Dec 1981	Mario de Jesus
1721	Tuguegarao Philippines	21 May 1989	Quirino Sumabat Donato
1558	Urdaneta Philippines	22 Sep 1985	Felino Caparas Ocampo
1571	Zamboanga Philippines	10 Nov 1985	Catalino A. Dugupan Sr.

Discontinued

1577	Munoz Philippines	24 Nov 1985	Juanito Wytangooy Tanedo
	31 May 1992		
1780	Ozamiz Philippines	25 Nov 1990	Wilfredo Tumampos Romero
	7 Nov 1993		

Missions — 13

(As of Oct. 1, 1994; shown with historical number. See MISSIONS.)

(110) PHILIPPINES BACOLOD MISSION
P.O. Box 660, Bacolod City
6100 Negros Occidental
Philippines
Phone: (011-63-34) 8-26-21

(172) PHILIPPINES BAGUIO MISSION
P.O. Box 380
Baguio City, Benguet 2600
Philippines
Phone: (011-63-74) 442-5951

(268) PHILIPPINES CABANATUAN MISSION
P.O. Box 176,
Cabanatuan City
3100 Nueva Ecija, Philippines
Phone: (011-63-44) 963-2406

(211) PHILIPPINES CAGAYAN DE ORO MISSION
Cor. Kauswagan Rd. & Faustina
Neri St., Block 1 RER Subd.
Kauswagan, Cagayan de Oro City
9000 Philippines
Phone: (011-63-88) 22 6531

(194) PHILIPPINES CEBU MISSION
P.O. Box 338
Cebu City
6000 Cebu, Philippines
Phone: (011-63-32) 311-153

(157) PHILIPPINES DAVAO MISSION
P.O. Box 82624
8000 Davao City,
Philippines
Phone: (011-63-82) 7-22-36

(256) PHILIPPINES ILAGAN MISSION
LDS Church
National Highway
Calamagui, Ilagan
3300 Isabela, Philippines
Phone: (011-63-2) 7623-62185

(76b) PHILIPPINES MANILA MISSION
P.O. Box 1997
Makati Central Post Office
Makati, Metro Manila
0714 Philippines
Phone: (011-63-2) 818-7749

(223) PHILIPPINES NAGA MISSION
P.O. Box 885
Naga City
4400 Camarines Sur, Philippines
Phone: (011-63-5421) 736209

(219) PHILIPPINES OLONGAPO MISSION
P.O. Box 1198, Ortigas Center
Emerald Avenue, Pasig
Metro Manila 1600, Philippines
Phone: (011-63-912) 302-8547

(192) PHILIPPINES QUEZON CITY MISSION
Ortigas Center P.O. Box 13873
Emerald Avene, Pasig
Metro Manila 1600, Philippines
Phone: (011-63-2) 631-5763

(250) PHILIPPINES SAN PABLO MISSION
P.O. Box 38
San Pablo City
4000 Laguna, Philippines
Phone: (011-63-93) 3771

(251) PHILIPPINES TACLOBAN MISSION
Diversion Road
Banezville, Maras Baras
Tacloban City, P.O. Box 69,
6500 Leyte, Philippines
Phone: (011-63-53) 321-3575

POLAND

Year-end 1993: Est. population, 38,500,000; Members, 500; Missions, 1; Districts, 1; Branches, 9; Europe Area.

On the Baltic Sea in east central Europe, Poland has a population that speaks Polish, and is mostly Roman Catholic.

In 1928, the Selbongen Branch meetinghouse was erected in Germany. After World War II, the town of Selbongen was part of the area ceded to Poland, and its name was changed to Zelbak.

President Ezra Taft Benson, then a member of the Council of the Twelve, was the first priesthood leader to visit Zelbak after the war. Upon his arrival, more than 100 members and friends gathered in a quickly convened meeting to bear their testimonies, sing and pray and receive his counsel.

While the branch struggled to stay alive during the subsequent years, the spirit of the Saints did not falter. In 1947, government officials ordered the Zelbak meetings discontinued on the grounds that only the Polish language could be spoken in public meetings of any kind. Three years later, the branch was re-opened. The branch continued until 1978, when priesthood leaders made the decision to discontinue the branch. The meetinghouse there still stands, but is no longer used for LDS functions.

President Spencer W. Kimball visited Poland Aug. 24, 1977, after official recognition of the Church by the Polish government, which came on May 30, 1977.

A number of couple missionaries served in Poland following 1977. The first elders arrived in January 1988. Sister Urzula Adamska, the first Polish missionary, was called in 1989.

On June 15, 1989, ground was broken for a meetinghouse in Warsaw. The ceremony was attended by more than 200 people, including government and religious leaders of different faiths. Elder Russell M. Nelson of the Council of the Twelve presided over and addressed the groundbreaking ceremony. The day after the groundbreaking, Elder Nelson and other Church leaders met with Poland's minister of religious affairs, who shared copies of a new law guaranteeing freedom of conscience and belief.

The meetinghouse was dedicated June 22, 1991, in a service attended by more than 400 people, including government leaders.

At the time work on the Warsaw meetinghouse was begun, Poland was part of the Austria Vienna East Mission. The Poland Warsaw Mission was created July 1, 1990.

Church Welfare Service workers served on a non-denominational consulting company helping Poland modernize its agriculture. The Church donated medical supplies, clothing and bedding to Poland in 1991. The Tabernacle Choir performed in Warsaw in 1991.

Sources: Swiss Mission manuscript history; *Church News*, July 13, Aug. 17, and Aug. 24, 1946; New Branch Organized in Red Poland," *Church News*, Oct. 1, 1966; "The Branch that Wouldn't Die," by Gilbert W. Scharffs, *Ensign*, 1971; *Church News*, Sept. 17, 1977; "Zelwagi survives," by Richard L. Jensen, *Church News*, June 30, 1979; "Church in Poland: Small but Strong," *Ensign*, August 1979; "Reunion revives spirit of Selbongen,'" *Church News*, Oct. 14, 1989; "The Book of Mormon in Polish," by Kerril Sue Rollins, *Ensign*, June 1982; *Church News*, July 1, 1989.

Mission — 1
(As of Oct. 1, 1994; shown with historical number. See MISSIONS.)

(252) POLAND WARSAW MISSION
ul. Wolska 142
P1-01-258 Warsaw, Poland
Phone: (011-48-22) 36-19-39

PORTUGAL

Year-end 1993: Est. population, 9,800,000; Members, 33,000; Stakes, 5; Wards, 24; Branches, 87; Missions, 3; Districts, 12; Percent LDS, 0.3, or one LDS in 297.

At the southwest corner of Europe, the Republic of Portugal is a parliamentary democracy. Its population is 97 percent Roman Catholic.

The first members of the Church in Portugal were members in the U.S. Armed Forces stationed in the country in the early 1970s. The first known regularly held Church meetings were conducted by military personnel John C. Peterson and Steven Lindsey, who in the spring of 1974 visited the Spain Madrid Mission to see if missionary work could begin in Portugal. Official recognition of the Church was not gained. However, a revolution in May 1974 led to a new government, which gave recognition to religious entities. Shortly thereafter, President Spencer W. Kimball and David M. Kennedy, special representative of the First Presidency, visited Portugal, and received assurances that the Church could enter the country.

In August 1974, Church member Ray E. Caldwell was assigned by the Canadian government to be first secretary of the Canadian embassy in Lisbon. He stopped en route in Salt Lake City, Utah, and was set apart as the group leader over any members he might find.

Church meetings were soon held in the Caldwell home. In November 1974, Pres. Wm. Grant Bangerter, later of the Presidency of the Seventy, arrived in Lisbon to preside over the newly created Portugal Lisbon Mission. Four missionaries were transferred from a mission in Brazil to begin the work, and they found many people who were interested in the gospel. By July 1975, there were 100 Portuguese members.

From those beginnings, the Church reached its first thousand members by July 1978, and has grown steadily since. The Lisbon Portugal Stake was created July 10, 1981, with Jose Manual da Costa Santos as president.

The Portugal Porto Mission was formed from the Portugal Lisbon Mission in July 1987. The Portugal Lisbon Mission was divided in 1989 to create the Lisbon North and Lisbon South Missions.

In September 1991, the first national Boy Scout encampment was held for members in Portugal, and some 60 young men participated. Portugal was among the nations that received general conference by satellite for the first time in 1993.

Sources: Culture for Missionaries: Portugal, 1984; "Discovering Gospel Riches in Portugal," by Don L. Searle, *Ensign,* October 1987; *Church News,* Feb. 16, 1989; "Brotherly Love," *Ensign,* August 1989.

AZORES AND MADEIRA ISLANDS

Year-end 1993: Est. population, 250,000; Members, 1,900; Districts, 3; Branches, 8; Europe/Mediterranean Area; Portugal Lisbon North Mission.

The Azores Islands, located 800 miles off the coast of Portugal in the North Atlantic, includes nine main islands that are populated.

Both archipelagos are Portuguese territories where Portuguese is spoken. The first branch was organized in Funchal on Sept. 4, 1983. In 1991 a group of Boy Scouts from Madeira took part in the Church's first Boy Scout encampment in Portugal. One district with four branches have been established in the Madeira Islands, and two districts in the Azores in the Europe Area.

Sources: French Mission correspondence; Portugal Lisbon North Mission; *Church News,* March 19, 1988; *Church News,* Oct. 5, 1991.

Stakes — 5
(Listed alphabetically as of Oct. 1, 1994.)

No.	Name	Organized	First President
Europe Mediterranean Area			
1276	Lisbon Portugal	10 Jun 1981	Jose Manuel da Costa Santos
1729	Lisbon Portugal Oeiras	25 Jun 1989	Vitor Manuel Pereira M.
1723	Matosinhos Portugal	28 May 1989	Alexandre Rocha Benidio
1613	Porto Portugal	2 Nov 1986	Alcino Pereira Da Silva
1652	Setubal Portugal	6 Sep 1987	Octavio Da Silva Melo

Missions — 3
(As of Oct. 1, 1994; shown with historical number. See MISSIONS.)

(253) PORTUGAL LISBON NORTH MISSION
Rua das Pedralvas
No 23, R/C-D
1500 Lisboa, Portugal
Phone: (011-351-1) 749-248

(115) PORTUGAL LISBON SOUTH MISSION
Largo Com. Augusto Madureira, 7-B
1495 Alges,
Portugal
Phone: (011-351-1) 410-2064

(203) PORTUGAL PORTO MISSION
Rua de Amalia Luazes 23 - Sala 1
4200 Porto,
Portugal
Phone: (011-351-2) 521-575

MACAU

Year-end 1993: Est. population, 400,000; Members, 700; Branches, 1; Asia Area; Hong Kong Mission.

An enclave at the mouth of the Canton River in China, Macau is administered by Portugal.

In 1964, Pres. Jay Quealey of the Southern Far East Mission sent Elders Darryl Thomander and Gilbert Montano to labor in Macau. They arrived July 2, 1964, and held the first LDS services July 12, in their rented quarters. Ten investigators were present. Their first convert was Gary Lau, baptized Aug. 21, 1964.

After an interlude, missionaries under Pres. Jerry D. Wheat of the Hong Kong Mission resumed work on Macau Sept. 6, 1976, after they learned of a constitutional amendment that allowed religious freedom to meet, teach and proselyte.

The Macau Branch of the Hong Kong Island Stake was organized Jan. 1, 1977, and had about 300 members in 1990, and increased to 640 members in 1993.

Sources: *Church News,* Dec. 4, 1976; Journal, correspondence from Darryl Thomander, Sept. 26, 1992.

PUERTO RICO

Year-end 1993: Est. population, 3,336,000; Members, 19,000; Districts, 8; Branches, 50; Missions, 1; Percent LDS, 0.5, or one LDS in 196.

The easternmost island of the Greater Antilles in the east Caribbean Sea, Puerto Rico is a U.S. commonwealth with a population that speaks Spanish. Most of the people are Roman Catholic.

Gardner H. Russell (who was called to the Seventy in 1986) began holding Church meetings with his family and LDS servicemen at Guajataca in 1947, and later in San Juan. For the first few years, those who attended the meetings were LDS servicemen. Later, other members moved to Puerto Rico.

Florida Mission Pres. Ned Winder visited Puerto Rico in October 1963 on a routine visit and felt inspired to send missionaries. In January 1964, Elders Verl Tolbert and Dwight K. Hunter arrived in Puerto Rico under his direction. They visited several branches in the Puerto Rico District, which had been organized ealier for military personnel. The first convert baptized in Puerto Rico was a serviceman, Dennis Wayne Hart, baptized Feb. 8, 1964. The first Puerto Rican baptized was Ilka Josephina Frau, baptized at the Naval Beach on March 2, 1964.

The next mission president was Pres. Glen L. Rudd (who was called to the Seventy in 1987), who sent Spanish-speaking missionaries to the island. The first Spanish-speaking branch was organized in 1970. On March 8 of that year, the first meetinghouse in the Caribbean District of the Florida Mission was dedicated in San Juan. On Oct. 17, home seminary was started. The Spanish branch became an independent branch a year later. Members' spirits were lifted March 8, 1981, by a visit from President Spencer W. Kimball.

The Puerto Rico San Juan Mission was created in 1979 with a membership of 1,892. The first stake was created in San Juan on Dec. 14, 1980, by President Ezra Taft Benson, then of the Council of the Twelve, at a meeting attended by 81 percent of the membership. Called to lead the stake was Pres. Herminio de Jesus.

New stakes were added in 1982, 1984 and 1985. President Benson visited again on April 12, 1987, and noted that membership had increased to more than 12,000. Four stakes were discontinued in December 1993 following the reduction of military personnel stationed in Puerto Rico.

Sources: "Puerto Rico organizes two branches," by Elder Delbert Goates, *Church News,* June 25, 1955; Florida Mission manuscript history; "The Saints in Puerto Rico," by Orson Scott Card, *Ensign,* March 1978; "Caribbean beginnings," by Gordon Irving, *Church News,* April 22, 1978; "First Puerto Rican stake organized," *Church News,* Dec. 27, 1980; "History is made: prophet visits Caribbean islands," by Gerry Avant, *Church News,* March 21, 1981; "President Benson visits Puerto Rico," by Gerry Avant, *Church News,* April 18, 1987; "Outline of Historical Events . . . in Caribbean Nations," *VASAA Newsletter,* by Virgil N. Kovalenko.

Stakes — 0
(Listed alphabetically as of Oct. 1, 1994.)

No.	Name	Organized	First President
North America Southeast Area			
		Discontinued	
1480	Carolina Puerto Rico 5 Dec 1993	17 Jun 1984	Jesus Nieves
1580	Mayaquez Puerto Rico 5 Dec 1993	1 Dec 1985	Heriberto Hernandez Vera
1349	Ponce Puerto Rico 5 Dec 1993	13 Jun 1982	Noah Jefferson Burns
1215	San Juan Puerto Rico 5 Dec 1993	14 Dec 1980	Herminio De Jesus

Mission — 1
(As of Oct. 1, 1994; shown with historical number. See MISSIONS.)

(157) PUERTO RICO SAN JUAN MISSION
Urb. Villa Andalucia
A14 Ronda Street #102
Rio Piedras, PR 00926
Phone: (809) 755-2670

ROMANIA

Year-end 1993: Est. population, 23,212,000; Members, 300; Missions, 1; Districts, 1; Branches, 4; Europe Area.

In July 1899, Mischa Markow, a prominent missionary to the Balkans, arrived in Constanta, Romania, with a Bulgarian companion, Argir Dimitrov, whom he baptized on Aug. 30, 1899. The pair traveled to Bucharest where they baptized another person. They made no further progress until Elder Markow had a dream about meeting a mother and daughter who would hear the gospel. The dream was realized in every detail and the mother and daughter were eventually baptized. Five others were later baptized as well and a branch organized.

Elder Markow was arrested a short time later. During his trial, Elder Markow defended the gospel and a dispute about the apostasy broke out in the courtroom. Elder Markow was confined to jail a for few days and banished.

In modern times, Elder Russell M. Nelson of the Council of the Twelve and Elder Hans B. Ringger of the Seventy met with the ministers of justice, health and religion, and other dignitaries, including the mayor of Bucharest and members of the district council on Feb. 8-9, 1990. Following this meeting, the Church began assisting with the Romanian orphanages and supplying medical supplies to the country.

Romania became part of the Austria Vienna East Mission in 1990, where it remained until the mission was discontinued in 1992. Missionaries serving in Romania provided humanitarian services under the Hungary Budapest Mission until the Romania Bucharest Mission was created July 1, 1993.

Assistance to Romania continued from European stakes through the early 1990s. By 1994, Romania had four branches in one district.

Sources: "Began with one," by William Slaughter, *Church News*, July 21, 1979; "Mischa Markow, Missionary to the Balkans," by William Hale Kehr, *Ensign*, June 1980; *Church News*, Aug. 18, 1990; Aug. 17, 1991, Dec. 7, 1991, Jan. 11, 1992, correspondence from Kahlile Mehr, Dec. 29, 1992.

Mission — 1

(292) ROMANIA BUCHAREST MISSION
B-Dul Unirii Nr. 10
BL. 7B Sc. 1 Et. 2 Apt. 5
Sector 4 Bucharesti,
Romania
Phone: 011-40-1 311-1928

RUSSIA

Year-end 1993: Est. population, 149,000,000; Members: 1,900; Missions, 3; Districts, 5; Branches: 33; Europe Area.

Russians speak Slavic languages, including Russian, and others. Non-religious or atheists make up 51 percent of the population, with Russian Orthodox 31 percent, and Moslem, 11 percent.

As early as 1843, Russia was considered a prospective mission field. Orson Hyde and George J. Adams were called to go to Russia by the Prophet Joseph Smith, but their mission was aborted by the Prophet's martyrdom a year later.

In 1895, Elder August Joel Hoglund, a native of Sweden, was sent to St. Petersburg where he arrived June 9. He met with the Johan M. Lindelof family and baptized Johan and his wife, Alma, on June 11 in the river Neva. The Lindelof family was visited periodically and in 1903, Elder Francis M. Lyman of the Council of the Twelve and then president of the European Mission, accompanied by Joseph J. Cannon, visited the family in St. Petersburg. The Lindelof family was later dispersed during the revolution of 1918.

On April 27, 1919, Andrew Hasberg, a member of the U.S. Expeditionary Forces in World War I, was baptized in a lake about four miles south of Vladivostok, Russia, by Thomas E. Hunsaker.

In 1959 Elder Ezra Taft Benson of the Council of the Twelve, then U.S. Secretary of Agriculture, visited the Central Baptist Church in Moscow and preached to an attentive congregation.

Missionary work resumed tentatively in 1989. Among the first to be baptized were Yuri, Liudmilla and Anna Terebenin, who heard about the Church and were baptized during a trip to Budapest, Hungary. Olga Smolyanova, then 18, was baptized in Italy. Others were baptized by Finnish member-missionaries. One of these was Leena Laitinen, who taught a group of investigators in her home in Leningrad. During this period, visits were made to Leningrad and Moscow by Elder Hans B. Ringger of the Seventy and mission presidents Steven R. Mecham of the Finland Helsinki Mission and Dennis B. Neuenschwander (now of the Seventy) of the Austria Vienna East Mission. In September of 1989, Pres. Neuenschwander authorized U.S. Embassy worker Dohn Thornton to begin holding group meetings in his apartment. Two missionaries, Elders David S. Reagan and Kevin A. Dexter, arrived in Leningrad on Jan. 26, 1990. They taught Sister Laitinen's investigators and baptized Anton Skripko Feb. 3, 1990, the first member baptized in Russia in modern times. He later became the first to serve a full-time mission from Russia, arriving at the Missionary Training Center July 26, 1991, and serving in the Utah Ogden Mission.

The first missionaries stationed in Leningrad were Elder Reagan and Elder Burt Dover. The Vyborg Branch was created in February 1990.

Elders Russell M. Nelson and Dallin H. Oaks of the Council of the Twelve, visited a number of times, and continued efforts to strengthen the Church in Russia and its neighboring countries.

By mid-summer 1990, the Leningrad Branch, which had been created Dec. 3, 1989, numbered 100 members, and the Vyborg Branch 25 members. In September, the St. Petersburg Branch was recognized by the government and in October, a religious freedom law was passed.

The Russia Moscow and Russia St. Petersburg missions were created Feb. 3, 1992, with the membership of Russia numbering about 750. The first Russian branch president was Andrei Petrov, sustained in March 1991. A year later, the Moscow Branch was divided into six branches, and in 1993, these became 15 branches. At that time, there were as many members in the Moscow area as in the whole of Russia a year earlier.

During 1991 and afterward, humanitarian relief to members in Russia was supplied by members in Europe and the United States. Tons of food clothing were distributed members and non-members.

In June 1991, the Tabernacle Choir received publicity "beyond its wildest expectations" as it performed in the Bolshoi Theater in Moscow, and in Leningrad (now St. Petersburg) and recorded songs later broadcast to a potential audience of 339 million. The Church was officially recognized by Russia on May 28, 1991, and announcement of this was made at a dinner following the Choir's Moscow performance on June 24.

A third mission, Russia Samara, was created July 1993, and two additional ones, Russia Novosibirsk and Russia Rostov na Donu, were created July 1, 1994.

Sources: *Times and Seasons,* 4:218; *Millennial Star,* Aug. 27, 1903; *Improvement Era,* November, 1903; "Mischa Markow, Missionary to the Balkans," by William Hale Kehr, *Ensign,* June 1980; *Journal of Mormon History,* Vol. 13, 1986-87; *Ezra Taft Benson, A Biography*; "Choir leaves trail of joyful tears," by Gerry Avant, *Church News,* July 7, 1991; *Church News,* Oct. 12, 1991; "Converts pioneer frontier in Russia," by Steve Fidel, *Church News,* Sept. 19, 1992; "1989-90, The Curtain Opens," by Kahlile Mehr, *Ensign,* December 1993 and correspondence from Kahlile Mehr, Dec. 29, 1992; "Growth of the Church in 'that vast empire,' " an address by Gary L. Browning, *Church News,* Nov. 6, 1993.

Missions — 5
(As of Oct. 1, 1994; shown with historical number. See MISSIONS.)

(272) RUSSIA MOSCOW MISSION
Rossiia, 101000 Moskova
Glavpochtampt a/ia 257
Russia
Phone: 011-7-502 220-4571

(301) RUSSIA NOVOSIBIRSK MISSION
Matsishenskoje Shosse 18
630123 Novosibirsk,
Russia
Phone: 011-7-3832 23-02-63

(302) RUSSIA ROSTOV NA DONU MISSION
Beregovaya/Ostrovskogo 17/1
344008 Rostov-na-Donu, Russia
Phone: 011-7-8632 65-96-40

(273) RUSSIA ST. PETERSBURG
Nab. Reki Moiki 11-11
St. Petersburg, Russia
Phone: 011-7-812 119-6148

(293) RUSSIA SAMARA MISSION
Studenchesky Periulok d 2a, kv 7
443001 Samara, Russia
Phone: 011-7-8462 386026

ST. KITTS AND NEVIS (ST. CHRISTOPHER-NEVIS)

Year-end 1993: Est. population, 40,000; Members, fewer than 100; Branches, 1; North America Southeast Area; West Indies Mission.

Located in the Eastern Caribbean in the Leeward Islands, St. Kitts and Nevis has a population that speaks English, and is mostly Protestant.

Pres. Kenneth Zabriskie of the West Indies Mission and his wife, LeOra, were introduced to the government officer of St. Kitts through a mutual acquaintance, Kutaba Alghanin, who sailed about the Caribbean in his yacht and employed two returned missionaries as tutors to his children.

In July 1984, Elders Douglas Myers and Robert J. Molina arrived on St. Kitts and were soon followed by Reuel and Alice Lambourn on Oct. 20, 1984. They adapted a home into a meetinghouse and the St. Kitts-Nevis Branch was organized on Sept. 10, 1985, with Elder Lambourn as the first president. On Feb. 2, 1985, Dianna Ermintude Johnson was baptized, the first convert on the island. A weekly open house was held on Thursdays where the newly baptized members and investigators could study together.

A local member, Carol Pamela Heather Thomas, became the first missionary from the islands when she was called June 14, 1991, to the New Jersey Morristown Mission. Three other missionaries served from St. Kitts and Nevis in the next two years. In 1994, the branch had about 70 members taking part in all the programs, including seminary. Two choirs regularly took part in the meetings.

Sources: Kenneth and LeOra Zabriskie journals; correspondence from West Indies Mission, 1994.

ST. VINCENT AND THE GRENADINES

Year-end 1993: Est. population, 100,000; Members, 200; Branches, 1; Percent LDS, 0.18, or one in 530; North America Southeast Area; West Indies Mission.

In the eastern Caribbean and part of the Windward Island chain, the Grenadines are a parliamentary democracy. Most of the population speaks English. Major religions are Methodist, Anglican and Roman Catholic.

The Grenadines were under the Puerto Rico San Juan Mission until 1983, when the islands were placed in the West Indies Mission. The Kingstown Branch was organized Oct. 22, 1980. Under the direction of Pres. Edmund Israel, the branch developed. Missionaries cleared the land for a meetinghouse and a site dedication was held June 16, 1985, and a building was subsequently constructed. A former prime minister of St. Vincent, Ebeneezer Joshua, joined the Church and served in the branch presidency. Sharon Nichols was the first local member called on a full-time mission in 1983.

When Brother Joshua died in 1991, from 30,000 to 40,000 people, including top government officials, viewed or attended his televised funeral in the Kingstown meetinghouse, and learned of the plan of salvation.

Sources: Kenneth and LeOra Zabriskie journals; correspondence from Pres. A. Dean Jeffs, West Indies Mission; Church News, March 30, 1991.

SCOTLAND
(See United Kingdom)

SERBIA

Year-end 1993: Est. population, 8,401,000; Members, fewer than 100; Districts, 1; Branches, 2; Europe Mediterannean Area; Austria Vienna Mission.

Located on the Balkan Peninsula in southeast Europe, Serbia is a republic made up of what was the easternmost internal division of Yugoslavia.

Mischa Markow, a Hungarian who had immigrated to Salt Lake City, Utah, arrived as a missionary in Belgrade, Yugoslavia, in June 1899. He was taken to court where he preached. Even his arresting officer pled his case. But one judge was so irate that he reportedly said the missionary should be "thrown in to the Danube to drown." Elder Markow was banished to Hungary. He wrote that he shed tears of joy that he was privileged to testify before a magistrate and a high court.

In modern times, missionary work has proceeded slowly. A few members live in Belgrade, where a branch was organized in 1988.

The Church provided members and non-members in Serbia with humanitarian supplies in 1992, which included food, clothing, blankets and medical supplies.

Sources: "Tears of joy," by Richard L. Jensen, Church News, Dec. 8, 1979; Yugoslavia, manuscript history; "Missionary to the Balkans, Mischa Markow," by William Hale Kehr, Ensign, June 1980; Zagreb Branch history, published by the branch at dedication of meetinghouse, Oct. 30, 1985; Church News, Sept. 26, 1992.

SIERRA LEONE

Year-end 1993: Est. population, 4,550,000; Members, 1,900; Districts, 3; Branches, 14; Africa Area; Ghana Accra Mission.

On the west coast of West Africa, the Republic of Sierra Leone has a population that speaks English and tribal languages, and is Moslem, 30 percent; Animist, 30 percent; and Christian, 10 percent.

Michael Samura, baptized in Holland in 1981, and later returned to Freetown, Sierra Leone, staying until 1984. He later returned permanently. Elizabeth Bangura and Monica Orleans were baptized in Ghana and formed a study group in Freetown in January 1988. Christian George was baptized outside the country and returned to preside over the first approved meeting, held Jan. 18, 1988, at Goderich, a suburb of Freetown. In May 1988, Elder and Sister Clair Fisher, and Elder and Sister Erwin Waite arrived and took part in a service on June 11, 1988, where the first 14 converts were baptized.

The Liberia Monrovia Mission, which included Sierra Leone, was created on March 1, 1988. The Goderich Branch was organized Aug. 7, 1988, with Michael Samura as a counselor in the branch presidency. On Oct. 6, 1989, Abu H. Conteh was called as the first full-time missionary and assigned to serve in Sierra Leone.

The Freetown District was created December 1990 by Elder Robert E. Sackley of the Africa Area presidency and a Seventy. Michael Samura was called as its president. Seminary was introduced into the country by 1991, and two more districts, Bo and Wellington, were created Aug. 25 of that year.

The Liberia mission offices were moved to Freetown, Sierra Leone, in May 1990 because of the unrest in Liberia. Later, as civil war developed, the Liberia mission was discontinued April 22, 1991, and the area transferred to the Ghana Accra Mission. In May and August 1992, two missionaries couples were temporarily removed from Sierra Leone because of unrest.

By year-end 1993, 89 Sierra Leonians were serving full-time missions, including 41 from the six branches of the Freetown Districts.

Sources: Pres. Miles Cunningham of the Liberia Monrovia Mission; *Church News*, Jan. 26, 1991; correspondence from Pres. Christopher N. Chukwurah, Ghana Accra Mission, March 14, 1994.

SINGAPORE

Year-end 1993: Est. population, 2,800,000; Members, 1,800; Missions, 1; Districts, 1; Branches, 6; Percent LDS, 0.06 or one LDS in 1,555; Asia Area.

On the tip of the Malay Peninsula in southeast Asia, Singapore is a parliamentary democracy. Its population speaks Chinese, Malay, Tamil and English (all are official languages). The people are Buddhist, Christian, Islam, Taoist and Hindu.

Members in the British military and Chinese members who moved from Hong Kong began holding meetings in Singapore in 1963. On March 19, 1968, four missionaries from the Southern Far East Mission arrived in Singapore. A branch was organized Oct. 13, 1968, with John McSweeney as president and Sheila Hsia, a member from Hong Kong, as Relief Society president. The Southeast Asia Mission was created Nov. 1, 1969.

About a year later the branch membership numbered approximately 100.

In 1970, the government restricted tracting and visas, and work progressed through the local members. By 1976, membership was 309. The Singapore Mission was re-opened Jan. 1, 1980. In 1985, membership increased to 960. Three meetinghouses were completed in 1990.

In August 1992, a returned missionary from Taiwan, Jon Huntsman Jr., was sworn in as U.S. ambassador to Singapore. He served until June 15, 1993, the youngest-ever U.S. ambassador to Singapore and the first to speak Mandarin.

By mid-1993, membership had increased to 1,750 members in seven branches.

Sources: LDS Scene, *Improvement Era*, June 1969; "Help from members," *Church News*, Aug. 18, 1979; *Church News*, March 10, 1985; Address by Elder Marion D. Hanks, Salt Lake Institute devotional April 5, 1981; *Church News*, Nov. 17, 1973, Nov. 16, 1991, Sept. 5, 1992; *Church News*, June 5, 1993; "Asia area: Welcome mat is out in several countries," by Sheridan R. Sheffield, *Church News*, June 19, 1993.

(89) SINGAPORE MISSION
253 Bukit Timah Road
Singapore 1025, Singapore
Phone: (011-65) 733-4410

SLOVAKIA

Year-end 1993: Est. Population, 5,300,000; Members, fewer than 100; Branches, 2; Europe Area; Czech Republic Prague Mission.

The east side of the former state of Czechoslovakia, Slovakia is a federal republic with a population that speaks Slovak, Czech and Hungarian, and which is mostly Roman Catholic, Protestant and Orthodox Jewish.

The first member in Slovakia was Valerie Ruzena Frantiska Zizkova, born to members in the Czech Republic and baptized July 1939, just before the missionaries departed prior to World War II. She regained contact with missionaries for a brief period after the war, and then, from the pressure of the Communist government, lost contact with the Church. She later married and moved to Central Slovakia and remained faithful, renewing contact with the Church in 1992. Other members who had been baptized as expatriates included Alzbeta Domotorova, who had been baptized in Germany in 1977; and Pavel Pirovits, who had requested political asylum in Germany prior to the fall of the Communist regime. Other influential converts were Peter and Hanka Vaclav. Brother Vaclav had been baptized in March 1991 stemming from contact with members in Moravia who were sponsoring a Yoga class. His wife joined several months later following an accident after which she began to have a deeper interest in God. The first Church meeting held in modern times in Slovakia was at the home of Brother and Sister Vaclav. The meeting was held in the latter part of October 1991 with visiting missionaries from the Czech Republic presiding. The family led to the establishment of the first branch in Slovakia, the Trencin Branch. This branch was created under the direction of Pres. Richard W. Winder of the Czechoslovakia Prague Mission on Jan. 24, 1993. A group of members began meeting in Bratislava, and a second branch was created there later in the year.

Elders David Backman and Christopher Williams arrived to work in Trencin on March 29, 1992, and they baptized Martin and Zuzana Blaskova on July 25, 1992, in Trencin.

On April 30, 1994, a translation team with Elder Marcello de Oliveira as coordinator began translating basic Church materials into Slovak.

Source: Unpublished history of the Church in Slovakia, courtesy Pres. Phil J. Bryson.

SLOVENIA

Year-end 1993: Est. Population, 2,000,000; Members, fewer than 100; Districts, 1; Branches, 3; Europe/Mediterranean Area; Austria Vienna Mission.

Located on the Balkan Peninsula in southeast Europe, Slovenia is a republic made up of what was the northernmost internal division of Yugoslavia.

Mischa Markow, a Hungarian who had immigrated to Salt Lake City, Utah, arrived as a missionary in Yugoslavia in May 1899. He was banished to Hungary a month later because government authorities objected to his preaching.

Some 70 years passed before members returned. By the early 1970s, a few Latter-day Saints were living in Yugoslavia, some of whom had joined the Church while working or studying abroad.

In early 1975, Neil D. Schaerrer, president of the Austria Vienna Mission, established the Church as a legal entity in Yugoslavia. He met with members in Ljubljana, a major city in central Slovenia, during the following months. In 1993, Elder Matjaz Juhart became the first full-time missionary called from the Republic of Slovenia. He was called to the Utah Salt Lake City Mission and entered the Missionary Training Center Sept. 15, 1993.

Boza Gardner, 22, and Albin Lotric, 24, president of the Ljubljana Branch, were to be the first couple to marry in the temple from Slovenia. They even found a wedding dress for her among clothing donated from members in other countries. The two were married in the Frankfurt Germany Temple July 8, 1992.

Sources: Yugoslavia, manuscript history; "Missionary to the Balkans, Mischa Markow," by William Hale Kehr, *Ensign*, June 1980; Zagreb Branch history, published by the branch at dedication of meetinghouse, Oct. 30, 1985; *Church News*, Sept. 26, 1992; "Cinderella story: A dress for bride-to-be," *Church News*, Feb. 6, 1993; *Church News*, Jan 22, 1994.

SOUTH AFRICA

Year-end 1993: Est. population, 39,040,000; Members, 23,000; Stakes, 5; Wards, 25; Branches, 72; Missions, 3; Districts, 8; Temples, 1; Percent LDS, 0.1, or one LDS in 1,697.

At the southern end of the continent of Africa, the Republic of South Africa is a tricameral parliament. Its people speak Afrikaans, English and Bantu, and are mainly Christian, with Hindu and Moslem minorities.

Elders Jesse Haven, Leonard L. Smith and William H. Walker began missionary labors in Cape Town, South Africa, on April 19, 1853. On May 23, 1853, the trio officially organized the Church in the Cape of Good Hope. Elder Haven was appointed the first mission president of the South African Mission. Despite immediate, heavy persecution, they baptized Henry Stringer, the first convert, on June 15, 1853.

On Aug. 16, 1853, the first branch of the Church in South Africa was organized at Mowbray, four miles from Cape Town. A second branch was organized Sept. 7, 1853, at Newlands, six miles from Cape Town. A third branch was organized Feb. 23, 1854, at Beaufort, Cape Colony. These branches later formed the the Cape Conference. At a conference held in Port Elizabeth on Aug. 13, 1855, the "Church in the Cape of Good Hope" (South African Mission) was reported to consist of three conferences, six branches and 126 members.

Due to proselyting restrictions and lack of knowledge of the Afrikaans language, the South African Mission was closed from 1865 to 1903. Elder Warren H. Lyon reopened and presided over the mission. The first LDS meetinghouse in South Africa was built in 1916-17 as an addition to the first mission home at Mowbray. In 1950, missionary work was extended to Rhodesia (now Zimbabwe), where several branches of the Church were established.

The first stake in South Africa, the Transvaal Stake, was organized on March 22, 1970, with Louis P. Hefer as president. The Afrikaans translation of the Book of Mormon was first introduced to the South African Saints on May 14, 1972.

The first-ever area conference in South Africa was held in Johannesburg Oct. 23-24, 1978, attended by 3,450 of the subcontinent's 7,200 members living in South Africa, Rhodesia (now Zimbabwe) and South West Africa (now Namibia). Five General Authorities attended the conference, the first time ever that more than one General Authority was in South Africa at the same time.

The Johannesburg South Africa Temple was completed and dedicated in 1982 and has been visited by members throughout the southern part of the continent.

The South African Mission was divided on July 1, 1984, creating the South Africa Johannesburg and South Africa Cape Town missions.

Work in townships and other areas in South Africa progressed significantly in the 1980s. At a regional conference held Feb. 8-9, 1992, in Johannesburg, attendance reached 4,200, including a choir of 140 youths from three area stakes. Membership in the Soweto township continued to grow as members and missionaries worked closely together. Following the abolition of aparthied (apartness), members of all origins worked together to overcome cultural barriers.

Sources: *Encyclopedic History of the Church,* by Andrew Jenson; South Africa, *Relief Society Magazine,* June 1969; "Mission Opening — 117 Years Ago," by Jack E. Jarrard, *Church News,* June 20, 1970; "The Saints in South Africa," by Lawrence E. Cummins, *Ensign,* March 1973; "South Africans greet prophet at conference," by Dell Van Orden, *Church News,* Nov. 4, 1978; Early Mormon imprints in South Africa, by David J. Whittaker, Brigham Young University Studies, spring 1980; Saints in South Africa, by Marjorie E. Woods, September 1986; *Church News,* Feb. 29, 1992, Sept. 26, 1992; "South Africa: Land of Good Hope," by R. Val Johnson, *Ensign,* February 1993.

Stakes — 5
(Listed alphabetically as of Oct. 1, 1994.)

No.	Name	Organized	First President
Africa Area			
1662	Benoni South Africa	29 Nov 1987	Jan G. Hugo
1470	Cape Town South Africa	6 May 1984	Otto Wilhelm Miessner
1314	Durban South Africa	29 Nov 1981	Percy E.A. Winstanley
506	*Johannesburg South Africa		
	†Transvaal (South Africa)	22 Mar 1970	Louis P. Hefer
969	*Pretoria South Africa 29 Nov 1987		
	†Sandton South Africa	22 Oct 1978	Johannes P. Brummer

(177a) SOUTH AFRICA CAPE TOWN MISSION
P.O. Box 217 Howard Place
Pinelands, 7450
Republic of South Africa
Phone: (011-27-21) 531-6903

(216) SOUTH AFRICA DURBAN MISSION
Suite 106 Ascot Park
3 Ascot Street
Greyville, Durban 4001
Republic of South Africa
Phone: (011-27-31) 309-2757

(14) SOUTH AFRICA JOHANNESBURG MISSION
Private Bag X27
Bryanston 2021
Republic of South Africa
Phone: (011-27-11) 463-4660

TRANSKEI

Year-end 1993: Est. population, 3,500,000; Members, fewer than 100; Branches, 1; Africa Area; South Africa Cape Town Mission.

Transkei, one of 10 homelands established for the Xhosa people by South Africa is on the southwest coast of South Africa. In March 1988, a member, Dr. Emmanuel Danso and his wife, Akosua Seiwa, moved to Port Saint Johns, where they met with missionaries and Akosua Seiwa was baptized. The Umtata Branch was organized with Dr. Danso as branch president on April 8, 1989. The branch is part of the East London South Africa District and part of the South Africa Cape Town Mission.

Sources: South Africa Johannesburg Mission manuscript history; "Gospel takes root in Africa's Wild Coast," by Jay H. Buckley, *Church News,* June 16, 1990.

SPAIN

Year-end 1993: Est. population, 39,100,000; Members, 25,000; Stakes, 3; Wards, 17; Branches, 127; Missions, 5; Districts, 18; Temples, 1 announced; Percent LDS, 0.1, or one LDS in 1,564.

Located in southwest Europe, Spain is a constitutional monarchy. Its people speak Spanish, Catalan, Galician and Basque, and 90 percent are Roman Catholic.

Regular Church services began in Spain among LDS servicemen after World War II when the United States established relations with that country. Two American branches were functioning in 1966, and a district presidency operated under the French Mission. One of the first converts in Spain, Jose Maria Oliveira, was baptized in France in March 1966.

The Spain Religious Liberty Law passed in 1967 paved the way for the organization of the Madrid Branch on the first Sunday in February 1968. Some 40 attended, including Spanish wives of American servicemen, other Spanish-speaking members, and investigators.

Official recognition for the Church in Spain was formalized on Oct. 22, 1968. A mission was organized July 11, 1970. During this period, many Spanish-speaking members were transferred by their businesses to Spain and helped strengthen the new branches. By 1974, 17 branches, with a total membership of 619, were operating in Spain.

Elder Gordon B. Hinckley, then of the Council of the Twelve, accompanied by Elder Neal A. Maxwell of the Presidency of the First Quorum of the Seventy, visited King Juan Carlos de Bourbon in August 1978.

Spain's first stake was created in Madrid on March 14, 1982, with Jose Oliveira as president. Additional stakes followed. When the Seville Spain Stake was created in 1988, one area within the stake reported 98 percent activity among Melchizedek Priesthood holders, and noted that 54 members of the stake were serving full-time missions.

President Hinckley visited King Juan Carlos I and Queen Sofia March 9, 1992, and presented the couple with a personalized, leather-bound copy of the Book of Mormon.

About that time, Spain was among the countries to receive satellite broadcasts of general conference. At the April 1993 general conference, President Gordon B. Hinckley announced that the Church was acquiring property for a temple in Spain, which will be the Church's fifth in continental Europe.

Sources: *Encyclopedic History of the Church,* by Andrew Jenson; "The Church Grows in Spain," by J Malan Heslop, *Church News,* Oct. 30, 1971; "Spain," *Ensign,* August 1973; "This is Spain," by Betty Ventura, *Ensign,* April 1975; "The Restored Church in Spain," unpublished history by David B. Timmons; "Relief Society Offers New Outlook for Spanish Women," by Gerry Avant, *Church News,* May 17, 1975;

"Mormons meet king of Spain," *Church News*, Oct. 14, 1978; "Lead their own," by Jill Mulvay Derr, *Church News*, Sept. 1, 1979; *Church News*, March 20, 1982; March 28, 1992.

Stakes — 3
(Listed alphabetically as of Oct. 1, 1994.)

No.	Name	Organized	First President
Europe/Mediterranean Area			
1370	Barcelona Spain	31 Oct 1982	Jose Lara Straube
1327	Madrid Spain	14 Mar 1982	Jose Mario Oliveira Aldamiz
1687	Seville Spain	14 Feb 1988	Jesus Manuel Benitez S.

Missions — 5
(As of Oct. 1, 1994; shown with historical number. See MISSIONS.)

(137) SPAIN BARCELONA MISSION
Calle Calatrava 10-12, bajos
08017 Barcelona, Spain
Phone: (011-34-3) 211-6558

(199) SPAIN BILBAO MISSION
c/Bidearte 6, 4o dcha
48930 Las Arenas (Vizcaya)
Spain
Phone 011-34-4 464-8687

(220) SPAIN LAS PALMAS MISSION
Avenida Rafael Cabrera 4-6oA
35002 Las Palmas de Gran Canaria
Spain
Phone: 011-34-28 36-87-62

(92) SPAIN MADRID MISSION
Calle San Telmo, 26
28016 Madrid (Madrid)
Spain
Phone: (011-34-1) 359-2634

(141) SPAIN MALAGA MISSION
Calle Virgen de Regla 1-1o,1
41011 Seville
Spain

CANARY ISLANDS

Year-end 1993: Est. population, 1,343,000; Members, 3,500; Districts, 3; Branches, 18; percent LDS, 0.26, or one LDS in 384 people; Africa Area; Spain Las Palmas Mission.

The Canary Islands, in the South Atlantic off the coast of Africa, are rugged, volcanic mountainous islands with rich soil and long beaches where sand from the western Sahara Desert has drifted.

The first converts on the Canary Islands were Francisco Dominguez Pena; his wife, Francisca; and their son, Javier; who were baptized June 13, 1979. They were introduced to the Church by Jesus Gomez y Vega, a resident of the islands who had moved to Spain and been baptized in 1973. Meetings were subsequently held in their home. The first missionaries were Elders David L. Gill and Scott C. Jensen.

The first branch was organized in Las Palmas on Jan. 29, 1980. The first district, Las Palmas Gran Canarias, was organized Oct. 2, 1984, with eight branches. The second district, Santa Cruz de Tenerife Canaria, was organized Aug. 8, 1989, with six branches. The Spain Las Palmas Mission, with headquarters in the Canary Islands, was created July 1, 1988, under the leadership of Pres. Marion K. Hamblin.

Sources: The Begininnings of the Church in the Canary Islands, by Maria Torio de Gomez Vega, unpublished; Spain Las Palmas Mission history; *Church News*, Nov. 10, 1990.

SURINAME

Year-end 1993: Est. population, 400,000; Members, 200; Branches, 1; North America Southeast Area; West Indies Mission.

Located on the Atlantic Coast at the top of South America, the Republic of Suriname has a population that speaks Dutch, Creole and English. They are Hindu, 27 percent; Moslem, 23 percent; and Christian, 25 percent.

Elder John Limburg and his wife, Beverly, arrived in Paramaribo in October 1988 and started the Paramaribo Branch. By the start of 1989, some 16 people were attending services. The first convert was baptized March 26, 1989, in services attended by about 25 people.

By 1990, attendance at the branch averaged about 100 people. Meetings were also held in the rural communities of Lelydorp and Uitkijk.

Sources: Interview with John M. and Beverly Limburg; manuscript history of Suriname; *Church News*, April 29, 1989, March 10, 1990; "Work flourishing among a people without guile," by Elayne Wells, *Church News*, Dec. 1, 1990.

SWAZILAND

Year-end 1993: Est. population, 801,000; Members, 700; Districts, 1; Branches, 5; Percent LDS, 0.09, or one LDS in 1,144; Africa Area; South Africa Johannesburg Mission.

The second smallest country in Africa, Swaziland is a mountainous kingdom located in southern Africa near the Indian Ocean. The people speak Siswati and English, and 57 percent of the people are Christian while 43 percent have indigenous beliefs.

A group of LDS non-Africans living in Swaziland in 1984 included the Herman Van Thiel Berghuijs, George Gardner and John Scott families. The Mbabane Branch was organized Nov. 5, 1985, with Brother Gardner as president. The Church was recognized by the government in February 1987, and Elder Kenneth Edwards and his wife, Betty, the first missionaries, arrived that year and converts came into the Church.

The first called on a mission from Swaziland was Elder Paulo Cipriano Zandamela, baptized July 31, 1988, a Mozambican. Sister Fikile Dlamini was the first Swazi to serve a full-time mission. By 1990, converts were serving full-time missions and of the 115 members, only Branch Pres. Larry Brown and his family were non-Africans.

On Feb. 24, 1991, three more branches were organized under local priesthood leadership. By then, several members from Swaziland had been through the temple, and seven local missionaries had been called. Swaziland's first meetinghouse was dedicated July 18, 1993, in a ceremony attended by government representatives, and presided over by Elder Richard P. Lindsay of the Seventy and president of the Africa Area. At the time, in Swaziland, there were 650 members in five branches. Other branches have been established in Ezulwini, Manzini and Nhlangano.

Sources: Manuscript history of South Africa Johannesburg Mission; correspondence from mission Pres. R.J. and Marilyn M. Snow; *Church News*, Jan. 27, 1990, and March 10, 1990.

SWEDEN

Year-end 1993: Est. population, 8,700,000; Members, 8,300; Stakes, 2; Wards, 14; Branches, 34; Missions, 1; Districts, 4; Temples, 1; Percent LDS, 0.1, or one LDS in 1,048.

In northern Europe on the east side of the Scandinavian Peninsula, the kingdom of Sweden is a constitutional monarchy; its population speaks Swedish and Finnish, and are 95 percent Lutheran.

The first missionary to Sweden was John E. Forsgren, a Swedish seaman who joined the Church in Boston, Mass., and then moved to Nauvoo, Ill., to be with the Saints.

After migrating to the Salt Lake Valley with the pioneers, he answered a mission call to Sweden. He went first to his hometown of Gavle, where his brother, Peter, was healed by the power of the priesthood. He then baptized Peter on July 26, 1850, as the first convert to the Church in Sweden.

After baptizing a few more converts, Elder Forsgren was arrested and banished from the country for preaching. Thereafter, missionaries occasionally visited Sweden from Denmark. In 1853, successful missionary operations were commenced in southern Sweden by Anders W. Winberg and others.

On April 24, 1853, the first branch of the Church was organized in Skonaback by Elder Winberg, and another branch was soon started in Malmo. From there, the Church extended northward, with many converts immigrating to the United States.

In 1905, Sweden was taken from the Scandinavian Mission and the Swedish Mission was organized.

Notable events of the Church in Sweden in recent times include the first Nordic area conference Aug. 16-18, 1974, in Stockholm; and organization of stakes in Stockholm on April 20, 1975, and in Goteborg Nov. 20, 1977. On March 17, 1984, ground was broken for a temple near Stockholm, which was dedicated July 2-4, 1985.

On March 24, 1988, President Thomas S. Monson, second counselor in the First Presidency, took part in Sweden's observance of the 350th anniversary of the first Swedish settlement in the United States. President Monson and his wife, Frances, exchanged greetings with King Carl XVI Gustaf and Queen Silvia. Also taking part was Gregory J. Newell, the U.S. ambassador to Sweden, a member of the Church.

As Eastern Europe opened to the preaching of the gospel, the temple in Sweden offered an opportunity for the Swedish members to host many visitors. The first group of Russian Saints to come to the temple arrived Aug. 30, 1993.

Sources: *Encyclopedic History of the Church*, by Andrew Jenson; *History of the Church in Sweden 1850-1905*, by A. Dean Wengreen, a BYU dissertation, August 1968; *History of the Swedish Mission of the*

Church, 1905-1973, by Carl-Erik Johansson, a BYU thesis August 1973; *Church News,* Nov. 21, 1987; *Church News,* Nov. 20, 1993.

Stakes — 2
(Listed alphabetically as of Oct. 1, 1994.)

No.	Name	Organized	First President
Europe North Area			
880	*Goeteborg Sweden 7 Jan 1991		
	†Goteborg Sweden	20 Nov 1977	Arne Lennart Hedberg
691	Stockholm Sweden	20 Apr 1975	Evert W. Perciwall

Mission — 1
(As of Oct. 1, 1994; shown with historical number. See MISSIONS.)

(145) SWEDEN STOCKHOLM MISSION
Box 2087
S-183 02 TABY, Sweden
Phone: (011-46-8) 768-03-35

SWITZERLAND

Year-end 1993: Est. population, 7,000,000; Members, 6,700; Stakes, 3; Wards, 16; Branches, 21; Missions, 2; Temples, 1; Percent LDS, 0.10, or one LDS in 1,044.

In central Europe, Switzerland is a federal republic with a population that speaks German, 65 percent; French, 18 percent; Italian, 12 percent; and Romansch, 1 percent. The Swiss people are 49 percent Roman Catholic and 48 percent Protestant.

Missionary work began in Switzerland on Nov. 24, 1850, as an outgrowth of the work in Italy. Elder Lorenzo Snow of the Council of the Twelve, laboring in Italy, set apart Thomas B.H. Stenhouse as the first president of the Swiss Mission. The *Millennial Star* reported that 20 converts were baptized in 1851 in Switzerland. Many Church members emigrated from Switzerland to America until the 1950s.

In August 1914 and again in September 1938, missionaries were evacuated from Switzerland due to World War I, and World War II, respectively, and during both wars, local priesthood holders were placed in leadership of the missions, branches, and districts in Switzerland.

After World War I, programs of the Church steadily developed in Switzerland as many Church publications and manuals were translated.

President David O. McKay visited in 1952 and a building site for the Swiss Temple was selected in Zollikofen, near Bern. The completed temple was dedicated in several sessions beginning Sept. 11, 1955, and served Church members in Western Europe and the Nordic countries, as well as Switzerland.

The first stake in Switzerland was organized Oct. 28, 1961, in Zurich. The first General Authority from Switzerland was Elder Hans B. Ringger, who was called to the Seventy in 1985.

European Saints from many countries attended the rededication after refurbishment of the Swiss Temple by President Gordon B. Hinckley on Oct. 23-25, 1992. At the dedication, he commented that while those of every nationality had different passports, their temple recommends were similar.

President Howard W. Hunter visited Switzerland Aug. 8-16, 1994, the first country he visited as Church president. He spoke to members, missionaries and attended to matters at the recently rededicated temple.

Sources: *Encyclopedic History of the Church,* by Andrew Jenson; *Church News,* Nov. 11, 1961; *History of the Church in Switzerland,* by Dale Z. Kirby, a BYU thesis, May 1971; "Switzerland," *Ensign,* April 1973; "Switzerland: land of peace, precision and great progress," by Gerry Avant, *Church News,* Dec. 22, 1979; "Thousands tour London and Swiss temples," and "LDS officials rededicate Swiss Temple," by Gerry Avant, *Church News,* Oct. 24, 1992; *Church News,* Aug. 20, 1994.

Stakes — 3
(Listed alphabetically as of Oct. 1, 1994.)

No.	Name	Organized	First President
Europe Area			
1261	Bern Switzerland	3 May 1981	Peter Lauener
341	*Zurich Switzerland		
	†Swiss (Switzerland, Germany)	28 Oct 1961	Wilhelm Friedrich Lauener

1352   Geneva Switzerland   20 Jun 1982   Denis Bonny

Missions — 2
(As of Oct. 1, 1994; shown with historical number. See MISSIONS.)

(59) SWITZERLAND GENEVA MISSION
8, chemin William Barbey
CH-1292 Chambesy (GE)
Switzerland
Phone: (011-41-22) 758-1535

(8) SWITZERLAND ZURICH MISSION
Pilatusstrasse 11
CH-8032 Zurich
Switzerland
Phone: (011-41-1) 252-5114

TAHITI
(See French Polynesia under FRANCE)

TAIWAN

Year-end 1993: Est. population, 20,900,000; Members, 21,000; Stakes, 3; Wards, 19; Branches, 29; Missions, 2; Districts, 4; Temples, 1; Percent LDS, 0.1, or one LDS in 995.

Off the southeast coast of China, the Republic of China has a population that speaks Mandarin Chinese and Taiwan and Hakka dialects. They mostly adhere to Buddhism, Taoism and Confucianism.

An American servicemen's group was functioning in Taipei when the first four missionaries departed from Hong Kong to open the work in Taiwan (then called Formosa). Elders Weldon J. Kitchen, Keith Madsen, Duane W. Dean and Melvin C. Fish arrived in June 1956. Progress was slow at first, and anti-American riots hindered the work in 1957. However, by the end of 1957 almost 50 people had been baptized. After another year, nearly 200 had been converted and 31 missionaries were working in six cities. By the end of 1959, eight branches had been organized. Two large meetinghouses were completed in the 1960s in Taipei and Kaohsiung. Translation of the Book of Mormon into Chinese in 1965 also helped the work. Local leadership presided over most of the branches. In 1975, 30 branches in three districts, with a membership of 7,000, had been reached. Church educational programs were established, and many young people grew up taking seminary and institute classes. Some 2,500 members attended an area conference held in Taipei Aug. 13-14, 1975 and in 1980.

The Taipei Taiwan Stake was created April 22, 1976. A temple was announced for Taiwan in April 1982 and was dedicated Nov. 17-18, 1984. At the time, membership numbered about 13,000. Membership in 1990 was 18,000.

Missionaries performing service projects in the 1990s have earned favorable publicity for the Church.

In 1993, some 20,300 members were in 57 units, three stakes and three districts in two missions. In December 1994, Jien-Nien Chen, a pharmacist and former branch president, became the first LDS elected governor in Taiwan.

Sources: "Mormon Missionaries Now Labor in Formosa," *Church News,* June 23, 1956; China and the Restored Church, by William Heaton, *Ensign,* August 1972; "My Sheep Know My Voice," *Church News,* April 28, 1973; "Taiwan: Steep Peaks and Towering Faith," by Janice Clark, *Ensign,* August 1975; Relative Freedom of Taiwan Allows Growth of Church," by Gerry Avant, *Church News,* Dec. 6, 1975; "Saints throng to area meetings in the Far East," by Dell Van Orden, *Church News,* Nov. 1, 1980; "First Temple in Chinese Realm," by Gerry Avant, *Church News,* Nov. 25, 1984; *Church News,* July 9, 1994.

Stakes — 3
(Listed alphabetically as of Oct. 1, 1994.)

No.	Name	Organized	First President
Asia Area			
1303	Koahsiung Taiwan	6 Nov 1981	Ho Tung Hai
1326	Taipei Taiwan East	14 Mar 1982	Yuan-Hu Yen
755	*Taipei Taiwan West 14 Mar 1982		
	†Taipei Taiwan	22 Apr 1976	I-Ch'ing Chang

Missions — 2
(As of Oct. 1, 1994; shown with historical number. See MISSIONS.)

(146) TAIWAN TAICHUNG MISSION
498-11 Wu Chuan Road
Taichung 40415
Taiwan ROC
Phone: (011-886-4) 226-7181

(94) TAIWAN TAIPEI MISSION
Floor 4, No. 24, Lane 183
Chin Hua Street
Taipei 10606, Taiwan ROC
Phone: (011-886-2) 393-3285

TANZANIA

Year-end 1993: Est. population, 27,800,000; Members, 100; Africa Area; Kenya Nairobi Mission.

On the east coast of Africa, Tanzania is a republic with its people speaking Swahili and English. The people are Moslem, 35 percent, Christian, 30 percent and the balance follow traditional beliefs.

One of the first families to hold Church meetings was D.E. Tapie Rohm Jr. from Los Angeles, Calif., a Fulbright scholar assigned to Dar es Salaam from 1988-1989. In August 1991, Bruce Wilson and his family from Smith Falls, Ontario, Canada, arrived in Dar es Salaam. He was employed by International Development Co. The Wilson family began holding meetings in September 1991.

The Kenya Nairobi Mission, which includes Kenya, Uganda and Tanzania, was created in July 1991.

Application for legal recognition was made March 15, 1992, and was approved Oct. 8, 1992. This recognition was assisted by a visit by Chief Judge J. Clifford Wallace of the U.S. Court of Appeals in San Diego, Calif., to Tanzania. An official who had been hosted by LDS members in Portland, Ore., facilitated Judge Wallace's request. Robert Muhile, a Tanzanian, was baptized in Cairo, Egypt, before the arrival of the missionaries.

On Dec. 15, 1992, the Daar es Salaam Branch was created, and Brother Muhile called as its president on March 13, 1994.

A missionary couple, Elder Lervae and Sister Joyce Cahoon, arrived in February, 1992. The first converts were Projest S. Captain, Dickson and Japhet Kiiza, Dishon Z. Makunge and Mariam Mohamed-Chui, all baptized March 15, 1992.

Sources: *Church News,* March 23, 1991; correspondence from Pres. Larry K. Brown, Kenya Nairobi Mission, April 12, 1994.

THAILAND

Year-end 1993: Est. population, 57,260,000; Members, 5,300; Districts, 4; Branches, 23; Missions, 1; Asia Area.

On the Indochinese and Malay Peninsula, Thailand is a constitutional monarchy. The Thai-speaking population is 95 percent Buddhist and 4 percent Moslem.

Elder Elam Luddington arrived in Bangkok, Thailand, April 6, 1854, as the first missionary to preach the gospel in the Asian country. Four elders had been assigned to preach the gospel in Thailand, then known as Siam, but only Elder Luddington reached the country. After laboring under difficult circumstances, he was able to baptize a ship's captain, James Trail, and his wife. When Elder Luddington left Thailand four months later, missionary work came to a halt for more than a century.

Six missionaries were transferred to Thailand from the Taiwan and Hong Kong zones of the Southern Far East Mission on Feb. 2, 1968. Thanks to the help of Anan Eldredge, a Thai who had been adopted by an American family and subsequently baptized, the elders were able to learn the language and teach the people the gospel. Brother Eldredge was the first Thai to hold the priesthood, the first to be a full-time missionary, and the first to be called as a mission president on July 1, 1988. Another early convert, Srilaksana Gottsche, was largely responsible for translating the Book of Mormon into Thai.

Thailand continued to grow as an important part of the Southern Far East Mission, which was divided Nov. 1, 1969. The new Southeast Asian Mission included Thailand with G. Carlos Smith as president. Under his direction, construction began on the country's first meetinghouse, located in Bangkok. Church leaders spent several years overcoming challenges and finally, on July 19, 1973, Thailand became its own mission with Paul D. Morris as president of the Thailand Bangkok Mission. The first sister missionaries arrived in the country in 1974, the same year that Elder David B. Haight of the Council of the Twelve dedicated the first meetinghouse in Thailand.

In 1987, three new meetinghouses were dedicated for the Bangnaa, Thonburi and Chiang Mai branches of the Church. The Church in Thailand noted a milestone in June 1990, when 201 Thai members went to the Manila Temple to receive their endowments or to be sealed to their families.

As of 1993, about 5,000 members live in four districts and 24 units of the Thailand Bangkok Mission. Long-term visas were recently extended to the Church by the government of Thailand.

Missionaries in the mission translated for the Utah Army National Guard in providing volunteer medical and dental services to residents near Ubon, Thailand, in 1993.

Sources: *Encyclopedic History of the Church,* by Andrew Jenson; Culture for Missionaries: *The Church Encounters Asia,* by Spencer J. Palmer, Deseret Book, 1970; "Thailand," prepared by Language Training

Mission, 1978; *Church News*, Jan. 16, 1988, Feb. 13, 1988, July 16, 1988; Sept. 3, 1988; *Church News*, May 23, 1993; "Asia Area: Welcome mat is out in several countries," by Sheridan R. Sheffield, *Church News*, June 19, 1993.

Mission — 1
(As of Oct. 1, 1994; shown with historical number. See MISSIONS.)

(109) THAILAND BANGKOK MISSION
50/829-832 Muang Thong Thani
Chaengwatana Road
T. Ban Mai, A Pakkret
Nonthaburi, Thailand 11120
Phone: (011-66-2) 503-3422

TONGA

Year-end 1993: Est. population, 103,000; Members, 38,000; Stakes, 10; Wards, 66; Districts, 1; Branches, 55; Missions, 1; Temples, 1; Percent LDS, 37, or one LDS in 3.

In the western South Pacific, the kingdom of Tonga is a constitutional monarchy whose population speaks Tongan and English. Tongans are Free Wesleyan, LDS, Roman Catholic, Church of Tonga, and Free Church of Tonga.

The first missionaries to Tonga were Brigham Smoot and Alva J. Butler, sent by the Samoan Mission Pres. William O. Lee. The missionaries arrived July 15, 1891, and soon visited King Jiaoji (George) Tubou and received permission to preach. They purchased property and erected a mission home and school, and also purchased a boat to travel between islands. The first convert was Alipate, baptized July 15, 1892. The mission made some progress, but was closed in 1897.

In 1907, the Tonga Mission was re-opened by Elders William O. Facer and Heber J. McKay. They opened a school in Nieafu on the island of Vava'u and by 1908, there were 28 day students and 13 night students. Elder Facer later was stationed in Ha'alaufuli where he found success, organizing a branch with 32 converts. Missionary work opened on the main island of Tongatapu on March 17, 1911, and by December 1912, a meetinghouse and school had been completed and a conference organized. A mission for Tonga was organized July 8, 1916, and more missionaries began serving.

Relationships with the government became strained as more people joined the Church. In 1921, Elder David O. McKay, then of the Council of the Twelve, visited, but was quarantined on a nearby island for 11 days before he was allowed to enter the country. Later, visas were denied to missionaries for two years. Local missionaries were called to do the work and served in positions of leadership.

Publication of the Book of Mormon in 1946 also helped strengthen the Church. All foreign missionaries were called home during World War II, but many LDS servicemen were stationed near Tonga and attended local meetings. After the war, foreign missionaries were once again restricted, with the exception of the mission president and his family. Membership in Tonga in 1946 was 2,422. From among them, mission presidents called local missionaries in what became one of the most successful local missionary programs in the Church.

Much of the progress on the islands has been through Church schools. The establishing of schools in 1892 and 1908 proved significant, and led to other schools starting. The Makeke School was opened Feb. 20, 1926, and it was the principal method of advancing the Church for many years. A new educational complex, the Liahona High School, was opened in 1952. Its building in 1949 was the beginning of the Church's labor missionary program and probably the catalyst for expansion of the Church.

In 1968, a jubilee celebration was held under the direction of mission Pres. John H. Groberg, now of the Seventy. Tonga's first stake was created Sept. 5, 1968. After that, the Church in Tonga became nearly all led by local members, including its mission, many of the schools and the stakes.

Membership reached 10,000 in 1967, and increased to 14,355 in 1970, 18,484 in 1980, and 27,400 in 1985.

A highlight came Aug. 9-11, 1983, when the Tonga Nuku'alofa Temple was dedicated. In 1991, LDS and other Tongans joined in celebrating the centennial of the Church in Tonga. Among the most significant parts of the lengthy celebration was a dance festival in which 3,000 youths performed for King Taufa'ahau Topou IV.

Sources: *Unto the Islands of the Sea,* by R. Lanier Britsch; *Mighty Missionary of the Pacific,* by David W. Cummings, Bookcraft, 1961; *Tongan Saints, Legacy of Faith,* translated and edited by Eric B. Shumway, Institute for Polynesian Studies, Laie, Hawaii; *From Tonga to Zion,* prepared by Ella Mae Judd from journals of Fa'aki K. A. Richter; "Celebrating 100 years in Tonga," *Church News,* Aug. 31, 1991.

No.	Name	Organized	First President
Pacific Area			
1430	Ha'apai Tonga	14 Jun 1983	Fanongonongo Vaitai
737	Neiafu Vava'u Tonga	4 Dec 1975	Mosese Hetau Langi
1172	Neiafu Vava'u Tonga North	27 Aug 1980	Mosese Hetau Langi
463	*Nuku'alofa Tonga		
	†Nuku'alofa	5 Sep 1968	Orson Hyde White
1986	Nuku'alofa Tonga Central	31 Jul 1994	Filimone Fie'eiki
550	*Nuku'alofa Tonga East		
	†Nuku'alofa East	21 Jul 1971	Viliami Pele Folau
1173	Nuku'alofa Tonga Liahona	31 Aug 1980	Vaikalafi Lutui
1445	Nuku'alofa Tonga North	9 Oct 1983	Sione Moala Fineanganofa
519	*Nuku'alofa Tonga South		
	†Nuku'alofa South	26 Jul 1970	Tevita Folau Mahuinga
1431	Nuku'alofa Tonga Vaini	15 Jun 1983	Samuela Iloa
520	*Nuku'alofa Tonga West		
	†Nuku'alofa West	26 Jul 1970	Orson H. White

Mission — 1
(As of Oct. 1, 1994; shown with historical number. See MISSIONS.)

(22c) TONGA NUKU'ALOFA MISSION
P.O. Box 58
Nuku'alofa, Tonga
Phone: (011-676) 21577

TRINIDAD AND TOBAGO

Year-end 1993: Est. population, 1,300,000; Members, 700; Districts, 1; Branches, 3; Missions, 1; Percent LDS, 0.05, or one LDS in 1,857; North America Southeast Area.

Off the east coast of Venezuela in the Caribbean Sea, Trinidad & Tobago is a parliamentary democracy where the people speak English as the official language. The major religions are Roman Catholic, 32 percent; Protestant, 29 percent; and Hindu, 25 percent.

Among the first converts to the Church were Blasil D. and Felicia Borde, baptized in 1977 by Elder Daniel Rector. A branch in Port of Spain was organized June 5, 1980, under the Venezuela Caracas Mission. The area was transferred to the West Indies Mission in September 1983. The first missionaries from the West Indies Mission were Elders Chris Doty, Doug Mathews, Randy Clark and David Roos, who helped organized a citywide cross country race that raised the Church's profile.

In 1991, Elder Newell Anderson and his wife, Cora Gene, taught agriculture and developed ways to grow row crops of vegetables. Sister Anderson taught sewing classes.

On Sept. 2-5, 1991, LDS basketball players Danny Ainge, Greg Kite, Jeff Chatman and Scott Runia held a series of basketball clinics on both islands of Trinidad and Tobago. They also appeared on television talk shows to discuss family values.

The Trinidad Tobago Mission was created July 1, 1991, but discontinued in 1994. That year, however, the West Indies Mission was headquartered in Trinidad.

Sources: Kenneth and LeOra Zabriskie journals; *Church News*, March 6, 1983, July 10, 1983, March 10, 1990, Sept. 21, 1991; *Church News*, March 26, 1994.

Mission — 1
(As of Oct. 1, 1994; shown with historical number. See MISSIONS.)

(178a) WEST INDIES MISSION
26-28 Murray Street, Suite 5
Woodbrook, Port of Spain
Trinidad, West Indies
Phone: (809) 627-3570

UGANDA

Year-end 1993: Est. population, 18,100,000; Districts, 2; Branches, 6; Members, 800; Africa Area; Kenya Nairobi Mission.

Uganda, in east central Africa, has a military government and a population that speaks English, Luganda and Swahili. Its people follow Christian, 63 percent; Moslem, 6 percent and traditional beliefs.

The first Ugandan to join the Church was Charles Osinde, who was baptized in Scotland, and returned to his homeland. Guy Denton and his wife, Peggy, arrived in Uganda in March 1990 as part of a USAID program. The Dentons held meetings in their home and Osinde and others joined them. The first Ugandan baptized was Mugisa James Collins, baptized Aug. 25, 1990, by Brother Denton.

A branch was soon created in Kampala and the people met in the Osinde's home. In December 1990, the first missionaries, Elder Lark and and Sister Arlea Washburn of Mesa, Ariz., arrived in Uganda. By March 1991, an average of 30 to 35 people attended branch meetings.

The Kenya Nairobi Mission, which includes Kenya, Uganda and Tanzania, was created in July 1991.

Sources: History provided by LuDean Worthen; *Church News*, March 30, 1991.

UKRAINE

Year-end 1993: Est. population, 51,900,000; Members, 1,700; Missions, 2; Districts, 3; Branches, 25; Europe Area.

Bordering the Black Sea, Ukraine is a member of the Commonwealth of Independent States.

Missionary work began in October 1991 in Ukraine under the direction of Pres. Gary L. Browning of the Finland Helsinki East Mission. The Ukraine Kiev Mission was created Feb. 3, 1992, under the direction of Pres. Howard L. Biddulph, formerly president of the Austria Vienna East Mission. The mission, with 35 missionaries in 1992, served the entire Ukraine population.

On Sept. 12, 1991, Elders Boyd K. Packer and Dallin H. Oaks of the Council of the Twelve visited Ukraine and met with about 40 people, including members, missionaries and investigators. The Kiev Branch was created in June 1991.

Humanitarian assistance to members in Kiev was offered by members in Germany and the United States, who shipped thousands of pounds of food and clothing to members and non-members in 1991, 1992 and 1993. In July 1993, Ukraine received its second mission in Donetsk as work moved forward rapidly.

Sources: *Church News*, Feb. 15, 1992, Feb. 29, 1992.

Missions — 2
(As of Oct. 1, 1994; shown with historical number. See MISSIONS.)

(295) UKRAINE DONETSK MISSION
P.O. Box 3494
340050 Donetsk,
Ukraine
Phone: 011-7-0622 63 91-99

(274) UKRAINE KIEV MISSION
P.O. Box 144
252001 Kiev,
Ukraine
Phone: 011-7-044 230-25-42

UNITED KINGDOM

Year-end 1993: Est. population, 58,000,000; Members, 161,000; Stakes, 41; Wards, 230; Branches, 114; Missions, 7; Temples, 1, 1 under construction; Percent LDS, 0.28, or one person in 358.

The United Kingdom consists of England, Scotland, Wales and Northern Ireland, and is located off the northwest coast of Europe. The population speaks English, Welsh, and Gaelic. Most belong to the Church of England or are Roman Catholics.

Sources: *Truth Will Prevail,* editors V. Ben Bloxham, James R. Moss and Larry C. Porter; A History of the Church in Cambridgeshire, unpublished history by Leonard Reed; *Church News,* July 6, 1974, Dec. 1, 1985; "Markers tell where history was made," by Dell Van Orden and Gerry Avant, *Church News,* Aug. 1, 1987, Aug. 8, 1987; *Church News,* Nov. 24, 1990; "Temples rededicated, lives renewed," by Gerry Avant, *Church News,* Oct. 31, 1992; "Ground broken for Preston temple," by Bryan J. Grant, *Church News,* June 18, 1994.

ENGLAND

Year-end 1993: Est. population, 46,293,000; Members, 123,000; Stakes, 33; Wards, 188; Branches, 77; Missions, 6; Temples, 1, 1 under construction; Percent LDS, 0.3, or one LDS in 376.

On July 1, 1837, seven Canadian and American missionaries set sail for England on the packet ship

Garrick. The seven, Elders Heber C. Kimball and Orson Hyde of the Council of the Twelve; and Willard Richards, Joseph Fielding, John Goodson, Isaac Russell and John Snider, arrived July 19, 1837. They preached at Preston on Sunday, July 23, and on July 30, a baptismal service was held at nearby River Ribble that was viewed by some 8,000 curious onlookers. Nine converts were baptized by Elder Kimball, the first of whom was George D. Watt. A week later, the number of converts reached 50. The first conference was held on Christmas. Missionaries began working in Alston and Bedford, where branches were established, but the greatest work was done in the Preston area. Opposition began to mount through ministers and the press, but within nine months, more than a thousand had been baptized.

From 1840-41, seven members of the Council of the Twelve labored in England, finding significant success. Some 800 converts emigrated during the apostles' stay. The flow of British converts was life-sustaining for the struggling Church in America.

By 1850, 42,316 people had been baptized, and 6,832 had emigrated; from 1851-60, 37,215 converts were baptized, and 12,972 had emigrated; from 1861-70, 14,977 had joined and 10,094 emigrated.

The Church faced considerable opposition during the next several decades and the work was slowed. Missionary work increased after the turn of the century. With the onset of World War I, local sisters took over missionary work. The Relief Society was particularly active during the war. After the war, missionary work increased and anti-Mormon activity waned. Membership increased and in the mid-1930s, a large building program began and local leadership and missionaries became stronger. Members were urged to stay in England rather than emigrate.

World War II again interrupted missionary work, and British Saints took charge of their affairs. Despite difficulties finding leaders, they persisted in "home missionary work." When American leadership resumed in 1944, the number of branches had increased from 68 to 75, although they were later consolidated into 29. After the war, the missionary force was bolstered and conversions increased. Many members immigrated to America.

The announcement of a temple for London Aug. 1, 1953, along with visits of authorities and the Tabernacle Choir during the next few years, lifted members' spirits. Many aspects of the Church were strengthened during this period. More than 12,000 members attended the dedication of the London Temple Sept. 7-9, 1958. On March 27, 1960, the Manchester Stake, under the leadership of Pres. Robert G. Larson, was created and the British Mission was divided. Growth continued, more missions were created, and a large building program started. By 1971, membership was nearly 70,000, increasing in 1980 to 91,000.

The celebration of the Church's 150th anniversary in Great Britain in 1987 underscored the maturity of the Church in this land. President Ezra Taft Benson and President Gordon B. Hinckley of the First Presidency joined former Prime Minister Edward Heath at a celebration which viewed a videotaped message from U.S. President Ronald Reagan. Eight public markers were dedicated honoring important Church sites in the British Isles. Membership in 1990 was 151,000.

In November 1990, Terry Rooney of the Bradford 2nd Ward, Huddersfield England Stake, became the first LDS member elected to Parliament.

In October 1991 area president Elder Jeffrey R. Holland of the Seventy presented to the Federation of Family History Societies microfiche containing the 1881 census of the British Isles, which had been placed on microfiche by members.

Natives of England who have been called as General Authorities through the years include John Taylor, president of the Church 1880-87; George Q. Cannon, John R. Winder, George Teasdale, James E. Talmage, John Longden, B. H. Roberts, George Reynolds, Joseph W. McMurrin and Derek A. Cuthbert. Elders Kenneth Johnson is currently serving in the Seventy.

The London Temple was rededicated Oct. 18, 1992. And another temple for England, to be built in the Preston area, was announced Oct. 19, 1992, by President Hinckley. Ground was broken for the Preston England Temple on June 12, 1994, by President Hinckley, with 10,500 in attendance.

Stakes — 33
(Listed alphabetically as of Oct. 1, 1994.)

No.	Name	Organized	First President
Europe North Area			
1345	Ashton England	6 Jun 1982	Brian Ashworth
760	*Billingham England 10 Jun 1986		
	†Hartlepool England	13 Jun 1976	Craig Lithgow Marshall
494	*Birmingham England		
	†Birmingham	14 Sep 1969	Derek A. Cuthbert
609	*Bristol England		
	†Bristol	29 Apr 1973	Donald V. Norris

1331	Cheltenham England	21 Mar 1982	Warrick N. Kear
1346	Chester England	6 Jun 1982	Peter Furniss Lee
1936	Coventry England	9 May 1993	Thomas William Phillips
856	Crawley England	19 Aug 1977	J.A. Casbon
327	*Huddersfield England		
	†Leeds	19 Mar 1961	Dennis Livesey
608	*Hull England		
	†Hull	26 Apr 1973	Ian David Swanney
1423	Ipswich England	29 May 1983	Brian Arthur Frank Watling
780	Leeds England	12 Nov 1976	Douglas Rawson
325	*Leicester England		
	†Leicester	5 Mar 1961	Derek A. Cuthbert
814	Lichfield England	20 Feb 1977	Robert James Mawle
748	Liverpool England	14 Mar 1976	Michael R. Otterson
	†London	26 Feb 1961	Donald W. Hemingway
928a	London England Hyde Park	28 May 1978	Wilford M. Farnsworth Jr.
	†London North	20 Sep 1970	Thomas Hill
929a	London England Wandsworth	28 May 1978	John Dodd
930	Maidstone England	28 May 1978	William J. Joliffe III
294	*Manchester England		
	†Manchester	27 Mar 1960	Robert G. Larson
677	Newcastle-Under-Lyme England	17 Jan 1975	James Kenneth Cork
810	Northampton England	13 Feb 1977	Michael J. Wade
549	*Norwich England 28 May 1978		
	*Ipswich England		
	†East Anglia	20 Jun 1971	Dennis R. Reeves
597	*Nottingham England		
	†Nottingham	4 Feb 1973	Ernest Hewitt
885	Plymouth England	27 Nov 1977	Leonard Eden
1343	Poole England	23 May 1982	Peter J. Crockford
600	*Portsmouth England 6 Feb 1990		
	*Southampton England		
	†Southampton	11 Feb 1973	Reginald V. Littlecott
762	Preston England	17 Jun 1976	Eric Cryer
615	*Reading England		
	†Thames Valley	24 May 1973	Peter B.C. Brighty
666	Romford England	24 Nov 1974	Arthur James Turvey
932	Saint Albans England	28 May 1978	Roland Edward Elvidge
1376	Sheffield England	14 Nov 1982	Kenneth Jones
931	Staines England	28 May 1978	Peter Benjamin C. Brighty
374	*Sunderland England		
	†Sunderland	17 Mar 1963	Fred W. Oates

Discontinued

323   *London England
      28 May 1978 ★London England Hyde Park (No. 928a), London
      England Wandsworth (No. 929a), Staines England (No. 931)

527   *London England North
      28 May 1978 ★Saint Albans England (No. 932), Romford
      England (No. 666), Staines England (No. 931), London
      England Hyde Park (No. 928a)

Missions — 6
(As of Oct. 1, 1994; shown with historical number. See MISSIONS.)

(183) ENGLAND BIRMINGHAM MISSION
185 Penns Lane
Sutton Coldfield, West Midlands B76
1JU England
Phone: (011-44-21) 384-2032

(68) ENGLAND BRISTOL MISSION
484 London Road
#2 Southfield Road, Westbury-on-Trym
Bristol BS9 3BH, England
Phone: (011-44-272) 621-939

(52) ENGLAND LEEDS MISSION
Techno Centre, Station Road
Horsforth, Leeds LS18 5BJ
West Yorkshire, England
Phone: (011-44-532) 584-221

(1) ENGLAND LONDON MISSION
88-92 Earls Court Road
London W8 6EG
England
Phone: (011-44-71) 938-1330

(79) ENGLAND LONDON SOUTH MISSION
Southfield House
Mitcham, Surrey CR4 4ED
England
Phone: (011-44-81) 640-6018

(138) ENGLAND MANCHESTER MISSION
Paul House
Stockport Road, Timperley
Altrincham, Cheshire WA15 7UP, England
Phone: (011-44-61) 980-8015

NORTHERN IRELAND

Year-end 1993: Est. population, 1,600,000; Members, 5,500; Stakes, 1; Wards, 7; Branches, 6; Percent LDS, 0.34, or one LDS in 290; Ireland Dublin Mission.

Located in the northeast corner of Ireland, Northern Ireland is part of the United Kingdom. About 66 percent of the people are Protestant and 33 percent are Roman Catholic.

Northern Ireland remained in the United Kingdom when Ireland became an independent republic in 1949. Most of the Church membership is centered in and around Belfast.

When the London Temple was dedicated in 1958, it marked a "new era" for the Saints in Northern Ireland, who then numbered 540 in 10 branches. The Irish Mission was organized July 7, 1962. Twelve years later, June 9, 1974, the Belfast Ireland Stake was organized with Andrew Renfrew, former president of the Ulster District, as president.

On Sept. 7, 1986, some 1,350 attended a regional conference in Belfast, the largest-ever gathering of Saints in this area.

Stake — 1
(As of Oct. 1, 1994)

No.	Name	Organized	First President
Europe North Area			
1647	*Belfast Northern Ireland 13 Jan 1987		
	†Belfast Ireland	9 Jun 1974	Andrew Renfrew

SCOTLAND

Year-end 1993: Est. population, 5,000,000; Members, 25,000; Stakes, 5; Wards, 24; Branches, 21; Missions, 1; Percent LDS, 0.5, or one LDS in 200.

Native Scots converted in Canada, Alexander Wright and Samuel Mulliner, were the first missionaries to Scotland, arriving in Glasgow Dec. 20, 1839. Alexander and Jessie Hay were baptized by Elder Mulliner in the River Clyde on Jan. 9, 1840. By May 3, membership had increased to 80. Elder Orson Pratt arrived and organized a branch at Paisley on May 8, and labored in Edinburgh, where he found a number of converts. During this period, he wrote an influential pamphlet, *An Interesting Account of Several Remarkable Visions*. By March 1841, more than 200 had joined the Church in Edinburgh. Another branch had been organized in Glasgow. By 1850, membership had risen to 3,257 in more than 50 branches. By 1855, four conferences had been organized. However, membership began a decline in the 1850s that lasted for many years.

One missionary about the turn of the century was Elder David O. McKay, who experienced little success; membership in the country was 338. Discouraged, he saw engraved in stone the words: "What e'er thou art, act well thy part." The inspiration from this had a great impact on his life, and the future of the Church as well.

Low conversions and frequent emigration reduced Church membership in Scotland. The Scottish-Irish Mission was created in 1961, and re-named Scottish Mission the following year. Scotland's first stake was created in Glasgow Aug. 26, 1962, with Archibald R. Richardson as president.

Members in Scotland celebrated the 150th anniversary of the Glasgow Branch as members of five Scotland stakes formed a chorus and took part in Glasgow's prestigious European Year of Culture 1990, receiving a standing ovation for their Oct. 21, 1990, performance.

Membership in Scotland was 12,000 in 1980, and 22,000 in 1990, 10,000 more than ever joined the Church during the 19th century.

In the 1990s, missionary work continued to progress as membership reached 25,000 by the end of 1993.

Stakes — 5
(Listed alphabetically as of Oct. 1, 1994.)

No.	Name	Organized	First President
Europe North Area			
1186	Aberdeen Scotland	12 Oct 1980	William Albert Wilson

734	Dundee Scotland	23 Nov 1975	John Keogh
1187	Edinburgh Scotland	12 Oct 1980	Alexander Mutter Clark
356	*Glasgow Scotland		
	†Glasgow	26 Aug 1962	Archibald R. Richardson
1188	Paisley Scotland	12 Oct 1980	Alexander Cumming

Mission — 1
(As of Oct. 1, 1994; shown with historical number. See MISSIONS.)

(61) SCOTLAND EDINBURGH MISSION
"Boroughfield," 32 Colinton Rd.
Edinburgh, EH10 5DG, Scotland
Phone: (011-44-31) 337-1283

WALES

Year-end 1993: Est. population, 2,947,000; Members, 7,100; Stakes, 2; Wards, 11; Branches, 9; Percent LDS, 0.24, or one LDS in 415; England Bristol Mission.

It is supposed that the first Welshman was converted at the lectures of Wilford Woodruff in Herfordshire in 1840, but records cannot confirm this. Possibly the first member to preach in Wales was James Morgan. The first known missionary was Elder Henry Royle and his companion, Frederick Cook. They met with immediate success in Flintshire in North Wales. Just three weeks after their arrival, a branch of 32 members was organized on Oct. 30, 1840. In four months, there were two congregations totaling 150 members, but the missionaries experienced active opposition from ministers. Evidently, most of these early converts promptly emigrated.

In South Wales, work proceeded more slowly at first. Elder James Palmer labored there with little success late in 1840. Two years later, 44 Welshmen had been baptized. In 1843, Elder William Henshaw began proselyting in the Merthyr Tydfil area, and a branch of 50 was eventually organized. In 1844, the first Welsh-language materials were printed and work began to progress. A converted Welshman and associate of the Prophet Joseph Smith, Dan Jones, arrived in 1845. After a disappointing year in North Wales, he found success in the south and by 1849, left for America as captain of 300 Saints. He was later called to a second mission in Wales, which he completed in 1856, again leaving with a company, this time of 560 members.

The work slowed considerably afterwards, but began to build up in the 1900s. By 1950, there were 1,500 members in two districts. The first stake was created Jan. 12, 1975, in Merthyr Tydfil. Membership in 1990 was 6,500.

Stakes — 2
(Listed alphabetically as of Oct. 1, 1994.)

No.	Name	Organized	First President
Europe North Area			
1341	Cardiff Wales	9 May 1982	Barry Derek Roy Whittaker
676	Merthyr Tydfil Wales	12 Jan 1975	Ralph Pulman

URUGUAY

Year-end 1993: Est. population, 3,200,000; Members, 61,000; Stakes, 11; Wards, 51; Branches, 80; Missions, 1; Districts, 8; Percent LDS, 1.9, or one person in 52.

On the eastern coast of South America, the Republic of Uruguay has a people who speak Spanish. Some 66 percent of the population is Roman Catholic.

The first Church contact in Uruguay came in 1940 when Elder Rolf L. Larson of the Argentina Mission starred on the championship Argentine basketball team in games held in Montevideo. His example and the publicity about him led to Uruguayan contacts.

The Montevideo Branch was organized June 25, 1944, by Frederick S. Williams, former president of the Argentine Mission, for his family and a few North Americans living here while on government service. Pres. Williams was called as mission president and opened the Uruguay Mission on Aug. 31, 1947. By the year's end, 24 missionaries were serving in Uruguay, though few spoke Spanish fluently. By the end of 1948 there were 14 branches, all well-attended by investigators.

The first converts in Uruguay were Avelino Juan Rodriguez and his wife, Maria Esther, baptized by Pres. Williams on Nov. 4, 1948. Baptismal services were held regularly after that, and eight new branches were created in 1949. By 1957, the mission was baptizing 500 converts a year. The Montevideo Stake was organized Nov. 12, 1967. At that time, there were 14,800 members in the country. In 1979, membership reached 26,000 members in Uruguay.

In 1990, Elder Luis Alvberto Ferrizo, a regional representative, was elected as national deputy in the Uruguayan government, equivalent to a governor in the United States. Membership in Uruguay in 1990 was 52,000.

Sources: *From Acorn to Oak Tree*, by Frederick S. Williams and Frederick G. Williams; *50 Anos de la Iglesia in Argentina — Cronologia*, by Nestor Curbelo, seminary system, 1986; *Church News*, Nov. 9, 1986, March 17, 1990.

Stakes — 11
(Listed alphabetically as of Oct. 1, 1994.)

No.	Name	Organized	First President
South America South Area			
1123	Artigas Uruguay	23 Mar 1980	Luis Gonzalez
1098	Durazno Uruguay	25 Jan 1980	Luis Alberto Ferrizo
1033a	Melo Uruguay	2 June 1979	Santiago Gonzalez
1944	Mercedes Uruguay	20 Jun 1993	Milton Jose Airala Perez
1058	Montevideo Uruguay Cerro	2 Sep 1979	Nester Rivera M.
631	Montevideo Uruguay East	17 Feb 1974	Ariel A. Fedrigotti
1034	Montevideo Uruguay Maronas	3 Jun 1979	Jorge Washington Ventura
890	Montevideo Uruguay North	12 Feb 1978	Ariel Omar Fedrigotti
444	*Montevideo Uruguay West 17 Feb 1974		
	*Montevideo Uruguay		
	†Montevideo	12 Nov 1967	Vincente C. Rubio
832	Rivera Uruguay	20 May 1977	Ormesindo Correa
1019	Salto Uruguay	22 Apr 1979	Atilio Silveiro
Discontinued			
836	Minas Uruguay	22 May 1977	Alberto E. Hernandez
	12 Nov 1989		
833	Paysandu Uruguay	21 May 1977	Atilio Silveira
	22 Oct 1989 ★Uruguay Montevideo Mission		
840	Santa Lucia Uruguay	23 May 1977	Hector Julio Vigo
	20 Aug 1989 ★Uruguay Montevideo Mission		

Mission — 1
(As of Oct. 1, 1994; shown with historical number. See MISSIONS.)

(40) URUGUAY MONTEVIDEO MISSION
San Carlos de Bolivar 6178
Carrasco, Montevideo
Uruguay 11.500
Phone: (011-598-2) 60-44-11

VENEZUELA

Year-end 1993: Est. population: 20,000,000; Members, 66,000; Stakes, 12; Wards, 67; Branches, 120; Missions, 3; Districts, 11; Percent LDS, 0.3, or one LDS in 303.

On the Caribbean coast of South America, Venezuela is a federal republic where the people speak Spanish and Indian languages, and are 96 percent Roman Catholic.

A group of members, most expatriates working in Venezuela, held Church meetings in the home of Carl C. Wilcox in 1966 and earlier. On Nov. 2, 1966, a branch of 45 members was organized by Elder Marion G. Romney, then of the Council of the Twelve. Pres. Wilcox, a top financial officer of Del Monte Corp., was called to preside. A week before the dedication, Pres. Ted E. Brewerton (now of the Seventy) of the Costa Rica Mission sent four missionaries to open Venezuela for missionary work. The first missionaries were Elders Floyd Baum, Neil Gruwell, David Bell and Fred Podlesny. Maracaibo was opened July 7, 1967, by Elders Baum and Bell, and Elders Steve Jensen and Stephen Edmunds.

Work progressed very slowly as missionaries at first sought out converts who had leadership ability, and tried to introduce the Church through the media and the family home evening program. On Feb. 12, 1967, Elders Fred Podlesny and David Bell baptized Hernan Sepulveda, the first convert. Though initial converts were few, work progressed to the point where the Colombia-Venezuela Mission was created in 1968. Soon the Caracas 1st, 2nd and 3rd branches in the Caracas District were organized with 150 members. Other small branches began in Merida, San Cristobal and Maracaibo in the Venoc District. The first district conference was held Oct. 15, 1968, with 28 missionaries then serving in Caracas and Maracaibo.

When the Venezuela Mission was created July 1, 1971, membership had reached 1,259, and the Church entered a new phase. Under the leadership of mission Pres. Clark D. Webb, the mission began to average 40 converts a month. Emphasis was placed on bringing in entire families, which greatly strengthened local branches.

In 1977, some 4,000 members were in 23 branches in five districts. Successive mission presidents emphasized building programs and leadership preparation. President Spencer W. Kimball visited Venezuela in January 1975.

On July 1, 1977, Alejandro Portal Campos, an early leader in Venezuela, became president of the Venezuela Caracas Mission.

The Church Educational System started in Venezuela in 1972, under the direction of Brother Portal, and has involved many youths continually since then. The Maracaibo Venezuela Mission was created in 1979, with membership at nearly 5,000. By 1986, membership was 23,516 in five stakes, two missions and eight districts. Within four years, that membership doubled.

Sources: Venezuela, *Ensign* 1977; "Perseverance pays," *Church News*, Nov. 10, 1979; *La Historia de la Iglesia en Venezuela 1966 a 1986*, published by the Church Educational System in Venezuela.

Stakes — 13
(Listed alphabetically as of Oct. 1, 1994.)

No.	Name	Organized	First President
South America North Area			
1724	Barcelona Venezuela	4 Jun 1989	Angel Luis Fajardo C.
1989	Barquisimeto Venezuela	28 Aug 1994	Julio Ramon Davila Duran
827	Caracas Venezuela	15 May 1977	Adolfo F. Mayer G.
1887	Caracas Venezuela Palo Verde	14 June 1992	Edgardo Angulo de la Paua
1717	Caracas Venezuela Urdaneta	7 May 1989	Hector Manuel Arraez R.
1787	Ciudad Ojeda Venezuela	24 Feb 1991	Juan Silfrido Carrizo C.
1585	Guayana Venezuela	15 Jan 1986	Luis A. Aguilar Guevara
1181	Maracaibo Venezuela	15 Sep 1980	Francisco Giminez S.
1862	Maracaibo Venezuela Central	17 May 1992	Ruben Dario Blanco Valles
1414	Maracaibo Venezuela South	24 Apr 1983	Omar Alvarez
1774	Maracay Venezuela	4 Nov 1990	Jairo R. Herrera
1885	Puerto La Cruz Venezuela	7 June 1992	Luis Jose Gonzalez
1050	Valencia Venezuela	19 Aug 1979	Teodoro Hoffman

Missions — 4
(As of Oct. 1, 1994; shown with historical number. See MISSIONS.)

(303) VENEZUELA BARCELONA MISSION
Avenida Intercomunal
Centro Comercial Colonia
Barcelona, Venezuela
Phone: 011-58-81 76-77-74

(95) VENEZUELA CARACAS MISSION
Apartado 62569
Caracas 1060-A
Venezuela
Phone: (011-58-2) 985-3431

(174) VENEZUELA MARACAIBO MISSION
Apartado 10020 Bella Vista
Maracaibo, Estada Zulia CP 4002A
Venezuela
Phone: 011-58-61 922-751

(267) VENEZUELA VALENCIA MISSION
Av. Bolivar - Edificio Torre Santos
Sect. El Recreo. Piso 4 Oficinas 5 Y 6
Valencia, Venezuela
Phone 011-58-14 238-478

VIETNAM

Year-end 1993: Est. population, 71,875,000,000; Members, fewer than 100; Asia Area.

LDS servicemen arrived in Vietnam in the early 1960s in sufficient numbers to establish groups. An LDS serviceman's group was organized as part of the Southern Far East Mission on June 30, 1962, by mission Pres. Robert D. Taylor with Cecil Cavender as president.

On Nov. 3, 1962, U.S. Air Force Capt. John T. Mullennex was baptized in Saigon by Maurice H. Lee of the Saigon Group presidency. Converts Nguyen Thi Thuy and Duong Thuy Van, baptized in early 1963 by Capt. Loring B. Bean, were the first Vietnamese to join the Church.

The size of the LDS group began to grow as the Vietnam War became more intense and more servicemen arrived. Other groups were added, and several General Authorities visited. A small meetinghouse was erected at Bien Hoa Air Base. By 1971, three districts had been organized under the Hong Kong Mission.

When the cease-fire was reached Jan. 27, 1973, the Saigon Branch numbered about 100 under branch Pres. Nguyen Van The. Elders were sent to Vietnam immediately afterward. Elders Colin B. Van Orman, James L. Christensen, David T. Posey and Richard C. Holloman were transferred to Saigon from Hong Kong, arriving April 6, 1973.

These elders and those who came later found success, but on April 30, 1975, South Vietnam fell. Many of the members in Vietnam were able to leave and were relocated in America by the Church. Some 83 members were assigned to sponsors in the United States and Canada by Church refugee workers, along with 672 of their relatives and friends. Following the relocation, many refugees joined the Church and a number of full-time missionaries came from their ranks.

LDS veterans from that period helped locate many former branch members and reunify families.

At the end of 1991, the Church donated medical equipment that enabled Vietnamese surgeons to use microsurgery. Presenting the gift was Elder Merlin R. Lybbert of the Seventy, the first General Authority to enter Vietnam since 1975.

A year later, two LDS couples entered Hanoi on Jan. 6, 1993, to teach English. The couples, Elder James L. and Sister Helen Ream Bateman, and Elder Stanley G. and Sister Mavis Lynnette Steadman, were warmly welcomed in ceremonies at Tran Hung Dao Hospital and at the Children's Palace. The couples taught English to many people and also set up the first-ever presentation of Handel's Messiah in Vietnam, an unusual event partly funded by professional Vietnamese musicians who donated 70 cents at each rehearsal.

Sources: *Church News,* March 30, 1963; history by Virgil N. Kovalenko; "Church donates medical gift to Vietnam," *Church News,* Jan. 11, 1992;"Asia Area: Welcome mat is out in several countries," by Sheridan R. Sheffield, *Church News*, June 19, 1993; "Vietnam: Musicians perform 'Messiah' " *Church News,* Dec. 4, 1993.

VIRGIN ISLANDS

Year-end 1993: Est. population, 104,000; Members, 200; Branches, 2; Percent LDS, 0.19, or one LDS in 520; North America Southeast Area; Puerto Rico San Juan Mission.

The Virgin Islands are made up of three large and 50 small islands located 70 miles east of Puerto Rico. The residents speak English and have a republican form of government that operates under the United States.

The first missionaries to St. Croix were Elders Thomas Williams, Eric Leach, Gregory Collier and Kurtis Gibbons, who arrived Jan. 28, 1981. They held meetings in the home of a member, Jack Cluett, with about 15 attending. A branch was organized Feb. 8, 1981, with Stephen L. Whitmer as the first president. Missionaries baptized several converts the first year. A meetinghouse was later built on the island. Branches have also been established on St. John and St. Thomas.

On St. Thomas, various expatriate families lived on the island. In 1969, one of these was the Earl Keele family. He arrived May 1969, and his wife, Celia, and two children followed in August. The family held a home Sunday School as part of the San Juan Branch in Puerto Rico. In 1970 another family, James and Carolyn Boykin, joined the group. Debra Rybacki, met with the family and received permission to be baptized in Brewer's Bay in January 1976. Other families arrived and the St. Thomas Branch was created Dec. 13, 1977. The first missionaries came in June 1978, Elders John Sorensen and D.E. Blomquist. They baptized the supervisor of Sister Rybacki, Aubrey Nelthropp, and his wife, Carol, on July 16, 1978. The first branch meetinghouse was used July 16, 1978.

A devastating hurricane, Hugo, struck St. Croix in September 1989, destroying the homes of many members. A shipment of food from the mainland and use of the branch meetinghouse helped alleviate emergency conditions. Damage to the islands was reported repaired within a year.

Sources: Kenneth and LeOra Zabriskie journals; *Church News,* Sept. 9, 1989; *Ensign,* November 1989; Unpublished historical sketch of the Church in St. Thomas, by Celia Keele.

WALES
(See United Kingdom)

WESTERN SAMOA

Year-end 1993: Est. population, 202,000; Members, 51,000; Stakes, 10; Wards, 69; Branches, 30; Missions, 1; Temples, 1; Percent LDS, 25, or one in 4.

Located in the South Pacific, Western Samoa is a parliamentary democracy. The people are Protestant, 45 percent; LDS, 29 percent; and Roman Catholic, 20 percent.

In 1863, two missionaries from Hawaii arrived in Samoa. The two, Kimo Pelia and Samuela Manoa, however, had been sent by an unauthorized leader, Walter Murray Gibson, excommunicated by the Church. The pair labored faithfully for nearly 20 years without the support of the Church.

Elder Joseph H. Dean and his wife, Florence, arrived June 21, 1888. The mission was organized June 17, 1888. The Deans found that Pelia had died but Manoa was still very supportive. He was re-baptized and re-ordained. The same day, Elder Dean baptized a woman named Malaea, who is considered his first convert. Within four months 40 others had joined, and Elder Dean received additional help as more missionaries arrived. Missionaries visited all the islands and baptized converts. A local member, Polonga, was called as the first local missionary.

By 1896, members began to join in greater number. Missionaries also helped educate youths in small chapel schools. As local members filled leadership positions, they were assigned to distant branches, a pattern unique to Samoa. Local members also served missions and contributed toward growth of the Church.

Proselyting continued, but was made difficult by internal political conflicts. In 1899, the Samoan islands were divided up between Germany and the United States. Western Samoa became a German colony. Soon, the Germans banned English-language schools, an act that temporarily slowed missionary work. The German control ended in 1914.

By June 1903, the Book of Mormon had been translated. At the end of 1920, membership numbered 3,500, about 5 percent of the total population of the islands.

A visit by Elder David O. McKay, then of the Council of the Twelve, in May 1921, had great impact upon the membership. Conversions increased afterward and some entire villages became LDS.

By 1950, membership had grown to more than 7,000, and by 1961, to more than 16,000. By 1974, the country had six stakes and became the first country of the world to be entirely covered by stakes.

On Oct. 15, 1977, a temple was announced to be built in Apia, Western Samoa, and was dedicated Aug. 5, 1983. At that time, membership reached an estimated 40,000, about 20 percent of the population of the islands. In 1980, membership was 27,000, increasing to 41,000 in 1990.

Members suffered considerable property losses and one member died during tropical storm in 1991. However, local units responded well to dealing with the disaster. A number of former missionaries to Samoa helped in preserving a 30,000-acre rain forest in Falealupo, and in restoring and preserving the historic home of Robert Louis Stevenson.

Sources: Encyclopedic History of the Church by Andrew Jenson; Unto the Isles of the Sea, by R. Lanier Britsch; Samoa Apia Mission History, 1888-1983, published by R. Carl Harris, president of the Samoa Apia Mission; "Samoan rain forest reprieved from ruin," Church News, Aug. 19, 1989; Deseret News, Oct. 14, 1990; "Stevenson's historic home and grave to get a face lift," Deseret News, July 24, 1994.

Stakes — 10
(Listed alphabetically as of Oct. 1, 1994.)

No.	Name	Organized	First President
Pacific Area			
353	*Apia Samoa		
	†Apia	18 Mar 1962	Percy John Rivers
1045	Apia Samoa East	5 Aug 1979	Daniel Afamasaga Betham
513	*Apia Samoa West		
	†Apia West	26 Apr 1970	Percy J. Rivers
538	*Savai'i Samoa		
	†Savai'i	8 Jan 1971	Amuia W. Hunt
1366	Savai'i Samoa South	17 Oct 1982	Malina Ropeti Ti'a
619	*Savai'i Samoa West		
	†Savai'i West	3 Jun 1973	Fa'afoi Tuitama
868	Upolu Samoa East	23 Oct 1977	Kovana Pauga
1909	Upolu Samoa North	25 Oct 1992	Sofeni Pilimai

645	Upola Samoa South	1 Jun 1974	William Richard Schwalger
545	*Upolu Samoa West		
	†Upolu West	25 Apr 1971	Tua'ifaiva O. Aiono

Mission — 1
(As of Oct. 1, 1994; shown with historical number. See MISSIONS.)

(13c) SAMOA APIA MISSION
P.O. Box 1865
Apia, Western Samoa
Phone: 011-685 20-311

ZAIRE

Year-end 1993: Est. population, 41,240,000; Members, 4,600; Districts, 6; Branches, 22; Missions, 1; Percent LDS, 0.01 percent, or one LDS in 8,965; Africa Area.

Formerly Belgian Congo in central Africa, Zaire became an independent republic in 1960 and was named Zaire in 1971. The people speak French and Bantu dialects, and are Christian, 70 percent; and Moslem, 10 percent.

Elder R. Bay and Sister Jean Hutchings arrived in Kinshasa in February 1986, when the Church received legal status through the efforts of David M. Kennedy, special representative of the First Presidency. Pres. Hutchings was soon called as president of the Zaire Kinshasa Mission, created July 1, 1987. Meetings were first held in the home of Michael S. Bowcutt, an employee of the U.S. Embassy, and later at the home of Nkita Bungi Mbuyi, a returned missionary from England, converted in Belgium. The Church purchased a villa and had it remodeled into a meetinghouse in September 1986. At the first meeting in the 200-seat facility, 208 attended. The first baptisms in Zaire were Banza Jr. and Philippe Muchioko, sons of Banza Muchioko, who were converted in Switzerland seven years earlier.

Many young men and young families were converted in the first year. In July 1987, membership reached 300. Some 20 of the new converts were to be called as local missionaries to extend the work.

The first full-time missionaries from Zaire were Banza Muchioko Jr., Diamany Ngalamulume, Mutombo Nkadi Thomas and Maly-malu Kanda, who began serving in their homeland before April 1991.

Church Educational System missionaries Phyll and Betty Hansen introduced seminary to Zaire in late 1991. Elder Hansen trained Kabwika Natambwe, a member of the Zaire mission presidency, who carried the work forward throughout the country.

Sources: *Church News,* April 25, 1987; "Zaire's people, thirsty for the gospel," *Church News,* July 18, 1987; "A new day dawns on African nations," by Dell Van Orden and Gerry Avant, *Church News,* Oct. 17, 1987; *Church News,* April 25, 1992, Sept. 9, 1992.

Mission — 1
(As of Oct. 1, 1994; shown with historical number. See MISSIONS.)

(198) ZAIRE KINSHASA MISSION
Service Centre
Clarion Quartier
Parcel #120, Section 1 Bloc
Brazzaville, Congo
Phone: (011-242) 837-313

ZAMBIA

Year-end 1993: Est. population, 8,700,000; Members, 200; Africa Area; Zimbabwe Harare Mission.

A republic in southcentral Africa, Zambia has a population that speaks English and local dialects. Most of the population follows Christian beliefs, with smaller numbers who have indigenous and Muslim beliefs.

In the 1960s, a meetinghouse was built in Kwekwe, Zimbabwe, for a branch composed almost totally of expatriates working in what was then northern Rhodesia in the copperbelt, and farmers from South Africa. Those original members left, presumably across the border into Zambia. However, when none were located, Pres. Vern Marble of the Zimbabwe Harare Mission went to Zambia in 1991 to search for members.

He searched for, but could not find, a man who had been baptized in England, Johnson Makombe, and his wife, Noria. However, a taxi driver in Lusaka offered to find them and deliver a message. When Pres. Marble returned a short time later, Noria Makombe went to the hotel where he was staying. When she met him in the lobby, her first words were, "Where can I pay my tithing?"

The first missionary couple, Elder Dean and Sister Ruth Harrison, were assigned to open the work in Zambia in April 1992, and the Church was formally registered July 10, 1992. When a branch of the Church was organized in Lusaka on July 14, 1992 by Pres. Marble, the congregation of about 50 was almost the same size as when the meetinghouse was built in Kwekwe in the early 1960s.

Sources: "Four nations in central, southern Africa," by Mary Mostert and Gerry Avant, *Church News* Sept. 26, 1992.

ZIMBABWE

Year-end 1993: Est. population, 10,715,000; Members, 5,300; Districts, 3; Branches, 24; Missions, 1; Percent LDS, 0.05, or one LDS in 2,022; Africa Area.

In southern Africa, Zimbabwe is a one-party socialist state where the people speak English (official language), Shona and Sindebele. Traditional tribal beliefs dominate, with a Christian minority.

Missionary work began in what was then Rhodesia in the early 1930s but soon slowed, continued by only short visits by missionaries from South Africa. In 1950, under the direction of mission Pres. Evan P. Wright, eight missionaries began working in Salisbury and Bulawayo. Hugh Hodgkiss was the first convert, baptized Feb. 1, 1951.

On April 17, 1951, the missionaries distributed 3,000 handbills, and a fairly large crowd attended an introductory meeting. The first services were held in a pre-school building and prospective members sat on tiny chairs. Later, they met in the cloak room of a primary school.

During that period, Sir John Kennedy, governor of Southern Rhodesia, invited the missionaries to teach square dancing. They attended four large dances and made many contacts, but few conversions, as they taught dancing.

In 1980, the government changed and the nation of Zimbabwe was formed. A new mission was established in Zimbabwe. At the time, membership was 1,014. Missionary work increased as local missionaries began serving full-time missions.

On July 26, 1990, mission president George T. Brooks died in a car-truck accident near Kwekwe, Zimbabwe. His wife, Sister Lillis Remington Brooks, was seriously injured.

Since 1988, the Church has had an ongoing humanitarian project in Zimbabwe that included funds, a mill for grinding grain, a dam near Masvingo, gardening materials, and two large shipments of new textbooks for Zimbabwe's school children.

Sources: A History of the South African Mission, by Evan P. Wright; "Preached by Dancing," *Church News,* July 14, 1979; *Church News,* March 14, 1987, March 23, 1991.

Mission — 1
(As of Oct. 1, 1994; shown with historical number. See MISSIONS.)

(204) ZIMBABWE HARARE MISSION
65 Enterprise Road
Highlands, Harare, Zimbabwe
Phone: 011-263-4 737-297

Editor's note: Information in this section has been gathered from a variety of sources and is believed to be the best available at the time of publication. Corrections, additional information and further country or state histories will be appreciated. Those with comments or information may write to: Church Almanac Histories, P.O. Box 1257, Salt Lake City, UT 84110.

MISSIONS, TEMPLES

FULL-TIME MISSIONS

Missions are listed here in chronological order and according to the name under which they were originally organized. On June 20, 1974, most mission names were changed under the Church's current naming system; these and other name changes are indicated on the lines beneath the "Name" column. * Denotes a name change; capital letters indicate the mission's new name.

The number immediately preceding the name of the mission indicates the total number of missions in existence at the time of its organization. A letter after the number indicates that the number was reached previously; the letter is added to clarify cross-references. This number is also placed with the mission in the "Worldwide Church" section.

By using this list it is possible to trace the "family tree" of each mission. Included in each mission entry is the number, in parenthesis, of the "parent" mission from which it was created, and, in the "See also" entry, the numbers of "offspring" missions that were created from divisions of this mission. Also included are the numbers of missions that this mission may have been transferred to when it was discontinued, and the number the mission was assigned when it was re-opened.

	NAME	ORGANIZED	FIRST PRESIDENT
1	BRITISH	20 Jul 1837	Heber C. Kimball
	*10 Jun 1970 ENGLAND EAST		
	*20 Jun 1974 ENGLAND LONDON		
	See also 4, 52, 62, 68, 79, 161		
2	EASTERN STATES	6 May 1839	John P. Greene
	Discontinued Apr 1850		
	Reopened 1854 (15)		
	Discontinued 1858		
	Reopened 1865 (9a)		
	Discontinued 1869		
	Reopened from Northern States Jan 1893 (15b)		
	*20 Jun 1974 NEW YORK NEW YORK		
	See also 23a, 29, 35, 54, 77, 202		
3	SOCIETY ISLANDS	30 Apr 1844	Noah Rogers
	Discontinued 15 May 1852		
	Reopened 29 Apr 1892 (13d)		
	*1907 TAHITIAN		
	*25 Nov 1959 FRENCH-POLYNESIAN		
	*10 Jun 1970 FRENCH-POLYNESIA		
	*20 Jun 1974 TAHITI PAPEETE		
4	WELSH	15 Dec 1845	Dan Jones
	Organized from British (1)		
	Discontinued 26 Mar 1854, transferred to British (1)		
5	CALIFORNIA	31 Jul 1846	Samuel Brannan
	Discontinued 1858		
	Reopened 23 Aug 1892 (14c)		
	*20 Jun 1974 CALIFORNIA LOS ANGELES		
	See also 37, 73a, 86, 159		
5a	SCANDINAVIAN	11 May 1850	Erastus Snow
	Discontinued 1 Apr 1920, transferred to Danish (23b), Norwegian (24)		
	See also 22a		
6	FRENCH	18 Jun 1850	John Taylor
	Discontinued 1864		
	Reopened 15 Oct 1912 (22b)		
	Discontinued 18 Sep 1914		
	Reopened 20 Aug 1923 (26) from Swiss-German (8)		
	*10 Jun 1970 FRANCE		
	*20 Jun 1974 FRANCE PARIS		
	See also 59, 76, 92, 121, 221a		
7	ITALIAN	1 Nov 1850	Lorenzo Snow
	Discontinued 1 Jan 1854, transferred to Swiss and Italian (8)		
	Reopened 2 Aug 1966 (74a) from Swiss (8)		
	*10 Jun 1970 ITALY		
	*1 Jul 1971 ITALY SOUTH		

```
        *20 Jun 1974 ITALY ROME
        See also 98, 123, 158, 244
8    SWISS                              24 Nov 1850   Thomas B.H. Stenhouse
        *1 Jan 1854 SWISS AND ITALIAN
        *1 Jan 1861 SWISS, ITALIAN AND GERMAN
        *1 Jan 1868 SWISS AND GERMAN
        *1 Jan 1898 SWISS
        *22 May 1904 SWISS-GERMAN
        *1 Jan 1938 SWISS AUSTRIAN
        *21 Nov 1938 SWISS
        *25 May 1946 SWISS AUSTRIAN
        *18 Sep 1960 SWISS
        *10 Jun 1970 SWITZERLAND
        *20 Jun 1974 SWITZERLAND ZURICH
        See also 6, 7, 13, 8a, 19, 26, 30, 53
9    SANDWICH ISLANDS                   12 Dec 1850   Hiram Clark
        Discontinued 1 May 1858
        Reopened 27 Mar 1864 (7a)
        *1900 HAWAIIAN
        *1 Apr 1950 HAWAII
        *20 Jun 1974 HAWAII HONOLULU
        See also 34, 178
10   AUSTRALIAN                         30 Oct 1851   John Murdock
        *1854 AUSTRALASIAN
        *1 Jan 1898 AUSTRALIAN
        *10 Jun 1970 AUSTRALIA EAST
        *20 Jun 1974 AUSTRALIA SYDNEY
        See also 20, 43c, 106
11   EAST INDIAN                            1851      Lorenzo Snow
        Discontinued 2 May 1856
        Reopened 1 Aug 1884 (12a)
        Discontinued 10 Jun 1885
12   MALTA                              26 Feb 1852   Lorenzo Snow
        Discontinued 1856
13   GERMAN                              3 Apr 1852   Daniel P. Garn
        Discontinued 1 Jan 1861, transferred to Swiss, Italian and German (8)
        Reopened 1 Jan 1898 (19) from Swiss and German (8)
        Discontinued 22 May 1904, transferred to Swiss-German (8)
        Reopened 23 Aug 1925 as German-Austrian (27) from Swiss-German (8)
        Discontinued 1 Jan 1938, transferred to West German (35a), East German
           (36), Swiss Austrian (8)
        See also 30
13a  GIBRALTAR                           7 Mar 1853   Edward Stevenson
        Discontinued 5 Jul 1854
14   SOUTH AFRICAN                      19 Apr 1853   Jesse Haven
        Discontinued 12 Apr 1865
        Reopened 25 Jul 1903 (23)
        *10 Jun 1970 SOUTH AFRICA
        *20 Jun 1974 SOUTH AFRICA JOHANNESBURG
        See also 177a, 204, 216
15   EASTERN STATES (See 2)                 1854      John Taylor
14a  SIAM                                6 Apr 1854   Elam Luddington
        Discontinued 12 Aug 1854
15a  EUROPEAN (Administrative)          28 Jun 1854   Franklin D. Richards
        Discontinued 14 Feb 1950
        Reopened 17 Jan 1960 (51)
        Discontinued 14 Sep 1965
        See also 64
14b  INDIAN TERRITORY                   26 Jun 1855   Henry W. Miller
        Discontinued 23 May 1860
        Reopened Mar 1877 (9b)
        Discontinued 12 Sep 1877
        Reopened 20 Apr 1883 (11a)
        *29 Mar 1898 SOUTHWESTERN STATES
```

```
            *4 Apr 1904 CENTRAL STATES
            *10 Jun 1970 KANSAS-MISSOURI
            *20 Jun 1974 MISSOURI INDEPENDENCE
            See also 31, 88, 140, 153
7a   SANDWICH ISLANDS (See 9)              27 Mar 1864   Joseph F. Smith
8a   NETHERLANDS                           1 Nov 1864    Joseph Weiler
            Organized from Swiss, Italian and German (8)
            *31 Jan 1891 NETHERLANDS-BELGIUM
            *15 May 1914 NETHERLANDS
            *20 Jun 1974 NETHERLANDS AMSTERDAM
            Discontinued 1 July 1994
            See also 135, 232
9a   EASTERN STATES (See 2)                      1865    William H. Miles
8b   SOUTHERN STATES                        Nov 1876     Henry G. Boyle
            *Jun 1971 GEORGIA-SOUTH CAROLINA
            *20 Jun 1974 GEORGIA ATLANTA
            See also 22, 29, 55, 130, 166a, 239
9b   INDIAN TERRITORY (See 14b)             Mar 1877     Matthew W. Dalton
9c   NORTHWESTERN STATES                    6 May 1878   Cyrus H. Wheelock
            *20 Jul 1889 NORTHERN STATES
            *1 Jul 1973 ILLINOIS
            *20 Jun 1974 ILLINOIS CHICAGO
            *1 Jul 1980 ILLINOIS CHICAGO NORTH
            *1 Jul 1983 ILLINOIS CHICAGO
            See also 23a, 26a, 43a, 46, 97, 167, 184
10a  MEXICAN                                16 Nov 1879  Moses Thatcher
            Discontinued Jun 1889
            Reopened 8 Jun 1901 (20a)
            *10 Jun 1970 MEXICO
            *20 Jun 1974 MEXICO MEXICO CITY
            *1 Jul 1978 MEXICO MEXICO CITY SOUTH
            See also 33, 43b, 45a, 75, 125, 163, 193
11a  INDIAN TERITORY (See 14b)              20 Apr 1883  George Teasdale
12a  EAST INDIAN (See 11)                   1 Aug 1884   William Willis
13b  TURKISH                                30 Dec 1884  Jacob Spori
            Discontinued 1 Oct 1909
            Reopened 6 Nov 1921 (25)
            *23 Jan 1924 ARMENIAN
            *12 Aug 1933 PALESTINE-SYRIAN
            Discontinued 1939
            Reopened 8 Nov 1947 (43)
            *25 Jan 1950 NEAR EAST
            Discontinued Jan 1951
13c  SAMOAN                                 17 Jun 1888  Joseph H. Dean
            *10 Jun 1970 SAMOA
            *20 Jun 1974 SAMOA APIA
            See also 22c, 57, 99
13d  SOCIETY ISLANDS (See 3)                29 Apr 1892  Joseph W. Damron
14c  CALIFORNIA (See 5)                     23 Aug 1892  John L. Dalton
15b  EASTERN STATES (See 2)                 Jan 1893     Job Pingree
16   MONTANA                                10 Sep 1896  Phineas Tempest
            Discontinued 12 Jun 1898, transferred to Northwestern States (18)
            See also 43a
17   COLORADO                               15 Dec 1896  John W. Taylor
            *1 Apr 1907 WESTERN STATES
            *10 Jun 1970 COLORADO-NEW MEXICO
            *10 Oct 1972 COLORADO
            *20 Jun 1974 COLORADO DENVER
            See also 26a, 33, 43a, 132
18   NORTHWESTERN STATES                    26 Jul 1897  George C. Parkinson
            *10 Jun 1970 OREGON
            *20 Jun 1974 OREGON PORTLAND
```

```
        See also 26a, 36a, 43a, 78a, 249
19  GERMAN (See 13)                         1 Jan 1898    Peter Loutensock
20  NEW ZEALAND                             1 Jan 1898    Ezra F. Richards
        Organized from Australasian (10)
        *10 Jun 1970 NEW ZEALAND NORTH
        *20 Jun 1974 NEW ZEALAND AUCKLAND
        See also 47, 99
20a MEXICAN (See 10a)                       8 Jun 1901    Ammon N. Tenney
21  JAPAN                                   12 Aug 1901   Heber J. Grant
        Discontinued 31 Jul 1924
        Reopened 6 Mar 1948 as Japanese (44)
        Discontinued 28 Jul 1955, transferred to Northern Far East (43d), Southern
            Far East (44a)
22  MIDDLE STATES                           28 Jun 1902   Ben E. Rich
        Organized from Southern States (8b)
        Discontinued 7 Aug 1903, transferred to Southern States (8b)
23  SOUTH AFRICAN (See 14)                  25 Jul 1903   Warren H. Lyon
22a SWEDISH                                 15 Jun 1905   Peter Matson
        Organized from Scandinavian (5a)
        *10 Jun 1970 SWEDEN
        *20 Jun 1974 SWEDEN STOCKHOLM
        See also 41, 145
22b FRENCH (See 6)                          15 Oct 1912   Edgar B. Brossard
22c TONGAN                                  8 Jul 1916    Willard L. Smith
        Organized from Samoan (13c)
        *10 Jun 1970 TONGA
        *20 Jun 1974 TONGA NUKU'ALOFA
        See also 99
23a CANADIAN                                1 Jul 1919    Nephi Jensen
        Organized from Eastern States (15b), Northern States (9c)
        *10 Jun 1970 ONTARIO-QUEBEC
        *1 Jul 1972 ONTARIO
        *20 Jun 1974 CANADA TORONTO
        See also 26a, 35, 99a
23b DANISH                                  1 Apr 1920    Carl E. Peterson
        Organized from Scandinavian (5a)
        *10 Jun 1970 DENMARK
        *20 Jun 1974 DENMARK COPENHAGEN
24  NORWEGIAN                               1 Apr 1920    Andrew S. Schow
        Organized from Scandinavian (5a)
        *10 Jun 1970 NORWAY
        *20 Jun 1974 NORWAY OSLO
25  TURKISH (See 13b)                       6 Nov 1921    Joseph Wilford Booth
26  FRENCH (See 6)                          20 Aug 1923   Russell H. Blood
26a NORTH CENTRAL STATES                    12 Jul 1925   John G. Allred
        Organized from Northern States (9c), Western States (17),
            Northwestern States (18), Canadian (23a)
        *10 Jun 1970 MANITOBA-MINNESOTA
        *1 Jul 1973 MINNESOTA-WISCONSIN
        *20 Jun 1974 MINNESOTA MINNEAPOLIS
        See also 36a, 43a, 167
27  GERMAN-AUSTRIAN (See 13)                23 Aug 1925   Fred Tadje
28  SOUTH AMERICAN                          6 Dec 1925    Melvin J. Ballard
        Discontinued 25 May 1935, transferred to Brazilian (31a), Argentine (32)
29  EAST CENTRAL STATES                     9 Dec 1928    Miles L. Jones
        Organized from Southern States (8b), Eastern States, (15b)
        *10 Jun 1970 KENTUCKY-TENNESSEE
        *20 Jun 1974 KENTUCKY LOUISVILLE
        See also 42, 131
30  CZECHOSLOVAK                            24 Jul 1929   Arthur Gaeth
        Organized from German-Austrian (27), Swiss (8)
        Discontinued 6 Apr 1950
        Reopened 1 Jul 1990, see 236
31  TEXAS                                   11 Jan 1931   Charles Elliott Rowan Jr.
```

Organized from Central States (11a)
*May 1945 TEXAS-LOUISIANA
*19 Jun 1955 GULF STATES
*20 Jun 1974 LOUISIANA SHREVEPORT
*1 Jul 1975 LOUISIANA BATON ROUGE
See also 60, 116, 171

31a BRAZILIAN   25 May 1935   Rulon S. Howells
Organized from South American (28)
*10 Jun 1970 BRAZIL CENTRAL
Discontinued 17 Oct 1972, transferred to Brazil North Central (101),
    Brazil South Central (102)
See also 48, 80

32   ARGENTINE   14 Aug 1935   W. Ernest Young
Organized from South American (28)
*10 Jun 1970 ARGENTINA SOUTH
*20 Jun 1974 ARGENTINA BUENOS AIRES NORTH
See also 40, 50, 73, 100, 112, 269

33   SPANISH-AMERICAN   28 Jun 1936   Orlando C. Williams
Organized from Mexican (20a)
Discontinued Dec 1967, transferred to Texas (60), Texas South (77b),
    Western States (17)
See also 46a, 77b

34   JAPANESE   24 Feb 1937   Hilton A. Robertson
Organized from Hawaiian (7a)
*14 May 1944 CENTRAL PACIFIC
Discontinued 1 Apr 1950, transferred to Hawaii (9)
(Administrative headquarters different from 21)

35   NEW ENGLAND   24 Sep 1937   Carl Eyring
Organized from Eastern States (15b), Canadian (23a)
*20 Jun 1974 MASSACHUSETTS BOSTON
See also 107, 169, 195, 299

35a WEST GERMAN   1 Jan 1938   Philemon M. Kelly
Organized from German-Austrian (27)
*10 Jun 1970 GERMANY WEST
*20 Jun 1974 GERMANY FRANKFURT
See also 49, 63, 240

36   EAST GERMAN   1 Jan 1938   Alfred C. Rees
Organized from German-Austrian (27)
*12 Sep 1957 NORTH GERMAN
*10 Jun 1970 GERMANY NORTH
*20 Jun 1974 GERMANY HAMBURG
See also 65

36a WESTERN CANADIAN   15 Sep 1941   Walter Miller
Organized from North Central States (26a), Northwestern States (18)
*10 Jun 1970 ALBERTA-SASKATCHEWAN
*20 Jun 1974 CANADA CALGARY
See also 58, 136

37   NORTHERN CALIFORNIA   2 Jan 1942   German E. Ellsworth
Organized from California (14c)
*15 Jul 1966 CALIFORNIA NORTH
*20 Jun 1974 CALIFORNIA SACRAMENTO
See also 85, 127, 187a

38   NAVAJO-ZUNI   7 Mar 1943   Ralph W. Evans
*1 Jan 1949 SOUTHWEST INDIAN
*10 Oct 1972 NEW MEXICO-ARIZONA
*20 Jun 1974 ARIZONA HOLBROOK
Discontinued 1 Jul 1984, transferred to Arizona Phoenix (179b)
See also 78, 128, 132

39   PACIFIC (Administrative)   7 Dec 1946   Matthew Cowley
Discontinued 27 Nov 1948

40   URUGUAY   31 Aug 1947   Frederick S. Williams
*10 Jun 1970 URUGUAY-PARAGUAY
*20 Jun 1974 URUGUAY MONTEVIDEO
See also 50, 155

41	FINNISH	1 Sep 1947	Henry A. Matis

Organized from Swedish (22a)
*10 Jun 1970 FINLAND
*20 Jun 1974 FINLAND HELSINKI
See also 238

42	CENTRAL ATLANTIC STATES	26 Oct 1947	Robert J. Price

Organized from East Central States (29)
*10 Jun 1970 NORTH CAROLINA-VIRGINIA
*1 Jul 1973 VIRGINIA
*20 Jun 1974 VIRGINIA ROANOKE
*25 Feb 1992 VIRGINIA RICHMOND
See also 105, 188

43	PALESTINE-SYRIAN (See 13b)	8 Nov 1947	Badwagan Piranian
44	JAPANESE (See 21)	6 Mar 1948	Edward L. Clissold
45	CHINESE	10 Jul 1949	Hilton A. Robertson

Discontinued 9 Feb 1953

46	GREAT LAKES	31 Oct 1949	Carl C. Burton

Organized from Northern States (9c)
*10 Jun 1970 INDIANA-MICHIGAN
*1 Jul 1973 INDIANA
*20 Jun 1974 INDIANA INDIANAPOLIS
See also 77a, 104

43a	WEST CENTRAL STATES	11 Nov 1950	Sylvester Broadbent

Organized from North Central States (26a), Northwestern States (18),
    Western States (17)
*10 Jun 1970 MONTANA-WYOMING
*20 Jun 1974 MONTANA BILLINGS
See also 111

43b	CENTRAL AMERICAN	16 Nov 1952	Gordon M. Romney

Organized from Mexican (20a)
*10 Jun 1970 CENTRAL AMERICA
*20 Jun 1974 COSTA RICA SAN JOSE
See also 76a, 79a, 177, 226

43c	SOUTH AUSTRALIAN	3 Jul 1955	Thomas S. Bingham

Organized from Australian (10)
*Nov 1958 SOUTHERN AUSTRALIAN
*1 Aug 1968 AUSTRALIA SOUTH
*20 Jun 1974 AUSTRALIA MELBOURNE
See also 82

43d	NORTHERN FAR EAST	28 Jul 1955	Hilton A. Robertson

Organized from Japanese (44)
Discontinued 31 Aug 1968, transferred to Japan (82a), Japan-Okinawa (83)
See also 71

44a	SOUTHERN FAR EAST	17 Aug 1955	Herald Grant Heaton

Organized from Japanese (44)
*1 Nov 1969 HONG KONG TAIWAN
*11 Jan 1971 HONG KONG
See also 76b, 89, 94

45a	NORTHERN MEXICAN	10 Jun 1956	Joseph T. Bentley

Organized from Mexican (20a)
*10 Jun 1970 MEXICO NORTH
*20 Jun 1974 MEXICO MONTERREY
See also 56, 81, 193, 218

46a	WEST SPANISH-AMERICAN	8 Mar 1958	Leland M. Perry

Organized from Spanish-American (33)
*10 Jun 1970 WEST SPANISH AMERICA
Discontinued 1 Jul 1970, transferred to California (5)
    California South (73a), Arizona (87)

47	NEW ZEALAND SOUTH	1 Sep 1958	Alexander P. Anderson

Organized from New Zealand (20)
*20 Jun 1974 NEW ZEALAND WELLINGTON
Discontinued 1 Jul 1981, transferred to New Zealand Christchurch (143),
    New Zealand Auckland (20)

48   BRAZILIAN SOUTH   20 Sep 1959   Asael T. Sorensen
       Organized from Brazilian (31a)
       *10 Jun 1970 BRAZIL SOUTH
       *20 Jun 1974 BRAZIL PORTO ALEGRE
       *1 Jul 1991 BRAZIL PORTO ALEGRE SOUTH
       See also 80, 181, 256a, 258

49   SOUTH GERMAN   4 Oct 1959   John A. Buehner
       Organized from West German (35a)
       *10 Jun 1970 GERMANY SOUTH
       *20 Jun 1974 GERMANY MUNICH
       See also 69, 240

50   ANDES   1 Nov 1959   J. Vernon Sharp
       Organized from Uruguay (40), Argentine (32)
       *10 Jun 1970 PERU-ECUADOR
       *1 Aug 1970 PERU
       *Feb 1971 PERU ANDES
       *Apr 1971 ANDES PERU
       *20 Jun 1974 PERU LIMA
       *1 Jan 1977 PERU LIMA SOUTH
       See also 67, 75a, 79a, 93, 149, 165, 300

51   EUROPEAN (Administrative) (See 15a)   17 Jan 1960   Alvin R. Dyer
52   NORTH BRITISH   27 Mar 1960   Bernard P. Brockbank
       Organized from British (1)
       *10 Jun 1970 ENGLAND NORTH
       *20 Jun 1974 ENGLAND LEEDS
       See also 61, 72, 138

53   AUSTRIAN   18 Sep 1960   W. Whitney Smith
       Organized from Swiss Austrian (8)
       *10 Jun 1970 AUSTRIA
       *20 Jun 1974 AUSTRIA VIENNA
       See also 205

54   EASTERN ATLANTIC STATES   16 Oct 1960   George B. Hill
       Organized from Eastern States (15b)
       *10 Jun 1970 DELAWARE-MARYLAND
       *20 Jun 1974 WASHINGTON D.C.
       *1 Jul 1986 WASHINGTON D.C. SOUTH
       See also 91a, 188b, 298

55   FLORIDA   1 Nov 1960   Karl R. Lyman
       Organized from Southern States (8b)
       *10 Jun 1971 FLORIDA SOUTH
       *20 Jun 1974 FLORIDA FT. LAUDERDALE
       Discontinued 20 Jun 1983, transferred to Florida Tampa (139), West Indies (178a)
       Reopened 1 Jul 1984 (178b)
       See also 96, 175

56   WEST MEXICAN   1 Nov 1960   Harold E. Turley
       Organized from Northern Mexican (45a)
       *10 Jun 1970 MEXICO WEST
       *20 Jun 1974 MEXICO HERMOSILLO
       See also 125, 247

57   RAROTONGA   20 Nov 1960   Joseph R. Reeder
       Organized from Samoan (13c)
       Discontinued 15 Apr 1966, transferred to New Zealand (20)

58   ALASKAN-CANADIAN   21 Nov 1960   Milton L. Weilenman
       Organized from Western Canadian (36a)
       *10 Jun 1970 ALASKA-BRITISH COLUMBIA
       *20 Jun 1974 CANADA VANCOUVER
       See also 114

59   FRENCH EAST   19 Jan 1961   Henry D. Moyle Jr.
       Organized from French (26)
       *10 Jun 1970 FRANCE-SWITZERLAND
       *20 Jun 1974 SWITZERLAND GENEVA
       See also 221a, 262

60 TEXAS   16 Feb 1961   Ralph J. Hill
      Organized from Gulf States (31)
      *10 Jun 1970 TEXAS NORTH
      *20 Jun 1974 TEXAS DALLAS
      See also 77b, 189
61 SCOTTISH-IRISH   28 Feb 1961   Bernard P. Brockbank
      Organized from North British (52)
      *8 Jul 1962 SCOTTISH
      *10 Jun 1970 SCOTLAND
      *20 Jun 1974 SCOTLAND EDINBURGH
      See also 70, 74, 147
62 CENTRAL BRITISH   6 Mar 1961   James A. Cullimore
      Organized from British (1)
      *10 Jun 1970 ENGLAND CENTRAL
      *20 Jun 1974 ENGLAND BIRMINGHAM
      Discontinued 1 Jul 1983, transferred to England Coventry (183)
63 CENTRAL GERMAN   15 Mar 1961   Stephen C. Richards
      Organized from West German (35a)
      *10 Jun 1970 GERMANY CENTRAL
      *20 Jun 1974 GERMANY DUSSELDORF
      Discontinued 1 Apr 1982, transferred to Germany Frankfurt (35a), Germany
          Munich (49)
      Reopened 1 Jul 1990, see 240
64 WEST EUROPEAN (Administrative)   30 Apr 1961   N. Eldon Tanner
      Organized from European (51)
      Discontinued 14 Sep 1965
65 BERLIN   14 Jul 1961   Percy K. Fetzer
      Organized from North German (36)
      Discontinued 31 May 1966, transferred to North German (36)
66 SOUTH AMERICA (Administrative)   25 Aug 1961   A. Theodore Tuttle
      Discontinued 17 Jul 1965
67 CHILEAN   8 Oct 1961   A. Delbert Palmer
      Organized from Andes (50)
      *10 Jun 1970 CHILE
      *20 Jun 1974 CHILE SANTIAGO
      *1 Jan 1977 CHILE SANTIAGO SOUTH
      See also 119, 148, 214
68 SOUTHWEST BRITISH   1 Feb 1962   A. Ray Curtis
      Organized from British (1)
      *10 Jun 1970 ENGLAND SOUTHWEST
      *20 Jun 1974 ENGLAND BRISTOL
      See also 79
69 BAVARIAN   4 Mar 1962   Owen Spencer Jacobs
      Organized from South German (49)
      Discontinued 10 Jun 1965, transferred to South German (49)
70 IRISH   8 Jul 1962   Stephen R. Covey
      Organized from Scottish-Irish (61)
      *10 Jun 1970 IRELAND
      *20 Jun 1974 IRELAND BELFAST
      *11 Sep 1976 IRELAND DUBLIN
71 KOREAN   8 Jul 1962   Gail Edward Carr
      Organized from Northern Far East (43d)
      *10 Jun 1970 KOREA
      *20 Jun 1974 KOREA SEOUL
      See also 124, 170
72 NORTHEAST BRITISH   1 Sep 1962   Grant S. Thorn
      Organized from North British (52)
      Discontinued May 1965, transferred to North British (52)
73 NORTH ARGENTINE   16 Sep 1962   Ronald V. Stone
      Organized from Argentine (32)
      *10 Jun 1970 ARGENTINA NORTH
      *20 Jun 1974 ARGENTINA CORDOBA
      See also 100, 206, 228

| 74 | NORTH SCOTTISH | 24 Nov 1962 | William N. Waite |

74 NORTH SCOTTISH   24 Nov 1962   William N. Waite
   Organized from Scottish (61)
   Discontinued 31 May 1965, transferred to Scottish (61)

75 SOUTHEAST MEXICAN   27 Mar 1963   Carl J. Beecroft
   Organized from Mexican (20a)
   *10 Jun 1970 MEXICO SOUTHEAST
   *20 Jun 1974 MEXICO VERACRUZ
   See also 126, 193

76 FRANCO-BELGIAN   1 Oct 1963   Joseph T. Edmunds
   Organized from French (26)
   *10 Jun 1970 FRANCE-BELGIUM
   *20 Jun 1974 BELGIUM BRUSSELS
   See also 135

77 CUMORAH   26 Jan 1964   N. Lester Petersen
   Organized from Eastern States (15b)
   *20 Jun 1974 NEW YORK ROCHESTER

78 NORTHERN INDIAN   8 Apr 1964   Grant Roper Farmer
   Organized from Southwest Indian (38)
   *1 Jul 1973 DAKOTA-MANITOBA
   *20 Jun 1974 SOUTH DAKOTA RAPID CITY
   See also 136

79 BRITISH SOUTH   27 Dec 1964   Don K. Archer
   Organized from British (1), Southwest British (68)
   *10 Jun 1970 ENGLAND SOUTH
   *20 Jun 1974 ENGLAND LONDON SOUTH

76a GUATEMALA-EL SALVADOR   1 Aug 1965   Terrance L. Hansen
   Organized from Central American (43b)
   *20 Jun 1974 GUATEMALA GUATEMALA CITY
   *29 Mar 1988 GUATEMALA GUATEMALA CITY SOUTH
   See also 137a, 152, 205a, 227

73a CALIFORNIA SOUTH   10 Jul 1966   D. Crawford Houston
   Organized from California (14c)
   *20 Jun 1974 CALIFORNIA ANAHEIM
   See also 86, 87, 113, 182

74a ITALIAN (See 7)   2 Aug 1966   John Duns Jr.

75a ANDES SOUTH   14 Nov 1966   Franklin Kay Gibson
   Organized from Andes (50)
   *1969 BOLIVIA
   *20 Jun 1974 BOLIVIA LA PAZ
   Discontinued 1 Feb 1982, transferred to Bolivia Cochabamba (150)
   Reopened 8 Jan 1988 (207)

76b PHILIPPINE   28 Jun 1967   Paul S. Rose
   Organized from Southern Far East (44a)
   *10 Jun 1970 PHILIPPINES
   *20 Jun 1974 PHILIPPINES MANILA
   See also 110, 172, 194, 250, 268

77a OHIO   31 Jul 1967   E. Garrett Barlow
   Organized from Great Lakes (46)
   *31 Aug 1972 OHIO-WEST VIRGINIA
   *20 Jun 1974 OHIO COLUMBUS
   See also 154, 188, 179a

77b TEXAS SOUTH   10 Dec 1967   Dean L. Larsen
   Organized from Texas (60), Spanish-American (33)
   *20 Jun 1974 TEXAS SAN ANTONIO
   See also 142, 224

78a PACIFIC NORTHWEST   1 Jan 1968   Joe E. Whitesides
   Organized from Northwestern States (18)
   *10 Jun 1970 WASHINGTON
   *20 Jun 1974 WASHINGTON SEATTLE
   See also 166, 255

79a COLOMBIA-VENEZUELA 1 Jul 1968 Stephen L. Brower
Organized from Central American (43b), Andes (50)
*1 Jul 1971 COLOMBIA
*20 Jun 1974 COLOMBIA BOGOTA
*1 Jul 1992 COLOMBIA BOGOTA NORTH
See also 95, 120, 215, 270

80 BRAZILIAN NORTH 7 Jul 1968 Hal Roscoe Johnson
Organized from Brazilian (31a), Brazilian South (48)
*10 Jun 1970 BRAZIL NORTH
*20 Jun 1974 BRAZIL RIO DE JANEIRO
See also 167a, 185a

81 MEXICO NORTH CENTRAL 5 Aug 1968 Arturo R. Martinez
Organized from Northern Mexico (45a)
*20 Jun 1974 MEXICO TORREON
See also 125, 208

82 AUSTRALIAN WEST 7 Aug 1968 Milton J. Hess
Organized from Southern Australian (43c)
*10 Jun 1970 AUSTRALIA WEST
*20 Jun 1974 AUSTRALIA ADELAIDE
See also 117

82a JAPAN 1 Sep 1968 Walter R. Bills
Organized from Northern Far East (43d)
*20 Jun 1974 JAPAN TOKYO
*1 Jul 1978 JAPAN TOKYO NORTH
See also 90, 108, 109a, 162

83 JAPAN-OKINAWA 1 Sep 1968 Edward Y. Okazaki
Organized from Northern Far East (43d)
*16 Mar 1970 JAPAN CENTRAL
*20 Jun 1974 JAPAN KOBE
See also 91, 108, 144, 185, 245

84 GERMANY DRESDEN 14 Jun 1969 Johannes Henry Burkhart
Discontinued Dec 1978
Reopened 1 Jul 1989, see 225

85 CALIFORNIA CENTRAL 1 Jul 1969 Wilbur Wallace Cox
Organized from California North (37)
*20 Jun 1974 CALIFORNIA OAKLAND
See also 118, 158a, 187a

86 CALIFORNIA EAST 7 Jul 1969 William L. Nicholls
Organized from California South (73a), California (14c)
*20 Jun 1974 CALIFORNIA ARCADIA
See also 182, 297

87 ARIZONA 1 Aug 1969 Clark M. Wood
Organized from California South (73a)
*20 Jun 1974 ARIZONA TEMPE
See also 127, 132, 179b, 231

88 SOUTH CENTRAL STATES 4 Aug 1969 Albert B. Crandall
Organized from Central States (11a)
*10 Jun 1970 OKLAHOMA
*20 Jun 1974 OKLAHOMA TULSA
See also 116, 248

89 SOUTHEAST ASIA 1 Nov 1969 G. Carlos Smith
Organized from Southern Far East (44a)
*20 Jun 1974 SINGAPORE
Discontinued 1 Jul 1978, transferred to Indonesia Jakarta (122)
Reopened 1 Jan 1980 (176)
See also 109

90 JAPAN EAST 15 Mar 1970 Russel N. Horiuchi
Organized from Japan (82a)
*20 Jun 1974 JAPAN SAPPORO

91 JAPAN WEST 18 Mar 1970 Kan Watanabe
Organized from Japan-Okinawa (83)
*20 Jun 1974 JAPAN FUKUOKA
See also 144

91a PENNSYLVANIA   1 Jul 1970   George M. Baker
     Organized from Delaware-Maryland (54)
     *20 Jun 1974 PENNSYLVANIA HARRISBURG
     See also 129, 156
92 SPAIN   11 Jul 1970   R. Raymond Barnes
     Organized from French (26)
     *20 Jun 1974 SPAIN MADRID
     See also 137, 141, 199
93 ECUADOR   1 Aug 1970   Louis W. Latimer
     Organized from Peru-Ecuador (50)
     *20 Jun 1974 ECUADOR QUITO
     See also 160
94 TAIWAN   11 Jan 1971   Malan R. Jackson
     Organized from Hong Kong-Taiwan (44a)
     *20 Jun 1974 TAIWAN TAIPEI
     See also 146
95 VENEZUELA   1 Jul 1971   Clark D. Webb
     Organized from Colombia-Venezuela (79a)
     *20 Jun 1974 VENEZUELA CARACAS
     *1 Jul 1991 VENEZUELA CARACAS EAST
     *25 Mar 1994 VENEZUELA
     See also 174, 267, 303
96 ALABAMA-FLORIDA   1 Jul 1971   Hartman Rector Jr.
     Organized from Florida (55)
     *20 Jun 1974 FLORIDA TALLAHASSEE
     See also 166a, 197
97 NAUVOO   1 Jul 1971   J. LeRoy Kimball
     Organized from Northern States (9c)
     Discontinued 1 Jul 1974, transferred to Illinois Chicago (9c)
98 ITALY NORTH   6 Jul 1971   Dan Charles Jorgensen
     Organized from Italy (74a)
     *20 Jun 1974 ITALY MILAN
     See also 244
99 FIJI   23 Jul 1971   Sherman A. Lindholm
     Organized from Samoa (13c), New Zealand North (20), Tonga (22c)
     *20 Jun 1974 FIJI SUVA
     See also 178
99a QUEBEC   14 Jul 1972   John K. M. Olsen
     Organized from Ontario-Quebec (23a)
     *20 Jun 1974 CANADA MONTREAL
100 ARGENTINA EAST   30 Jul 1972   Joseph T. Bentley
     Organized from Argentina North (73), Argentina South (32)
     *20 Jun 1974 ARGENTINA ROSARIO
     See also 229
101 BRAZIL NORTH CENTRAL   17 Oct 1972   Leroy A. Drechsel
     Organized from Brazil Central (31a)
     *20 Jun 1974 BRAZIL SAO PAULO NORTH
     See also 190, 257
102 BRAZIL SOUTH CENTRAL   17 Oct 1972   Owen Nelson Baker
     Organized from Brazil Central (31a)
     *20 Jun 1974 BRAZIL SAO PAULO SOUTH
     See also 181, 257
103 INTERNATIONAL   9 Nov 1972   Bernard P. Brockbank
     Organized for "unattached" members worldwide
     Discontinued 15 Aug 1987
     See also 179, 205
104 MICHIGAN   3 Jul 1973   C. Russell Hansen
     Organized from Indiana-Michigan (46)
     *20 Jun 1974 MICHIGAN LANSING
     See also 164
105 NORTH CAROLINA   18 Jul 1973   Charles M. Alexander
     Organized from North Carolina-Virginia (42)
     *20 Jun 1974 NORTH CAROLINA GREENSBORO
     *1 Jul 1980 NORTH CAROLINA CHARLOTTE
     See also 186

106 AUSTRALIA NORTHEAST   26 Jul 1973   J. Martell Bird
Organized from Australia East (10)
*20 Jun 1974 AUSTRALIA BRISBANE
See also 275
107 CANADA-MARITIMES   27 Jul 1973   Thurn J. Baker
Organized from New England (35)
*20 Jun 1974 CANADA HALIFAX
108 JAPAN-NAGOYA   1 Aug 1973   Satoru Sato
Organized from Japan (82a), Japan Central (83)
*20 Jun 1974 JAPAN NAGOYA
109 THAILAND   1 Aug 1973   Paul D. Morris
Organized from Southeast Asia (89)
*20 Jun 1974 THAILAND BANGKOK
109a JAPAN SENDAI   1 Jul 1974   Walter Teruya
Organized from Japan Tokyo (82a)
110 PHILIPPINES CEBU CITY   1 Jul 1974   Carl D. Jones
Organized from Philippines Manila (76b)
*3 Aug 1984 PHILIPPINES CEBU
*1 Jul 1988 PHILIPPINES BACOLOD
See also 157, 194, 223
111 IDAHO POCATELLO   1 Jul 1974   Ernest Eberhard Jr.
Organized from Montana Billings (43a)
*29 May 1979 IDAHO BOISE
See also 132, 264
112 ARGENTINA BUENOS AIRES SOUTH   22 Jul 1974   Juan Carlos Avila
Organized from Argentina South (32)
See also 180, 269
113 CALIFORNIA SAN DIEGO   1 Aug 1974   Frank M. Bradshaw
Organized from California Anaheim (73a)
114 ALASKA ANCHORAGE   15 Oct 1974   Weston F. Killpack
Organized from Canada Vancouver (58)
115 PORTUGAL LISBON   19 Nov 1974   Wm. Grant Bangerter
* 1 Jul 1990 PORTUGAL LISBON SOUTH
See also 203, 253
116 ARKANSAS LITTLE ROCK   1 Jul 1975   Richard M. Richards
Organized from Louisiana Shreveport (31), Oklahoma Tulsa (88)
117 AUSTRALIA PERTH   1 Jul 1975   Bruce James Opie
Organized from Australia Adelaide (82)
118 CALIFORNIA FRESNO   1 Jul 1975   Robert B Harbertson
Organized from California Oakland (85)
119 CHILE CONCEPCION   1 Jul 1975   Lester D. Haymore
Organized from Chile Santiago (67)
See also 151
120 COLOMBIA CALI   1 Jul 1975   Jay E. Jensen
Organized from Colombia Bogota (79a)
121 FRANCE TOULOUSE   1 Jul 1975   George W. Broschinsky
Organized from France Paris (26)
Discontinued 1 Jul 1982, transferred to France Paris (26), Switzerland Geneva (59)
122 INDONESIA JAKARTA   1 Jul 1975   Hendrik Gout
Organized from Singapore (89)
Discontinued 1 Jan 1981, transferred to Singapore (89)
Reopened 1 Jul 1985 (182a)
Discontinued 1 Jul 1989
123 ITALY PADOVA   1 Jul 1975   John Anthony Grinceri
Organized from Italy Rome (7)
Discontinued 1 Jul 1982, transferred to Italy Milan (98)
Reopened 1 Jul 1990, see 244
124 KOREA PUSAN   1 Jul 1975   Han In Sang
Organized from Korea Seoul (71)
See also 191
125 MEXICO GUADALAJARA   1 Jul 1975   Isauro Gutierrez
Organized from Mexico Mexico City (20a), Mexico Torreon (81),
Mexico Hermosillo (56)
See also 201

126 MEXICO VILLAHERMOSA   1 Jul 1975   Abraham Lozano
    Organized from Mexico Veracruz (75)
    *1 Jul 1978 MEXICO MERIDA
    See also 193, 209
127 NEVADA LAS VEGAS   1 Jul 1975   Ronald M. Patterson
    Organized from Arizona Tempe (87), California Sacramento (37)
128 NEW MEXICO ALBUQUERQUE   1 Jul 1975   Stanley D. Roberts
    Organized from Arizona Holbrook (38)
    See also 231
129 PENNSYLVANIA PITTSBURGH   1 Jul 1975   Kenneth W. Godfrey
    Organized from Pennsylvania Harrisburg (91a)
    See also 188
130 SOUTH CAROLINA COLUMBIA   1 Jul 1975   Ronald L. Knighton
    Organized from Georgia Atlanta (8b)
    See also 239
131 TENNESSEE NASHVILLE   1 Jul 1975   Emerson Taylor Cannon
    Organized from Kentucky Louisville (29)
132 UTAH SALT LAKE CITY   1 Jul 1975   Ernest Eberhard Jr.
    Organized from Idaho Pocatello (111), Colorado Denver (17),
      Arizona Tempe (87), Arizona Holbrook (38)
    *1 Jul 1980 UTAH SALT LAKE CITY NORTH
    *1 Jan 1989 UTAH OGDEN
    See also 187, 222
133 YUGOSLAVIA ZAGREB   1 Jul 1975   Gustav Salik
    Discontinued 1 Jul 1976
134 IRAN TEHRAN   4 Jul 1975   Dean Burton Farnsworth
    Discontinued 1 Jan 1979
135 BELGIUM ANTWERP   16 Jul 1975   Larry Hyde Brim
    Organized from Belgium Brussels (76), Netherlands Amsterdam (8a)
    Discontinued 1 Jul 1982, transferred to Netherlands Amsterdam (8a)
    Reopened 1 Jul 1990, see 232
136 CANADA WINNIPEG   15 Feb 1976   Howard L. Lund
    Organized from Canada Calgary (36a), South Dakota Rapid City (78)
137 SPAIN BARCELONA   8 May 1976   Smith B. Griffin
    Organized from Spain Madrid (92)
    See also 199
137a EL SALVADOR SAN SALVADOR   1 Jul 1976   Eddy L. Barillas
    Organized from Guatemala Guatemala City (76a)
    Discontinued 1 Apr 1981, transferred to Guatemala Guatemala City (76a)
    Reopened 1 Oct 1984 (181a)
138 ENGLAND MANCHESTER   1 Jul 1976   O. Louis Alder
    Organized from England Leeds (52)
139 FLORIDA TAMPA   1 Jul 1976   A. Sterling Workman
    Organized from Florida Ft. Lauderdale (55)
    See also 178a, 197
140 IOWA DES MOINES   1 Jul 1976   Erwin E. Wirkus
    Organized from Missouri Independence (11a), Illinois Chicago (9c)
141 SPAIN SEVILLE   3 Jul 1976   Hugo A. Catron
    Organized from Spain Madrid (92)
    13 Jan 1993 SPAIN MALAGA
    See also 220
142 TEXAS HOUSTON   3 Jul 1976   George L. Merrill
    Organized from Texas San Antonio (77b)
    See also 254
143 NEW ZEALAND CHRISTCHURCH   5 Jul 1976   Ivan G. Radman
    Organized from New Zealand Wellington (47)
    *15 Jan 1991 NEW ZEALAND WELLINGTON
144 JAPAN OKAYAMA   9 Jul 1976   William H. Nako
    Organized from Japan Fukuoka (91), Japan Kobe (83)
145 SWEDEN GOTEBORG   26 Jul 1976   Paul Kent Oscarson
    Organized from Sweden Stockholm (22a)
    Discontinued 1 Jul 1982, transferred to Sweden Stockholm (22a)

146 TAIWAN KAOHSIUNG 3 Aug 1976 P. Boyd Hales
   Organized from Taiwan Taipei (94)
   *28 Sep 1983 TAIWAN TAICHUNG
   See also 173
147 SCOTLAND GLASGOW 1 Nov 1976 Roy W. Oscarson
   Organized from Scotland Edinburgh (61)
   Discontinued 1 Jul 1981, transferred to Scotland Edinburgh (61)
148 CHILE SANTIAGO NORTH 1 Jan 1977 Berkley A. Spencer
   Organized from Chile Santiago (67)
   See also 168, 214
149 PERU LIMA NORTH 1 Jan 1977 Jose A. Sousa
   Organized from Peru Lima (50)
   See also 165, 184a, 210, 300
150 BOLIVIA SANTA CRUZ 1 Jul 1977 DeVere R. McAllister
   Organized from Bolivia La Paz (75a)
   *1 Feb 1982 BOLIVIA COCHABAMBA
151 CHILE OSORNO 1 Jul 1977 Lester D. Haymore
   Organized from Chile Concepcion (119)
152 GUATEMALA QUETZALTENANGO 1 Jul 1977 John F. O'Donnal
   Organized from Guatemala Guatemala City (76a)
153 MISSOURI ST. LOUIS 1 Jul 1977 Norman W. Olsen
   Organized from Missouri Independence (11a)
   See also 176a
154 OHIO CLEVELAND 1 Jul 1977 Donald S. Brewer
   Organized from Ohio Columbus (77a)
   See also 179a
155 PARAGUAY ASUNCION 1 Jul 1977 Mearl K. Bair
   Organized from Uruguay Montevideo (40)
156 PENNSYLVANIA PHILADELPHIA 1 Jul 1977 Lewis K. Payne
   Organized from Pennsylvania Harrisburg (91a)
157 PHILIPPINES DAVAO 1 Jul 1977 Layton B. Jones
   Organized from Philippines Cebu City (110)
   See also 211
158 ITALY CATANIA 10 Jul 1977 Leopoldo Larcher
   Organized from Italy Rome (7)
158a CALIFORNIA SAN JOSE 1 Jul 1978 Lysle R. Cahoon
   Organized from California Oakland (85)
159 CALIFORNIA VENTURA 1 Jul 1978 Hyrum S. Smith
   Organized from California Los Angeles (14c)
   See also 182, 297
160 ECUADOR GUAYAQUIL 1 Jul 1978 William J. Mitchell
   Organized from Ecuador Quito (93)
   *1 Jul 1991 ECUADOR GUAYAQUIL SOUTH
   See also 261
161 ENGLAND LONDON EAST 1 Jul 1978 Carl D. Jones
   Organized from England London (1)
   Discontinued 1 Jul 1983, transferred to England London (1), England
   London South (79)
162 JAPAN TOKYO SOUTH 1 Jul 1978 Delbert H. Groberg
   Organized from Japan Tokyo (82a)
163 MEXICO MEXICO CITY NORTH 1 Jul 1978 John B. Dickson
   Organized from Mexico Mexico City (20a)
   See also 193, 218, 222a
164 MICHIGAN DEARBORN 1 Jul 1978 William R. Horton
   Organized from Michigan Lansing (104)
   * 1 Dec 1989 MICHIGAN DETROIT
165 PERU AREQUIPA 1 Jul 1978 Norval C. Jesperson
   Organized from Peru Lima North (149), Peru Lima South (50)
166 WASHINGTON SPOKANE 1 Jul 1978 Norwood C. McKoy
   Organized from Washington Seattle (78a)
167 WISCONSIN MILWAUKEE 1 Jul 1978 L. Flake Rogers
   Organized from Minnesota Minneapolis (26a), Illinois Chicago (9c)
166a ALABAMA BIRMINGHAM 1 Jan 1979 William J. Attwooll
   Organized from Georgia Atlanta (8b), Florida Tallahassee (96)

167a BRAZIL RECIFE 1 Jul 1979 Harry Eduardo Klein
   Organized from Brazil Rio de Janeiro (80)
   See also 200, 234
168 CHILE VINA DEL MAR 1 Jul 1979 Gerald J. Day
   Organized from Chile Santiago North (148)
   See also 214
169 CONNECTICUT HARTFORD 1 Jul 1979 Gerald L. Ericksen
   Organized from Massachusetts Boston (35)
   See also 195, 299
170 KOREA SEOUL WEST 1 Jul 1979 D. Brent Clement
   Organized from Korea Seoul (71)
171 MISSISSIPPI JACKSON 1 Jul 1979 Frank W. Hirschi
   Organized from Louisiana Baton Rouge (31)
172 PHILIPPINES QUEZON CITY 1 Jul 1979 Robert E. Sackley
   Organized from Philippines Manila (76b)
   *1 Jan 1981 PHILIPPINES BAGUIO
   *11 Feb 1991 PHILIPPINES LA UNION
   *22 Aug 1991 PHILIPPINES BAGUIO
   See also 192, 219
173 TAIWAN T'AICHUNG 1 Jul 1979 Frederick W. Crook
   Organized from Taiwan Kaohsiung (146)
   Discontinued Jul 1982, transferred to Taiwan Kaohsiung (146), Taiwan Taipei (94)
174 VENEZUELA MARACAIBO 1 Jul 1979 Alejandro Portal
   Organized from Venezuela Caracas (95)
175 PUERTO RICO SAN JUAN 7 Jul 1979 Richard L. Millett
   Organized from Florida Ft. Lauderdale (55)
   See also 178a, 188a
176 SINGAPORE (See 89) 1 Jan 1980 J. Talmage Jones
177 HONDURAS TEGUCIGALPA 1 Feb 1980 Samuel Flores
   Organized from Costa Rica San Jose (43b)
   See also 242
178 MICRONESIA GUAM 1 Apr 1980 Ferron C. Losee
   Organized from Hawaii Honolulu (7a), Fiji Suva (99)
179 AFRICA WEST 1 Jul 1980 Bryan Espenschied
   Organized from International (103)
   *1 Jul 1985 NIGERIA LAGOS
   See also 183a, 221, 276
180 ARGENTINA BAHIA BLANCA 1 Jul 1980 Allen B. Oliver
   Organized from Argentina Buenos Aires South (112)
   See also 230
181 BRAZIL CURITIBA 1 Jul 1980 Dixon D. Cowley
   Organized from Brazil Sao Paulo South (102), Brazil Porto Alegre (48)
182 CALIFORNIA SAN BERNARDINO 1 Jul 1980 Howard C. Sharp
   Organized from California Anaheim (73a), California Arcadia (86),
      California Ventura (159)
   See also 235, 297
183 ENGLAND COVENTRY 1 Jul 1980 Quinn G. McKay
   Organized from England Birmingham (62)
   *22 Aug 1991 ENGLAND BIRMINGHAM
184 ILLINOIS CHICAGO SOUTH 1 Jul 1980 Charles E. Petersen
   Organized from Illinois Chicago (9c)
   Discontinued 1 Jul 1983, transferred to Illinois Chicago (9c)
185 JAPAN OSAKA 1 Jul 1980 Shigeki Ushio
   Organized from Japan Kobe (83)
186 NORTH CAROLINA RALEIGH 1 Jul 1980 Joel N. Gillespie
   Organized from North Carolina Greensboro (105)
187 UTAH SALT LAKE CITY SOUTH 1 Jul 1980 Jonathan W. Snow
   Organized from Utah Salt Lake City (132)
   *1 Jan 1989 UTAH SALT LAKE CITY
   See also 222
188 WEST VIRGINIA CHARLESTON 1 Jul 1980 O. Rex Warner
   Organized from Ohio Columbus (77a), Virginia Roanoke (42),
      Pennsylvania Pittsburgh (129)

188a DOMINICAN REPUBLIC SANTO DOMINGO   1 Jan 1981   John A. Davis
Organized from Puerto Rico San Juan (175)
*1 Jul 1991 DOMINICAN REPUBLIC SANTO DOMINGO WEST
See also 178a, 196, 260
178a WEST INDIES   20 Jun 1983   Kenneth L. Zabriskie
Organized from Florida Tampa (139), Dominican Republic Santo
Domingo (188a), Puerto Rico San Juan (175)
See also 180a, 186a, 266
176a ILLINOIS PEORIA   1 Jul 1983   Brent Reed Rigtrup
Organized from Missouri St. Louis (153)
177a SOUTH AFRICA CAPE TOWN   1 Jul 1984   G. Philip Margetts
Organized from South Africa Johannesburg (23)
178b FLORIDA FT. LAUDERDALE (See 55)   1 Jul 1984   Claud Darwin Mangum
179a OHIO AKRON   1 Jul 1984   Stanley M. Smoot
Organized from Ohio Columbus (77a)
Discontinued 1 Jul 1989, transferred to Ohio Cleveland (154)
179b ARIZONA PHOENIX   1 Jul 1984   Francis M. Bay
Organized from Arizona Holbrook (38), Arizona Tempe (87)
See also 231
180a HAITI PORT-AU-PRINCE   1 Aug 1984   James S. Arrigona
Organized from West Indies (178a)
181a EL SALVADOR SAN SALVADOR (See 137a)   1 Oct 1984   Manuel Antonio Diaz
*1 Jul 1990 EL SALVADOR SAN SALVADOR WEST
See also 237
182a INDONESIA JAKARTA (See 122)   1 Jul 1985   Effian Kadarusman
183a GHANA ACCRA   1 Jul 1985   Miles H. Cunningham
Organized from Africa West (179)
184a PERU TRUJILLO   1 Jul 1985   Roberto Vidal
Organized from Peru Lima North (149)
185a BRAZIL BRASILIA   1 Jul 1985   Demar Staniscia
Organized from Brazil Rio de Janeiro (80), Brazil Recife (167)
See also 213, 233
186a JAMAICA KINGSTON   1 Jul 1985   Richard L. Brough
Organized from West Indies (178a)
187a CALIFORNIA SANTA ROSA   1 Jul 1985   Robert C. Witt
Organized from California Sacramento (37), California Oakland (85)
188b WASHINGTON D.C. NORTH   1 Jul 1986   Dennis E. Simmons
Organized from Washington D.C. (54)
See also 298
189 TEXAS LUBBOCK   1 Jul 1986   Lyle L. Wasden
Organized from Texas Dallas (60)
*20 Jan 1988 TEXAS FT. WORTH
190 BRAZIL CAMPINAS   1 Jul 1986   Sheldon R. Murphy
Organized from Brazil Sao Paulo North (101)
See also 213
191 KOREA TAE JON   1 Jul 1986   Moo-Kwang Hong
Organized from Korea Pusan (124)
192 PHILIPPINES QUEZON CITY   1 Jul 1986   Joel E. Leetham
Organized from Philippines Baguio (172)
See also 219, 256, 268
193 MEXICO MEXICO CITY EAST   1 Jan 1987   Enrique Moreno
Organized from Mexico Mexico City North (163), Mexico Mexico City South (20a),
Mexico Monterrey (45a), Mexico Merida (126), Mexico Veracruz (75)
See also 217
194 PHILIPPINES CEBU EAST   1 Jul 1987   C. Elliott Richards
Organized from Philippines Cebu (110), Philippines Manila (76b)
*1 Jul 1988 PHILIPPINES CEBU
See also 251
195 NEW HAMPSHIRE MANCHESTER   1 Jul 1987   Lynn E. Thomsen
Organized from Massachusetts Boston (35), Connecticut Hartford (169)
196 DOMINICAN REPUBLIC SANTIAGO   1 Jul 1987   Michael D. Stirling
Organized from Dominican Republic Santo Domingo (188a)

197 FLORIDA JACKSONVILLE   1 Jul 1987   Douglas W. DeHaan
    Organized from Florida Tampa (139), Florida Tallahassee (96)
198 ZAIRE KINSHASA   1 Jul 1987   R. Bay Hutchings
199 SPAIN BILBAO   1 Jul 1987   Garth J. Wakefield
    Organized from Spain Madrid (92), Spain Barcelona (137)
200 BRAZIL FORTALEZA   1 Jul 1987   Helvecio Martins
    Organized from Brazil Recife (167a)
    See also 233
201 MEXICO MAZATLAN   1 Jul 1987   Samuel Lara M.
    Organized from Mexico Guadalajara (125)
202 NEW JERSEY MORRISTOWN   1 Jul 1987   Dan J. Workman
    Organized from New York New York (15b)
203 PORTUGAL PORTO   1 Jul 1987   Dan Copeland
    Organized from Portugal Lisbon (115)
    See also 220
204 ZIMBABWE HARARE   1 Jul 1987   Joseph Hamstead
    Organized from South Africa Johannesburg (23)
205 AUSTRIA VIENNA EAST   1 Jul 1987   Dennis B. Neuenschwander
    Organized from Austria Vienna (53), International (103)
    *3 Feb 1992 UKRAINE KIEV
    See also 236, 241, 243, 252, 259, 274
205a GUATEMALA GUATEMALA CITY NORTH   1 Jan 1988   Gordon W. Romney
    Organized from Guatemala Guatemala City South (76a)
206 ARGENTINA SALTA   8 Jan 1988   Francisco Jose Vinas
    Organized from Argentina Cordoba (73)
207 BOLIVIA LA PAZ (See 75a)   8 Jan 1988   Steven R. Wright
208 MEXICO CHIHUAHUA   8 Jan 1988   Victor M. Cerda
    Organized from Mexico Torreon (81)
209 MEXICO TUXTLA-GUTIERREZ   8 Jan 1988   Alberto D. Gamboa
    Organized from Mexico Merida (126)
    See also 246
210 PERU LIMA EAST   8 Jan 1988   Douglas K. Earl
    Organized from Peru Lima North (149)
    See also 300
211 PHILIPPINES CAGAYAN DE ORO   8 Jan 1988   Rufino A. Villanueva Jr.
    Organized from Philippines Davao (157)
212 LIBERIA MONROVIA   1 Mar 1988   J. Duffy Palmer
    Discontinued 12 Feb 1991, transferred to Ghana Accra (183a)
213 BRAZIL BELO HORIZONTE   1 Jul 1988   Nivio Varella Alcover
    Organized from Brazil Brasilia (185a), Brazil Campinas (190)
    See also 295a
214 CHILE ANTOFAGASTA   1 Jul 1988   Carlos Ramon Espinola
    Organized from Chile Santiago North (148), Chile Santiago South (67),
       Chile Vina del Mar (168)
215 COLOMBIA BARRANQUILLA   1 Jul 1988   Frank Berrett
    Organized from Colombia Bogota (79a)
216 MASCARENE ISLANDS   1 Jul 1988   Gerard Giraud-Carrier
    Organized from South Africa Johannesburg (23)
    *22 Apr 1991 SOUTH AFRICA DURBAN
217 MEXICO PUEBLA   1 Jul 1988   George G. Sloan
    Organized from Mexico Mexico City East (193)
218 MEXICO TAMPICO   1 Jul 1988   Hector Ceballos
    Organized from Mexico Mexico City North (163), Mexico Monterrey (45a)
    *16 June 1992 MEXICO MONTERREY EAST
219 PHILIPPINES QUEZON CITY WEST   1 Jul 1988   Robert J. Kennerley
    Organized from Philippines Baguio (172), Philippines Quezon City (192)
    *1 Jul 1991 PHILIPPINES SAN FERNANDO
220 SPAIN LAS PALMAS   1 Jul 1988   M. K. Hamblin
    Organized from Spain Seville (141), Portugal Porto (203)
221 NIGERIA ABA   1 Jul 1988   Arthur W. Elrey Jr.
    Organized from Nigeria Lagos (179)
    See also 277

222 UTAH PROVO   1 Jan 1989   George E. Magnusson
     Organized from Utah Salt Lake City South (187)
221a FRANCE BORDEAUX   1 Jul 1989   Neil L. Andersen
     Organized from France Paris (6), Switzerland Geneva (59)
     See also 262
222a MEXICO QUERETARO   1 Jul 1989   Scott T. Lyman
     Organized from Mexico Mexico City North (163)
     *24 Mar 1992 MEXICO LEON
223 PHILIPPINES NAGA   1 Jul 1989   Augusto A. Lim
     Organized from Philippines Cebu (110)
224 TEXAS CORPUS CHRISTI   1 Jul 1989   S. Gibbons Frost
     Organized from Texas San Antonio (77b)
225 GERMAN DEMOCRATIC REPUBLIC DRESDEN 1 Jul 1989   Wolfgang Paul
     Reopened, see 84
     *1990 GERMANY DRESDEN
     See also 263
226 PANAMA PANAMA CITY   1 Jul 1989   Pedro E. Abularach
     Organized from Costa Rica San Jose (43b)
227 NICARAGUA MANAGUA   15 Oct 1989   Luis A. Alvarez O.
     Organized from Guatemala Guatemala City South (76a)
228 ARGENTINA MENDOZA   1 Jul 1990   Charles W. Eastwood
     Organized from Argentina Cordoba (73)
229 ARGENTINA RESISTENCIA   1 Jul 1990   Wilfredo R. Lopez G.
     Organized from Argentina Rosario (100)
230 ARGENTINA TRELEW   1 Jul 1990   Antonio Cappi
     Organized from Argentina Bahia Blanca (180)
     *25 May 1993 ARGENTINA NEUQUEN
231 ARIZONA TUCSON   1 Jul 1990   James E. Mangum
     Organized from Arizona Tempe (87), Arizona Phoenix (179b), New
       Mexico Albuquerque (128)
232 BELGIUM ANTWERP   1 Jul 1990   R. Bruce Barrett
     Reopened; see 135; organized from Netherlands Amsterdam (8a)
     Discontinued 1 Jul 1994; transferred to Netherlands Amsterdam (8a)
233 BRAZIL MANAUS   1 Jul 1990   Claudio R. Mendes C.
     Organized from Brazil Brasilia (185a), Brazil Fortaleza (200)
     See also 294a
234 BRAZIL SALVADOR   1 Jul 1990   Jairo Massagardi
     Organized from Brazil Recife (167a)
     See also 296
235 CALIFORNIA RIVERSIDE   1 Jul 1990   Jerry M. Hess
     Organized from California San Bernardino (182)
236 CZECHOSLOVAKIA PRAGUE   1 Jul 1990   Richard W. Winder
     Reopened, see 30; organized from Austria Vienna East (205)
237 EL SALVADOR SAN SALVADOR EAST   1 Jul 1990   Ramon E. Turcios D.
     Organized from El Salvador San Salvador (181a)
238 FINLAND HELSINKI EAST   1 Jul 1990   Gary L. Browning
     Organized from Finland Helsinki (41)
     *3 Feb 1992 RUSSIA MOSCOW
     See also 272, 273, 293
239 GEORGIA MACON   1 Jul 1990   John H. Cox
     Organized from South Carolina Columbia (130), Georgia Atlanta (8)
240 GERMANY DUESSELDORF   1 Jul 1990   Edgar Wolferts
     Reopened, see 63; organized from Germany Frankfurt (35a), Germany Munich (49)
241 GREECE ATHENS   1 Jul 1990   R. Douglas Phillips
     Organized from Austria Vienna East (205)
242 HONDURAS SAN PEDRO SULA   1 Jul 1990   Lehi Gracia
     Organized from Honduras Tegucigalpa (177)
243 HUNGARY BUDAPEST   1 Jul 1990   James L. Wilde
     Organized from Austria Vienna East (205)
244 ITALY PADOVA   1 Jul 1990   Vicenzo Conforte
     Reopened, see 123; organized from Italy Milan (98), Italy Rome (7)
245 JAPAN OKINAWA   1 Jul 1990   Evan Allan Larsen
     Organized from Japan Kobe (83)

| 246 | MEXICO OAXACA | 1 Jul 1990 | Miguel Hidalgo N. |

246 MEXICO OAXACA   1 Jul 1990   Miguel Hidalgo N.
Organized from Mexico Tuxtla-Gutierrez (209)
247 MEXICO TIJUANA   1 Jul 1990   Arturo de Hoyos
Organized from Mexico Hermosillo (56)
248 OKLAHOMA OKLAHOMA CITY   1 Jul 1990   Duane Beazer
Organized from Oklahoma Tulsa (88)
249 OREGON EUGENE   1 Jul 1990   Lloyd M. Rasmussen
Organized from Oregon Portland (18)
250 PHILIPPINES SAN PABLO   1 Jul 1990   Dean O. Peck
Organized from Philippines Manila (76b)
251 PHILIPPINES TACLOBAN   1 Jul 1990   Leonardo S. Mina
Organized from Philippines Cebu (194)
252 POLAND WARSAW   1 Jul 1990   Walter Whipple
Organized from Austria Vienna East (205)
253 PORTUGAL LISBON NORTH   1 Jul 1990   Vitor Martins
Organized from Portugal Lisbon (115)
254 TEXAS HOUSTON EAST   1 Jul 1990   Allen S. Farnsworth
Organized from Texas Houston (142)
255 WASHINGTON TACOMA   1 Jul 1990   Sidney R. Henderson
Organized from Washington Seattle (78)
256 PHILIPPINES ILAGAN   1 Sep 1990   Reynaldo Ibanez Vergara
Organized from Philippines Quezon City (192)
256a BRAZIL PORTO ALEGRE NORTH   1 Jul 1991   Larry Memmott
Organized from Brazil Porto Alegre (48)
257 BRAZIL SAO PAULO EAST   1 Jul 1991   Willis C. Fails
Organized from Brazil Sao Paulo North (101) , Brazil Sao Paulo South (102)
258 BRAZIL SAO PAULO INTERLAGOS   1 Jul 1991   Frederick G. Williams
Organized from Brazil Sao Paulo South (102)
259 BULGARIA SOFIA   1 Jul 1991   Kiril P. Kiriakov
Organized from Austria Vienna East (205)
260 DOMINICAN REPUBLIC SANTO DOMINGO EAST 1 Jul 1991   Mark Allen Jarman
Organized from Dominican Republic Santo Domingo (188a)
261 ECUADOR GUAYAQUIL NORTH   1 Jul 1991   Daniel L. Johnson
Organized from Ecuador Guayaquil (160)
262 FRANCE MARSEILLE   1 Jul 1991   Richard W. Thatcher
Organized from Switzerland Geneva (59), France Bordeaux (221a)
263 GERMANY BERLIN   1 Jul 1991   Manfred H. Schutze
Organized from Germany Dresden (225)
264 IDAHO POCATELLO   1 Jul 1991   Wayne W. Probst
Organized from Idaho Boise (111)
265 KENYA NAIROBI   1 Jul 1991   Larry King Brown
266 TRINIDAD TOBAGO   1 Jul 1991   J. Richard Toolson
Organized from West Indies (178a)
Discontinued 1 Jul 1994, transferred to West Indies (178a)
267 VENEZUELA CARACAS WEST   1 Jul 1991   Charles M. Hunter
Organized from Venezuela Caracas (95)
25 Mar 1994 VENEZUELA VALENCIA
See also 303

268 PHILIPPINES CABANATUAN   1 Jan 1992   Martin D. Openshaw
Organized from Philippines Quezon City (192),Philippines Manila (76b)
269 ARGENTINA BUENOS AIRES WEST   27 Jan 1992   Lloyd H. Richmond
Organized from Buenos Aires North (32) Buenos Aires South (112)
270 COLOMBIA BOGOTA SOUTH   27 Jan 1992   Jerry P. Cahill
Organized from Colombia Bogota (79a)
271 CAMAROON YAOUNDE   1 Jul 1992   Robert L. Mercer
*18 May 1993 IVORY COAST ABIDJAN
272 RUSSIA ST. PETERSBURG   3 Feb 1992   Thomas S. Rogers
Organized from Finland Helsinki East (238)
273 PAPUA NEW GUINEA PORT MORESBY   13 Feb 1992   Joseph Jones Grigg
Organized from Australia Brisbane Mission (106)
274 NIGERIA ILORIN   1 Jul 1992   John A. Ehanire
Organized from Nigeria Lagos (179)

275	NIGERIA JOS	1 Jul 1992	Ato Kwamina Dadson

Organized from Nigeria Aba (221)

| 276 | MEXICO MONTERREY SOUTH | 3 Nov 1992 | Garry R. Flake |

Organized from Mexico Monterrey East (218)

| 277 | INDIA BANGALORE | 1 Jan 1993 | Gurcharan Singh Gill |

Organized from Singapore (89)

| 278 | AUSTRALIA SYDNEY NORTH | 1 Jan 1993 | Glenn L. Pace |

Organized from Australia Sydney (10)

| 279 | BRAZIL RIBEIRO PRETO | 1 Feb 1993 | Cesar A. Seiquer Milder |

Organized from Brazil Campinas

| 280 | BRAZIL RIO DE JANEIRO NORTH | 1 Feb 1993 | Moises Barreiro Damasceno |

Organized from Brazil Rio de Janeiro (80)

| 281 | BRAZIL FLORIANOPOLIS | 1 Jul 1993 | Jose Benjamin Puerta |

Organized from Brazil Curitiba (181)

| 282 | BRAZIL RECIFE SOUTH | 1 Jul 1993 | Jorge Moreira |

Organized from Brazil Recife (167a)

| 283 | CALIFORNIA CARLSBAD | 1 Jul 1993 | Merlyn K. Jolley |

Organized from California San Diego (113)

| 284 | CALIFORNIA ROSEVILLE | 1 Jul 1993 | John Hoybjerg |

Organized from California Sacramento (37)

| 285 | CANADA TORONTO EAST | 1 Jul 1993 | Harold Roger Boyer |

Organized from Canada Toronto (23a)

| 286 | COLORADO DENVER NORTH | 1 Jul 1993 | Lynn M. Paulson |

Organized from Colorado Denver (17)

| 287 | GUATEMALA CITY GUATEMALA CENTRAL | 1 Jul 1993 | Denis Roy Morrill |

Organized from Guatemala City North (205a), Guatemala City South (294),
Guatemala Quetzaltenango (152)

| 288 | LATVIA RIGA MISSION | 1 Jul 1993 | Robert W. Blair |

Organized from Russia St. Petersburg (272)

| 289 | NEBRASKA OMAHA | 1 Jul 1993 | Reed B. Maw |

Organized from Missouri Independence (14b)

| 290 | NEW YORK NEW YORK NORTH | 1 Jul 1993 | Parley L. Howell |

Organized from New York New York (2)

| 291 | PERU CHICLAYO | 1 Jul 1993 | Rene Loli |

Organized from Peru Trujillo (184a) and Peru Lima North (149)

| 292 | ROMANIA BUCHAREST | 1 Jul 1993 | John Rolph Morrey |

Organized from Hungary Budapest (243)

| 293 | RUSSIA SAMARA | 1 Jul 1993 | Arlo R. Nelson |

Organized from Russia Moscow (238)

| 294 | TENNESSEE KNOXVILLE | 1 Jul 1993 | Richard Karl Sager |

Organized from Tennessee Nashville (131)

| 295 | UKRAINE DONETSK | 1 Jul 1993 | Leo Merrill |

Organized from Ukraine Kiev (205)

| 294a | BRAZIL BELEM | 1 Jul 1994 | Pedro J. D. Penha |

Organized from Brazil Manaus (233)

| 295a | BRAZIL BELO HORIZONTE SOUTH | 1 Jul 1994 | Thomas P. Smith |

Organized from Brazil Belo Horizonte (213)

| 296 | BRAZIL SALVADOR SOUTH | 1 Jul 1994 | Marcos A.C. Prieto |

Organized from Brazil Salvador (234)

| 297 | CALIFORNIA SAN FERNANDO | 1 Jul 1994 | Steven E. Snow |

Organized from California Arcadia (86), California
San Bernardino (182), California Ventura (159)

| 298 | MARYLAND BALTIMORE | 1 Jul 1994 | Bruce M. Ballard |

Organized from Washington D.C. North (188b), Washington D.C. South (54)

| 299 | NEW YORK UTICA | 1 Jul 1994 | Robert Noel Hatch |

Organized from Connecticut Hartford (169), Massachusetts Boston (35)

| 300 | PERU LIMA CENTRAL | 1 Jul 1994 | Carlos A. Cuba Q. |

Organized from Peru Lima North (149), Peru Lima East (210),
Peru Lima South (50)

301	RUSSIA NOVOSIBIRSK	1 Jul 1994	Jerald C. Sherwood
302	RUSSIA ROSTOV NA DONU	1 Jul 1994	Vladimir Siwachok
303	VENEZUELA BARCELONA	1 Jul 1994	Ned B. Roueche

Organized from Venezuela Caracas East (95), Venezuela Caracas West (267)

FIRST STAKE IN EACH STATE OF THE UNITED STATES

STATE	NAME OF STAKE	DATE ORGANIZED	CURRENT NAME
ALABAMA	Alabama (452)	3 Mar 1968	Huntsville Alabama
ALASKA	Alaska (331)	13 Aug 1961	Anchorage Alaska
ARIZONA	Little Colorado (21)	27 Jan 1878	†18 Dec 1887
	*Maricopa (24)	10 Dec 1882	Mesa Arizona Maricopa
ARKANSAS	Arkansas (484)	1 Jun 1969	Little Rock Arkansas
CALIFORNIA	San Bernardino (4a)	6 Jul 1851	†By 1857
	*Hollywood (98)	22 May 1927	Los Angeles California
COLORADO	San Luis (26)	10 Jun 1883	Manassa Colorado
CONNECTICUT	Hartford (421)	18 Sep 1966	Hartford Connecticut
DELAWARE	Wilmington Delaware (673)	8 Dec 1975	Same
DIST. OF COLUMBIA	Washington (131)	30 Jun 1940	Washington D.C.
FLORIDA	Florida (163)	19 Jan 1947	Jacksonville Florida West
GEORGIA	Atlanta (241)	5 May 1957	Tucker Georgia
HAWAII	Oahu (113)	30 Jun 1935	Laie Hawaii
IDAHO	Bear Lake (8a)	20 Jun 1869	Paris Idaho
ILLINOIS	Nauvoo (2a)	5 Oct 1839	†By 1846
	*Chicago (118)	29 Nov 1936	Wilmette Illinois
INDIANA	Indianapolis (283)	17 May 1959	Indianapolis Indiana
IOWA	Iowa (3a)	5 Oct 1839	†6 Jan 1842
	*Cedar Rapids (419)	29 May 1966	Cedar Rapids Iowa
KANSAS	Wichita (355)	24 Jun 1962	Wichita Kansas
KENTUCKY	Louisville (540)	17 Jan 1971	Louisville Kentucky
LOUISIANA	New Orleans (221)	19 Jun 1955	New Orleans Louisiana
MAINE	Maine (461)	23 Jun 1968	Augusta Maine
MARYLAND	Chesapeake (526)	13 Sep 1970	Silver Spring Maryland
MASSACHUSETTS	Boston (354)	20 May 1962	Boston Massachusetts
MICHIGAN	Detroit (197)	9 Nov 1952	Bloomfield Hills Michigan
MINNESOTA	Minnesota (317)	29 Nov 1960	Minneapolis Minnesota
MISSISSIPPI	Jackson (404)	2 May 1965	Jackson Mississippi
MISSOURI	Clay-Caldwell (2)	3 Jul 1834	†By 1839
	*Kansas City (234)	21 Oct 1956	Kansas City Missouri
MONTANA	Butte (208)	28 Jun 1953	Butte Montana
NEBRASKA	Winter Quarters (318)	11 Dec 1960	Omaha Nebraska
NEVADA	Carson Valley (7a)	4 Oct 1856	†By 1858
	*Moapa (64)	9 Jun 1912	Logandale Nevada
NEW HAMPSHIRE	Merrimack (507)	22 Mar 1970	Nashua New Hampshire
NEW JERSEY	New Jersey (292)	28 Feb 1960	Morristown New Jersey
NEW MEXICO	Young (63)	21 May 1912	Farmington New Mexico
NEW YORK	New York (110)	9 Dec 1934	New York New York
NORTH CAROLINA	North Carolina (332)	27 Aug 1961	Kinston North Carolina
NORTH DAKOTA	Fargo North Dakota (852)	7 Aug 1977	Same
OHIO	Kirtland (1)	17 Feb 1834	†24 May 1841
	*Cincinnati (270)	23 Nov 1958	Cincinnati Ohio
OKLAHOMA	Tulsa (298)	1 May 1960	Tulsa Oklahoma
OREGON	Union (49)	9 Jun 1901	La Grande Oregon
PENNSYLVANIA	Philadelphia (304)	16 Oct 1960	Philadelphia Pennsylvania
RHODE ISLAND	Providence Rhode Island (818)	20 Mar 1977	Same
SOUTH CAROLINA	South Carolina (169)	19 Oct 1947	Columbia South Carolina
SOUTH DAKOTA	Rapid City (592)	10 Dec 1972	Rapid City South Dakota
TENNESSEE	Memphis (403)	18 Apr 1965	Memphis Tennessee
TEXAS	El Paso (194)	21 Sep 1952	El Paso Texas
UTAH	Salt Lake (1a)	3 Oct 1847	Same
VERMONT	Montpelier Vermont (753)	11 Apr 1976	Same
VIRGINIA	Virginia (245)	30 Jun 1957	Richmond Virginia
WASHINGTON	Seattle (124)	31 Jul 1938	Seattle Washington
WEST VIRGINIA	West Virginia (522)	23 Aug 1970	Charleston West Virginia
WISCONSIN	Milwaukee (367)	3 Feb 1963	Milwaukee Wisconsin
WYOMING	Star Valley (33)	14 Aug 1892	Afton Wyoming

( ) Chronological number of stake; † Discontinued; * First permanent stake

FIRST STAKE ORGANIZED
IN COUNTRIES OF THE WORLD

COUNTRY	NAME OF STAKE	DATE ORGANIZED	CURRENT NAME
AMERICAN SAMOA	Pago Pago (488)	15 Jun 1969	Pago Pago Samoa
ARGENTINA	Buenos Aires (423)	20 Nov 1966	Buenos Aires Argentina East
AUSTRALIA	Sydney (293)	27 Mar 1960	Sydney Australia Greenwich
AUSTRIA	Vienna Austria (1126)	20 Apr 1980	Same
BELGIUM	Brussels Belgium (813)	20 Feb 1977	Same
BOLIVIA	Santa Cruz Bolivia (993)	14 Jan 1979	Santa Cruz Bolivia Canoto
BRAZIL	Sao Paulo (417)	1 May 1966	Sao Paulo Brazil
CANADA	Alberta (35)	9 Jun 1895	Cardston Alberta
CHILE	Santiago (590)	19 Nov 1972	Santi. Chile Quinta Normal
COLOMBIA	Bogota Colombia (805)	23 Jan 1977	Same
COSTA RICA	San Jose Costa Rica (803)	20 Jan 1977	Same
DENMARK	Copenhagen Denmark (648)	16 Jun 1974	Same
DOMINICAN REPUBLIC	Santo Domingo Dominican Republic (1593)	23 Mar 1986	Same
ECUADOR	Guayaquil Ecuador (939)	11 Jun 1978	Guayaquil Ecuador West
EL SALVADOR	San Salvador (618)	3 Jun 1973	San Salvador El Salvador
ENGLAND	Manchester (294)	27 Mar 1960	Manchester England
FIJI	Suva Fiji (1428)	12 Jun 1983	Same
FINLAND	Helsinki Finland (865)	16 Oct 1977	Same
FRANCE	Paris France (731)	16 Nov 1975	Same
GERMANY	Berlin (334)	10 Sep 1961	Berlin Germany
GHANA	Accra Ghana (1791)	21 Apr 1991	same
GUATEMALA	Guatemala City (436)	21 May 1967	Guatemala City Guatemala
HONDURAS	San Pedro Sula Honduras (820)	10 Apr 1977	Same
HONG KONG	Hong Kong (756)	25 Apr 1976	Hong Kong Island
ITALY	Milan Italy (1274)	7 Jun 1981	Same
JAPAN	Tokyo (505)	15 Mar 1970	Tokyo Japan
KOREA	Seoul (604)	8 Mar 1973	Seoul Korea
MEXICO	Juarez (37)	9 Dec 1895	Colonia Juarez Mexico
NETHERLANDS	Holland (326)	12 Mar 1961	The Hague Netherlands
NEW ZEALAND	Auckland (264)	18 May 1958	Auckland N.Z. Mt. Roskill
NICARAGUA	Managua Nicaragua (1246)	22 Mar 1981	†15 Oct 1989
NIGERIA	Aba Nigeria (1695)	15 May 1988	Same
NORTHERN IRELAND	Belfast Ireland (647)	9 Jun 1974	Belfast Northern Ireland
NORWAY	Oslo Norway (835)	22 May 1977	Same
PANAMA	Panama City Panama (1081)	11 Nov 1979	Same
PARAGUAY	Asuncion Paraguay (1002)	25 Feb 1979	Same
PERU	Lima (503)	22 Feb 1970	Lima Peru Limatambo
PHILIPPINES	Manila (613)	20 May 1973	Manila Philippines
PORTUGAL	Lisbon Portugal (1276)	10 Jun 1981	Same
PUERTO RICO	San Juan Puerto Rico (1215)	14 Dec 1980	Same
SCOTLAND	Glasgow (356)	26 Aug 1962	Glasgow Scotland
SOUTH AFRICA	Transvaal (506)	22 Mar 1970	Johannesburg South Africa
SPAIN	Madrid Spain (1327)	14 Mar 1982	Same
SWEDEN	Stockholm Sweden (691)	20 Apr 1975	Same
SWITZERLAND	Swiss (341)	28 Oct 1961	Zurich Switzerland
TAHITI	Tahiti (573)	14 May 1972	Papeete Tahiti
TAIWAN	Taipei Taiwan (755)	22 Apr 1976	Taipei Taiwan West
TONGA	Nuku'alofa (463)	5 Sep 1968	Nuku'alofa Tonga
UNITED STATES	Kirtland (1)	17 Feb 1834	†24 May 1841
	*Salt Lake (1a)	3 Oct 1847	Same
URUGUAY	Montevideo (444)	12 Nov 1967	Montevideo Uruguay West
VENEZUELA	Caracas Venezuela (827)	15 May 1977	Same
WALES	Merthyr Tydfil Wales (676)	12 Jan 1975	Same
WESTERN SAMOA	Apia (353)	18 Mar 1962	Apia Samoa

( ) — Existing number at time of stake's creation   † Disorganized   * First permanent stake

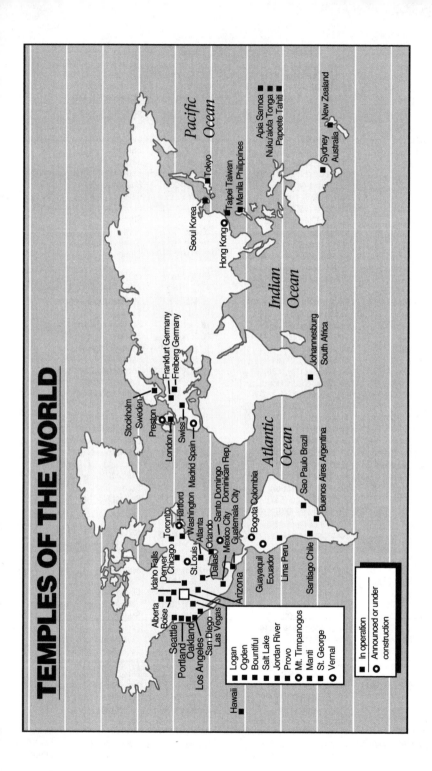

TEMPLES OF THE WORLD

Pacific Ocean

Apia Samoa
Nuku'alofa Tonga
Papeete Tahiti

Sydney
New Zealand
Australia

Tokyo
Taipei Taiwan
Manila Philippines
Seoul Korea
Hong Kong

Indian Ocean

Johannesburg South Africa

Stockholm Sweden
Frankfurt Germany
Freiberg Germany
Preston
London
Swiss
Madrid Spain

Atlantic Ocean

Toronto
Hartford
Washington
Atlanta
Orlando
Santo Domingo Dominican Rep.
St. Louis
Mexico City
Guatemala City
Dallas
Arizona
Bogota Colombia
Guayaquil Ecuador
Lima Peru
Sao Paulo Brazil
Santiago Chile
Buenos Aires Argentina

Alberta
Idaho Falls
Boise
Denver
Chicago
Seattle
Portland
Oakland
Los Angeles
San Diego
Las Vegas

Hawaii

Logan
Ogden
Bountiful
Salt Lake
Jordan River
Provo
Mt. Timpanogos
Manti
St. George
Vernal

■ In operation
○ Announced or under construction

TEMPLES OF THE CHURCH
Listed by order of completion

	TEMPLE	LOCATION	DEDICATED	BY WHOM
	Kirtland*	Kirtland, Ohio	27 Mar 1836	Joseph Smith
	Nauvoo**	Nauvoo, Ill.	30 Apr 1846	Joseph Young (private)
			1 May 1846	Orson Hyde (public)
1	St. George	St. George, Utah	6 Apr 1877	Daniel H. Wells
	Rededicated after remodeling		11 Nov 1975	Spencer W. Kimball
2	Logan	Logan, Utah	17 May 1884	John Taylor
	Rededicated after remodeling		13 Mar 1979	Spencer W. Kimball
3	Manti	Manti, Utah	17 May 1888	Wilford Woodruff (private)
			21 May 1888	(His prayer read by Lorenzo Snow; public)
	Rededicated after remodeling		14 Jun 1985	Gordon B. Hinckley
4	Salt Lake	Salt Lake City, Utah	6 Apr 1893	Wilford Woodruff
5	Hawaii	Laie, Oahu, Hawaii	27 Nov 1919	Heber J. Grant
	Rededicated after remodeling		13 Jun 1978	Spencer W. Kimball
6	Alberta	Cardston, Alberta, Canada	26 Aug 1923	Heber J. Grant
	Portions rededicated after remodeling		2 Jul 1962	Hugh B. Brown
	Rededication after remodeling		22 Jun 1991	Gordon B. Hinckley
7	Arizona	Mesa, Ariz.	23 Oct 1927	Heber J. Grant
	Rededicated after remodeling		15 Apr 1975	Spencer W. Kimball
8	Idaho Falls	Idaho Falls, Idaho	23 Sep 1945	George Albert Smith
9	Swiss	Zollikofen, near Bern, Switzerland	11 Sep 1955	David O. McKay
	Rededicated after remodeling		23 Oct 1992	Gordon B. Hinckley
10	Los Angeles	Los Angeles, Calif.	11 Mar 1956	David O. McKay
11	New Zealand	Hamilton, New Zealand	20 Apr 1958	David O. McKay
12	London	Newchapel, Surrey, England	7 Sep 1958	David O. McKay
	Rededicated after remodeling		18 Oct 1992	Gordon B. Hinckley
13	Oakland	Oakland, Calif.	17 Nov 1964	David O. McKay
14	Ogden	Ogden, Utah	18 Jan 1972	Joseph Fielding Smith
15	Provo	Provo, Utah	9 Feb 1972	Joseph Fielding Smith (His prayer read by Harold B. Lee)
16	Washington	Kensington, Md.	19 Nov 1974	Spencer W. Kimball
17	Sao Paulo	Sao Paulo, Brazil	30 Oct 1978	Spencer W. Kimball
18	Tokyo	Tokyo, Japan	27 Oct 1980	Spencer W. Kimball
19	Seattle	Bellevue, Wash.	17 Nov 1980	Spencer W. Kimball
20	Jordan River	South Jordan, Utah	16 Nov 1981	Marion G. Romney
21	Atlanta Georgia	Sandy Springs, Ga.	1 Jun 1983	Gordon B. Hinckley
22	Apia Samoa	Apia, Western Samoa	5 Aug 1983	Gordon B. Hinckley
23	Nuku'alofa Tonga	Nuku'alofa, Tonga	9 Aug 1983	Gordon B. Hinckley
24	Santiago Chile	Santiago, Chile	15 Sep 1983	Gordon B. Hinckley
25	Papeete Tahiti	Pirae, Tahiti	27 Oct 1983	Gordon B. Hinckley
26	Mexico City	Mexico City, Mexico	2 Dec 1983	Gordon B. Hinckley
27	Boise Idaho	Boise, Idaho	25 May 1984	Gordon B. Hinckley
28	Sydney Australia	Carlingford, Australia	20 Sep 1984	Gordon B. Hinckley
29	Manila Philippines	Quezon City, Philippines	25 Sep 1984	Gordon B. Hinckley
30	Dallas Texas	Dallas, Texas	19 Oct 1984	Gordon B. Hinckley
31	Taipei Taiwan	Taipei, Taiwan	17 Nov 1984	Gordon B. Hinckley
32	Guatemala City	Guatemala City, Guatemala	14 Dec 1984	Gordon B. Hinckley
33	Freiberg Germany	Freiberg, Germany	29 Jun 1985	Gordon B. Hinckley
34	Stockholm Sweden	Vasterhaninge, Sweden	2 Jul 1985	Gordon B. Hinckley
35	Chicago Illinois	Glenview, Ill.	9 Aug 1985	Gordon B. Hinckley
36	Johannesburg South Africa	Johannesburg, South Africa	24 Aug 1985	Gordon B. Hinckley
37	Seoul Korea	Seoul, Korea	14 Dec 1985	Gordon B. Hinckley
38	Lima Peru	Lima, Peru	10 Jan 1986	Gordon B. Hinckley
39	Buenos Aires Argentina	Buenos Aires, Argentina	17 Jan 1986	Thomas S. Monson
40	Denver Colorado	Littleton, Colo.	24 Oct 1986	Ezra Taft Benson
41	Frankfurt Germany	Friedrichsdorf, Germany	28 Aug 1987	Ezra Taft Benson

42	Portland Oregon	Lake Oswego, Ore.	19 Aug, 1989	Gordon B. Hinckley
43	Las Vegas Nevada	Las Vegas, Nev.	16 Dec 1989	Gordon B. Hinckley
44	Toronto Ontario	Brampton, Ontario, Canada	25 Aug 1990	Gordon B. Hinckley
45	San Diego California	San Diego, Calif.	25 Apr 1993	Gordon B. Hinckley
46	Orlando Florida	Windermere, Fla.	9 Oct. 1994	Howard W. Hunter
47	Bountiful Utah	Bountiful, Utah	8 Jan. 1995	Howard W. Hunter

Temples announced or under construction:

Bogota Colombia	Madrid Spain	Recife Brazil
Boston Massachusetts	Monterrey Mexico	St. Louis Missouri
Cochabamba Bolivia	Mount Timpanogos Utah	Santo Domingo Dominican Republic
Guayaquil Ecuador	Nashville Tennessee	Vernal Utah
Hong Kong	Preston England	White Plains New York

* No longer in use by the Church   **No longer stands

TEMPLES OF THE CHURCH
(Listed alphabetically)

ALBERTA TEMPLE

Location: Cardston, about 185 miles south of Calgary in southern Alberta; 348 3rd St. West, Cardston, Alberta. Telephone: (403) 653-3552.

Site: In 1887, eight-acre site laid out and given to the Church by Charles Ora Card, leader of the first group of Mormons to Canada. It was then called the Tabernacle Block.

Exterior finish: White granite quarried near Kootenai Lakes in Nelson, British Columbia. Each stone was hand-hewn at the quarry or temple site.

Temple design: Octagonal shape, similar to Maltese cross, with no spire.

Architects: Hyrum C. Pope and Harold W. Burton.

Number of rooms: Approximately 40 in original structure; 4 ordinance, 5 sealing.

Total floor area: Originally 29,471 square feet, now 65,000 square feet.

Dimensions of building: 100 feet by 100 feet; height, 85 feet.

District: Alberta, Saskatchewan, Manitoba, southeastern British Columbia, northern Montana; 23 stakes.

Groundbreaking, site dedication: July 27, 1913, President Joseph F. Smith dedicated site in the presence of about 1,500 people. Ground broken Nov. 9, 1913, by Daniel Kent Greene of Glenwoodville, Alberta.

Dedication: Aug. 26-29, 1923, by President Heber J. Grant; 11 sessions. Rededicated after remodeling July 2, 1962, by President Hugh B. Brown of the First Presidency; closed for remodeling May, 1988-June 1991; toured by 101,000 people during an open house June 6-15, 1991. Rededicated by President Gordon B. Hinckley June 22-24, 1991; 12 sessions.

Rededicatory prayer excerpt: *"Bless the Latter-day Saints of Canada that they may be good citizens of the nation, men and women of integrity worthy of the respect of the people of this nation, and contributing of their talents and strength to its well-being."*

APIA SAMOA TEMPLE

Location: Near the school and mission home in Pesega; P.O. Box 1621, Apia, Western Samoa, Telephone: (011-685) 21964.

Site: 1.7 acres.

Exterior finish: "R-wall" exterior finish and insulation system on concrete block; split cedar shake shingles on roof.

Temple design: Modern.

Architect: Emil B. Fetzer, Church architect.

Construction advisers: Dale Cook and Richard Rowley.

Contractor: Utah Construction and Development.

Number of rooms: Three sealing rooms, two ordinance rooms; 31 total rooms.

Total floor area: 13,020 square feet.

Dimensions of building: on top spire, 75 feet high.

District: Western Samoa and American Samoa; 13 stakes.

Groundbreaking, site dedication: Feb. 19, 1981, by President Spencer W. Kimball, assisted by the head of state, Malieotoa Tanumafil II. Nearly 4,000 people attended.

Dedication: Aug. 5-6, 1983, by President Gordon B. Hinckley; 7 sessions.

Dedicatory prayer excerpt: *"We pray for thy blessings upon those who govern these islands and the people who dwell here that principles of peace and equity may prevail and that the citizens of these islands may have cause to rejoice in the liberty that is theirs."*

ARIZONA TEMPLE

Location: In Mesa, 16 miles east of Phoenix, in central Arizona's Valley of the Sun. Mesa's Main Street passes the site on the north; 101 S. LeSueur, Mesa, AZ. 85204. Telephone: (602) 833-1211.

Site: 20-acre site selected Feb. 1, 1920, by President Heber J. Grant, Apostles David O. McKay and George F. Richards. Purchased in 1921.

Exterior finish: Concrete reinforced with 130 tons of steel. Exterior is faced with a terra cotta glaze that is egg-shell in color and tile-like in finish.

Temple design: Modification of the classic style, suggestive of pre-Columbian temples and even the Temple of Herod.

Architects: Don C. Young and Ramm Hansen.

Construction supervisor: Arthur Price.

Construction chairman: Executive building committee: J.W. LeSueur, chairman; O.S. Stapley, John Cummard, Andrew Kimball.

Number of rooms: 4 ordinance, 9 sealing; 193 total rooms.

Total floor area: 72,712 square feet.

Dimensions of building: 128 feet by 184 feet, and 50 feet in height above the foundation.

District: Most of Arizona and New Mexico; El Paso Texas region; 72 stakes.

Site dedication, groundbreaking: Site dedicated Nov. 28, 1921; ground broken April 25, 1922, by President Heber J. Grant.

Dedication: Oct. 23, 1927, by President Heber J. Grant; services broadcast by radio. Rededicated after extensive remodeling April 15-16, 1975, by President Spencer W. Kimball; 8 sessions.

Dedicatory prayer excerpt: *"Accept the dedication of this house, and these grounds, which we have dedicated unto thee by virtue of the Priesthood of the Living God which we hold."*

ATLANTA GEORGIA TEMPLE

Location: In Sandy Springs, on the northeastern outskirts of Atlanta; 6450 Barfield Rd.; Atlanta, GA 30328. Telephone: (404) 393-3698.

Site: 5.9 acres.

Exterior finish: Pre-cast stone walls, built-up roof.

Temple design: Modern.

Architect: Emil B. Fetzer, Church architect.

Construction adviser: Michael Enfield and Ronald Prince.

Contractor: Cube Construction Company.

Number of rooms: Five sealing rooms, four ordinance rooms; 54 total rooms.

Total floor area: 27,360 square feet.

Dimensions: 187 feet 8 inches by 166 feet 3 inches; statue of Angel Moroni on top spire.

District: Most of southeastern U.S. except Florida, and extreme south of Georgia; 54 stakes (10 of these stakes will be included in the St. Louis Missouri Temple District when that temple is completed).

Groundbreaking, site dedication: March 7, 1981, by President Spencer W. Kimball, attended by 10,000 people.

Dedication: June 1-4, 1983, by President Gordon B. Hinckley; 11 sessions.

Dedicatory prayer excerpt: *"May the very presence of this temple in the midst of thy people become a reminder of the sacred and eternal covenants made with thee. May they strive more diligently to banish from their lives those elements which are inconsistent with the covenants they have made with thee.*

"May all who enter these holy precincts feel of thy spirit and be bathed in this marvelous, sanctifying influence. May they come . . . in a spirit of love and dedication."

BOGOTA COLOMBIA TEMPLE

Announced: April 7, 1984, by President Gordon B. Hinckley. Site announced May 28, 1988, by the First Presidency.

Site: 3.75 acres; Located in the Niza section of Bogota, about 10 miles from downtown.

District: Colombia, Venezuela and Panama; 25 stakes.

Groundbreaking, site dedication: June 26, 1993, by Elder William R. Bradford of the First Quorum of the Seventy and president of the South America North Area.

BOISE IDAHO TEMPLE

Location: Just off Interstate 84 on South Cole Road in the west end of Boise; 1211 S. Cole Road, Boise, ID 83709-1781. Telephone: (208) 322-4422.

Site: 4.8 acres.

Exterior finish: Faced with light colored marble and has a slate roof. It is surrounded by three detached towers on each end; 8-foot statue of the Angel Moroni tops highest spire.

Temple design: Modern adaptation of six-spire design.

Architects: Church architectural staff, with assistance from Ron Thurber & Associates of Boise.

Construction adviser: Jerry Sears.

Contractor: Comtrol Inc. of Midvale, Utah.

Number of rooms: Four ordinance rooms, three sealing rooms, 42 total rooms.

Total floor area: 32,269 square feet, following 1987 addition.

Dimensions of building: 236 feet by 78 feet; statue of Angel Moroni on top spire.

District: Southwestern Idaho, eastern Oregon; 33 stakes.

Groundbreaking, site dedication: Dec. 18,

1982, by Elder Mark E. Petersen of the Council of the Twelve.

Dedication: May 25-30, 1984, by President Gordon B. Hinckley; 24 sessions. Addition dedicated by Elder James E. Faust of the Council of the Twelve, May 29, 1987.

Dedicatory prayer excerpt: *"May thy faithful Saints of this and future generations look to this beautiful structure as a house to which they will be made welcome . . . for the making of eternal covenants with thee, for inspiration and sanctification, as they serve unselfishly. . . ."*

BOUNTIFUL UTAH TEMPLE

Location: In the Bountiful foothills on east bench, 600 S. Bountiful Blvd. (1650 East).

Site: 9 acres.

Exterior finish: Granite.

Temple design: Modern, with single spire.

Architect: Church architectural staff.

Contractor: Okland Construction Co.

Construction adviser: Michael Enfield.

Number of rooms: Four endowment rooms, eight sealing rooms.

Total floor area: 104,000 square feet.

Dimensions: 195 feet by 157 feet; statue of Angel Moroni on top spire; 176 feet high.

Temple district: Most of Davis County, Utah; 28 stakes.

Groundbreaking: May 2, 1992, by President Ezra Taft Benson, with 10,000 participating.

Dedication: Scheduled for Jan. 8-14, 1995, in 28 sessions.

BUENOS AIRES ARGENTINA TEMPLE

Location: On southwest outskirts of Buenos Aires; Autopista Richieri y Puente 13, 1778 Ciudad Evita, Buenos Aires, Argentina. Telephone: (011-54-1) 620-3980.

Site: 3 acres.

Exterior finish: Light gray native granite.

Temple design: Modern adaptation of earlier six-spire design.

Dimensions: 178 by 71 feet. Angel Moroni statue is atop tallest spire, 112 feet.

Architects: Church architectural staff; local architect Ramon Paez.

Construction adviser: Gary Holland.

Contractor: Benito Roggio and Sons.

Number of rooms: Four ordinance rooms, three sealing rooms.

Total floor area: 11,980 square feet.

District: Argentina, Uruguay; 48 stakes.

Groundbreaking, site dedication: April 20, 1983, by Elder Bruce R. McConkie of the Council of the Twelve.

Dedication: Jan. 17-19, 1986, by President

Thomas S. Monson; 11 sessions.

Dedicatory prayer excerpt: *"We remember that it was in this very city of Buenos Aires, on Christmas Day in the year 1925, just 60 years ago, that* Elder Melvin J. Ballard, an apostle of the Lord, dedicated all of South America for the preaching of the gospel. What a fulfillment to an inspired prayer is evident today."

CHICAGO ILLINOIS TEMPLE

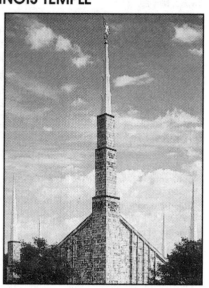

Location: 20 miles north of Chicago; 4151 West Lake Ave., Glenview, IL 60025. Telephone: (708) 299-6500.

Site: 13 acres.

Exterior finish: Gray buff marble, gray slate roof.

Temple design: Modern adaptation of earlier six-spire design.

Architects: Church architectural staff; local architect, Wight & Co.

Construction adviser: Virgil Roberts.

Contractor: Pora Construction Co., Des Plaines, Ill., with Utah Construction and Development Co.

Number of rooms: Five ordinance rooms, three sealing rooms.

Total floor area: Originally 17,850 square feet; 37,060 square feet following addition.

Dimensions of building: 236 feet by 78 feet; seven-foot-tall Angel Moroni statue is atop tallest spire, 112 feet high.

District: Michigan, Minnesota, Wisconsin; parts of Illinois, Iowa, Indiana, North Dakota, South Dakota; and Ohio; 53 stakes (15 of these stakes will be in the St. Louis Missouri Temple District when that temple is completed).

Groundbreaking, site dedication: Aug. 13, 1983, by President Gordon B. Hinckley.

Dedication: Aug. 9-13, 1985, by President Gordon B. Hinckley; 19 sessions.

Dedicatory prayer excerpt: *"We are mindful* that thy Prophet Joseph, and his brother Hyrum, were martyred in Carthage, Ill., at a time of terrible conflict and persecution. May there now be peace and goodwill in the land. Bless the officers of this state and nation that they shall stand firmly for those principles of freedom and equity which were written into the Constitution of the United States under thine inspiration."

DALLAS TEXAS TEMPLE

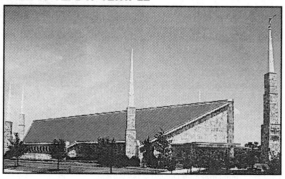

Location: 12 miles north of the downtown area, at 6363 Willow Lane, Dallas, TX 75230. Telephone: (214) 991-1273.

Site: 6 acres.

Exterior finish: Light-colored marble tile walls, dark gray slate roof.

Temple design: Modern adaptation of earlier six-spire design.

Architects: Church architectural staff, with assistance from West & Humphries of Dallas.

Construction adviser: Virgil Roberts.

Contractor: Comtrol Inc. of Midvale, Utah.

Number of rooms: Five ordinance rooms, three sealing rooms, total rooms 43.

Total floor area: Originally 17,850 square feet; 42,383 square feet following addition.

Dimensions of building: 236 by 78 feet; tower, 95 feet; statue of Angel Moroni on top spire.

District: Texas (except El Paso region) and parts of Oklahoma, Arkansas, and Louisiana; 59 stakes (3 of these will be in the St. Louis Missouri Temple District when that temple is completed).

Groundbreaking, site dedication: Jan. 22, 1983, by President Gordon B. Hinckley.

Dedication: Oct. 19-24, 1984, by President Gordon B. Hinckley; 23 sessions.

Dedicatory prayer excerpt: *"May this beautiful temple, standing in this community, become a declaration to all who shall look upon it, of the faith of thy Saints in the revealed things of eternity, and may they be led to respect that which is sacred unto us, thy people."*

DENVER COLORADO TEMPLE

Location: In Littleton, a suburban community in Arapahoe County, about 20 miles south of Denver, at County Line Road and South University Boulevard; 2001 E. Phillips Circle, Littleton, CO 80122. Telephone: (303) 730-0220.

Site: 7.5 acres.

Exterior finish: Modern design, similar to Atlanta Georgia Temple; precast stone walls and built-up roof.

Dimensions: 187 by 160 feet; single 90-foot spire capped with statue of Angel Moroni.

Temple design: Modern.

Architects: Church architectural staff.

Supervising architect: Local architect, Bobby R. Thomas.

Construction adviser: Michael Enfield.

Contractor: Langley Constructors.

Number of rooms: Four ordinance rooms, six sealing rooms; total of 54 rooms.

Total floor area: 29,117 square feet.

District: Most of Colorado, eastern Wyoming, western North and South Dakota; part of Kansas, Nebraska, Oklahoma and New Mexico; 31 stakes (1 of these stakes will be included in the Vernal Utah Temple District when that temple is completed).

Groundbreaking, site dedication: May 19, 1984, by President Gordon B. Hinckley.

Dedication: Oct. 24-28, 1986, by President Ezra Taft Benson; 18 sessions.

Dedicatory prayer excerpt: *"Touch the hearts of thy people that they may look to this temple as a refuge from the evil and turmoil of the world. May they ever live worthy of the blessings here to be found. May they be prompted to seek the records of their forebears and to serve here in their behalf, under that plan which thou has revealed for the salvation and exaltation of thy children of all generations."*

FRANKFURT GERMANY TEMPLE

Location: In the center of Friedrichsdorf, a small town nine miles north of Frankfurt; Talstrasse # 10, D-61381 Friedrichsdorf/TS, Germany. Telephone: (011-49-61) 72-72066.

Site: 5.2 acres.

Exterior finish: White granite, copper roof.

Architects: Church architectural staff; local architect, Borchers-Metzner-Kramer; project architect, Hanno Luschin.

Construction adviser: Henry Haurand.

Contractor: Hochtief AG.

Number of rooms: Four ordinance rooms, five sealing rooms; total rooms, 63.

Total floor area: 24,757 square feet.

Dimensions of building: 93 feet by 232 feet; statue of Angel Moroni on top spire, 82 feet high.

District: Belgium, the Netherlands, Luxembourg, northern France, much of Germany, and a small part of Austria; 19 stakes.

Groundbreaking, site dedication: July 1, 1985, by President Gordon B. Hinckley.

Dedication: Aug. 28-30, 1987, by President Ezra Taft Benson; 11 sessions.

Dedicatory prayer excerpt: *"The presence of this house, on the soil of this nation, is an answer to the prayers of thy people."*

FREIBERG GERMANY TEMPLE

Location: In Freiberg, about 120 miles south of Berlin; Hainchener strasse 64, 009599 Freiberg, Germany. Phone: (011-49-3) 731-23546.

Site: 1 acre.

Exterior finish: Exterior white German stucco over 24-inch thick brick walls, blue gray slate stone slab roof.

Temple design: Modern design with Geman influence; two high arches, reminicent of Gothic style, are parallel with front of building and bisected by two similar arches to form a single spire.

Architect: Emil B. Fetzer.

Government construction adviser: Dr. Dieter Hantzche, architect director of Bauakademie of Dresden.

Number of rooms: One ordinance room, two sealing rooms; 32 total rooms.

Total floor area: 7,840 square feet.

Dimensions of building: Square, 98 feet by 98 feet.

District: Eastern Germany and most of eastern Europe; 3 stakes.

Groundbreaking, site dedication: April 23, 1983, by Elder Thomas S. Monson.

Dedication: June 20-30, 1985, by President Gordon B. Hinckley, 7 sessions.

Dedicatory prayer excerpt: *"On this day of dedication our hearts turn to thee. We thank thee for this holy temple in this land and nation. We thank thee for all who have made possible its building — the officers of the government who have who have given encouragement and made available land and materials, the architects and the builders, and all who have made possible this glorious day of dedication."*

GUATEMALA CITY TEMPLE

Location: At the base of hills in southeastern Guatemala City; 24 avenida 2-20, Zona 15, Vista Hermosa 1, Guatemala City, Guatemala. Telephone: (011-502) 269-3425.

Site: About 1.4 acres.

Exterior finish: Natural white Guatemala marble.

Temple design: Modern adaptation of earlier six-spire design.

Architects: Church archectural staff, assisted by Jose Asturias, Guatemala City.

Construction adviser: David Judd.

Contractor: Isa Constructors Aires Y Cia Ltd.

Number of rooms: Four ordinance rooms, three sealing rooms, 32 total rooms.

Total floor area: 11,610 square feet.

Dimensions of building: 178 feet by 72 feet, six spires; statue of Angel Moroni tops 126-foot spire.

District: Guatemala, Nicaragua, Cost Rica, El Salvador, Honduras, Belize, southern Mexico; 54 stakes.

Groundbreaking, site dedication: Sept. 12, 1982, by Elder Richard G. Scott of the First Quorum of the Seventy.

Dedication: Dec. 14-16, 1984, by President Gordon B. Hinckley; 10 sessions.

Dedicatory prayer excerpt: *Bless our land, O Father, this nation of Guatemala where stands thy holy house. May those who govern do so in righteousness. . . .'' Bless them as they act to preserve the liberties. . . and enhance the prosperity of the people. May there be peace in the land.''*

GUAYAQUIL ECUADOR TEMPLE

Announced: March 31, 1982, by President Gordon B. Hinckley.

Status: Pending government approvals.

District: Ecuador, 16 stakes.

HARTFORD CONNECTICUT TEMPLE

On Sept. 30, 1995, President Gordon B. Hinckley announced that two temples would replace the one announced previously for Hartford, Conn. New temples will be built in White Plains, N.Y., and Boston, Mass. During the years of searching for a suitable temple site in the Hartford area, the Church grew appreciably in the areas to the north and south of Hartford.

HAWAII TEMPLE

Location: In Laie, on the northeast side of the island of Oahu, formerly a 6,000-acre plantation purchased by the Church in 1865, 32 miles from Honolulu; P.O. Box BB, 55-600 Naniloa Loop, Laie, HI 96762.

Site: 11.4 acres, a portion of original property purchased by Church.

Exterior finish: Built of concrete made of the crushed lava rock of the area, reinforced with steel. After hardening, it was dressed on the exterior by pneumatic stone cutting tools that produced a white cream finish.

Temple design: The first of three temples built with no tower; shaped like a Grecian cross and suggestive of the ancient temples found in South America.

Architects: Hyrum C. Pope and Harold W. Burton.

General superintendent: Samuel E. Woolley. Much of the work on this temple was done by the Polynesian Saints.

Number of rooms: Three ordinance rooms, six sealing rooms; total rooms after remodeling, 163.

Total floor area: 10,500 square feet originally; approximately 40,971 square feet after remodeling.

Dimensions of building: 140 feet by 282 feet, rising to a height of 50 feet above the upper terrace. Very similar "cubical contents" as ancient temple of Solomon.

District: Hawaii and some central Pacific islands, 13 stakes.

Groundbreaking, site dedication: June 1, 1915, site dedicated by President Joseph F. Smith.

Dedication: Thanksgiving Day, Nov. 27, 1919, by President Heber J. Grant.

Rededicated June 13-15, 1978, by President Spencer W. Kimball after extensive remodeling; nine sessions.

Dedicatory prayer excerpt: *"May all who come upon the grounds which surround this temple, in the years to come, whether members of the Church or not, feel the sweet and peaceful influence of this blessed hallowed spot."*

HONG KONG TEMPLE

Location: At the Hong Kong mission home in Kowloon Tong on the Kowloon Peninsula.

Announced: Oct. 3, 1992, by President Gordon B. Hinckley.

Site: 0.3 acres.

Exterior finish: Polished granite.

Temple design: Hong Kong colonial.

Architects: Liang Peddle Thorpe Architects.

Project architect: Jon Yu.

Number of rooms: Two endowment rooms, two sealing rooms.

Total floor area: 22,600 square feet.

Dimensions of building: 70 feet by 92 feet; statue of Angel Moroni is 135 feet above main floor.

District: Hong Kong and Macau; 5 stakes.

Groundbreaking, site dedication: Jan. 22, 1994, by Elder John K. Carmack of the First Quorum of the Seventy and Asia Area president.

Status: Under construction.

IDAHO FALLS TEMPLE

Location: In northwestern Idaho Falls on the banks of the Snake River; 1000 Memorial Drive, Idaho Falls, ID 83402. Telephone: (208) 522-7669.

Site: 7 acres.

Exterior finish: Built of reinforced concrete. A mixture of white quartz aggregate and white cement called cast stone covers the 16-inch thick exterior walls in slabs two inches thick.

Temple design: Modern-contemporary.

Architects: Church board of temple architects: Edward O. Anderson, Georgius Y. Cannon, Ramm Hansen, John Fetzer, Hyrum C. Pope, Lorenzo S. Young.

Construction adviser: Arthur Price.

Contractor: Birdwell Finlayson of Pocatello, Idaho.

Number of rooms: 1 ordinance room, 9 sealing rooms; total of 38 rooms in original plans; 84 following various additions.

Total floor area: 86,972 square feet.

Dimensions of building: 175 feet by 190 feet; tower 148 feet high. Two annexes added 7,700 square feet. A 12-foot statue of Angel Moroni was added to the tower Sept. 5, 1983.

District: Most of eastern Idaho, parts of Montana and Wyoming; 64 stakes.

Groundbreaking, site dedication: Dec. 19,

1939, ground broken by David Smith, North Idaho Falls Stake president. Site dedicated Oct. 19, 1940, by President David O. McKay of the First Presidency.

Dedication: Sept. 23-25, 1945, by President George Albert Smith.

Dedicatory prayer excerpt: *"We pray that thou wilt accept this temple as a freewill offering from thy children, that it will be sacred unto thee."*

JOHANNESBURG SOUTH AFRICA TEMPLE

Location: 2 miles north of city center; 7 Jubilee Rd., Parktown, Johannesburg, 2193, South Africa. Telephone: (011-27-11) 642-4952.

Site: One acre.

Exterior finish: Masonry exterior.

Temple design: Modern adaptation of earlier six-spire design.

Architects: Church architectural staff; local architect, Halford & Halford.

Construction adviser: Stanley G. Smith.

Contractor: Tiber Bonvac.

Number of rooms: Four ordinance rooms, three sealing rooms.

Total floor area: 13,025 square feet.

Dimensions of building: 178 feet by 71 feet; Angel Moroni statue is atop tallest spire at 112 feet.

District: Africa south of the Sahara; 10 stakes.

Groundbreaking, site dedication: Nov. 27, 1982, by Elder Marvin J. Ashton of the Council of the Twelve.

Dedication: Aug. 24-25, 1985, by President Gordon B. Hinckley; 4 sessions.

Dedicatory prayer excerpt: *"Almighty God, wilt thou overrule for the blessing and safety of thy faithful Saints. We pray for peace in this troubled land. Bless this nation which has befriended thy servants. May those who rule in the offices of government be in-spired to find a basis for reconciliation among those who now are in conflict one with another. May the presence of thy house on the soil of this land bring blessings to the entire nation."*

JORDAN RIVER TEMPLE

Location: About 15 miles south of Salt Lake City in South Jordan, with access from Redwood Road and 13th West; 10200 S. 1300 West, South Jordan, UT 84065. Telephone: (801) 254-2030.

Site: 15 acres, announced Feb. 3, 1978, by the First Presidency.

Exterior finish: Cast stone containing white marble chips. Tower appears same as the rest of the building, but in order to reduce weight it contains fiberglass in a product called cemlite.

Temple design: Modern.

Architect: Emil B. Fetzer, Church architect.

Resident project inspector: Jerry Sears.

Construction superintendent: Lawrence O. Dansie for Layton Construction Co.

Number of rooms: Six ordinance rooms, 17 sealing rooms.

Total floor area: 153,641 square feet.

Dimensions of building: Basement and main floor, 211 by 218 feet; two upper levels, 140 by 166 feet. Height to square is 58 feet, to top of tower, 199½ feet. Tower topped with a 20-foot figure of the Angel Moroni.

District: Southern Salt Lake County in Utah; 91 stakes.

Groundbreaking, site dedication: June 9, 1979, by President Spencer W. Kimball.

Dedication: Nov. 16-20, 1981, by President Marion G. Romney; 15 sessions.

Dedicatory prayer excerpt: *"May all who enter have clean hands and pure hearts, and may they participate with faith in the ordinances to be given herein."*

KIRTLAND TEMPLE*

*No longer in use by the Church.

Location: Kirtland, Ohio, 25 miles east of Cleveland, on a hill west of the Chagrin River.

Site: Selected March 1833; deed recorded Aug. 4, 1834.

Exterior finish: Sandstone covered with stuccoed plaster.

Temple design: Adaptation of Federal Georgian and New England Colonial.

Architect: Joseph Smith.

Building committee: Hyrum Smith, Reynolds Cahoon and Jared Carter.

Master builder: Artemis Millett.

Number of rooms: Originally 15.

Total floor area: Approximately 15,000 square feet.

Dimensions of building: 79 feet by 59 feet; walls 50 feet high; tower height above ground, 110 feet.

Start of work: Hauling of sandstone to site began June 5, 1833.

Cornerstones: July 23, 1833.

Dedication: March 27, 1836, by President Joseph Smith.

Dedicatory prayer excerpt: *"And we ask thee, Holy Father, that thy servants may go forth from this house, armed with thy power and that thy name may be upon them. . . ."*

LAS VEGAS NEVADA TEMPLE

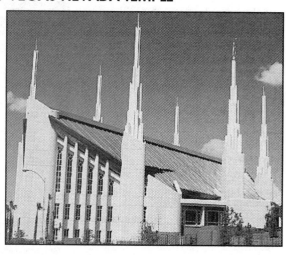

Location: On the east side of Las Vegas at edge of a residential area on the slope of Frenchman Mountain, 827 Temple View Drive, Las Vegas, NV 89110. Telephone: (702) 452-5011.

Site: 10.3 acres; announced April 7, 1984.

Exterior finish: White prescast stone walls and copper roof and detailing.

Temple design: Six spires

Architects: Tate & Snyder.

Construction adviser: Gary Holland

Contractor: Hogan & Tingey.

Number of rooms: 4 ordinance rooms, 6 sealing rooms.

Total floor area: 80,900 square feet.

Dimensions of building: 260 feet by 127 feet; statue of Angel Moroni on top spire, 119 feet.

District: Southern Nevada, parts of Arizona and California; 21 stakes.

Groundbreaking, site dedication: Nov. 30, 1985, by President Gordon B. Hinckley.

Dedication: Dec. 16-18, 1989, by President Gordon B. Hinckley; 11 sessions.

Dedicatory prayer excerpt: *"Within its walls are to be tasted the refreshing waters of living and eternal truth. For all who enter the portals of thy house may this be an oasis of peace and life and light, in contrast with the clamor and evil and darkness of the world."*

LIMA PERU TEMPLE

Location: Southwest part of Lima, in the Molina district; Avenida Javier Prado Este y Av. de Los Ingenieros, La Molina, Lima, Peru. Telephone: (011-51-14) 36-1284.

Site: 4.5 acres.

Exterior finish: Local granite, Oriental design.

Temple design: Modern adaptation of earlier six-spire design.

Dimensions of building: 178 by 71 feet. Angel Moroni statue is atop tallest spire at 112 feet.

Architects: Church architectural staff; local architect Jose Asturias.

Construction adviser: Sergio Gomez.

Number of rooms: Four ordinance rooms, three sealing rooms.

Total floor area: 10,052 square feet.

District: Peru and most of Bolivia, Colombia, Ecuador and Venezuela; 104 stakes until Guayaquil Ecuador and Bogota Colombia temples are completed.

Groundbreaking, site dedication: Sept. 11, 1982, by Elder Boyd K. Packer.

Dedication: Jan. 10-12, 1986, by President Gordon B. Hinckley; 11 sessions.

Dedicatory prayer excerpt: *"We are particularly mindful this day of the sons and daughters of Lehi. They have known so much of suffering and sorrow in their many generations. They have walked in darkness and in servitude. Now thou hast touched*

them by the light of the everlasting gospel. The shackles of darkness are falling from their eyes as they embrace the truths of thy great work."

LOGAN TEMPLE

Location: On eastern bench overlooking Cache Valley; 175 N. 300 East, Logan, UT 84321. Telephone: (801) 752-3611.

Site: 9 acres, selected by Brigham Young, May 18, 1877.

Exterior finish: Dark-colored, siliceous limestone, extremely hard and compact in texture, was used for the major portion of the temple. Buff-colored limestone, more easily carved, was used wherever intricate shaping was necessary.

Temple design: Castellated style.

Architect: Truman O. Angell.

Construction heads: Superintendent of construction, Charles O. Card; master mason, John Parry; plastering foreman, William Davis. Labor needs met by 25,000 people who worked on Logan Temple.

Number of rooms: 4 ordinance rooms, 11 sealing rooms; five stories, total rooms, 60.

Total floor area: Originally 59,130 square feet; 115,507 square feet after remodeling.

Dimensions of building: 171 feet by 95 feet; 86 feet high. The east tower is 170 feet high; west tower, 165 feet high; four octagonal towers, each 100 feet high.

District: Northern Utah, southeastern Idaho; 39 stakes.

Groundbreaking, site dedication: May 17, 1877; site dedicated by Elder Orson Pratt, ground broken by President John W. Young of the First

Presidency.

Dedication: May 17-19, 1884, by President John Taylor; 3 sessions.

On March 13-15, 1979, after extensive remodeling, the temple was rededicated by President Spencer W. Kimball; 9 sessions.

Dedicatory prayer excerpt: *"We ask that in this house a more full knowledge of thee and thy laws may be developed. . . . And, as all wisdom dwells with thee, and, as all light, truth and intelligence. . . we humbly seek unto thee for thy learning under thy guidance, direction and inspiration."*

LONDON TEMPLE

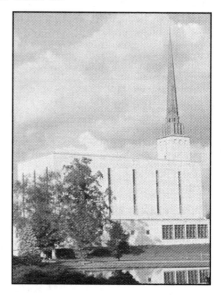

Location: 25 miles south of London, formerly Elizabethan farm; Newchapel, Nr. Lingfield, Surrey, England, RH7 6HW. Telephone: (011-44-342) 83-2759.

Site: In June 1952, President David O. McKay and Elder Stayner Richards, president of the British Mission, selected site at Newchapel. Purchased several months later in 1953; 32 acres.

Exterior finish: Reinforced concrete and structural steel skeleton, walls of brick masonry faced with cut Portland limestone, white in color. Spire sheathed in lead-coated copper.

Temple design: Modern-contemporary.

Architect: Edward O. Anderson, Church architect.

Supervising architects: T.T. Bennett and Son, London.

Contractor: Kirk and Kirk, Ltd., London.

Number of rooms: 4 ordinance rooms, 7 sealing rooms, total rooms, 64.

Total floor area: Originally 34,000 square feet; now 42,652 square feet.

Dimensions of building: 84 feet wide, 159 feet long, 56 feet to the square. The tower rises 156 feet 9½ inches from ground level, spire 33 feet above that.

District: England, Scotland, Wales, Northern Ireland, Ireland, and the Canary Islands; 41 stakes (20 of these will be in the Preston England Temple District when that temple is completed).

Groundbreaking, site dedication: Aug. 10, 1953, site dedicated by David O. McKay, who broke ground on Aug. 27, 1955.

Dedication: Sept. 7-9, 1958, by President David O. McKay; 6 sessions. Rededicated Oct. 18-20 1992, by President Gordon B. Hinckley; 10 sessions.

Dedicatory prayer excerpt: *"With humility and deep gratitude we acknowledge thy nearness, thy divine guidance and inspiration. Help us, we pray thee, to become even more susceptible in our spiritual response to thee."*

"Temples are built to thy holy name as a means of uniting thy people, living and dead, in bonds of faith, of peace and of love throughout eternity."

LOS ANGELES TEMPLE

Location: Atop a hill near Westwood Village, two miles west of Beverly Hills in Los Angeles, Calif.; 10777 Santa Monica Blvd., Los Angeles, CA 90025. Telephone: (310) 474-5569.

Site: On 13 of the original 24.23 acres purchased from the Harold Lloyd Motion Picture Company on March 23, 1937, by President Heber J. Grant.

Exterior finish: The exterior is covered with 146,000 square feet of Mo-Sai stone facing, a mixture of crushed quartz and white Portland cement quarried in Utah and Nevada. Wainscot around exterior is Rockville granite from Minnesota.

Temple design: Modern.

Architect: Edward O. Anderson, Church architect. (Millard F. Malin, sculptor of 15-foot statue of Angel Moroni on spire.)

Superintendent: Vern Loder.

Contractor: Soren N. Jacobsen.

Number of rooms: 4 ordinance rooms, 10 sealing rooms, total rooms, 90.

Total floor area: 190,614 square feet, or approximately 4½ acres.

Dimensions of building: 364 feet by 241 feet; overall height is 257 feet 1½ inches.

District: Part of Southern California; 76 stakes.

Groundbreaking, site dedication: Sept. 22, 1951, by President David O. McKay.

Dedication: March 11-14, 1956, by President David O. McKay; 8 sessions.

Dedicatory prayer excerpt: *"May all who come within these sacred walls feel a peaceful, hallowed influence. Cause, O Lord, that even people who pass the grounds, or view the temple from afar, may lift their eyes from the groveling things of sordid life and look up to thee and thy providence."*

MADRID SPAIN TEMPLE

Announced: Country announced at general conference on April 4, 1993, by President Gordon B. Hinckley; city announced at groundbreaking of Mt. Timpanogos Utah Temple on Oct. 9, 1994.

Status: Pending groundbreaking.

District: Spain, Portugal, Azores and Canary Islands; specific district not determined.

MANILA PHILIPPINES TEMPLE

Location: In Quezon City; 13 Temple Drive, Greenmeadows Subdivision, Quezon City, Metro Manila, Philippines 1110. Telephone: (011-63-2) 635-0954.

Site: About 3.5 acres.

Exterior finish: Ceramic tile.

Temple design: Modern adaptation of earlier six-spire design.

Architect: Church architectural staff, with assistance from Felipe M. Mendoza & Partners, Manila.

Construction adviser: Wayne Tuttle.

Contractor: A. C. K. Construction of Manila.

Number of rooms: 4 ordinance rooms, three sealing rooms, 34 total rooms.

Total floor area: 19,388 square feet.

Dimensions of building: 200 feet by 75 feet, six spires; tallest is 115 feet high, including statue of Angel Moroni.

District: Philippines, Micronesia, Indonesia, Singapore, Thailand, India, and part of Burma; 46 stakes.

Groundbreaking, site dedication: Aug. 25, 1982, by President Gordon B. Hinckley. Despite the threat of a typhoon, 2,000 members attended groundbreaking.

Dedication: Sept. 25-27, 1984, by President Gordon B. Hinckley; 9 sessions.

Dedicatory prayer excerpt: *"Lift the blight of poverty from which so many suffer. Particularly bless thy faithful Saints who live honestly with thee in the payment of their tithes and offerings. Bless*

them that neither they nor their generations after them will go hungry, nor naked, nor without shelter from the storms that beat about them.

"We thank thee for this beautiful edifice and for all who have worked to make it possible. May it stand as a pillar of truth and as an invitation to all who look upon it to learn of the purposes for which it has been created."

MANTI TEMPLE

Location: Hill above U.S. Highway 89 in Sanpete Valley in Manti, Utah, 120 miles south of Salt Lake City; Temple Hill, Manti, UT 84642. Telephone: (801) 835-2291.

Site: 27 acres. "Manti Stone Quarry" had been prophesied as site for a temple since area's settlement in 1849. President Brigham Young on June 25, 1875, announced the temple would be built there. It then became known as "Temple Hill."

Exterior finish: Fine-textured, cream-colored oolite limestone obtained from quarries in hill upon which it is built.

Temple design: The castellated style reflecting influence of Gothic Revival, French Renaissance Revival, French Second Empire and colonial architecture.

Architect: William H. Folsom.

Construction heads: William H. Folsom from Oct. 15, 1877, to Aug. 7, 1888, when Daniel H. Wells took his place as supervisor; master mason, Edward L. Parry.

Number of rooms: Four floors including basement, 1 ordinance room and 8 sealing rooms; 43 total rooms.

Total floor area: 86,809 square feet.

Dimensions of building: 171 feet by 95 feet; 86 feet high. The east tower is 179 feet high, west tower 169 feet high, building at ground level 60 feet above highway below.

District: Central and southeastern Utah and southwestern Colorado; 28 stakes.

Groundbreaking, site dedication: April 25, 1877, by President Brigham Young.

Dedication: May 17, 1888, private dedication held; dedicated by President Wilford Woodruff.

Three public dedicatory services held May 21-23, 1888; Elder Lorenzo Snow, then of the Council of the Twelve, read prayer.

Rededicated June 14-16, 1985, by President Gordon B. Hinckley; 9 sessions.

Dedicatory prayer excerpt: *"May this holy temple be to them as one of the gates of heaven, opening into the straight and narrow path that leads to endless lives and eternal dominion."*

MEXICO CITY TEMPLE

Location: Near Aragon public park and zoological gardens, bounded by Calle Ignacio Allende and Calle Emiliano Capata; Avenida 510 #90, Col. San Juan de Aragon, Mexico D.F. 07950. Telephone: (011-52-5) 551-4347.

Site: 7 acres.

Exterior finish: White cast stone, ornate with adaptations of ancient Mayan designs, especially on upper portion of the structure.

Temple design: Modern adaptation of ancient Mayan architecture.

Architect: Emil B. Fetzer, Church architect.

Resident project inspector: Ricardo Espiriti.

Construction superintendent: Jose Ortiz for Urbec Construction Co.

Number of rooms: Four ordinance rooms, 11 sealing rooms.

Total floor area: 117,133 square feet.

Dimensions of building: Basement and first floors, 178 by 214½ feet; two upper levels, 119½ by 157 feet. Height to square, 70 feet; to top of tower, 152 feet. Statue of Angel Moroni stands on top tower.

District: Most of Mexico; 121 stakes.

Groundbreaking, site dedication: Nov. 25, 1979, by Elder Boyd K. Packer of the Council of the Twelve, 10,000 people attended.

Dedication: Dec. 2-4, 1983, by President Gordon B. Hinckley; 9 sessions.

Dedicatory prayer excerpt: *"Bless thy Saints in this great land and those from other lands who will use this temple. Most have in their veins the blood of Father Lehi. Thou hast kept thine ancient promises."*

MOUNT TIMPANOGOS UTAH

Location: At 900 East and 700 North in American Fork, Utah.

Announced: A temple was announced for Utah County, Utah, Oct. 3, 1992, by President Gordon B. Hinckley and President Thomas S. Monson.

Site: 16.7 acres, part of a larger parcel of land that was once a welfare farm.

Groundbreaking, site dedication: Oct. 9, 1993, with President Gordon B. Hinckley presiding.

Exterior finish: Granite.

Temple design: Modern, with a single spire.

Architect: Church architectural staff.

Contractor: Okland Construction Company.

Number of rooms: Four ordinance rooms, eight sealing rooms.

Total floor area: more than 104,000 square feet.

Dimensions of building: 195 feet by 157 feet; 190-foot spire, including statue of Angel Moroni.

District: Northern Utah County and Wasatch County in Utah; 38 stakes.

Status: Under construction, completion expected by 1996.

NAUVOO TEMPLE**

****No longer stands; burned by arson fire in 1848; walls later destroyed by a tornado.

Location: In Nauvoo, Ill., on a high bluff on the east side of the Mississippi River. Temple block bounded by Woodruff, Mulholland, Knight and Wells streets.

Site: Selected in October 1840 by Joseph Smith on property known as the Wells addition, slightly less than 4 acres.

Exterior finish: Light gray limestone quarried to the north and south of the city.

Temple design: Incorporated several types of architecture, no single style dominating.

Architect: William Weeks.

Temple building committee: Alpheus Cutler, Elias Higbee and Reynolds Cahoon. After the death of Elias Higbee in 1843, Hyrum Smith replaced him until his own death.

Number of rooms: Approximately 60.

Total floor area: Approximately 50,000 square feet.

Dimensions of building: Approximately 128 feet by 88 feet; and 65 feet high, with the tower and spire reaching to 165 feet.

Cornerstones: April 6, 1841, President Joseph Smith presiding.

Dedication: Portions of the temple were dedicated and used as soon as completed. To avoid possible violence, a private dedication was held April 30, 1846, with Orson Hyde and Joseph Young officiating. The temple was dedicated publicly, May

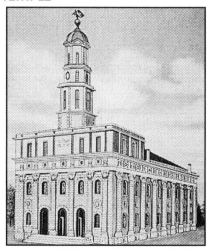

1-3, 1846, with the dedicatory prayer offered by Orson Hyde.

Dedicatory prayer excerpt: *"We thank thee that thou hast given us strength to accomplish the charges delivered by thee. Thou hast seen our labors and exertions to accomplish this purpose. By the authority of the Holy Priesthood now we offer this building as a sanctuary to thy worthy name. We ask thee to take the guardianship into thy hands and grant thy spirit shall dwell here and may all feel a sacred influence on their hearts that His Hand has helped this work."*

NEW ZEALAND TEMPLE

Location: At site of Church College of New Zealand in Temple View, outside of Hamilton, New Zealand. Hamilton is 75 miles south of Auckland; Private Bag 3003, Hamilton, New Zealand. Telephone: (011-64-7) 847-7169.

Site: Temple site and college grounds, 86 acres.

Exterior finish: Reinforced concrete block, manufactured at site, structural steel; painted white.

Temple design: Modern-contemporary. Plan and lines similar to Swiss and London Temples, but with different dimensions and exterior designs.

Architect: Edward O. Anderson, Church architect.

Construction chairman: Wendell B. Mendenhall.

Construction supervisor: E. Albert Rosenvall and George R. Biesinger.

Number of rooms: 1 ordinance room, 3 sealing rooms, 75 total rooms.

Total floor area: 34,000 square feet.

Dimensions of building: 159 feet by 84 feet; total height of tower, 215 feet above highway, 157 feet above ground line.

District: New Zealand and nearby South Pacific islands; 17 stakes.

Groundbreaking, site dedication: Dec. 21, 1955. First sod turned by Ariel Ballif, Wendell B. Mendenhall, and George R. Biesinger.

Dedication: April 20, 1958, by President David O. McKay.

Dedicatory prayer excerpt: *"We invoke thy blessing particularly upon the men and women who have so willingly and generously contributed their means, time and effort to the completion of this imposing and impressive structure. Especially we mention all those who have accepted calls as labor missionaries and literally consecrated their all upon the altar of service."*

NUKU'ALOFA TONGA TEMPLE

Location: At site of Church's Liahona College, several miles outside of Nuku'alofa; Loto Rd., Tongatapu, Nuku'alofa, Tonga. Telephone: (011-676) 29-255.

Site: 5 acres.

Exterior finish: "R-wall" exterior finish and insulation system on concrete block; split cedar shake shingles on roof.

Temple design: Modern.

Architect: Emil B. Fetzer, Church architect.

Construction adviser: Richard Westover and Richard Rowley.

Contractor: Utah Construction & Development.

Number of rooms: Three sealing rooms, two ordinance rooms; 31 total rooms.

Total floor area: 13,020 square feet.

Dimensions of building: 142.88 feet by 115.32 feet; statue of Angel Moroni on top spire, 75 feet high.

District: Tongan islands, Fiji; 12 stakes.

Groundbreaking, site dedication: Feb. 18, 1981, by President Spencer W. Kimball with Tonga's King Taufa'ahau Tupou IV. Nearly 7,000 people attended.

Dedication: Aug. 9-11, 1983, by President Gordon B. Hinckley; 7 sessions.

Dedicatory prayer excerpt: *"We ask that thou wilt accept this temple as the gift of thy people presented unto thee with love for the accomplishments of thy holy purposes with reference to thy children. It is thy house. It is the house of thy Son. May it always be held in reverence by thy people."*

OAKLAND TEMPLE

Location: On hill overlooking Oakland, Berkeley, San Francisco and the Bay, near intersection of Lincoln Avenue and Warren Freeway; 4700 Lincoln Ave., Oakland, CA 94602.Telephone: (510) 531-3200.

Site: Inspected and approved by President David O. McKay in 1942; 14½ acres purchased Jan. 28, 1943; additional land acquired later to make 18.3 acres;

Exterior finish: Reinforced concrete faced with Sierra white granite from Raymond, Calif.

Temple design: Modern, with an Oriental motif.

Architect: Harold W. Burton. Resident architect supervisor, Arthur Price.

Construction chairman: W. B. Mendenhall.

Construction supervisor: Robert C. Loder. Contractors: Leon M. Wheatley Co., Palo Alto, Calif., and Jacobsen Construction Co., Salt Lake City.

Number of rooms: 4 ordinance rooms, 7 sealing rooms, 265 total rooms.

Total floor area: 82,417 square feet.

Dimensions of building: Temple proper, 210 feet by 190 feet with a central tower rising 170 feet; other towers 96 feet.

District: Northern California and western Nevada; 67 stakes.

Groundbreaking, site dedication: May 26, 1962, by President David O. McKay.

Dedication: Nov. 17-19, 1964, by President David O. McKay, 6 sessions.

Dedicatory prayer excerpt: *"This temple . . . is a monument testifying to the faith and loyalty of the members of thy Church in the payment of their tithes and offerings. We thank thee for every effort that has been put forth by the members, from every sacrifice that has been made by the young boys and girls who have given of their dimes and dollars, to the millionaire who gave of his thousands."*

OGDEN TEMPLE

Location: In downtown Ogden, between Grant Avenue and Washington Boulevard; 350 22nd Street, Ogden, UT 84401. Telephone: (801) 621-6880.

Site: Approved by President David O. McKay and announced Aug. 14, 1967; 18.3 acres.

Exterior finish: White cast stone with a fluted appearance, gold anodized aluminum grillwork, gold directional glass windows; similar to Provo Temple.

Temple design: Modern and functional.

Architect: Emil B. Fetzer, Church architect.

Construction chairman: Mark B. Garff and Fred A. Baker, vice chairman.

Contractor: Okland Construction Company.

Number of rooms: 6 ordinance rooms, 11 sealing rooms, 4 floors, 283 total rooms.

Total floor area: 115,000 square feet.

Dimensions of building: 200 feet by 184 feet;

tower 180 feet above ground level; single tower of 180 feet.

District: Part of northeastern Utah, southwestern Wyoming; 65 stakes (2 of these will be included in the Vernal Utah Temple District when that temple is completed).

Groundbreaking, site dedication: Sept. 8, 1969, President N. Eldon Tanner conducted; prayers given by President Alvin R. Dyer and President Joseph Fielding Smith; ground broken by President Hugh B. Brown.

Dedication: Jan. 18-20, 1972, by President Joseph Fielding Smith; 6 sessions.

Dedicatory prayer excerpt: *"It has been our privilege, as guided by the whisperings of thy Spirit, to build unto thee this temple, which we now present unto thee as another of thy holy houses."*

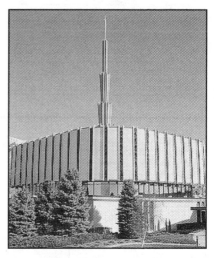

ORLANDO FLORIDA TEMPLE

Location: On a knoll overlooking Butler chain of lakes at Apopka-Vineland Road on the edge of Orlando suburb of Windermere, five miles southwest of Orlando near Florida Turnpike and Interstate 4. 9000 Windy Ridge Road, Windermere, FL 34786. Telephone: (407) 876-0022.

Site: 13 acres.

Exterior finish: White precast concrete with marble chips.

Temple design: Classic modern with one spire.

Architects: Scott partnership architects.

Church project manager: Ralph Cluff.

Contractor: Brice Building Company.

Number of rooms: Four endowment rooms, five sealing rooms.

Total floor area: 70,000 square feet.

Dimensions of building: 180 feet by 182 feet, tower with statue of Angel Moroni is 165 feet high.

District: Florida, part of southern Georgia; 33 stakes (10 of these will be included in the Santo Domingo Dominican Republic Temple District when temple is completed).

Groundbreaking, site dedication: June 20, 1992, by Elder James E. Faust of the Council of the Twelve.

Dedication: Oct. 9-11, 1994, by President Howard W. Hunter; 12 sessions.

Dedicatory prayer excerpt: *"To all who look upon it, including those who reside in this area, may it ever present a picture of peace and beauty, a structure partaking of thy divine nature."*

PAPEETE TAHITI TEMPLE

Location: In Pirae, adjacent to Papeete, on Rua de Pierri Loti; B.P. 5682, (Allee Pierre Loti, Titioro) Pirae, Tahiti. Telephone: (011-689) 43-9118.

Site: 5 acres.

Exterior finish: Stucco, using imported white sand.

Temple design: Shows some European elements of French influence as well as Polynesian

culture.

Architect: Emil B. Fetzer, Church architect; adapted by Temples and Special Projects Architecture.

Construction adviser: George Bonnet.

Contractor: Comtrol Inc., a Midvale, Utah, construction firm.

Number of rooms: 2 ordinance rooms, 2 sealing

rooms; 29 total rooms.

Total floor area: 10,658 square feet.

Dimensions of building: 125 feet by 105 feet, with an eight-foot statue of Angel Moroni on a 66-foot spire.

District: French Polynesia; 4 stakes.

Groundbreaking, site dedication: Feb. 13, 1981, by President Spencer W. Kimball, who also offered a prayer of dedication that the temple would be "a light to all in these islands."

Dedication: Oct. 27-29, 1983, by President Gordon B. Hinckley; 6 sessions.

Dedicatory prayer excerpt: *"We ask that thou wilt preserve [the temple]. . . as thy house. May it be protected by thy power from any who would defile it. May it stand against the winds and the rains. . ."*

PORTLAND OREGON TEMPLE

Location: In a wooded suburb about 10 miles southwest of downtown Portland, in the northwest corner of Oswego, adjacent to Interstate 5; 13600 SW Kruse Oaks Blvd., Lake Oswego, OR 97035. 97035. Telephone: (503) 639-7066.

Site: The land was purchased by the Church in mid-1960s for a junior college, but 7.3 acres was later chosen as a temple site.

Exterior finish: White marble walls and slate roof.

Temple design: 6 spires.

Architects: Leland A. Gray, architect; Lee/Ruff/Waddle, site and local architects.

Construction adviser: Michael Enfield

Contractor: Zwick Construction Co.

Number of rooms: 4 ordinance, 14 sealing rooms.

Total floor area: 65,000 square feet.

Dimensions of building: 270 feet by 183 feet, four towers 124 feet tall; statue of Angel Moroni on east spire, 169 feet tall.

District: Includes most of Oregon and parts of Washington and California; 36 stakes.

Groundbreaking, site dedication: Sept. 20, 1986, by President Gordon B. Hinckley.

Dedication: Aug. 19-21, 1989, by President Gordon B. Hinckley; 11 sessions.

Dedicatory prayer excerpt: *"May a spirit of solemnity rest upon all who enter herein. Open to their vision a glimpse of thy great and everlasting designs."*

PRESTON ENGLAND TEMPLE

Location: In rural Chorley, Lancashire, England.

Announced: Oct. 19,1992, by President Gordon B. Hinckley. and Northern Ireland; 20 stakes.

Groundbreaking, site dedication: June 12, 1994, by President Gordon B. Hinckley.

Status: Under construction.

PROVO TEMPLE

Location: At the entrance of Rock Canyon on the east bench of Provo; 2200 Temple Hill Drive, Provo, UT 84604. Telephone (801) 375-5775.

Site: 17 acres. Announced by President David O. McKay on Aug. 14, 1967.

Exterior finish: White cast stone, gold anodized aluminum grilles, bronze glass panels, and single spire finished in gold and anodized aluminum; similar to Ogden Temple.

Temple design: Modern and functional.

Architect: Emil B. Fetzer, Church architect.

Construction chairman: Mark B. Garff, with Fred A. Baker, vice chairman.

Construction supervisor: Hogan and Tingey, general contractors.

Number of rooms: 6 ordinance, 12 sealing rooms, 283 total rooms.

Total floor area: 115,000 square feet.

Dimensions of building: 200 by 184 feet; 175 feet high with a 118-foot spire on top of the building.

District: Central and eastern Utah; 94 stakes (47 of these will be included in the Mt. Timpanogos and Vernal Utah temple districts when those temples are completed).

Groundbreaking, site dedication: Sept. 15, 1969, ground broken by President Hugh B. Brown.

Dedication: Feb. 9, 1972; dedicatory prayer written by President Joseph Fielding Smith and read by

President Harold B. Lee; 2 sessions.

Dedicatory prayer excerpt: *"We dedicate this temple to thee, the Lord. We dedicate it as a house of baptism, a house of endowment, a house of marriage, a house of righteousness for the living and the dead."*

SALT LAKE TEMPLE

Location: On Temple Square in the center of Salt Lake City; 50 W. North Temple St., Salt Lake City, UT 84150. Telephone: (801) 240-2640.

Site: 10 acres. Selected July 28, 1847, by Brigham Young.

Exterior finish: Granite from Little Cottonwood Canyon, 20 miles to the southeast of Salt Lake City. The chapel and office annex is reinforced concrete faced with Utah granite.

Temple design: Suggestive of Gothic and other classical styles, but unique and distinctive.

Architect: Truman O. Angell, Church architect, worked out plans under direction of Brigham Young. During Angell's illness, William Folsom temporarily filled his post. After Angell's death in 1887, Don Carlos Young completed work on the temple.

Construction supervisor: Daniel H. Wells supervised construction; "Public Works," was organized Jan. 26, 1850, to provide labor and materials.

Number of rooms: 1 ordinance room, 14 sealing rooms, 177 total rooms.

Total floor area: 253,015 square feet in the temple, including the annex.

Dimensions of building: 118 feet 6¾ inches by 181 feet 7¼ inches. At east end of the building, the height of the center pinnacle is 210 feet. The center of the three towers on the west end is 204 feet high.

District: Tooele County and part of Salt Lake and Summit counties in Utah; 57 stakes.

Groundbreaking, site dedication: Feb. 14, 1853, President Brigham Young broke ground and Heber C. Kimball dedicated the site.

Dedication: April 6-24, 1893, by President Wilford Woodruff; 31 sessions.

On April 5, 1893, more than 600 non-LDS residents of Salt Lake City toured the temple, which had taken more than 40 years to complete.

Dedicatory prayer excerpt: *"When thy people. . . are oppressed and in trouble . . . we beseech thee, to look down from thy holy habitation in mercy and tender compassion. . . ."*

SAN DIEGO CALIFORNIA TEMPLE

Location: In the northern part of city of San Diego near the suburb of La Jolla on a ridge above the San Diego Freeway; 7474 Charmant Dr., San Diego, CA 92122. Telephone: (619) 622-0991.

Site: 7.2 acres.

Exterior finish: Marble chips in plaster.

Temple design: Modern, with two major towers.

Architects: Deems, Lewis & McKinnley-William Lewis, and Hyndman & Hyndman.

Project representative: Stanley G. Smith.

Contractor: Okland Construction Co.

Number of rooms: Four ordinance and eight sealing rooms.

Total floor area: 82,447 square feet.

Dimensions of building: 165 feet by 194 feet; roof 62 feet high; statue of Angel Moroni on top spire, 200 feet high.

Groundbreaking, site dedication: Ground broken Feb. 27, 1988, by President Ezra Taft Benson; site dedicated the same day by President Thomas S. Monson of the First Presidency.

District: Parts of Southern California and northwestern Mexico; 26 stakes.

Dedicated: April 25-30, 1993, by President Gordon B. Hinckley in 23 sessions.

Dedicatory prayer excerpt: *"We thank thee that hundreds of thousands of men and women of various faiths and philosophies have had the opportunity of walking through this sacred house prior to this time of dedication. May an attitude of respect and reverence grow within them. May very many of them be stirred to seek and learn the truths of thy restored work that they too might become eligible to enjoy the blessings offered herein. May any voices of criticism be stilled and any words of disrespect be silenced."*

SANTIAGO CHILE TEMPLE

Location: At site of former Church school headquarters in Santiago suburb of Providencia on Pedro de Valdivia 1423; Pocuro #1940 Providencia, Santiago, Chile. Telephone: (011-56-2) 223-9976.

Site: 2.61 acres.

Exterior finish: Stucco on concrete block.

Temple design: Modern.

Architect: Emil B. Fetzer, Church architect.

Construction adviser: Gary Holland.

Contractor: H. Briones Y Cia & The Church of Jesus Christ of Latter-day Saints.

Number of rooms: 2 ordinance rooms, 3 sealing rooms; 31 total rooms.

Total floor area: 13,020 square feet.

Dimensions of building: 142.88 feet by 115.32 feet; statue of Angel Moroni on top spire, 76.5 feet high.

District: Chile; 67 stakes.

Groundbreaking, site dedication: May 30, 1981, by President Spencer W. Kimball, in a cold rain, attended by 6,000 members.

Dedication: Sept. 15-17, 1983, by President Gordon B. Hinckley; 10 sessions.

Dedicatory prayer excerpt: *"Bless thy work upon this great continent of South America which is part of the land of Zion. Bless thy work in this nation of Chile. May all that has been done in the past be but a prologue to a far greater work in the future. May thy people be recognized for the virtue of their lives."*

SANTO DOMINGO DOMINICAN REPUBLIC TEMPLE

Announced: Dec. 4, 1993, by the First Presidency.

Status: Pending groundbreaking.

Temple district: The Caribbean; 10 stakes.

SAO PAULO TEMPLE

Location: In the Butanta section of Sao Paulo; Av. Prof. Francisco Morato 2390, CEP 05512, Sao Paulo, Brazil. Telephone: (011-55-11) 813-9622.

Exterior finish: Reinforced concrete faced with cast stone composed of quartz and marble aggregates set in special white-base cement.

Temple design: Modern design with Spanish influence.

Architect: Emil B. Fetzer, Church architect.

Construction chairman: Christiani Nielsen, general contractor.

Construction supervisor: Ross Jensen and James Magleby.

Number of rooms: 2 ordinance rooms, 4 sealing rooms, 76 total rooms.

Total floor area: 51,279 square feet.

Dimensions of building: 116 feet by 256 feet, with tower reaching 101 feet, 4 inches.

District: Brazil, Paraguay, part of Bolivia; 111 stakes.

Groundbreaking, site dedication: March 20, 1976; by Elder James E. Faust, then an Assistant to the Twelve; attended by 2,000 Church members.

Dedication: Oct. 30-Nov. 2, 1978, by President Spencer W. Kimball; 10 sessions.

Dedicatory prayer excerpt: *"Our Father, may peace abide in all the homes of thy saints. May holy*

angels guard them. May prosperity shine upon them and sickness and disease be rebuked from their midst. May their land be made fruitful. May the waters be pure and the climate tempered to the comfort and well-being of thy people.

"Bless the poor of thy people, that the cry of want and suffering may not ascend unto thy saints."

SEATTLE TEMPLE

Location: Across from Bellevue Community College, near the Eastgate Interchange on Interstate 90; 2808 148th Ave. SE, Bellevue, WA 98007. Telephone: (206) 643-5144.

Site: 23.5 acres, selected June 1975.

Exterior finish: Reinforced concrete faced with white marble aggregate and cast stone.

Temple design: Modern.

Architect: Emil B. Fetzer, Church architect.

Project representative: Michael Enfield.

Construction superintendent: Kent Carter for Jacobsen Construction Co. of Salt Lake City.

Number of rooms: 4 ordinance rooms, 12 sealing rooms.

Total floor area: 110,000 square feet.

Dimensions of building: Ground level is 142 feet by 194 feet; upper levels are 117 feet by 163 feet. Height to square is 70 feet; to top of the Angel Moroni, 179 feet.

District: Most of Washington, British Columbia, Alaska, northern Idaho, 58 stakes.

Groundbreaking, site dedication: May 27, 1978, by President Marion G. Romney of the First Presidency.

Dedication: Nov. 17-21, 1980, by President Spencer W. Kimball; 13 sessions.

Dedicatory prayer excerpt: *"Bless, we pray*

thee, the presidency of this temple and the matron and all the officiators herein. Help them to create a sublime and holy atmosphere so that all ordinances may be performed with love and a sweet, spiritual tone that will cause the members to greatly desire to be here, and to return again and again."

SEOUL KOREA TEMPLE

Location: 500-23 Chang Chun-dong, Seodaemun-Ku, Seoul, Korea 120-180. Telephone: (011-82-2) 332-9526.

Site: 1 acre.

Exterior finish: Granite exterior.

Temple design: Modern adaptation of earlier six-spire design.

Dimensions of building: 178 feet by 71 feet; Angel Moroni statue is atop tallest spire at 112 feet.

Architects: Church architectural staff; local architect, Komerican Architects.

Construction adviser: Calvin Wardell.

Contractor: Woo Chang.

Number of rooms: Four ordinance rooms, three sealing rooms.

Total floor area: 12,780 square feet.

District: South Korea; 16 stakes.

Groundbreaking, site dedication: May 9, 1983,

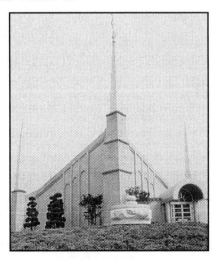

by Elder Marvin J. Ashton of the Council of the Twelve.

Dedication: Dec. 14-15, 1985, by President Gordon B. Hinckley; 6 sessions.

Dedicatory prayer excerpt: *"Our hearts are filled with gratitude for this long-awaited day. This is the first such house of the Lord ever constructed on the mainland of Asia, this vast continent where dwell more than a billion of thy sons and daughters, and where through the generations of the past have lived unnumbered hosts whose lives have not been touched by the saving principles of the gospel."*

ST. GEORGE TEMPLE

Location: near the center of St. George; 250 E. 400 South, St. George, UT 84770. Telephone: (801) 673-3533.

Site: 6 acres, selected by Brigham Young in 1871.

Exterior finish: Native red sandstone quarried north of the city was used for the temple which was then plastered white.

Temple design: Castellated Gothic style.

Architect: Truman O. Angell.

Construction superintendent: Miles P. Romney, Edward L. Parry, head stone mason.

Number of rooms: 3 ordinance rooms, 8 sealing rooms, 64 rooms in original structure; 135 rooms after remodeling.

Total floor area: 56,062 square feet in original building; 110,000 square feet after remodeling completed in 1975.

Dimensions of building: 142 feet by 96 feet. To the top of the buttresses, the height is 80 feet, and to the top of the vane, 175 feet.

District: Southwestern Utah, small part of Nevada, Arizona; 28 stakes.

Groundbreaking, site dedication: Nov.9, 1871, by President Brigham Young; site dedication prayer by George A. Smith.

Dedication: Jan. 1, 1877, completed portions were dedicated. Final dedication, April 6-8, 1877, President Brigham Young presiding, and Daniel H. Wells offered prayer.

On Nov. 11-12, 1975, after extensive remodeling, the temple was rededicated by President Spencer W. Kimball; 5 sessions.

Dedicatory prayer excerpt: *"We implore thy blessings upon the various congregations of thy people who may assemble in this house from time to time."*

ST. LOUIS MISSOURI TEMPLE

Location: in the city of Town and Country, a suburb of St. Louis, about 10 miles west of the city center, near Interstate 64, near the interchange of I-270, the area's principal belt route.

Announced: Dec. 29, 1990, in a letter from the First Presidency to local Church leaders.

District: Missouri, parts of Iowa, Nebraska, Kansas, Illinois, Indiana, Kentucky, Tennessee, Mississippi and Arkansas; 26 stakes.

Groundbreaking, site dedication: Oct. 30, 1993, by President Gordon B. Hinckley and President Thomas S. Monson.

Status: Under construction.

STOCKHOLM SWEDEN TEMPLE

Location: Vasterhaninge, about 13 miles southeast of Stockholm; Box 153, (Tempelvagen 5) S-13732 Vasterhaninge, Sweden. Telephone: (011-46-7) 501-26-70.

Exterior finish: Masonry exterior, copper roof.

Temple design: Modern adaptation of earlier six-spire design.

Architects: Church architectural staff; local architect, John Sjostrom.

Construction adviser: Henry Haurand.

Contractor: Johnson Construction Co.

Number of rooms: Four ordinance rooms; three sealing rooms.

Total floor area: 14,508 square feet.

Dimensions of building: 178 feet by 71 feet; Angel Moroni statue is atop tallest spire at 112 feet.

District: Sweden, Finland, Denmark, Norway; 7 stakes.

Groundbreaking, site dedication: March 17, 1984, by Elder Thomas S. Monson of the Council of the Twelve.

Dedication: July 2-4, 1985, by President Gordon B. Hinckley; 11 sessions.

Dedicatory prayer excerpt: *"Bless this nation where is found thy temple, and its sister nations. . . .*

"Save these nations from war and oppression, and may their people look to thee and open their

doors and hearts to thy messengers of eternal truth."

SWISS TEMPLE

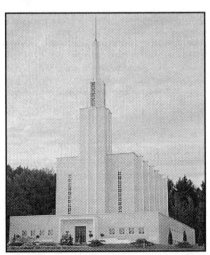

Location: A northern suburb of Bern in a setting with the Alps on the south, and the Jura Mountains on the west and north; Tempelstrasse 4, Ch - 3052 Zollikofen, Switzerland. Telephone: (011-41-31) 911-0912.

Site: 7 acres, selected July 1952, by President David O. McKay and President Samuel E. Bringhurst of the Swiss-Austrian Mission.

Exterior finish: Built of reinforced concrete with a creamish gray terra cotta facing trimmed in white. Tower is white base and spire is gold-colored.

Temple design: Modern-contemporary, but similar to lines of early Church temples.

Architect: Edward O. Anderson, Church architect. Re-drawn into German specifications by Wilhelm Zimmer of Bercher and Zimmer Architects.

Contractor: Hans Jordi of Bern.

Number of rooms: 4 ordinance, 7 sealing; total rooms, 82.

Total floor area: Originally 34,750 square feet; now 39,063 square feet.

Dimensions of building: 152 feet by 84 feet; top of tower rises 140 feet.

District: Switzerland, Austria, Spain, Portugal, It-

aly, southern France; 18 stakes.

Groundbreaking, site dedication: Aug. 5, 1953, by President David O. McKay.

Dedication: Sept. 11-15, 1955, by President David O. McKay; 10 sessions, Tabernacle Choir participated. Rededicated Oct. 23-25, 1992, by President Gordon B. Hinckley; 10 sessions.

Dedicatory prayer excerpt: *"Increase our desire, O Father, to put forth even greater effort towards the consummation of thy purpose to bring to pass the immortality and eternal life of all thy children. This edifice is one more means to aid in bringing about this divine consummation."*

SYDNEY AUSTRALIA TEMPLE

Location: In suburban Carlingford, 15 miles northwest of downtown Sydney; Pennant Hill Road & Moseley Street, Carlingford, NSW Australia 2118. Telephone: (011-61-2) 873-0471.

Area of site: 3 acres.

Exterior finish: Precast panels, white quartz finish, terra cotta roof tiles.

Temple design: Modern.

Architect: Emil B. Fetzer, Church architect, and R. Lindsay Little.

Construction adviser: D. Crosbie and Richard Rowley.

Contractor: J.P. Cordukes Pty. Ltd.

Number of rooms: Three sealing rooms, two ordinance rooms; 31 total rooms.

Total floor area: 13,020 square feet.

Dimensions of building: 145.11 feet by 115.14 feet; statue of Angel Moroni added to top spire.

District: Australia and Papua New Guinea; 18 stakes.

Groundbreaking, site dedication: Aug. 13, 1982, by Elder Bruce R. McConkie of the Council of the Twelve.

Dedication: Sept. 20-23, 1984, by President Gordon B. Hinckley; 14 sessions.

Dedicatory prayer excerpt: *"May this temple with its grounds be a place of beauty to all who look upon it. May they be touched by thy spirit. . . ."*

TAIPEI TAIWAN TEMPLE

Location: In the Taipei business district; 256 Ai Kuo East Road, Taipei, Taiwan, R.O.C. Telephone: (011-886-2) 351-0218.

Site: 0.5 acres.

Exterior finish: White ceramic tile.

Temple design: Modern adaptation of earlier six-spire design.

Architect: Church architectural staff with assistance from Philip Fei & Associates of Taipei.

Construction adviser: Harold Smith.

Contractor: I. Cheng Construction & Development Corp.

Number of rooms: 4 ordinance rooms, 3 sealing rooms; 32 total rooms.

Total floor area: 16,214 square feet.

Dimensions of building: 178 feet by 72 feet, six spires; statue of Angel Moroni rises to height of 126 feet.

District: Taiwan and Hong Kong; 8 stakes (5 of these will be included in the Hong Kong Temple District when that temple is completed 1996-97).

Groundbreaking, site dedication: Aug. 27, 1982, by President Gordon B. Hinckley.

Dedication: Nov. 17-18, 1984, by President Gordon B. Hinckley; 5 sessions.

Dedicatory prayer excerpt: "We thank thee for the firm foundation on which thy Church is now established in this part of the earth. We thank thee for this day when those who will use this temple may turn their hearts to their fathers, participating in this thy holy house in those ordinances which will make it possible for their deceased forebears to move forward on the way that leads to eternal life."

TOKYO TEMPLE

Location: Opposite the Arisugawa Park; 5-8-10 Minami Azabu, Minato-Ku, Tokyo, Japan 106. Telephone: (011-81-33) 442-8171.

Site: 18,000 square feet (about 0.5 acre).

Exterior finish: Structural steel and reinforced concrete faced with 289 panels of precast stone, having the appearance of light gray granite.

Architect: Emil B. Fetzer, Church architect. Architect's local representative, Masao Shiina.

Resident engineer: Sadao Nagata.

Construction superintendent: Yuji Morimura for the Kajima Corporation.

Number of rooms: Two ordinance rooms, five sealing rooms.

Total floor area: 58,000 square feet.

Dimensions of building: Ground floor is 103 feet by 134 feet; upper levels are 103 by 105 feet. Height to square is 70½ feet, to top of tower, 178½ feet.

Design: Modern, one spire.

District: Japan; 25 stakes.

Groundbreaking, site dedication: Neither were held.

Dedication: Oct. 27-29, 1980, by President Spencer W. Kimball.

Dedicatory prayer excerpt: "Kind Father, bless all those who come to this temple, that they may do so with humble hearts, in cleanliness, and honor, and integrity. We are grateful for these Saints, for

their devotion and their faith, for their worthiness and their determination to be pure and holy.

"We are jubilant this day, our Holy Father, and have hearts filled with praise to thee that thou hast permitted us to see the completion of this temple and to see this day for which we have so long hoped and toiled and prayed."

TORONTO ONTARIO TEMPLE

Location: On the outskirts of Brampton, about 20 miles west of Toronto; 10060 Bramalea Rd, Brampton, Ontario, Canada L6R 1A1. Telephone: (905) 799-1122.

Site: Announced April 15, 1984; 13.4 acres.

Exterior finish: White cast stone.

Temple design: Modern.

Architects: Allward-Gouinlock Inc.

Supervising architects: Alfred T. West Jr. and Dagmar Wertheim.

Construction adviser: Jerry Sears

Contractor: Milne & Nicholls Ltd.

Number of rooms: 4 ordinance rooms, 6 sealing rooms.

Total floor area: 56,000 square feet.

Dimensions of building: 154 feet by 208 feet; spire, 105 feet high with 11-foot statue of Angel Moroni.

District: Northeastern Canada and parts of Ohio, Michigan, New York, Pennsylvania, Maine and Vermont; 25 stakes.

Groundbreaking, site dedication: Oct. 10, 1987, by President Thomas S. Monson.

Dedication: Aug. 25-27, 1990, by President Gordon B. Hinckley; 11 sessions.

Dedicatory prayer excerpt: *"This nation has become a gathering place for people from scores of other lands. In their veins flows the blood of Israel. Many have hearkened to the testimony of thy servants and been favored with a knowledge of the principles and ordinances of thine everlasting gospel."*

VERNAL UTAH TEMPLE

Location: The temple will be remodeled from the renovated 87-year old Uintah Stake Tabernacle, at 100 South and 500 West, Vernal, Utah, some 180 miles east of Salt Lake City.

Site: 1.6 acres

Announced: Feb. 13, 1994, in a letter to local Church leaders from the First Presidency.

Status: Under construction.

District: East central Utah and parts of Wyoming and Colorado; 12 stakes.

WASHINGTON TEMPLE

Location: Wooded site in Kensington, Md., near Exit 20 of the Capital Beltway (Interstate 495), a half-hour drive from downtown Washington, D.C.; 9900 Stoneybrook Dr., Kensington, MD 20895. Telephone: (301) 588-0650.

Site: Selected in 1962; 52 acres.

Exterior finish: Reinforced concrete sheathed in 173,000 square feet of Alabama white marble.

Temple design: The total design portrays the Church as "a light to the world," with three towers to the east representing the Melchizedek Priesthood leadership, and those to the west, the Aaronic Priesthood leadership, said principal architect Keith W. Wilcox.

Architects: Fred L. Markham, Henry P. Fetzer, Harold K. Beecher, Keith W. Wilcox, under general

direction of Church architect Emil B. Fetzer.

Contractor: Jacobsen, Okland, and Sidney

Foulger construction companies.

Number of rooms: 6 ordinance rooms, 14 sealing rooms, seven floors, 294 total rooms.

Total floor area: 160,000 square feet.

Dimensions of building: 248 feet long, 136 feet wide, not including annex or bridge to temple proper. Statue of Angel Moroni on highest spire 288 feet above ground.

District: Most of eastern United States, including some of New England; 62 stakes.

Groundbreaking, site dedication: Dec. 7, 1968, by President Hugh B. Brown.

Dedication: Nov. 19-22, 1974, by President Spencer W. Kimball; 10 sessions.

Dedicatory prayer excerpt: *"We are so grateful, our Father, that thy Son has thrown wide open the doors of the prisons for the multitudes who are waiting in the spirit world."*

Total Microfilm Rolls in Posession at Granite Mountain Records Vault

Year	Total rolls	Year	Total rolls
1978	1,301,914	1986	1,551,722
1979	1,338,982	1987	1,607,583
1980	1,363,735	1988	1,607,583*
1981	1,390,094	1989	1,664,174
1982	1,431,400	1990	1,712,400
1983	1,469,622	1991	1,788,816
1984	1,494,624	1992	1,887,530
1985	1,519,886	1993	1,970,452

* Estimated

Temples in use

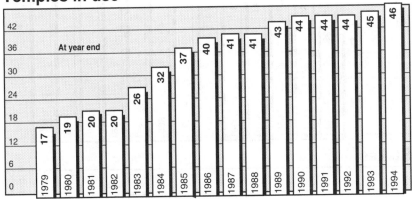

Church growth

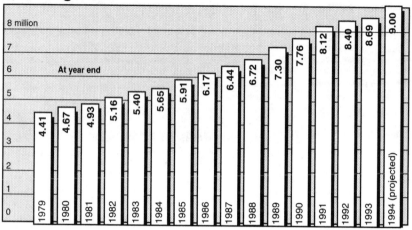

At year end

Year	Value
1979	4.41
1980	4.67
1981	4.93
1982	5.16
1983	5.40
1984	5.65
1985	5.91
1986	6.17
1987	6.44
1988	6.72
1989	7.30
1990	7.76
1991	8.12
1992	8.40
1993	8.69
1994 (projected)	9.00

Nations, Territories

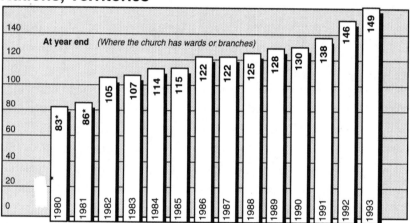

At year end   *(Where the church has wards or branches)*

Year	Value
1980	83*
1981	86*
1982	105
1983	107
1984	114
1985	115
1986	122
1987	122
1988	125
1989	128
1990	130
1991	138
1992	146
1993	149

Stakes

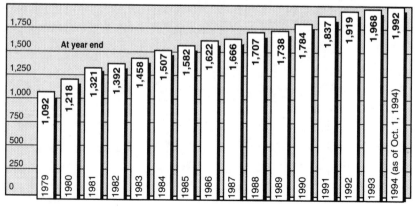

At year end

Year	Value
1979	1,092
1980	1,218
1981	1,321
1982	1,392
1983	1,458
1984	1,507
1985	1,582
1986	1,622
1987	1,666
1988	1,707
1989	1,738
1990	1,784
1991	1,837
1992	1,919
1993	1,968
1994 (as of Oct. 1, 1994)	1,992

CHRONOLOGY,
NEWS IN
REVIEW

HISTORICAL CHRONOLOGY OF THE CHURCH

This chronology gives a selected listing of important dates in Church history. Among the items excluded are many that can be found elsewhere in this Almanac, including information on General Authorities and the establishment of stakes and missions. Italicized entries are secular events that were taking place during the time.

1805

April 27 — *The U.S. Marines captured the port city of Derna in the Tripolitan War; the phrase, "To the shores of Tripoli," in the official Marine hymn comes from this campaign.*

Dec. 23 — Joseph Smith Jr. was born in Sharon, Windsor County, Vt., the fourth child of Joseph and Lucy Mack Smith.

1816

After living in several villages in central Vermont and New Hampshire, the Joseph Smith Sr. family moved to Palmyra, N.Y., and a couple of years later to a farm in nearby Manchester, N.Y.

1820

Spring — In Joseph Smith's First Vision, the Father and Son answered his question about which church to join. Joseph had prayed for guidance in response to a religious revival in the area.

March 3 — *The Missouri Compromise, allowing slavery in Missouri but not anywhere else west of the Mississippi and north of Missouri, was passed by Congress.*

1823

Sept. 21-22 — In five visits with Joseph Smith, the resurrected Moroni revealed the existence of ancient gold plates and instructed him on his role in restoring the gospel and translating the Book of Mormon.

Dec. 2 — *The Monroe Doctrine, stating opposition to European intervention in the Americas, was announced by President James Monroe in his annual message to Congress.*

1827

Jan. 18 — Joseph Smith married Emma Hale in South Bainbridge, N.Y. The couple met while Joseph was working in Harmony, Pa., for Josiah Stowell and boarding with Emma's father, Isaac Hale.

Aug. 6 — *The United States and Great Britain signed a treaty, continuing joint occupation of the Oregon country, which extended from the California border to Alaska.*

Sept. 22 — Joseph Smith received the plates of the Book of Mormon from the Angel Moroni at the Hill Cumorah. He also received the Urim and Thummim, which was used to assist in translation.

1828

February — Martin Harris took a transcript and partial translation of the Book of Mormon to Professor Charles Anthon of Columbia College and to Dr. Samuel L. Mitchell of New York. In June, Harris borrowed and lost 116 manuscript pages.

July 4 — *The age of railroading began in the United States when the first passenger railroad in the country, the Baltimore & Ohio, started operation.*

1829

May 15 — Joseph Smith and Oliver Cowdery received the Aaronic Priesthood from John the Baptist along the banks of the Susquehanna River, near Harmony, Pa. (See D&C 13.) The two baptized one another, as instructed.

May/June — Peter, James and John conferred the Melchizedek Priesthood upon Joseph Smith and Oliver Cowdery near the Susquehanna River between Harmony, Pa., and Colesville, N.Y.

June — The Book of Mormon translation was completed, and the three witnesses — Oliver Cowdery, David Whitmer and Martin Harris — viewed the plates in a vision. (See D&C 17.) Soon afterward, the plates were shown to eight other witnesses — J. Christian Whitmer, Jacob Whitmer, Peter Whitmer Jr., John Whitmer, Hiram Page, Joseph Smith Sr., Hyrum Smith and Samuel H. Smith.

1830

First covered wagons, led by Jedediah Smith and William Sublette of the Rocky Mountain Fur Company, made the trek from the Missouri River to the Rocky Mountains.

March 26 — The Book of Mormon was published in Palmyra, N.Y., by Joseph Smith. E.B. Grandin printed 5,000 copies for $3,000.

April — The revelation on Church government (See D&C 20) outlined procedures for organizing the Church, duties of members and officers, need for recordkeeping and procedures for baptism and sacrament administration.

April 6 — Joseph Smith organized the "Church of Christ" at the Peter Whitmer Sr. home in Fayette, N.Y. — with six incorporators as required by law — Joseph Smith, Oliver Cowdery, Hyrum Smith, Peter Whitmer Jr., David Whitmer and Samuel H. Smith.

April 11 — Oliver Cowdery preached the first public discourse of the new Church at a meeting in the Peter Whitmer home.

June — The "Words of Moses," later incorporated in the Pearl of Great Price, were revealed to Joseph Smith. The prophecy of Enoch was revealed to the Prophet in December.

June — Joseph Smith was arrested on charges of disorderly conduct but was acquitted in a trial at South Bainbridge, N.Y. This was the first of what would be many trumped-up charges against the Prophet.

June 9 — The first conference of the Church, which now numbered 27 members, convened in Fayette.

June 30 — Samuel H. Smith left on a mission to neighboring villages, including Mendon, where the Young and Kimball families resided.

Oct. 17 — Following a revelation received by the Prophet Joseph Smith (See D&C 32), Parley P. Pratt, Oliver Cowdery, Peter Whitmer Jr. and Ziba Peterson began a mission to the Lamanites, leaving copies of the Book of Mormon with the Cattaraugus Indians in New York, the Wyandots in Ohio and the Shawnees and Delawares on the Missouri frontier. They stopped en route to teach and baptize Sidney Rigdon and a congregation of his followers in the Kirtland, Ohio area.

Dec. 30 — The Saints were commanded in a revelation (See D&C 37) to gather in Ohio, the first commandment concerning a gathering in this dispensation.

1831

Feb. 4 — Edward Partridge was named "bishop unto the Church." (See D&C 41.) This was the first revelation given through the Prophet Joseph Smith at Kirtland, Ohio.

June 3-6 — At a conference in Kirtland, the first high priests were ordained, and elders were called to go to Jackson County, Mo. (See D&C 52.)

Aug. 2 — During a ceremony in Kaw Township, 12 miles west of Independence in Jackson County, Mo., Sidney Rigdon dedicated the Land of Zion for the gathering of the Saints. Joseph Smith dedicated a temple site the following day on Aug. 3.

Dec. 12 — *The Republican Party held the first nominating convention of a major party in the United States.*

1832

Jan. 25 — Joseph Smith was sustained president of the high priesthood at a conference at Amherst, Ohio. Sidney Rigdon and Jesse Gause were named counselors in

March 1832. Gause's service in this capacity is unconfirmed by historical records. Frederick G. Williams was called by revelation (See D&C 81) to replace him.

Feb. 16 — While working on the inspired revision of the Bible, Joseph Smith and Sidney Rigdon received a vision of the three degrees of glory. (See D&C 76.)

May 21 — *The Democratic Party formally adopted its present name at a convention in Baltimore, Md.*

June — Elders began teaching in Canada, the first missionary effort outside the United States.

June 1 — The *Evening and Morning Star*, the first LDS publication, was issued at Independence, Mo., with William W. Phelps as editor.

Dec. 25 — Revelation and prophecy on war (See D&C 87), commencing with the Civil War some 28 years later, was given to the Prophet Joseph Smith.

Dec. 27 — The revelation known as the "Olive Leaf" (D&C 88) was presented to the Church. Included were instructions leading to the organization of the School of the Prophets.

Dec. 28 — *John Calhoun became the first U.S. vice president to resign. Afterward, he won an election to fill a vacant Senate seat representing South Carolina.*

1833

Feb. 27 — The revelation known as the "Word of Wisdom" (D&C 89) was received at Kirtland, Ohio.

March 18 — The First Presidency of the Church was organized when Sidney Rigdon and Frederick G. Williams were appointed and set apart by Joseph Smith to be his counselors in the Presidency of the Church.

May 6 — The Saints were commanded by revelation to build a House of the Lord at Kirtland. (See D&C 94.) Further instructions concerning the building of the temple were given by revelation on June 1. (See D&C 95.)

July 2 — The Prophet Joseph Smith finished the translation of the Bible.

July 20 — A mob destroyed the *Evening and Morning Star* printing office in Independence, Mo., interrupting the printing of the Book of Commandments. The *Evening and Morning Star* began publication again on Dec. 18 in Kirtland.

Oct. 5 — The Prophet Joseph Smith left Kirtland, Ohio, for Canada, the only country outside the United States where the Prophet preached.

November — The Saints left Jackson

County, Mo., in response to mob threats and attacks.

Dec. 3 — *Oberlin College in Ohio opened, becoming the first co-educational college in the U.S.*

Dec. 18 — The Prophet Joseph Smith gave the first patriarchal blessings in this dispensation to his parents, three of his brothers and Oliver Cowdery. Joseph Smith Sr. was ordained the first Patriarch to the Church.

1834

Feb. 17 — The first high council of the Church was organized by revelation (See D&C 102) for the stake in Kirtland, Ohio, which was created on the same day. The Kirtland Stake was the first stake organized in the Church. A similar organization was created in Missouri on July 3, 1834.

May 3 — At a conference of elders in Kirtland, the Church was first named "The Church of Jesus Christ of Latter-day Saints."

May 8 — Zion's Camp commenced its march from New Portage, Ohio, to Clay County, Mo., to assist the exiled Missouri Saints. The camp dispersed June 30.

June 30 — *The Indian Territory was created by an act of Congress.*

October — The *LDS Messenger and Advocate* began publication at Kirtland and continued until the Mormon evacuation of Ohio in 1837.

1835

The Church published a collection of hymns and sacred songs selected by Emma Smith. She had been appointed to the work in July 1830 (See D&C 25), but destruction of the Independence, Mo., printing press in 1833 had delayed publication.

Feb. 14 — The three witnesses to the Book of Mormon selected 12 apostles at a meeting of the members of Zion's Camp in Kirtland, Ohio, and the Quorum of the Twelve was organized.

Feb. 28 — The First Quorum of the Seventy was organized in Kirtland, and its first seven presidents named.

March 28 — A revelation in which various priesthood offices and powers were defined (See D&C 107) was received during a meeting of the First Presidency and Twelve in Kirtland.

May 4 — The Twelve left Kirtland for the Eastern states on their first mission as apostles.

July 3 — Michael H. Chandler arrived in Kirtland to exhibit four Egyptian mummies and some scrolls of papyrus. Joseph Smith's work with the scrolls resulted in the Book of

Abraham, later included in the Pearl of Great Price.

Aug. 17 — A general assembly of the Church in Kirtland accepted the revelations selected for publication as the Doctrine and Covenants. This volume contained the revelations gathered for the Book of Commandments in 1833 and others received since that time, along with articles on marriage and government and a series of Lectures on Faith written for the School of the Prophets.

1836

March 27 — The Kirtland Temple, the first temple built in this dispensation, was dedicated after being under construction for nearly three years. The dedicatory prayer was given to the Prophet Joseph Smith by revelation. (See D&C 109.)

April — Apostle Parley P. Pratt was set apart for a mission to upper (eastern) Canada, the first area outside the United States opened for the preaching of the gospel.

April 3 — The Savior and also Moses, Elias and Elijah appeared in the Kirtland Temple and committed the keys of their respective dispensations to Joseph Smith and Oliver Cowdery. (See D&C 110.)

June 29 — A mass meeting of citizens at Liberty, Mo., passed a resolution to expel the Saints from Clay County. By December many had relocated on Shoal Creek (later known as Far West) in the newly established Caldwell County, located northeast of Clay County.

1837

Parley P. Pratt issued his pamphlet *Voice of Warning,* the first tract published for missionary use in the Church.

June 13 — Apostles Heber C. Kimball and Orson Hyde and Elders Willard Richards and Joseph Fielding left Kirtland, Ohio, on their missions to England — opening up the missionary work outside North America. They and three brethren from Canada, Joseph Fielding, John Goodson and Isaac Russell, left New York on July 1 aboard the ship *Garrick.*

June 20 — *Victoria became Queen of Great Britain.*

July 30 — Nine persons were baptized in the River Ribble at Preston, England, the first converts to the Church in Great Britain. By December, there were 1,000 LDS members in England.

1838

April 23 — *The first transatlantic steamship service began, although scheduled service was not established until 1840.*

May 19 — Joseph Smith and others visited a place on Grand River, about 25 miles north of Far West, Mo., called Spring Hill by the Saints, which by revelation was named Adam-ondi-Ahman because "it is the place where Adam shall come to visit his people, or the Ancient of Days shall sit, as spoken of by Daniel the prophet." (See D&C 116, Dan. 7:9-14.)

July 6 — The exodus from Kirtland, Ohio, began under the direction of the First Council of the Seventy, as planned three months earlier. The Kirtland Camp arrived at Far West, Mo., Oct. 2, and at Adam-ondi-Ahman two days later.

July 8 — Revelation on law of tithing (See D&C 119) was given at Far West, Mo.

Aug. 6 — A scuffle at the polls at Gallatin, Daviess County, Mo., intensified the mounting tension between Latter-day Saints and other area settlers.

Oct. 27 — Acting upon reports of civil war and rebellion among the Mormons, Gov. Lilburn W. Boggs issued an order to exterminate or expel the Saints from Missouri.

Oct. 30 — Seventeen Latter-day Saints were killed in the Haun's Mill Massacre at a small settlement on Shoal Creek, 12 miles east of Far West. The attack, by the Livingston County militia, was a reaction to the extermination order of Gov. Boggs.

Oct. 31 — Joseph Smith and others were made prisoners of the militia. The next day, a court-martial ordered the Prophet and the others shot, but Brig. Gen. A.W. Doniphan refused to carry out the order.

Nov. 9 — Joseph Smith and the other prisoners arrived in Richmond, Mo., where they were put in chains and suffered much abuse by the guards. An arraignment and a two-week trial followed, resulting in their imprisonment in the Liberty Jail in Liberty, Mo., on Nov. 28.

1839

Jan. 26 — Brigham Young and the Twelve organized a committee to conduct the removal of the Saints from Missouri.

March 20 — While in Liberty Jail, Joseph Smith wrote an epistle to the Saints, which contained fervent pleadings with the Lord regarding the suffering of the Saints and words of prophecy. (See D&C 121.) A few days later, he continued the epistle, parts of which became Sections 122 and 123 of the Doctrine and Covenants.

April 16 — Joseph Smith and four other prisoners were allowed to escape while being transferred from Daviess to Boone counties under a change of venue in their case.

April 20 — The last of the Saints left Far West, Mo. A whole community, numbering about 15,000, had been expelled from their homes on account of their religion.

April 25 — Commerce, Ill., was selected as a gathering place for the Church. On May 1, two farms were purchased by Joseph Smith and others, the first land purchased in what later became Nauvoo.

June 11 — Joseph Smith began the task of compiling his *History of the Church*. He had the help of scribes and, later, Church historians. Segments of his history were published in Church periodicals in Nauvoo and later in Salt Lake City, and appeared in book form beginning in 1902.

Oct. 29 — Joseph Smith left Illinois for Washington, D.C., to seek redress from the president of the United States for wrongs suffered by the Saints in Missouri.

November — The first issue of the *Times and Seasons* was published in Nauvoo.

Nov. 29 — In a meeting with U.S. President Martin Van Buren in Washington, D.C., Joseph Smith was told by the president that he [Van Buren] could do nothing to relieve the oppressions in Missouri. Petitions were also presented to Congress, and a second interview was held with Van Buren, all to no avail.

1840

January — *Wilkes expedition discovered the Antarctic continent.*

April 15 — The Twelve in England named Parley P. Pratt editor of a proposed monthly periodical to be named the *Latter-day Saints Millennial Star*. The first issue was published in Manchester, England, on May 27; the publication would continue until 1970.

June 6 — Forty-one members of the Church sailed for the United States from Liverpool, England, on the ship *Britannia*, being the first Saints to gather from a foreign land. By 1890, some 85,000 LDS emigrants crossed the Atlantic in about 280 voyages.

Dec. 16 — Gov. Thomas Carlin of Illinois signed a bill creating a charter for Nauvoo, defining the city boundaries and establishing its government. Provisions included a university and a militia, the Nauvoo Legion.

1841

Jan. 19 — A revelation (See D&C 124) given at Nauvoo outlined instructions for building a temple in Nauvoo. Baptism for the dead was introduced as a temple ordinance.

Oct. 24 — At a site on the Mount of Olives in Jerusalem, Orson Hyde dedicated Palestine for the gathering of the Jews.

1842

Elder Lorenzo Snow presented a British edition of the Book of Mormon to Queen Victoria of England, the first head of government in the world to receive a copy of the Book of Mormon. The book, printed in Liverpool in 1841, is now in the Royal Library at Windsor.

March 1 — The Articles of Faith were published for the first time in the *Times and Seasons,* a publication of the Church in Nauvoo, Ill. Joseph Smith, in response to a request from John Wentworth, editor of the *Chicago Democrat,* wrote a summary of the Church's history, ending with 13 declarations of LDS belief.

March 17 — Joseph Smith organized the Female Relief Society of Nauvoo, with Emma Smith, Sarah M. Cleveland and Elizabeth Ann Whitney as its presidency, to look after the poor and sick.

May 4 — Joseph Smith introduced the temple endowment to seven men at a meeting in the room over his store in Nauvoo. A few others received endowments before completion of a temple.

Aug. 6 — Joseph Smith prophesied that the Saints would be driven to the Rocky Mountains, but that he would not go with them.

1843

Jan. 10 — *The first impeachment resolution was introduced in Congress; Virginian John Botts charged President John Tyler with corruption, misconduct in office and high crimes. It was rejected 127-83.*

May 3 — The *Nauvoo Neighbor* began publication and was voice for the Church for 2½ years.

June 21 — Illinois agents, armed with a warrant from Gov. Thomas Ford, arrested Joseph Smith at Dixon, Lee County, Ill. He was released July 1, 1843, under a writ of habeas corpus.

July 12 — A revelation received in Nauvoo, Ill., on the "Eternity of the Marriage Covenant and Plural Marriage" (See D&C 132) was recorded, giving fuller meaning to the "new and everlasting covenant," which had been mentioned as early as 1831.

1844

Jan. 29 — A political convention in Nauvoo nominated Joseph Smith as a candidate for the United States presidency.

Feb. 20 — Joseph Smith instructed the Twelve to organize an exploratory expedition to locate a site for the Saints in California or Oregon. A group of volunteers was organized

for the trip in meetings over the next several days.

March 26 — Joseph Smith prepared a message for Congress asking for a law protecting United States citizens immigrating to the unorganized territories, known as California and Oregon, and offered volunteers to serve in such a protective force.

May 11 — Joseph Smith organized the Council of Fifty, a secret political body that directed the westward migration of the Saints and served as a "shadow government" in Utah during the 19th century.

May 24 — *Samuel Morse transmitted the first public message by telegraph from Washington, D.C. to Baltimore, opening the way for development of the first means of rapid communications.*

June 7 — The first and only edition of the *Nauvoo Expositor* appeared. The city council declared the paper a nuisance three days later, and the city marshal forced entry to the print shop and destroyed the type and papers.

June 11 — Joseph Smith and the city council were charged with riot in the destruction of the *Expositor* press. A Nauvoo court absolved them of the charge, but the complainant asked for the issue to be examined by the Carthage court.

June 22 — Joseph and Hyrum Smith crossed the Mississippi River to flee to the Great Basin. Gov. Ford had promised the Prophet safety, and so, at the pleadings of others, the pair returned to Nauvoo and turned themselves over to government agents.

June 27 — Joseph and Hyrum Smith were killed by a mob that rushed the Carthage jail in Carthage, Ill. John Taylor was injured in the attack; Willard Richards escaped injury.

Aug. 4 — Sidney Rigdon advocated appointment of a guardian for the Church at a meeting in Nauvoo.

Aug. 8 — At a meeting designated for the appointment of a guardian, Rigdon again stated his views, after which Brigham Young announced an afternoon meeting. During the latter session, Young claimed the right of leadership for the Twelve and was sustained by vote of the Church.

1847

Jan. 14 — Brigham Young presented instructions at Winter Quarters for the westward trek, including patterns for organizing the wagon companies (See D&C 136).

March 3 — *Congress passed an act providing for adhesive postage stamps.*

April 7 — The first pioneer company, numbering 143 men, 3 women and 2 children, left

150 YEARS AGO: 1845-1846

1845

January — The Illinois Legislature repealed the city charter of Nauvoo.

April 14 — A wall was started around the Nauvoo Temple Block.

May — The nine accused murderers of Joseph and Hyrum Smith were acquitted upon instructions of the court.

May 18 — The attic story was begun on the Nauvoo Temple.

Fall — A limestone baptismal font replaced temporary wooden font in basement of Nauvoo Temple.

Sept. 9 — Church leaders stated their intent to move to the Rocky Mountains to establish a refuge for the Saints.

Sept. 22 — Citizens at a mass meeting in Quincy, Ill., endorsed a proposal requesting that the Saints leave Illinois as quickly as possible. The Twelve's reply reiterated the Latter-day Saints' intention to move to a remote area and asked for cooperation and an end of molestation in order to prepare for the move early the following summer.

Sept. 23 — *The first U.S. baseball club, the New York Knickerbocker Club, was organized.*

Dec. 10, 1845-Feb. 7, 1846 — Some 5,000 endowments were performed in the Nauvoo Temple.

1846

Jan. 30 — A wind vane in the shape of an angel was put on the tower of the Nauvoo Temple.

Feb. 4 — The Mormon migration from Nauvoo began. The same day, the ship *Brooklyn* left New York for California under the direction of Samuel Brannan.

April 24 — A temporary settlement of the westward-moving Saints was established at Garden Grove, Iowa. Other permanent camps were established at Mount Pisgah, Iowa, on May 18; at Council Bluffs, Iowa, on June 14; and at Winter Quarters, Neb., in September.

May 1 — The Nauvoo Temple was dedicated by Apostle Orson Hyde in public services.

Mid-June — Brigham Young and advance vanguard reached the Missouri River at Council Bluffs, Iowa Territory.

July 7 — *Annexation of California was proclaimed by the United States after the surrender of Mexico in the Mexican War.*

July 13 — The first of the volunteer companies of the Mormon Battalion was enlisted in response to a request delivered to Brigham Young two weeks earlier by Capt. James Allen of the United States Army. The battalion left for Fort Leavenworth on July 20, and arrived in San Diego, Calif., on Jan. 29, 1847.

August — *The Donner party blazed a trail from Henefer to Salt Lake Valley that was used the following summer by Brigham Young's party. The delay to build the road cost the Donner party 42 lives when they became snowbound in the Sierra Nevada.*

Sept. 17 — The remaining Saints in Nauvoo were driven from the city in violation of a "treaty of surrender" worked out with a citizens' committee from Quincy, Ill. The siege became known as the Battle of Nauvoo.

Winter Quarters under the leadership of Brigham Young.

July 22-24 — Brigham Young's pioneer company arrived in the Great Salt Lake Valley to select a settlement site for the Saints. Eleven companies arrived in the valley in 1847.

July 28 — Brigham Young selected a site for the Salt Lake Temple and instructed surveyors to lay out a city on a grid pattern square with the compass.

Dec. 5 — The First Presidency was reorganized by the Quorum of the Twelve in Kanesville, Iowa, with Brigham Young sustained as president, and Heber C. Kimball and Willard Richards as counselors. The action was ratified in a conference in Kanesville three weeks later.

1848

Jan. 24 — Gold was discovered in Sutter's millrace in California, which was dug up by members of the Mormon Battalion.

Feb. 2 — *The Treaty of Guadalupe Hidalgo ended the war between Mexico and the United States that had begun in 1846. By terms of the treaty, Mexico gave up what are now the states of California, Nevada, Utah, most of Arizona, and parts of New Mexico, Colorado and Wyoming, and relinquished all rights to Texas north of the Rio Grande.*

May — Millions of crickets descended into Salt Lake Valley and devoured the crops of the Pioneers. The "miracle of the sea gulls" saved what was left of the crops by devouring the crickets.

1849

March 3 — *Congress authorized coinage of the gold dollar and $20 gold piece (double eagle).*

March 5 — A provisional State of Deseret was established and appeals made for self-government.

October — A Perpetual Emigrating Fund was established during general conference to assist the poor. The system, which was incorporated one year later, continued until it was disincorporated by the Edmunds-Tucker Act in 1887.

Dec. 9 — The Sunday School was started by Richard Ballantyne in Salt Lake City. George Q. Cannon became the first general superintendent in November 1867.

1850

Missionary work took on a wider scope as missions were opened overseas in Scandinavia, France, Italy, Switzerland and Hawaii; most were discontinued after a few years.

June 15 — The first edition of the *Deseret News* was published in Salt Lake City.

September — Brigham Young was appointed governor of the Territory of Utah.

Sept. 18 — *The U.S. Congress passed the Fugitive Slave Act, permitting slave owners to reclaim slaves who had escaped into other states.*

1851

The Book of Mormon was published in Danish, the first language other than English in which the book was printed.

March 24 — A company of 500 settlers bound for California departed from Payson, Utah. The group settled in San Bernardino, Calif., which became the first Mormon colony outside the Great Basin since the arrival of the pioneers in 1847.

Aug. 12 — *Isaac Singer was granted a patent for his sewing machine. Singer set up business in Boston with $40 capital.*

September — Three federally appointed officials, Judge Lemuel C. Brandebury, Judge Perry C. Brochus and Secretary Broughton D. Harris left Utah in protest against plural marriage, as well as what they considered unjustified influence of the Church in political affairs in the territory.

1852

March 20 — *Harriet Beecher Stowe's influential novel about slavery, "Uncle Tom's Cabin," was published.*

Aug. 28-29 — At a special conference in Salt Lake City, the doctrine of plural marriage was first publicly announced, although several of the leading brethren of the Church had been practicing the principle privately since it had been taught to them by Joseph Smith in Nauvoo.

1853

April 6 — The cornerstones were laid for the Salt Lake Temple.

June 29 — *The U.S. Senate ratified the $10 million Gadsden Purchase from Mexico, which completed the modern geographical configuration of the United States.*

July 18 — The so-called Walker War began near Payson, Utah. This was one of several incidents of tension between Mormons and Indians in Utah territory. The war ended in May 1854.

1854

Jan. 19 — The official announcement adopting the Deseret Alphabet was made in the *Deseret News.*

May 26 — *The Kansas-Nebraska bill passed, giving territories or states freedom of choice on the question of slavery.*

1855

Feb. 17 — *Congress authorized construction of a telegraph line from the Mississippi River to the Pacific.*

May 5 — The Endowment House in Salt Lake City was dedicated.

July 23 — The foundation of the Salt Lake Temple was finished.

Oct. 29 — In a general epistle, the First Presidency proposed that Perpetual Emigration Fund immigrants cross the plains by handcart.

1856

During this year a general "reformation" took place throughout the Church, in which Church members were admonished forcefully from the pulpit to reform their lives and rededicate themselves to the service of the Lord. As a symbol of renewed dedication, many members renewed their covenants by rebaptism. The reformation movement continued into 1857.

Feb. 10 — *An important change in U.S. citizenship laws provided that all children born abroad to U.S. citizens were assured of citizenship.*

June 9 — The first handcart company left Iowa City, Iowa. Later that year two handcart companies, captained by James G. Willie and Edward Martin, suffered tragedy due to an early winter. More than 200 in the two companies died along the trail.

1857

March 6 — *The U.S. Supreme Court handed down its landmark ruling that a slave, Dred Scott, could not sue in federal court for his freedom.*

March 30 — Territorial Judge W.W. Drummond, who had earlier left the Territory of Utah, wrote a letter to the attorney general of the United States, charging Mormon leaders with various crimes.

May 13 — Elder Parley P. Pratt of the Council of the Twelve was assassinated while on a mission in Arkansas.

May 28 — Under instructions from President James Buchanan, the United States War Department issued orders for an army to assemble at Fort Leavenworth, Kan., to march to Utah. It was assumed that the people of Utah were in rebellion against the United States. This was the beginning of the so-called "Utah War."

July 24 — While participating in the 10th anniversary celebration in Big Cottonwood Canyon of the arrival of the Pioneers, Brigham Young received word that the army, under the command of Gen. Albert S. Johnston, was approaching Utah.

Sept. 7 — The Mountain Meadows Massacre took place, in which Arkansas immigrants on their way to California were killed by a group of misguided Mormons in Southern Utah. Twenty years later, John D. Lee was executed for his part in the crime.

Sept. 15 — Brigham Young declared Utah to be under martial law and forbade the approaching troops to enter the Salt Lake Valley. An armed militia was ordered to go to various points to harass the soldiers and prevent their entry. Brigham Young also called the elders home from foreign missions and advised the Saints in many outlying settlements to return to places nearer the headquarters of the Church.

1858

June 26 — After having been stopped for the winter by the delaying tactics of the Mormons, Gen. Johnston's army finally entered the Salt Lake Valley, but peacefully. The army's permanent encampment, until 1861, was at Camp Floyd in Cedar Valley in Utah County. Meanwhile, most of the Saints north of Utah County had moved south, but they returned to their homes when peace seemed assured.

Aug. 5 — *The first trans-Atlantic cable was completed.*

1859

July 13 — Horace Greeley, founder and editor of the *New York Tribune*, had a two-hour interview with Brigham Young, covering a variety of subjects from infant baptism to plurality of wives. The substance of his interview was published a year later in his *Overland Journey From New York to San Francisco.*

Aug. 27 — *The first oil well in the United States was drilled near Titusville, Pa.*

1860

April 3 — *The Pony Express mail service began.*

Sept. 24 — The last of 10 groups of Saints to cross the plains by handcarts entered Salt Lake City.

1861

April 12 — *The Civil War began, as Confederate forces fired on Ft. Sumter in South Carolina.*

April 23 — The first of several Church wagon trains left the Salt Lake Valley with provisions for incoming Saints, whom they would meet at the Missouri River. This was the beginning of a new program to help immigrating Saints that lasted until the railroad came in 1869.

Oct. 1 — The first baptisms in the Netherlands took place near the village of Broek-Akkerwoude in the northern province of Friesland. A monument marking the site was erected in 1936.

1862

March 6 — The Salt Lake Theater, which became an important cultural center for Mormon people in the area, was dedicated. It was opened to the public two days later.

May 20 — *The Homestead Act, granting free family farms to settlers, was passed.*

July 8 — A federal law was passed defining plural marriage as bigamy and declaring it a crime. Mormons considered the law unconstitutional and refused to honor it.

1863

March 10 — President Brigham Young was arrested on a charge of bigamy and placed under a $2,000 bond by Judge Kinney. He was never brought to trial, however.

April 14: *A continuous roll printing press was patented, the first press to print both sides of a sheet.*

1864

April 5 — A small group of Saints bound for Utah sailed form Port Elizabeth, South Africa. Five days later another group set sail for Utah from South Africa.

1865

A war with the Indians in central Utah, known as the Black Hawk War, began. It lasted until 1867.

Feb. 1 — *Abraham Lincoln signed the document abolishing the institution of slavery in the United States. After ratification by 27 states, the necessary three-fourths, the measure became the 13th Amendment to the Constitution on Dec. 18, 1865.*

April 10 — In a special conference, the Church agreed to build a telegraph line connecting the settlements in Utah. The line was completed in 1867.

April 14 — *U.S. President Abraham Lincoln was assassinated by John Wilkes Booth in Ford's Theatre in Washington, D.C., while watching a performance of "Our American Cousin."*

1866

Jan. 1 — The first edition of the *Juvenile Instructor*, the official organ of the Sunday School, was published. Its name was changed to the *Instructor* in 1930, and it continued publication until 1970.

July 27 — *The first permanent transatlantic cable between the United States and Great Britain was completed.*

1867

July 1 — *The Dominion of Canada was created.*

Oct. 6 — The first conference to be conducted in the newly completed Tabernacle on Temple Square in Salt Lake City began. The building was dedicated eight years later on Oct. 4, 1875.

Dec. 8 — Brigham Young requested that bishops reorganize Relief Societies within their wards. The societies had been disbanded during the Utah War.

1868

Jan. 29 — The name Great Salt Lake City was changed to simply Salt Lake City.

May 26 — *President Andrew Johnson was acquitted of impeachment charges by one vote. Johnson had been accused of "high crimes and misdemeanors."*

1869

March 1 — ZCMI opened for business. The Church-owned institution was the forerunner of several cooperative business ventures in Utah territory.

May 10 — The transcontinental railroad was completed with the joining of the rails at Promontory Summit, Utah. The railroad had great impact in immigration policy and on the general economy of the Church in Utah.

Nov. 17 — *The Suez Canal, linking the Mediterranean Sea and the Red Sea, was opened.*

Nov. 28 — The Young Ladies' Retrenchment Association, later renamed the Young Women's Mutual Improvement Association, was organized by Brigham Young in the Lion House in Salt Lake City. The first president, called June 19, 1880, was Elmina Shepherd Taylor. This was the forerunner of today's Young Women.

1870

Jan. 13 — A large mass meeting was held by the women of Salt Lake City in protest against certain anti-Mormon legislation pending in Congress. This and other such meetings demonstrated that, contrary to anti-Mormon claims, Mormon women were not antagonistic to the ecclesiastical power structure in Utah.

February — The "Liberal Party" was formed, which generally came to represent the anti-Mormon political interests, as opposed to the "People's Party," which generally represented Church interests until the end of the century.

Feb. 12 — An act of the Territorial Legislature giving the elective franchise to the women of Utah was signed into law. Utah became one of the first American states or territories to grant woman's suffrage.

July 24 — *The first railroad car from the Pacific Coast reached New York City, opening the way for transcontinental train service.*

1871

February — Judge James B. McKean, who had arrived in Utah in August 1870, made several rulings regarding naturalization that began a bitter and antagonistic relationship between himself and Church members.

Oct. 2 — President Brigham Young was arrested on a charge of unlawful cohabitation. Various legal proceedings in the court of Judge James B. McKean lasted until April 25, 1872, during which time President Young was sometimes kept in custody in his own home. The case was dropped, however, due to a U.S. Supreme Court decision that overturned various judicial proceedings in Utah for the previous 18 months.

Oct. 8 — *Fire broke out in Patrick O'Leary's*

barn, which later became known as the Chicago fire, and before the blaze was put out 27 hours later, 300 persons died, 18,000 buildings were destroyed and 90,000 were left homeless.

1872

June — The first edition of the *Woman's Exponent*, a paper owned and edited by Mormon women, was published. This periodical continued until 1914.

Nov. 5 — *Susan B. Anthony was fined $100 for voting in the presidential election, because women didn't then have the right to vote.*

1873

April 6 — Due to failing health, President Brigham Young called five additional counselors in the First Presidency.

1874

May 8 — *Massachusetts enacted the first effective 10-hour day law for women.*

May 9 — At general conference, which began on this date, the principal subject discussed was the "United Order." This resulted in the establishment of several cooperative economic ventures, the most notable of which were communities such as Orderville, Utah, where the residents owned no private property but held all property in common.

June 23 — The so-called Poland Bill became a federal law. It had the effect of limiting the jurisdiction of probate courts in Utah. These courts had been authorized to conduct all civil and criminal cases and were generally favorable toward members of the Church, but now Mormons accused of crimes had to be tried in federal courts.

1875

March 18 — Judge James B. McKean, with whom the Mormons had been unhappy, was removed from office by U.S. President Ulysses S. Grant.

May 19 — *The first Kentucky Derby was run at Louisville, Ky.*

June 10 — The first Young Men's Mutual Improvement Association was organized in the Thirteenth Ward in Salt Lake City. On Dec. 8, 1876, a central committee was formed to coordinate all such associations. Junius F. Wells was the first superintendent. This was the forerunner of today's Young Men organization.

Oct. 16 — Brigham Young Academy, later to become Brigham Young University, was founded in Provo, Utah.

1876

March 7 — *The patent was issued for Alexander Graham Bell's telephone.*

March 23 — Advance companies of Saints from Utah, who were called to settle in Arizona, arrived at the Little Colorado. This was the beginning of Mormon colonization in Arizona.

1877

April 6 — The St. George Temple was dedicated by President Daniel H. Wells in connection with the 47th Annual Conference of the Church that was held in St. George. This was the first temple to be completed in Utah. The lower portion of the temple had been dedicated earlier, on Jan. 1, 1877, and ordinances for the dead had commenced.

April 24 — *Northern post-Civil War rule in the South ended as federal troops were removed from New Orleans.*

Aug. 29 — President Brigham Young died at his home in Salt Lake City at age 76.

Sept. 4 — The Council of the Twelve, with John Taylor as president, publicly assumed its position as the head of the Church.

1878

May 19 — The Church had previously provided for the purchase of land in Conejos County, Colo., for settlements of Saints from the Southern states. On this date the first settlers arrived, thus opening Mormon settlements in Colorado.

Aug. 25 — The Primary, founded by Aurelia Rogers, held its first meeting at Farmington, Utah. The movement spread rapidly and on June 19, 1880, a Churchwide organization was established, with Louie B. Felt as the first president.

Dec. 1 — *The first telephone was installed in the White House.*

1879

Jan. 6 — The Supreme Court of the United States, in the important Reynolds case, upheld the previous conviction of George Reynolds under the 1862 anti-bigamy law. With the ruling, the court paved the way for more intense and effective prosecution of the Mormons in the 1880s.

Oct. 4 — The first edition of the *Contributor*, which became the official publication of the Young Men's Mutual Improvement Association, was issued. It was published until 1896.

Oct. 21 — *Thomas Edison tested an electric incandescent light bulb in Menlo Park, N.J., that burned for 13½ hours, marking the beginning of a new era of electric lighting.*

1880

April 6 — At general conference, a special jubilee year celebration was inaugurated. Charitable actions, reminiscent of Old Testament jubilee celebrations, included rescinding half the debt owed to the Perpetual Emigration Fund Company, distribution of cows and sheep among the needy and advice to the Saints to forgive the worthy poor of their debts.

Oct. 10 — The First Presidency was reorganized and John Taylor was sustained as third president of the Church, with George Q. Cannon and Joseph F. Smith as counselors.

Dec. 20 — *One mile of Broadway Street in New York City was electrically illuminated by arc lighting.*

1881

May 21 — *The American Red Cross was organized, with Clara Barton as president.*

1882

Jan. 8 — The Assembly Hall on Temple Square in Salt Lake City was dedicated.

March 22 — The Edmunds Anti-Polygamy bill became law when U.S. President Chester A. Arthur added his approval to that of the Senate and House of Representatives. The law defined polygamous living as "unlawful cohabitation" and made punishable the contracting of plural marriage as well as disenfranchisement of those who continued to live it. Serious prosecution under this law began in 1884.

July 17 — The Deseret Hospital, the second hospital in Utah and the first Church hospital, was opened by the Relief Society in Salt Lake City.

Aug. 18 — The Utah Commission, authorized in the Edmunds law, arrived in the territory. The five members of the commission, appointed by the U.S. president, had responsibility of supervising election procedures in Utah. Since the result of its activities was to enforce the disfranchisement of much of the Mormon population, Church members considered its work unfair.

Sept. 30 — *The first hydroelectric power station in the United States was opened at Appleton, Wis.*

1883

January — *The Pendleton Act established the U.S. Civil Service System.*

June 21 — The Council House, the first public building erected in Salt Lake City, was destroyed by fire. The structure was completed in December 1850 and was designed as a "general council house" for the Church, but was also used by the provisional State of Deseret as a statehouse. It also housed the University of Deseret for a number of years.

Aug. 26 — The first permanent branch of the Church among the Maoris in New Zealand was organized at Papawai, Wairarapa Valley, on the North Island. The first baptism of a Maori in New Zealand was on Oct. 18.

1884

May 1 — *Work began in Chicago on a 10-story building called a "skyscraper."*

May 17 — The Logan Temple, the second temple constructed after the Saints came west, was dedicated by President John Taylor.

June 9 — The building known as the "Cock Pit," in Preston, England, in which the first Mormon missionaries to England held meetings in 1837, tumbled down.

1885

Extensive prosecution under the Edmunds law continued in both Utah and Idaho. Many who practiced polygamy were imprisoned, while others fled into exile, some to Mexico in 1885 and to Canada in 1887. Most of the Church leaders went into hiding, which was referred to as the "underground." Similar conditions continued for the next few years. These years are sometimes called the years of the "Crusade."

Feb. 1 — President John Taylor delivered his last public sermon in the Tabernacle in Salt Lake City. It was also his last appearance in public before he went to the "underground."

Feb. 3 — An Idaho law was approved by the governor that prohibited all Mormons from voting through the device of a "test oath." The Idaho "test oath" was upheld five years later by the U.S. Supreme Court on Feb. 3, 1890.

Feb. 21: *The 555-feet high Washington Monument was dedicated 37 years after the cornerstone was laid.*

March 22 — The U.S. Supreme Court annulled the "test oath" formulated by the Utah Commission, thus restoring the right to vote to a number of Saints in the territory.

May 13 — A delegation, appointed by a mass meeting held in the Tabernacle in Salt Lake City on May 2, met with U.S. President Grover Cleveland in the White House in Washington D.C. They presented to the president a "Statement of Grievances and Protest" concerning injustices brought about because of the Edmunds law.

1886

Jan. 31 — The first Church meeting was held in the first meetinghouse built in Mexico on the Piedras Verdes River in a settlement named Colonia Juarez.

March 6 — A mass meeting of 2,000 LDS women assembled in the Salt Lake Theater to protest the abuse heaped upon them by the federal courts and to protest the loss of their vote.

Oct. 28 — *The Statue of Liberty, a gift from the French people symbolizing the friendship between the United States and France, was dedicated in New York Harbor.*

1887

Feb. 17-18 — The Edmunds-Tucker Act passed Congress, and it became law without the signature of the U.S. president, Grover Cleveland. Among other stringent provisions, the law disincorporated the Church, dissolved the Perpetual Emigration Fund Company and escheated its property to the government, abolished female suffrage and provided for the confiscation of practically all the property of the Church.

June 3 — Charles O. Card, leading a contingent of eight families, pitched camp on Lee's Creek in southern Alberta, marking the beginning of the Mormon colonies in Canada. Under instructions from President John Taylor, a gathering place for Latter-day Saints in Canada was selected, and on June 17 a site was chosen for what later became Cardston.

July 25 — President John Taylor died while in "exile" at Kaysville, Utah, at age 78. The Quorum of Twelve Apostles assumed leadership of the Church until 1889.

July 30 — Under provisions of the Edmunds-Tucker Act, suits were filed against the Church and the Perpetual Emigration Fund Company, and Church property was confiscated. A receiver for the property was appointed in November 1887, but the government allowed the Church to rent and occupy certain offices and the temple block.

Aug. 31 — *Thomas A. Edison was awarded a patent for a device he called a "kinetoscope," used to produce pictures representing objects in motion.*

1888

March 11 — *More than 400 people died as a snowstorm crippled the eastern United States during the legendary "Blizzard of '88," the most noted snowstorm in U.S. history.*

May 17 — The Manti Temple was dedicated in a private service by President Wilford Woodruff; a public service was held May 21.

June 8 — The Church General Board of Education sent a letter instructing each stake to establish an academy for secondary education. From 1888 to 1909, 35 academies were established in Utah, Idaho, Wyoming, Arizona, Mexico and Canada. The academy in Rexburg, Idaho, later became Ricks College.

June 21 — The first authorized missionary, Elder Joseph Dean, accompanied by his wife, arrived on the island of Anunu'u in Samoa.

1889

April 6 — The first Relief Society general conference was held in the Assembly Hall in Salt Lake City. Twenty stakes were represented.

April 7 — Wilford Woodruff was sustained fourth president of the Church, with George Q. Cannon and Joseph F. Smith as counselors.

May 6 — *The Eiffel Tower in Paris was officially opened.*

October — The *Young Women's Journal*, official organ of the Young Ladies' Mutual Improvement Association, began publication. It was merged with the *Improvement Era* in 1929.

November — The Endowment House in Salt Lake City was torn down.

1890

Sept. 24 — President Wilford Woodruff issued a "Manifesto," now included in the Doctrine and Covenants as "Official Declaration - 1," that declared that no new plural marriages had been entered into with Church approval in the past year, denied that plural marriage had been taught during that time, declared the intent of the president of the Church to submit to the constitutional law of the land and advised members of the Church to refrain from contracting any marriage forbidden by law.

Oct. 6 — The "Manifesto" was unanimously accepted by vote in the general conference of the Church. This marked the beginning of reconciliation between the Church and the United States, which effectively paved the way to statehood for Utah a little more than five years later.

Oct. 25 — The First Presidency sent a letter to stake presidents and bishops directing that a week-day religious education program be established in every ward where there was not a Church school. It was recommended that classes be taught, under the direction of the Church's General Board of Education, after school hours or on Saturdays .

Dec. 31 — *Ellis Island in New York Harbor was opened as an immigration depot.*

1891

March — At the first triennial meeting of the National Council of Women of the United States, the Relief Society attended and became a charter member of that council.

1892

Jan. 4 — The new Brigham Young Academy building at Provo, Utah, was dedicated.

April 19 — *Three million acres of Cheyenne and Arapaho lands in Oklahoma were opened for settlement by presidential proclamation.*

Oct. 12 — Articles of incorporation for the Relief Society were filed, after which it became known as the National Women's Relief Society. The name was again changed in 1945 to Relief Society of The Church of Jesus Christ of Latter-day Saints.

1893

Jan. 4 — The President of the United States, Benjamin Harrison, issued a proclamation of amnesty to all polygamists who had entered into that relationship before Nov. 1, 1890. The Utah Commission soon ruled that voting restrictions in the territory should be removed.

April 6 — The Salt Lake Temple was dedicated by President Wilford Woodruff. The dedicatory services were repeated almost daily until April 24 with a total of 31 services held.

May 23 — The first ordinance work, baptism for the dead, was performed in the Salt Lake Temple. On May 24, the first endowment work and sealings were performed.

June 27 — *The stock market crashed, resulting in four years of economic depression.*

Sept. 8 — The Salt Lake Tabernacle Choir, while competing in the choral contest at the Chicago World's Fair won second prize, ($1,000). While on this tour, the choir also held concerts at Denver, Colo.; and Independence, Kansas City and St. Louis in Missouri; and Omaha, Neb. The First Presidency, consisting of Wilford Woodruff, George Q. Cannon and Joseph F. Smith, accompanied the Choir.

Oct. 25 — President Grover Cleveland signed a resolution, passed by Congress, for the return of the personal property of the Church. Three years later, on March 28, 1896, a memorial passed by Congress and approved by the president provided for the restoration of the Church's real estate.

1894

January — *The railroad age continued with railroad building by far the nation's single largest economic enterprise.*

April — President Wilford Woodruff announced in General Conference that he had received a revelation that ended the law of adoption. The law of adoption was the custom of being sealed to prominent Church leaders instead of direct ancestors. He re-emphasized the need for genealogical research and sealings along natural family lines. With the termination of this type of sealings, genealogical work to trace the direct

---

100 years ago: 1895-1896

1895

March 4 — The Utah Constitutional Convention met in Salt Lake City. John Henry Smith, a member of the Council of the Twelve, was elected president of that convention.

Nov. 5 — By a vote of 31,305 to 7,687, the people of Utah ratified the constitution and approved statehood. The documents were later hand-delivered to President Grover Cleveland.

Nov. 28 — *The first automobile race in the U.S. took place from the heart of Chicago to its suburbs, 54 miles at 7½ miles an hour.*

1896

Jan. 4 — President Grover Cleveland signed the proclamation that admitted Utah to the Union as the 45th state. Up to statehood, the affairs of the Church in the Utah territory had been closely associated with the affairs of the civil government. With statehood and the rights of self-government secured to the people, the Church could become separate from political struggles.

Aug. 12 — *Gold was discovered in Alaska on the Klondike River, sparking the second great gold rush in U.S. history.*

Nov. 5 — The First Presidency issued a formal letter of instruction directing that the first Sunday in each month be observed as fast day, rather than the first Thursday, which had been observed as fast day since the early days of the Church in the Utah territory.

ancestry increased among the members of the Church.

July 14 — President Grover Cleveland signed an act that provided for statehood for Utah. This culminated 47 years of effort on the part of Mormons in Utah to achieve this status.

Aug. 27 — President Grover Cleveland issued a proclamation granting pardons and restoring civil rights to those who had been disfranchised under anti-polygamy laws.

Nov. 13 — The genealogical society of the Church, known as the Genealogical Society of Utah, was organized.

1897

July 5 — *Soft coal miners, as ordered by the United Mine Workers, went on strike, eventually winning an 8-hour day and abolition of the company store.*

July 20-25 — The Jubilee anniversary of the arrival of the Pioneers into the Salt Lake Valley was held in Salt Lake City for six days. The celebration began with the dedication by President Wilford Woodruff of the Brigham Young Monument at the intersection of Main and South Temple streets on July 20, and ended with a celebration for the Pioneers in the Tabernacle on July 24 and memorial services honoring all deceased Pioneers on July 25.

November — The *Improvement Era* began publication as the official organ of the Young Men's Mutual Improvement Association. Other Church organizations later joined in sponsoring the monthly magazine, which continued as the official voice of the Church until 1970. It was replaced by the *Ensign* magazine.

1898

April 24 — *Spain declared war on the United States, and the Spanish-American War began. The war formally ended on Feb. 10, 1899.*

April 28 — A First Presidency statement encouraged Latter-day Saint youths to support the American War effort in the Spanish-American War. This placed the Church firmly on the side of the war declarations of constituted governments and ended a policy of selective pacifism.

Sept. 2 — President Wilford Woodruff died at age 91 in San Francisco, Calif., where he had gone to seek relief from his asthma problems.

Sept. 13 — Lorenzo Snow became fifth president of the Church. He chose George Q. Cannon and Joseph F. Smith as counselors. Both had served as counselors to President John Taylor and President Wilford Woodruff.

1899

May 8 — President Lorenzo Snow announced a renewed emphasis concerning the payment of tithing, which members had been neglecting for some time, at a conference in St. George, Utah. "The time has now come for every Latter-day Saint . . . to do the will of the Lord and pay his tithing in full," President Snow told the conference.

July 2 — A solemn assembly was held in the Salt Lake Temple, attended by the Church's 26 General Authorities and presidencies of the 40 stakes and bishops of the 478 wards of the Church. The solemn assembly accepted the resolution that tithing is the "word and will of the Lord unto us."

Oct. 14 — *The U.S. declared an "Open Door Policy" toward China, opening it as an international market.*

1900

Jan. 8 — President Lorenzo Snow issued an official statement reaffirming the Church ban on polygamy.

Jan. 25 — The U.S. House of Representatives voted to deny Utahn B.H. Roberts of the First Council of the Seventy his seat in Congress following an investigation of the right of polygamists to hold office under the Constitution.

Aug. 14 — *Anti-saloon agitator Carry Nation began attacking bars with a hatchet.*

1901

Aug. 12 — Elder Heber J. Grant of the Council of the Twelve dedicated Japan and opened a mission there as a first step in renewed emphasis on preaching the gospel in all the world.

Sept. 6 — *U.S. President William McKinley was shot by Leon Czolgosz; he died eight days later.*

Oct. 10 — President Lorenzo Snow died at his home in the Beehive House in Salt Lake City at age 87.

Oct. 17 — Joseph F. Smith was ordained the sixth president of the Church, with John R. Winder and Anthon H. Lund as counselors.

1902

The Church published in book form the first volume of Joseph Smith's *History of the Church,* edited by B.H. Roberts. Publication continued over the next decade, with a seventh volume added in 1932.

January — The *Children's Friend* began publication as an organ for Primary Association teachers. The magazine later widened its audience to include children, then eliminated the teachers' departments. It was published until 1970 when it was replaced by the *Friend* magazine.

March 6 — *The Bureau of the Census was created by an act of Congress.*

Aug. 4 — The First Council of the Seventy opened a Bureau of Information and Church Literature in a small octagonal booth on Temple Square. It was replaced by a larger building in March 1904 and by the present visitors centers in 1966 and 1978.

1903

Nov. 5 — The Church announced purchase of the Carthage Jail as a historic site.

Dec. 17 — *Orville and Wilbur Wright became the first men to fly when they managed to get their powered airplane off the ground near Kitty Hawk, N.C., for 12 seconds. They made four flights that day, the longest lasting for 59 seconds.*

1904

April 5 — President Joseph F. Smith issued an official statement upholding provisions of the 1890 Manifesto and invoking excommunication against persons violating the "law of the land" by contracting new plural marriages.

July 23 — *The first Olympic games to be held in the U.S. opened as part of the St. Louis, Mo., Exposition.*

1905

Jan. 1 — The Dr. William S. Groves Latter-day Saints Hospital opened in Salt Lake City and was dedicated three days later, the first in the Church hospital system. In 1975, the Church divested itself of its hospitals and turned them over to a private organization.

Sept. 5 — *The Treaty of Portsmouth ended the Russian-Japanese War.*

Oct. 28 — Elders John W. Taylor and Matthias F. Cowley, finding themselves out of harmony with Church policy on plural marriage, submitted resignations from the Council of the Twelve that were announced to the Church April 6, 1906.

Dec. 23 — President Joseph F. Smith dedicated the Joseph Smith Memorial Cottage and Monument at Sharon, Windsor County, Vt., the site of the Prophet's birth 100 years earlier.

1906

The Sunday School introduced a Church-wide parents' class as part of an increased emphasis on the importance of the home and of the parents' role in teaching their children the gospel.

April 18 — *San Francisco was hit by a major earthquake, measuring 8.25 on the Richter scale, which leveled 490 city blocks.*

Summer — President Joseph F. Smith traveled to Europe, the first such visit of a serving president to the area. President Smith also visited Hawaii, Canada and Mexico during his presidency.

1907

Jan. 10 — President Joseph F. Smith announced payment of the last two $500,000 bond issues sold by President Lorenzo Snow in December 1899 to fund the Church debt. The first had been paid in 1903.

February — The United States Senate agreed to seat Utah Sen. Reed Smoot, a member of the Council of the Twelve. The vote culminated a three-year investigation, during which Church officials testified concerning polygamy and Church involvement in politics.

April 5 — A vote of the general conference approved the First Presidency's 16-page summary statement of the Church position in the Smoot hearings.

Aug. 1 — *An aeronautical division, consisting of one officer and two enlisted men, was established by the U.S. Army, the forerunner of the U.S. Air Force.*

1908

April 8 — The First Presidency created a General Priesthood Committee on Outlines, which served until 1922. In fulfillment of its assignment, the committee created definite age groupings for Aaronic Priesthood offices, provided systematic programs for year-round priesthood meetings, and in other ways reformed, reactivated and systematized priesthood work.

Oct. 1 — *Henry Ford introduced his famous Model-T Ford automobile.*

1909

April 6 — *The North Pole was discovered by an expedition led by Robert E. Peary.*

November — The First Presidency issued an official statement on the origin of man.

1910

The Bishop's Building, an office building for the Presiding Bishopric and auxiliary organizations at 50 N. Main St., opened. It was used for more than 50 years.

January — The first issue of the *Utah Genealogical and Historical Magazine* was published. This quarterly publication served as the voice of the Genealogical Society of Utah. It was discontinued in October 1940.

Feb. 8 — *The Boy Scouts of America was*

founded. It was chartered by the U.S. Congress in 1916.

1911

The Church adopted the Boy Scout program and has since become one of the leading sponsors of this movement for young men.

April 15 — *Collier's magazine published a letter from Theodore Roosevelt refuting many charges made against Utah Sen. Reed Smoot and the Church. This action helped defuse an anti-Mormon propaganda surge of 1910-11.*

Dec. 14 — *Norwegian explorer Roald Amundsen became the first man to reach the South Pole.*

1912

Aug. 14 — *The United States sent Marines to Nicaragua, which was in default of loans from the U.S. and Europe.*

Fall — A seminary at Granite High School in Salt Lake City opened, marking the beginning of a released-time weekday education program for young Latter-day Saints. As the seminary program grew, the Church phased out its involvement in academies, which were Church-sponsored high schools or junior colleges. By 1924, only the Juarez Academy in Mexico remained.

Nov. 8 — The First Presidency created a Correlation Committee, headed by Elder David O. McKay, and asked it to coordinate scheduling and prevent unnecessary duplication in programs of Church auxiliaries. A Social Advisory Committee of the General Boards was merged with it in 1920. The combined committee issued a major report April 14, 1921, offering proposals for correlating priesthood and auxiliary activities; many of its recommendations were thereafter adopted.

1913

The Church established the Maori Agricultural College in New Zealand. It was destroyed by an earthquake in 1931 and was never rebuilt.

Feb. 25 — *The 16th Amendment, creating the income tax, became a part of the U.S. Constitution, the first constitutional amendment adopted in the 20th century.*

May 21 — The Boy Scout program was officially adopted by the Young Men's Mutual Improvement Association and became the activity program for boys of the Church.

1914

January — The *Relief Society Magazine* appeared as a monthly publication containing lesson material for use in the women's auxil-

iary of the Church. The magazine carried stories, poetry, articles, homemaking helps, news and lesson material until it ceased publication in December 1970, when the *Ensign* magazine became the magazine for adults in the Church.

The Relief Society also introduced its first uniform courses of study, organized around four general themes. The pattern was altered in 1921 to include theology, work and business meetings, literature and social service.

Aug. 15 — *The Panama Canal, connecting the Atlantic Ocean to the Pacific, was officially opened. Twelve days before, on Aug. 3, an ocean steamer, the SS Acon, passed through the canal.*

1915

May 7 — *A German submarine sank the British liner Lusitania, enroute from New York to Liverpool, off the coast of Iceland, killing 1,198 persons.*

September — James E. Talmage's influential book *Jesus the Christ* was published.

1916

Feb. 21 — *The longest and bloodiest battle of World War I, the Battle of Verdun, began in France, resulting in the death of 1 million soldiers.*

June 30 — The First Presidency and Council of the Twelve issued a doctrinal exposition clarifying the use of the title "Father" as it is applied to Jesus Christ.

1917

Oct. 2 — The Church Administration Building at 47 E. South Temple was completed.

Nov. 7 — *Nikolai Lenin and the Bolsheviks overthrew the Kerensky regime in Russia.*

1918

May — Wheat that Relief Society sisters had been gathering and storing since 1876 was sold to the U.S. government at a government price, with approval of the First Presidency and the Presiding Bishopric, to alleviate shortages during World War I.

Oct. 3 — While contemplating the meaning of Christ's atonement, President Joseph F. Smith received a manifestation on the salvation of the dead and the visit of the Savior to the world of spirits after His crucifixion. A report of the experience was published in December and was added to the Doctrine and Covenants June 6, 1979, as Section 138.

Nov. 11 — *World War I ended, as the Allies signed an armistice with Germany.*

Nov. 19 — President Joseph F. Smith died six days after his 80th birthday. Because of an epidemic of influenza, no public funeral was held for the Church president.

Nov. 23 — Heber J. Grant was sustained and set apart as the seventh president of the Church during a meeting of the Twelve in the Salt Lake Temple. He selected Anthon H. Lund and Charles W. Penrose as counselors.

1919

January — The 18th Amendment to the United States Constitution established prohibition. Church leaders supported the movement toward nationwide prohibition and opposed the amendment's repeal in 1933.

April — The April general conference of the Church was postponed due to the nationwide influenza epidemic. The conference was held June 1-3.

May 27 — *The first transatlantic flight (with two stopovers) was completed by a U.S. Navy seaplane.*

Nov. 27 — President Heber J. Grant dedicated the temple at Laie, Hawaii, the first Latter-day Saint temple outside the continental United States. Construction had begun soon after the site was dedicated in June 1915.

1920

Jan. 10 — *The League of Nations, the first permanent international body encompassing many of the nations of the world, was established as the World War I Treaty of Versailles went into effect.*

1920-1921

Elder David O. McKay of the Council of the Twelve and President Hugh J. Cannon of the Liberty Stake in Salt Lake City traveled 55,896 miles in a world survey of Church missions for the First Presidency. The pair visited the Saints in the Pacific Islands, New Zealand, Australia and Asia, and then made stops in India, Egypt and Palestine, before visiting the missions of Europe.

1921

The M-Men and Gleaner departments in the MIA were introduced Churchwide to serve the special needs of young people from ages 17 to 23.

Oct. 5 — *The World Series was broadcast on radio for the first time.*

1922

May — The Primary Children's Hospital opened in Salt Lake City.

Nov. 26 — *King Tutankhamen's tomb was opened in Egypt.*

1923

The Church purchased a part of the Hill Cumorah. Additional acquisitions in 1928 gave the Church possession of the entire hill

and adjacent lands.

Aug. 26 — President Heber J. Grant dedicated the Alberta Temple, in Cardston, Alberta, which had been under construction for nearly a decade.

Sept. 29 — *Britain began to rule Palestine under a mandate from the League of Nations.*

1924

March 21 — A First Presidency statement answered criticism of unauthorized plural marriages by once again confirming the Church's policy against the practice. Polygamist cliques within the Church were excommunicated when discovered.

June 2 — *The U.S. Congress granted citizenship to all American Indians.*

Oct. 3 — Radio broadcast of general conference began on KSL, the Church-owned station. Coverage was expanded into Idaho in 1941.

1925

July 24 — *In the famous "Scopes Monkey Trial," John T. Scopes, a Tennessee school teacher, was found guilty of teaching evolution in a public school.*

Dec. 6 — Elder Melvin J. Ballard of the Council of the Twelve established a mission in South America with headquarters in Buenos Aires, Argentina, opening the Church's official work in South America.

1926

Weekday religious education was expanded to include college students with the building of the first institute of religion adjacent to the University of Idaho at Moscow.

May 9 — *Richard Byrd and Floyd Bennett became the first men to make an airplane flight over the North Pole.*

1927

May 21 — *Charles Lindbergh, aboard his "Spirit of St. Louis" monoplane, completed the first transatlantic solo flight from New York City to Paris, a distance of 3,610 miles, in 33½ hours.*

Oct. 23 — President Heber J. Grant dedicated the Arizona Temple at Mesa, completing a project begun six years before.

1928

The YMMIA introduced a Vanguard program for 15- and 16-year-old boys. After the National Boy Scout organization created the Explorer program in 1933, patterned in part after the Vanguards, the Church adopted Explorer Scouting.

January — Priesthood quorums began

meeting during the Sunday School hour for gospel instruction under a correlated experiment lasting 10 years. This priesthood Sunday School experiment included classes for all age groups, with Tuesday evening reserved as an activity night for both priesthood and young women.

May 11 — *The first regularly scheduled television programs were begun by Station WGY in Schenectady, N.Y.*

1929

July 15 — The Tabernacle Choir started a weekly network radio broadcast on NBC. Richard L. Evans joined the program with his sermonettes in June 1930. "Music and the Spoken Word" eventually switched with KSL Radio to the CBS network and has since become one of the longest continuing programs in broadcasting history.

Oct. 29 — *The New York Stock Market collapsed in frantic trading, a dramatic beginning of the Great Depression.*

1930

April 6 — The centennial of the Church's organization was observed at general conference in the Tabernacle in Salt Lake City. B.H. Roberts prepared his *Comprehensive History of The Church of Jesus Christ of Latter-day Saints* as a centennial memorial.

July 21 — *The U.S. Veterans Administration was established.*

1931

March 21 — A 10-reel film of the history of the Church was completed.

April 6 — The first edition of the *Church News* was printed by the Church's *Deseret News.*

May 1 — *The Empire State Building was opened in New York City.*

June — The Church Music Committee outlined a proposal to have better choirs in every ward and stake in the Church.

1932

Jan. 10 — The first missionary training classes began, which were to be organized in every ward throughout the Church.

February — The Lion House, home of Brigham Young and a noted landmark of Salt Lake City, was turned over to the Young Ladies Mutual Improvement Association by the Church for a social center for women and young ladies. The Beehive House was previously placed under the direction of the YLMIA as a girls' home.

April 2 — A campaign against the use of tobacco was launched by the Church.

May 12 — *Charles Lindbergh Jr., kid-napped on March 1, was found dead.*

May 15 — Utah Gov. George H. Dern proclaimed a special fast day in the depths of the Great Depression to gather funds for the poor.

June 12 — A marker at the site of the "Great Salt Lake Base and Meridian," was dedicated on the southeast corner of Temple Square. Apostle Orson Pratt on Aug. 3, 1847, established the base line from which all government measurements and surveys began for the West.

July 16 — The first of the Mormon Trail markers were unveiled in Henefer, Utah, and Casper, Wyo.

1933

Jan. 30 — *Adolf Hitler was named chancellor of Germany, capping a phenomenal 10-year rise to power. He soon became absolute dictator.*

Feb. 21 — The Church began a six-day commemoration of the 100th anniversary of the Word of Wisdom revelation with special observances in every ward throughout the Church.

June 1 — The Church opened a 500-foot exhibit in the Hall of Religions at the Century of Progress World's Fair in Chicago, Ill. The exhibit was prepared by famed LDS sculptor Avard Fairbanks.

July 26 — The first effort to mark the historic spots in Nauvoo, Ill., was made by the Relief Society when it placed a monument at the site of its organization in 1842 in Joseph Smith's store.

Nov. 5 — The First Presidency and four members of the Council of the Twelve participated in the dedication of the Washington D.C. chapel, which was adorned by a statue of the Angel Moroni atop its 165-foot spire.

1934

The general board of the Sunday School officially recognized the Junior Sunday School, which had been part of some ward programs for many years.

Jan. 17 — New headquarters of the Genealogical Society of Utah, located in the Joseph F. Smith Memorial Building on North Main Street in Salt Lake City, was formally opened. The building previously was part of the campus of the LDS College.

Feb. 3 — Stake seventies were instructed in a letter from the First Council of the Seventy that they have a duty, under the direction of the stake president, to do missionary work in the stakes.

Aug. 2 — *Adolf Hitler took control of Germany after the death of President Paul von Hindenburg.*

1935

Jan. 11 — *American aviatrix, Amelia Earhart, became the first woman to fly over the Pacific, from Hawaii to California.*

Feb. 24 — The YMMIA general superintendency was released to allow the General Authorities serving in those posts more time for other duties. In April, Albert E. Bowen, George Q. Morris and Franklin West were sustained as the new superintendency.

March 3 — First of a series of six "Church of the Air" broadcasts was carried nationwide by the Columbia Broadcasting Co.

July 21 — President Heber J. Grant dedicated the Hill Cumorah Monument near Palmyra, N.Y.

1936

A separate Aaronic Priesthood program for adults, recommended by the General Priesthood Committee on Outlines 20 years earlier, was introduced.

Jan. 29 — *Ty Cobb, Walter Johnson, Christy Mathewson, Babe Ruth and Honus Wagner became the first five men to be elected to the Baseball Hall of Fame.*

April — The Church introduced a formal welfare program to assist needy Church members and those unemployed in emergency situations. Called the Church Security Program at first, it was renamed the Church Welfare Program in 1938 and has continued to expand its services with the addition of local production programs.

Also in April, supervision of stake missions was given to the First Council of the Seventy, and stake missions were soon organized in all stakes. The work had previously been under stake presidency direction.

1937

January — The First Presidency officially adopted the practice widely utilized over several preceding decades of ordaining young men in the Aaronic Priesthood at specific ages. The recommended ages for advancement from deacon to teacher to priest to elder changed from time to time since 1937.

Feb. 20 — A portion of the Nauvoo Temple lot in Nauvoo, Ill., returned to Church ownership when Wilford C. Wood, representing the Church, purchased the property.

April 27 — *The first Social Security payment in the U.S. was made.*

July — The Hill Cumorah pageant, "America's Witness for Christ," began on an outdoor stage on the side of the Hill Cumorah in New York. A Bureau of Information opened at the base of the hill.

Sept. 12 — President Heber J. Grant returned to Salt Lake City after a three-month tour of Europe, where he visited with Church members and missionaries in 11 countries. He dedicated nine meetinghouses and gave some 55 addresses, including the principal address at the British Mission Centennial Conference at Rochdale, England, on Aug. 1.

1938

Aug. 14 — The first Deseret Industries store opened in Salt Lake City to provide work opportunities for the elderly and handicapped. Part of the Welfare Program, a growing network of stores still offers used furniture, clothing, and other items.

Oct. 30 — *Orson Welles' fantasy radio program "War of the Worlds," was so realistic that it caused nationwide panic.*

1939

Feb. 18 — A miniature Salt Lake Tabernacle, with a seating capacity of about 50 persons, was built by the Church for its exhibit at the San Francisco World's Fair. The exhibit attracted 1,400 persons on opening day.

June 19 — Wilford Wood purchased the Liberty Jail in Missouri on behalf of the Church.

Aug. 24 — The First Presidency directed all missionaries in Germany to move to neutral countries. Later the missionaries were instructed to leave Europe and return to the United States. The last group arrived in New York Nov. 6, 1939.

Sept. 1 — *World War II began when Nazi Germany invaded Poland. Britain and France declared war on Germany two days later.*

Oct. 6 — The First Presidency message on world peace was delivered in general conference by President Heber J. Grant.

1940

Jan. 28 — The Mormon Battalion Monument was dedicated in San Diego, Calif.

Sept. 16 — *U.S. President Franklin D. Roosevelt signed the Selective Service Act, setting up the first peacetime military draft in the nation's history.*

1941

The Presiding Bishopric inaugurated a new membership record system. Under the new system, a master record for each member was established in the Presiding Bishopric's Office, eliminating the need for personal membership certificates.

April 6 — In general conference, the First Presidency announced the new position of Assistant to the Twelve, and the first five Assistants were called and sustained.

May — The First Presidency appointed Hugh B. Brown as the Church Army coordinator. His work with the LDS servicemen and military officials led to the development of the Church servicemen's program.

Dec. 7 — *The Japanese bombed Pearl Harbor, killing 2,403 Americans and wounding 1,178. The next day, President Franklin D. Roosevelt asked Congress for a declaration of war against Japan. Four days later, Germany and Italy declared war on the United States, and on the same day the U.S. declared war on the European dictatorships.*

1942

The Girls' Activity Program of the Church was introduced.

Jan. 4 — The Church observed a special Fast Sunday in conjunction with a national day of prayer called by President Franklin D. Roosevelt.

Jan. 17 — The First Presidency asked all general boards and auxiliary organizations to discontinue institutes, conventions and auxiliary stake meetings to help members meet wartime restrictions on travel and to help reduce personal expenses under increased war taxes.

Feb. 28 — It was announced that due to World War II, the Relief Society general conference scheduled for April, which had been planned to commemorate the centennial anniversary of the founding of the Relief Society, along with centennial celebrations in the stakes, would not be held. Rather, celebrations were to be held on the ward and branch level.

March 23 — The First Presidency announced that for the duration of World War II it would call only older men who have been ordained high priests and seventies on full-time missions.

March 23 — *The forced movement of Japanese-Americans from their homes on the U.S. West Coast to inland camps during World War II began.*

April 4-6 — Because of limitations on travel, the annual April general conference was closed to the general Church membership and confined to General Authorities and presidencies of the 141 stakes. The First Presidency on April 5, 1942, closed the Tabernacle for the duration of the war. Conference sessions were held in the Assembly Hall on Temple Square and in the assembly room of the Salt Lake Temple.

April 18 — May Green Hinckley, general president of the Primary Association, announced that the presiding officers of the Primary on all levels would henceforth be known

as "presidents" rather than "superintendents."

July — Church Welfare leaders urged members to plant gardens, to bottle as many fruits and vegetables as they could utilize, and to store coal.

Aug. 17 — *The USS Brigham Young was christened. It was of the Liberty ship class.*

1943

March 7 — The Navajo-Zuni Mission was formed, the first mission designated only for Indians.

May — The Church announced that a pocket-size Church directory had been printed for distribution in the armed forces, along with a pocket-size Book of Mormon and a compilation titled *Principles of the Gospel.*

May 22 — *USS Joseph Smith,* a Liberty class ship, was launched in Richmond, Calif. Ceremonies included a tribute to Joseph Smith and a description of the Church's part in the war effort.

July 24 — The M.I.A. completed a war service project to purchase aircraft rescue boats by purchasing war bonds. The project began May 11 and ended with 87 stakes raising a total of $3.1 million, enough to purchase 52 boats, which cost $60,000 each.

Sept. 9 — *United States troops invaded Italy.*

1944

March — The Church announced the purchase of the Spring Hill in Missouri, known in Church history as Adam-ondi-Ahman. Final deeds for the purchase were dated June 27, 1944, the 100th anniversary of the martyrdom of the Prophet Joseph Smith. The deed to the land was passed on to the Church by Eugene Johnson, whose family had been in possession of the property for a century.

May 15 — A 12-page monthly *Church News* for the 70,000 LDS servicemen was inaugurated by the First Presidency in order to keep more closely in touch with the servicemen. This edition contained inspirational material, vital messages, answers to questions and a summary of important news in the Church.

June 6 — *Allied forces, numbering 130,000 men, invaded Europe at Normandy, France, on "D-Day," and broke the Nazi stranglehold on the Continent and led to the eventual surrender of Germany.*

June 25 — Memorial services were held in each ward to commemorate the 100th anniversary of the martyrdom of the Prophet Joseph Smith and Hyrum Smith. Special services were also held in Carthage Jail on June 27.

50 years ago: 1945-1946

1945

May 14 — President Heber J. Grant died in Salt Lake City at age 88.

May 21 — At a special meeting of the Council of the Twelve in the Salt Lake Temple, the First Presidency was reorganized with George Albert Smith sustained and set apart as the eighth president of the Church. Presidents J. Reuben Clark Jr. and David O. McKay, counselors to President Grant, were called also as counselors to President Smith.

July 16 — The First Presidency authorized monthly priesthood and auxiliary leadership meetings if they could be held without violating government restrictions concerning use of gas and rubber.

September — The First Presidency began calling mission presidents for areas vacated during the war. This process continued through 1946. The sending of missionaries soon followed the appointment of mission presidents. By the end of 1946, 3,000 missionaries were in the field.

Also, the Tabernacle was opened to the general public for the first time since March 1942.

Sept. 2 — *Formal ceremonies of surrender, ending World War II — history's deadliest and most far-reaching conflict — were held aboard the battleship Missouri in Tokyo Bay. Japan had surrendered on Aug. 14, (V-J Day); Germany on May 8 (V-E Day).*

Sept. 23 — The Idaho Falls Temple was dedicated by President George Albert Smith.

Oct. 5-7 — The first general, unrestricted conference of the Church in four years was held in the Tabernacle in Salt Lake City. During World War II, general conferences were limited to general, stake and ward priesthood leaders.

Nov. 3 — President George Albert Smith met with U.S. President Harry S. Truman in the White House and presented the Church's plans to use its welfare facilities to help relieve the suffering of Latter-day Saints in Europe.

1946

January — The Church began sending supplies to the Saints in Europe. This continued for the next several years.

Jan. 7 — *The United Nations General Assembly held its first session in London.*

Feb. 4 — Elder Ezra Taft Benson of the Council of the Twelve left New York for Europe to administer to the physical and spiritual needs of members there. He traveled throughout Europe for most of the year, visiting Saints who had been isolated by the war, distributing Church welfare supplies and setting the branches of the Church in order.

May — President George Albert Smith became the first president of the Church to visit Mexico. While in the country, he met with Manuel Arvilla Camacho, president of Mexico, and presented to him a copy of the Book of Mormon.

May 2 — The First Presidency instructed local Church leaders that in meetings where the the sacrament is passed, it should be passed to the presiding officer first.

December — The Relief Society announced the creation of an enlarged social service and child welfare department.

July — The Church organized the Committee on Publications comprised of General Authorities to supervise the preparation and publication of all Church literature. This committee controlled all auxiliary lessons and all publications published by and for the Church.

November — The name of the Genealogical Society of Utah was changed to the Genealogical Society of The Church of Jesus Christ of Latter-day Saints.

Nov. 28 — Young Women's Mutual Improvement Association celebrated its 75th anniversary. A plaque was dedicated by President Heber J. Grant and placed in the Lion House where the initial organization had taken place.

1947

April 11 — *Jackie Robinson broke baseball's previous all-white color barrier when he began playing for the Brooklyn Dodgers.*

July 24 — Church members celebrated the 100th anniversary of the Pioneers' arrival in Salt Lake Valley.

December — Fast Day was set aside for the relief of those in need of Europe. About $210,000 was collected and then distributed to Europeans of all faiths by an agency not connected with the Church.

Also in December, more than 1 million people visited Temple Square in one year for the first time.

1948

May 14 — *Britain ended its rule in Palestine, and the independent state of Israel was proclaimed.*

June — It was announced that Ricks College in Rexburg, Idaho, would become a four-year college in the 1949-50 school year.

1949

April 5 — At a special welfare meeting held in conjunction with general conference, the Welfare Program was declared a permanent program of the Church.

May 12 — *The Berlin Blockade ended, as the Soviet Union announced reopening of East German land routes.*

October — For the first time, general conference was broadcast publicly over KSL television, although since April 1948 it had been carried by closed-circuit television to other buildings on Temple Square.

Also in October, the centennial conference of the Deseret Sunday School Union was held.

1950

July 1 — The responsibility of the LDS girls' program was transferred from the Presiding Bishopric to the Young Women's Mutual Improvement Association, where it remained until 1974.

September — Early morning seminaries were inaugurated in Southern California. This was the beginning of a movement that spread seminary throughout the Church on an early morning, nonreleased-time basis.

Nov. 8 — *American jets were attacked by North Korean MIGs in the opening days of the Korean War.*

1951

A new edition of the Servicemen's Directory was published. In addition, it was announced that the United States armed forces had authorized the use of special "LDS" identification tags (called "dog tags") for Church members in the service.

March 29 — *Julius Rosenberg and his wife, Ethel, were convicted of wartime espionage. They were executed June 19.*

April 4 — President George Albert Smith died in Salt Lake City at age 81.

April 9 — David O. McKay was sustained as ninth president of the Church, with Stephen L Richards and J. Reuben Clark Jr. as counselors.

July 20 — *Because the Korean War reduced the number of young elders being called as missionaries, the First Presidency issued a call for seventies to help fill the need. Many married men subsequently served full-time missions.*

1952

A Systematic Program for Teaching the Gospel was published for use by the missionaries of the Church. This inaugurated the use of a standard plan of missionary work throughout the Church, although the specific format of the various lessons was modified from time to time after this.

March 2 — The new Primary Children's Hospital in Salt Lake City was dedicated. Half the cost of the building had been raised by children of the Church through the continuing Primary penny drive.

April 5 — The Church began carrying the priesthood session of general conference by direct wire to buildings beyond Temple Square.

June — President David O. McKay took a six-week tour of European missions and branches in Holland, Denmark, Sweden, Norway, Finland, Germany, Switzerland, Wales, Scotland and France. During this trip he announced the selection of Bern, Switzerland, as site of the first European temple.

Oct. 6 — A letter from the Presiding Bishopric introduced a new Senior Aaronic Priesthood program, with men over 21 years of age organized into separate Aaronic Priesthood quorums. Subsequently, special weekday classes were encouraged in each stake to prepare these brethren for the Melchizedek Priesthood and temple ordinances.

Nov. 1 — *The United States announced "satisfactory" experiments in developing the world's first hydrogen bomb.*

Nov. 25 — Elder Ezra Taft Benson of the Council of the Twelve was chosen Secretary of Agriculture by Dwight D. Eisenhower, newly elected president of the United States. Elder Benson served in that capacity for eight years.

Dec. 31 — A letter from the First Presidency announced that the Primary Association had been assigned the duty of establishing the Cub Scout program of the Boy Scouts of America for boys of the Church.

1953

March 25 — The First Presidency announced that returning missionaries would no longer report directly to General Authorities but, rather, to their stake presidency and high council.

May 29 — *Sir Edmund Hillary of New Zea-*

land became the first person to reach the top of Mount Everest.

July 9 — Organization of the United Church School System, with Ernest L. Wilkinson as administrator, was publicly announced.

October — The semiannual conference of the Church was broadcast by television for the first time outside the Intermountain area.

1954

Utahns debated the question of ownership of Dixie, Snow and Weber State Colleges, which had once been owned by the Church. Though the Church expressed a willingness to resume control, and the state was hard-pressed financially to operate them, voters rejected the transfer in a referendum.

Jan. 2 — President David O. McKay left Salt Lake City on a trip to London, England; South Africa; and South and Central America. He returned in mid-February, and at that point had officially visited every existing mission of the Church. He was the first president of the Church to visit the South African Mission.

April 7 — The Church Board of Education announced that Ricks College, which had been a four-year college since 1949-50, would revert back to being a junior college, effective fall semester 1956. The final graduation of a four-year class was Aug. 10, 1956.

May 17 — *The U.S. Supreme Court ruled that racial segregation in public schools was unconstitutional.*

July — The Church announced the inauguration of the Indian Placement Program, whereby Indian students of elementary and secondary age would be placed in foster homes during the school year in order for them to take advantage of better educational opportunities.

July 21 — The First Presidency announced the establishment of the Church College of Hawaii. The college commenced operation Sept. 26, 1955.

Aug. 31 — The First Presidency approved a plan to ordain young men to the office of teacher at age 14 and priest at age 16. The previous ages were 15 and 17.

1955

A special program of missionary work among the Jewish people was organized. It continued until 1959.

January-February — President David O. McKay took a trip covering more than 45,000 miles to the missions of the South Pacific, selected a site for the New Zealand Temple and discussed plans for the building of a Church college in New Zealand.

April 5 — *British Prime Minister Winston Churchill resigned.*

July — The Church Building Committee was organized to supervise the now-vast building program of the Church throughout the world.

August-September — The Tabernacle Choir made a major concert tour of Europe.

Sept. 11 — The Swiss Temple, near Bern, was dedicated by President David O. McKay.

Dec. 27 — A letter from the Presiding Bishopric announced that students at BYU would be organized into campus wards and stakes, commencing Jan. 8, 1956. This move set the pattern for student wards to be organized at Church colleges and institutes of religion wherever their numbers warranted it.

1956

March 11 — President David O. McKay dedicated the Los Angeles Temple.

Oct. 3 — The new Relief Society Building in Salt Lake City was dedicated.

December — A new program for training priesthood leaders was inaugurated. It included quarterly stake priesthood meetings, quarterly leadership meetings and various special leadership sessions in connection with stake conferences.

1957

Ward education committees were organized throughout the Church to encourage and enroll young people in a seminary, organize their transportation and encourage them to attend a Church college or a college with an institute of religion. These committees functioned until 1964, when their duties were transferred to home teachers.

April — The First Presidency announced plans to move Ricks College from Rexburg to Idaho Falls, Idaho. This created much local concern and started a long debate that ended in a reversal of the decision and the announcement on April 26, 1962, of a major expansion program for the Rexburg campus.

July — The Pacific Board of Education was organized to supervise all Church schools in the Pacific area.

October — For the first time in the history of the Church, the semiannual general conference was canceled due to a flu epidemic.

Oct. 4 — *The Space Age began when the Soviet Union put the first man-made satellite into orbit around the earth.*

1958

A new program for convert integration was adopted during the year, having been previously tried on a pilot basis in several stakes.

April 20 — The New Zealand Temple was dedicated by President David O. McKay.

Aug. 3 — *The world's first atomic-powered submarine, the USS Nautilus, made the first voyage underneath the North Pole.*

Sept. 7 — The London Temple was dedicated by President David O. McKay.

1959

Aug. 21 — *Hawaii was admitted as the 50th state; Alaska had been added to the United States Jan. 3.*

November — The Tabernacle Choir received a Grammy award for its recording of the "Battle Hymn of the Republic."

1960

January — The First Presidency inaugurated a three-month series of weekly Sunday evening "fireside" programs for youth. They were carried to 290 stake centers of the Church by closed-circuit radio.

Also in January, the Church began setting up the administrative framework for a large building program in Europe. By early 1961, administrative building "areas" outside North America had been established for all parts of the world where the Church existed, and the labor missionary program, which originated in the South Pacific in the early 1950s, was utilized in each area.

March — The First Presidency requested the General Priesthood Committee, with Elder Harold B. Lee of the Council of the Twelve as chairman, make a study of Church programs and curriculum with the object of providing for better "correlation."

May 1 — *A U.S. U-2 reconnaissance airplane was shot down over the Soviet Union, typifying worsening relations between the two superpowers.*

1961

March 12 — The first non-English-speaking stake of the Church was organized at The Hague in The Netherlands.

June-July — A number of significant developments took place that revamped the missionary program of the Church. The first seminar for all mission presidents was held June 26-July 27 in Salt Lake City, at which new programs were outlined. Also, a new teaching plan of six lessons to be used in every mission of the Church was officially presented, as was the "every member a missionary" program. The missions of the world were divided into nine areas, and a General Authority was called to administrate each area.

Aug. 13 — *The Soviet Union began building the Berlin Wall, dividing East and West Germany.*

November — A Language Training Institute was established at Brigham Young University for missionaries called to foreign countries. In 1963, it became the Language Training Mission.

1962

Feb. 20 — *John Glenn became the first American to orbit the earth, a feat he accomplished in one hour and 37 minutes aboard the Friendship 7 space capsule.*

March — The age at which young men became eligible for missions was lowered from 20 to 19.

April — At the 132nd Annual Conference, the first seminar of General Authorities and presidents of stakes outside North America was held.

October — The Church purchased a shortwave radio station, WRUL, with a transmitter in Boston and studios in New York City. It was subsequently used to transmit Church broadcasts to Europe and South America.

Dec. 3 — The first Spanish-speaking stake was organized, headquartered in Mexico City.

1963

July — The labor missionary program was expanded to include the United States and Canada.

Oct. 12 — The Polynesian Cultural Center, located near the temple in Laie, Hawaii, was dedicated.

Nov. 22 — *John F. Kennedy became the fourth U.S. president to be assassinated; he was fatally wounded while riding in a motorcade in Dallas, Texas.*

December — Church storage vaults for records in Little Cottonwood Canyon were completed. They were dedicated on June 22, 1966.

1964

January — A new program of home teaching was officially inaugurated throughout the Church after having been presented in stake conferences during the last half of 1963.

Jan. 28 — Temple Square and the Lion House were recognized as National Historic Landmarks by the federal government.

March — Two LDS schools were opened in Chile, one in Santiago and the other in Vina del Mar. During the early 1970s, the Church opened an elementary school in Paraguay, one in Bolivia and one in Peru.

April — The Mormon pavilion opened at the New York World's Fair. The Church also built elaborate pavilions for subsequent expositions in San Antonio, Texas (1968); Japan (1970); and Spokane, Wash.(1974).

July 31 — *The U.S. Ranger VII spacecraft transmitted to earth the first close-up pictures of the moon.*

October — The Pacific Board of Education was discontinued. Schools under its direction became part of the Unified Church School System.

Nov. 17 — The Oakland Temple was dedicated by President David O. McKay.

1965

January — The home evening program was inaugurated. A weekly home evening had been encouraged before by Church leaders, but now the Church published a formal home evening manual, which was to be placed in every LDS home. In October 1970, Monday was designated for home evening throughout the Church; no other Church activity was to be scheduled during that time.

Jan. 18 — The Tabernacle Choir sang at the inauguration of U.S. President Lyndon B. Johnson in Washington D.C.

February — The Italian government gave permission for LDS missionaries to proselyte in the country. No missionary work had been done there since 1862.

March — The three-generation genealogical family group-sheet program was initiated.

June 3 — *Astronaut Ed White made the first American "walk" in space during the Gemini 4 orbital flight.*

September — Because of the war in Vietnam, a missionary quota of two per ward was established within the United States to comply with Selective Service requests.

October — With the appointment of President Joseph Fielding Smith and Elder Thorpe B. Isaacson as counselors, President David O. McKay announced that the First Presidency would be increased to five, instead of three.

1966

May 1 — The first stake in South America was organized at Sao Paulo, Brazil.

June 29 — *North Vietnam's capital, Hanoi, and principal seaport, Haiphong, were bombed for the first time by the U.S. in the Vietnam War.*

August — A new visitors center on Temple Square was opened to tourists in August. While this would be the most elaborate center, it represented a trend of building new visitors centers at historic sites and temples, and at various other locations during the 1960s and 1970s.

1967

April — For the first time, seven Mexican television and radio stations carried a session of general conference.

June 10 — *The Six-Day War in the Middle East ended with Israel holding conquered Arab territory four times its own size.*

Sept. 1 — The beginning of the Church year was changed to Sept. 1 instead of Jan. 1 in the Southern Hemisphere, to coincide with the public school year.

Sept. 29 — The new administrative position of regional representative of the Twelve was announced, and 69 regional representatives were called and given their initial training.

November — Part of the Egyptian papyri owned by Joseph Smith while he was translating the Pearl of Great Price was given to the Church by the New York Metropolitan Museum of Art.

1968

Jan. 22 — *The USS Pueblo and its 83 crew members were seized in the Sea of Japan by North Korea.*

August — A large LDS educational complex was dedicated in Mexico City. The school, Benemerito de las Americas, contained 11 grades for more than 1,200 students.

Oct. 17 — Relief Society Gen. Pres. Belle S. Spafford was named president of the National Council of Women for a two-year term.

1969

January — Two-month language training missions began. Language training for missionaries prior to their departure to their mission field first began during the early 1960s for Spanish, Portuguese, and German language missions.

Jan. 20 — The Tabernacle Choir sang at U.S. President Richard M. Nixon's inauguration in Washington D.C.

June — The first missionaries were sent to Spain.

July 20 — *U.S. astronaut Neil Armstrong became the first man to walk on the moon when he descended from the lunar module "Eagle"; he was followed 18 minutes later by Edwin Aldrin, pilot of the lunar module.*

Aug. 3-8 — A world conference on records was held in Salt Lake City, sponsored by the Church's Genealogical Society.

Nov. 1 — The Southeast Asia Mission formally opened, with headquarters in Singapore. In January 1970, the first missionaries were sent to Indonesia, which was part of the mission.

1970

January — A computerized system for recording and reporting Church contributions went into operation.

Jan. 18 — President David O. McKay died in Salt Lake City at age 96.

Jan. 23 — Joseph Fielding Smith became the 10th president of the Church and chose Harold B. Lee and N. Eldon Tanner as his counselors.

March 15 — The first stake in Asia was organized in Tokyo, Japan.

March 22 — The first stake in Africa was organized in Transvaal, South Africa.

April 22 — *Earth Day, organized to call attention to environmental concerns, was first celebrated.*

May — The Beehive House was placed on the register of National Historic Sites.

September — A new Aaronic Priesthood Personal Achievement Program was started, which gave young men the opportunity to set their own goals in consultation with their bishop. A similar program for young women commenced in January 1971.

1971

January — Distribution of the new Church magazines began: the *Ensign* for adults, the *New Era* for youth, and the *Friend* for children.

Also in January, a bishops' training program conducted by stake presidents commenced, and a new correlated teacher development program began operation.

July — The medical missionary program (later called the health missionary program) began.

Aug. 27-29 — The first Area Conference of the Church was held in Manchester, England. Before the program of holding large area conferences ended, 44 were held throughout the world.

September — All LDS women were automatically enrolled as members of the Relief Society; dues were eliminated.

Sept. 30 — *The United States and the Soviet Union signed pacts designed to avoid accidental nuclear war.*

1972

Church sports tournaments and dance festivals were directed to be held on a regional basis, instead of on an all-Church basis.

Jan. 14 — The Church Historical Department was formed in a reorganization of the Church Historian's Office. Church library, archives and history divisions were created within the new department.

Jan. 18 — The Ogden Temple was dedicated by President Joseph Fielding Smith.

Feb. 9 — The Provo Temple was dedicated by President Joseph Fielding Smith.

Feb. 27 — J. Spencer Kinard became the commentator for the Tabernacle Choir's "Music and the Spoken Word," succeeding Elder Richard L. Evans of the Council of the Twelve, who had been the program's spokesman for nearly 40 years.

July 2 — President Joseph Fielding Smith died in Salt Lake City at age 95.

July 7 — Harold B. Lee became the 11th president of the Church, with N. Eldon Tanner and Marion G. Romney as his counselors.

Sept. 5 — *Eleven Israeli athletes, and five of their assailants, were killed in an attack on the Olympic Village at Munich, West Germany, by Arab terrorists.*

November — The MIA was realigned into the Aaronic Priesthood and Melchizedek Priesthood MIA and placed directly under priesthood leadership.

Nov. 4 — Church departments began moving into the newly completed 28-story Church Office Building at 50 E. North Temple in Salt Lake City.

1973

A new set of missionary lessons was completed for use in all missions. It was the first change in missionary lessons since 1961.

February — The first Church agricultural missionaries to leave the United States were sent to the Guatemala-El Salvador Mission.

Feb. 4 — The Marriott Activities Center at BYU was dedicated. It was the largest such arena on any university campus in the United States.

March 8 — The first stake on mainland Asia was organized in Seoul, Korea.

April 7 — The creation of the Welfare Services Department was announced in general conference. The new organization brought the three welfare units — health services, social services, and welfare — into full correlation.

Sept. 20 — *The British-French supersonic airliner, Concorde, made its first landing in the United States at the Dallas-Fort Worth International Airport.*

Dec. 26 — President Harold B. Lee died in Salt Lake City at age 74.

Dec. 30 — Spencer W. Kimball was set apart as the 12th president of the Church, with N. Eldon Tanner and Marion G. Romney as counselors.

1974

Jan. 14 — Names of stakes Churchwide were changed to reflect a consistent style identifying them with the geographical area served. Mission names were changed June 20, 1974.

March 23 — In an exchange of pioneer homes, the Church traded the Brigham Young Forest Farm home in Salt Lake City to the state of Utah for use in the state's Pioneer State Park. The Church acquired the Brigham Young winter home in St. George and the Jacob Hamblin home in Santa Clara, Utah, for use as visitor and information centers.

May 9 — *Impeachment hearings began against U.S. President Richard M. Nixon.*

June 23 — MIA was dropped from the name of Church youth programs, and further modifications were implemented in the administrative structure of the Aaronic Priesthood and the Young Women organizations.

Sept. 1 — Church College of Hawaii became a branch of Brigham Young University and was given the name Brigham Young University-Hawaii Campus.

Oct. 3 — Seventies quorums were authorized in all stakes, and all quorums in the Church were renamed after the stake. Stake mission presidencies were also reorganized, with all seven presidents of seventies serving in the calling, instead of three of the presidents.

Nov. 19-22 — President Spencer W. Kimball dedicated the Washington Temple at Kensington, Md. Visitors during pre-dedication tours September through November totaled 758,327, topping the previous record of 662,401 at the Los Angeles Temple in 1956.

1975

March 21 — The Church completed legal steps to divest itself of 15 hospitals operated by its Health Service Corporation in three Western states. A nonprofit, non-Church organization, Intermountain Health Care Inc., assumed ownership.

April 20 — *South Vietnam unconditionally surrendered to North Vietnam, and the Vietnam War was officially at an end.*

May 3 — The First Presidency announced the creation of an Area supervisory program and the assignment of six Assistants to the Twelve to oversee Church activities while residing outside of the United States and Canada. The number of these foreign areas was increased to eight later in the year.

May 17 — A supervisory program for missions in the United States and Canada was announced, along with the assignment of

members of the Council of the Twelve as advisers and other General Authorities as supervisors of the 12 areas.

June 27 — The end of auxiliary conferences was announced during the opening session of the 1975 June Conference. These conferences would be replaced with annual regional meetings for priesthood and auxiliary leaders.

July 24 — The 28-story Church Office Building was dedicated by President Spencer W. Kimball.

Oct. 3 — President Spencer W. Kimball announced in general conference the organization of the First Quorum of the Seventy, and three members of the quorum were sustained.

Oct. 6-11 — Brigham Young University observed its 100th anniversary during homecoming week.

Nov. 18 — The Church Genealogical Department was organized with five divisions, two of which were formerly known as the Genealogical Society.

1976

April 3 — Members attending general conference accepted Joseph Smith's Vision of the Celestial Kingdom and Joseph F. Smith's Vision of the Redemption of the Dead for addition to the *Pearl of Great Price*. The scriptures on June 6, 1979, became part of the Doctrine and Covenants.

June 5 — The First Presidency published an official statement reaffirming the Church policy against abortion. The statement supplemented a filmstrip placed in distribution in March.

June 25 — Missouri Gov. Christopher S. Bond signed an executive order rescinding the extermination order issued in 1838 by Gov. Lilburn W. Boggs.

July 4 — President Spencer W. Kimball spoke at a Church-sponsored U.S. Bicentennial devotional attended by more than 23,000 people at the Capitol Centre in Landover, Md. Numerous additional activities involved Church members in the United States during the year-long Bicentennial observance.

Sept. 3 — *Viking 2, an American spaceship, made a successful landing on Mars.*

Oct. 1 — Members of the First Council of the Seventy and the Assistants to the Twelve were released in general conference and called to the new First Quorum of the Seventy. Franklin D. Richards was named the first presiding president.

1977

Jan. 1 — The First Presidency announced a new format for general conferences, with general sessions on the first Sunday of each April and October and on the preceding Saturday, and regional representative seminars on the preceding Friday.

Jan. 14 — The first Presiding Bishopric area supervisor, called to direct temporal affairs of the Church in Mexico, began work in Mexico City. Presiding Bishopric area supervisors for eight other areas outside the United States and Canada were announced June 4.

Feb. 5 — The First Presidency announced that the Council of the Twelve would oversee ecclesiastical matters, and the Presiding Bishopric would have responsibility for temporal programs.

Feb. 21-March 11 — President Spencer W. Kimball met with heads of state in Mexico, Guatemala, Chile, and Bolivia during a tour of Latin America to attend area conferences, and then visited at the White House with U.S. President Jimmy Carter March 11.

March 27 — *The worst airline disaster in history killed 581 people, as two jumbo jets collided on a runway in the Canary Islands.*

May 14 — A bishops central storehouse, the second in the Church and first outside of Salt Lake City, opened at Colton, Calif. Also, the Young Men program was restructured. The Young Men presidency and general board were given responsibility for Aaronic Priesthood curriculum, leadership training and quorum work.

May 22 — Formation of a new Church Activities Committee, with responsibility for coordinating cultural arts and physical activities, was announced. Similar groups were organized on the stake and local level.

July 1 — In response to continued growth in membership worldwide, the geographic subdivisions of the Church, previously known as areas, were renamed zones, and the 11 zones were subdivided into areas. Members of the First Quorum of the Seventy were assigned as zone advisers and area supervisors.

July 30 — The Church Educational System was placed in the ecclesiastical line organization of the Church through an Education Executive Committee of the Council of the Twelve.

Oct. 1 — The Church published *A Topical Guide to the Scriptures of The Church of Jesus Christ of Latter-day Saints,* the first product of a continuing scriptural-aids project established by the First Presidency.

1978

March 31 — President Spencer W. Kimball announced in a regional representative seminar that, to simplify workloads of local leaders, semiannual rather than quarterly stake

conferences would be held, starting in 1979.

April — The Church published an eight-page removable insert about Church programs in the *Reader's Digest,* the first of a series aimed at nearly 50 million *Digest* readers.

April 1 — President Spencer W. Kimball emphasized the four-generation program, which later became the basis for the Church's computerized Ancestral File.

June 9 — In a letter dated June 8 and made public the following day, the First Presidency announced the revelation that worthy men of all races would be eligible to receive the priesthood. On Sept. 30, members accepted the revelation by sustaining vote at general conference. The First Presidency's announcement is now "Official Declaration - 2" in the Doctrine and Covenants.

July 1 — The Relief Society Monument to Women was dedicated in Nauvoo, Ill., by President Spencer W. Kimball.

July 22 — The United States Senate passed a bill, earlier approved by the House of Representatives, designating the Mormon Trail from Nauvoo, Ill., to Salt Lake City as a national historic trail.

Sept. 9 — A new missionary training program was announced: Missionaries to English-speaking missions will receive four weeks training while those learning other languages will continue to receive eight weeks training at the new Missionary Training Center in Provo, Utah, which replaced the Language Training Mission and the Mission Home in Salt Lake City.

Sept. 16 — Women and girls 12 years of age and over gathered for a first-ever special closed-circuit audio conference, similar to general conference priesthood broadcasts.

Sept. 30 — A new special emeritus status for General Authorities was announced in general conference, and seven members of the First Quorum of the Seventy were so designated.

Oct. 22 — *Pope John Paul II formally assumed the papal throne.*

Oct. 30 — The Sao Paulo Temple in Brazil was dedicated by President Spencer W. Kimball.

1979

Jan. 1 — *The United States and China established diplomatic relations after decades of animosity.*

Feb. 3 — The Church Genealogical Department announced a new "family entry system" to allow submissions of names of deceased ancestors for temple work whose birthplaces and birthdates are unknown.

Feb. 18 — The Church's 1,000th stake was created at Nauvoo, Ill., by President Ezra Taft Benson.

June 6 — Joseph Smith's Vision of the Celestial Kingdom and Joseph F. Smith's Vision of the Redemption of the Dead were transferred from the Pearl of Great Price to the Doctrine and Covenants, becoming Sections 137 and 138, respectively.

Sept. 12-14 — The Tabernacle Choir, which celebrated the golden anniversary of its nationally broadcast radio program in July, toured Japan and Korea.

Sept. 29 — A new 2,400-page edition of the King James version of the Bible, with many special features, including a topical guide, a Bible dictionary and a revolutionary footnote system, was published by the Church.

Oct. 24 — President Spencer W. Kimball, on a tour of the Middle East, dedicated the Orson Hyde Memorial Gardens on the Mount of Olives in Jerusalem.

1980

Feb. 22 — The Presidency of the First Quorum of the Seventy was reorganized to strengthen the lines of administration at Church headquarters. The executive directors of the Missionary, Curriculum, Priesthood and Genealogy departments replaced former members of the presidency.

March 2 — U.S. and Canadian members began a new consolidated meeting schedule that put priesthood, sacrament and auxiliary meetings into one three-hour time block on Sundays.

April 6 — To celebrate the Church's 150th anniversary, President Spencer W. Kimball conducted part of general conference from the newly restored Peter Whitmer farmhouse at Fayette, N.Y., the site where the Church was organized. The proceedings in Fayette were linked with the congregation in the Tabernacle in Salt Lake City via satellite, the first time a satellite was used in the Church for transmitting broadcasts of general conference.

May 18 — *Mt. St. Helens in Washington, one of the few active volcanoes in the United States, erupted in a violent explosion that left 10 dead and scores of others homeless.*

Oct. 27 — The Tokyo Temple was dedicated by President Spencer W. Kimball.

Nov. 17 — The Seattle Temple was dedicated by President Spencer W. Kimball.

1981

Jan. 20 — The Tabernacle Choir participated in the inaugural festivities for President Ronald Reagan.

April 1 — Plans to build nine smaller temples in the United States, Central America, Asia, Africa and Europe were announced by President Spencer W. Kimball: Chicago, Ill.; Dallas, Texas; Guatemala City, Guatemala; Lima, Peru; Frankfurt, Germany; Stockholm, Sweden; Seoul, Korea; Manila, Philippines; and Johannesburg, South Africa.

May 5 — The First Presidency publicly voiced its opposition to the proposed basing of the MX missile system in the Utah-Nevada desert.

July 23 — Elder Gordon B. Hinckley was called as a counselor in the First Presidency, the first time since the administration of President David O. McKay that a president had more than two counselors.

Sept. 12 — A smaller, less-expensive ward meetinghouse, called the Sage Plan, was announced by the First Presidency.

Sept. 26 — The first copies of a new version of the Triple Combination (Book of Mormon, Doctrine and Covenants and Pearl of Great Price), with extensive scripture helps, were made available to the public.

Oct. 3 — A network of 500 satellite dishes for stake centers outside of Utah was announced. The receivers linked Church headquarters in Salt Lake City with members in the United States and Canada.

Nov. 16 — The Jordan River Temple was dedicated by President Marion G. Romney of the First Presidency.

1982

March 9 — The Spencer W. Kimball Tower, the tallest building on the BYU campus, was dedicated during ceremonies that featured President Kimball's first public appearance in six months because of illness.

March 18 — Three Church executive councils were created: the Missionary Executive Council, the Priesthood Executive Council and the Temple and Genealogy Executive Council.

April 1 — It was announced that Church membership had reached the 5-million member mark.

April 2 — At general conference, major changes in financing Church meetinghouses were announced, shifting construction costs to general Church funds and utility costs to local units. Also, the term of service for single elders serving full-time missions was reduced from two years to 18 months.

June 30 — *The Equal Rights Amendment was defeated after a 10-year struggle for ratification.*

Sept. 5 — The Mormon Tabernacle Choir

celebrated 50 years of continuous weekly broadcasts over the CBS radio network.

Sept. 10 — U.S. President Ronald Reagan visited Utah to tour a Church cannery and see the Church Welfare Program in action.

Oct. 3 — Elder Boyd K. Packer of the Council of the Twelve and a member of the Scriptures Publication Committee announced that a subtitle was being added to the Book of Mormon: "Another Testament of Jesus Christ."

Oct. 30 — A visitors center and historic site opened its doors in the three-story Grandin printing building in Palmyra, N.Y., where the first copies of the Book of Mormon were printed in 1830.

1983

Feb. 27 — The 150th anniversary of the Word of Wisdom was observed throughout the Church and at the Newel K. Whitney store in Kirtland, Ohio, where the original revelation was received in 1833.

June 1 — The Atlanta Georgia Temple was dedicated by President Gordon B. Hinckley of the First Presidency.

Aug. 5, 9 — For the first time in Church history, two temples were dedicated within a week's time: the Apia Samoa Temple on Aug. 5, and the Nuku'alofa Tonga Temple on Aug. 9; both by President Gordon B. Hinckley.

Sept. 15 — The Santiago Chile Temple was dedicated by President Gordon B. Hinckley.

Oct. 16 — The first of a series of multi-stake (later known as regional) conferences was held in London, England.

Oct. 25 — *U.S. Marines and Rangers invaded the Caribbean island of Grenada, deposing the island's Marxist government.*

Oct. 27 — The Papeete Tahiti Temple was dedicated by President Gordon B. Hinckley.

Dec. 2 — The Mexico City Temple was dedicated by President Gordon B. Hinckley.

1984

Jan. 7 — Premier Zhao Ziyang of the People's Republic of China visited the BYU-Hawaii campus and the adjacent Polynesian Cultural Center during the first visit of a Chinese premier to the United States since the People's Republic of China was formed in 1949.

March 25 — A new program — the Four-Phase Genealogical Facilities Program — was announced to allow wards and branches to establish genealogical facilities in their meetinghouses.

April 7 — The first members of the First Quorum of the Seventy called for temporary three- to five-year terms, were sustained. These Brethren were later sustained to the Second Quorum of the Seventy, created in 1989, and their term of service standardized at five years.

May 10 — *A federal judge in Salt Lake City ruled that the U.S. government was negligent in its above-ground testing of nuclear weapons at the Nevada test site in the 1950s and early 1960s.*

May 25 — President Gordon B. Hinckley dedicated the Boise Idaho Temple.

June 24 — Members of the First Quorum of the Seventy were appointed to serve as area presidencies in 13 major geographical areas of the Church — seven in the United States and Canada and six in other parts of the world.

Sept. 20 — The Sydney Australia Temple was dedicated by President Gordon B. Hinckley.

Sept. 25 — The Manila Philippines Temple was dedicated by President Gordon B. Hinckley.

Oct. 19 — The Dallas Texas Temple was dedicated by President Gordon B. Hinckley.

Oct. 28 — The Church's 1,500th stake was created 150 years after the first stake was organized in Kirtland, Ohio. The landmark stake was the Ciudad Obregon Mexico Yaqui Stake.

Nov. 17 — The Taipei Taiwan Temple was dedicated by President Gordon B. Hinckley.

Nov. 26 — The First Presidency announced that, beginning Jan. 1, the term of full-time missionary service for single elders would again be 24 months. It had been shortened from two years to 18 months in April 1982.

Dec. 14 — The Guatemala City Temple was dedicated by President Gordon B. Hinckley.

1985

Jan. 2 — BYU's football team was voted No. 1 in the nation for the 1984 season by every major poll, and for the first time ever, was named national champions. The Cougars had just completed a perfect 13-0 season.

Jan. 27 — Latter-day Saints in the United States in Canada participated in a special fast to benefit victims of famine in Africa and other parts of the world. The fast raised more than $6 million.

April 12 — U.S. Senator Jake Garn became the first Church member to fly in space. He was aboard the space shuttle Challenger. Another Church member, Don Lind, was a crew member on a space shuttle mission that blasted off April 29.

June 29 — The Freiberg Temple, located in the German Democratic Republic, then communist-controlled, was dedicated by President Gordon B. Hinckley.

July 2 — The Stockholm Sweden Temple was dedicated by President Gordon B. Hinckley.

July 31 — Li Xiannian, president of the People's Republic of China, and his wife, Madame Lin Jiamei, toured the Church's Polynesian Cultural Center in Hawaii as part of his tour of the United States and Canada.

Aug. 2 — A new LDS hymnbook, the first revision in 37 years, came off the presses.

Aug. 9 — The Chicago Illinois Temple was dedicated by President Gordon B. Hinckley.

Aug. 24 — The Johannesburg South Africa Temple was dedicated by President Gordon B. Hinckley. With the dedication of this building, there was now a temple on every continent except Antarctica.

Oct. 23 — The Church Genealogical Library was dedicated by President Gordon B. Hinckley. It was renamed Family History Library in 1987.

Nov. 5 — President Spencer W. Kimball died in Salt Lake City at age 90.

Nov. 10 — President Ezra Taft Benson was set apart as the 13th president of the Church, with President Gordon B. Hinckley and President Thomas S. Monson as counselors.

Dec. 14 — The Seoul Korea Temple was dedicated by President Gordon B. Hinckley.

1986

Jan. 10 — The Lima Peru Temple was dedicated by President Gordon B. Hinckley.

Jan. 17 — The Buenos Aires Argentina Temple was dedicated by President Thomas S. Monson.

Jan. 28 — *The space shuttle Challenger exploded shortly after liftoff, killing all seven people aboard, including Christa McAuliffe, the first teacher in space.*

April 30 — Church membership was estimated to have reached the 6-million member milestone.

June 22 — The 1,600th stake of the Church was created by President Thomas S. Monson in Kitchener, Ontario.

July 6 — New missionary discussions, which focus on "teaching from the heart," were approved for use in all English-speaking missions.

Aug. 10 — An archaeological dig at a pioneer cemetery in Salt Lake City turned up the remains of 22 children and nine adults. The site, where a large apartment complex was planned, was thought to be the pioneers' first cemetery in the Salt Lake Valley.

Aug. 31 — A major organization adjustment in the Relief Society eliminated stake boards and allowed for ward Relief Society boards to meet local needs and resources.

Oct. 4 — Seventies quorums in stakes throughout the Church were discontinued. Brethren serving as seventies returned to elders quorums or were ordained high priests.

Oct. 5 — The First Presidency issued a statement opposing the legalization of gambling and government sponsorship of lotteries.

Oct. 11 — In the first Churchwide Young Women activity, an estimated 300,000 gathered at sites around the world to release helium-filled balloons containing personal messages from the young women.

Oct. 24 — The Denver Colorado Temple was dedicated by President Ezra Taft Benson.

1987

Jan. 23 — Documents dealer Mark Hofmann was imprisoned after a plea bargain arrangement in which he admitted responsibility for the bombing deaths of two people in Salt Lake City in October 1985. He also confessed that he had forged the so-called Martin Harris "salamander letter" and other documents relating to the Church.

Jan. 27 — *Soviet Union leader Mikhail Gorbachev proposed a series of economic and social reforms that signaled the start of an era of "glasnost," or openness, in the Communist country.*

Feb. 15 — The Tabernacle Choir marked its 3,000th radio broadcast in a series that had become the longest-running network program in the free world.

March 12 — It was announced that the Church-owned Hotel Utah, a landmark in downtown Salt Lake City for 76 years, would close as a hotel Aug. 31 and be renovated as a meetinghouse and office building.

April 25 — The First Presidency announced a realignment of the Church's worldwide administrative areas, including creation of four new areas.

June 20 — The First Presidency sent a letter to priesthood leaders defining the organizational structure of ward Young Women presidencies and calling for consistent midweek activities for young women.

July 15 — The Genealogical Library celebrated the conversion of the last card from its card catalog to computer.

July 24-26 — LDS throughout Britain commemorated the 150th anniversary of the first missionary work in Great Britain. Thirteen General Authorities, including President Ezra Taft Benson and President Gordon B. Hinckley, attended various events, which included dedication of historical sites, firesides and conferences.

Aug. 15 — The Church's Genealogical Department was renamed the Family History Department.

Aug. 25 — A national Emmy award, the first-ever awarded to a public service spot, was given to the Church by the National Academy of Television Arts and Sciences.

Aug. 28 — The Frankfurt Germany Temple was dedicated by President Ezra Taft Benson.

Sept. 4 — A letter from the First Presidency announced the discontinuance of the International Mission. Responsibility for its areas reverted to the respective area presidencies of the Church.

Oct. 6 — A letter from the First Presidency to local priesthood leaders encouraged increased contributions to the General Missionary Fund, which provides assistance to those who otherwise would not be able to fund their own missions.

December — More than 3.4 million people visited Temple Square in 1987, an all-time annual high by 800,000.

1988

March 24: President Thomas S. Monson, second counselor in the First Presidency, and his wife, Frances, were guests of the king and queen of Sweden at a dinner commemorating the 350th year of the first Swedish settlement in the United States.

April 2 — Ricks College officially inaugurated its centennial celebration.

May 15 — Elder Neal A. Maxwell organized the Aba Nigeria Stake, the first Church stake in West Africa.

May 28 — The First Presidency issued a statement on the subject of AIDS, stressing chastity before marriage, fidelity in marriage and abstinence from homosexual behavior.

June 1 — The Church was granted legal recognition in Hungary, the first of several such steps in Eastern European nations during the next two years.

July 4 — The Tabernacle Choir completed a 21-day, 19-concert tour of Hawaii, Australia and New Zealand.

July 16 — Monuments commemorating where the Mormon Battalion was mustered and where LDS pioneers established Nebraska's first community were dedicated near Council Bluffs, Iowa, and Florence, Neb.

Mid-August — The Church reached the milestone of having completed 100 million endowments for the dead.

Sept. 17 — The Church joined an interfaith television network (VISN) sponsored by 18 religious organizations.

Also, the BYU Folk Dancers were the only North American dance company that performed at Opening Ceremonies of the 1988 Olympic Games in Seoul, Korea, viewed by an estimated 1 billion people worldwide.

Oct. 16 — Elder David B. Haight created the 1,700th stake of the Church. The new stake was in Manaus, Brazil, a city of 1.5 million in the heart of the Amazon jungle.

Oct. 24-28 — President Thomas S. Monson, second counselor in the First Presidency, led a delegation of Church leaders that met with the German Democratic Republic's top government officials. It was announced Nov. 12 that the Church had been granted rights to send missionaries to the DDR and for LDS members from the DDR to serve as missionaries in other countries.

Nov. 12 — Ricks College celebrated its 100th birthday when Pres. Joe J. Christensen cut a huge 450-pound birthday cake at Founder's Day festivities. The previous day, a memorial was dedicated, honoring 38 Ricks students and alumni killed in battle from World War I on.

1989

Jan. 19 — The Mormon Tabernacle Choir, called "The Nation's Choir," performed at events during the inauguration of President George Bush.

Jan. 28 — Elders Russell M. Nelson and Dallin H. Oaks of the Council of the Twelve completed an eight-day visit to China and were assured by high-level Chinese leaders that people are free to practice religious beliefs in that country.

Feb. 15 — One hundred fifty years after Quincy, Ill., residents gave aid to Church members forced to flee from Missouri, the city's mayor presented Elder Loren C. Dunn of the First Quorum of the Seventy with a key to the city and proclaimed this date "Latter-day Saints Day."

March 24 — *The Exxon Valdez struck a reef in Alaska's Prince William Sound and spilled 240,000 barrels of oil, the largest oil spill in U.S. history.*

April 1 — The Second Quorum of the Seventy was created and all General Authorities serving under a five-year call were sustained as members, along with another eight newly called General Authorities.

May 16 — The BYU Jerusalem Center for Near Eastern Studies was dedicated by President Howard W. Hunter.

May 24 — Two missionaries in the Bolivia La Paz Mission, Elders Jeffrey B. Ball, 20, and Todd R. Wilson, 20, were killed by terrorists.

Early June — The Church surpassed 100 million names processed in the 12-year-old stake record extraction program.

June 14 — LDS missionaries and those of the Jehovah's Witnesses were expelled from Ghana, a western Africa nation where 6,000 Church members live. The Church had no advance notice of the ban. The LDS missionaries were able to return to Ghana in 1990.

June 15 — Ground was broken for the first LDS meetinghouse in Poland.

June 25 — The 100th stake in Mexico was created in Tecalco. Mexico became the first country outside the United States with 100 or more stakes.

June 27 — The renovated Carthage Jail complex in Illinois, where the Prophet Joseph Smith was martyred, was dedicated by President Gordon B. Hinckley, highlighting activities commemorating the 150th anniversary of the Mormon settlement of Nauvoo, Ill.

Aug. 19 — The Portland Oregon Temple was dedicated by President Gordon B. Hinckley.

Sept. 9 — Because of threats expressed against Americans in Colombia during increasing drug-related violence, Church leaders decided to give early releases or transfers to North American missionaries serving in that country.

Sept. 30 — The first General Authorities called under a plan to serve for five years were released in general conference.

Oct. 17 — The first LDS meetinghouse in the Republic of Hungary, located in the capital city of Budapest, was dedicated by President Thomas S. Monson, second counselor in the First Presidency.

Nov. 9 — *The Berlin Wall came down, paving the way for eventual unification of East and West Germany.*

Nov. 25 — A major change in policy for financing local Church units in the United States and Canada was announced by the First Presidency. Ward members would no longer have stake and ward budget assessments.

Dec. 16 — The Las Vegas Nevada Temple was dedicated by President Gordon B. Hinckley.

1990

Jan. 19-23 — Elder Dallin H. Oaks of the Council of the Twelve met with Chinese leaders and delivered a 90-minute address about the Church to the Chinese Academy of Social Sciences.

Jan. 21 — David Hsiao Hsin Chen, a professor at BYU-Hawaii who was born and raised in China, was sustained as the Church's "traveling elder" to oversee Church affairs in China.

April 2 — A new Church software package called FamilySearch, designed to simplify the task of family history research, was released by the Church.

April 27-29 — Soviet Union's ambassador to the United States, Yuri V. Dubinin, made a historic visit to Utah Church sites and spoke at a conference of the Salt Lake Monument Park Stake.

May 21 — The U.S. Supreme Court handed down a unanimous decision that money given directly to missionaries is not a deductible donation under federal tax law. The Church encouraged members to follow established procedures of contributing through their wards.

July — New missions in the Eastern European countries of Czechoslovakia, Hungary and Poland highlighted the record 29 missions created in 1990.

Aug. 7 — *International forces of Operation Desert Shield left for Saudi Arabia following the invasion of Kuwait by Iraq.*

Aug 25 — The Toronto Ontario Temple was dedicated by President Gordon B. Hinckley.

Sept. 13 — Registration of the Leningrad Branch of the Church was approved by the Council on Religious Affairs of the Council of Ministers in the Soviet Union.

Sept. 15 — President Gordon B. Hinckley spoke at a memorial service at Cedar City, Utah, that brought together descendants of the pioneers involved with and the victims of the Mountain Meadows Massacre. He also dedicated a monument that had recently been erected at the site.

Sept. 19 — President Ezra Taft Benson underwent surgery to remove two subdural hematomas. After a recurrence of problems, President Benson was operated on again Sept. 23.

November — The First Presidency announced in November a new policy for United States and Canada, effective Jan. 1, 1991, that would equalize contributions required to maintain a full-time missionary.

Nov. 30 — The government of Ghana gave

permission for the Church to resume activities in that West African country.

1991

Jan. 15. — Latter-day Saints were among the servicemen and women who were mobilized as part of the war in the Persian Gulf, "Operation Desert Storm." More than 100 LDS groups, spread out across the Arabian Peninsula, saw to the spiritual needs of LDS servicemen and women.

Late February — Delivery of 1,800 packages of food and vitamins, designated for Church members and non-members in the Soviet Union republics of Russia and Estonia, was completed.

April 19 — Recognition of the Church in the Ivory Coast, the center of French West Africa, was announced at a special meeting of Church members in Abidjan. The announcement was made by Elder Richard P. Lindsay, a member of the Seventy and president of the Africa Area.

April 27 — Fifty years after the Church began keeping individual membership records, it computerized membership records worldwide.

May 1 — The 500,000th full-time missionary in this dispensation was called.

May 26 — The 1,800th stake in the Church, the San Francisco de Macoris Dominican Republic Stake, was created.

June 8 — The Tabernacle Choir embarked on a historic, 21-day tour of eight European countries, including five countries in which the choir had not performed before: Hungary, Austria, Czechoslovakia, Poland and the Soviet Union.

June 22-24 — The Alberta Temple, after three years of renovation, was rededicated by President Gordon B. Hinckley, first counselor in the First Presidency, in 12 sessions.

June 24 — The Russian Republic, the largest in the Soviet Union, granted formal recognition to the Church following the Tabernacle Choir's concert in Moscow's Bolshoi Theater.

Aug. 13-27 — The 100th anniversary of the founding of the Church in Tonga was observed with events in Tonga. King Taufa'ahau Tupou IV attended the major events on the main island of Tongatapu.

Sept. 1 — Membership in the Church reached 8 million, about two years after membership hit the 7 million mark in December 1989.

Nov. 5 — Twenty-two members of the Church were killed in the Philippines when a typhoon unleashed flash floods, sending a wall of mud and water through the central Philippine city of Ormoc.

December — The *Encyclopedia of Mormonism,* promoted by its New York publisher as "a landmark reference work," was published. A 13-member board of editors at BYU compiled the encyclopedia under commission from Macmillan Publishing Co.

1992

March 14 — The sesquicentennial of the founding of the Relief Society on March 17, 1842, was celebrated beginning with an international satellite telecast.

May 2-3 — In the aftermath of rioting and looting in Los Angeles, Calif., sparked by the April 29 acquittal of four policemen charged in the beating of a motorist, hundreds of Church members joined thousands of volunteers in clean-up and relief efforts.

May 13 — Elder Dallin H. Oaks of the Council of the Twelve appeared before the U.S. House Subcommittee on Civil and Constitutional Rights advocating legislation that would restore freedom of religion that was diminished in a 1990 Supreme Court decision. He testified Sept. 18 before the Senate advocating the same legislation.

May 31 — Attending specially called meetings in four Utah cities, six members of the Council of the Twelve and three members of the Seventy counseled stake presidents and regional representatives on moral issues.

June 9 — The new Social Hall Memorial and walkway — featuring the recently unearthed foundation of the historic Social Hall of Brigham Young's era — was dedicated by President Gordon B. Hinckley, first counselor in the First Presidency, in downtown Salt Lake City.

Aug. 15 — Commemorating the "second rescue" of the ill-fated Willie and Martin handcart pioneers, President Gordon B. Hinckley, first counselor in the First Presidency, dedicated three monuments near South Pass, Wyo. The Riverton Wyoming Stake researched family histories and performed temple ordinances for those pioneers whose work was not previously done.

Aug. 23-26 — Hurricane Andrew, the most powerful hurricane in more than 60 years, caused $30 billion in damage, including homes of Church members and some Church buildings, particularly in the the Homestead Florida Stake near Miami.

Aug. 30 — The Church's 1,900th stake, the Orlando Florida South Stake, was organized by Elder Neal A. Maxwell of the Council of the Twelve.

Sept. 26 — The First Presidency authorized the use of humanitarian relief funds to be sent to Somalia and other African nations in the grip of the drought of the century." In an initial response, 1 million pounds of food was shipped.

NEWS IN REVIEW
October 1992-September 1994

October 1992

During Semiannual General Conference **Oct. 3-4,** Elders Henry B. Eyring and Glenn L. Pace, released as first and second counselors in the Presiding Bishopric, were sustained to the First Quorum of the Seventy. Sustained as counselors in the Presiding Bishopric were Bishop H. David Burton and Bishop Richard C. Edgley.

In addition, plans were announced for temples in Hartford, Conn.; Hong Kong; and an undesignated location in Utah County, Utah.

Sustained as Sunday School president was Elder Merlin R. Lybbert, with Elders Clinton L. Cutler and Ronald E. Poelman, all of the Seventy, as his counselors.

Called as counselors in the Young Men general presidency to Elder Jack H Goaslind, president since 1990, were Elders Stephen D. Nadauld and L. Lionel Kendrick, all of the Seventy.

Emeritus status was granted to Elder Marion D. Hanks and Elder Robert L. Backman of the Presidency of the Seventy.

Six members of the Second Quorum of the Seventy were released: Elders George R. Hill III, John R. Lasater, Douglas J. Martin, Glen L. Rudd, Douglas H. Smith and Lynn A. Sorensen.

Also in the news in October 1992:

Oct. 17: The First Presidency issued a statement urging Sabbath day observance. The statement read in part, "We sense that many Latter-day Saints have become lax in their observance of the Sabbath day. We should refrain from shopping on the Sabbath and participating in other commercial and sporting activities that now commonly desecrate the Sabbath.

"We urge all Latter-day Saints to set this holy day apart from activities of the world and consecrate themselves by entering into a spirit of worship, thanksgiving, service, and family-centered activities appropriate to the Sabbath."

Oct. 18-20: The London Temple was

Oct. 23, 1992: Hermann Batjer and daughters Tamara, Tanja leave Swiss Temple following rededicatory session.

rededicated following extensive remodeling and refurbishing. Ten dedicatory sessions were held, with some 13,200 members attending.

Oct. 19: A temple site in the general area of Preston, England, was announced by President Gordon B. Hinckley, first counselor in the First Presidency, during the second day of ceremonies at the London Temple rededication.

Oct. 23-25: The Swiss Temple was rededicated following extensive remodeling and refurbishing. Ten dedicatory sessions were held with nearly 9,000 members attending.

Oct. 25: A new videocassette production, *On the Way Home,* depicting a family's joy in finding the gospel, premiered over the Church satellite network as part of missionary open houses in Church meetinghouses throughout North America.

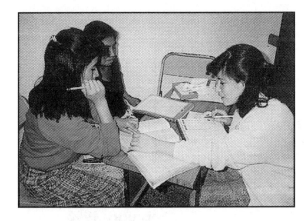

Dec. 15, 1992: Following the announcement of Relief Society's worldwide literacy effort, member in Guatemala City, Guatemala, tutors others to read.

November 1992

Elaine L. Jack, Relief Society general president, made the first visit to India by a Church auxiliary president on **Nov. 8.** She attended a home-centered sacrament meeting in Bangalore, where 11 adults and three children were present, and a fireside, where 65 people attended. Bangalore is the headquarters of the new India Bangalore Mission.

Also in the news in November 1992:

Nov. 14: Stephen K. Woodhouse, 52, was installed as the 12th president of LDS Business College in Salt Lake City. President Thomas S. Monson, second counselor in the First Presidency, issued the charge to the new president.

Nov. 21: Young women throughout the Church joined in a day of service for the Young Women Worldwide Celebration: "Walk in the Light." Previous worldwide celebrations were held in 1986 and 1989.

Nov. 27: Elder Richard G. Scott of the Council of the Twelve turned on 250,000 Christmas lights on Temple Square. It was the 27th year for the traditional lighting of the Square.

Nov. 28: Creation of the Australia Sydney North Mission — the sixth in the that nation — was announced. It began operation Jan. 1, 1992.

December 1992

The Church reached a milestone of 20,000 wards and branches with the creation of the Harvest Park Ward in the Salt Lake Granger South Stake on **Dec. 6.**

Also in the news in December 1992:

Dec. 1: Diplomats from many nations, including ambassadors from the African diplomatic corps in the U.S., attended ceremonies to switch on 250,000 Christmas lights on the Washington Temple grounds. Elder Dallin H. Oaks of the Council of the Twelve and Cameroon Ambassador Paul Pondi turned on the lights.

Dec. 6: President Thomas S. Monson, second counselor in the First Presidency, gave the annual message in the First Presidency Christmas Devotional, saying, "To catch the real meaning of the Spirit of Christmas, we need only drop the last syllable, and it becomes the Spirit of Christ."

Dec. 7: The Central American nation of Belize, located on the Yucatan Peninsula, was dedicated by Elder Russell M. Nelson of the Council of the Twelve for the preaching of the gospel. It completed the dedication of all seven nations in Central America.

Dec. 15: A gospel literacy effort sponsored by the Relief Society to help increase literacy throughout the Church was announced in a letter from the First Presidency to priesthood and Relief Society leaders.

Dec. 26: The Tabernacle Choir left on a tour of the Holy Land. Concerts were later held in Jerusalem, Tel Aviv and Haifa.

January 1993

The Tabernacle Choir concluded a 12-day tour to the Holy Land on **Jan. 6.** During the history-making tour, the choir sang in five public concerts in Haifa, Tel

Jan. 3, 1993: On the Mount of Beatitudes overlooking the Sea of Galilee, Tabernacle Choir sings during history-making visit to Holy Land.

Aviv and Jerusalem and one private concert in Jerusalem. Audiences and critics alike gave the choir accolades for its performances.

Also in the news in January 1993:

January: A yearlong effort by the Genealogical Society of Utah to commemorate its centennial began with an emphasis on strengthening and expanding the partnership between the society and others worldwide in compiling records and automating information for the benefit of all mankind. The society was organized Nov. 13, 1894.

Jan. 6: Four Church service missionaries entered Hanoi, Vietnam, to give humanitarian service, teaching English to doctors and staff at a children's hospital and to teachers, staff and children at a school for young children.

Jan. 8-12: Church members rendered service to those in need in the aftermath of record snowfalls in central and northern Utah and severe flooding in Tijuana, Mexico.

February 1993

A BYU 19-stake fireside address **Feb. 7** by President Howard W. Hunter of the Council of the Twelve was disrupted for about 10 minutes when a man walked up to the podium threatening to detonate a bomb. The man was subdued by security officers and members of the congregation, and taken into custody. President Hunter then finished his address.

Also in the news in February 1993:

Feb. 20: The First Presidency issued a statement discouraging the translation of the Book of Mormon into modern English, even though those who do so may be well-intentioned. Such a translation likely will introduce errors and obscure the ancient origins of the book, the First Presidency said.

Feb. 20: Elder M. Russell Ballard of the Council of the Twelve announced that a committee under his direction has begun plans for a global celebration in 1997 of the sesquicentennial of the ar-

Jan. 6, 1993: Students in Hanoi, Vietnam, welcome Elder John K. Carmack and English teachers Stanley G. and Mavis Steadman and J. LaVar and Helen R. Bateman.

rival of the Mormon Pioneers in Utah.

Feb. 22: Elder Robert E. Sackley of the Second Quorum of the Seventy died while on a Church assignment in Australia.

March 1993

Seventeen new missions were announced for areas throughout the world on **March 6** and **March 13**. The new missions will be in:

Brazil Florianopolis, Brazil Recife South, Brazil Ribeirao Preto, Brazil Rio de Janeiro North, California Carlsbad, California Roseville, Canada Toronto West, Colorado Denver North, Guatemala Guatemala City Central, Latvia Riga, Nebraska Omaha, New York New York South, Peru Chiclayo, Romania Bucharest, Russia Samara, Tennessee Knoxville and Ukraine Donetsk.

Also in the news in March 1993:

March 17: Elder James E. Faust of the Council of the Twelve dedicated Latvia for the preaching of the gospel.

April 1993

At the 163rd Annual General Conference **April 3-4**, three members of the Second Quorum of the Seventy were sustained to the First Quorum of the Seventy: Elders F. Melvin Hammond, Kenneth Johnson and Lynn A. Mickelsen. Also, two more leaders were sustained to the First Quorum of the Seventy: Elders Neil L. Andersen and D. Todd Christofferson. At the conference, it was announced that property is being acquired for a temple in Spain "and at least three other nations."

Also in the news in April 1993:

April 6, 1993: Scene from Salt Lake Temple centennial video "Mountain of the Lord" portrays President Wilford Woodruff arriving to dedicate Salt Lake Temple in 1893.

April 3: "The Mountain of the Lord" a new motion picture produced by the Church about the building of the Salt Lake Temple, premiered between sessions of conference, part of a yearlong commemoration of the centennial of the Salt Lake Temple.

April 6: The centennial of the Salt Lake Temple was observed at a Tabernacle Choir special program, and a special mural was placed in the temple. In addition, a major exhibit opened March 27 in the Museum of Church History and Art on commemoration of the sesquicentennial of the Salt Lake Temple, fea-

April 25, 1993: At cornerstone ceremony for San Diego California Temple, are, from left, President Gordon B. Hinckley, President Thomas S. Monson with Susana Elizabeth Cardenas Vargas, representing the youth, President Howard W. Hunter and Elder Boyd K. Packer.

turing the building of the temple.

April 7: A site was announced for a planned new temple in Utah County in central Utah. The temple will be built in American Fork, the First Presidency announced.

April 9: Ground was broken for the new Ezra Taft Benson Science Building on the BYU campus.

April 15: Elder Neal A. Maxwell of the Council of the Twelve dedicated Mongolia for the preaching of the gospel.

April 23: Elder Dallin H. Oaks dedicated Albania for the preaching of the gospel.

April 25-30: The San Diego California Temple was dedicated by President Gordon B. Hinckley, in the first of 23 dedicatory sessions.

April 26-28: Five influential Mexican legislators visited Church headquarters to learn more about the operations of the Church.

May 1993

The Tabernacle Choir performed **May 2** in the newly renovated Catholic Cathedral of the Madeleine in Salt Lake City. The performance was so popular, more people were turned away than were seated. And on **May 12,** industrialist Jon M. Huntsman, regional representative and philanthropist, was greeted by Pope John Paul II at the Vatican in Rome.

Also in the news in May 1993:

May: A wide range of LDS medical professionals performed voluntary service in Bulgarian hospitals and other former eastern bloc nations.

May 11: Elder Russell M. Nelson dedicated Belarus for the preaching of the gospel.

May 15: Church typesetters announced that the Church has all but five of the world's alphabets ready for printing the scriptures.

May 20: Elder M. Russell Ballard dedicated Lithuania for the preaching of the gospel.

June 1993

Following a six-year closure for major renovation, the former Hotel Utah in Salt Lake City was dedicated **June 27** and

June 27, 1993: President Gordon B. Hinckley and President Thomas S. Monson stand by heroic-sized statue of Joseph Smith that is in lobby of newly refurbished Joseph Smith Memorial Building.

renamed the Joseph Smith Memorial Building, housing office and meeting facilities for the Church; a theater showing the new film "Legacy"; and the Family-Search Center, a facility to introduce novices to family history.

Also in the news in June 1993:

June 5: BYU's Young ambassadors returned from a monthlong tour of Russia, Latvia, Lithuania and Estonia, where they helped strengthen members of the Church in an area where the Church is new.

June 12: Three General Authorities were called to the Presidency of the Seventy, effective Aug. 15: Elders Joe J. Christensen, Monte J. Brough and W. Eugene Hansen.

June 22-27: A training seminar for 136 new mission presidents was held at the Missionary Training Center in Provo, Utah.

June 26: Elder William R. Bradford of the Seventy broke ground for the Bogota Colombia Temple.

June 29, 1993: Agricol Lozano H. speaks for Church at ceremony officially registering Church by the government of Mexico.

June 29: The government of Mexico formally registered the LDS Church, granting it all the rights of a religious organization, including the right to own property.

July 1993

Flooding in the midwestern United States provided extensive opportunity for service to Church members in Missouri, North Dakota, South Dakota, Iowa and Illinois from **July 18-26.**

Also in the news in July 1993:

July: The FamilySearch Center in the Joseph Smith Memorial Building was opened to help tourists and others discover their ancestors.

July 10: Tongan King Taufa'ahau Tupou IV attended festivities for the 30th anniversary of the Polynesian Cultural Center.

July 17: President Thomas S. Monson, second counselor in the First Presi-

dency, presided at reinterment services for the remains of Apostle Abraham O. Woodruff, who died June 20, 1904, in El Paso, Texas, and his wife, Helen May Winters Woodruff, who died in the Mormon colonies in Mexico on June 7, 1904. The remains of both were buried side by side in the Salt Lake City Cemetery.

July 26: President Ezra Taft Benson observed the 50th anniversary of his being called as an apostle.

July 30: Midwest flooding led to the cancellation of the annual "City of Joseph" pageant at Nauvoo, Ill.

August 1993

More than 16 tons of clothing and shoes arrived in St. Petersburg, Russia, in **August** as part of the Church's humanitarian aid efforts continuing throughout the nations that made up the former Soviet Union.

Also in the news in August 1993:

Aug. 1: A letter from the First Presidency re-emphasized "the need for all adult members to focus on our children in an ongoing effort to help them learn to follow the teachings of the Savior." The effort, "Focus on Children," is to help children achieve their divine potential.

Aug. 4-10: Some 3,000 LDS Scouts took part in the National Scout Jamboree at Fort AP Hill, Va.

Aug. 6: Iceland's highest honor, the Order of the Falcon, was presented by the ambassador of Iceland to Byron T. Geslison, who re-opened missionary work in Iceland in 1975, and who has served three missions in the country.

Aug. 11-15: More than 100 LDS vol-

August, 1993: In St. Petersburg, Russia, Yaroslav Kuznetsov and Boris Shapovalov, in truck, and on ground, Roman Leus, Pavel Anishenko, Victor Burkov and Pavel Stozhkov unload bales of clothing donated by Church.

unteers joined a community effort to help with the Catholic World Youth Day in Denver, Colo., and a visit by Pope John Paul II.

Aug. 20-21: The Tabernacle Choir performed concerts at the 1993 Grand Teton Music Festival at Teton Village near Jackson, Wyo.

Aug. 25: One of the Church's Homefront Junior spots, "Splash," was presented an Emmy award by the National Academy of Television Arts and Sciences at New York City.

Aug. 27: Elder James E. Faust of the Council of the Twelve broke ground for a new Brazil Area missionary training center, expected to be the second largest in the Church.

Aug. 28-Sept. 5: Elder Russell M. Nelson of the Council of the Twelve represented the Church at the 1993 Parliament of the World's Religions in Chicago, Ill.

September 1993

The First Presidency announced **Sept. 25** that Sunday School opening exercises and the hymn practice would no longer be held. "In the spirit of simplification and a continuing desire to strengthen all members, we announce a change in the Sunday meeting schedule," a letter from the First Presidency stated.

Also in the news in September 1993:

Sept. 14: Elder Joseph B. Wirthlin of the Council of the Twelve dedicated the Mediterranean island of Cyprus for the preaching of the gospel.

Sept. 15: Liberty, Mo., Mayor Robert Saunders took part in commemorating the 30th anniversary of the Liberty Jail Visitors Center.

Sept. 25: Elder Richard G. Scott of the Council of the Twelve announced that the Family Record Extraction Program, started in 1987 to computerize the Church's temple records, is expected to be complete shortly. This will allow immediate local clearance of names for temple work.

October 1993

Three General Authorities were granted emeritus status at the 163rd Semiannual General Conference on **Oct. 2:** Elders Jacob de Jager, Adney Y. Komatsu and H. Burke Peterson. Three new members of the Presidency of the Seventy, Elders Joe J. Christensen, Monte J. Brough and W. Eugene Hansen, called in June, were sustained. They succeed Elders Dean L. Larsen, James M. Paramore, and J. Richard Clarke, now serving as area presidents. Also, Elder Vaughn J Featherstone was sustained as second counselor in the Young Men general presidency.

Also in the news in October 1993:

Oct. 9: Ground was broken by President Gordon B. Hinckley, first counselor in the First Presidency, and President Thomas S. Monson, second counselor in the First Presidency, for the Mt. Timpanogos Temple in American Fork, Utah, to be the Church's 49th temple.

Oct. 9: Ambassadors and other diplomats, representing 33 countries, from Washington, D.C.'s diplomatic commu-

Oct. 9, 1993: Gregory Newell, a Church member and former ambassador to Sweden, visits with India's deputy ambassador Kanwal Sibal and wife, Elisabeth Sibal, during a western picnic for diplomats by the Women's International Committee of the Church's International Affairs Office.

Nov. 8, 1993: Kim and LaRae Sayer of Sandy, Utah, learn about TempleReady software from Cindy Ogden, standing. The new software clears names locally for temple work.

nity enjoyed a western-style picnic at the Marriott farm in Hume, Va., sponsored by the Church.

Oct. 13: A new 100,000-square-foot Museum of Art was dedicated at BYU by President Gordon B. Hinckley, first counselor in the First Presidency. It opened with a traveling exhibit on the lost Etruscan civilization, on loan from the Vatican Museums.

Oct. 17: The First Presidency issued a statement reaffirming the Church policy on discipline. The statement was in light of extensive publicity given to six recent Church disciplinary councils in Utah.

Oct. 25: The statue of Brigham Young was moved from its vantage point of nearly 100 years at the intersection of South Temple and Main streets in Salt Lake City to a location 82 feet to the north.

Oct. 26-Nov. 6: More than a dozen separate wildfires charred parts of Southern California, destroying eight LDS homes in the process. Church members joined relief efforts.

Oct. 30: Ground was broken by President Gordon B. Hinckley, first counselor in the First Presidency, and President Thomas S. Monson, second counselor in the First Presidency, for the St. Louis Missouri Temple, scheduled to be the Church's 50th temple.

November 1993

An LDS worship service was held in the Kirtland Temple **Nov. 6** in connection with an area priesthood leadership training meeting and mission presidents seminar. It was believed to be the first LDS service in the temple in 140 years.

Also in the news in November 1993:

Nov. 1: Richard A. Searfoss, the first Church member to pilot a space shuttle, successfully landed the spaceship Columbia following a 14-day voyage, the shuttle's longest flight to date.

Nov. 8: TempleReady, a long-awaited software making it possible to rapidly clear names from family history research for temple work, was announced in a letter to priesthood leaders from the First Presidency.

Nov. 14: A regional welfare center with multiple facilities was dedicated in Las Vegas, Nev., by Bishop H. David Burton of the Presiding Bishopric.

Nov. 16: Church leaders hailed the Religious Freedom Restoration Act passed Oct. 27 by the U.S. Senate and by the House of Representatives on May 11. This act was signed into law by the U.S. President on this date — as "the most historic piece of legislation dealing with religious freedom in our lifetime."

Nov. 22: Pres. Jose M. Jimenez and his counselor Julio Afre of the Guatemala City North Mission died in an airplane accident in Guatemala.

December 1993

The First Presidency announced **Dec. 4** that a temple will be built in the Caribbean at a site in Santo Domingo, Dominican Republic. This makes a total of 55 temples in use, under construction or announced.

Also in the news in December 1993:

December: Members in Spanish-speaking countries received the Triple Combination of the scriptures with the scripture aids in their language. The Book of Mormon with scripture aids was published in 1992.

Dec. 1: Ambassadors from 17 countries attended the annual lighting ceremony at the Washington Temple, hosted by Elder James E. Faust of the Council of the Twelve.

Dec. 18: The historic Grandin Building in Palmyra, N.Y., where the Book of Mormon was printed, will be restored to better present the story of the coming forth of the Book of Mormon.

Dec. 19: A choir of LDS missionaries serving in Rome sang at St. Peter's Basilica in the Vatican, which was broad-

January 1994

A yearlong commemoration of the 100th anniversary of the Church's Genealogical Society of Utah — now the Family History Department — began in **January** with an effort to invite the non-member international genealogical community to join the effort in preserving, automating, and sharing genealogical information for the benefit of all mankind.

Also in the news in January 1994:

January: Church members in southern Utah stitched more than 1,000 quilts for the relief of persons affected by the Midwestern floods in the summer of 1993.

Jan. 1: The First Presidency endorsed the designation by the United Nations of 1994 as the International Year of the Family.

Jan. 11: Members in Australia escaped danger in 30 bush fires that burned 1.5 million acres and 300 homes.

Jan. 17: An earthquake in Los Angeles, Calif., measuring 6.6 on the Richter Scale, destroyed 15 homes of Church members, displacing some 500-600 members. Damage of $15 billion was done by the temblor. The Church and its members donated many tons of supplies and hours of service in the clean-up effort.

Jan. 22: Ground was broken for the Hong Kong Temple by Elder John K. Carmack of the Seventy and president of the Asia Area.

February 1994

The First Presidency announced **Feb. 13** that the 87-year-old Unitah Stake Tabernacle in Vernal, Utah, will be renovated and dedicated as Utah's 10th temple. It is the first existing building to be renovated into a temple.

Also in the news in February 1994:

February: In conjunction with Black History Month, African-American choirs from various denominations combined for performances at the Los Angeles Temple Visitors Center.

Feb. 5: The Church announced it has launched a television series that will make LDS programs available in 85 percent of the English-speaking homes across Canada during 1994 over the

March 10, 1994: Flags fly over one of three new buildings dedicated at Missionary Training Center in Provo, Utah.

May 8, 1994: Elder Russell M. Nelson prepares to dedicate French Polynesia during commemoration of Church's 150th anniversary of the arrival of missionaries on these South Pacific islands.

VISION/TV network.

Feb. 19: The First Presidency issued a statement opposing efforts to legalize same-gender marriages.

Feb. 25: Elder Marvin J. Ashton, a member of the Council of the Twelve for 22 years, died following surgery. He was eulogized in funeral services March 2 as a "champion of love."

March 1994

In a letter to priesthood leaders, President Howard W. Hunter of the Council of the Twelve announced in **March** that the Stake Record Extraction and Family History Record Extraction programs would become a single, simplified organization called Family Record Extraction. The change has partly been the result of many more families submitting names to the temple, reducing the need for record extraction.

Also in the news in March 1994:

March 5: Elder Joseph B. Wirthlin of the Council of the Twelve dedicated a new missionary training center near the temple in Buenos Aires, Argentina.

March 6: The government of Cambodia officially recognized the Church, announced President Gordon B. Hinckley, first counselor in the First Presidency. Missionary couples would be sent to Cambodia to perform humanitarian service in the country but not proselyte, he said.

March 10: Three new buildings at the Missionary Training Center in Provo, Utah, were dedicated by President Gordon B. Hinckley, first counselor in the First Presidency.

March 24: Jane Partridge, an LDS

student in McLean, Va., testified before an U.S. Congressional Committee in support of a bill against drunk driving. She spoke of an automobile accident the previous year in which a young woman at her school had been killed.

March 26: A display of the Museum of Church History and Art's third international art competition opened and included works from 26 nations and 18 states of the United States, the most international exhibit to date.

April 1994

Elder Robert D. Hales, Presiding Bishop, was sustained **April 2** to fill the vacancy in the Council of the Twelve created by the death of Elder Marvin J. Ashton. Other sustainings at general conference included Elder Cree-L Kofford from the Second Quorum of the Seventy to the First Quorum of the Seventy, and Elders Claudio R.M. Costa, W. Don Ladd, James O. Mason, Dieter F. Uchtdorf, and Lance B. Wickman to the Second Quorum of the Seventy.

Sustained as Presiding Bishop was Elder Merrill J. Bateman of the Second Quorum of the Seventy. Sustained as his counselors were Bishops H. David Burton and Richard C. Edgley, who served as counselors to Bishop Hales.

Also in the news in April 1994:

April 9: Elder Clinton L. Cutler of the Second Quorum of the Seventy and second counselor in the Sunday School general presidency, died at his home.

April 16: Elder David B. Haight of the Council of the Twelve, mayor of Palo Alto, Calif., from 1961-63, was honored as the city's oldest living former mayor.

April 27: President Thomas S. Monson, second counselor in the First Presi-

June 6, 1994: Newly organized First Presidency, with members of the Council of the Twelve seated to the sides, issues statements to media.

dency, represented the Church at funeral services for former U.S. President Richard M. Nixon in Yorba Linda, Calif.

April 28-May 2: Some 18,800 people attended an open house at the 87-year-old Uintah Stake Tabernacle. The building will be renovated to become the Vernal Utah Temple.

April 29: The 59th annual American Mothers National Convention was held in Salt Lake City, under the leadership of Barbara B. Smith, former Relief Society general president.

May 1994

President Ezra Taft Benson, 94, president of the Church for 8½ years, died at his apartment **May 30** in Salt Lake City of congestive heart failure. He was eulogized at funeral services June 4 by admirers from around the world for his great contributions to mankind.

Also in the news in May 1994:

May 10: President Gordon B. Hinckley, first counselor in the First Presidency, and President Thomas S. Monson, second counselor in the First Presidency, spoke at a ceremony at Promontory Summit on the 125th anniversary of the completion of the intercontinental railway.

May 5: Elder Russell M. Nelson of the Council of the Twelve addressed the opening ceremonies in Papeete, Tahiti, of festivities marking the 150th anniversary of the arrival of LDS missionaries in Tahiti. The events ranged from the anniversary date of April 30 to May 11.

May 8: As part of the celebration of the 150th year of the Church in French Polynesia, Elder Russell M. Nelson dedicated the islands of French Polynesia.

May 13: President Ezra Taft Benson was inducted into the University of Idaho's Alumni Hall of Fame in honor of his humanitarian and professional contributions.

May 14: Thousands of members and leaders took part in a statewide clean-up effort endorsed by the Church in preparation of Utah's upcoming centennial in 1996.

May 21: President Gordon B. Hinckley, first counselor in the First Presidency, dedicated the renovated Cove Fort in south central Utah, which was built by his grandfather, Ira Hinckley.

June 1994

President Howard W. Hunter was ordained and set apart as the Church's 14th president of the Church on **June 5**. At a press conference in the Church Administration Building on **June 6,** President Hunter pledged his life and the full measure of his soul to his new calling, and invited members to live with "evermore attention to the life and example of the Lord Jesus Christ," and to "establish

June 26, 1994: President Howard W. Hunter speaks during telecast from Carthage Jail site on 150th anniversary of martyrdom of Joseph and Hyrum Smith.

the temple of the Lord as the great symbol of their membership and the supernal setting for their most sacred covenants." President Gordon B. Hinckley and President Thomas S. Monson were called as his first and second counselors, respectively.

President Gordon B. Hinckley was called and set apart as president of the Council of the Twelve. President Boyd K. Packer was called as Acting President of the Council of the Twelve.

Also in the news for June 1994:

June 12: Ground was broken at Chorley, England, for the Preston England Temple by President Gordon B. Hinckley, first counselor in the First Presidency.

June 21: President Howard W. Hunter delivered his first major address at the annual Mission President's Seminar at the Missionary Training Center in Provo, Utah. He emphasized that the atonement of the Savior is the foundation for missionary work.

June 23: Elder Jeffrey R. Holland of

the First Quorum of the Seventy was called to be a member of the Council of the Twelve. He filled the vacancy in the quorum created when President Howard W. Hunter became president of the Church following the death of President Ezra Taft Benson.

June 26: President Howard W. Hunter, President Gordon B. Hinckley and Elder M. Russell Ballard spoke at three separate commemorative events in Nauvoo and Carthage, Ill., on the 150th anniversary of the martyrdom of the Prophet Joseph Smith. The Prophet and his brother Hyrum were killed while incarcerated in Carthage Jail June 27, 1844.

July 1994

Massive relief efforts by the Church and LDS volunteers helped in the aftermath of the worst flooding in history **July 2-12** in 43 counties in Georgia that killed 31 people, inundated 300,000 acres and caused about $1 billion in damages. The homes of 35 LDS families were dam-

July 2-12, 1994: Among the more than 6,000 volunteers from Southern States, workers begin flood clean-up efforts in Albany, Ga., with prayer.

July 1994: Elder Kwok Yuen Tai, in suit, presents rice to officials of Front D'Edification Nationale Lao at Vientiane, Laos.

aged. Elder M. Russell Ballard of the Council of the Twelve delivered a message form the First Presidency as he visited the ravaged sites July 17.

Also in the news in July 1994:

July 22: A donation of rice to Laos by the Church received a public expression of thanks through the Laos media.

July 23: President Howard W. Hunter addressed a gathering at the centennial of the Salt Lake City and County building, congratulating those who had been instrumental in preserving it.

July 23: Hundreds gathered on the high plains of Wyoming at Rock Creek, 65 miles southwest of Riverton, as President Gordon B. Hinckley dedicated a monument and burial site of 15 handcart pioneers of the Willie company who died of freezing and starvation during their trip.

July 25: An heroic-sized statue of a younger, vigorous Brigham Young was unveiled at the Utah Capitol, the first full length statue of Utah's first governor to be placed in the rotunda. President Gordon B. Hinckley, first counselor in the First Presidency, spoke at the unveiling ceremony.

July 25: An historic agreement between BYU and the University of Jordan will help develop cooperation between the two institutions through possible academic, cultural and personnel exchanges.

July 28: The First Presidency announced that a $760,000 relief package would be sent to Rwanda, including emergency supplies and funds to deliver the supplies. The First Presidency also announced that Church assistance has

been distributed to more than 50 countries during recent years.

July 30: Hundreds gathered for commemorative services at a mountain peak in eastern California, which last October had been named for Melissa Coray, the wife of a Mormon Battalion soldier. She had accompanied the battalion on its 1,000-mile trek.

August 1994

Fully one-third of the population of the United States has been visited by Church representatives, and 36 percent have friends or relatives that are LDS, it was announced **Aug. 6** by the Missionary Department. In addition, the Church's paid media announcements on the Savior and the Book of Mormon are striking a responsive chord among many non-members.

Also in the news in August 1994:

August: BYU's Young Ambassadors were well-received as they performed in Morocco, Tunisia and Spain.

Aug. 5: A marker was dedicated in honor of Iowaville, a town on the Mormon Trail that no longer exists but where Mormon pioneers who left Nauvoo in 1846 often stopped and where some are buried.

Aug. 8-16: President Howard W. Hunter visited Switzerland on his first trip out of the United States since he became president of the Church, and praised the people of that nation for their "haven of peace." He also met with Church leaders at the Swiss Temple and addressed Lausanne Ward members.

Aug. 30: The First Presidency issued a statement reaffirming "the promised blessings to those who faithfully hold family home evenings."

September 1994

In a first-ever address of a Church president to missionaries over the Church's satellite system on **Sept. 13**, President Howard W. Hunter instructed missionaries to make their calling of teaching and baptizing the focus of their missions. The address of President Hunter and other instruction were to go to every LDS missionary in the world.

Also in the news for September 1994:

Sept. 7: The old Lafayette School building, the last mission training home in Salt Lake City, was razed to make way for a parking lot. It was used as a mission home from 1971-78.

Sept. 8: VIPs were the first to attend the open house of the Orlando Florida Temple, and were followed by some 90,000 other visitors. Many positive comments were made of their experiences. The open house continued through Sept. 30.

Sept 14: Elder Dallin H. Oaks of the Council of the Twelve dedicated the Republic of Cape Verde, a string of 10 rugged islands and five islets located 400 miles west of Senegal on the African coast.

Sept. 18: President Howard W. Hunter addressed 13,000 people at a regional conference in Tucson, Ariz., the first at which he presided since he became Church president June 5.

Sept. 24: President Howard W. Hunter asked the women of the Church to stand with and for the Brethren in stemming the "tide of evil that surrounds us, and in moving forward the work of our Savior" at the annual General Relief Society Meeting.

October 1994

In a solemn assembly **Oct. 1**, President Howard W. Hunter was sustained as the 14th president of the Church. Also sustained were his first counselor, President Gordon B. Hinckley, and his second counselor, President Thomas S. Monson.

Elder Jeffrey R. Holland, ordained an apostle on June 23, was sustained a member of the Council of the Twelve.

Called from the Second Quorum of the Seventy to the First Quorum was Elder Dennis B. Neuenschwander. Two others called to the First Quorum of the Seventy were Elders Andrew W. Peterson and Cecil O. Samuelson Jr.

Elder Hartman Rector Jr. of the First Quorum of the Seventy, a General Authority since 1968, was given emeritus status. Members of the Second Quorum of the Seventy who were released at the conclusion of their five-year term of service were: Elders Albert Choules Jr., Lloyd P. George, Malcolm S. Jeppsen, Richard P. Lindsay, Merlin R. Lybbert, Gerald E. Melchin and Horacio A. Tenorio.

Sustained as the new Sunday School general president was Elder Charles Didier of the presidency of the Seventy. His first and second counselors, respectively, are Elders J Ballard Washburn and F. Burton Howard of the Seventy. They succeed Elder Merlin R. Lybbert, former Sunday School general president, and his second counselor, Ronald E. Poelman. Elder Clinton L. Cutler, former first counselor, died April 9, 1994.

Sustained as new Primary general

Sept. 14, 1994: Elder Dallin H. Oaks, second from right, listens to Policarpo Gomes speak at meeting at which Elder Oaks dedicated Cape Verde.

president was Patricia Peterson Pinegar, formerly second counselor in the Young Women general presidency. Her first and second counselors, respectively, are Anne Goalen Wirthlin and Susan Carol Lillywhite Warner.

Bonnie Dansie Parkin was sustained as second counselor in the Young Women General presidency, succeeding Sister Pinegar.

Sister Michaelene P. Grassli and her counselors, Sisters Betty Jo N. Jepsen and Ruth B. Wright, were released.

Also in the news in late 1994:

Transcription of the 1881 British Census Project is a joint venture of the Church and the British Genealogical Record Users Committee that began in 1988 to produce microfiche indexes for all counties in England, Wales, and the Channel Islands, Isle of Man and Scotland. The records, provided by Her Majesty's Stationery Office and the Public Record Office, include some 30.2 million names.

The combining of all Church resources into one data base was made possible by the Family Record Extraction Program volunteers. The information will be available in future editions of the International Genealogical Index.

PROGRESS DURING ADMINISTRATIONS OF THE PRESIDENTS

	At beginning		At end	
	Stakes	Members*	Stakes	Members*
JOSEPH SMITH	0	280	2	26,146
BRIGHAM YOUNG	2	34,694	20	115,065
JOHN TAYLOR	23	133,628	31	173,029
WILFORD WOODRUFF	32	180,294	40	267,251
LORENZO SNOW	40	267,251	50	292,931
JOSEPH F. SMITH	50	292,931	75	495,962
HEBER J. GRANT	75	495,962	149	954,004
GEORGE ALBERT SMITH	149	954,004	184	1,111,314
DAVID O. MCKAY	184	1,111,314	500	2,807,456
JOSEPH FIELDING SMITH	500	2,807,456	581	3,218,908
HAROLD B. LEE	581	3,218,908	630	3,306,658
SPENCER W. KIMBALL	630	3,306,658	1,570	5,920,000
EZRA TAFT BENSON	1,570	5,920,000	1,980	8,688,511
HOWARD W. HUNTER	1,980	8,688,511		

* Nearest year-end total

FACTS,
STATISTICS

MEMBERSHIP STATISTICS

Membership and units by Church area

(As of Dec. 31, 1993; Area boundaries do not necessarily follow country, state or province boundaries. Individual Area, Country/land, State and Province membership numbers are rounded. Total membership listed at the bottom of the columns are from exact numbers and then rounded. Therefore, column totals may not agree with the sum of individual entries. (Utah North and Utah Central totals have been combined.)

Area	Stakes	Wards	Stake branches	Missions	Districts	Mission branches	Total wards, branches	Membership
Africa	10	55	53	12	51	287	395	77,000
Asia	7	43	14	6	17	99	156	54,000
Asia North	41	220	99	14	25	128	447	167,000
Brazil	104	639	233	19	39	241	1,113	474,000
Central America	51	302	185	11	44	259	746	303,000
Europe	21	115	131	21	20	148	394	61,000
Europe North	48	274	147	12	13	60	481	184,000
Europe Mediterranean	20	104	131	18	53	305	540	110,000
Mexico North	60	343	110	10	29	193	646	341,000
Mexico South	65	437	148	8	18	152	737	347,000
North America Central	102	705	253	14	11	79	1,037	389,000
North America Northeast	102	660	334	24	7	62	1,056	396,000
North America Northwest	182	1,310	154	9	5	32	1,496	666,000
North America Southeast	83	548	265	23	22	170	983	394,000
North America Southwest	150	1,060	273	13	0	0	1,333	635,000
North America West	173	1,272	188	15	0	5	1,465	773,000
Pacific	61	410	182	13	33	188	780	297,000
Philippines/ Micronesia	46	276	146	14	92	558	980	321,000
South America North	106	654	319	18	84	584	1,557	591,000
South America South	115	651	324	18	84	493	1,468	627,000
Utah North	275	1,982	71	2	0	0	2,053	1,002,000
Utah South	146	1,195	41	1	0	0	1,236	478,000
Total in U.S., Canada Areas	**1,213**	**8,732**	**1,574**	**101**	**45**	**348**	**10,659**	**4,734,000**
Total other areas	**755**	**4,523**	**2,222**	**194**	**602**	**3,695**	**10,440**	**3,955,000**
Worldwide total	**1,968**	**13,255**	**3,801**	**295**	**647**	**4,043**	**21,099**	**8,689,000**

Membership and units by lands

* Denotes fewer than 100 members; # denotes fewer than 1 LDS per 10,000)

Country/land	Stakes	Wards	Stake branches	Missions	Districts	Mission branches	Total wards, branches	Membership	Per cent LDS	1 LDS in:
AFRICA										
Botswana	0	0	0	0	1	3	3	300	0.00	#
Cameroon	0	0	0	0	0	1	1	*	0.00	#
Cape Verde	0	0	0	0	3	13	13	2,000	0.00	#
Central Africa Republic	0	0	0	0	0	2	2	*	0.00	#
Congo	0	0	0	0	1	5	5	800	0.00	#
Egypt	0	0	0	0	1	1	1	*	0.00	#
Ethiopia	0	0	0	0	0	1	1	*	0.00	#
Ghana	2	13	9	1	4	24	46	12,000	0.01	1,375
Ivory Coast	0	0	0	1	2	12	12	1,500	0.00	#
Kenya	0	0	0	1	2	11	11	1,400	0.00	#
Lesotho	0	0	0	0	0	1	1	300	0.00	#
Liberia	0	0	0	0	1	7	7	1,400	0.02	#
Madagascar	0	0	0	0	0	1	1	100	0.00	#
Mauritius	0	0	0	0	0	2	2	200	0.02	#
Namibia	0	0	0	0	1	2	2	100	0.00	#
Nigeria	3	17	16	4	15	93	126	22,000	0.02	4,322
Reunion (France)	0	0	0	0	1	4	4	500	0.09	1,150
Sierra Leone	0	0	0	0	3	14	14	1,900	0.04	2,395
South Africa	5	25	28	3	8	44	97	23,000	0.1	1,697
Swaziland	0	0	0	0	1	5	5	700	0.09	1,144
Tanzania	0	0	0	0	0	1	1	100	0.00	#
Tunisia	0	0	0	0	0	1	1	*	0.00	#
Uganda	0	0	0	0	2	6	6	800	0.00	#
Zaire	0	0	0	1	6	22	22	4,600	0.01	8,965
Zambia	0	0	0	0	0	2	2	200	0.00	#
Zimbabwe	0	0	0	1	3	24	24	5,300	0.05	2,022
Africa total	**10**	**55**	**53**	**12**	**55**	**302**	**410**	**79,000**	**0.00**	**#**
ASIA										
Bangladesh	0	0	0	0	0	1	1	*	0.00	#
China	0	0	0	0	0	2	2	100	0.00	#
Cyprus	0	0	0	0	0	1	1	*	0.00	#
Diego Garcia	0	0	0	0	0	1	1	*	0.00	#
Hong Kong (U.K.)	4	24	8	1	0	0	32	18,000	0.3	322
India	0	0	0	1	4	14	14	1,300	0.00	#
Indonesia	0	0	0	0	3	18	18	4,600	0.00	#
Japan	25	132	54	10	21	103	289	103,000	0.1	1,208
Korea, Republic	16	88	45	4	4	25	158	65,000	0.15	686
Macau (Portuguese)	0	0	1	0	0	0	1	700	0.06	1,670
Malaysia	0	0	0	0	1	4	4	600	0.00	#
Mongolia	0	0	0	0	0	1	1	*	0.00	#
Myanmar (Burma)	0	0	0	0	0	1	1	*	0.00	#
Papua New Guinea	0	0	0	1	2	16	16	3,300	0.08	1,184
Philippines	46	276	146	13	83	521	943	314,000	0.5	205
Singapore	0	0	0	1	1	6	6	1,800	0.06	1,555
Sri Lanka	0	0	0	0	0	1	1	100	0.00	#
Taiwan	3	19	5	2	4	24	48	21,000	0.1	995
Thailand	0	0	0	1	4	23	23	5,300	0.00	#
Turkey	0	0	0	0	1	4	4	200	0.00	#
Asia total	**94**	**539**	**259**	**34**	**129**	**771**	**1,569**	**540,000**	**0.00**	**#**

Country/land	Stakes	Wards	Stake branches	Missions	Districts	Mission branches	Total wards, branches	Membership	Per cent LDS	1 LDS in:
CARIBBEAN										
Antigua (U.K.)	0	0	0	0	0	1	1	*	0.00	#
Aruba (Netherlands)	0	0	0	0	0	1	1	*	0.00	#
Bahamas	0	0	0	0	0	2	2	300	0.1	1,006
Barbados	0	0	0	1	0	4	4	400	0.17	604
Bermuda (U.K.)	0	0	0	0	0	1	1	*	0.00	#
Bonaire (Netherlands)	0	0	0	0	0	1	1	*	0.00	#
Cayman Islands (Jamaica)	0	0	0	0	0	1	1	*	0.00	#
Cuba	0	0	0	0	0	1	1	*	0.00	#
Curacao	0	0	0	0	0	2	2	300	0.00	#
Dominican Republic	7	43	25	3	9	57	125	47,000	0.6	163
Grenada	0	0	0	0	0	1	1	*	0.00	#
Guadeloupe (France)	0	0	0	0	0	1	1	*	0.00	#
Haiti	0	0	0	1	2	18	18	5,000	0.1	1,312
Jamaica	0	0	0	1	2	14	14	3,000	0.1	747
Martinique (France)	0	0	0	0	0	1	1	*	0.00	#
Netherlands Antilles	0	0	0	0	0	1	1	*	0.00	#
Puerto Rico (U.S.)	0	0	0	1	8	50	50	19,000	0.50	196
St. Kitts-Nevis (U.K.)	0	0	0	0	0	1	1	*	0.00	#
Saint Lucia (U.K.)	0	0	0	0	0	1	1	*	0.00	#
Saint Martin (France)	0	0	0	0	0	1	1	*	0.00	#
Saint Vincent & Grenadines	0	0	0	0	0	1	1	200	0.18	530
Trinidad & Tobago	0	0	0	1	0	3	3	700	0.05	1,857
Virgin Islands (U.S.)	0	0	0	0	0	2	2	200	0.19	520
Caribbean total	**7**	**43**	**25**	**8**	**21**	**166**	**234**	**77,000**		
MEXICO										
Mexico	125	780	258	18	47	345	1,383	688,000	0.8	130
CENTRAL AMERICA										
Belize	0	0	0	0	3	8	8	1,400	0.7	145
Costa Rica	4	20	14	1	6	28	62	22,000	0.70	151
El Salvador	10	56	43	2	1	13	112	50,000	1.0	105
Guatemala	24	151	87	4	18	100	338	140,000	1.4	72
Honduras	9	53	21	2	6	35	109	53,000	0.9	106
Nicaragua	0	0	0	1	8	59	59	13,000	0.30	316
Panama	4	22	20	1	2	16	58	23,000	0.9	109
Central America total	**51**	**302**	**185**	**11**	**44**	**259**	**746**	**303,000**	**0.54**	**182**
SOUTH AMERICA										
Argentina	34	194	126	10	54	305	625	205,000	0.6	164
Bolivia	12	75	26	2	10	78	179	78,000	1.0	102
Brazil	104	639	233	19	39	241	1,113	474,000	0.3	320
Chile	67	391	151	6	16	90	637	345,000	2.6	39
Colombia	13	85	42	4	21	135	262	98,000	0.3	356
Ecuador	17	99	58	3	12	91	248	115,000	1.1	90
French Guiana	0	0	0	0	0	2	2	100	0.00	#

Country/ land	Stakes	Wards	Stake branches	Missions	Districts	Mission branches	Total wards, branches	Membership	Per cent LDS	1 LDS in:
Guyana	0	0	0	0	0	1	1	300	0.00	#
Paraguay	3	15	8	1	6	52	75	16,000	0.4	263
Peru	52	328	163	6	30	185	677	234,000	1.0	97
Suriname	0	0	0	0	0	1	1	200	0.04	2,040
Uruguay	11	51	39	1	8	41	131	61,000	1.9	52
Venezuela	12	67	30	3	11	90	187	66,000	0.3	303
South America total	**325**	**1,944**	**876**	**55**	**207**	**1,318**	**4,138**	**1,692,000**	**0.49**	**204**
SOUTH PACIFIC										
Australia	18	118	35	6	16	69	222	82,000	0.5	217
Cook Islands	0	0	0	0	1	6	6	800	4.44	22
Fiji	1	5	10	1	2	10	25	9,500	1.2	85
French Polynesia (Tahiti)	4	25	14	1	2	17	56	13,000	6.4	16
Guam (U.S.)	0	0	0	1	1	4	4	1,200	.73	136
Johnson Atoll	0	0	0	0	0	1	1	*	0.00	#
Kiribati	0	0	0	0	1	17	17	4,600	6.5	15
Marshall Islands	0	0	0	0	2	9	9	2,200	4.2	24
Micronesia Federated States	0	0	0	0	5	20	20	2,400	2.3	42
Nauru	0	0	0	0	0	1	1	*	0.00	#
New Caledonia (France)	0	0	0	0	1	5	5	1,000	0.5	200
New Zealand	16	108	48	2	5	28	184	80,000	2.3	43
Niue	0	0	0	0	1	3	3	300	17.00	6
Northern Mariana Islands	0	0	0	0	0	2	2	400	.92	108
Palau	0	0	0	0	1	2	2	300	2.22	45
Samoa, American (U.S.)	2	19	4	0	0	0	23	12,000	25	4
Samoa, Western	10	69	30	1	0	0	99	51,000	25	4
Tonga	10	66	41	1	2	14	121	38,000	37	3
Tuvalu	0	0	0	0	0	1	1	*	0.00	#
Vanuatu	0	0	0	0	0	1	1	400	0.13	750
South Pacific total	**61**	**410**	**182**	**13**	**40**	**210**	**802**	**300,000**	**1.25**	**80**
UNITED KINGDOM AND IRELAND										
England	33	188	77	6	0	0	265	123,000	0.3	376
Northern Ireland	1	7	6	0	0	1	14	5,500	0.34	290
Scotland	5	24	18	1	0	3	45	25,000	0.5	200
Wales	2	11	9	0	0	0	20	7,100	0.24	415
United Kingdom total	**41**	**230**	**100**	**7**	**0**	**4**	**344**	**161,000**	**0.28**	**358**
Ireland	0	0	0	1	2	12	12	2,200	0.06	1,636
EUROPE										
Albania	0	0	0	0	0	3	3	100	0.00	#
Austria	1	7	13	1	0	1	20	3,900	0.05	2,027
Belgium	1	8	6	2	1	12	26	5,600	0.05	1,867
Bulgaria	0	0	0	1	1	10	10	700	0.00	#
Corsica	0	0	0	0	0	1	1	*	0.00	#
Croatia	0	0	0	0	1	3	3	100	0.00	#
Czech Republic	0	0	0	1	2	13	13	1,000	0.00	#
Estonia	0	0	0	0	0	2	2	200	0.00	#
France	7	34	44	3	6	28	106	25,000	0.04	2,308
Germany	15	85	85	6	1	7	177	36,000	0.04	2,253
Greece	0	0	0	1	1	7	7	200	0.00	#
Hungary	0	0	0	1	2	18	18	1,400	0.01	7,357
Italy	2	10	15	4	10	78	103	16,000	0.03	3,612

Country/land	Stakes	Wards	Stake branches	Missions	Districts	Mission branches	Total wards, branches	Membership	Percent LDS	1 LDS in:
Latvia	0	0	0	1	0	2	2	*	0.00	#
Luxembourg	0	0	1	0	0	0	1	100	0.00	#
Malta	0	0	0	0	0	1	1	*	0.00	#
Netherlands	3	13	21	1	0	0	34	7,000	0.05	2,171
Poland	0	0	0	1	1	9	9	500	0.00	#
Portugal	5	24	27	3	12	60	111	33,000	0.3	297
Romania	0	0	0	1	1	4	4	300	0.00	#
Russia	0	0	0	3	5	33	33	1,900	0.00	#
Serbia	0	0	0	0	1	2	2	*	0.00	#
Slovakia	0	0	0	0	0	2	2	*	0.00	#
Slovenia	0	0	0	0	1	3	3	*	0.00	#
Spain	3	17	19	5	18	108	144	25,000	0.1	1,564
Switzerland	3	16	20	2	0	0	36	6,700	0.10	1,044
Ukraine	0	0	0	2	3	25	25	1,700	0.00	#
Europe total	**40**	**214**	**250**	**39**	**67**	**432**	**896**	**167,000**	**0.00**	**#**
NORDIC COUNTRIES										
Denmark	2	12	11	1	0	0	23	4,400	0.09	1,155
Finland	2	11	6	1	3	11	28	4,400	0.09	1,159
Iceland	0	0	0	0	1	3	3	200	0.10	999
Norway	1	7	2	1	3	14	23	4,000	0.1	1,075
Sweden	2	14	18	1	4	16	48	8,300	0.1	1,048
Nordic total	**7**	**44**	**37**	**4**	**11**	**44**	**125**	**21,000**	**0.09**	**1,100**

Membership and units in the United States, Canada

(As of Dec. 31, 1993; membership numbers are rounded off;
totals are from original, not rounded, numbers)

United States

State	Stakes	Wards	Stake branches	Missions	Districts	Mission branches	Total wards, branches	Membership	Percent LDS	1 LDS in:
Alabama	6	39	32	1	0	0	71	24,000	0.6	176
Alaska	5	32	16	1	3	20	68	23,000	3.7	26
Arizona	62	452	55	3	0	0	507	256,000	6.4	16
Arkansas	4	25	24	1	0	0	49	15,000	0.6	162
California	160	1,169	180	14	0	4	1,353	719,000	2.3	43
Colorado	25	167	34	2	0	1	202	95,000	2.6	38
Connecticut	3	20	6	1	0	0	26	10,000	0.3	363
Delaware	1	6	2	0	0	0	8	3,300	0.5	215
District of Columbia	0	1	3	0	0	0	4	1,000	0.2	575
Florida	21	144	36	4	0	0	180	93,000	0.7	149
Georgia	11	76	32	2	1	5	113	49,000	0.7	142
Hawaii	13	103	11	1	0	0	114	53,000	4.4	23
Idaho	97	691	38	2	0	0	729	316,000	28.5	4
Illinois	10	74	25	2	0	0	99	41,000	0.3	286
Indiana	8	54	21	1	0	0	75	29,000	0.5	197
Iowa	3	26	12	1	0	0	38	13,000	0.4	216
Kansas	4	35	16	0	1	7	58	21,000	0.8	121
Kentucky	3	30	30	1	0	0	60	19,000	0.5	201
Louisiana	7	37	28	1	0	0	65	23,000	0.5	187
Maine	2	16	8	0	0	0	24	7,500	0.6	166
Maryland	7	51	15	1	0	0	66	29,000	0.5	173
Massachusetts	3	26	13	1	0	0	39	15,000	0.2	334
Michigan	8	51	26	2	1	5	82	30,000	0.3	323
Minnesota	5	33	16	1	0	0	49	18,000	0.4	252
Mississippi	4	25	16	1	0	0	41	15,000	0.5	178
Missouri	10	72	31	2	0	0	103	40,000	0.8	132

State	Stakes	Wards	Stake bran- ches	Miss- ions	Dist- ricts	Miss- ion bran- ches	Total wards, bran- ches	Mem- ber- ship	Per cent LDS	1 LDS in:
Montana	10	61	36	1	1	10	107	37,000	4.4	23
Nebraska	4	24	16	1	0	4	44	14,000	0.9	116
Nevada	26	196	28	1	0	0	224	117,000	8.2	12
New Hampshire	3	12	5	1	0	0	17	6,400	0.6	177
New Jersey	4	26	17	1	0	2	45	17,000	0.2	467
New Mexico	12	81	31	1	0	0	112	51,000	3.1	32
New York	9	57	50	3	2	22	129	44,000	0.2	414
North Carolina	12	74	34	2	0	0	108	48,000	0.7	147
North Dakota	1	3	3	0	1	9	15	4,800	0.7	133
Ohio	11	68	31	2	0	0	99	40,000	0.3	287
Oklahoma	7	42	27	2	0	1	70	29,000	0.9	113
Oregon	34	218	36	2	0	0	254	121,000	4.0	25
Pennsylvania	9	60	25	3	2	17	102	32,000	0.3	377
Rhode Island	1	5	1	0	0	0	6	2,000	0.2	558
South Carolina	4	38	14	1	0	0	52	24,000	0.7	154
South Dakota	2	10	8	1	3	15	33	8,100	1.1	89
Tennessee	8	43	20	2	0	0	63	25,000	0.5	206
Texas	38	273	110	6	0	0	383	170,000	0.9	108
Utah	405	3,046	104	3	0	0	3,150	1,425,000	76	1.3
Vermont	1	6	5	0	0	0	11	3,200	0.5	181
Virginia	15	93	31	1	0	0	124	59,000	0.9	113
Washington	50	385	45	3	0	0	430	203,000	3.8	26
West Virginia	3	16	18	1	0	0	34	11,000	0.6	166
Wisconsin	3	22	16	1	1	7	46	15,000	0.3	337
Wyoming	16	118	14	0	0	0	132	54,000	11.5	9
Total	1,169	8,433	1,451	86	16	129	10,013	4,520,000	1.7	58

Canada

Prov- ince/ Terri- tory	Stakes	Wards	Stake bran- ches	Miss- ions	Dist- ricts	Miss- ion bran- ches	Total wards, bran- ches	Mem- ber- ship	Per cent LDS	1 LDS in:
Alberta	17	129	35	1	1	7	171	58,000	2.2	45
British Columbia	6	42	19	1	2	14	75	25,000	0.7	136
Manitoba	1	5	6	1	0	0	11	3,800	0.3	290
New Brunswick	1	5	3	0	0	0	8	2,100	0.3	347
Newfoundland	0	0	0	0	0	4	4	600	0.1	947
Northwest Territories	0	0	0	0	0	1	1	100	0.1	600
Nova Scotia	1	6	5	1	1	4	15	4,000	0.3	324
Ontario	8	53	23	2	2	8	84	32,000	0.3	324
Prince Edward Island	0	0	0	0	0	3	3	300	0.2	437
Quebec	2	11	5	1	1	5	21	7,400	0.1	944
Saskatchewan	1	5	7	0	1	4	16	4,400	0.5	226
Yukon	0	0	0	0	0	1	1	100	0.3	290
Canada total	37	256	103	7	8	51	410	138,000	0.5	202

CHURCH STATISTICS

As of Dec. 31	Members, stakes	Members, missions	Total members	Stakes	Wards, branches	Missions	Mission branches
1830							
Apr. 6	0	0	6	0	0	0	0
Dec. 31	280	0	280	0	4	0	0
1831	680	0	680	0	6	0	0
1832	1,318	1,313	2,661	0	27	0	6
1833	1,805	1,335	3,140	0	23	0	17
1834	3,050	1,322	4,372	2	22	0	18
1835	7,500	1,335	8,835	2	22	0	26
1836	12,000	1,293	13,293	2	25	0	29
1837	14,400	1,882	16,282	2	25	1	42
1838	15,300	2,581	17,881	2	26	1	65
1839	13,700	2,760	16,460	3	16	2	70
1840	11,962	4,903	16,865	10	18	2	69
1841	12,475	7,381	19,856	2	19	2	84
1842	13,549	10,015	23,564	2	26	2	199
1843	15,601	10,379	25,980	2	31	2	238
1844	16,374	9,772	26,146	2	33	3	239
1845	17,020	13,312	30,332	1	34	4	277
1846	18,960	15,033	33,993	0	30	5	311
1847	17,263	17,431	34,694	1	48	5	357
1848	16,749	23,728	40,477	1	55	5	426
1849	17,654	30,506	48,160	1	75	5	515
1850	18,756	33,083	51,839	1	61	9	637
1851	16,069	36,096	52,165	4	60	11	717
1852	15,627	37,013	52,640	5	65	13	795
1853	25,537	38,617	64,154	5	75	14	885
1854	30,817	37,612	68,429	6	79	13	859
1855	28,654	35,320	63,974	6	99	14	858
1856	31,762	32,119	63,881	7	124	12	841
1857	32,529	22,707	55,236	6	77	12	742
1858	33,880	21,875	55,755	4	81	9	661
1859	36,481	20,557	57,038	4	98	9	635
1860	39,338	21,744	61,082	4	110	8	611
1861	42,417	23,794	66,211	4	126	7	588
1862	45,565	23,215	68,780	4	135	7	563
1863	49,283	22,487	71,770	4	143	7	524
1864	53,006	21,342	74,348	4	161	8	471
1865	56,562	20,209	76,771	4	164	8	436
1866	59,803	18,081	77,884	4	167	8	420
1867	63,071	18,053	81,124	4	175	8	407
1868	66,589	18,033	84,622	5	178	8	385
1869	70,157	18,275	88,432	9	187	7	383
1870	73,747	16,383	90,130	9	195	7	363
1871	78,458	17,138	95,596	9	200	7	342
1872	81,821	16,331	98,152	9	206	7	347
1873	85,194	16,344	101,538	9	213	7	348
1874	88,567	15,349	103,916	10	216	7	309
1875	91,992	15,175	107,167	10	222	7	302
1876	95,773	15,338	111,111	10	230	8	307
1877	99,780	15,285	115,065	20	252	8	285
1878	109,894	15,152	125,046	21	254	9	272
1879	112,705	15,681	128,386	22	263	10	289
1880	117,773	15,855	133,628	23	272	10	287
1881	123,918	16,815	140,733	23	283	10	293
1882	128,779	16,825	145,604	24	292	10	291
1883	135,128	16,465	151,593	27	317	11	292

As of Dec. 31	Members, stakes	Members, missions	Total members	Stakes	Wards, branches	Missions	Mission branches
1884	142,417	15,825	158,242	29	340	13	296
1885	147,557	16,573	164,130	29	348	12	311
1886	150,602	16,051	166,653	30	342	12	315
1887	155,654	17,375	173,029	31	360	12	326
1888	162,424	17,830	180,294	32	373	13	336
1889	164,834	18,310	183,144	32	388	12	339
1890	170,653	17,610	188,263	32	395	12	330
1891	177,489	17,956	195,445	32	409	12	332
1892	182,623	18,338	200,961	33	439	14	350
1893	194,352	20,182	214,534	34	451	15	356
1894	201,047	21,322	222,369	34	457	15	356
1895	208,179	22,937	231,116	37	479	15	356
1896	215,514	25,913	241,427	37	489	17	348
1897	222,802	32,934	255,736	37	493	18	374
1898	229,428	37,823	267,251	40	516	20	401
1899	229,734	41,947	271,681	40	506	20	412
1900	236,628	47,137	283,765	43	529	20	438
1901	243,368	49,563	292,931	50	577	21	442
1902	249,927	49,178	299,105	50	595	22	481
1903	257,661	47,240	304,901	51	612	23	477
1904	275,681	48,608	324,289	55	619	21	475
1905	281,162	50,886	332,048	55	627	22	514
1906	289,377	55,637	345,014	55	636	22	541
1907	298,847	59,066	357,913	55	634	22	558
1908	307,308	64,164	371,472	59	666	22	595
1909	308,094	69,185	377,279	60	684	21	590
1910	327,017	71,461	398,478	62	699	21	611
1911	334,643	72,648	407,291	62	706	21	632
1912	341,278	76,277	417,555	65	716	22	647
1913	350,321	81,286	431,607	66	749	22	650
1914	371,729	82,989	454,718	68	772	21	601
1915	381,336	84,902	466,238	72	783	21	608
1916	390,449	86,872	477,321	73	808	22	559
1917	397,933	90,105	488,038	75	875	22	578
1918	404,030	91,932	495,962	75	893	22	559
1919	413,563	94,398	507,961	79	888	23	554
1920	426,167	99,820	525,987	83	904	24	623
1921	441,472	107,331	548,803	86	933	25	665
1922	451,762	114,596	566,358	87	946	25	661
1923	463,578	112,318	575,896	90	962	26	697
1924	479,498	118,363	597.861	94	969	25	716
1925	490,688	122,884	613,572	94	985	28	720
1926	494,536	129,373	623,909	96	992	28	739
1927	510,910	133,835	644,745	99	1,005	28	758
1928	516,986	138,700	655,686	101	1,004	29	813
1929	520,339	143,313	663,652	104	1,004	30	823
1930	532,877	137,140	670,017	104	1,000	30	868
1931	544,453	143,982	688,435	104	1,004	31	861
1932	554,462	149,487	703,949	104	1,012	31	867
1933	564,042	153,577	717,619	105	1,014	31	875
1934	579,118	151,620	730,738	110	1,035	31	892
1935	595,071	151,313	746,384	115	1,064	32	900
1936	607,202	153,488	760,690	118	1,081	33	933
1937	616,088	151,664	767,752	118	1,101	35	951
1938	632,994	151,770	784,764	126	1,137	36	947
1939	645,618	157,910	803,528	129	1,154	35	1,002
1940	703,017	159,647	862,664	134	1,191	35	728

As of Dec. 31	Members, stakes	Members, missions	Total members	Stakes	Wards, branches	Missions	Mission branches
1941	736,544	155,536	892,080	139	1,224	36	757
1942	754,826	162,889	917,715	143	1,242	37	776
1943	774,161	162,889	937,050	146	1,261	38	807
1944	792,362	161,642	954,004	148	1,273	38	773
1945	811,045	168,409	979,454	153	1,295	38	909
1946	823,819	172,686	996,505	161	1,340	39	959
1947	843,021	173,149	1,016,170	169	1,425	43	1,149
1948	854,099	187,871	1,041,970	172	1,451	44	1,323
1949	876,661	202,010	1,078,671	175	1,501	46	1,327
1950	898,478	212,836	1,111,314	180	1,541	43	1,370
1951	933,792	213,365	1,147,157	191	1,666	42	1,414
1952	974,118	214,935	1,189,053	202	1,767	43	1,551
1953	1,034,381	211,981	1,246,362	211	1,884	42	1,399
1954	1,079,583	222,657	1,302,240	219	1,993	42	1,476
1955	1,126,265	213,009	1,357,274	224	2,082	44	1,471
1956	1,177,856	238,875	1,416,731	239	2,210	45	1,854
1957	1,233,397	254,917	1,488,314	251	2,362	45	1,740
1958	1,292,098	263,701	1,555,799	273	2,513	47	1,757
1959	1,336,675	279,413	1,616,088	290	2,614	50	1,895
1960	1,408,722	284,408	1,693,180	319	2,882	58	1,811
1961	1,514,551	309,110	1,823,661	345	3,143	67	1,872
1962	1,626,965	335,821	1,965,786	364	3,423	74	1,802
1963	1,736,567	380,884	2,117,451	389	3,615	77	1,782
1964	1,801,571	433,345	2,234,916	400	3,749	79	2,016
1965	1,977,418	418,514	2,395,932	412	3,897	76	2,137
1966	2,032,359	448,540	2,480,899	425	4,022	75	2,053
1967	2,144,766	469,574	2,614,340	448	4,166	77	1,987
1968	2,207,976	476,097	2,684,073	473	4,385	83	2,112
1969	2,344,635	462,821	2,807,456	496	4,592	88	2,016
1970	2,485,525	445,285	2,930,810	537	4,922	92	1,943
1971	2,645,419	445,534	3,090,953	562	5,135	98	1,942
1972	2,794,731	424,177	3,218,908	592	5,394	101	1,891
1973	2,904,244	402,414	3,306,658	630	5,707	108	1,817
1974	2,999,536	410,451	3,409,987	675	5,951	113	1,822
1975	3,188,062	384,140	3,572,202	737	6,390	134	1,761
1976	3,352,535	390,214	3,742,749	798	6,903	149	1,422
1977	3,618,331	350,889	3,969,220	885	7,486	157	1,694
1978	3,829,385	337,469	4,166,854	990	8,064	165	1,790
1979	4,059,044	345,077	4,404,121	1,092	9,365	175	1,121
1980	4,328,521	311,301	4,639,822	1,218	10,324	188	2,267
1981	4,621,688	298,761	4,920,449	1,321	11,063	188	2,030
1982	4,832,158	330,461	5,162,619	1,392	11,492	180	1,979
1983	5,013,541	338,183	5,351,724	1,458	11,952	178	1,991
1984	5,278,192	362,862	5,641,054	1,507	12,422	182	2,046
1985	5,555,407	364,074	5,919,483	1,582	12,939	188	2,068
1986	5,785,324	381,650	6,166,974	1,622	13,318	193	2,064
1987	5,974,239	420,075	6,394,314	1,666	13,727	205	2,307
1988	6,271,311	449,889	6,721,210	1,707	14,069	222	2,470
1989	6,794,686	514,016	7,308,702	1,739	14,534	228	2,758
1990	7,141,487	619,625	7,761,112	1,784	15,003	256	3,079
1991	7,423,061	666,417	8,089,878	1,837	15,513	267	3,325
1992	7,673,985	730,107	8,404,092	1,919	16,293	276	3,819
1993	7,910,975	777,536	8,688,511	1,968	17,056	295	4,043

INDEX

A

Abrea, Angel 23
Africa Area 98
Alabama 108-9
Alabama Birmingham Mission 319
Alaska. 109-10
Alaska Anchorage Mission 317
Albania 192,12,400
Alberta, Canada 207-8
Alberta Temple. 330
Aldrich, Hazen 58
Alvarez, Lino 33
Amado, Carlos H. 23
American Samoa. 192-93
Andersen, H. Verlan 71
Andersen, Neil L.. 23
Anderson, Joseph 67
Anderson, May. 89
Antigua and Barbuda 193
Apia Samoa Temple. 330-31
Archibald, Dallas N. 33
Areas
  membership statistics. 412
  maps 98-106
Argentina 193-95
Argentina Buenos Aires North Mission   310
Argentina Buenos Aires South Mission   317
Argentina Buenos Aires West Mission.   324
Argentina Cordoba Mission 313
Argentina Mendoza Mission 323
Argentina Neuquen Mission. 323
Argentina Resistencia Mission 323
Argentina Rosario Mission 316
Argentina Salta Mission 322
Arizona 110-13
Arizona Phoenix Mission 321
Arizona Tempe Mission 315
Arizona Temple 331
Arizona Tucson Mission. 323
Arkansas 113-14
Arkansas Little Rock Mission. 317
Armenia. 195
Arno (island) 257
Artifacts
  '79:292-93,
  '83:280-81
Asay, Carlos E.. 21
Ashby, Armis Joseph 11
Ashton, Marvin J. 56,9
Ashton, Marvin O. 77
Asia Area. 98
Asia North Area 99
Assistant Presidents of the Church. . . 44
Assistants to the Twelve 63-65
Assistants to the Twelve, chart
  '74:142,
  '75:B42,
  '76:B39
Atlanta Georgia Temple. 331-32
Australia. 195-97,404
Australia Adelaide Mission 315
Australia Brisbane Mission 317
Australia Melbourne Mission 311
Australia Perth Mission 317
Australia Sydney Mission 307
Australia Sydney North Mission . 325,397
Austria. 197-98
Austria Vienna Mission 312
Ayala, Eduardo. 33
Azores Islands 278

B

Backman, Robert L. 66
Bahamas 198
Ballard, M. Russell, Jr.. 19
Ballard, Melvin J.. 54
Bangerter, Wm. Grant 65-66
Bangladesh. 198
Banks, Benjamin B. 23
Barbados 198-99
Bateman, Merrill J.. 41
Bavarian Mission. 313
Belarus 199,12,400
Belgium 199
Belgium Antwerp Mission 318,,323
Belgium Brussels Mission. 314
Belize 200,11,397
Bennett, Archibald F. 10
Bennett, John C.. 48-49
Bennett, Wallace F. 11
Bennett, William H. 67
Bennion, Adam S. 56
Bennion, Milton. 83
Bennion, Samuel O. 62
Benson, Ezra T. 52
Benson, Ezra Taft 44
  death. 9,406
  honors 10,406
  tributes 401
Bentley, Joseph T.. 10-11,86
Berlin Mission 313
Bermuda 200
Berrett, William E. 11
Bevell, Darrell 10
Billings, Titus 77-78
Bishops, long-term
  '80:277,
  '81:257
Bogota Colombia Temple. 332,400
Boise Idaho Temple 332-33
Bolivia. 200-201
Bolivia Cochabamba Mission 319
Book of Mormon, editions/translations . . .
  '93/94:401-02
  modern English translation 398
  translations. . . . . '93/94:401-02
  translations chart
  '85:303
Botswana. 201-2
Bountiful Utah Temple. 333
Bowen, Albert E.. 55

Boy Scouts 401
Boynton, John F.. 51
Bradford, William R. 24
Bradley, Shawn 10
Brazil 202-5,402
Brazil Area 101
Brazil Belem Mission 325
Brazil Belo Horizonte Mission. 322
Brazil Belo Horizonte South Mission . . 325
Brazil Brasilia Mission 321
Brazil Campinas Mission 321
Brazil Curitiba Mission 320
Brazil Florianopolis Mission 325
Brazil Fortaleza Mission 322
Brazil Manaus Mission. 323
Brazil Porto Alegre North Mission . . 324
Brazil Porto Alegre South Mission . . . 312
Brazil Recife Mission 320
Brazil Recife South Mission. 325
Brazil Ribeiro Preto Mission. 325
Brazil Rio de Janeiro Mission. 315
Brazil Rio de Janeiro North Mission . . 325
Brazil Salvador Mission 323
Brazil Salvador South Mission 325
Brazil Sao Paulo East Mission 324
Brazil Sao Paulo Interlagos Mission . . 324
Brazil Sao Paulo North Mission. . . . 316
Brazil Sao Paulo South Mission . . . 316
Brewerton, Ted E. 24
Brigham Young Monument (Salt Lake
City) 403
Brigham Young University
and University of Jordan 408
awards. 10
bomb threat 11,398
buildings 400
'75:F33, '76:G46, '77:294, '78:296

degrees offered: '79:294-98
enrollment, '75:F32, '76:G45, '77:293,
'78:296
Museum of Art 403
Young Ambassadors 400,408
Brigham Young University-Hawaii Campus
enrollment and presidents
'75:F34, '76:G47, '77:295, '78:298
British-born members,
'74:255, '80:276, '81:256
British Census Project 409
British Columbia, Canada 208-9
British Mission 306
Brockbank, Bernard P. 67
Brough, Monte J.. 22
Brown, Hugh B. 46
Brown, S. Kent 9
Brown, Victor L. 76
Buehner, Carl W.. 78
Buenos Aires, Argentina. 405
Buenos Aires Argentina Temple . . 333-34
Bulgaria. 205-6,400
Bulgaria Sofia Mission 324
Bullock, Hart 9
Burton, H. David 41
Burton, Robert T.. 77

Burton, Theodore M.. 67
Burundi 206
Busche, F. Enzio. 24
Butterfield, Josiah 59

C

Calendar, perpetual
'82:298-99,
'83:300-301
Caldwell, C. Max 33
California 114-20
California Anaheim Mission 314
California Arcadia Mission. 315
California Carlsbad Mission 325
California Fresno Mission 317
California Los Angeles Mission. 306
California Oakland Mission 315
California Riverside Mission. 323
California Roseville Mission. 325
California Sacramento Mission 310
California San Bernardino Mission . . . 320
California San Diego Mission 317
California San Fernando Mission. . . . 325
California San Jose Mission. 319
California Santa Rosa Mission 321
California Ventura Mission 319
Call, Waldo P. 70
Callis, Charles A.. 55
Camargo, Helio R. 70
Cambodia. 12,405
Cameroon 206-7
Canada 207-15,404
Canada Calgary Mission. 310
Canada Halifax Mission 317
Canada Montreal Mission. 316
Canada Toronto East Mission 325
Canada Toronto Mission 309
Canada Vancouver Mission. 312
Canada Winnipeg Mission. 318
Canadians, '79:255, '80:281, '81:255
Canary Islands 287
Cannon, Abraham H. 53
Cannon, Elaine A. 93
Cannon, George I.. 71
Cannon, George Q. 45
Cannon, John Q. 78
Cannon, Lucy Grant 92
Cannon, Sylvester Q. 55
Cape Verde, Republic of 215,12,409
Carmack, John K. 24
Carrington, Albert 49
Carthage Jail 407
Cathedral of the Madeleine 400
Catholic Church 402,404
Celebrations, historical
'80:316-20, '81:298-302
Central Africa Republic 215-16
Central America Area 100
Checketts, David W.. 10
Chicago Illinois Temple 334
Children, focus on 401
Chile. 216-18
Chile Antofagasta Mission 322

Chile Concepcion Mission. 317
Chile Osorno Mission 319
Chile Santiago North Mission. 319
Chile Santiago South Mission. 313
Chile Vina del Mar Mission 320
China 218
Chinese Mission 311
Choules, Albert, Jr.. 72
Church growth charts 359-60
Christensen, Joe J. 22
Christiansen, ElRay L. 64
Christmas Devotional 397
Christofferson, D. Todd 25
Chronology, historical 362-95
Chuuk (island) 262
Circuit, Richard K. 9
'City of Joseph' pageant 401
Clapp, Benjamin L.. 59
Clark, J. Reuben, Jr.. 46
Clarke, J. Richard 25
Clawson, Rudger. 48
Clyde, Aileen H. 94-95
Coleman, Gary J. 34
Colombia 219
Colombia Barranquilla Mission 322
Colombia Bogota North Mission . . . 315
Colombia Bogota South Mission . . . 324
Colombia Cali Mission. 317
Colonization, '80:321-25
Colorado 120-22
Colorado Denver Mission 308
Colorado Denver North Mission . . . 325
Coltrin, Zebedee 58
Commemorative celebrations, '80:316-20,
'81:298-302
Condie, Spencer J.. 25
Congo. 220
Connecticut. 122-23
Connecticut Hartford Mission. 320
Cook, Gene R.. 25
Cook Islands 220
Coray, Melissa 408
Corrill, John. 77
Costa, Claudio R. M.. 34
Costa Rica 220-21
Costa Rica San Jose Mission. 311
Council of the Twelve 16-20,50-57
    Assistants to the. 63-65
    chart, '74:129-31, '75:B28-31, '76:B29-31
    leadership changes 8
    length of service. 79-80
Cove Fort. 406
Cowdery, Oliver 44
Cowley, Matthew. 55
Cowley, Matthias F. 53
Craven, Rulon G.. 34
Critchlow, William J., Jr.. 64
Croatia 221
Cullimore, James A. 67
Curriculum, uniform 8
Curtis, Elbert R. 86
Curtis, LeGrand R. 34
Cuthbert, Derek A.. 69
Cutler, Clinton L. 74,9,405

Cyprus 221-22,12,402
Czech Republic 222
Czechoslovak Mission. 309
Czechoslovakia Prague Mission 323

D

Dallas Texas Temple 334-35
Davila, Julio E. 35
de Jager, Jacob 69
Delaware 123
Dellenbach, Robert K.. 26
Denmark 223
Denmark Copenhagen Mission. 309
Denver, Colorado 402
Denver Colorado Temple 335
Derrick, Royden G.. 66
Dickson, John B.. 35
Didier, Charles 21
Discipline policy 7,403
District of Columbia 124-25
Divorce clearance 8
Doctrine and Covenants
    biographies, '89/90:196-202
    translations, '85:315, '89/90:202
Dominican Republic 223-24
Dominican Republic Santiago Mission. 321
Dominican Republic Santo Domingo East
Mission 324
Dominican Republic Santo Domingo West
Mission 321
Doxey, Graham W.. 35
Dunn, Loren C.. 26
Dunn, Paul H.. 65
Durham, G. Homer. 66
Durham, Lowell M.. 10
Dyer, Alvin R.. 49-50

E

Earthquakes 12,404
East Indian Mission 287
Eastern States Mission 306
Ebeye (island) 257
Ecuador. 224-26
Ecuador Guayaquil North Mission . . . 324
Ecuador Guayaquil South Mission . . . 319
Ecuador Quito Mission 316
Edgley, Richard C.. 41
Education, statistics 6
Egypt 226
El Salvador 226-27
El Salvador San Salvador East Mission 323
El Salvador San Salvador Mission . . . 318
El Salvador San Salvador West Mission 321
Eldredge, Horace S.. 60
Eldredge, W. Jay. 86
Engar, Keith M.. 11
England. 294-97
England Birmingham Mission. 320
England Bristol Mission 313
England Leeds Mission 312
England London Mission 306
England London South Mission 314

England Manchester Mission 318
Equatorial Guinea 227
Estonia 227
Ethiopia. 228
Europe Area 103
Europe/Mediterranean Area 102
Europe North Area. 102
European-born members, '79:256, '80:276-77, '81:256-57
European Mission (Administrative) . . . 307
Evans, Richard L. 56
Eyestone, Ed 10
Eyring, Henry B. 26

F

Family, International Year 404
Family history, handbook 7
Family home evening 409
Family Record Extraction program . . . 7-
. . . . 8,402,405
Faust, James E. 18
Featherstone, Vaughn J. 26
Felt, Louie B. 88
Fiji 228-29
Fiji Suva Mission 316
Finland 229
Finland Helsinki Mission. 311
Fires. 403-4
First Council of the Seventy. 58-63
First Presidency . . . .
  assistant counselors 50
  counselors, other 48-50
  first counselors 44-47
  first counselors, chart
  '74:122, '75:B22, '76:B24
  length of service. 79-80
  second counselors 47-48
  second counselors, chart, '74:125,
  '75:B25, '76:B27
First Quorum of the Seventy . 23-32,66-73
  chart, '76:B47
  leadership changes 8
Fjelsted, Christian D.. 60
Flags, '80:334, '81:297
Floods. 12,398,401,404,407
Florida. 125-26
Florida Ft. Lauderdale Mission 321
Florida Jacksonville Mission 322
Florida Tallahassee Mission 316
Florida Tampa Mission 318
Foster, James 58
Fowler, John E. 35
Fox, Ruth May 92
France 230-31
France Bordeaux Mission. 323
France Marseille Mission 324
France Paris Mission 306
Frankfurt Germany Temple 335-36
Freiberg Germany Temple 336
French Guiana 231
French Mission. 306
French Polynesia. 231-32,12,406
Funk, Ruth Hardy 92

Fyans, J. Thomas 65

G

Gabon. 233-34
Gates, Jacob 60
Gause, Jesse. 48
Gaylord, John 59
Gee, Salmon 59
Genealogical Department, Field Service
  Centers
  '85:293-94
Genealogical Society, microfilms
  centennial commemoration . . . 398,404
  received, '74:212, '75:F13
General Authorities
  emeritus members 8
  leadership changes 8-9
General Conference . 396,399,402,405,409
George, Lloyd P. 72
Georgia 126-28,12,407
Georgia Atlanta Mission. 308
Georgia Macon Mission 323
German Mission 307
Germany 234-36
Germany Berlin Mission. 324
Germany Dresden Mission 323
Germany Duesseldorf Mission 323
Germany Frankfurt Mission 310
Germany Hamburg Mission 310
Germany Munich Mission 312
Geslison, Byron T. 401
Ghana. 236
Ghana Accra Mission 321
Gibbons, Francis M. 71
Gibraltar Mission 307
Goaslind, Jack H. 27
Gould, John 58
Government officials (U.S.), '85:319-20
Grandin Building 404
Granite Mountain Records Vault
  microfilm reel storage 359
Grant, Heber J. 43
Grant, Jedediah M. 47
Grant, Josh. 10
Grassli, Michaelene P.. 89
Greece 237
Greece Athens Mission 323
Greenland 223
Grassli, Michaelene P.. 89
Greece 237
Greece Athens Mission 323
Greenland 223
Grenada 237
Grenadines (islands). 282
Groberg, John H.. 27
Guadeloupe 232
Guam 237-38
Guatemala 238-39
  airplane accident 403
Guatemala City Guatemala
  Central Mission 325
Guatemala City Temple 336-37
Guatemala Guatemala City
  North Mission 322

Guatemala Guatemala City
  South Mission 314
Guatemala Quetzaltenango Mission . . 319
Guayaquil Ecuador Temple 337
Guyana 239-40

H

Haight, David B. 17,405
Haiti 240
Haiti Port-Au-Prince Mission 321
Hales, Janette C. 91
Hales, Robert D. 20
Hammond, F. Melvin. 27
Han, In Sang 36
Hancock, Levi W. 58
Handcart pioneers 408
Hanks, Marion D. 65
Hansen, W. Eugene 22
Harbertson, Robert B. 69
Hardy, Leonard W. 76-77
Hardy, Rufus K. 62
Harriman, Henry 59
Harris, Devere 70
Hart, Charles H. 61
Hartford Connecticut Temple 337
Harvest Park Ward (California) . . . 11,397
Hawaii 128-29
Hawaii Honolulu Mission 307
Hawaii Temple 337
Haycock, D. Arthur. 11
Hill, George R. 83
Hill, George R., III 71
Hillam, Harold G. 27
Hinckley, Alonzo A. 55
Hinckley, Gordon B. 15
Hinckley, May Green 89
Historic sites, '80:300-313, '83:273-74
Historical chronology 362-95
Historical chronology index, '76:A72-A73
Holland, Jeffrey R. 20,407
Homefront Junior TV spots 402
Homosexual marriages 7,405
Honduras 241
Honduras San Pedro Sula Mission . . . 323
Honduras Tegucigalpa Mission 320
Hong Kong 241-42
Hong Kong Temple 338,404
Hong Kong Mission 311
Howard, F. Burton 28
Howells, Adele Cannon 89
Humanitarian aid projects 12,401
Hungary 242-43
Hungary Budapest Mission 323
Hunter, Edward. 76
Hunter, Howard W. 14
  addresses 409
  bomb threat 11,398
  sustained president 409
  travels 408
Hunter, Milton R. 62
Huntsman, Jon M. 400
Hyde, Orson 51

I

Iceland 243-44,401
Iconography
  '80:335-36
Idaho 129-33
Idaho Boise Mission 317
Idaho Falls Temple 338
Idaho Pocatello Mission 324
Illinois 134-35
Illinois Chicago Mission 308
Illinois Peoria Mission 321
India 244-45,11,397
India Bangalore Mission 325
Indian Territory Mission 307
Indiana 135-36
Indiana Indianapolis Mission 311
Indonesia 245
Indonesia Jakarta Mission 321
International Mission 316
Iowa 136-37
Iowa Des Moines Mission 318
Iran Tehran Mission 318
Ireland 245-46
Ireland Dublin Mission 313
Isaacson, Henry Thorpe B. 49
Italian Mission 306-7
Italy 246-47,11
Italy Catania Mission 319
Italy Milan Mission 316
Italy Padova Mission 323
Italy Rome Mission 306-7
Ivins, Anthony W. 46
Ivins, Antoine R. 62
Ivory Coast 247-48
Ivory Coast Abidjan Mission 324

J

Jack, Elaine L. 94-95,397
Jacobsen, Florence S. 92
Jamaica 248
Jamaica Kingston Mission 321
Japan 248-50
Japan Fukuoka Mission 315
Japan Kobe Mission 315
Japan Mission 309
Japan Nagoya Mission 317
Japan Okayama Mission 318
Japan Okinawa Mission 323
Japan Osaka Mission 320
Japan Sapporo Mission 315
Japan Sendai Mission 317
Japan Tokyo North Mission 315
Japan Tokyo South Mission 319
Japanese Mission 310
Jensen, Jay E. 36
Jensen, Marlin K. 28
Jeppsen, Malcolm S. 74
Jepsen, Betty Jo N. 9
Johannesburg South Africa Temple 338-39
Johnson, Kenneth 28
Johnson, Luke 51
Johnson, Lyman E. 51-52

Jordan, University of 408
Jordan River Temple 339
Joseph Smith Memorial Building 12,400-401
Judy, Cody 11,398

K

Kansas 137-38
Kapp, Ardeth G. 93
Kawjalein (island) 257
Kay, F. Arthur. 70
Kendrick, L. Lionel 28
Kentucky 138-39
Kentucky Louisville Mission. 309
Kenya 250-51
Kenya Nairobi Mission. 324
Kikuchi, Yoshihiko 29
Kimball, Heber C. 45
Kimball, J. Golden 61
Kimball, J. LeRoy 10
Kimball, Spencer W.. 44
Kiribati. 251
Kirkham, Oscar A. 62
Kirtland Temple 339-40,403
Kofford, Cree-L. 29
Komatsu, Adney Y. 68
Korea 252-53
Korea Pusan Mission 317
Korea Seoul Mission. 313
Korea Seoul West Mission 320
Korea Taejon Mission 321
Kosrae (island) 262

L

LDS Business College. 397
   enrollment and presidents ,'75:F35,
   '76:G48, '77:296, '78:299
Ladd, W. Don. 36
Lafayette School. 409
Landmarks, Church historic, '82:282-83
Languages in the Church, '82:276-77,
   '83:252-53
Laos. 408
Larsen, Dean L. 29
Las Vegas, Nevada 403
Las Vegas Nevada Temple 340
Lasater, John R. 71
Latvia 253,11,399
Latvia Riga Mission 325
Law, William 47
Lawrence, W. Mack 36
Leaders, Church see Church leaders
Lee, George P. 68
Lee, Harold B. 43
'Legacy' film 400
Lesotho. 253
Lewis, Theodore B. 60
Liberia. 254
Liberty Jail 402
Libraries, Mormon research, '79:301
Lim, Augusto A. 37
Lima Peru Temple 340-41
Lindsay, Richard P. 74

Lines of authority, ecclesiastical, '87:18
Literacy education 11,397
Lithuania 254,12,400
Little, Jesse C. 78
Logan Temple 341
Logos, Church
   '82:278-81,
   '83:254-57
London Temple 342,11,396
Longden, John 64
Los Angeles Temple. 342-43
   Visitors Center 404
Louisiana 139-40
Louisiana Baton Rouge Mission 310
Lund, Anthon H. 45
Luxembourg 254-55
Lybbert, Merlin R. 74
Lyman, Amasa M. 49
Lyman, Amy Brown 96
Lyman, Francis M. 53
Lyman, Richard R. 54

M

Macau. 278
Madagascar 255
Madeira Islands 278
Madrid Spain Temple 343
Madsen, John M.. 37
Maine 140-41
Majuro. 256-57
Malaysia 255-56
Malta 256
Malta Mission. 307
Manila Philippines Temple 343
Manitoba, Canada 209-10
Manti Temple. 343-44
Marriage, same-gender 405
Marsh, Thomas B. 50
Marshall Islands 256-57
Martin, Douglas J. 71
Martinique 232
Martins, Helvecio. 37
Maryland 141-42
Maryland Baltimore Mission. 325
Mason, James O. 37
Massachusetts 142-43
Massachusetts Boston Mission. 310
Mauritius 257
Maxwell, Neal A. 18
McConkie, Bruce R. 56
McKay, David Lawrence. 11,83
McKay, David O.. 43
McKay, Thomas E.. 63
M'Lellin, William E.. 51
McMurrin, Joseph W. 61
Melchin, Gerald E. 72
Membership, by area by decade, '74:E5-E13,
   '76:E5-E13
   during president's administrations. . . 410
   outside North America, '75:E14-E15,
   '76:E14-E15
      statistics 6,412-20
Merrell, V. Dallas. 38

Merrill, Joseph F.. 55
Merrill, Marriner W.. 53
Mexican Mission 308
Mexico 257--62,12,400-401
Mexico Chihuahua Mission 322
Mexico City Temple 344
Mexico Guadalajara Mission 317
Mexico Hermosillo Mission 312
Mexico Leon Mission 303
Mexico Mazatlan Mission 322
Mexico Merida Mission 318
Mexico Mexico City East Mission. . . . 321
Mexico Mexico City North Mission . . . 319
Mexico Mexico City South Mission . . . 308
Mexico Monterrey East Mission 322
Mexico Monterrey Mission 311
Mexico Monterrey South Mission. . . . 325
Mexico North Area. 100
Mexico Oaxaca Mission 324
Mexico Puebla Mission 322
Mexico South Area 100
Mexico Tijuana Mission 324
Mexico Torreon Mission. 315
Mexico Tuxtla-Gutierrez Mission 322
Mexico Veracruz Mission 314
Michigan 143-44
Michigan Detroit Mission 319
Michigan Lansing Mission. 316
Mickelsen, Lynn A.. 29
Microfilm chart 359
Microfilming. 10,422
Micronesia 262-63
Micronesia Guam Mission. 320
Middle States Mission 309
Miles, Daniel S.. 59
Mili (island) 257
Miller, George 75
Miller, Orrin P. 77
Minnesota 145-46
Minnesota Minneapolis Mission 309
Mission presidents, seminar . . . 400,407
Mission Representatives, '74:196
Missionaries
  satellite broadcast 12,409
  statistics . . . . 6,'93-94:399-400
Missionary Training Centers
  Argentina 405
  Brazil. 402
  Provo 405
Missions, chronological list 306-25
Mississippi 146-47
Mississippi Jackson Mission 320
Missouri 147-49
Missouri Independence Mission . . . 307-8
Missouri St. Louis Mission. 319
Money, 80:326-32, '81:290-96
Mongolia 263,12,400
Monson, Thomas S.. 15
Montana 149-50
Montana Billings Mission 311
Montana Mission. 308
Morgan, John. 60
Morley, Isaac 76
Mormon Tabernacle Choir, see Salt Lake

Mormon Tabernacle Choir
Mormon Trail. 408
  sites '89/90:186-87
Morris, George Q.. 56
Morrison, Alexander B. 30
Morocco 408
Mothers, national convention. 406
Motion pictures, Church
  '77:300-306
Mt. Timpanogos Utah Temple 345,400,402
The Mountain of the Lord (motion picture)399
Mountains. 408
Moyle, Henry D. 46
Muren, Joseph C. 38
Museum of Church History and Art 399,405

N

Nadauld, Stephen C.. 38
Namibia. 263
Nauvoo Mission 316
Nauvoo Temple 345
Nebraska 150-51
Nebraska Omaha Mission. 325
Nelson, Russell M.. 18,12
Netherlands 263
Netherlands Amsterdam Mission. . . . 308
Neuenschwander, Dennis B. 30
Nevada 151-53
Nevada Las Vegas Mission. 318
Nevis (island) 281-82
New Brunswick, Canada 210
New Caledonia. 233
New Hampshire 153-54
New Hampshire Manchester Mission . 321
New Jersey. 154-55
New Jersey Morristown Mission 322
New Mexico 155-56
New Mexico Albuquerque Mission . . . 318
New York 156-57
New York New York Mission 306
New York New York North Mission . . 325
New York Rochester Mission. 314
New York Utica Mission. 325
New Zealand. 265-66
New Zealand Auckland Mission 309
New Zealand Temple 346
New Zealand Wellington Mission. . . . 318
Newfoundland, Canada 210
Newspapers, Church, '75:F39, '76:F43,
  '77:299, '89/90:191
Nibley, Charles W.. 48
Nicaragua. 266-67
Nicaragua Managua Mission 323
Nigeria 267-68
Nigeria Aba Mission 322
Nigeria Ilorin Mission. 324
Nigeria Jos Mission 325
Nigeria Lagos Mission. 320
Niue (island) 268
Nixon, Richard M. 406
North America Central Area 106
North America Northeast Area 105
North America Northwest Area. 104

North America Southeast Area 104
North America Southwest Area. 105
North America West Area. 106
North Carolina 157-58
North Carolina Charlotte Mission. . . . 316
North Carolina Raleigh Mission. 320
North Dakota 159
Northern Far East Mission 311
Northern Ireland 297
Northern Mariana Islands 268-69
Northwest Territory, Canada 215
Norway 269-70
Norway Oslo Mission 309
Nova Scotia, Canada 211
Nuku'alofa Tonga Temple. 346-47

O

Oakland Temple 347
Oaks, Dallin H. 19
Ogden Temple 347-48
Ohio 159-60
Ohio Cleveland Mission 319
Ohio Columbus Mission 314
Okazaki, Chieko N. 94-95
Oklahoma. 161-62
Oklahoma Oklahoma City Mission . . . 324
Oklahoma Tulsa Mission 315
Olympians, LDS,
'89/90:192-93
On the Way Home (video) 396
Ontario, Canada 211-12
Oregon 162-64
Oregon Eugene Mission. 324
Oregon Portland Mission 308-9
Organization of the Church, '80:333, '83:281
Orlando Florida Temple 348,409
Orton, Roger 59
Osborn, Spencer H. 70
Osmond, Amy 10

P

Pace, Glenn L. 30
Pacific Area. 99
Pacific (Administrative) Mission. 310
Pacific Northwest Mission. 314
Packer, Boyd K. 17
Page, John E. 52
Panama 270
Panama Panama City Mission 323
Papeete Tahiti Temple 348-49
Papua New Guinea 271
Papua New Guinea
    Port Moresby Mission. 324
Paraguay 271-72
Paraguay Asuncion Mission. 319
Paramore, James M.. 30
Parkin, Bonnie D. 91
Parliament of World's Religions . . 12,402
Parmley, LaVern Watts 89
Partridge, Edward 75
Partridge, Jane. 405

Patriarchs to the Church 57
    chart
    '74:140-41,
    '75:B41
Patten, David W. 50
Pearce, Virginia H. 91
Pearl of Great Price, translations,
    '89/90:202
Pennsylvania 164-65
Pennsylvania Harrisburg Mission 316
Pennsylvania Philadelphia Mission . . . 319
Pennsylvania Pittsburgh Mission 318
Penrose, Charles W. 46
Perciwall, Evert Wilford 11
Periodicals, Church, '74:200-204, '75:F28-32,
    '76:G38-42, '89/90:187-90
Perpetual calendar, '82:298-99, '83:300-301
Perry, L. Tom. 17
Peru 272-74
Peru Arequipa Mission. 319
Peru Chiclayo Mission. 325
Peru Lima Central Mission 325
Peru Lima East Mission 322
Peru Lima North Mission 319
Peru Lima South Mission 312
Peru Trujillo Mission 321
Petersen, Mark E. 55
Peterson, Andrew W. 31
Peterson, H. Burke. 70
Peterson, Tom 10
Philippines 274-76
Philippines Cebu Mission 321
Philippines Davao Mission 319
Philippines Ilagan Mission. 324
Philippines Manila Mission 314
Philippines Naga Mission 323
Philippines Quezon City Mission 321
Philippines San Fernando Mission . . . 322
Philippines San Pablo Mission 324
Philippines Tacloban Mission 324
Philippines/Micronesia Area 99
Photographs, historic, '80:122-35
Pinegar, Patricia P.. 88
Pinegar, Rex D. 21
Pinnock, Florence B.
Pinnock, Hugh W. 31
Pioneers, companies, chart, '89/90:172
    companies, crossing plains, '76:G8-22,
    '77:278-92, '89/90:173-86
    emigrants, crossing ocean, '75:F18-24,
    '76:G2-8, '77:272-78, '89/90:166-72
    sesquicentennial celebration . . . 398-99
Poelman, Ronald E. 31
Pohnpei. 262
Poland 276-77
Poland Warsaw Mission. 324
Polish Genealogical Society 10
Polynesian Cultural Center 401
Porter, L. Aldin 22
Portland Oregon Temple 349
Portugal. 277-78
Portugal Lisbon North Mission 324
Portugal Lisbon South Mission 317
Portugal Porto Mission 322

Pratt, Orson. 51
Pratt, Parley P. 51
Pratt, Rey L. 62
Presidency of the Quorums of
　the Seventy 21-22
Presidency of the Seventy 65-66
Presidents of the Church 42-44
　Assistant 44
　milestones, '87:10-16
　progress chart 410
Presiding Bishopric 41
Presiding Bishops 75-76
　chart, '74:150, '75:B51, '76:B48
　first counselors, chart
　'74:153, '75:B52, '76:B49
　first counselors 76-77
　leadership changes 9
　second counselors, chart,
　'74:153, '75:B53, '76:B50
　second counselors 77-78
Preston England Temple . . . 349,396,407
Preston, William B. 76
Priesthood, lines of authority
　'76:B51-56
Primary, general officers. 87-89
Prince Edward Island, Canada . . . 212-13
Promontory, Utah 406
Provo Temple 350
Przekurat, Carolyn B. 9-10
Puerto Rico. 279
Puerto Rico San Juan Mission 320
Pulsipher, Zera 59
Pyper, George D. 83

Q

Quebec, Canada. 213-14
Quilts 404

R

Rarotonga 220
Rarotonga Mission. 312
Record extraction program 7-8
Rector, Hartman, Jr. 68
Reeder, Bertha S. 92
Reeve, Rex C., Sr. 69
Regions, '78:130-40
Relief Society
　chronology, '75:F24-F25, '76:G32-G33,
　'83:275-76
　General Meeting 409
　general officers 93-96
　gospel literacy program 11,397
Relief work 398,401,403-4,407
Religious Freedom Restoration Act 12,403
Religious liberty efforts 12
Reunion (island) 233
Reynolds, George 61
Rhode Island 165-66
Rich, Charles C. 52
Rich, Leonard 58
Richards, Franklin D. 65
Richards, Franklin Dewey. 52

Richards, George F. 54
Richards, LeGrand. 56
Richards, Stayner 63
Richards, Stephen L. 46
Richards, Willard. 47
Richmond, Virginia
Ricks College, anniversary,
　'75:F34-35, '76:G47-48, '77:295-96,
　'78:298-99
　presidents, '75:F34, '76:G47, '77:295,
　'78:298
Rigdon, Sidney. 44-45
Ringger, Hans B. 31
Roberts, Brigham H. 61
Roberts, William 11
Robison, Louise Y. 96
Rockwood, Albert P. 59
Rojas, Jorge A. 38
Romania 280
Romania Bucharest Mission 325
Rome, Italy 404
Romney, Marion G. 47
Rota (island) 269
Rudd, Glen L. 71
Russell, Gardner H. 71
Russia. 280-81,12,400-401
Russia Moscow Mission. 323
Russia Novosibirsk Mission. 325
Russia Rostov Na Donu Mission . . . 325
Russia St. Petersburg Mission 324
Russia Samara Mission 325
Rwanda. 12,408

S

Sabbath Day, statement on. 7,396
Sackley, Robert E. 72,9,399
Saipan (island) 269
St. George Temple. 354
St. Kitts (island) 281-82
St. Louis Missouri Temple. 354,403
St. Maarten (island) 263
St. Martin 233
St. Vincent 282
Salt Lake City, historic photographs,
　'80:130-132
　original ward boundaries map,
　'85:317
Salt Lake City and County Building. . . 408
Salt Lake Mormon Tabernacle Choir,
　history, '76:F18
　tours . 11,397-98,402, '75:F38, '76:G51,
　'77:298-99
Salt Lake Tabernacle organ, '87:327
Salt Lake Temple 350-51,11,399
Samoa Apia Mission. 308
Samuelson, Cecil O., Jr. 32
San Diego California Temple . . 351,12,400
Sandwich Islands Mission. 307
Santiago Chile Temple 351-52
Santo Domingo
　Dominican Republic Temple. 352,12,403
Sao Paulo Temple 352
Saskatchewan, Canada 214-15

Scandinavian Mission 306
Scandinavians, '79:256, '80:275, '81:255-56
Schaerrer, Neil D. 86
Schools, Church, '83:285-86
Scotland 297-98
Scotland Edinburgh Mission 313
Scott, Richard G.. 20
Scriptures, Spanish language. 404
typesetting. 400
Searfoss, Richard A.. 403
Seattle Temple. 353
Second Quorum
of the Seventy 33-41,73-75
Seminaries, enrollment, '75:F36-37, '76:F49
'77:297-98, '78:300-301, '83:279-80
Seoul Korea Temple. 353-54
Serbia 282
Seventy, First Council of the 58
First Quorum of the 23-32,66-73
Presidency of the 65-66
Presidency of the Quorums of the. 21-22
Second Quorum of the . . . 33-41,73-75
Sherman, Lyman R.. 58
Shimabukuro, Sam K.. 39
Shumway, Eric B. 9
Shumway, Naomi M.. 89
Siam Mission 307
Sierra Leone 283
Sill, Sterling W.. 67,9
Simpson, Robert L. 68
Singapore. 283-84
Singapore Mission 315
Slovakia. 284
Slovenia. 284
Smith, Barbara B. 96,406
Smith, Bathsheba W. 95
Smith, David A.. 77
Smith, Douglas H. 71-72
Smith, Eldred G. 58
Smith, Emma Hale. 95
Smith, G. Carlos 86
Smith, George A.. 45
Smith, George Albert 43
Smith, Hyrum. 44
Smith, Hyrum G. 57
Smith, Hyrum Mack 54
Smith, John. 50
Smith, John (patriarch) 57
Smith, John Henry 48
Smith, Joseph 42
children, '83:283
martyrdom commemoration 12,407
Smith, Joseph, Sr. 50
Smith, Joseph F.. 42-43
Smith, Joseph Fielding 43
Smith, Joseph Fielding (patriarch) . . 57-58
Smith, Nicholas G.. 63
Smith, Sylvester 58
Smith, William 51,57
Smoot, Reed 54
Snow, Eliza R. 95
Snow, Erastus 52
Snow, Lorenzo 42
Society Islands Mission 306

Sonne, Alma 67
Sonnenberg, John 70
Sonntag, Philip T. 70
Sorensen, David E. 39
Sorensen, Lynn A.. 72
South Africa 285-86
South Africa Cape Town Mission.. . . 321
South Africa Durban Mission 322
South America (administrative) Mission 313
South America North Area 100
South America South Area 101
South American Mission 309
South Carolina 166-67
South Carolina Columbia Mission . . . 318
South Dakota. 167-68
South Dakota Rapid City Mission. . . . 314
Southern Far East Mission 311
Spafford, Belle S. 96
Spain 286-87
Spain Barcelona Mission 318
Spain Bilbao Mission 322
Spain Las Palmas Mission 322
Spain Madrid Mission 316
Spain Malaga Mission 318
Spanish-American Mission 310
Stakes, chronological list . '91-92:176-222
first in each country 327
first in each state 326
Stanley, F. David. 39
Stapley, Delbert L.. 55
Statistics 6,412-22
Stevenson, Edward 61
Stockholm Sweden Temple. 355
Stone, O. Leslie 68
Sunday School, anniversary
appointments 9
general officers 81-83
opening exercises 7,402
Suriname 287
Swaziland. 288
Sweden 288-89
Sweden Stockholm Mission. 309
Swiss Temple 355-56,11,396
Switzerland 289-90,408
Switzerland Geneva Mission 312
Switzerland Zurich Mission 307
Sydney Australia Temple 356
Symbols, Mormon
'80:335-36

T

Tabernacle Choir see Salt Lake Mormon
Tabernacle Choir
Tahiti see French Polynesia
Tahiti Papeete Mission 306
Tai, Kwok Yuen 39
Taipei Taiwan Temple 356-57
Taiwan 290
Taiwan Taichung Mission 319
Taiwan Taipei Mission. 316
Talmage, James E. 54
Tanner, N. Eldon. 47
Tanzania 291

Taylor, Elmina S. 92
Taylor, Henry D. 67
Taylor, John 42
Taylor, John H. 62
Taylor, John W. 53
Taylor, Russell C. 69
Taylor, William W. 60
Teasdale, George 53
Teenagers, early-day, '81:289, '83:283
Television programs
Temple presidents, '85:289-91
Temple Square. 397
Temple work, handbook. 7
TempleReady software 12,403
Temples. 330-59
    chronological list. 329-30,
    '89/90:191-92
    cornerstone ceremonies, '85:292
    dedications chart, '87:302
    languages used at, '87:301
    ordinance chart, '85:13
    ordinance chronology, '74:210-11, '75:F4-
5, '76:G34-35
    presidencies, '75:F6-12, '76:F11-17
    world map, '85:8
Tennessee 168-69
Tennessee Knoxville Mission. 325
Tennessee Nashville Mission. 318
Tenorio, Horacio A. 74
Texas 169-71
Texas Corpus Christi Mission. 323
Texas Dallas Mission 313
Texas Ft. Worth Mission 321
Texas Houston East Mission 324
Texas Houston Mission 318
Texas San Antonio Mission. 314
Thailand. 291-92
Thailand Bangkok Mission 317
Thatcher, Moses 52-53
Tijuana, Mexico 398
Tingey, Burton S. 10
Tingey, Earl C. 32
Tingey, Martha Horne 92
Tinian (island) 269
Tokyo Temple 357
Tonga 292-93,401
Tonga Nuku'alofa Mission. 309
Toronto Ontario Temple. 357-58
Transkei. 286
Trinidad and Tobago. 293
Tucson, Arizona 409
Turkish Mission. 308
Tuttle, A. Theodore 65
Twelve Apostles, see Council of the Twelve

U

Uchtdorf, Dieter F. 40
Uganda 293-94
Ukraine 294
Ukraine Donetsk Mission 325
Ukraine Kiev Mission 322
United Kingdom 294-98

United States
    membership statistics 416
    missionary work. 408
Unwed parents 7
Uruguay 298-99
Uruguay Montevideo Mission 310
Utah, centennial celebration 406
    history 172-73
    stakes/missions. 173-84
    state capitol 408
Utah Central Area 12
Utah North Area 107
Utah Ogden Mission. 318
Utah Provo Mission 323
Utah Salt Lake City Mission. 320
Utah South Area 107

V

Van Cott, John 60
Van Dam, Ada S.. 11
Vandenberg, John H. 76
Vatican 404
Venezuela 299-300
Venezuela Barcelona Mission 325
Venezuela Maracaibo Mission 320
Venezuela Mission. 316
Venezuela Valencia Mission 324
Vermont. 184-85
Vernal Utah Temple 358,12,404,406
Vietnam 300-301,11,398
Virgin Islands 301
Virginia 185-86
Virginia Richmond Mission 311
VISION/TV network 404-5
Visitors centers, statistics
'75:F16-17,
'76:B36-37

W

Waite, Michelle Kay 10
Wales 298
Wards. 397
Warner, Susan Lillywhite 88
Washburn, J Ballard 40
Washington. 186-88
    diplomatic community 397,402-4
Washington D.C. North Mission 321
Washington D.C. South Mission 312
Washington Spokane Mission 319
Washington Tacoma Mission 324
Washington Temple 358-59,397,404
Wells, Daniel H. 47-48
Wells, Emmeline B. 95
Wells, John 78
Wells, Robert E. 32
Wells, Rulon S. 61
Welsh Mission 306
West European (Administrative) Mission 313
West Indies Mission 321
West Spanish-American Mission 311
West Virginia 188-89
West Virginia Charleston Mission. . . . 320
Western Canadian Mission 310

Western Samoa 302-3
Whitney, Newel K. 75
Whitney, Orson F. 54
Wickman, Lance B. 40
Widtsoe, John A. 54
Wight, Lyman. 52
Wilcox, Keith W. 70
Williams, Clarissa Smith 95
Williams, Frederick G. 47
Winder, Barbara W. 96
Winder, John R. 45
Wirthlin, Anne Goalen 88
Wirthlin, Joseph B. 19
Wirthlin, Joseph L. 76
Wisconsin. 189-90
Wisconsin Milwaukee Mission 319
Women, prominent, '81:258-60
Wood, Lowell D. 40
Woodhouse, Stephen K. 397
Woodruff, Abraham O. 53,401
Woodruff, Wilford 42
Woolsey, Durrel A. 41
Word of Wisdom, statistics charts, '85:304-5
Wright, Ruth B. 9
Wyoming 190-91,408

Y

Yap (island). 262

Young Men
  general officers 84-87
Young Women
  general officers 90-93
  worldwide celebrations. 397
Young, Brigham 42
Young, Brigham, Jr. 49
Young, Clifford E. 63
Young, Dwan J. 89
Young, John W. 45
Young, Joseph 58
Young, Joseph A. 57
Young, Levi Edgar 61
Young, S. Dilworth 68
Young, Seymour B. 60
Young, Steve. 10
Young, Zina D. 95
Yugoslavia Zagreb Mission 318
Yukon Territory. 215

Z

Zaire. 303
Zaire Kinshasa Mission 322
Zambia 303-4
Zimbabwe. 304
Zimbabwe Harare Mission 322

Changes in area presidency assignments

(Effective Aug. 15, 1995)

First Quorum of the Seventy

Elder Carlos H. Amado — Second counselor, Mexico South Area
Elder Neil L. Andersen — First counselor, Europe West Area
Elder William R. Bradford — President, North American Central Area
Elder F. Enzio Busche — First counselor, North America Southwest Area
Elder John K. Carmack — Second counselor, North America Southeast Area
Elder D. Todd Christofferson — President, Mexico South Area
Elder Spencer J. Condie — President, North America Northwest Area
Elder Gene R. Cook — Second counselor, Utah South Area
Elder Robert K. Dellenbach — Second counselor, Utah North Area
Elder John B. Dickson — President, South America South Area
Elder Vaughn J Featherstone — President, North America Northeast Area
Elder John H. Groberg — First counselor, Asia Area
Elder F. Melvin Hammond — First counselor, South America South Area
Elder Marlin K. Jensen — Second counselor, North America Northeast Area
Elder Kenneth Johnson — Second counselor, Philippines/Micronesia Area
Elder L. Lionel Kendrick — Second counselor, North America Central Area
Elder Cree-L Kofford — Second counselor, Pacific Area
Elder Dean L. Larsen — President of the Europe West Area (name change)
Elder Lynn A. Mickelsen — Second counselor, North America Southwest Area
Elder Alexander B. Morrison — President, Utah North Area
Elder Dennis B. Neuenschwander — President, Europe East Area (name change)
Elder Glenn L. Pace — First counselor, North America Northwest Area
Elder James M. Paramore — First counselor, Utah South Area
Elder Andrew W. Peterson — Second counselor, Mexico North Area
Elder Hugh W. Pinnock — First counselor, North America Central Area
Elder Cecil O. Samuelson Jr. — Second counselor, Europe North Area
Elder Robert E. Wells — First counselor, Utah North Area
Elder W. Craig Zwick — First counselor, Brazil Area

Second Quorum of the Seventy

Elder Lino Alvarez — First counselor, Central America Area
Elder Dallas N. Archibald — President, Brazil Area
Elder C. Max Caldwell — Second counselor, North America West Area
Elder Claudio R.M. Costa — Second counselor, Brazil Area
Elder Rulon G. Craven — Second counselor, Asia Area
Elder Graham W. Doxey — President, Europe North Area
Elder John E. Fowler — First counselor, Europe North Area
Elder W. Don Ladd — First counselor, North America Northeast Area
Elder John M. Madsen — First counselor, Mexico North Area
Elder Joseph C. Muren — President, Central America Area
Elder Bruce D. Porter — Second counselor, Europe East Area
Elder Jorge A. Rojas — Second counselor, Central America Area
Elder Sam K. Shimabukuro — First counselor, Asia North Area
Elder Kwok Yuen Tai — President, Asia Area
Elder Dieter F. Uchtdorf — Second counselor, Europe West Area

AREA AUTHORITIES

The position of regional representative has been discontinued. In its place is a new administrative position, the area authority. The change was announced by President Gordon B. Hinckley at general priesthood meeting April 1, 1995. All regional representatives were released Aug. 15, 1995, the day that the terms of service for 117 newly called Area Authorities became effective.

They are "high priests chosen from among past and present experienced Church leaders." The new leaders will continue their current employment, reside in their own homes, and serve on a Church-service basis. The term of their call will be flexible, generally, for a period of approximately six years. They will be closely tied to the Area Presidencies.

Deseret News

1995-96 CHURCH ALMANAC

— ADDENDUM —

Featuring the new First Presidency

Center, President Gordon B. Hinckley; left, President Thomas S. Monson, first counselor; and right, President James E. Faust, second counselor.

Selected changes since the almanac was printed in November, 1994

THE CHURCH OF JESUS CHRIST OF LATTER-DAY SAINTS